ALSO BY JEFFRY D. WERT

General James Longstreet

Mosby's Rangers

*From Winchester to Cedar Creek:
The Shenandoah Campaign of 1864*

THE CONTROVERSIAL LIFE OF GEORGE ARMSTRONG CUSTER

JEFFRY D. WERT

.

A Touchstone Book

Published by Simon & Schuster

C U

STER

TOUCHSTONE
Rockefeller Center
1230 Avenue of the Americas
New York, NY 10020

First Touchstone Edition 1997

TOUCHSTONE and colophon are registered trademarks
of Simon & Schuster Inc.

Designed by Karolina Harris

Manufactured in the United States of America

1   2   3   4   5   6   7   8   9   10

Library of Congress Cataloging-in-Publication Data
Wert, Jeffry D.
Custer : the controversial life of George Armstrong
Custer / Jeffry D. Wert.
p.   cm.
Includes index.
1. Custer, George Armstrong, 1839–1876.
2. Generals—United States—Biography.
3. United States. Army—Biography. I. Title.
E467.1.C99W47   1996
973.8′2′092—dc20
96-7290
[B]   CIP

ISBN 0-684-81043-3
0-684-83275-5 (Pbk.)

To our parents:
Merle and Kathleen Wert
Ralph and Ethel Long

PREFACE

George Armstrong Custer has been the subject of more books and articles than any American except Abraham Lincoln. More has been written about the Battle of Little Big Horn than about the Battle of Gettysburg. His mythic "Last Stand" remains one of the nation's alluring enigmas. He is a rare figure in the country's past, an individual assured of immortality. He is as fascinating as he is controversial.

Justification for another book about Custer seemingly strains credulity. My biography, however, is the first full-scale study of his entire life in over three decades. Its purpose is to present a fresh reexamination of his life based upon recent scholarship and archival research. While many biographers or historians have chosen to concentrate either on the Civil War years or the postwar decade, my work embraces both periods. Understanding of the man and of the soldier requires inclusiveness. He strides across both eras, and both eras help to define him.

Any written work such as this requires collective effort. For those individuals who offered their assistance, I extend my sincere appreciation and gratitude. Their knowledge and insight have made this a better book, but all errors are solely the responsibility of the author.

First of all, I wish to thank the archivists and librarians at the institutions cited in the bibliography for their understanding, expertise, and patience with my requests for materials.

Other individuals deserve my particular recognition:

Michael Musick, archivist, National Archives; Dr. Richard Sommers and David Keogh, archivists, and Michael Winey, photograph curator, United States Army Military Institute; Kitty Deernose, curator, Little Big Horn Battlefield National Monument; Ted Alexander and Paul Chiles, historians, Antietam National Battlefield; Karl Katafiasz, special collections librarian, Monroe County Library System; and the Licensed

Guides, Gettysburg National Battlefield, for supplying me with important manuscripts and guiding my research.

Marshall Krolick, an expert on cavalry operations at Gettysburg, for sharing with me material from his collection.

Todd Kern, historian on operations in the Shenandoah Valley, for walking the ground with me at Locke's Ford and arranging an interview with members of the Locke family.

Clark B. "Bud" Hall, an authority on Civil War cavalry operations, for reading several of my chapters and sharing material with me.

Tom and Alice O'Neil, Custer scholars, for reading the entire manuscript, offering perceptive comments, and correcting errors, above and beyond the call of duty.

Brian Pohanka, Civil War and Custer historian and author, for reading my chapters on Little Big Horn, answering questions, and sharing material from his collection.

Allan Tischler, longtime friend and fellow Civil War historian, for reading chapters on the Shenandoah Valley campaign, walking the ground with me at Tom's Brook, finding numerous sources, and for his friendship.

Nick, Sr.; Kathy; and Nick Picerno, Jr., dear family friends, for their generosity in sharing their home with us for research visits, for escorting me around Vermont and New Hampshire, and for their support and kindness.

Robert Gottlieb, my agent, for the idea and the counsel.

Bob Bender, my editor, for his endless patience, understanding, and commitment.

Jason and Natalie, our son and daughter, for their love, the richest of life's gifts.

Gloria, my wife, for sharing with me the work of this book, from beginning to end, for her love, and for giving meaning and fulfillment to my life.

Merle and Kathleen Wert, my parents, and Ralph and Ethel Long, Gloria's parents, for their encouragement, support, and love, and to whom this book is dedicated.

Jeffry D. Wert
Centre Hall, Pennsylvania
July 14, 1995

CONTENTS

12 ▪ CONTENTS

"YELLOW-HAIRED LADDIE"

■ It was a Sabbath day—and men waited. Despite the sound of artillery fire and musketry, many of them believed that the long road of civil war could go no farther. For four years, a divided nation sought such a time and place, and now on April 9, 1865, Palm Sunday, near Appomattox Court House, Virginia, the stillness appeared to be at hand.

Although anticipated for months, this final collision had come swiftly during the past week. On April 2, the Union Army of the Potomac, under the direction of Lieutenant General Ulysses S. Grant, overwhelmed the enemy lines around Petersburg, Virginia, and seized the vital railroad center. For ten months, the Confederate entrenchments and General Robert E. Lee's Army of Northern Virginia had defied the Federals. But desertion and death had reduced Lee's ranks to a shadow, and when the Northerners rolled forward, the Southern veterans stood one last time long enough for Lee to extricate his units. Into the night Lee marched the remnants, guiding them westward. Behind the Confederates, their capital, Richmond, roughly twenty miles north of Petersburg, surrendered the next day.

The Federals pursued, relentlessly, sensing that Petersburg had been a mortal wound. It became a race that Lee's men had to win, but could not. In the forefront of Grant's army rode the cavalry. The Union horsemen gnawed at the edges and ripped apart the fleeing columns. "Our cavalry were untiring," remembered a general, and the Rebels no longer could match them. Finally, on the evening of April 8, the Third Cavalry Division knifed into the van of Lee's army and barred its path.

The cavalrymen of the Third Division belonged to twenty-five-year-old Brevet Major General George Armstrong Custer. He had been their commander since the previous autumn, and under his leadership, the troopers had become one of the finest combat units in the army. Personally fearless, Custer had instilled an aggressiveness in his veterans that often had placed them in the forefront. Once again, they had paced the army, bringing them here to a Virginia crossroads, perhaps only a day from victory.

At daylight on April 9, Confederate infantry, supported by artillery, advanced against the Yankees. Proud, defiant, the once seemingly invincible Rebels came on for a final time. Federal units who had reached the front during the night opened fire, while Custer hurried his brigades forward. Behind Custer, troopers carried a cluster of captured Confederate battle flags, a dramatic gesture typical of the general. His men repulsed an enemy sortie and prepared to charge.

From a ridge, George Custer watched as his regiments wheeled into formation. For the renowned "Boy General" of the Union army, he was where he wanted to be, where he had dreamed of being since he had been a youth. He had been in the debacle at First Bull Run in 1861, and now, he would be in at the end. At one time, he was the youngest general in the army, and his name became a household word in the North. He attained a combat record as a cavalry officer nearly unmatched, while the fame he enjoyed was reserved for few others in the army.

For Custer, however, there was no acclaim without controversy. Even on this day of Union victory, his brashness and flair would generate eventual disagreement. With him, there seemed to be no middle ground. While his men were devoted to him and his superiors praised him, fellow officers resented—perhaps envied—his fame, his showmanship, his loudly proclaimed "luck." He was a soldier encased in an image; a man shaped by his times, when the country redefined itself and concluded a continental mission.

George Custer moved within that era, defined by it, and in part, defining it. Because of that he remains a disturbing and controversial presence within American history. In life, he fascinated a nation; in death, he haunted its soul. If his military career had ended on the ridge near Appomattox Court House, he would be remembered as one of the country's finest horse soldiers, a warrior hero, standing at ease, in a front rank of fellow soldiers. But his passage would come instead on a ridge above a Montana river on another Sabbath day when men also waited.[1]

George Armstrong Custer was born in New Rumley, Harrison County, Ohio, on December 5, 1839, the third child of Emanuel H. and Maria Ward Kirkpatrick Custer. His father owned a blacksmith shop and served as the local justice of the peace. Like many of the town's adults, Emanuel and Maria had come to New Rumley from elsewhere. Home and family roots lay to the east.[2]

Emanuel's family were Marylanders of German descent. His great-great-great-grandfather was Paulus Kuster or Kuester, who may have been the first of the lineage to settle in America. By the 1750s, the family was established in Maryland and spelled its name "Custer." Emanuel Custer, George Armstrong's great-grandfather, was born in Allegany County in 1754, served as a sergeant in the militia during the Revolutionary War, and married Anna Maria Fadley, with whom he had seven children.[3]

Emanuel and Anna's second child and son was John, born on February 26, 1782. At the age of twenty, John married eighteen-year-old Catherine Valentine and began housekeeping in Cresaptown in Allegany County. Here they raised seven children to maturity, with John dying in the 1830s, and Catherine in 1877.

Their oldest son was Emanuel Henry, born on December 10, 1806, and named for his grandfather. Generations of Custer men evidently made their living by blacksmithing, and Emanuel Henry learned the trade from either his father or an uncle. In 1824, Emanuel headed west to the hill country of southeastern Ohio to join his father's brother, Jacob Custer, who most likely wrote to John and asked for his nephew.[4]

Jacob Custer had been in Ohio for over a decade, following that characteristic westering itch of Americans. Once General Anthony Wayne defeated the Indian tribes in the mid-1790s, Ohio became the new magnet, with its promise of virgin land and with the hope of a new beginning. Jacob Custer stopped at a tiny settlement, Rumley Town, founded by a squatter, John Rumley. But the Marylander had ideas and some money, and had the village plotted and rechristened New Rumley. The village lay about eleven miles from Cadiz, the growing county seat of Harrison County, and was on the stage road from Steubenville to New Philadelphia.[5]

When Emanuel arrived in New Rumley, the village boasted twenty-four families as residents, an increase of nearly fivefold since Jacob surveyed the plots. The townsfolk soon must have learned that the teenaged Emanuel was an impulsive, intense, and outspoken young man. Men with business at the blacksmith shop and loafers could readily engage the blond-haired Marylander in an argument on nearly any subject. He relished such debates, and in his loud voice held forth, with each point perhaps emphasized by the clang of hammer on anvil. Within a year or so of Emanuel's arrival, Jacob turned over the business to his nephew and moved to a farm outside of town.[6]

On August 7, 1828, Emanuel married twenty-four-year-old Matilda Viers, daughter of New Rumley's justice of the peace, Bruce Viers, and his wife, Hannah. Emanuel and Matilda lived in the log house next to the blacksmith shop, and Matilda gave birth to three children—Hannah in 1830; Brice W. in 1831; and John A. in 1833. Their daughter, however, lived for only a year, and on July 18, 1835, Matilda died of unknown causes. Widowed, with two young sons, Emanuel did not wait long to marry again.[7]

Emanuel undoubtedly knew Maria Ward Kirkpatrick from the time he came to New Rumley. She was the daughter of the town's tavern keeper and wife, James and Catherine Ward. The Wards had relocated from Washington County, Pennsylvania, in 1816. A tailor and tavern keeper in his native state, James Ward opened an unlicensed public house soon after his arrival, which resulted in a conviction and fine. By the summer of 1817, he had a license and had built a two-story log house, with attached kitchen, on a corner lot of the town square. It must have been a rowdy establishment because Ward was a foul-tempered man, and with his sons, James, Jr., and Joseph, would be involved in a number of assaults on fellow townsmen.[8]

A frequent customer at the tavern was Israel R. Kirkpatrick, a merchant in town. He and Maria Ward, who was not quite sixteen years old and twelve years younger than Israel, were married on January 8, 1823. A son, David, was born to the couple within a year, followed by a daughter, Lydia Ann, in 1825. The family lived in Israel's house until 1830, when it moved into the tavern. James Ward had died in 1824, and Andrew Thompson, a shoemaker, managed the business until Catherine

Ward died, probably in 1829. In January 1830, Israel Kirkpatrick closed the tavern, and with his wife, two children, and his sister-in-law, Margaret Ward, made it the family home.[9]

Like Emanuel Custer, Maria Kirkpatrick lost her spouse in 1835, with Israel dying on March 6, four months before Matilda Custer. Because of their shared losses and common needs, Emanuel and Maria gravitated toward each other. They were less than a year apart in age, both with young children, and on February 23, 1836, were married, with Emanuel and his two sons moving into Maria's home. Jacob Custer still owned the log house and blacksmith shop, so Emanuel joined Maria in the larger house. Unfortunately for them, Maria's father and her first husband had died intestate, and it would not be until Israel Kirkpatrick's estate was settled in 1848 that the couple secured ownership of the property.[10]

Tragedy, however, remained a companion of Emanuel and Maria for the first three years of their marriage. Five months after their marriage, in July 1836, Emanuel's three-year-old son John died. Later in the year, Maria gave birth to their first child, James, but he survived only a few months. In 1838, another son, Samuel, was born, but he also died in infancy. By the summer of 1839, Maria was pregnant with their third child.[11]

Those months also marked other significant changes in the household. For years, Emanuel had been one of the town's most boisterous Jacksonian Democrats. Around the forge, he railed against any politician or supporter opposed to "Old Hickory." He was later described as a "staunch, uncompromising Democrat." But during his fifteen years in New Rumley, he had earned his fellow townsmen's respect, and in August they elected him to the first of four successive terms as justice of the peace.[12]

The couple also joined the Methodist Church during this period. Emanuel had been a Presbyterian; Maria, a Lutheran, but they must have found Methodism's doctrine more comforting. Both of them embraced the faith devoutly, often boarding itinerant preachers in their home. As was her wont, Maria was a quiet, dedicated follower; not so Emanuel—quiet fitted him like a poor Sunday suit. In church, his voice boomed in song; in the blacksmith shop, his arguments were enlivened by the Methodist catechism. He was as intensely and passionately loyal to his church as he was to his political party.[13]

Three weeks before Christmas, on December 5, in the back room of the first story of their house, Maria gave birth to their third child, George Armstrong, named for one of Emanuel's younger brothers. The parents doted over the curly-headed, blue-eyed, healthy baby, whom they called Armstrong. As he grew and began talking, he garbled his name as Autie, and to his family he was Autie for the rest of his life.[14]

Autie was the first of five children born to Emanuel and Maria during a thirteen-year span. Nevin Johnson followed Autie, born on July 29, 1842. A frail, sickly child whom Autie protected, Nevin seemed misplaced among the Custer clan. The third child, Thomas Ward, born on March 15, 1845, would shadow his oldest brother and strive to emulate everything Autie did. Boston followed three years later, born on October 31, 1848. To Boston, Autie was a hero, an older brother to brag about and to worship. The final child was a daughter, Margaret Emma, born June 5, 1852, whose life, even as an adult, would be entwined with her brothers'.[15]

The Custer household vibrated with life and with love. To outsiders, there seemed to be no difference between the Custer brood and the three children from the previous marriages and, indeed, there was none among the children. Family meant inclusiveness, devotion, and loyalty, a lesson never forgotten.[16]

Although both parents lavished affection upon their offspring, Maria was the quiet, steady counterpoint to the loud, impulsive Emanuel. After the Civil War, when Autie was a famous general, she wrote a revealing letter to him about herself as a mother. "My loveing son," she began it. "When you speak about your boyhood home in your dear letter I had to weep for joy that the recollection was sweet in your memory. Many a time I have thought there was things my children needed it caused me tears. Yet I consoled myself that I had done my best in making home comfortable." The family had little money, she reminded him, and added, "So I tried to fill the empty spaces with little acts of kindness. Even when there was a meal admired by my children it was my greatest pleasure to get it for them." [17]

Of all the children, however, Autie was special, both to his parents and to his siblings. Bright and impulsive, he "was irrepressible as a boy," according to one of his teachers. Mischief clung to Autie; in the words of a schoolmate, "George was a wide awake boy full of all kinds of pranks and willing to take all kinds of chances." As he grew older, Autie emulated his father as a practical joker. Usually with Tom in tow, Autie eagerly sought victims for their tricks. The boys especially enjoyed ones that involved their father. It would be a lifelong practice relished by the Custer brothers.[18]

Emanuel sought to rein in his frisky sons. He assigned them chores and every Sunday marched them to church: "His boys was just as punctual as he was," Nevin remembered, "but not of their own free will." Autie was a constant presence in the blacksmith shop, listening to town gossip, hearing his father discuss the political sins of Whigs, watching him give shape to metal, and riding newly shod horses so his father could examine the fit. Whenever the chance came, Autie was on horseback, sitting bareback, guiding an animal around the shop. He was "very fond of horses," a cousin remarked.[19]

Despite his efforts at discipline, Emanuel could not stop bragging about and showing off Autie, whom he called his "yellow-haired laddie." When Autie was four years old, his mother, apparently at Emanuel's insistence, made a soldier's uniform for the boy. Periodically, in town, the local militia unit, the New Rumley Guards, whom the residents snidely referred to as "the Invincibles," held musters. At these gatherings, Emanuel had Autie, dressed in his uniform and carrying a toy musket or wooden sword, march down the street with the citizen soldiers. The spectacle delighted onlookers and the Guards, many of whom were drunk, and some enjoyed putting the young warrior through the manual of arms.[20]

At one muster, according to family tradition, Autie had a toothache, and Emanuel gathered him up and hauled him to a dentist in another town. As the dentist prepared to extract the tooth, Emanuel told Autie that he "must be a good soldier." On the way home, Autie suddenly blurted out, "Pa, we can whip all of Michigan," referring to a border dispute between it and Ohio. His father roared with laughter and spent the next several months retelling the story to anyone who came to the shop.[21]

At the age of six, Autie began attending the one-room log school in town. The school provided him with fertile ground for his mischievousness and new victims for his pranks, and he soon emerged as the leader among his classmates. "He was rather a bad boy in school," claimed the teacher's son, "but one thing would be said of him, he *always* had his lessons, yet he was not considered an unusually bright lad." In fact, he was bright, hated homework, and seldom completed the lessons beforehand, skimming over them before the recitations. Once he learned to read well, he smuggled novels into the class and placed them inside a textbook during reading periods.[22]

In the spring of 1849, Emanuel and Maria sold their house and shop in town and bought an eighty-acre farm three miles from New Rumley. Emanuel still did blacksmithing work while trying to scratch an income from the hilly, thin soil of the new place. In turn, the children attended Creal School, apparently a subscription school taught by A. B. Creal. Perhaps because of the cost of the school or because of Autie's dislike for the schoolwork, the parents apprenticed him to Joseph R. Hunter, a furniture maker in Cadiz. But the apprenticeship failed; Autie was extremely unhappy, and the Custers decided to send him to school in Monroe, Michigan.[23]

Maria's daughter, Lydia Ann, lived in that southeastern Michigan community, having married a Monroe resident, David Reed. How Ann —as she was familiarly called—met Reed is uncertain, but the Custers had had connections to Monroe for a decade. In 1842, Emanuel had uprooted the family from New Rumley and moved to Monroe, where he rented a farm about a mile south of town. The new beginning failed miserably—their horses were stolen, and within six months the family had returned to New Rumley. A year or so later, Emanuel's brother, George Custer, married Sidney Reed, David's sister. This may have brought Ann and David together. They were married on December 1, 1846, in New Rumley.[24]

Autie must have been excited about the decision for him to live with the Reeds—he adored Ann. Since he had been an infant, Ann had assisted her mother with his care. Her marriage to Reed and departure for Michigan was surely a sad time for the seven-year-old boy. She had become a surrogate mother to him, and in time, a friend and confidante.[25]

Monroe was one of the oldest settlements in Michigan, located on the western shore of Lake Erie, near the mouth of River Raisin, roughly thirty-five miles south of Detroit. Originally established as a trading post by French-Canadian trappers in 1785, it was called Frenchtown once American settlers entered the territory. In 1813, a British and Indian force massacred a contingent of Kentucky riflemen along the river. After President James Monroe visited four years later, the town was renamed in his honor. Monroe boomed as Americans poured into the old Northwest Territory during the next decades, and in 1852 it had 4,800 residents. It is believed that the Reeds lived at the corner of Fifth and Monroe streets, where David Reed had a drayage business and loaned money in real estate transactions.[26]

Autie spent most of the next three years with the Reeds in Monroe, attending the New Dublin School and later the Stebbins Academy for Boys. Whether he was a more serious student in these schools is speculative; what is reasonably to be assumed was that his impulsive behavior and penchant for practical jokes continued. The minister of Monroe Methodist Church, which the Reeds attended, remembered Autie as the instigator of devilish plots both during the service and in Sunday school. On the surface, he appeared attentive and respectful, but underneath, the mind boiled with disruptive ideas. During prayer meetings, the boys rifled birdshot with their thumbs through the congregation. "We knew who was the promoter of such schemes," asserted the minister, "for George was easily their leader."[27]

When the Stebbins Academy closed in early 1855, Autie returned to the family farm outside of New Rumley. Monroe, however, had become his adopted home and would increasingly be so as the years passed. Back in Ohio, his education resumed at the McNeely Normal School at Hopedale. McNeely was a boarding school, with the students residing in small cottages. Autie attended it intermittently during the next eighteen months. At sixteen years of age, increasingly his attention turned toward young women, with whom, his cousin alleged, he was "quite a favorite." A fellow student remembered him: "Custer was what he appeared. There was nothing hidden in his nature. He was kind and generous to his friends; bitter and implacable towards his enemies."[28]

Autie interrupted his education at McNeely to accept a teaching position at the Beech Point School in Athens Township. He earned $28 a month and evidently used the money to pay for his own schooling. He roomed with a William Dickerson and walked to the school. A friend of the time described him as a "big-hearted, whole-souled fellow," and with his zest for life and fun-loving disposition, he proved to be a popular teacher. "What a pretty girl he would have made," thought one of his female students. Ironically, perhaps fittingly, he became the target of student pranks. At Christmas in 1855, the students locked him out of the schoolhouse. When the boys went outside for wood, he sneaked inside. Upon their return, a scuffle ensued, and they shoved him out the door. Finally, he sought assistance from school board members, who reopened the building. He apparently did not finish the winter term at Beech Point.[29]

In the spring of 1856, Autie returned to McNeely while also securing a teacher's certificate. By midsummer he had finished at McNeely, and a month later he accepted a teaching position in District Number Five in Cadiz Township, near the county seat. He boarded with the Alexander Holland family. Holland was superintendent of an infirmary that consisted of three log houses. The Hollands lived in one of the houses, and there Autie came in the late summer.[30]

Controversy, caused in part by lack of creditable evidence, gnaws at various aspects of Custer's life. The lack of documentation, the irretrievable silence of the past, the motives of contemporaries—friend and enemy alike—and the biases of later chroniclers conspire against the historic record. A prime example of such dispute is the events that transpired in the Holland household.

What is certain is that Autie fell passionately in love with teenaged Mary Jane, or Mollie, Holland; what is uncertain is the nature of the relationship. Was it sexually consummated? And how far did Alexander Holland go in ridding himself and Mollie of the suitor? The attraction was mutual, and undoubtedly the first such emotional experience for each of them. The couple spent as much time together as possible, and after a day in school with twenty-five students, Autie surely raced back to the Holland home.[31]

The love-struck young man let his feelings flow on to paper. Throughout his life he would be comfortable expressing his thoughts in writing. "To Mary," he titled a poem:

> I've seen and kissed that crimson lip
> With honied smiles o'erflowing
> Enchanted watched the opening rose
> Upon thy soft cheek flowing
> Dear Mary, thy eyes may prove less blue,
> Thy beauty fade tomorrow,
> But oh, my heart can ne'er forget
> Thy parting look of sorrow.[32]

They talked about marriage and a future together—at least Autie did. He ended one letter to her with the words, "Farewell my only love

until we meet again from your true & faithful Lover, 'Bachelor Boy.' "
A few days later, he wrote again, "You occupy the first place in my
affections and the only place as far as love is concerned. . . . If any power
which I possess or control can aid in or in any way hasten our marriage
it shall be exerted for that object." [33]

The couple sometimes met in or on a trundle bed. Whether or not
Autie and Mollie were sexually involved remains elusive. One biographer alleges that he shared a bed with her and at least three other
women before the age of twenty, but that claim seems to be only
reasonable speculation. As a married man, Autie enjoyed sex, as is
evident in his correspondence with his wife. At seventeen years old,
healthy, virile, and impulsive by nature, he surely wanted to explore the
mystery. If Mollie shared the ache and accepted the risks, their relationship was more than kisses and poetry. Regardless, when Alexander
Holland learned of the trundle bed, he banished the schoolteacher from
his home. [34]

Autie moved nearby, residing in the home of Henry Boyle. Despite
her father's wishes, Mollie continued to see Autie, meeting when they
could at a neighbor's house. The arrangement did not cool the youthful
romance. Mollie had a daguerreotype taken of herself and gave it to
Autie, who posed for one of himself, holding Mollie's in his hand.
Fortunately for her parents, a solution to the Custer problem was at
hand. [35]

In the spring of 1856, Autie decided to try for an appointment to
the United States Military Academy at West Point, New York—an
aspiration he often spoke of to Mollie as they planned a future. The
academy offered a number of attractions for Autie. His boyish dreams
of military glory might be fulfilled—he had enjoyed reading books on
generals and campaigns—the education provided there was one of the
best in the country, and as he wrote to Ann Reed, a graduate of the
institution might obtain a lucrative civilian position. Autie said he knew
of a local man who had attended West Point and was now reportedly
worth $200,000. Money would always entice him. [36]

The appointment, however, would be a difficult task for him. The
local congressman was John A. Bingham, an antislavery, even abolition-
ist, Republican. His politics were anathema to Emanuel Custer, who
refused to intercede on behalf of his son. It probably would not have
mattered if Emanuel had tried, because the Republican Party was barely

two years old and preparing for its first presidential campaign. Appointments to the academy were political patronage that rewarded new Republican supporters.[37]

Undaunted by the prospects, Autie wrote to Bingham on May 27,
1856. "I am desirous of going to West Point," he began, "and I think
my age and tastes would be in accordance with its requirements. But I
must forbear on that point for the present. I am now in attendance at
the McNeely Normal School in Hopedale, and could obtain from the
principal, if necessary, testimonials of moral character. I would also say
that I have the consent of my parents in the course which I have in
view. Wishing to hear from you as soon as convenient."[38]

Bingham replied within a week or so, stating that he had already
appointed one man and had promised a second appointment to a Jefferson County resident. With the letter, he enclosed the qualifications for
admission. Autie wrote back on June 11, asserting that he appeared
qualified as to age and height, and added that he was "of remarkably
strong constitution and vigorous frame." He continued, "If that young
man from Jeff. County of whom you spoke does not push the matter,
or if you hear of any other vacancy, I should be glad to hear from you."
A month later, the congressman interviewed Autie in his Cadiz home.[39]

Bingham knew of the Custer family's political affiliation, and it would
have been prudent for Autie to remain aloof from the campaign of
1856. But he was Emanuel's son, and as the father later boasted about
him, "Of course he was a democrat. My boys were all democrats. I
would not raise any other kind." In August, Autie participated in a rally
for Democratic presidential candidate James Buchanan at the McNeely
Normal School. Six weeks later, at a Republican rally for John C.
Frémont in Cadiz, he joined a group of young Democrats who marched
past the gathering, dressed in turned-out coats and stovepipe hats as
"border ruffians" in reference to the fighting in Kansas. The Republicans, including Bingham, were annoyed by the spectacle.[40]

About this time, Alexander Holland learned about the trundle bed.
It would appear that Holland, a Republican and an old friend of Bingham's, went to the congressman and requested that his daughter's suitor
be given the appointment. Holland knew that a cadet could not be
married, and with Autie in New York for five years, Mollie's and his
passions should subside. It is also speculated that John Wirt, a merchant
in New Rumley and a friend of Emanuel Custer's, despite their polar

views on politics, interceded with Bingham. The intervention worked —whoever's it may have been—and in November, Bingham wrote to Secretary of War Jefferson Davis requesting the appointment and noting that the candidate was five feet nine and three-fourths inches tall and academically qualified.[41]

In January 1857, the secretary of war notified Bingham of the appointment, and on the twenty-ninth Autie accepted in writing and his father signed his permission. The consent of his parents came only after his mother had been persuaded. At one time, she had entertained the idea that Autie might be a minister, but she had probably abandoned that thought long ago. With her son, David Kirkpatrick, and David and Ann Reed supporting Autie, she acquiesced. A cadet needed two hundred dollars for admission, so in the spring Emanuel borrowed that amount with a lien against the farm.[42]

Davis had included with the notification a form letter that warned candidates of the academy's rigorous academic standards. To Autie, it should have been a sobering message, for he had been an indifferent student at best. He possessed the intellectual ability, but did he have sufficient preparation? The academy presented a daunting challenge, but he never hesitated—hesitation seemed not to be a part of him. He saw Mollie Holland for the final time, still speaking of marriage. On a June day, in Scio, Ohio, he boarded a train for New York. The farewells to his family were difficult; they would never be otherwise, especially to his mother.[43]

The train clanged eastward, from out of the country's heartland to the bustling Atlantic coast. He probably thought little of it, but the future soldier was more than Emanuel and Maria Custer's "yellow-haired laddie." He was from a place and a time, from a country that put shoulders to wagons, gazed at the road ahead, not behind, and honored heroes. It would be a journey from here to there.

Chapter

2

WEST POINT

■ George Armstrong Custer, Cadet, Twenty-first Congressional District of Ohio, reported to the adjutant's office in the Library at the United States Military Academy in early June 1857. Like his fellow plebes, or new cadets, he had finished his trip to West Point by steamer up the Hudson River. After days of instruction by upperclassmen, over one hundred candidates underwent the entrance examinations before a board of staff and faculty in the Academic Building. On June 20, the Class of 1862, composed of sixty-eight members, was admitted to the academy.[1]

For over half a century, the academy had trained officers for the Regular Army. Since its founding in 1802, the institution had measured men. Discipline, classwork, routine, and tradition proscribed a cadet's existence. The education provided equaled or excelled that offered in most of the country's colleges and universities. Its graduates had constructed forts, designed coastal defenses, built levees along rivers, explored and mapped vast stretches of the frontier, and fought wars.

Permanence and solidity marked the academy and its grounds. Located on a high bluff above the Hudson River where Revolutionary forts had guarded the narrows of the river, it was a place of granite, limestone, and brick. The buildings edged the center of the grounds, a forty-acre swath of grass known as the Plain.[2]

Within this setting, authorities regulated cadet behavior with a strict code of conduct, enumerated in a system of demerits. Called "skins" by cadets, demerits were issued for various breaches of the codes. The corps members earned demerits for carelessness in attire; for tardiness, absence, or inattention at roll calls for drill, inspections, chapel, and meals; for unkempt hair and unshaven faces; for dirty quarters and equipment; for visiting without permission or after taps; for neglect of duty; for disturbances during study hours; for throwing food in the Mess Hall; for altercations or fights with fellow cadets; and for unmilitary behavior toward academy and cadet officers. If a cadet received two hundred "skins" in a year, he could be expelled from the institution.[3]

"At West Point all is monotony," grumbled a cadet a decade earlier. "What is said of one day will answer for it almost years after." Cadets of the 1850s would have shared his sentiments. Routine still measured time. In the classroom, on the drill field, in the barracks, even in the Mess Hall, the sameness of each day blended into weeks and months. The exuberance of youth confronted an institution governed by order, discipline, and tradition.[4]

For plebes, introduction to academy life began with the annual summer camp held in July and August. After commencement in June, the corps moved from the barracks to the open ground south of the West Point Hotel, where old Fort Clinton had stood, and erected a camp comprising of eight rows of white tents. In each tent, cadets slept on blankets on wooden floors with a gun rack as the only piece of furniture.[5]

Camp instruction focused on soldierly conduct and military drill, under the direction of officers and upperclass cadets. Each day began with reveille at 5 A.M., followed by policing of grounds, drill, breakfast, drill, dinner, policing, drill, dress parade, supper, and tattoo at 9:30 P.M. Mistakes sent cadets to the guard tent. "If my hat or even my head was falling off," claimed one of the novice soldiers, "I would have no right to raise my hand to save it." Fortunately, dances on Saturday nights, visits by military personnel, politicians, and civilians enlivened the weeks spent in tents.[6]

In the middle of his first encampment, George Custer wrote to a friend: "I like West Point as well if not better than I did at first. I think it is the most romantic spot I ever saw." He was becoming accustomed to the discipline, he added, relating how some of his fellow corpsmen sneaked off the post to visit the town of Buttermilk Falls, about a mile south of the academy. Some of them were caught and would be punished, perhaps even dismissed. "This seems hard," he asserted, "but military law is very severe and those who overstep its boundaries must abide the consequences."[7]

For Custer, the latter was a curious statement, for he had already begun to "overstep its boundaries." "Fanny," as his fellow cadets had nicknamed him because of his blond hair and fair complexion, had compiled ten demerits by the time he wrote the letter on August 7. Most were minor infractions—"not casting eyes to front: at parade," late for parade, "not keeping dressed" in ranks, and "no collar visible" on uniform. Before the month had ended, however, he received another seventeen demerits for carelessness, inattention, "boyish conduct," improper attire, unbuttoned coat, falsely stating a report, and "not carrying" his musket properly at drill. It was only a beginning for Fanny Custer.[8]

With his fellow plebes and the upperclassmen, Custer moved into the barracks at the end of summer camp. Finished in 1850, the Cadet Barracks was a four-story, L-shaped stone building with distinctive Gothic turrets. Eight divisions of rooms divided the interior of the building, with a company assigned to two divisions. Two or four cadets shared a room, depending on the time of year. During the cold months, only two cadets lived in the spartan quarters. Each room had a window, a fireplace with a white-painted mantel, a gun rack, a clothes press, a table, two chairs, two beds with thin mattresses on slats, a washstand, and an oil lamp. A water bucket and a "slop bucket" completed the furnishings. In warm weather, four cadets roomed together, sleeping on blankets on the floor, an experience a corpsman described later: "My bones ached in the morning as if I had been pounded all night."[9]

Academy authorities assigned cadets to companies according to individual heights, an innovation begun by former superintendent Robert E. Lee. Companies A and D, the flank companies in formations, had the taller men; Companies B and C, the shorter ones. Although the institution's staff endeavored to limit the practice, by the 1850s, cadets preferred an assignment to a company either of fellow Northerners or fellow Southerners. Height remained the official policy, but as the nation divided along sectional lines, so did the corps. Custer, in contrast, served in a predominantly Southern company.[10]

In fact, Custer gravitated toward Southerners—among their ranks he would find his closest friends. His roommate that fall was James Parker of Missouri, a stout, slow-moving, rugged young man, almost the physical opposite of Custer. Others in his class who soon shared in his escapades and merriment were William Dunlap and George Watts of Kentucky, John "Gimlet" Lea of Mississippi, Pierce M. B. Young of Georgia, and Lafayette "Lafe" Lane, a Southern sympathizer who was the son of the territorial delegate to Congress from Oregon. In the

Class of 1861, Alabamian John Pelham and Texan Thomas Rosser were kindred spirits. In particular, the tall, powerful, dark-complexioned Rosser may have been Custer's best friend in the corps. Among third classmen, Stephen Dodson Ramseur, a serious North Carolinian, was often in the company of the Ohioan.[11]

Custer's friendships extended across sectional lines, however. Among his classmates from the North, he counted as friends Alonzo "Lon" Cushing and Patrick H. O'Rorke of New York, George A. Woodruff of Michigan, Leroy S. Elbert of Ohio, and Henry E. Noyes of Massachusetts. Others who were his acquaintances and whose future became linked with his included Judson Kilpatrick, Henry DuPont, Orville Babcock, Wesley Merritt, James H. Wilson, Alexander C. M. Pennington, and Horace Porter. In time, as new classes entered, Custer would add Tully McCrea, Morris Schaff, and Peter Michie to his group.[12]

There was a "joyousness" to Custer, proclaimed a cadet, that attracted others to him. Personable, fun-loving, and loyal, Custer possessed a personality that few could resist. "He was beyond a doubt," a friend claimed, "the most popular man in his class." "West Point has had many a character to deal with," insisted another one, "but it may be a question whether it ever had a cadet so exuberant, one who cared so little for its serious attempts to elevate and burnish, or one on whom its tactical officers kept their eyes so constantly and unsympathetically searching as upon Custer. And yet how we all loved him."[13]

In him, the cadets saw a spirit and zest for life that even the academy's disciplinary rigor could not smother. Custer's defiance of rules, night-time adventures, indifference to schoolwork, and pranks resulted in laughter in barracks rooms and probably secret admiration. He remained immature, impetuous, and rebellious. Authority was meant to be tested, whether it was at a prayer meeting in the Monroe Methodist Church or at a drill on the Plain at West Point.

As he stated in his summer camp letter, however, Custer understood that breaches meant consequences. While "his boyish, but harmless frolics kept him in constant hot water," according to a cadet, Custer could abide by the rules, not earning a single skin for several months, when his demerit total reached levels that could result in dismissal. He even had minor infractions removed by walking extra duty tours. In fact, by his own estimate, he spent sixty-six Saturdays during his academy years on such tours.[14]

Nevertheless, Custer accumulated demerits in numbers unequaled by any other cadet in his class. With him, "the great difficulty," believed Tully McCrea, a roommate, "is that he is too clever for his own good. He is always connected with all the mischief that is going on and never studies any more than he can possibly help." To Peter Michie, Custer "was always in trouble with authorities." Whenever he saw an officer and suspected that he was the subject of the officer's search, he darted away "to delay the well-known formula: 'Sir, you are hereby placed in arrest and confined to quarters, by direction of the superintendent.' " "He had more fun," argued Michie, "gave his friends more anxiety, walked more tours of extra duty, and came nearer to being dismissed more often than any other cadet I have ever known." [15]

The nature of some of his demerits and the daring of some of his pranks elicited howls of laughter as they were recounted in barracks rooms and became a part of academy lore. Frequently, he wore a tan-colored wig to conceal his long hair, but on one occasion, after receiving demerits for its length, he had the post barber shave his head. For weeks afterward, either at inspections or whenever seen on the grounds, cadets shouted, "Hair out of uniform." During a summer camp, he and Henry Noyes were caught hazing a plebe. When the officer approached, both of them ran, covering their heads with their uniform capes. The ruse failed as the officer shouted, "It's no use for you to try to escape. The knock knees of one and the bow legs of the other belong only to two, Noyes and Custer." The friends were punished together. [16]

Moreover, his pranks possessed variety and a richness of imagination. He tied tin pans to the tail of a dog that belonged to a professor's family. He painted an ankle with iodine and feigned a limp to be excused from drills. He killed, cooked, and ate Lieutenant Henry Douglas's rooster. Often at night, he and George Watts or another culprit sneaked into plebes' rooms and yanked the sleeping underclassmen out of their beds and then fled. Finally, during his third year, one day in Spanish class he asked the instructor, Professor Patrice de Janon, to translate "Class dismissed" into Spanish. When de Janon responded as requested, Custer stood up and led the members out of the room. [17]

The pattern of Custer's disciplinary and academic record at the academy began during his initial term in September 1857. When the corps returned to the barracks from summer camp, the academic year commenced. Since 1854, at the instigation of Secretary of War Jefferson Davis, the course of study had been extended from four to five years.

When the decision was announced, the corps nearly mutinied. It remained unsettled into 1859, but when the candidates reported in June 1857, they expected to spend five years at the institution.[18]

The addition of a year allowed for the expansion of the curriculum, with emphasis on military courses. The curriculum stressed both the education of the man and of the soldier. The classes were rigorous. Underclassmen studied mathematics, English, French, Spanish, drawing, electrics, mineralogy, geology, chemistry, natural and experimental philosophy, geography, history, ethics, and grammar. Military subjects included infantry, artillery, and cavalry tactics, ordnance, gunnery, military and civil engineering, fortification, military science and art, equitation, veterinary science and art, military police, discipline and administration, and the use of a sword. Semiannual examinations in January and June determined whether a cadet passed or failed a course and his class rank. The academic requirements challenged the best of the corpsmen and could overwhelm the mediocre, ill-prepared, or ill-disciplined members.[19]

Custer settled in comfortably into the latter group. He once informed Peter Michie that there were only two positions in a class, "head and foot," and since he was disinclined to strive for the "head," he aspired for the "foot." "It was all right with him," recalled a roommate, "whether he knew his lesson or not: he did not allow it to trouble him." In the words of another cadet, "Custer's course at West Point may be described in the remark that he merely scraped through. . . . He was anything but a good student."[20]

During the 1857–1858 academic year, Custer studied mathematics, which embraced algebra, geometry, and trigonometry, and English, including grammar. After his January 1858 examinations, and with his demerit record, he ranked fifty-eighth in the class of sixty-eight. At year's end in June, he stood fifty-second in mathematics, and fifty-seventh in English. The class, however, now stood at sixty-two, as six members were deficient and were either dismissed or resigned.[21]

His overall class rank reflected, in part, his mounting delinquency record. From September through December 1857, Custer received a total of ninety demerits. Most of the infractions were minor and typical—visiting after hours, inattention, tardiness, dirty oil can, throwing snowballs. On November 28, he and two others were caught playing cards, and given twelve extra tours of Saturday guard duty. In one day,

December 19, he received fifteen demerits for five separate incidents.[22] Custer added eighty-two more skins during the second term. The most serious infraction occurred on February 13, 1858, when he and four cadets were charged with "allowing gross violations of military propriety in their sections" for failure to keep their section at attention during a formation. Each man received four demerits and all were stripped of their positions as squad marchers. In the special orders citing the incident and punishment, Superintendent Richard Delafield, a tough career officer, admonished them that "being faithless to a military trust confided to him is the greatest reproach to the soldier." By June 1858, his total of 151 was the highest in his class.[23]

Despite his dismal first-year record, Custer wrote to Ann and David Reed on June 30, that "I would not leave this place for any amount of money because I would rather have a good education and no money, than to have a fortune and be ignorant." He described the month's examination period as lasting "unremittingly" and thought that his efforts during it did "honor not only to myself but to my instructors also."[24]

His efforts in the classroom did not represent his intellectual abilities and literary interests, however. In the spring, he checked out his first book from the West Point Library, *Swallow Barn,* a novel about Southerners by Pendleton Kennedy. The book's magnolia interpretation of plantation life and its hero, Ned Hazard, a dashing, romantic figure, appealed to Custer and probably influenced his view of American slaves and their masters. He then read James Fenimore Cooper's Leatherstocking Tales of the frontier and American Indians. For his ethics instructor, he wrote an essay on "The Red Man," a composition reflective of Cooper's "noble savage." It was his initial effort, but not his last. In time, he became a skillful and rather prolific writer. As one of his biographers has noted, he possessed "that burning need to write, to set down for posterity his own experiences." West Point seeped into the characters and souls of men in unexpected ways.[25]

Custer and his classmates' second academic year commenced in September 1858, at the conclusion of the summer encampment. Custer's course work consisted of English, French, mathematics, drawing, and equitation. Except for drawing, in which he ranked twenty-third, and horsemanship, in which he excelled, he stood near the bottom of his class in the other subjects. Although he had new victims for his mischief with the arrival of the plebes, he had no serious breaches of conduct throughout the year. Nevertheless, he compiled an even more dismal delinquency record with 192 demerits, only 8 short of the 200 that could result in dismissal. At year's end, he ranked overall fifty-sixth in a class now comprising sixty members.[26]

With the conclusion of examinations in June, the members of the Class of 1862 departed for their first furlough since they had entered the academy two years earlier. It had been eagerly anticipated for weeks, probably for months, by the third-classmen. For Custer, it could mean a reunion with Mollie Holland, who had been in his thoughts for a long time. During the year, he and she had exchanged letters, the contents of which intrigue as to the nature of their relationship.[27]

On November 13, 1858, Custer wrote to Mollie, recounting activities at West Point and discussing his visit to Ohio in the summer. Although he knew from her that her parents still objected to their relationship, he warned that he was "as full of mischief as ever." Then, evidently replying to a letter from Mollie, he added, "By the way I will see if we are not well enough acquainted to have a 'sleep' when I come home. Please say yes to it in your next and *you may impose any condition upon me.*"[28]

Mollie answered Custer's letter with two of her own, "two sweet and encouraging letters," as he described them. From his response, dated New Year's Day, Mollie apparently mentioned the "sleep," and supplied him with gossip about other young persons.[29]

Custer's letter of January 1 was lengthy and frank. There were couples back home, he said, who had allegedly been in bed together. "Tell me whether I can come and see you or not when I come home," he asked. "At your house what room do you have as your own, and tell what plan you can make up so that we can have that great 'sleep' now do not put me off by saying that you cannot think of any but tell me some one and another thing." This time he made no mention of any conditions about their "sleep" together as he had in the previous letter.[30]

Whether Custer and Mollie Holland had the "great 'sleep'" together when he returned to Ohio during the summer eludes historical inquiry. Undoubtedly, he visited her town, dashing in his cadet uniform. If he saw her, it was probably the last time. He never forgot Mollie, regarded her affectionately, and during the Civil War sent her a photograph of himself as a brigadier general and a silver star taken from the uniform of a captured Confederate general. Mollie Holland had been his first love, a memory that always lingered softly.[31]

Custer spent much of his two-month furlough at his family home in New Rumley and at the Reed home in Monroe. His parents, three brothers, and sister certainly celebrated his homecoming. Autie was special, and deeply missed. Emanuel had much more to brag about, and Maria to fret about. When the time came for his departure, at least Autie and his mother cried—it would always be that way. He reported for duty at West Point by 2 P.M., August 28, 1859, as specified by orders.[32]

On Monday, August 29, Custer was admitted to the Post Hospital at West Point. A three-story stone building, with two-story wings, the hospital was located behind the barracks near the South Gate. Commissioned Regular Army officers served as surgeons, and to one of them Custer reported that day. The surgeon diagnosed his illness as gonorrhea, an infectious disease caused by the gonococcus bacterium. With an incubation period of seven to ten days, gonorrhea causes a painful urethral discharge in men. Custer contracted the disease while on furlough, either from an infected female acquaintance or, more likely, from a prostitute, probably in New York City. It was a common malady among cadets who had been on furlough.[33]

During the era, treatment consisted of various metallic solutions— chlorate of potash, sulfate of zinc, nitrate of silver, sugar of lead, or mercury—injected urethrally. Any such treatment, however, was palliative only; the disease and its painful effects would have to run their course. For some victims, there would be little or no lasting harm. But since the treatment did not destroy the bacterium, which lodged in the prostate gland, seminal vesicles, and vas deferens, a victim could be rendered sterile by scarring and fibrousness of the urethral tract and of the sperm passageway. If the fibrousness was severe and persistent, a surgeon inserted a metal rod and scraped the tract.[34]

In Custer's case, the severity of the disease and the duration of the symptoms cannot be determined. He never wrote about it, and if his cadet friends knew of it, they maintained a subsequent silence. In two letters he wrote that fall, however, he noted that he had been ill for some time and that "I was detained in the hospital during the beginning of the present term." In time, like others so afflicted, he would be free of the disease. If the illness persisted, as he seemed to indicate in the letters, the possibility increased significantly that the infection caused sterility.[35]

The illness affected his classwork, or as he stated in a letter, put him "behind in studies." With the increase in his course load, Custer struggled throughout the academic year. He studied French, Spanish, drawing, swordsmanship, infantry drill, natural philosophy, astronomy, optics, and acoustics. At the conclusion of examinations in June 1860, Custer ranked again near the bottom of his class, which now consisted of fifty-seven members. In general merit, which included a cadet's disciplinary record, he was last in the class.[36]

His demerits totaled 191 for the year, one less than during the previous twelve months. The 1859–1860 record, however, contained a three-month period in which Custer received no demerits. He had compiled skins at a faster pace than in the past, with his final ones earned on March 19, 1860. Confronted with the reality of dismissal if he did not alter his behavior, Custer obeyed the rules, finishing the academic year without another demerit. In July, authorities rewarded him and others for their conduct by allowing them off the post for one day.[37]

The 1860–1861 academic year at West Point began as usual after summer encampment. On September 8, Major John F. Reynolds replaced Lieutenant Colonel William H. Hardee as commandant of cadets. It was a welcome change, as Hardee was "disliked by all the cadets." A month later, the entire corps passed in review for Albert Edward, Prince of Wales, and an estimated 6,000 spectators. The British royal visitor, wrote Tully McCrea, "is a grand humbug in the shape of a well dressed Dutch boy with monstrous big feet." McCrea's unflattering opinion of the prince may have been influenced by the fact that he and his comrades waited three hours in ranks with muskets for the prince to arrive. But the corps marched with precision for the crowd which afterward termed it the "best review that they ever saw," in McCrea's words.[38]

The uniform stride of the corpsmen on the Plain could not mask the discordant voices in the barracks. Few, if any, cadets avoided discussion of the forthcoming presidential election. Politicians in the slaveholding states had warned of the consequences if the outcome favored Republican Abraham Lincoln, and their predictions of secession meant difficult choices for the cadets from that region. As the election neared, a group of Southern cadets hanged a figure of Lincoln in effigy in front of the barracks. They removed it before daylight, so few others knew of the act. But in early November, Lincoln and the Republicans won an electoral victory.[39]

A few days after the news reached West Point, Custer wrote to his sister, Ann Reed. "The election has passed," he began. "I fear that there will be much trouble." All the Southern cadets, he informed her, had decided to resign from the academy when their states seceded. Two of them had submitted resignations already. "You cannot imagine how sorry I will be to see this happen," he continued, "as the majority of my best friends and all my roommates except one have been from the South." Duties at the academy might be suspended, he thought, but he knew that if war resulted the country "would be impoverished." "I sincerely hope we may be spared this Sorrow."[40]

As Custer noted, a handful of Southerners departed before their states withdrew from the Union. South Carolina initiated the secession movement on December 20, 1860, followed during the next several weeks by Georgia, Florida, Alabama, Mississippi, Louisiana, and Texas. The decisions of these states accelerated the resignations of cadets. By year's end, Custer's friend John "Gimlet" Lea of Mississippi was gone. One Saturday morning while walking an extra duty tour, Custer saw two classmates, John Kelly and Charles Ball, being carried on the shoulders of friends toward South Gate. They were leaving, and Custer stopped and saluted them with his musket at present arms.[41]

Most of the Southerners hesitated, however. They were torn by conflicting allegiances and personal interest. For members of the Class of 1861, in particular, a resignation meant that over four years of rules, discipline, classwork, and all the other sacrifices demanded by the academy would be lost. If war could be avoided until after commencement, they could then leave as graduates. They wrote home for advice, conversed with friends, and waited. At least in January, midyear examinations consumed their time.[42]

The previous months of excitement and discord had evidently affected study habits, as the examination board declared thirty-three cadets academically deficient, including Custer. Most of them were allowed to take a reexamination, but they still panicked. The ones who failed French tried to bribe the instructor's servant for a copy of the test. When that ploy failed, they sneaked into his office, pried open a locked desk, took the exam back to the barracks, copied it, and returned it to the desk. Custer, meanwhile, "in a desperate fix," according to Tully McCrea, entered an instructor's room at the hotel and began copying the test until he heard someone approaching. He ripped the page from the book and fled. But the professor discovered it and prepared a different one.[43]

"He has narrowly escaped several times before," McCrea grumbled about Custer, "but unluckily he did not take warning, and now it is too late, and he will always have cause to repent of his folly." But for reasons neither Custer nor McCrea understood, the former was reinstated, the only one in the class. He was declared "not proficient" only in ethics, while passing infantry and cavalry tactics, chemistry, and drawing.[44]

February brought the formation of the Confederate States of America, with Jefferson Davis as president, in Montgomery, Alabama. At West Point, Superintendent P. G. T. Beauregard, a Louisianan, was relieved, after holding the post for barely a fortnight. Additional Southerners started for home to volunteer for military service in the rapidly organizing units. On February 22, in honor of George Washington's birthday, authorities declared a holiday. At one point during the day, the academy band played songs. When it struck "The Star-Spangled Banner," Northern cadets, listening from barracks windows, cheered, while "Dixie" elicited a similar response from Southerners. It became a contest between the two groups. At one window stood Custer; at another, Rosser. It would be a long time until these best of friends stood shoulder-to-shoulder again, listening to music, as comrades.[45]

With Lincoln's inauguration on March 4, the national crisis quickened. If there was to be war, it appeared that it could ignite at either of two forts in South Carolina and Florida, where Confederate officials demanded their abandonment by the federal government.

In an April 10 letter to Ann Reed, Custer described "the excitement" at West Point as "so great." Everyone spoke of war, and "I have scarcely thought of anything else." The post's enlisted personnel were leaving for duty with the army. "When war is once begun between the north & south," he asserted, "it will be beyond the power of human foresight to predict when and where it will terminate or what will be the consequences." The professors told the corps that they should be prepared to leave, without graduating, to drill the recruits that would pour into the army in the event of war.[46]

Two days after Custer wrote the letter, Southern artillerymen opened fire on Fort Sumter in the harbor of Charleston, South Carolina, the cannon's roar echoing across the nation. The fort's commander surrendered on the fourteenth, and Lincoln reacted with a call for volunteers to save the Union. Within a week, thirty-seven Southern cadets, including Tom Rosser and John Pelham, chose allegiance to their states and boarded a steamer for home. West Point's academic staff recommended that the remaining members of the Class of 1861 be graduated at once, and that the course work of the Class of 1862 be accelerated so its members could graduate in May.[47]

The recent events moved Custer to write to his sister again on April 26. Earlier she had corresponded with him, hoping that he would be spared from the conflict, "but in times like the present," he responded, "we should discard all private and personal desires and consider nothing but the prosperity and welfare of our country." All citizens must "reflect upon the obligations we are under to the government." Because of the education he had received at the academy, if he refused to volunteer, he would be guilty of "the basest ingratitude." In fact, he had already offered his services to the governor of Ohio, he informed his sister. If the secretary of war allowed a transfer from regular to volunteer service, he preferred to be in a unit from his native state. Duty with volunteers, he added, would also mean a higher rank for himself.[48]

On May 6, an order from the War Department was read to the corps at West Point, directing the forty-five members of the Class of 1861 to report to the adjutant general's office in Washington, D.C., for duty with the army. The instructions also designated the Class of 1862 as the First Class and appointed its commissioned and noncommissioned officers. That same day, the class members began an intense abbreviated course of instruction that would substitute for their fifth year. By month's end, Custer noted that "the class are beginning to look thin and pale," from the lack of sleep and amount of study. "We are all so anxious to be prepared fully for the duties of our calling," he explained. Then: "If it is my lot to fall in the defence of my countrys rights, I will lay down my life as freely as if I had a thousand lives at my disposal."[49]

The second Class of 1861 was graduated on June 24. Custer's Irish friend, Patrick H. O'Rorke, ranked first in the class of thirty-four members, while Custer stood last. As the Ohioan joked later, "only thirty-four graduated, and of these thirty-three graduated above me." He had compiled another 192 demerits during the year, for a four-year total of 726, the most in the class. His best subject his final year was artillery tactics; his worst, cavalry tactics.[50]

The graduates filtered away from West Point to various assignments as orders were received. Custer's orders had not arrived by June 29, when he was appointed officer of the day for the summer encampment. During the evening, Cadet William Ludlow and two others taunted Cadet Peter M. Ryerson, a plebe. After Ryerson threatened them with a bayonet, the three upperclassmen walked away. Ryerson then reported the incident to Custer at the guard tent, and while there, Ludlow appeared and called Ryerson a coward. Ludlow was "a damned fool," Ryerson shot back, and Ludlow punched him in the face. The two antagonists grabbed each other, stumbling into the tent ropes. As other cadets gathered to witness the fracas, Custer exclaimed, "Stand back boys, let's have a fair fight," or words to that effect. Finally, several of the onlookers separated the pair. When two academy officers approached, the crowd dispersed. The next morning, Custer reported to Commandant Reynolds and was placed in arrest.[51]

The court-martial convened on July 5, with nine officers comprising the board. First Lieutenant Stephen Benét served as judge advocate. The charges, each with a specification, were neglect of duty and "conduct to the prejudice of good order and military discipline." In the specifications, Custer failed to "suppress a quarrel between two cadets," and "did give countenance to a quarrel." Cadets Ludlow and Ryerson testified that it was not a serious matter, only a "scuffle." First Lieutenant William B. Hazen, an assistant instructor of tactics and one of the two officers who ended the affair, acted as a character reference for the defendant.[52]

In his defense, Custer submitted a four-page statement to the court on the sixth. He argued that he had regarded the fight as a "trifling" matter. Continuing, he asked for the court's understanding. "I plodded my way for four long years," he averred, and now all he wanted to do was join his classmates in the conflict. The court considered his statement, and then found him guilty on both charges. Benét released the sentence, to be "reprimanded in orders," on July 15, adding that "the court was lenient in the sentence, owing to the peculiar situation of Cadet Custer represented in his defense, and in consideration of his general good conduct as testified to by Lieutenant Hazen, his immediate commander."[53]

In Washington, meanwhile, Congressman John A. Bingham, who

had appointed Custer to the academy, interceded on his behalf at the War Department. Custer or someone else at West Point probably apprised him of the incident. Bingham's efforts resulted in orders for Custer to report for duty at the capital. On July 18, the last member of the class boarded a steamer for New York City. He surely looked back as the boat churned into the current, for West Point would always be a special place for him—as his wife related afterward, "its traditions were dear to him."[54]

In New York City, he purchased a lieutenant's uniform, a sword, a pistol, and spurs at Horstmann's, and posed for a photograph for his sister. He then boarded a train for Washington, and for an obligation demanded of all a divided nation's citizenry.[55]

A BEGINNING

■ Brevet Lieutenant General Winfield Scott was older than the capital itself. A teenager when President John Adams moved into the new Executive Mansion, he had received his appointment to the army from Adams's successor, Thomas Jefferson, in 1808. Since then, the army had been his life, and in it, he had fashioned one of the most distinguished careers in American military history. In 1847, his army had captured Mexico City in a brilliant campaign, ending the conflict with Mexico. When the Civil War began, Scott was the country's most respected soldier, a legend.

At seventy-five years of age, however, his once magnificent six-foot five-inch frame was now little more than a tired hulk, ravaged by time and obesity. Proud and vain, "Old Fuss and Feathers," as his men had dubbed him, could neither work long hours nor sit on a horse. Field command was physically impossible, but from his office at the War Department, he could use his ample abilities and experience as Abraham Lincoln's chief military advisor. He had no illusions or romantic notions about the forthcoming nightmare, predicting that it would require four years and incalculable manpower to subdue the rebellious states. His words, however, went unheeded.[1]

Since Fort Sumter, the two sections had raced toward a bloodletting, convinced that one battle would settle the issue. Scott and other professionals knew better. The thousands of recruits flooding into regiments required training and time, a seasoning, to make of them an army. But in a democracy, soldiers' voices could be silenced by the clamor of politicians and citizens. Northerners demanded an advance on Richmond, Virginia, the relocated Confederate capital, a scant hundred miles south of Washington. A Union army went forth into the Old Dominion in mid-July. By Saturday, the twentieth, twenty-five miles southwest of Washington, Northerner and Southerner confronted each other across a creek called Bull Run.

That Saturday afternoon, Second Lieutenant George A. Custer reported to the adjutant general's office at the War Department. Custer had arrived early in the morning in Washington, D.C., visited briefly at a hotel with his former roommate, James Parker, and then went to the military headquarters. He wrote later that the building boiled with activity as everyone waited for news of fighting at the front. In the adjutant general's office, he learned that he had been assigned to Company G, Second United States Cavalry, Major Innes Palmer commanding. The regiment, he was told, was with Brigadier General Irvin McDowell's army at Centreville, Virginia, just east of Bull Run.[2]

The adjutant general then ushered Custer into the office of General Scott. The old warrior, whom Custer had seen only from a distance at West Point during a visit, was surrounded by officers and members of Congress, all of whom were studying maps. The interview was brief, with Scott asking the second lieutenant what he preferred. Custer, as he recalled, "stammered" that he wanted to join his company at once. Scott issued the order, but cautioned him that he might not find a horse in the city. If he succeeded in locating a mount, Scott added, he should report back at 7 P.M. for dispatches the general wanted delivered to McDowell.[3]

Custer spent the next few hours searching stables for a horse, but discovered none. With little hope left, he stumbled upon an enlisted man he had known at West Point. The soldier explained that he had been sent into the city by Captain Charles Griffin to secure a spare horse that Griffin's battery had left behind when it advanced with the army. The man offered Custer the use of the animal—ironically, it was a mount named Wellington that the former cadet had ridden at the academy. About nightfall, with the dispatches, Custer and his companion crossed the Potomac River on the Long Bridge. The pair rode most of the night, arriving at Centreville about 3 A.M. Custer delivered the correspondence at army headquarters, ate breakfast, and learned that the army would attack that morning. No one knew with certainty his regiment's location, but Custer rode forward, weaving through the columns of infantry and artillery batteries that would implement McDowell's offensive.[4]

Custer overtook the Second United States Cavalry near the army's van, was introduced to its commander and various officers, and then joined his company. It had been less than four days since he had de-

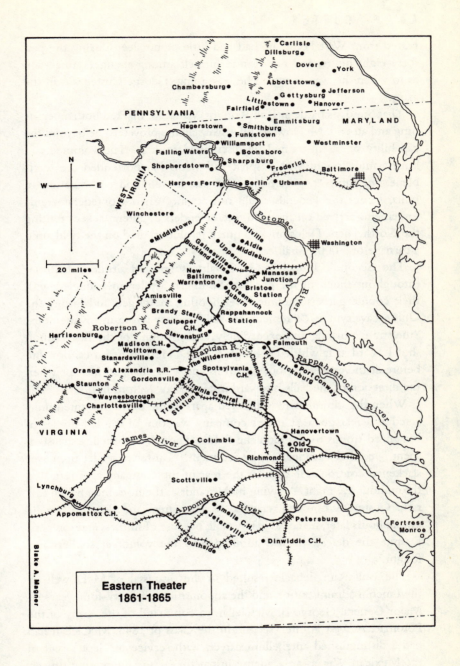

**Eastern Theater
1861–1865**

Blake A. Magner

parted from West Point; he had had little or no sleep during the past forty-eight hours, and now found himself among strangers, uncertain as to where he was or where he was going. George Custer was in the army.[5]

That Sunday's battle at Bull Run, or Manassas, marked both a beginning and an end. McDowell's offensive scheme proved to be beyond the capability of his ill-trained, ill-disciplined soldiers. The volunteers in both armies fought with a spirit and valor that portended the terribleness of future engagements. But attacks required coordination of units, tactics the Federals could not attain. When Confederate reinforcements arrived on the field, the defenders counterattacked, routing the Northerners. Delusions of a quick resolution died on the field amid a carnage of 5,000 casualties.

The Second United States Cavalry supported artillery batteries throughout much of the combat. Southern artillerymen dueled with their counterparts, sometimes overshooting the targets and hitting the Union cavalrymen. "I remember well," Custer wrote in his memoirs, "the strange hissing and exceedingly vicious sound of the first cannon shot I heard as it whirled through the air." He had heard cannon fire before at the academy, "but a man listens with changed interest when the direction of the balls is toward instead of away from him."[6]

When the Union army splintered apart, some of the mounted units acted as a rear guard. Custer's company was one of the last bodies of organized troops to abandon the field. "Though famished, exhausted, spent," recalled a trooper in the regiment, "Custer never let up, never slackened control." He rode in the rear of the company as it retreated throughout the night. Arriving in Alexandria, the horsemen halted in a rain. Custer dismounted, crawled under a tree, and slept. When he awoke hours later, he could barely walk because of stiffness and soreness. Despite the defeat, he had admired how the volunteer soldiers had fought.[7]

The Bull Run debacle resulted in the dismissal of McDowell by the Lincoln administration and the appointment of thirty-four-year-old Major General George B. McClellan to command of the Army of the Potomac. A West Pointer, second in the Class of 1846, McClellan had had a distinguished antebellum career, with service on Scott's staff in the Mexican War, as an academy instructor, as an engineering officer, as an observer during the Crimean War in Europe, and as the inventor

of the "McClellan saddle," which became standard equipment for officers and mounted units. In 1857, he resigned his commission to enter
the railroad industry. When Fort Sumter fell, Governor William Den-
nison of Ohio appointed him major general of state volunteers. A
month later, Lincoln commissioned him a major general in the Regular
Army, assigning him to command of troops in a department that embraced Kentucky and western Virginia.[8]

In June and July, McClellan's troops won minor victories in the
mountains of western Virginia, protecting the vital Baltimore & Ohio
Railroad and fostering the allegiance of the citizens that eventually led
to the creation of West Virginia. With the North clamoring for success
after Bull Run, Lincoln summoned McClellan to Washington. The
general possessed ability in the administrative and organizational aspects
of an army and began at once to restore morale and reforge the Union
command.[9]

Each element of the army underwent reorganization. On August 3,
Congress enacted a law that reorganized all mounted Regular Army
units into a uniform command designated as "Cavalry." The antebellum
dragoon, mounted rifle, and cavalry regiments were either renamed
or renumbered. The Second United States Cavalry, Custer's regiment,
became the Fifth and was attached to the brigade of Brigadier General
Philip Kearny.[10]

Like McClellan, Kearny had joined the army after Bull Run, and
when he assumed command of New Jersey regiments, he needed staff
officers. As the junior lieutenant in the Fifth United States Cavalry,
Custer was assigned to the general's staff. Custer served with Kearny,
who had lost his left arm in the Mexican War, for several weeks, rising
from aide-de-camp to assistant adjutant general. In his memoirs, Custer
described Kearny as "a very peculiar, withal a very gallant leader," and
as "the strictest disciplinarian" of all the generals he knew in the war.
Custer's duty on the staff ended when an order was issued forbidding
Regular Army officers from serving under volunteer officers.[11]

On October 3, Custer was granted a leave of absence because of
illness until December 2. Although the nature or seriousness of his
affliction is unknown, the leave was extended until February 1862.
When he returned to the army, he wrote to Tully McCrea, stating that
he had been so sick at one time that he was not expected to live. If he
passed through such a crisis, he apparently fully recovered.[12]

As he had during his academy furlough in 1859, Custer divided his time during the leave between his parents' home and David and Ann Reed's in Monroe, Michigan. In the spring of 1861, Emanuel and Maria Custer had left New Rumley and purchased an eighty-acre farm in Wood County in northwestern Ohio. Nineteen-year-old Nevin and thirteen-year-old Boston helped their father, while sixteen-year-old Tom, whose hero was his older brother Autie, had enlisted as a private in the Twenty-first Ohio a month before Autie returned home. Tom was tempered in the same forge as his soldier-brother.[13]

Monroe, however, attracted Custer more than his family's farm in rural Ohio. For a young man in an officer's uniform, the community's inducements were evident. Here were old friends and eligible young women, and he embraced the social life during the winter weeks. On one occasion, however, he and a male companion were publicly drunk, stumbling along a street together. When he reached the Reed home, Ann—"my darling sister," as he called her—was embarrassed and angered by the spectacle and secured a promise from him that he would never drink alcoholic beverages again. He never did.[14]

By the first week of February 1862, Custer had rejoined the army. Since his departure four months earlier, no major engagement had occurred along the Virginia front. While the Confederates were encamped around Centreville, with outposts and detachments pushed toward Washington, the Federals remained behind their works outside of the capital. Recruits swelled the army's ranks, and when weather permitted, the fields bristled with regiments on drill. President Lincoln had prodded for a movement, an advance that might silence the criticism of the administration. McClellan, however, deflected such advice or interference. A man of obsessive caution, he accepted as accurate inflated estimates of Rebel strength. The army required time and training —Scott had said as much before Bull Run—before it met the enemy again. The lumbering beast that he commanded would not move until McClellan, not civilians, gave the order.[15]

While McClellan may have refused to unsheathe the weapon, he had recast an amalgam of regiments, brigades, and batteries into an army. He labored long hours with the details of organization, supply, drill, and morale. His skill as a commander became evident throughout the command. With the cavalry, however, McClellan limited its role. Although the mounted arm had problems with arms and equipment and with untrained recruits, McClellan further crippled its effectiveness by his interpretation of its function. To him, cavalry acted as outpost guards, as mounted sentries to prevent surprise enemy attacks. When it performed scouting duty, it did so in small numbers and within limited areas.

More important, McClellan failed to organize the cavalry into an independent arm. While his counterpart at Centreville, Confederate General Joseph E. Johnston, was forming a cavalry brigade that could operate on its own under the brilliant James Ewell Brown "Jeb" Stuart, McClellan was attaching individual mounted regiments to infantry units. His cavalry commander, Brigadier General George Stoneman, acted only as an administrator, not as a tactical commander. The result was that, in the words of a Pennsylvania trooper, "the cavalry were for the most part scattered about and used as escorts, strikers, dog-robbers and orderlies for all the generals and their numerous staff officers from the highest in rank down to the second lieutenants." In time, Jeb Stuart would demonstrate the capabilities of a unified mounted force.[16]

For cavalry officers like Custer, routine duty marked the days during February. He secured a pass to visit the capital, and enjoyed a day of serenading friends and young women with a former academy classmate, Leroy Elbert. "Everywhere," he informed Ann Reed, "we were offered fashionable wine and liquors, but *nowhere did I touch a drop.*" They spent some time with Elbert's "sweetheart," prodding Custer to joke to his sister that "I am not blessed with such a treasure (?)."[17]

On March 9, 1862, the Confederates abandoned their lines around Centreville, marching south toward central Virginia and behind the Rappahannock and Rapidan rivers. Johnston had anticipated for weeks some movement by McClellan, believing that if the Federals undertook an offensive, his position was indefensible. Without informing President Jefferson Davis, and destroying a hugh stockpile of foodstuffs, Johnston directed his army out of its winter encampment.[18]

When Union scouts reported the empty works, McClellan ordered the cavalry to trail the retreating enemy and to probe for information. The mounted units began the pursuit immediately, including the Fifth United States. About twenty miles south of Manassas Junction, the Yankees collided with Johnston's rear guard. Stoneman, who was directing the Federal horsemen, instructed Lieutenant Colonel William Grier of the Fifth to select an officer and a detachment to drive in the enemy pickets. Custer volunteered for the assignment, and Grier gave him fifty men, with another company as support.[19]

When Custer saw the enemy videttes, he ordered a charge at a gallop, riding at the column's head. The Rebels fired a few shots and fled southward across a bridge over a small stream. The Yankees pursued until they encountered an enemy force of about 300. They opened with carbines—"the bullets rattled like hail several whizzed close to my head," Custer asserted to his parents. Before Custer could retire, three of his men were wounded and a horse was killed. In camp, he reported directly to Stoneman and then was interviewed by three newspapermen. In his letter to his parents that described the action, he told them he was well, weighed 176 pounds, had not changed clothing in a week, and had secured a black foxhound as a companion in the deserted Rebel camps. For the first time, he had led cavalry in an attack.[20]

In this March 17 letter, Custer also reported that because of the Confederate withdrawal the Union army expected to move southward on transports down the Potomac River. With McClellan in command, he assured his parents, victory would result. "I have more confidence in him than any man living," Custer stated. "I am willing to forsake everything and follow him to the ends of the earth and would lay down my life for him if necessary. He is here now, I wish you could see him, every one officer & private worship him, & would fight any one who would say anything against him."[21]

On that same day, the Federal units began filing onto transports in the river. An exasperated President Lincoln had finally succeeded in getting McClellan to act. While he and the general differed on details of the operation, Lincoln approved McClellan's plan to advance on Richmond from the east, up the Virginia Peninsula between the York and James rivers. "I had hoped, let me say," the general argued later, "by rapid movements to drive before me or capture the enemy on the Peninsula, open the James River, and press on to Richmond before he should be materially re-enforced from other portions of his territory." At the Peninsula's tip lay Fortress Monroe and toward there McClellan's vast host came by water.[22]

Almost 400 vessels—steamers, barges, schooners—hauled over 120,000 men, 15,000 horses, 44 batteries, and 1,150 wagons from Washington to the Peninsula in twenty days. Custer described it as "the greatest expedition ever fitted out" as he prepared to board the *Adele*

Felicia on March 26. The river brimmed with ships, he noted, and all of the officers and troops were confident of victory because they were "going south under the greatest and best of men, Genl. McClellan." He repeated that he would sacrifice his life for the "just cause" in which they were engaged. By month's end, Custer and his regiment had disembarked at Fortress Monroe.[23]

While authorities in Richmond had learned of the massive operation soon after it began, Johnston's army was still positioned behind the Rappahannock River, approximately fifty miles north of the Confederate capital. On the Peninsula, roughly 12,000 troops under Major General John B. Magruder held Yorktown, twenty miles up the York River from Fortress Monroe. If Davis and Johnston expected Magruder to delay the Yankees, the general needed reinforcements. Fortunately for the Southerners, McClellan preferred maneuver to battle, and when he studied Magruder's works behind the Warwick River, he began siege operations, planning to plummet the defenses with heavy cannon. That would take time—the commodity that the Confederates needed to transfer Johnston's units to the Peninsula.[24]

Twice during the siege Custer came under fire on reconnaissance missions. In one of them, he and another officer crawled up a hill to locate a Rebel battery. In the other, he accompanied infantry and encountered enemy sharpshooters. For one hour, the skirmish flared; "everyone got behind a tree and blazed away as hard as he could," wrote Custer. "I got awful tired of my hiding-place" until reinforcements scattered the Confederates. The next day they buried the dead in blankets. "It seemed hard," he related, "but it could not be helped. Some were quite young and boyish, and, looking at their faces, I could not but think of my own younger brother."[25]

His accounts of combat brought responses from the family. His father wrote, describing his mother's concern: "she troubles hir self so much about you and Thomas and she doant like to here of you being so venturesom. she thinks that there is no caul for you to throw your self in so much danger." Ann Reed also cautioned him: "My dear Brother I want you to be very careful of yourself. Don't expose yourself you know how much your parents depend on you and how much we all love you."[26]

Before he received the letters, Custer assured his sister that he was in "excellent health" and "in as good spirits as it is possible." "It is said," he continued, "that there is no real or perfect happiness during this life, this may be true but I often think that I am perfectly happy." His optimism he attributed to his "disposition."[27]

Not long afterward, Custer reported for staff duty. The circumstances of the transfer are unclear, but the evidence suggests that he was appointed an assistant engineer on the staff of Brigadier General Andrew A. Humphreys, the army's chief of topographical engineers. Although he served under Humphreys's orders, Custer was detached to the staff of Brigadier General William F. Smith, commander of the Second Division, Fourth Corps. His prior service with Philip Kearny the previous autumn had not prepared him for the onerous tasks a staff officer may perform during a campaign in the field.[28]

Custer's initial mission for "Baldy" Smith, as the general was known in the army, was unexpected and beyond his previous experience. Accompanying the army was a balloon corps, under the direction of "Professor" Thaddeus S. C. Lowe, who had developed a portable hydrogen generator for the gas required for the balloons. McClellan had utilized them from the campaign's outset whenever the weather permitted. Confederate artillerists enjoyed firing shots at the potlike targets above the trees, although they never hit one of them. On April 11, Brigadier General Fitz-John Porter, commander of the Fifth Corps, ascended in a balloon that broke from its moorings, floating toward Confederate lines until a wind shift shoved it back to safety.[29]

As Custer recounted his first trip up in a balloon, he sat in the bottom of the basket, gripping both sides as it climbed into the air. One of Lowe's assistants worked the balloon as the lieutenant surveyed the Confederate works. "I had the finest view I ever had in my life & could see both armies at once," he declared in a letter. Smith sent him up, alone, three more times. On the night of May 3, while in the balloon, Custer detected the Confederate abandonment of Yorktown and retreat up the Peninsula. He notified Smith, who telegraphed McClellan's headquarters.[30]

The Yankees entered the empty works on the fourth. Custer and another staff officer dashed across a dam on the river and were the first Federals into that sector of the lines. McClellan ordered a pursuit. Both armies crawled westward during the day as rain and marching men churned the muddy roads into muck that mired wagons and artillery pieces. Infantrymen shouldered the vehicles forward; teamsters cursed and whipped the animals. On the morning of the fifth, the Northerners collided with Johnston's rear guard at Williamsburg, the old colonial capital of Virginia.[31]

The Battle of Williamsburg began before 7 A.M., when Union Brigadier General Joseph Hooker's division, following Lee's Mill Road, approached Fort Magruder, an earthen redoubt a mile and a half east of the town. The fighting started fitfully in the wet woodlands, but once Hooker deployed his brigades and posted the artillery, the combat escalated into a fierce engagement. On Hooker's right, Baldy Smith's division covered Yorktown Road. Here Smith learned from a black contraband that a road cut through the woods, crossed a dam on Cub Creek, and continued on toward Williamsburg, beyond the enemy flank. The Confederates had built a redoubt at the dam, but no troops manned it. Smith sent Custer to ascertain the accuracy of the man's story.[32]

When Custer returned with the confirmation, Smith requested permission from Brigadier General Edwin V. Sumner, McClellan's designated commander in the field, to advance across the dam with his entire division. Sumner denied the request—Smith held the center of the Union line. Smith prodded, and Sumner relented, agreeing to one brigade. Smith selected Brigadier General Winfield Scott Hancock's brigade, bolstering its strength with two regiments and two batteries. Smith assigned Custer to Hancock.[33]

Hancock was an aggressive brigadier, the best in the division. He rode to his leading regiment, the Fifth Wisconsin, Colonel Amasa Cobb commanding. Pointing to Custer, Hancock told Cobb, "He says that he had found a place where he can cross the stream and turn the enemy's left flank; you will follow him with your regiment and effect a crossing if possible. Keep a sharp lookout for surprises and keep me advised of everything of importance. I will be near you with the brigade." Cobb formed the regiment, and Custer led it on an "obscure wagon track through heavy timber," in Cobb's words. When the Wisconsin men cleared the trees, Custer took them across the dam. Cobb shifted his companies into a battle line, while Custer rode back to report to Hancock.[34]

Hancock closed to within almost a mile of Fort Magruder, aligning his 3,400 men and cannon on a rise above a wheatfield. The Confederates countered this threat with a brigade that advanced to the attack.

The Southern regiments did not charge in concert, and Hancock's troops and guns ripped the units apart, turning the wheatfield into a slaughter pit. The Federals counterattacked, pushing into woods beyond the field. Custer rode in front of the line, capturing a captain and five soldiers himself. He claimed that he also seized an enemy battle flag—white with a red cross, made of silk—although none of the Confederate regiments reported the loss. He "was in the thickest of the fight from morning till night," he boasted to Ann Reed. Hancock cited Custer in his report.[35]

Among the Confederate prisoners was John "Gimlet" Lea, a classmate of Custer's, who had been wounded in the leg. When the Mississippian met his academy friend, he hugged Custer and cried. Custer received permission to attend to Lea, and while the army resumed the pursuit, he remained behind for two days. As the two friends separated, Custer gave Lea stockings and some money. The Confederate officer scribbled in Custer's notebook that if the Federal was captured the Southerners should treat him well. With that, Lea said. "God bless you old boy."[36]

Custer overtook the army as it marched leisurely up the Peninsula. A soldier in the ranks described the pursuit as "marked by genuine enjoyment." By May 20, advance elements of McClellan's command reached the Chickahominy River, a stream that flowed southeasterly across the region, emptying into the James River. Normally forty feet wide, the river had overrun its banks because of the recent rains, inundating the forested bottomlands along its course. Beyond the Chickahominy, the Confederates manned old fieldworks about three miles from Richmond.[37]

When the Rebels had passed the river, Johnston ordered the bridges burned and detached units to guard the crossings. While the Union army closed on the river, details of engineering officers reconnoitered along the stream's northern bank for crossing sites. Custer accompanied Brigadier General John G. Barnard, the army's chief engineer, wading into the waters on several occasions to test the depth at various locations. It was dangerous duty—enemy sharpshooters could be hidden anywhere in the woods beyond the river—but Custer never hesitated. He possessed an absolute fearlessness that had attracted the attention of superior officers.[38]

On May 24, the Federals attempted crossings at several sites on the

Chickahominy. At New Bridge, seven miles below Mechanicsville, Lieutenant Nicolas Bowen and a number of staff officers, including Custer, conducted the operation with a force of infantry and cavalry. At a signal, Companies A and B of the Fourth Michigan, led by Bowen and Custer, dashed to a ford located one half mile above the burned span that the two officers had discovered the day before. While one company crossed the river, the second company moved downstream where the remainder of the regiment engaged the Confederates at New Bridge. The Southerners—Louisianans and Georgians—repulsed the sortie at the bridge until the Yankees on their side of the stream plowed into their flank.[39]

The Rebels turned to meet this threat when Custer plunged his chestnut mare into the river and recrossed to the north bank. Four companies of the Fourth Michigan charged down the slope. As they neared the bank, Custer met them, shouting, "Go in Wolverines, give them hell." With rifles and cartridge belts above their heads, they waded through the water, scrambled up the opposite bank, and triggered a volley into the enemy ranks. The Confederates fell back about a mile to their main position, losing roughly fifty men to capture. Bowen deployed the Michiganders in a ditch while Custer advanced with a line of skirmishers. For the next three hours, the opponents exchanged gunfire until Bowen ordered a withdrawal. In his report of the action, Bowen noted that Custer was the first man across the river and the last to leave.[40]

The results of the reconnaissance were relayed to McClellan, who described the affair in a message as "very gallant." Either Humphreys, Smith, or both of them commended Custer to McClellan. The army commander sent for the staff officer, and as McClellan recalled the meeting: "He was then a slim, long-haired boy, carelessly dressed. I thanked him for his gallantry, and asked him what I could do for him. He replied very modestly that he had nothing to ask, and evidently did not suppose that he had done anything to deserve extraordinary reward." McClellan then inquired if Custer would be interested in serving on his personal staff as an aide-de-camp. "Upon this," wrote McClellan, "he brightened up, assured me that he would regard such service as the most gratifying he could perform; and I at once gave the necessary orders."[41]

Custer's appointment to the staff was dated May 28. For months, he had written of his admiration for McClellan and of his willingness to "follow him to the ends of the earth." Perhaps no other superior officer would Custer have deeper affection for than "Little Mac," as the men called him. According to his future wife, "Autie adored General McClellan. It was the hero worship of a boy." In turn, McClellan described Custer "in those days" as "simply a reckless, gallant boy, undeterred by fatigue, unconscious of fear; but his head was always clear in danger, and he always brought me clear and intelligible reports of what he saw when under the heaviest fire. I became much attached to him." [42]

Staff duty at army headquarters entailed a myriad of responsibilities. Aides-de-camp conducted reconnaissances, delivered written and oral messages, relayed intelligence from subordinate commanders, acted as the commander's representative with units in action, and oversaw troop movements. The duty could mean hours in the saddle, infrequent meals, and exposure to enemy fire. It was training that would prove invaluable for an officer like Custer.

Custer had barely joined the staff when the campaign took a dramatic shift. Since the Confederate withdrawal from Yorktown, McClellan had conducted operations with his characteristic calculation. He shifted his supply base to White House on the Pamunkey River, reorganized the army's corps, and burned the telegraph wires to Washington with requests for reinforcements. In his mind, the Union force at Fredericksburg, Virginia, fifty miles north of Richmond, was critical to his plans for the final advance on the Rebel capital. Lincoln approved the strategy until Confederate Major General Thomas J. "Stonewall" Jackson threatened Federal units in the Shenandoah Valley. On May 24, McClellan learned that Lincoln had suspended the movement. The next day, the president wired that Jackson had captured Winchester and was threatening to march to the Potomac. "I think the time is near when you must either attack Richmond or give up the job and come to the defence of Washington," Lincoln advised. "Let me hear from you instantly." [43]

Although McClellan reacted furiously to the message—for a long time he had believed that Lincoln and Secretary of War Edwin Stanton had deliberately undermined his operations—he replied that "the time is near when I shall attack Richmond." Already units of the army had crossed to the south side of the Chickahominy and halted near the crossroads of Seven Pines and Fair Oaks Station on the Richmond &

York River Railroad. To the north, on the army's right flank, Union troops held Mechanicsville, from where the spires of Richmond could be seen by the Yankees. It appeared that the "one desperate blow" McClellan had predicted to his wife was now approaching.[44]

The blow came on May 31, not from McClellan, but from his opponent, Joseph Johnston. Like McClellan, the Confederate commander had his own difficulties with his president, Jefferson Davis, who had been urging an offensive against the enemy. With the Union army divided by the river, Johnston acted. The attack targeted the Yankees at Seven Pines and Fair Oaks, and for two days the combat was the fiercest of the campaign. Johnston's plan of assaults along converging roads faltered because of misunderstandings, the terrain, and command errors that allowed the Federals to hold the ground but only after reinforcements crossed the flooded stream.[45]

One of the Confederate prisoners at Seven Pines/Fair Oaks was Lieutenant James B. Washington, an aide-de-camp of Johnston. On the thirty-first, Washington stumbled into Federal pickets while carrying messages from his commander. Taken to McClellan's headquarters, the great-grandnephew of George Washington met Custer, an acquaintance from the academy. Washington once said that Custer was "the rarest man I knew at West Point." As he had with Gimlet Lea, Custer befriended the officer, sitting together for photographs and giving him some money before he was sent to the rear. Washington and his family never forgot the kindness.[46]

During the battle, Johnston fell wounded, and on June 1, Davis assigned General Robert E. Lee to command of the army. The war in the East now followed a different road. In time, Lee proved to be one of the finest generals in American military history. He possessed all the attributes of a great chieftain, none more important than his audacity, his willingness to accept risks in the struggle against long odds. Within less than four weeks, Lee had fashioned an offensive against McClellan. Jeb Stuart's cavalry rode around the Union army, confirming that McClellan's right flank was vulnerable. Lee brought Jackson's troops from the Shenandoah Valley and on June 26 attacked the Federals at Mechanicsville.[47]

The Northerners repulsed the assaults, but Lee's aggressiveness convinced McClellan that he must withdraw from Richmond. On the twenty-seventh, while the army's Fifth Corps fought the Confederates at Gaines's Mill, north of the Chickahominy, McClellan abandoned his base at White House and prepared for a retreat across the Peninsula to the James River. For the next four days, the Army of the Potomac was in a race for its life. McClellan's staff was involved in nearly all phases of the operation.[48]

When the Confederates struck at Mechanicsville, McClellan sent Custer to report on the situation. The aide complied, returned to army headquarters, and was hurried back with a message for the commander of the Pennsylvania Reserves to "maintain the honor of Pennsylvania." After he informed the officer of McClellan's words, he rode along the battle line, repeating them to each regiment, which brought cheers from the men. Later in the day, Custer assisted Chief Engineer Barnard in preparing a retreat route across the river. During the night of June 27–28, as the Federals abandoned their position at Gaine's Mill, Custer was on horseback, guiding brigades and directing the removal of the wounded.[49]

Custer spent four consecutive days in the saddle, snatching a few hours of sleep when he could. He generally ate one meal each day, breakfast of hard bread crumbled into coffee. Although of slender build, he was physically strong, with remarkable stamina. A few months earlier, his regimental commander had stated that Custer "can eat and sleep as much as anyone when he has the chance. But he can do without either when necessary!" The so-called Seven Days' Campaign ended on July 1, when the Federals repulsed Confederate assaults at Malvern Hill. McClellan then withdrew the army to Harrison's Landing, where Union gunboats on the James River shielded the troops with their armament.[50]

While the Confederates failed to destroy a portion of the Union army, Lee's offensive relieved Richmond and secured for him the strategic initiative in Virginia. McClellan remained entrenched at Harrison's Landing and blistered the Lincoln administration with demands for more men, blaming the officials for the campaign's outcome. In a letter of July 13, Custer reflected opinion at army headquarters by asserting that they had been outnumbered two to one. Despite the Southern victory in the operations, Federal morale held. McClellan had reviews of corps, and whenever he rode through the camps, the troops cheered, in the words of one of them, "for country, cause & leader." Near month's end, Custer wrote that "nothing interesting or exciting is transpiring here."[51]

On August 5, Custer accompanied a 300-man detachment on a reconnaissance toward Southern lines. He was now a first lieutenant in the Regular Army, dating from July 17, with the brevet, or temporary, rank of captain. Near White Oak Swamp, Custer located Rebel cavalry while scouting ahead. The Yankees charged, and in the fighting, Custer shot an enemy officer, the first man he killed in combat. He captured another one and a "splendid double-barreled" shotgun, which he sent home to his brother Boston. The detachment's commander, Colonel William W. Averell, cited Custer in his report for "gallant and spirited conduct." [52]

Two days prior to the reconnaissance, orders from Washington arrived at Harrison's Landing, directing McClellan to begin the withdrawal of the army from the Peninsula. For the better part of a fortnight, the administration and McClellan had debated future operations. The general proposed the renewal of an advance on Richmond, but only after he received 50,000 additional troops. The litany was all too familiar to the president and his advisors. Instead, Lincoln recalled McClellan's corps to combine them with the newly created Army of Virginia under Major General John Pope. Together, the forces could protect the capital while advancing overland against the Confederates. The orders were telegraphed on August 3. [53]

McClellan opposed the plan, and it was not until August 14 that the first contingent marched for Fortress Monroe and transport ships. A week later, he was at the embarkation point, overseeing the loading of units. During the withdrawal, McClellan granted Custer a brief leave to attend a wedding. Custer's friend Gimlet Lea, while recuperating from his wound in Williamsburg, had fallen in love with a young woman who had nursed him in her family's home. Before being exchanged and returned to duty, Lea wanted to be married, asking Custer to act as groomsman. During the ceremony, Custer in his blue uniform stood beside Lea in his gray uniform. The Federal officer was treated with hospitality and enjoyed himself. The friends parted, each bound by duty to be enemies on a battlefield. [54]

McClellan and his staff boarded a steamer on August 23, a general without an army. Six days later, Lee's army collided with Pope's, which included elements of the Army of the Potomac, on the old killing ground along Bull Run. The Second Battle of Bull Run, or Manassas, resulted in a Union defeat, with the Rebels caving in Pope's flank on August 30. By September 3, Lee's troops were approaching fords on the

Potomac River, preparatory to a raid with the entire army into Maryland. Reluctantly, the day before, Lincoln restored McClellan to command of the beaten forces. The news electrified the ranks—"the army idolized McClellan," claimed a New Yorker—and when he rode out of the capital to join them, cheers of "Little Mac is back!" rolled over the columns like one, long sustained volley of musketry. "Boys, go back to your camps," he said to them.[55]

Once Lee's veterans crossed into Maryland, they occupied Frederick until September 10, when the invaders marched west beyond South Mountain. The Federals followed cautiously, entering Frederick on the twelfth. Here two soldiers discovered a lost copy of Lee's orders, and with the information, McClellan advanced toward the mountain range. On the fourteenth, units of both armies fought for gaps, with the Southerners retiring after dark. The pursuit resumed the next day, with McClellan assigning Custer to the army's van to report developments to army headquarters. The Yankees found the enemy on hills between Antietam Creek and the village of Sharpsburg. It took McClellan another day to close his units and prepare for battle. On September 17, the fury was unleashed. From a signal station on the mountain to the east, a Union soldier described the scene in his diary: "It was the prettiest sight I ever beheld—shells flying in all directions, houses burning, musketry cracking & altogether the grandest sight imaginable." But within the cauldron, the carnage was staggering—24,000 casualties, the bloodiest day in American history. Lee's army clung to the field by the slimmest of margins.[56]

The opponents faced each other across the ravaged landscape for another day. Shielded by the darkness, the Confederates recrossed into Virginia. On the twentieth, McClellan pushed two divisions over the Potomac, igniting a rearguard clash at Shepherdstown. While Lee could claim a tactical victory at Antietam, his return to the Old Dominion was a strategic success for the Federals. Lincoln seized the opportunity to issue his preliminary Emancipation Proclamation on September 22. In Ohio, when the news of Lincoln's action arrived, the old Democrat, Emanuel Custer, fumed.[57]

For the next month, the Union army healed and rested in the vicinity of Sharpsburg. Once more, the president urged action, even visiting with McClellan during the first four days of October. The conference resolved little. During a review of the army, Lincoln sarcastically remarked to a friend that the troops were "only McClellan's bodyguard." The commanding general had reasons to want more time: the army needed rest, and supply problems had not been resolved. The president's patience, however, was draining away like the warmth of the autumn weather.[58]

Like most members of the army, Custer must have welcomed the respite. Duties at headquarters slowed. On September 26, he escorted paroled Confederate prisoners across the Potomac River under a flag of truce and enjoyed a "chat" of an hour with a few Southerners who knew some of his academy friends. When Lincoln visited, Custer's work increased, for he spent the entire day on horseback during the review. "After I get back to Monroe," he grumbled in a letter to Ann Reed, "I do not intend to eat hard bread, salt pork, nor drink coffee without milk—fashionable dishes in the army."[59]

On October 3, with the president in camp, Custer wrote a revealing letter to a cousin. "You ask me if I will not be glad when the last battle is fought," he stated, "so far as my country is concerned I, of course, must wish for peace, and will be glad when the war is ended, but if I answer for myself *alone,* I must say that I shall regret to see the war end I would be willing, yes glad, to see a battle every day during my life. Now do not misunderstand me. I only speak of my own *interests* and *desires,* perfectly regardless of all the world besides, but as I said before, when I think of the pain & misery produced to individuals as well as the miserable sorrow caused throughout the land I cannot but earnestly hope for peace, and at an early date. Do you understand me?"[60]

These words were from a man who had been at Gaines's Mill, Malvern Hill, and Antietam, places that redefined war and its costs. He understood the long silences that had visited thousands of homes, but warfare offered possibilities for a young man. Danger could be defied; glory could be seized. To Custer, the romance of martial pageantry was a trumpet calling. Before the stillness, he wanted his chance.

A few weeks after he wrote the letter, however, Custer was an officer without assignment. Although McClellan began a movement into Virginia on October 26, Lincoln's tolerance for the general's delays and complaints had dissipated. On November 5, the president replaced McClellan with Major General Ambrose Burnside. McClellan received the order on the night of November 7, and four days later, after emotional farewells and a final review, the general and his staff members boarded a special train for Washington. The War Department ordered him to Trenton, New Jersey.[61]

George Custer returned to Ohio to await orders. Like McClellan, he believed that the general had failed because of the opposition to him in the administration. A Democrat, McClellan had not shared the government's war aims and the course the conflict would take after the Emancipation Proclamation went into effect on January 1, 1863. Custer overlooked, even denied, McClellan's flaws as an army commander. Although Custer's relish for fighting would be the antithesis of McClellan's caution, his affection and respect for his superior was deep and unending. He had witnessed while on the staff the bond that could be fused between a general and his men. He would remember.[62]

LIBBIE

■ Elizabeth Clift Bacon could walk through a doorway and change a room. Twenty years old in the autumn of 1862, she was a very attractive woman, with a slender figure, brown hair, and blue eyes. She was properly educated for the era, refined, and comfortable amid conversation with both sexes. Vivacious and appealing, she understood the nuances of flirtation, of the shifting currents of attention or affection between a man and a woman. To family, friends, and acquaintances, she was Libbie.[1]

Libbie Bacon was the daughter of one of Monroe, Michigan's most respected citizens, Daniel S. Bacon, circuit court judge. Like many of the community's residents, he had come from elsewhere. In the fall of 1822, at the age of twenty-four, Daniel left his family's Onondaga County, New York, homestead with a teacher's certificate and some money, uncertain of his destination. He stopped in Monroe.[2]

Bacon secured a teaching position and purchased ten acres of land, planting a nursery. Ambitious and hardworking, he read law books at night, passed his examination, and opened an office. Eventually, he formed a partnership in a real estate business with Levi S. Humphrey, a transplanted Vermonter whom Bacon had taught to read and write. Humphrey managed a stage line and the Exchange Hotel, and as the town's first land registrar, he and Bacon bought government land, platted lots, and prospered. Bacon also embraced politics, winning elections as county supervisor, school inspector, and territorial legislator. With statehood, he failed as the Whig candidate for lieutenant governor. By 1837, he served as president of the newly instituted Merchants & Mechanics Bank and as assistant judge of the Monroe County Circuit Court.[3]

That same year, Bacon married Eleanor Sophia Page, the twenty-three-year-old daughter of a successful Grand Rapids nursery owner.

On June 9, 1839, their first child, Edward Augustus, was born. Months later, the bank closed because of a national economic depression, with Bacon, Humphrey, and other investors suffering losses. Bacon, however, was elected to the state senate, and in 1840 was elected an associate judge. Despite personal financial constraints, Bacon built a house on South Monroe Street in the center of town. Here three daughters were born—Libbie on April 8, 1842, and Sophia and Harriet, both of whom died in infancy. Here, too, Edward Augustus, their son, died on April 11, 1848, from a contagious disease after having spent nearly a year in bed with a spinal injury. Six-year-old Libbie, named for her paternal grandmother, was the Bacons' only surviving child.[4]

Daniel and Sophia doted on Libbie. Both parents punished her for misdeeds but covered her with love and protection. A quiet, devout woman, Sophia taught Libbie a sense of right and wrong that came from within a person. Although strong-willed, Libbie was an obedient child, eager to secure her parents' approval and that of their friends. When her father gave her a journal on her ninth birthday with the admonition that her handwriting must be neat, she waited another year to begin her entries.[5] When she confided personal thoughts to the journal, she focused on her behavior and the struggles of a young Christian girl. She enjoyed copying poetry, favoring lines that could be guides for future conduct. For her eleventh birthday, she received a piano.[6]

Tragedy revisited the Bacon home, however, in the summer of 1854, when Libbie was twelve years old. On August 12, Sophia Bacon died of "bloody dysentery" after lapsing into a coma. She had never been healthy since her pregnancy with Harriet, and with the loss of a son and daughter within a year, her physical ailments had been compounded by emotional depression. To his family in New York, Daniel wrote: "My poor wife is no more. Her physicians were unacquainted with the nature of her disease. She bore her sufferings with great composure and Christian fortitude. . . . Elizabeth bears her affliction well, but the poor girl does not realize the overdevotion of her mother."[7]

But the father misunderstood the daughter and the depths of her grief. Libbie knew her mother's "overdevotion" and her love for her child. On August 27, Libbie turned to her journal: "Alas! my poor diary you have been sadly neglected. When I last wrote you my Mother sat comfortably in her dear rocking chair by the fire. My dear mother is sleeping her last great sleep from which she never will awake no never! Not even to correct my numerous mistakes." Continuing: "Two weeks ago my mother was laid in the cold cold ground & as I stood by that open grave & felt Oh! God and know what anguish filled my heart. Oh! why did they put my mother in that great Black coffin & screw the lid down so tight. Oh! what was it for?" Before the funeral, Libbie had removed her mother's wedding ring and cut a locket of hair.[8]

A short time later, Daniel sent Libbie for a visit to Sophia's sister, Loraine Richmond, in Grand Rapids, hoping that the company of Loraine's daughters, Rebecca and Mary, could assuage some of the sorrow. Libbie stayed with the Richmonds until November, when her father brought her back to Monroe. He had vacated their home, renting a room at the Exchange Hotel, and had enrolled Libbie in the Young Ladies' Seminary and Collegiate Institute, a boarding school founded in 1849. The Reverend Erasmus Boyd served as principal. Libbie had been a student in its primary school.[9]

Libbie spent the next four years at Boyd's Seminary, as it was commonly called, or as she subsequently jotted in her journal, "I went there a *child*—but came away a *woman*. God be praised." Reverend Boyd and his wife Sarah granted Libbie special privileges at first, allowing her to room with a teacher, Miss Thompson. But Libbie soon learned that as "poor motherless Libbie Bacon" she could extract other favors from sympathetic adults and schoolmates. "How shamelessly I traded on this," she admitted years later. "What an excuse I made of it for not doing anything I didn't want to do! And what excuses were made for me on that score."[10]

Bright, serious, and competitive, Libbie excelled as a student. The curriculum emphasized the development of a woman, or as the seminary's catalog stated, the school sought to "cultivate, not only the mind, but the taste and heart—to make Woman what she should be, not *masculine,* coarse and unlovely, but *educated,* and at the same time refined, and ready for every good work that becomes her." The young women studied French, literature, and "Fine Arts." Social activities were organized by Sarah Boyd. Parents were permitted weekly visits. Upon graduation, the educated young lady should be able to take her place alongside a husband, assisting him in his life's work and making their home comfortable.[11]

Despite the attention of the Boyds, the schoolwork and activities at the seminary, and her friends, the pain of her mother's death healed slowly. Libbie remained lonely and sad: "No one knows how much I lost but myself, when mother died," she wrote in the winter of 1858. Before the semester ended, her father withdrew her from the school and took her east to stay with his family. Libbie spent the summer with Daniel's sister, Mary, and her husband, John Case. In the fall, she attended the Young Ladies Institute in Auburn, New York, boarding there for the entire school year before returning to Monroe.[12]

Daniel Bacon, meanwhile, had remarried. He had approached Libbie with the idea in January 1858, in what she described as "a long talk." "I told him," she noted in her journal, "if he found a person with whom he could be suited and I would be suited too, and so I will for even if I did feel so averse to his marriage a year ago I have undergone a great change since and I now feel if it would add to my father's happiness to be married again, I would advise it."[13]

Daniel had met Rhoda Wells Pitts, a widow, through a mutual friend about the time he and Libbie discussed the subject. Her husband, the Reverend Samuel Pitts, had died in 1855 while serving a Presbyterian church in Tecumseh, Michigan. Daniel and Rhoda courted for a year before marrying in Orange, New Jersey, on February 23, 1859—he was sixty years old; she was forty-eight. They boarded with friends until the Bacon house could be repaired and refurbished. Libbie arrived home in June, and by summer's end, the family had moved into their home.[14]

Rhoda Bacon possessed qualities that would, in time, endear her to Libbie. Like the deceased Sophia, Rhoda was a devout Christian, laboring in the Presbyterian church. But she had a sense of humor, enjoyed laughter, in contrast to her more sober husband. Libbie later joked to her cousin that "Mother and I laugh and grow fat." In turn, Rhoda described her stepdaughter as "never so well and fleshy and full of fun and wit." After visits to the Bacon home and letters from Libbie, Rebecca Richmond asserted that Rhoda "thinks as much of Libbie as Libbie does her." A friend of the judge told him, as Daniel recalled it, that "my wife governed me, and that Libbie governed both."[15]

Libbie resumed her studies at Boyd's Seminary in the fall of 1859. During the semester, however, she became seriously ill and had to withdraw for the year. The nature of her illness is uncertain, but her stepmother ministered to Libbie during the months, undoubtedly contributing to the growing relationship between the two of them.[16]

Fully recovered by September 1860, Libbie reentered the seminary and would spend the next two years there, until her graduation in June 1862. Once again, she excelled at schoolwork, competing for the coveted rank of class valedictorian. "She mourns past time misapplied," her stepmother wrote of Libbie in 1861, "and fears she will not get first honors in examinations." By her graduation, she stood first in the class and delivered the customary farewell address. Rebecca Richmond attended the ceremony and wrote home: "Libbie has a splendid disposition and lovely temperament. I never saw her superior in qualities that go to make up a noble woman. Her parents never restrain her, but encourage her mimicries, drolleries and schoolgirl gaieties." [17]

Her years at the seminary, particularly the final two, secured for Libbie lifelong friendships. Libbie and friends Nettie Humphrey and Fanny Fifield drew the attentions of many young men. Seminary women belonged to Monroe's upper social class and offered prospective beaux acceptance within the city's most respected families. Libbie's physical attractiveness and spirited personality lured a variety of attentive men. [18]

As it had throughout the nation, the war summoned many eligible young men from Monroe. When they returned on leave, they drew attention in their uniforms from their female friends. Libbie dreamed of marrying a soldier and of accompanying him to the battlefield. Her father did not approve of the visitors in uniform, writing to his sister in 1862: "Libbie like her Aunt Harriet has many suitors, many of the mustached, gilt-striped and Button kind, more interesting to her than to me. My wife and I have a great deal of anxiety about her, but I expect this is true of all parents of fanciful girls." [19]

At a party given by the Boyds at the seminary on Thanksgiving Day, 1862, Libbie Bacon was introduced to Brevet Captain George Armstrong Custer. Each knew of the other, but the Reeds and Custer did not socialize in the same circles as the Bacons. In fact, Libbie and her father had witnessed Custer's drunken stumble through the streets the year before. When Conway Noble, a brother of one of Libbie's best friends, introduced them to each other at the party, the conversation was brief. Libbie remarked, "I believe your promotion has been very rapid?" "I have been very fortunate," he replied, and that ended the polite meeting. [20]

That night, as he recounted it, Custer returned to the Reeds', went to bed, and dreamed of Libbie Bacon. If his subsequent letters to her are to be accepted as sincere—and there is no evidence to suggest otherwise—he fell in love with her that evening at the seminary. His impulsiveness, kindled by his romantic nature, may have contributed to his initial emotions. He may also have viewed her as a challenge, a local belle who had spurned numerous suitors. If either or both were true, he never indicated it. Furthermore, if he had not known already, he would learn shortly that her father did not welcome attention to his daughter from a lowly captain with an unsavory reputation. In his subsequent words, he confronted "well-nigh insurmountable obstacles," but that did not deter him. They seldom did, as Libbie soon discovered.[21]

On the day following the party, Libbie visited a millinery shop. As she stood at the door, ringing the bell, Custer approached her, stopped, and watched her as she entered the shop. "Oh, how pleased I was," Libbie admitted later. The captain began attending the Presbyterian church, sitting so he could see her and she him. During the services, "You looked *such things* at me," she jokingly scolded him afterward. Every day, he passed by the Bacon residence, but when he came to the door, she refused to talk with him. A week before Christmas, Custer returned to the army. When her father mentioned his departure— Daniel Bacon was evidently still unaware of the situation—Libbie put her thoughts in her journal, writing: "I could almost have given way to the melting mood. I feel so sorry for him. I think I had something to do with his going." She confided that she would miss his strolls by the house, but it all had been "in too much haste tho' I admire his perseverance."[22]

Custer was back in Monroe by Christmas, however. Why he journeyed to Virginia for such a brief period of time is not in the record. Since McClellan's removal, he had been trying to secure the colonelcy of the Seventh Michigan Cavalry, a regiment being organized in the state. Initially, he contacted Congressman John Bingham, who recommended that he approach Isaac P. Christiancy, justice of the Michigan Supreme Court and founder of the Republican Party in the state. A Monroe resident, Christiancy agreed to intercede with Governor Austin Blair on Custer's behalf.[23]

Blair, however, was unwilling to give the colonelcy, a political patronage appointment, to an officer of Custer's views and associations. "Custer is using you to his own advantage, just as he used Bingham," the governor responded to Christianity. "His people are Rebel Democrats. He himself is a McClellan man; indeed McClellan's fair-haired boy, I should say. Sorry, your Honor, but I cannot place myself . . . whatever his qualification." [24]

Custer, meanwhile, was trying to secure a staff appointment for Justice Christiancy's son Henry, a company captain in a Michigan infantry regiment. Custer agreed to write to members of generals Daniel Butterfield's and Andrew Humphreys's staffs. "I have had experience in company duty and staff duty," he stated to Christiancy. "The opportunities are infinitely greater in the latter." Furthermore, Henry would join "with a class of men whom it would be an honor and a pleasure to know." [25]

Custer's efforts succeeded, with Henry Christiancy assigned as aide-de-camp to Humphreys in December. While he was in Virginia, Custer visited Humphreys's headquarters and perhaps sought a reappointment to the general's staff. He may also have decided simply to renew friendships, but this seems unlikely, since it required several days of railroad travel between Monroe and Fredericksburg. He may have been seeking assistance or recommendations in his quest for command of the cavalry regiment. Whatever the reasons for the trip, he spent only a few days with the army. [26]

Once back in Monroe, Custer renewed his daily walks in front of the Bacon home; Libbie thought he passed by "forty times a day." Libbie expected "a renewal of the attack soon," but even she had to be surprised at his tenacity. "Whenever I put my nose out of doors," she informed Rebecca Richmond, Custer was there to meet her. "I *don't care for him* except as an escort," Libbie argued to her close friend Laura Noble. "He just passed the house and I couldn't forbear making a sketch of him." [27]

Sometime between Christmas and New Year's, Custer discussed marriage with Libbie, exclaiming his willingness to "sacrifice every earthly hope to gain my love," as she entered his words in her journal. "I tell him if I could I would give it to him," she wrote. "I told him to forget me and he said he *never could* forget me and I told him I never should forget *him* and I wished to be his true friend through life but it is no use to offer myself as a friend for he will never think of me otherwise than his wife." But what he had asked was impossible. By now, her father had heard rumors and was adamantly opposed to any relationship between Libbie and Custer. He had forbidden her to invite him into the house and to be seen in his company. "Oh, *Love, love,* how many are made miserable as well as happy by the all powerful influence," she wondered in her journal.[28]

Libbie's turmoil intensified during the next several weeks. Although Custer continued the pursuit, he began escorting Libbie's seminary friend and rival, Fanny Fifield, to parties and walking with her in public. With friends, Libbie joked about the army officer and Fanny, but it is evident that his attentions to her troubled Libbie. She was confused about her feelings toward Custer and concerned about her father's insistent views about him. At a party, she secretly gave him her ring, but days afterward, informed him that he could not see her again—it was what both she and her father wanted.[29]

At her father's urging, Libbie visited family friends in Toledo, Ohio, twenty miles south of Monroe, during February. On the day she left, Custer came to the railroad station, assisting her with baggage and boarding. He had suggested that he accompany her, but she rejected the idea. When Judge Bacon saw him at the station with Libbie, he seethed with anger. Once in Toledo, Libbie wrote home, requesting a dress to wear to a party. Her parents forwarded it, but the judge included a letter, lecturing his daughter about dances and about Custer.[30]

"Father," Libbie replied with frustration and anger, "I told Mother to tell you of my interview with Captain Custer. I never had a trial that made me feel so badly. I did it *all for you.* I like him very well, and it is pleasant always to have an escort to depend on. But I am sorry I have been with him so much, and you will never see me in the street with him again, and never at the house except to say Good-bye. I told him never to meet me, and he has the sense to understand. But I did not promise *never* to see him again. But I will not cause you any more trouble, be sure."

Continuing, she asked her father not to "blame Captain Custer." "He has many fine traits," she added, "and Monroe will yet be proud of him." Finally: "You have never been a girl, Father, and you cannot tell how hard a trial this was for me. . . . And Monroe people will please mind their own business, and let me alone. If the whole world Oh'd and Ah'd it would not move me as does your displeasure. . . . I wish the gossipers sunk in the sea. It would give me great pleasure to know that you place entire confidence in me—Your affectionate daughter Libbie."[31]

Libbie returned to Monroe by month's end. Once at home, however, she could no longer resist the deepening affection she had for Custer. While he was seen publicly in the company of Fanny Fifield, Custer and Libbie were able to share moments together at social affairs. He still attended church on Sunday, sitting in a pew near her. Using Nettie Humphrey as a liaison, Libbie passed notes to him and gave him an ambrotype of herself. It was the passion of the man that enticed and reassured. "He acts it, speaks it from his eyes, and tells me every way *I love you*," she confided in her journal.[32]

Nevertheless, Libbie appeared to be trapped in a maze of emotions —her yearnings for him, her pledge to her father. At night, before she slept, Libbie turned to her journal—"A SAFETY VALVE," she called it—to recount a day's events, to seek understanding, perhaps comfort. In one entry, she wrote: "I was not in love—yes I was, perhaps, but I am sure that the deep feelings which I know have not been stirred by anyone—the chords of my heart were not swept by him. Yes, I like him so much now—no one knows how much—but I feel that it is proof that I do not really love for how could I silence so soon feelings that are always so deep."[33]

On another day, after she had resisted his efforts to kiss her—she believed for the four thousandth time—Libbie confessed, "I long so to put my arms about his neck and kiss him and how often I lay my head on his breast—in imagination—and feel how sweet it would be to make him entirely happy." Then after they had sat together on a sofa at the Humphrey House, a hotel opened by Nettie's father in 1860, she avowed, "Darkness reigned. That hand, that tenant hand! He would not let go but held it and kissed *oh so passionately*." "I have everything I wish," she continued, "and have had nearly all my life and now one thing is refused me I sometimes almost rebel. But I shall conquer. In time I'll learn not to regret or reprove."[34]

A week after the incident in the Humphrey House, April 8, Libbie's twenty-first birthday, Custer boarded a train for Washington, D.C. Orders for a return to duty had been anticipated for some time, and he undoubtedly used the prospects of his departure in his courting of Libbie. The thought that he might fall on a battlefield gave urgency to his desires and requests, but Libbie—if her journal entries can be accepted as accurate—was not swayed, refusing still to allow him to kiss her. Much uncertainty marked their relationship when he left Monroe.[35]

Libbie thought frequently about Custer and evaluated her feelings toward him, as evidenced by her diary entries. Custer, meanwhile, had reported for duty in the capital on April 10. At the War Department, he learned that George B. McClellan had requested his assistance in the preparation of the general's reports on the campaigns of 1862. He arrived in New York City, where McClellan was posted, the following day, renting a room at the Metropolitan Hotel and visiting with his former commander and the commander's wife. McClellan and Custer were pleased to see each other again, with McClellan telling his aide that he would have sent for him sooner if he had known where he had been staying.[36]

Custer worked with the general in the latter's residence—a "magnificently furnished" house presented to the McClellans for their use—from ten o'clock in the morning until three o'clock in the afternoon. McClellan sought vindication for his generalship and prepared a lengthy report of the operations. Custer's assistance, however, was limited, as he soon received orders, reassigning him to the Fifth United States Cavalry, his former regiment. By the end of April, First Lieutenant Custer was at the War Department, temporarily posted to office duty, which he described as "idleness and theatregoing."[37]

Monroe, however, never strayed far from his thoughts, nor did Libbie Bacon.

5

"COME ON,

YOU

WOLVERINES"

■ During the first five days of May 1863, the Yankees found themselves caught in a nightmarish landscape in Virginia known locally as the Wilderness, around a crossroads village called Chancellorsville. When the Confederates assailed the advance elements of the Federal army, Major General Joseph Hooker pulled his army into the confines of the Wilderness, negating his numerical and artillery superiority. Lee and Lieutenant General Stonewall Jackson seized the opportunity, brilliantly utilizing tactics that crushed a flank of Hooker's army and pushed the Federals back across the river. The elation in Confederate ranks was tempered, however, by the loss of Jackson, mortally wounded by his own troops.[1]

The defeat created acrimony within the Union army. Yet another commander had boasted of victory, only to be outgeneraled by Lee. Much had been expected of Hooker after he assumed command in January 1863. The rank and file festered with discontent that winter because Major General Ambrose Burnside, George McClellan's successor, had led the army into a firestorm of death at Fredericksburg on December 13, 1862, and in a failed offensive in January, ignominiously dubbed the "Mud March." In its wake, President Abraham Lincoln replaced Burnside with Hooker, who had lobbied for Burnside's dismissal. Ambitious but capable, "Fighting Joe" Hooker restored morale by attending to the men's needs—granting furloughs, insuring that rations and supplies reached the troops, and assigning distinctive badges to each corps. He brimmed with confidence, and it seeped into the ranks—until Chancellorsville.[2]

George Custer rejoined the army as it withdrew from the bloody ground around Chancellorsville. Except for his brief visit before Christmas 1862, he had been away from the army for nearly six months. He had been pulled from his desk job at the War Department with the assignment of aide-de-camp on the staff of Brigadier General Alfred Pleasonton, commander of the First Cavalry Division. While on McClellan's staff, Custer had served with Pleasonton during the Seven Days' and Antietam campaigns. Although the record is undocumented, it would appear that Pleasonton requested the appointment. The records indicate that the assignment was as of June 6, but in all likelihood, the date was misrecorded, May 6 being the correct date.[3]

Upon his return, Custer learned of the details of the recent defeat and listened to the criticism about Hooker's performance. "To say that everything is gloomy and discouraging does not express the state of affairs here," he wrote to George McClellan on May 6. "Hooker's career is well exemplified by that of a rocket, he went up like one and came down like a stick." Camp rumor percolated that Hooker, who had a fondness for liquor, was drunk at some point during the operations, added Custer. "Even Hooker's best friends are clamoring for his removal," he confided to his old commander, "saying that they are disappointed in him. . . . You will not be surprised when I inform you that the universal cry is 'Give us McClellan.'"[4]

Despite the sullenness within the army, Custer welcomed the assignment to staff duty. While he enjoyed his extended furlough in Monroe, he probably chafed at the inactivity, at the prospect that others were advancing in rank and he appeared to be shelved temporarily. First and foremost, he was a soldier, a man who viewed the conflict as an unparalleled opportunity for advancement and fame. He wanted to be a part of it, and with the orders to report to the army, he hurried to the front. Before long, he wrote to his sister of the "good table" set at Pleasonton's headquarters, of the camaraderie among the staff members, and of the serenades by the general's band. Custer seemingly never tired of army life—he was back where he belonged.[5]

Within days of Custer's return to the army, Hooker ordered personnel changes in the cavalry command as a result of his assessment of performances during the campaign. When Hooker replaced Burnside, one of his initial reforms was the consolidation of the cavalry units into one corps under Major General George Stoneman. As noted previously, the War Department had done little with mounted units, except to redesignate them as cavalry. In turn, George McClellan had frittered away their combat worth by assigning regiments to infantry brigades. When Federal cavalry units were used in combat, they followed the Napoleonic tradition of a mounted attack against infantry. While Lee's cavalry commander, Jeb Stuart, demonstrated the prowess and possibilities of the mounted arm, the Federals were plagued by tactical orthodoxy, crippling organization, and misuse by commanders.[6]

The role of cavalry in the Civil War demanded organization and flexibility. The mounted arm performed reconnaissance and counterreconnaissance operations, harried the advance elements of an enemy force, pursued and harassed retreating enemy units, conducted raids, added force to infantry and artillery units in offensive actions, and fought dismounted in defensive struggles. Cavalry operations demanded initiative and daring, even recklessness, from leaders, qualities that Stuart and his subordinates possessed. For two years, the Confederates rode as dashing, invincible knights in Virginia, their supremacy in mounted warfare unchallenged by the Federals.[7]

The imbalance between the opposing horse soldiers had been narrowing when Hooker reorganized the army's cavalry into a corps, composed of three divisions and a Reserve Brigade of Regular Army regiments. Even before the consolidation, numbers of Union troopers believed that they could match the enemy if given the chance and if properly led. The initial challenge came within a fortnight of the corps's creation when the Yankees attacked Stuart's men at Kelly's Ford on the Rappahannock. Although the Federals withdrew, they fought the Confederates on even terms, inflicting more casualties than they suffered. During the Chancellorsville Campaign, however, Hooker ordered Stoneman with part of the corps on a raid against Lee's communication links to Richmond. While the raiders burned and wrecked, the absence of the mounted units hampered Hooker's operations and contributed to his defeat. At the campaign's conclusion, the Union cavalry remained a command searching for an identity within the army.[8]

Before the campaign had ended, Hooker removed Brigadier General

William W. Averell, commander of the Second Cavalry Division, ordering him to Washington for reassignment, on May 3. While Averell's
failure to protect the army's flank was not entirely his fault, Hooker
blamed him and sent him away from the army, giving Pleasonton command of both his own and Averell's division. Once the army recrossed
the Rappahannock, Hooker's dissatisfaction with the results of Stoneman's raid led to the cavalry commander's departure with a leave of
absence granted officially because of ill health on May 20. Two days
later, Hooker appointed Pleasonton to temporary command of the
cavalry corps.[9]

A West Pointer, class of 1844, Pleasonton spent much of his antebellum career in the dragoons, heavily armed mounted troops. When the
war began, he was in Utah, with the Second Dragoons. He commanded
the regiment during its march to the East, spending the winter of 1862
in the defenses of Washington, his native city. At the end of the Seven
Days' Campaign, he was promoted to brigadier and led a division of
five regiments at Antietam. With the formation of the cavalry corps,
Pleasonton assumed command of the First Cavalry Division, remaining
with the army during the Chancellorsville operations.[10]

A short, slender man, Pleasonton exuded self-confidence. He dressed
fastidiously, complete with white kid gloves, and strutted through cavalry camps, a cowhide riding whip constantly in hand. A newspaperman
thought him to be "keen-eyed," "polished and affable," with a pale face,
prematurely graying brown hair, and "features sharply chiseled." Fellow
officers who knew him better described him as a "nice little dandy,"
whose vanity was "over-weening."[11]

In fact, many officers in the cavalry corps had little regard, even had
disdain, for Pleasonton. An ambitious self-promoter, he possessed a
reputation for untruthfulness and shameless ingratiation with superiors.
In his Chancellorsville report, for instance, the brigadier claimed that
his units repulsed Stonewall Jackson's entire corps when the troopers
only routed a Confederate patrol. "I can't call any cavalry officer good
who can't see the truth and tell the truth," groused Colonel Charles
Russell Lowell of the Second Massachusetts Cavalry about Pleasonton.
"With an infantry officer this is not so essential, but cavalry are the eyes
and ears of the army and ought to see and hear and tell truly; and yet it
is the universal opinion that P's own reputation and P's late promotions
are bolstered by systematic lying."[12]

Another Massachusetts officer was even less charitable than Lowell, asserting to his mother that Pleasonton "is the bete noire of all cavalry officers." "He is pure and simple a newspaper humbug," stated Charles Francis Adams, Jr. "You always see his name in the papers, but to us who have served under him he is notorious as a bully and a toady. . . . Yet mean and contemptible as Pleasonton is, he is always *in* at Head Quarters." A third officer alleged that he was a tyrannical, cruel disciplinarian, given to "illegal exercise of military authority." [13]

Questions also persisted about Pleasonton's combat skill as an officer and his courage as a man in battle. His conduct under fire was "notorious" among those "who have served under him and seen him under fire." Furthermore, he was neither a prudent nor capable reconnaissance officer, as Lowell rightly claimed, favoring rumor and speculation in his dispatches to reliable, active scouting against enemy units. He may have been nothing more than a competent administrator and bureaucrat who looked like a cavalry officer and enjoyed the confidence of superiors. [14]

The cavalry corps numbered roughly 10,000 officers and men present for duty, organized into three divisions of seven brigades. The division commanders were Brigadier Generals John Buford and David Gregg, and Colonel Alfred Duffié. A Kentuckian, Buford was a West Pointer, Regular Army, a quiet, unassuming man, as tough as worn leather, and tireless on duty and in attending to his men's needs. He was regarded, as an officer argued, as "decidedly the best cavalry general we had." Like Buford, Gregg was academy-trained, experienced, reliable, a steady influence in combat, and a popular officer. Duffié was a Frenchman, educated at St. Cyr, decorated for service in the Crimean War, but an officer perhaps promoted beyond his capabilities. Among brigade commanders, Colonels Benjamin "Grimes" Davis, Thomas C. Devin, Judson Kilpatrick, and John Irvin Gregg combined experience with promise. [15]

Custer, meanwhile, had settled in at cavalry headquarters. He wrote to Isaac Christiancy that Pleasonton "is an excellent cavalry officer" and that "my position is a desirable one to a person fond of excitement." He interceded with Pleasonton to secure the appointment of First Lieutenant George W. Yates to the staff, and by month's end, Yates was named an inspector general. A native New Yorker, Yates had enlisted in the Fourth Michigan in 1861, suffered a wound at Fredericksburg, and while recuperating in Monroe, met Custer in January 1863. A stocky blond, Yates became a close friend of Custer. [16]

On May 20, Pleasonton ordered a reconnaissance of a section of the

Northern Neck of Virginia between the Potomac and Rappahannock rivers. The general assigned Custer to accompany a squadron, or two companies of seventy-five men each, of the Third Indiana Cavalry on the raid. The detachment left that night on two steamers, onloading at Moon's Landing on the Potomac on the morning of the twenty-second. Crossing the neck on horseback, they reached the Rappahannock River opposite Urbanna, repaired boats, chased a Rebel sailing vessel, and then landed at Urbanna. Surprising some Confederate troops, the Yankees grabbed a dozen prisoners, fifteen horses, and two boxes of footwear. Custer kept one of the mounts for himself, a blooded iron-gray stallion that he named Roanoke. By the morning of the twenty-fourth, the squadron rejoined the army, without the loss of a man, and Hooker personally complimented Custer.[17]

Several days after the raid, Governor Austin Blair visited the camps of Michigan troops. While duty prevented Custer from speaking with Blair, the staff officer had been at work again through intermediaries to secure an appointment to command of a cavalry regiment. Earlier, in his letter to Christiancy about his position with Pleasonton, Custer stated that "I would rather be in command of the 5th Michigan Cavalry or 8th Regiment if that were possible." Christiancy approached the governor, but Blair replied that although he was willing to help, no vacancy existed.[18]

Custer also asked for assistance from Pleasonton, who agreed to write a letter of recommendation to Blair. "Captain Custer," the general stated, "will make an excellent commander of a cavalry regiment and is entitled to such promotion for his gallant and efficient services in the present war of rebellion. I do not know anyone that I could recommend to you with more confidence than Captain Custer." The brigadier forwarded the letter to Hooker, who endorsed it with "I cheerfully concur in the recommendation of Brig Genl Pleasonton. He is a young officer of great promise and of uncommon merit." Custer mailed it to Blair on May 31, enclosing it with additional letters he had received earlier from Ambrose Burnside, Andrew Humphreys, and George Stoneman. "If the Governor refuses to appoint me," he asserted to Judge Christiancy, "it will be for some other reason than a lack of recommendations."[19]

Furthermore, according to a lieutenant of the Fifth Michigan Cavalry, Custer visited their camp, seeking the support of the unit's officers.

The regiment's commander, Colonel Russell A. Alger, was temporarily absent on leave, and Custer asked the officers to sign a petition to Governor Blair that requested the appointment of himself to the colonelcy. First Lieutenant Samuel A. Harris remembered the staff officer as "a slim young man with almost flaxen hair, looking more like a big boy . . . with the cheek of a government mule." The officers refused, in the words of Harris, "as we considered him too young." If Custer did as Harris related years afterward, it was a brazen act on his part to secure a command by having a colonel removed while on furlough, using the latter's subordinates in the effort.[20]

Across the Rappahannock River, meanwhile, Lee's veterans were stirring. Since Chancellorsville, Lee had refitted and reorganized the army and secured approval from the administration in Richmond to undertake a full-scale raid into Pennsylvania, similar to the operation into Maryland the previous autumn. The victory at Chancellorsville had given the Confederates the strategic initiative in the East, and Lee planned to exploit it. On June 3, units of the army filed from the lines around Fredericksburg, marching westward. By June 8, advance elements of infantry, artillery, and Jeb Stuart's cavalry were halted at Culpeper Court House, approximately thirty miles upriver from Fredericksburg.[21]

Federal signal officers detected the Confederate movement, but Hooker could not determine the scale of the operation or the units involved and so was uncertain whether Lee had shifted troop positions or had begun an offensive. Infantry probes on June 5 and 6 gathered little information, so the next day Hooker ordered Pleasonton to advance against Stuart's horsemen, reported to be in the Culpeper Court House area. The commanding general augmented the three divisions of cavalry with two infantry brigades. Believing that the enemy cavalry were preparing for a raid, Hooker directed Pleasonton "to disperse and destroy the rebel force assembled in the vicinity of Culpeper, and to destroy his trains and supplies of all description to the utmost of your ability."[22]

After nightfall on June 8, the Union cavalrymen closed on Beverly and Kelly's fords—Buford's command at the former, Gregg's and Duffié's at the latter. The troopers unsaddled the horses and lay down for a few hours' sleep. Pleasonton established headquarters at the home of William Bowen, Sr., located about a mile from Beverly Ford. Before he rested, Custer wrote to Ann Reed from the Bowen house, "I never was in better spirits than I am at this moment." If "something happens to me," he told her, he had given instructions for his trunk and articles to be sent to Monroe. "If such an event occurs," he admonished, "I want all my letters burned." [23]

The Yankees marched at 4 A.M., June 9. Custer accompanied Grimes Davis's brigade of Buford's division across Beverly Ford. The Eighth New York Cavalry led the brigade, with Davis riding in front of his former regiment. Rebel pickets fired shots, and Davis ordered a charge. "When Colonel Davis found the rebels he did not stop at anything, but went for them heavy," asserted a New York trooper. "I believe he liked to fight the rebels as well as he liked to eat." A Mississippian who had remained loyal to the Union, Davis plunged ahead, saber drawn. He and his men galloped toward a Confederate battery when they were attacked by the Sixth Virginia Cavalry. The Federals stopped and tumbled rearward. Davis sat his horse in the road, emptying his pistol, before using his sword. Lieutenant R. O. Allen of the Sixth Virginia dueled with the Union colonel, firing three pistol shots at close range. The final shot struck Davis in the forehead, killing him before he hit the ground. [24]

A biographer of Custer has asserted that upon Davis's fall, the staff officer assumed command of the brigade. Other historians have repeated the story, but it is inaccurate. Temporary command of the brigade devolved upon Major William McClure of the Third Indiana Cavalry until Colonel Thomas Devin received orders to direct his and Davis's brigade. But Custer distinguished himself in the fighting, once being knocked from his horse when the mount could not leap a stone wall. Later in the day, he joined Pleasonton, whose headquarters during the battle were at the Mary Emily Gee house near St. James Church. After the Federals recrossed the river, Custer delivered the captured flag of the Twelfth Virginia Cavalry to Hooker's headquarters. In his report, Pleasonton cited the staff officer for "gallantry throughout the fight." [25]

The Battle of Brandy Station was the largest cavalry engagement of the war. The Union troopers fought with a tenacity and skill that nearly secured a victory. The combat flowed across the fields and woodlots around and on Fleetwood Hill near the railroad station east of Culpeper. They and Rebel horsemen hammered each other in mounted charges and countercharges. Although Stuart's veterans held the field, it had been a close call, and the Confederates knew it. Soon afterward, a Federal artillery officer argued correctly that "the affair at Brandy Station certainly did a great deal to improve the morale of our cavalry, so that they are not now afraid to meet the 'rebs' on equal terms."[26]

While the Federals surprised the Rebels at Brandy Station, Stuart's men had prevented them from learning about the presence of Confederate infantry in the area. On June 10, Lee resumed the army's movement, and within a week, the Southerners had routed a Union force at Winchester in the Shenandoah Valley and were preparing to cross the Potomac River. To the east of the gray-clad columns, Stuart's troopers guarded the gaps of the Blue Ridge, screening the march. On June 16, the advance contingent of the Army of Northern Virginia waded the Potomac.[27]

The Union Army of the Potomac slowly started northward in pursuit. Unconvinced of the magnitude of the Southern offensive, Hooker hesitated to withdraw from the Rappahannock. Once Winchester fell, units of the army began filling the Virginia roads east of the Blue Ridge. To locate the Confederates, Hooker sent Pleasonton and the cavalry toward the mountain range. The opposing horsemen clashed in spirited engagements in the Virginia Piedmont at Aldie on the seventeenth, at Middleburg on the nineteenth, and at Upperville on the twenty-first. Once again, the Yankees fought well, but Stuart's men protected the gaps.[28]

At Aldie, on June 17, Custer accompanied David Gregg's division, which spearheaded Pleasonton's corps. When Gregg and his staff reached the Little River, east of the village, Custer plunged his mount into the stream to give it a drink. He then rode downstream, and as he spurred the horse up a bank, the animal fell over backward, tumbling his rider into the water. It was a hot, dusty day, and in the words of one of Gregg's staff members, when the dust "settled on his wet clothes and wet hair, Custer was an object that one can better imagine than I can describe."[29]

Late in the action west of Aldie, Custer joined the brigade of Brigadier General Judson Kilpatrick, an academy acquaintance. Kilpatrick's regiments were heavily engaged, and Custer could not resist being along the battle line. "He was always in the fight," an orderly on Pleasonton's staff recalled, "no matter where it was." When one Union regiment broke, Custer rode with the First Maine Cavalry in a counterattack that ended the combat. A Michigan newspaper subsequently reported that he was surrounded by Rebels in the swirling fighting and only escaped because the enemy mistook him for one of their own with his broad-brimmed hat. Although Custer wore such a hat to protect his fair complexion from sunburn, the account seems dubious.[30]

Stuart's defense of the gaps insured an unhindered passage of Lee's army down the Shenandoah Valley and kept Hooker searching for reliable information. By June 26, Confederate units were spreading across southern Pennsylvania, creating panic among the citizenry and the state government in Harrisburg. East of the mountain ranges, Hooker led his infantry corps en route to Maryland, keeping his army between the Southerners and Washington. At cavalry headquarters, Pleasonton had been fuming about rumors that Major General Julius Stahel, commander of the capital's cavalry forces, would be given overall direction of the army's cavalry corps. Stahel outranked Pleasonton, and his units were now attached to Hooker's army.[31]

Pleasonton turned to a political ally in the capital, Congressman John F. Farnsworth, whose nephew, Captain Elon Farnsworth, served on the general's staff. "Our cavalry business is badly managed & will lead us into trouble unless speedily corrected," Pleasonton grumbled to the congressman in a June 23 letter. "We have too many detachments independent of each other scattered over this country." If Stahel, a native of Hungary, was appointed to command, Pleasonton would resign. "I have no faith in foreigners saving our Government or country," he affirmed. "Stahel has not shown himself a cavalry man."[32] Pleasonton followed with a second letter later in the day imploring Farnsworth that "the cavalry [be] consolidated and Stahel left out for Gods sake do it."[33]

Five days later, on June 28, Stahel was removed in a command reorganization that included Hooker. The commanding general had been in a dispute with the War Department and President Lincoln over the Union garrison at Harpers Ferry, Virginia, and the overall conduct of the campaign against Lee. When Hooker submitted his resignation, Lincoln accepted it, replacing the army commander with Major General George G. Meade, commander of the Fifth Corps. A Pennsylvanian, Meade had a reputation as a solid, cautious, but combative general and as a man with a fearsome temper. With Lee's troops in Meade's native state, Lincoln burdened the new commander and army with enormous responsibility.[34]

The order appointing Meade, dated June 27, arrived at 3 A.M. on the twenty-eighth, at Frederick, Maryland. Meade reported to army headquarters and conferred with Hooker and his chief of staff, Major General Daniel Butterfield. The generals discussed the strategic situation and the location of the army's corps. When Meade departed, he sent a wire to Major General Henry W. Halleck, general-in-chief, accepting the command and stating that "I can only now say that it appears to me I must move toward the Susquehanna, keeping Washington and Baltimore well covered." [35]

Meade spent the next several hours issuing orders and meeting with subordinate officers. When Pleasonton consulted with Meade, the cavalry commander recommended a reorganization of the corps that Meade accepted, evidently to increase the mounted arm's performance. Lincoln had granted Meade the authority to replace any officer and promote others. At Pleasonton's request, Meade relieved Stahel and Brigadier General Joseph Copeland, commander of the Michigan Brigade. "To organize with efficiency the cav'lry force now with this army," Meade then telegraphed Halleck, "I require three Brig. Generals." He requested the promotion to that rank of Elon Farnsworth, Wesley Merritt, and George Custer, all staff members. The names surely startled Halleck, an old Regular Army officer—Farnsworth and Merritt were captains; Custer, a first lieutenant with the brevet rank of captain. Meade issued the order announcing the appointments later that day, with confirmation from the War Department coming on June 29, the official date of rank.[36]

Custer wrote an account of his promotion to Isaac Christiancy a month later. Although some of the details he related in the letter cannot be documented, his version must be accepted as the most reliable. Like so many aspects of his life and career, accounts of his promotion to brigadier general have been a mixture of fact and legend.[37]

As Custer recounted the events in his letter to Christiancy, dated July 26, 1863, he reported to cavalry headquarters at Pleasonton's request about three o'clock on the afternoon of June 28. Once together, Pleasonton informed Custer that he and Meade had recommended the staff officer to Lincoln for a brigadiership, because as Custer wrote, "the Cavalry was to set out next day in search of the rebel Army and leaders were needed." The news stunned Custer: "I had not the most remote idea that the president would appoint me, because I considered my youth, my low rank and what is of great importance at times & recollected that I have not a single 'friend at Court.' "

Pleasonton then told Custer that he had relieved Copeland of command, because he did not know the general's abilities and wanted as subordinates only men on whom he could rely. He asked Custer which command he preferred, and the latter requested the Michigan Brigade. Confirmation of the promotion in orders from Meade was not issued until that evening. "To say I was elated would faintly express my feelings," Custer wrote.[38]

He slept little, if at all, during the night of June 28–29. According to a memoir of Private Joseph Fought, the new brigadier spent much of the time readying a uniform for the next day. Fought had served under Custer in the Fifth United States Cavalry, and when the latter joined Pleasonton's staff, he had Fought appointed as an orderly and bugler. The private was devoted to Custer and must have appeared to be his shadow to other staff members. Fought's respect and affection for him never wavered, and his version of events and his assessment of the general's personality and achievements must be accepted judiciously.[39]

Custer, in Fought's recounting, needed a pair of stars, the insignia of a brigadier general, to complete his uniform. The orderly left headquarters, searching for the items. Eventually, Fought located an army sutler who had silver cloth stars. Returning to Custer, he sewed the stars on a blue, wide-collared, navy-style shirt that had been given to Custer by a Potomac River gunboat officer. Fought placed the insignia, at Custer's direction, on the points of the collar so the stars could be clearly seen.[40]

What is missing from Fought's reminiscences is any detail about Custer's uniform. It was a striking uniform, unlike any other worn by a general in the army. Custer possessed undeniable flair and a craving for attention. But when asked subsequently why he wore such distinctive attire—a conspicuous target for an enemy in combat—Custer replied that he wanted his men to see and to know him during combat. If the uniform were unmistakable, they could recognize him upon sight, reassured by his presence along a battle line, to him a necessary attribute of leadership.[41]

The best description of Custer and his uniform comes from Captain James H. Kidd of the Sixth Michigan Cavalry, who saw his new commander for the first time on June 30. Kidd remembered:

Looking at him closely, this is what I saw: An officer superbly mounted who sat his charger as if to the manor born. Tall, lithe, active, muscular, straight as an Indian and as quick in his movements, he had the fair complexion of a school girl. He was clad in a suit of black velvet, elaborately trimmed with gold lace, which ran down the outer seams of his trousers, and almost covered the sleeves of his cavalry jacket. The wide collar of a blue navy shirt was turned down over the collar of his velvet jacket, and a necktie of brilliant crimson was tied in a graceful knot at the throat, the long ends falling carelessly in front. The double rows of buttons on his breast were arranged in groups of twos, indicating the rank of brigadier general. A soft, black hat with wide brim adorned with a gilt cord, and rosette encircling a silver star, was worn turned down on one side giving him a rakish air. His golden hair fell in graceful luxuriance nearly or quite to his shoulders, and his upper lip was garnished with a blonde mustache. A sword and belt, gilt spurs and top boots completed his unique outfit.[42]

Questions intrigue. Did Custer have the uniform made and tailored to his specifications beforehand? If so, had Pleasonton confided earlier to him that if the opportunity arose, he would recommend him for a generalship? Did Custer purchase the uniform from a sutler in Frederick or buy the cloth and have a tailor sew it together during the night? Or, did he acquire it weeks earlier while attempting to secure the colonelcy of the Fifth Michigan Cavalry? No definite answer can be given, because he never wrote about it. It would have been extremely difficult in Frederick for him to have purchased such a unique uniform, with the gold braid on the sleeves, or to find a tailor who had the material. Most likely, he had had it made earlier, stashed it in his trunk, and awaited the opportunity to wear it. If that were the case, then Custer had thought much about his appearance and had readied himself should he be given the chance to lead men in battle.

Dressed like the night, Custer rode northward from Frederick to assume command of the Michigan Brigade on the morning of June 29. In Pleasonton's reorganization of the cavalry corps, Stahel's former division was designated the Third Cavalry Division, with Judson Kilpatrick commanding. Custer assumed command of the Michigan Brigade.[43]

The entire Union army marched toward Pennsylvania on the twenty-ninth. The cavalry was instructed to guard the army's flanks and rear and continue the search for Confederate units. A report had been received that enemy cavalry were operating east of Frederick, between that city and Washington and Baltimore, and Pleasonton directed his commanders to be alert to the Southerners' presence. Although the information identified only one brigade, the Confederate horsemen comprised three brigades under Jeb Stuart. Since one o'clock on the morning of June 25, Stuart had passed to the rear of the Federal army, before turning north toward the Keystone State. Like the Yankees, Stuart was seeking Lee's infantry corps.[44]

Custer found part of his brigade a few miles north of Frederick. On June 28, Copeland had taken the Fifth and Sixth Michigan Cavalry on a reconnaissance to Gettysburg, Pennsylvania. It was a Sunday, and the two regiments passed through the town as church bells rang and residents filled the streets. The blue-jacketed troopers were a welcome sight as Confederate units had marched through during the previous days. The townsfolk offered water and apple butter sandwiches to the troopers—"It was a gala day," recalled an officer. The cavalrymen prowled the surrounding countryside before camping for the night. The next morning, they resumed the scout, circling south and east of Gettysburg.[45]

While the Fifth and Sixth conducted the reconnaissance, the First and Seventh Michigan Cavalry remained posted beyond Frederick. It was these latter two regiments Custer met on the morning of the twenty-ninth. The Fifth, Sixth, and Seventh regiments, recruited successively in the summer and fall of 1862, were organized as a brigade on December 12, 1862. In the spring of 1863, the First, organized in September 1861, joined the brigade. It had served in the Shenandoah Valley and in the Second Manassas Campaign in 1862. It possessed some combat experience while the other three regiments had been assigned to the defenses of Washington, duty that involved plenty of scouting and little combat. Battery M, Second United States Artillery, had just been attached to the brigade.[46]

The irony of his appointment to command of the Michigan Brigade did not escape Custer. A few weeks later, he wrote to Ann Reed, noting: "I have certainly great cause to rejoice. I am the youngest General in the U S Army by over two years, which of itself is something to be proud of. . . . My brigade is composed entirely of Michigan troops except my Artillery which belongs to the regular Army. The regiment of which I endeavored to obtain the Colonelcy (5th) belongs to my brigade so that I rather outwitted the Governor who did not see fit to give it to me."[47]

As for the officers and men of the First and Seventh Michigan, they were not sure what to make of their new commander in his resplendent, velvet uniform. Numbers of the men began joking:

"Who is the child?"
"Where is his nurse?"
"It's our new general, boys."
"General?—Oh, Sugar."

One of them jotted in his diary that the brigadier "is light complexion has blue eyes & yellow hair which rests in ringlets on his shoulders." Almost at once, he added, the men were calling him "the boy General of the Golden Lock."[48]

Custer soon mounted the regiments and artillery battery, marching them north toward Emmitsburg, several miles south of the Pennsylvania line. Turning northeast, the command proceeded to Littlestown, Pennsylvania, where it joined Elon Farnsworth's First Brigade and bivouacked for the night. The Fifth and Sixth Michigan joined the brigade the next morning. A scant eight to twelve miles to the southeast on the Gettysburg-Baltimore Pike, Stuart's three brigades bedded down between Union Mills and Westminster, Maryland.[49]

Rain fell on June 30, as Kilpatrick's cavalrymen rode out of Littlestown toward Hanover, seven miles to the northeast. Custer's two regiments and battery led the march, with Farnsworth's brigade following an hour or so later. Kilpatrick and Custer entered Hanover about eight o'clock, halted at the home of Jacob Wirt, and mentioned that the men needed food. A local minister notified the residents, and soon the troopers had bread, meat, and coffee. With gratitude, the Federals started for Abbottstown and York, searching for the elusive Confederates. Behind them, Farnsworth's men filtered into the town, and were greeted with similar offerings by the citizens.[50]

South of Hanover, unknown to the Yankees, Stuart's three Confederate brigades were approaching, strung out in a long column, slowed by over one hundred captured wagons seized in Maryland. Stuart wanted to evade Federal units, but before he learned of enemy horsemen in

Hanover, the column's advance guards fired on the Yankees. The Confederate general spurred to the front, saw only one Union regiment south of town, and ordered an attack. Artillerymen rolled two cannon into a field, rammed in the charges, and discharged the pieces. Minutes later, the Thirteenth Virginia Cavalry of Colonel John R. Chambliss, Jr.'s brigade surged ahead in a mounted charge.[51]

The Virginians slammed into the Eighteenth Pennsylvania Cavalry, Farnsworth's rearguard unit. The Pennsylvanians wavered and then splintered apart when the Second North Carolina Cavalry attacked. The Yankees raced for Hanover, pursued by the Rebels. The gunfire alerted Farnsworth, who reeled around the Fifth New York Cavalry, personally leading it in a counterattack. The opposing horsemen collided in the streets of Hanover, the tumult spreading beyond the town square. When the Pennsylvanians rallied and reentered the action, the Confederates retreated. Stuart had found more Yankees than he wanted.[52]

While Stuart regrouped on a ridge southeast of town and waited for his two other brigades—Wade Hampton's and Fitzhugh Lee's—to come up, Kilpatrick galloped into Hanover. Reining in before the Central Hotel—his horse collapsed from exhaustion—the division commander made the building his headquarters and learned of the situation. There was not much to Kilpatrick physically, but what there was always seemed to be at a boil. "He was of a highly excitable and nervous temperament," argued a cavalry officer. If Pleasonton sought spirit and combativeness in commanders, he had found them in Kilpatrick. Stuart had ruffled a bantam rooster's feathers.[53]

Custer soon rode into town. When Kilpatrick raced back to Hanover upon hearing the combat, Custer turned around his column and followed. Riding ahead of his men, the brigadier reported to the hotel for orders. He tied his mount, this time a bay, to a maple tree in front of a residence on the southwest corner of Centre Square, and for years afterward townsfolk referred to it as "Custer's Tree." Inside the hotel, Kilpatrick instructed the subordinate to position the division's two six-gun batteries on a rise north of town, known locally as Bunker Hill, and deploy his regiments in support. Farnsworth's regiments covered the eastern and southern approaches, opposite Stuart's troopers.[54]

South and west of Hanover, along the Littlestown Road, meanwhile, the Fifth and Sixth Michigan Cavalry had become entangled with Fitz

Lee's Confederate brigade. The two regiments had reached Littlestown shortly after daylight, spending much of the morning resting in town. The Fifth departed first, scouting on a back road to Hanover. When a local man reported Rebels toward Hanover, the Sixth marched on the Littlestown Road. About a mile from their destination, they struck Lee's troopers, who were deploying to cover Stuart's left flank.[55]

The Southerners formed for an attack. Colonel George Gray of the Sixth Michigan realized that his regiment had little chance against an entire brigade. Forming Companies B and F, under Major Peter Weber, into a skirmish line to delay the Rebels, Gray detoured the remaining companies to the northwest, and in the words of a disgruntled sergeant, "was obliged to skedaddle not very creditably." Twice Lee's veterans attacked Weber's squadron and were repulsed by the Northerners, who were armed with Spencer rifles. The Spencer was a .56-caliber weapon, with a seven-shot magazine, or cylindrical tube, that fit into the stock. A squadron of men could deliver firepower beyond their numbers, and the Michiganders raked the Southerners. A third assault settled it, however, as Weber retired, losing approximately 20 men as prisoners. Cut off from their comrades, the squadron did not rejoin the Sixth until the next morning.[56]

The Fifth Michigan Cavalry grazed by the action along the Littlestown Road, exchanging shots with Lee's men before entering Hanover. With the two regiments' arrival, Custer commanded the entire brigade, roughly 2,300 troopers. It was past noon, with the opponents stalking each other across the farmland outside of town. A dozen cannon on each side dueled, highlighted by the explosion of a Federal caisson from a direct hit that licked flames into the air and seared the ground with shards of metal and wood, killing one gunner and two horses.[57]

The stalemate lengthened until late in the afternoon when the Sixth Michigan advanced, supported by the Seventh, against the Rebel artillery. Dismounted, the troopers crossed the fields of the Carl Forney farm southwest of town. The fire of the Spencer rifles drove the gun crews away from their pieces, forcing Lee and Chambliss to counterattack. Custer rallied his men, sending them in a second time. Once again, the Southerners repulsed the thrust, but the Yankees withdrew a short distance, still threatening Stuart's flank.[58]

At sundown, the Confederates disengaged, swinging eastward beyond the Federal left flank. Hanover cost Stuart precious hours, and all night he pushed his columns to elude the Federals and to locate the main units of General Lee's army. Kilpatrick pursued, but darkness shielded the Rebels. By the morning of July 1, the Yankees had lost contact with the enemy horsemen. While Stuart's exhausted men and horses swung along a wide arc through Jefferson, Dover, and Dillsburg to Carlisle, Kilpatrick marched from Hanover to East Berlin and bivouacked. To the south and west, Lee's and Meade's armies had followed the roads to Gettysburg.[59]

The collision at Gettysburg on July 1 resulted in the rout of two Union infantry corps. The Federals regrouped, however, on a ridge and hills south of town, and there they made a stand. Meade ordered a concentration of the army. Kilpatrick received the message during the night and started for Gettysburg about 6 A.M. on the second. The cavalrymen passed through "beautiful country," in the words of a Michigander, arriving east of town in midafternoon. Here, on Hanover Road, Kilpatrick met David Gregg, commander of the Second Division, and received orders to guard the army's flank toward Abbottstown. The division backtracked north to York Pike, turned east for a short distance, and then filed into a narrow country lane that led to the village of Hunterstown. Custer's brigade marched in front.[60]

It was about 4:30 P.M. when the Sixth Michigan met Confederate pickets south of Hunterstown. The Southerners retreated through town, riding out the Gettysburg Road to the brick farmhouse of John Gilbert, where their comrades of Cobb's Legion were deployed at the edge of woods across the road. The Georgians belonged to the brigade of Brigadier General Wade Hampton, en route from Carlisle to Gettysburg. A handsome, wealthy South Carolinian, Hampton was an excellent officer whose duty on this day was to serve as rear guard for Stuart's cavalry. He had six regiments, roughly 1,750 men, and when the Federals scattered the pickets, he ordered back Phillips Legion and the Second South Carolina Cavalry to support the Georgians at the Gilbert farmstead.[61]

The Sixth Michigan chased the Confederates into Hunterstown, halting at the town's southwestern edge on the Gettysburg Road at the brick house and barn of John Felty, the local magistrate. Kilpatrick rode up, established headquarters at the Grass Hotel, and without either he or Custer determining the strength of the enemy, ordered the brigade commander to charge the Rebel position. Custer joined his troopers at the Felty farm, posting the artillery on a knoll and the Sixth Michigan among the farm buildings, with the First and Seventh Michigan on foot and the Fifth Michigan mounted in reserve. Fields of corn and wheat hemmed the rail fences on both sides of the road.[62]

Company A, Sixth Michigan, Captain H. E. Thompson commanding, formed a column in the road for the attack. Custer rode to the front, turned to the men, and shouted that he would lead them. It was not a place for a brigade commander, but if Custer wanted to demonstrate his personal bravery to the Michiganders, he picked the right time. Ahead, at the Gilbert farm, Colonel Pierce M. B. Young of Cobb's Legion watched the Yankees deploy. Young and Custer had been friends at the academy, and before Young returned to Georgia in the winter of 1861, he told his Ohio friend that they would meet as enemies in a cavalry engagement. Although neither man yet knew it, the rendezvous was at hand.[63]

With a yell, and with their new general dressed in black at their head, Thompson's men charged down the road. The Georgians triggered a volley and then scattered. But Young met his friend's thrust with his reserves, and the fighting swirled in the road and around the Gilbert house. Capt. Thompson was wounded, and Lieutenant S. H. Ballard's horse was killed, resulting in the officer's capture. When Custer's mount went down, he tumbled to the ground. A Confederate aimed his carbine at the brigadier, but Private Norvill Churchill of the First Michigan, who had joined in the attack, shot the enemy rider and pulled Custer onto his horse. The Confederates pressed forward, routing the Yankees. The attack cost the Union company 1 killed, 34 wounded, and 9 captured.[64]

Young's men pursued toward the Felty farm and met a wall of rifle fire and cannon blasts. Horses and riders collapsed in the roadbed. The Southerners reeled, fleeing to the rear. Hampton brought up some artillery, and the combat subsided. After dark, Hampton withdrew. In his report, Kilpatrick praised the Michiganders, asserting that they "fought most handsomely." As for Custer, his rashness nearly cost him his life, but his conduct impressed the men. The Northerners camped at Hunterstown for the night.[65]

Before midnight, however, orders arrived for the division to march to Two Taverns, south of Gettysburg. At Gettysburg, July 2 had been

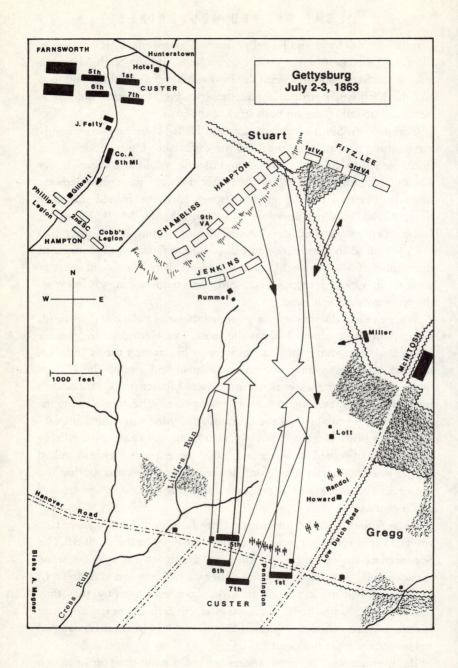

FARNSWORTH

Hunterstown

Hotel

5th

1st

6th

CUSTER

7th

J. Felty

Co. A
6th MI

Phillip's
Legion

Gilbert

2nd SC

Cobb's
Legion

HAMPTON

Gettysburg
July 2-3, 1863

Stuart

1st VA

FITZ. LEE

3rd VA

HAMPTON

CHAMBLISS

9th
VA

JENKINS

Rummel

Miller

N

W ——— E

S

1000 feet

McINTOSH

Little's Run

Lott

Randol

Howard

Hanover
Road

Gregg

Low Dutch Road

5th

6th

Pennington

1st

Cress Run

Blake A. Magner

CUSTER

another day of slaughter, more fearful than on the first, in places that would resonate in America's memory—the Peach Orchard, the Wheatfield, Devil's Den, the Valley of Death, Little Round Top, and Culp's Hill. The Federals held amid a fury that decimated units. On both sides, it seemed as if the soldiers fought for the nation's fate—and it may have been so. Meade expected a renewal of the battle on the third, and wanted all units on the field. A courier found Kilpatrick in Hunterstown.[66]

Kilpatrick's troopers rode south through much of the night, with the division halting near Two Taverns before daylight of the third. With little sleep, Farnsworth's brigade resumed the march that morning toward the southern flank of the army near Big Round Top. Before Custer could follow, however, an order came from Pleasonton to send one brigade to David Gregg's division, which protected the army's right flank and rear on Hanover Road. Kilpatrick detached Custer, and before ten o'clock Custer reported to Gregg near the intersection of Hanover Road and Low Dutch Road, approximately four miles east of Gettysburg's town square. Worried about the gap between his two brigades and Union infantry and artillery, Gregg shifted his units toward the Baltimore Pike and posted Custer at the intersection.[67]

Fertile farmland and woodlots of the Rummel, Lott, Spangler, and Howard families spread north from Hanover Road. Rail fences defined boundaries, while Little's Run flowed from a springhouse on the Rummel farm. Behind Rummel's house and barn, wooded Cress Ridge rose, over a mile from the intersection. It had been a place of peace, of farmers scything grain from the limestone soil—until this day.[68]

Skirmishers from the Fifth and Sixth Michigan—the two regiments armed with Spencer rifles—spread out behind fences and along Little's Run. Already, the July sun had heated the air, "a hot day all around," recalled a Federal. Their wait was brief. Shortly after ten o'clock, Confederate cannon wheeled out of the woods on Cress Ridge and fired three shots. Behind them, gray-jacketed skirmishers on foot filtered down the slope to the Rummel outbuildings. They were Virginians, part of Jeb Stuart's cavalry that had been ordered by Robert E. Lee to hold the army's left flank. Stuart had come from York Road, marching across country. He had ordered the firing of the cannon, perhaps to flush out any Yankees, but the blasts alerted Custer and Gregg to his presence.[69]

Desultory skirmishing characterized the action for the remainder of the morning. About noon, however, Custer received an order from Kilpatrick, through Gregg, to rejoin the division. Within an hour, Colonel John McIntosh began relieving Custer's men. McIntosh reported to Custer, who summarized the situation, and then pointing toward Cress Ridge, jokingly remarked, "I think you will find the woods out there . . . full of them." While the Michiganders filed into columns, troopers from three of McIntosh's regiments pushed into the fields, igniting an exchange of skirmish fire.[70]

The escalation in the combat concerned Gregg, who knew that if the Confederates pressed an attack, McIntosh would need reinforcements. With Colonel John Irvin Gregg too far away to be of assistance, David Gregg countermanded Kilpatrick's order to Custer, who "was well pleased to remain with his brigade," in Gregg's words. Custer positioned his regiments south of Hanover Road and added the six cannon of Battery M, Second United States Artillery, to First United States Artillery Captain Alanson M. Randol's four guns. Battery M belonged to Lieutenant Alexander C. M. Pennington, an academy friend of Custer's in the Class of 1860.[71]

About two o'clock, McIntosh advanced the First New Jersey and Third Pennsylvania toward the Rummel farm. The Virginians of Brigadier General Micah Jenkins's brigade, armed with Enfield rifles, blistered the Federals. With ammunition running low, the New Jerseymen and Pennsylvanians asked for help. Custer hurried the Fifth Michigan forward on foot, and they formed behind a stake-and-rail fence along a lane in front of the Rummel farm. To their left, companies of the Sixth Michigan reoccupied the ground along Little's Run. What had smoldered for hours now flamed.[72]

The Ninth Virginia charged dismounted down the slope of Cress Ridge, only to be pounded back. On its left, the Third Virginia started, stopped, and retreated. Stuart had enough, ordering the First Virginia forward in a mounted charge to sever the Union line into two pieces. The regiment cleared the trees, a lance in Confederate gray pointed toward the Fifth Michigan and McIntosh's troopers. "A more determined and vigorous charge than that made by the 1st Virginia," wrote an admiring Union captain, "it was never my fortune to witness."[73]

The Yankees scattered, running for their mounts and safety. Gregg, however, had seen the Confederate deployment and had ordered the

Seventh Michigan forward on horseback. The Seventh was the smallest and least experienced of the regiments in the brigade. As Colonel William D. Mann formed the regiment into a column, Custer galloped up. Drawing his sword, the brigadier shouted, "Come on, you Wolverines," waving them forward. The Seventh bolted ahead, charging diagonally across the fields toward the oncoming First Virginia. Members of the Fifth Michigan, spilling rearward, "stopped to see that charge."[74]

The opponents met at the post-and-rail fence previously held by the Fifth Michigan, southeast of the Rummel farm. The fence withstood the collision, "breaking our columns into jelly," stated a captain of the Seventh, "and mixing us up like a mass of pulp." The Virginians and Michiganders flailed at each other with sabers and fired their pistols. Along the edges of the mounted mass, Confederates on foot raked the Federals with carbine fire. According to Mann, it was "a desperate, but unequal, hand-to-hand conflict."[75]

A number of the Michiganders leveled a section of the fence, and a contingent of the regiment poured through, up the slope toward the Rummel buildings. "At them we went every man for himself," boasted Captain George Armstrong. They did not go far, as Stuart hurled four more mounted regiments into the fighting. One dismounted Virginian, standing over a wounded Union officer, asked him who was his commander. "He told me it was Gen. Custer," the Rebel wrote later. "That was the first time I had ever heard his name, but, afterwards, I had occasion to become very familiar with it."[76]

The Confederate reinforcements drove the Seventh Michigan from the fence, sending the Federals rearward. Colonel McIntosh rode toward the Michiganders, shouting, "For God's sake, men, if you are ever going to stand, stand now, for you are on your free soil!" Colonel Russell A. Alger of the Fifth Michigan mounted a squadron of the regiment, ordering it into the flank of the pursuing Southerners. Major Luther Trowbridge led the two companies, stating that they attacked "with a thrilling shout for Michigan." Dismounted clusters of McIntosh's troopers seared the edges of Stuart's forces with carbine and rifle fire. When the Seventh Michigan cleared the front of the Union artillery, the gun crews lashed the front. The Southerners recoiled and withdrew to the shelter of Cress Ridge.[77]

The Confederates were not finished. Before long, ranks of horsemen emerged from the trees on Cress Ridge. Their drawn sabers glistened "like silver in the bright sunlight—the spectacle called forth a murmur of admiration" from the Yankees. The Southerners, Wade Hampton's troopers, began at a trot and then increased to a canter. The ranks kept their alignment, "as if in review." Officers reminded them, "Keep to your sabers, men, keep to your sabers." "It was an inspiriting and an imposing spectacle," asserted Captain James Kidd of the Sixth Michigan.[78]

For several minutes, the gray-clad horsemen ruled the fields as every Yankee in their path scattered. Hampton pointed them toward the Union gun crews, who were ramming double charges of canister— one-inch balls, packed in cylinders—into their cannon. The gait increased to a gallop. "On came the rebel cavalry, yelling like demons, right toward the battery we were supporting apparently sweeping everything before them," Kidd told his parents in a letter six days later. Pennington's and Randol's gunners unleashed their gale of death, making "dreadful havoc," Kidd thought, in the Confederate ranks. But Hampton's men kept coming.[79]

Gregg had already reacted to the attack by ordering the First Michigan forward. The regiment emerged from a hollow south of Hanover Road and deployed into a column of squadrons. Colonel Charles H. Town, who was ill with consumption or tuberculosis and needed assistance to mount, moved to the head of the regiment. Here, Custer joined Town, and the two officers waved the men forward at a trot. "They advanced to the charge of a vastly superior force with as much order and precision as if going upon parade," reported Custer.[80]

When the Michiganders passed in front of the cannon, the gun crews stood and gazed. The Rebels were less than one hundred yards away when Custer signaled the gallop and shouted once again, "Come on, you Wolverines." The Yankees were "wild furious men" as they closed on the Rebels. The columns barreled into each other, "suddenly a crash, like the falling of timber." Horses and riders collapsed, with men crushed beneath the animals. Sabers clanged against sabers; pistols exploded into the faces of opponents. It was a struggle beyond description. From the Michiganders' right, Captain William E. Miller led a detachment of the Third Pennsylvania that knifed into the mass of Rebel horsemen, cutting a swath through the ranks. On the left, a squadron of the First New Jersey hit the Southerners. With Hampton wounded and headed toward the rear, the Confederates spurred toward

Cress Ridge. The Northerners pursued beyond the Rummel buildings before pulling back. Neither side had more to give, and the battle ended.[81]

"I challenge the annals of warfare," Custer declared in his report, "to produce a more brilliant or successful charge of cavalry" than that of the First Michigan. He had reason to be proud of its conduct and of the entire brigade's. He had emerged unscathed, but two of his horses had been wounded. Casualties in the brigade numbered 29 killed, 123 wounded, and 67 captured or missing, for a total of 219. In all, the Federals suffered 254 casualties, while the Confederates placed theirs at 181.[82]

Like Custer, members of the Michigan Brigade reacted with pride to their role in the fighting. "This is the most furious dragoon fight I ever saw or engaged in," an enlisted man of the Sixth scribbled into his diary. A comrade in the same regiment termed it "the hardest Battle of the war," while a trooper of the Seventh boasted in a letter to his family that "cavalry never did such fighting before in America." Edward Corselius of the Fifth avowed to his mother that "such fighting I never saw before," adding, "It is an honor to belong to Mich Cavalry."[83]

About midnight, the Yankees bedded down for the night. Earlier they had learned that a Confederate infantry assault, preceded by a massive artillery bombardment that they had heard, had been repulsed. Their comrades in the infantry and artillery still held the killing ground at nearby Gettysburg. They were probably too exhausted to speculate about its meaning.[84]

Chapter

6

"FIGHTING

WAS HIS

BUSINESS"

■ George Custer was sitting on a log, chatting and joking with members of the Michigan Brigade on the morning of July 4, when orders arrived to rejoin the division at Gettysburg. Regimental commanders filtered the directive down to the ranks; sergeants barked commands, and before long, sets of fours filled the roads. Southwest the troopers clattered, riding with the knowledge that they were now combat veterans, men of a brotherhood. Hanover, Hunterstown, Gettysburg—the war had been redefined for them. Experience shared their saddles on this morning.[1]

While Custer reported to Judson Kilpatrick, his men procured corn for their mounts. It was probably at this time that the brigade learned of the deaths of Elon Farnsworth and over sixty other men in a senseless charge ordered by Kilpatrick on the third. Farnsworth had protested the order, but Kilpatrick would not be swayed. Farnsworth obeyed and led two battalions into what a Confederate described as "wholesale slaughter." Kilpatrick's order had been inexplicable, almost irrational, and the men of the brigade did not forgive him for it. There was a disturbing quality to the general's judgment.[2]

When the Michigan Brigade arrived at the Gettysburg battlefield, little had changed from the previous night. Both armies maintained their respective positions, but neither side sought a renewal of the fearful carnage of the previous three days. Union commander George G.

Meade rejected Alfred Pleasonton's advice of an assault against the Rebels and settled for sending most of his cavalry to the south and west. If the enemy stayed at Gettysburg, the horsemen could operate against Robert E. Lee's supply and communication lines. If the Southerners retreated, as was most likely, the Yankees could harass the columns.[3]

Kilpatrick's and John Buford's divisions marched south, the former to Emmitsburg, the latter to Frederick. While they were en route, a rainstorm rolled in, unleashing a downpour that continued through the afternoon and night. At Emmitsburg, Colonel Pennock Huey's brigade of David Gregg's division joined Kilpatrick. Between three and five o'clock, pickets brought C. H. Buhrman, a civilian, to headquarters. Buhrman lived near Monterey Springs, northwest of Emmitsburg, and reported that a Confederate wagon train was moving south toward Hagerstown, Maryland. Lee had started the army's wagons and ambulances before the infantry and artillery withdrew from Gettysburg. The train sighted by Buhrman had passed through Fairfield Gap in South Mountain, following the so-called Furnace Road.[4]

Buhrman guided the cavalrymen. When they approached Fairfield Gap, Kilpatrick ordered the First Michigan to attack the rear of the train while the other units moved to intercept it at Monterey Pass. A battalion of the regiment, under Lieutenant Colonel Peter Stagg, charged the Confederates in the gap. The Rebels belonged to Brigadier General William E. Jones's brigade, and they hammered back the Federals, killing two officers and seventeen enlisted men. Stagg suffered a severe injury when his horse was shot from under him.[5]

The night was pitch dark, and it was "raining in torrents" when Kilpatrick and Custer halted at the Monterey House just below the crest of Monterey Pass. Kilpatrick had detached the First Vermont Cavalry to swing southwest to Smithsburg, Maryland, to cut off the van of the train if the Southerners were moving in that direction. Inside the Monterey House, the generals learned from the tenant's son that Rebel cavalrymen were posted beyond the crest and that the Furnace Road lay about a half-mile to the west. Alexander Pennington's gun crews slogged cannon into position on the road in front of the house and began shelling the darkness. Dismounted skirmishers from the Sixth Michigan plodded through mud toward the pass. "This was a night never to be forgotten," wrote an officer of the regiment a few days later.[6]

Beyond a narrow, plank bridge over a stream on the gap road, the Confederates—a few dozen Marylanders and North Carolinians—concealed themselves. When the Michiganders advanced, stumbling through underbrush and woods, the Rebel carbines flashed in the blackness, the gunfire stopping the Yankees. Custer's men could hear the wagons as they creaked past, but the Southerners could not be budged. Behind the Sixth, Colonel Russell A. Alger massed the Fifth Michigan in support. When Alger learned that the bridge was intact, he sent a message to Custer for a mounted charge as he attacked on foot. "With a rush," as Alger described it, his men crossed the bridge into what one of them thought was "a boiling pot of hell." The Southerners triggered a volley and then disappeared into the woods and the darkness.[7]

The First West Virginia Cavalry on horseback followed Alger's troopers, slicing into the column of wagons with a "whoop and yell." Panicked drivers whipped the teams, but the Federals were among them, threatening the teamsters with sabers. Some of the wagons and ambulances overturned amid the screams of the wounded inside. Kilpatrick reported the capture of 1,360 prisoners, mostly wounded men. He gathered the wagons and ambulances together, assigned guards to the Rebels who could walk, and started the brigades toward Smithsburg. Through "mud and rain," the column marched, arriving at the Maryland village about daylight on July 5. Details escorted the prisoners to Boonsboro, Maryland, and burned the vehicles.[8]

By the morning of the fifth, the entire Confederate army was on the move from Gettysburg to Virginia. The rain had abated, but roads remained troughs of mud, slowing the march. At Gettysburg, Meade reacted cautiously to Lee's withdrawal, pushing only one corps forward in a reconnaissance. It would be another two days before the Union infantry marched in full pursuit of the enemy. The duty of slowing and harassing Lee's units fell to Pleasonton's cavalrymen as the Rebels closed on Hagerstown and Williamsport, Maryland.[9]

For Kilpatrick's exhausted troopers, the initial contact occurred on the afternoon of the fifth, at Smithsburg, when two brigades of Confederate cavalry, under Jeb Stuart, approached from the east. The skirmish lasted for two hours, before Kilpatrick—for reasons not altogether clear—withdrew to Boonsboro for the night. On the sixth, his and Buford's units probed toward Hagerstown and Williamsport. While Colonel Nathaniel P. Richmond led Farnsworth's men against Rebel horsemen in

Hagerstown, Custer's troopers supported Buford at Williamsport along the Potomac River. The fighting was limited.[10]

The opposing cavalry units skirmished with each other for the next three days. On July 10, Union infantry and artillery units approached the Confederate lines north of the Potomac. Lee's fieldworks extended in a long arc, encasing a bend in the river from Williamsport to Falling Waters, where engineers constructed a pontoon bridge. The recent rainstorms had raised the Potomac above fordable levels, and until the water subsided and the bridge was completed, the Confederates were stranded in Maryland. But they constructed a formidable network of earthworks and gun emplacements. Meade and his generals studied the line, discussed the merits of an assault, and probed the works with infantry, sparking skirmishes. Finally, on the thirteenth, Meade ordered a reconnaissance in force for the next day.[11]

The Union cavalry, meanwhile, roamed along the front and on the army's flanks. Kilpatrick's division clashed with Stuart's units at Funkstown on the eleventh and cleared the enemy from Hagerstown on the twelfth. On both days, the Michigan Brigade led the advance. On Monday, the thirteenth, the horsemen marched south on the Hagerstown-Williamsport Road. A thunderstorm, with heavy rain, had struck during the previous night, and as one of them noted in his diary, "I never saw a muddier lot of men than we were" on this morning. When they struck Confederate pickets, Pennsylvania militiamen engaged the enemy. "It is very amusing to see the malicia fight," thought a cavalryman, "they scatter ralley yell & shout but do not get up much of a fight." The troopers supported the novice soldiers, but the fighting dissolved into sporadic skirmishing.[12]

As a part of Meade's reconnaissance in force on July 14, Kilpatrick's division closed on Williamsport, where it discovered abandoned works and a handful of rearguard troops. During the night, shielded by more heavy rain and the darkness, Lee evacuated his position, crossing the ford at Williamsport and the pontoon bridge at Falling Waters. Most of the Confederates had passed into Virginia by daylight, except for infantry units at Falling Waters. Local residents alerted Kilpatrick to the presence of these troops, five miles downstream, and the Union general hurried his division to the location in what an officer described as "a wild ride."[13]

Custer halted the Michigan Brigade in a woodlot. Beyond the tree line, a large, cultivated field rose to a knoll, where "crescent-shaped" enemy works could be seen. Uncertain of the Rebel strength, Custer instructed Major Peter Weber to advance Companies B and F of the Sixth Michigan, dismounted, into the field as skirmishers. Kilpatrick, however, reined up, briefly studied the works, and countermanded the order, directing Weber to mount the companies and attack. "Gen. Kilpatrick don't wait for infantry or orders when the rebels are in places as that, retreating across a river," a staff officer boasted about the general on this day.[14]

Regarded as "the best officer in the regiment," Weber formed the two companies—fifty-seven men—into a column. Emerging from the trees, they crossed the muddy field at a trot. Fortune rode with them for a few minutes as the Southerners mistook them for their own cavalry. Before the Alabamians and Tennesseans realized that they were Federals, Weber's men had plunged into the works, sabers slashing and pistols firing. The surprised Confederates belonged to Major General Henry Heth's division and numbered in the hundreds. They blasted the horsemen at point-blank range and swung muskets or fence rails. Weber pitched from the saddle, dead; Lieutenant Charles E. Bolza was killed, and Lieutenant George Crawford's leg was shattered, necessitating subsequent amputation. Caught in a vise, the Michiganders never had a chance. Of the fifty-eight officers and men, fifteen were killed, twelve wounded, and thirteen captured. "It cost us Some of our Bravest & Best men," complained a surgeon in the brigade.[15]

As the survivors fled to the woods, Custer rushed the remaining companies of the Sixth Michigan into the field. The Confederates counterattacked, driving the Northerners back until the First Michigan and a squadron of the Eighth New York repulsed them. The Southerners remained in the works, covering the crossing of Heth's brigades. Before the final regiments could withdraw, however, Custer attacked with the First and Seventh regiments on foot. The Yankees poured over the works, grabbing scores of prisoners, three battle flags, and a cannon. A trooper claimed in a letter to his wife that he saw Custer drive a saber into the abdomen of an infantryman who was trying to shoot him. "You can guess," he added, "how bravely soldiers fight for such a general."[16]

"We gave the Rebs the finishing touch," bragged a member of the First Michigan. "I think old Lee will remember Gen Killpatrick's cavalry for some time." Reports conflict as to the number of prisoners captured. John Buford, whose brigades hit the Southerners on the right, claimed 500 captives, while Kilpatrick stated that his troopers grabbed almost 1,500. But as an artillery officer asserted, "the fact that Kilpatrick makes the report leads to some doubt to its accuracy." Custer placed his brigade's total at 400, which was much closer to the truth than Kilpatrick's figure. Regardless, the Union cavalry embarrassed and stung the Southerners at Falling Waters, including the mortal wounding of Brigadier General J. Johnston Pettigrew by Weber's squadron. When Lee's men cut the ropes of the pontoon bridge, the Gettysburg Campaign ended.[17]

The Third Cavalry Division bivouacked outside of Boonsboro on the night of the fourteenth. Custer and his staff lodged in the village at the home of "an old copperhead," or antiwar Democrat. "The Gen'l did not get a very warm reception," claimed one of his orderlies. The next morning, Kilpatrick requested and was granted a leave of absence for medical reasons. As he noted, he had a "severe pain in my side." Evidence indicates that he suffered from inflammation of the kidneys, or nephritis. He complained frequently of back pain and rode stooped or bent over. Eventually, he died of Bright's disease, or chronic nephritis, and was probably afflicted with it in its early stages during the war. He would not return until August 4. Until then, Custer commanded the division.[18]

Kilpatrick's departure was not unwelcome news to the members of the command. Already, they were calling him "Kill-Cavalry" because of the needless slaughter of Farnsworth's men at Gettysburg and the sacrifice of Weber's companies at Falling Waters. Captain James Kidd later summarized well the sentiments of the troopers about Kilpatrick when he wrote: "He had begun to be a terror to foes, and there was a well-grounded fear he might become a menace to friends as well. He was brave to rashness, capricious, ambitious, reckless in rushing into scrapes, and generally full of expedients in getting out, though at times he seemed to lose his head entirely when beset by perils which he himself, had invited. He was prodigal of human life, though to do him justice he rarely spared himself."[19]

By contrast, Custer emerged from the campaign with the confidence and admiration of the entire brigade. In contemporary writings and in postwar memoirs, his men praised him. Despite his youth and his appearance, Custer removed any questions about his bravery, his leadership qualities, and his skill in combat. On the road at Hunterstown, in the fields at Gettysburg, and on the knoll at Falling Waters, he led them, not from a distance behind a battle line, but at the very forefront of combat. In slightly over a fortnight, he had instilled in the brigade an aggressiveness and a belief in themselves as fighting men that transformed the command.

Their words resonate with devotion and respect. On July 9, a trooper in the brigade wrote that "Gen. Custerd. He is a glorious fellow, full of energy, quick to plan and bold to execute, and with us he had never failed in any attempt he has yet made." On the same day, in a letter to his family, Andrew Newton Buck of the Seventh boasted that "our cavalry is doing mighty things whereof we are glad." Custer, reasoned another, "was not afraid to fight like a private soldier . . . and that he was ever in front and would never ask them to go where he would not lead." After Gettysburg, Lieutenant S. H. Ballard of the Sixth claimed, "The command perfectly idolized Custer. The old Michigan Brigade adored its Brigadier, and all felt as if he weighed about a ton." To a private, the general had put "the very devil" into the brigade.[20]

Superior officers shared the men's estimation of the brigadier. Kilpatrick cited him for Hanover, Hunterstown, and the engagements during the Confederate retreat to Virginia. Writing of Custer and Wesley Merritt, Alfred Pleasonton stated in his report that both generals "have increased the confidence entertained in their ability and gallantry to lead troops on the field of battle." Unofficially, Pleasonton allegedly remarked that "Custer is the best cavalry general in the world and I have given him the best brigade to command." In Washington, the War Department promoted him to brevet major in the Regular Army, to rank from July 3, 1863.[21]

The Gettysburg Campaign tested Custer as a general, revealing attributes of the man and of the soldier that merited his men's loyalty and his superiors' commendation. "Fighting was his business," said James Kidd of him, and he demonstrated a remarkable aptitude for it during the operations. In the confusing madness of combat—a veteran once described it as a "hell carnival"—Custer reacted instinctively to its fluidity, or as Kidd argued, "his perceptions were intuitions." He was self-confident, fearless, and resourceful, leading the brigade as if he had done it for months.[22]

Custer's aggressiveness in action, however, was not intemperate. Except for Hunterstown, he directed his units as prescribed in textbooks, deploying skirmishers, probing for enemy strength and position before committing them to attack. At Falling Waters, Kilpatrick countermanded his order to use dismounted skirmishers to test the Rebel works. Custer, reported a Michigan lieutenant, "always displayed excellent judgment in handling his troops. He was different from Kilpatrick, who was rash. His [Kilpatrick's] standing order was 'Charge, God damn them,' whether they were five or five thousand."[23]

Custer understood that battles develop, take form according to terrain and dispositions, but offer moments that favor the opponent prepared and willing to seize them. He sought the edge, an advantage that could be exploited and that could result in victory. Custer preferred the mounted charge, the thunder of hooves, the flash of sabers, believing that cavalry tactics required boldness. At Gettysburg, on July 3, he met Stuart's thrusts on horseback with his own. To him, combat rewarded audacity.

To be sure, glory trailed the daring, the indomitable. Custer was, as Kidd admitted, "eager for laurels." His ambition and desire for renown impelled, but they did not govern. The engagements indicated that he was neither "a reckless commander" nor "regardless of human life." He relished combat, drawn to it not for its terribleness, but for its possibilities. In his own distinctive velvet coat of arms, Custer was a knight errant, trapped within a conflict shorn of romance—on a personal quest within a national tragedy. The men of the Michigan Brigade had judged him and then filed into column behind the banner.[24]

The warriors' road led out of Boonsboro, Maryland, on the morning of July 16, as the Third Cavalry Division marched south along the Potomac River. The next day, the command crossed the river on a pontoon bridge opposite Berlin (now Brunswick), Maryland, bivouacking for the night at Purcellville, in Loudoun County, Virginia. Here the troopers mustered for pay, before heading south on the nineteenth, riding through the Piedmont, east of the Blue Ridge Mountains. On July 23, the division forded the Rappahannock River and camped near Amissville. "I have had," Custer proudly informed Ann Reed, "the post of honor ever since the Army crossed into Virginia that is I have held the advance with my division."[25]

When the Confederates crossed the Potomac on the night of July

13–14, they carried the war with them back to the Old Dominion. In Washington, Lincoln was bitterly disappointed that Lee had escaped unharmed, except for the action at Falling Waters, blaming George Meade for the failure. The president's criticism had some merit, but from the distant capital, he misread the situation at Williamsport. In his memorable words—"We had them within our grasp. We had only to stretch forth our hands and they were ours. And nothing I could say or do could make the Army move"—Lincoln did a disservice to Meade and his veterans. In fact, Lee was neither surrounded nor trapped, and his troops manned a strong defensive position. Meade acted cautiously, but a frontal assault on the works could have resulted in heavy casualties. After Lee reentered Virginia, Meade shifted the army east of the mountains. By July 20, the Yankees had completed the river's passage, advancing south through the Piedmont.[26]

For the next four days, skirmishes ignited in the gaps of the Blue Ridge as Meade attempted to interdict Lee's march from the Shenandoah Valley. By July 24, one corps of Lee's army reached Culpeper Court House, south of the Rappahannock River. During the day, Custer's horsemen clashed with Lee's infantry, forcing some Rebel units to deploy. Lee had won the race, and Meade ordered a concentration of his army around Warrenton, north of the Rappahannock. As more Confederate divisions arrived, Lee stretched his lines along the river's southern bank. On July 31, Custer withdrew, under orders, across the Rappahannock.[27]

With the armies divided by the river, operations settled into a summer languor that would stretch through August into September. Soldiers on both sides needed a respite from the two months of campaigning. Meade and Lee wrestled with supply shortages and the replenishing of thinned ranks. In the Union cavalry, the need for serviceable mounts became so acute that Lincoln issued an executive order that forbade the export of horses. The Gettysburg Campaign had exacted a toll that required weeks of recovery.[28]

Custer busied himself during these weeks, attending to the men's needs and refitting the brigade. He was pleased with and proud of the command, telling his sister that "I would not exchange it for any other brigade in the Army." He visited the picket posts frequently, seemingly always at hand when gunfire erupted. Restless and energetic by nature, Custer labored long hours, either in camp or on horseback. He used scouts as often as he could to gather information. Nothing exasperated him more, however, than local civilians whom he had arrested for disloyal activities but who then returned to the area when they were paroled. He complained to headquarters about the practice, only to be reminded that his authority extended only to arrests, not paroles.[29]

Tully McCrea, a Union artillery officer and former academy roommate of Custer's, visited him in mid-August. McCrea had not seen his friend since September 1862, when the latter passed through the capital during the Antietam Campaign. When McCrea arrived at headquarters, the brigadier greeted him with "a hearty smile on his face." "He is the same careless, reckless fellow that he was" at West Point, McCrea wrote home. "He is the most romantic of men and delights in something odd. Last summer when he was on the Peninsula, he vowed that he would not cut his hair until he entered Richmond. He has kept his vow and now his hair is about a foot long and hangs over his shoulders in curls just like a girl."

McCrea then described Custer's uniform in detail, adding that "you may think from this that he is a vain man, but he is not; it is nothing more than his penchant for oddity. . . . But he is a gallant soldier, a whole-souled generous friend, and a mighty good fellow, and I like him and wish him every success in his new role of Brigadier."[30]

Custer valued few traits in individuals more than friendship and loyalty. His efforts on the Peninsula in 1862, on behalf of Gimlet Lea and James Washington, and McCrea's letters indicated the kindness and generosity he extended to friends. Those individuals who shared it with him never wavered in their affection for him. Such friendships became lifelong bonds.

In turn, the staff changes implemented during these weeks reflected Custer's preference for men he knew personally and trusted. For assistant adjutant general, or chief of staff, he selected Jacob Greene of Monroe, Michigan. Greene had served as a lieutenant in the Seventh Michigan Infantry before resigning his commission in January 1862. Custer met him while on leave, and together they enjoyed a number of parties, with Custer courting Libbie Bacon and Greene, Nettie Humphrey. Greene was commissioned a captain in the Sixth Michigan Cavalry and joined the staff by early August 1863.[31]

Soon after Greene reported for duty, Custer had the chief of staff accompany him to the front, where a skirmish ensued. They sat their horses near the pickets. "I tried him the other day," Custer wrote afterward to Nettie Humphrey of her beau, "took him where the bullets flew thick and fast. I watched him closely. He never faltered, was as calm and collected as if sitting at his dinner." Greene passed the initial test, and as Custer added, "succeeds beyond expectation" as adjutant general.[32]

James Christiancy, the nineteen-year-old son of Judge Isaac Christiancy and brother of Henry, also joined the staff in August. He had originally enlisted in the Seventeenth Michigan before transferring to the Ninth Michigan Cavalry as a first lieutenant in January 1863. Custer secured his appointment to the staff probably as a favor to the judge. Young Christiancy had a problem with alcohol, and it appears that his father hoped that Custer, who did not imbibe, could change his son's habits. While Christiancy proved to be a fine aide-de-camp, he continued to drink liquor, causing his family much despair.[33]

Other members appointed to the staff included Captain Robert F. Judson and Second Lieutenant Edward G. Granger of the Fifth Michigan Cavalry as aides-de-camp, and Private Frederick Nims, a Monroe lad, and Private Gustavus Lange of the First Michigan Cavalry as orderlies. Custer also selected Sergeant Michael Bellior as his personal color bearer and designated Company C, Fifth Michigan Cavalry as the color company or, as he called the members, his "Guard of Honor."[34]

Sometime during August, a group of runaway slaves, or contrabands, entered the army's camps. Seeking a cook for himself and the staff, Custer approached a young woman among the ragged runaways and asked her if she would serve in the position. She agreed, returning with the general to his headquarters. She identified herself as Eliza Denison Brown, and in time, would "become a figure of no minor importance in the Custer story," according to a biographer of Custer.[35]

Little is known about Eliza's background, except that she had fled a plantation in Virginia. Subsequently, she explained that "everybody was excited over freedom, and I wanted to see how it was. Everybody keeps asking me why I left. I can't see why they can't recollect what war was for, and that we was all bound to try and see for ourselves how it was." When she hired on with Custer, however, she had misgivings: "Oh, how awful lonesome I was at first, and I was afraid of everything in the shape of war. I used to wish myself back on the plantation with my mother."[36]

While Eliza never overcame her fear of "everything in the shape of war," she soon began to rule headquarters as effectively and firmly as Custer commanded on a battlefield. In her soft voice, she scolded the staff members and Custer, whom she called "the Ginnel," when they were late for meals or when their antics at headquarters became too boisterous. During quiet periods at headquarters, particularly when Custer was not present, the officers chatted with Eliza about personal or nonmilitary matters. She kept their money and personal items when they left on a raid or when combat appeared imminent. She became a constant presence with the command, and throughout the brigade she was called "the Queen of Sheba." [37]

As with numerous facets of Custer's life, his relationship with Eliza has produced questions and controversy. He had affection for her, but did he share his bed with her? According to Frederick W. Benteen, an officer in Custer's postwar regiment, the Seventh Cavalry, "it was notorious" throughout the Cavalry Corps of the Army of the Potomac that Custer "used to sleep with his cook." Benteen claimed that he learned of it from a Virginia "classmate of mine." The problem with Benteen's assertion is twofold—it is based upon hearsay, and he loathed Custer. No other evidence that supports Benteen's charge has been uncovered, and his private correspondence is replete with falsehoods, half-truths, and venom about Custer. [38]

Benteen also alleged that Libbie Custer knew of the relationship between her husband and Eliza. If it were true and she knew of it, Libbie concealed it with consummate skill. Her writings describe Eliza in the kindest and fondest terms. More important, for Libbie to have retained in her household for six years a woman who shared a sexual relationship with her husband defies reason. Eliza was a servant and expendable at any time. When Eliza left their employ, she remained attached to the Custers. As Eliza once told Libbie: "There's many folks says that a woman can't follow the army without throwing themselves away, but I know better. I went in, and I cum out with the respect of the men and of the officers." Her words echo with more credibility than those of a man consumed with hatred. [39]

While Custer reorganized the staff and left the housekeeping at head-quarters in Eliza's care, he continued to drill the brigade and to address the command's supply needs. On August 17, the brigade moved down-stream to a camp outside of Falmouth, across the river from Fredericksburg. Three days later, in a reorganization of the division, the First Vermont Cavalry was assigned to the brigade, and Colonel Henry E. Davies assumed command of Elon Farnsworth's First Brigade. The Vermonters were veterans, members of the first complete cavalry regiment organized from New England, and the Michiganders welcomed them to the brigade.[40]

On August 25, the division conducted a reconnaissance downriver from Falmouth. Between Port Conway and King George Court House the cavalry collided with Confederate infantry. The Michigan Brigade led the division, and Custer dismounted the First and Sixth Michigan, sending them forward against the Rebels posted in woods. He and his staff remained on horseback on the road between the two regiments. In James Christiancy's words, they were in the "most exposed" position on the field. It was the first time Christiancy saw the commander in action, and he marveled at his poise and bravery. "Through all that sharp and heavy firing," the aide wrote two days later to Daniel S. Bacon, Libbie's father, "the General gave his orders as though conducting a parade or review, so cool and indifferent that he inspired us all with something of his coolness and courage."[41]

The Federals cleared the woods of the enemy, pushing them back to their reserve line, and pressing ahead until Confederate artillery, anchoring a third position, stopped them. Custer withdrew, and the cavalry returned to Falmouth. "To say that General Custer is a brave man is unnecessary," concluded Christiancy. "He has proven himself to be not only that but also a very cool and self possessed man. It is indeed difficult to disturb his mental Equilibrium."[42]

Kilpatrick's division remained in the Falmouth area until September 12, when ordered upriver to Kelly's Ford. Meade had received reports that Lee had detached infantry divisions from the army and ordered Pleasonton to cross the Rappahannock with the cavalry corps to conduct a reconnaissance in force. At 6 A.M., on the thirteenth, the horsemen splashed across, with Kilpatrick's two brigades advancing as the left wing at Kelly's Ford. Davies's brigade marched in front, shoving aside Confederate cavalry and reaching Brandy Station about 7:30 A.M. Here John Buford's and David Gregg's divisions joined Kilpatrick's, and the combined units rode toward Culpeper Court House.[43]

The Yankees followed the tracks of the Orange & Alexandria Railroad, halting on a ridge three-fourths of a mile north of Culpeper. In town, Virginians of Colonel Lunsford Lomax's brigade were posted behind the bank of a swollen Mountain Run, among buildings, and around the railroad station. Three cannon of horse artillery braced the dismounted Rebels. If the Federals meant business, Lomax's men would be hard-pressed against three divisions. Pleasonton was serious and ordered Kilpatrick to attack.[44]

The Second New York Cavalry of Davies's brigade spurred down the ridge, veered to the west along the stream, and, locating a crossing point, surged into the town. The Virginians resisted, but they were caught between the mounted New Yorkers and the rifle fire of the dismounted Sixth Michigan Cavalry north of Mountain Run. Before the artillerists could extricate two of the guns, the New Yorkers were among them, slashing those who would not surrender.[45]

While the New Yorkers secured the cannon and bagged prisoners, a train steamed into town, stopping at the station. From the ridge, Custer saw the prize and reacted at once. Gathering a color sergeant and orderlies around him, he formed a battalion of the First Vermont Cavalry into a column and signaled the charge. With the brigadier and his men in the lead, the attackers swept into Culpeper, firing at the train, whose crew had reversed the engine, shoving the cars down the track. The train outraced the pursuing horsemen, but Custer's detachment seized the other cannon and cleared the town of Rebels.[46]

Lomax's Virginians withdrew to Greenwood Hill, a wooded knoll southwest of Culpeper, and deployed. Jeb Stuart, who was in overall command, sent forward additional cannon as support for the cavalrymen. Before long, the Fifth New York Cavalry attacked on horseback, but the Confederate gunners blasted them back with canister. Kilpatrick arrived, took command, bringing up artillery and advancing skirmishers on foot. Custer added the First Vermont and Seventh Michigan to the line, and the Federals pressed forward. Stuart's gun crews arced shells over the Yankees, the explosions hurling iron shards into the enemy ranks. A piece of a shell ripped into Custer's foot, causing a painful wound, while another piece killed his horse. Staff officers carried the general to the rear.[47]

A surgeon attended to Custer's wound, and as it was subsequently reported, the brigade commander rode up to Pleasonton, exclaiming, "How are you, fifteen-days'-leave-of-absence? They have spoiled my boots but they didn't gain much there, for I stole 'em from a Reb."

Pleasonton surely laughed at the remark, but granted the request. A week earlier, Custer had asked for a leave, citing the serious illness of his mother. Pleasonton approved it at the time, but operations prevented Custer from leaving the brigade. Now the brigadier would need some time for his foot to heal, and Pleasonton approved a twenty-day furlough.[48]

The Union officer who recorded in his diary the encounter of Custer and Pleasonton described the former's attack at Culpeper as "a really handsome charge." He then confessed in his diary: "This officer is one of the funniest-looking beings you ever saw, and looks like a circus rider gone mad! He wears a huzza jacket and tight trousers, of faded black velvet trimmed with tarnished gold lace. His head is decked with a little, gray felt hat; high boots and gilt spurs complete the costume, which is enhanced by the General's coiffure, consisting in short, dry, flaxen ringlets! His aspect, though highly amusing, is also pleasing as he has a very merry blue eye, and a devil-may-care style!"[49]

A captain of the Second New York Cavalry, who had witnessed Custer in action for the first time at Culpeper, admitted later that "it seemed to be the general impression that he would not have the nerve to 'Face the music' with his bandbox equipment, but he soon proved himself equal to the occasion. . . . No soldier who saw him on that day . . . ever questioned his right to wear a star, or all the gold lace he felt inclined to wear." A Michigan trooper, who had already seen him in battle, put it bluntly to his wife in a letter: "He is a bully general and brave too. He is a very odd man but he understands his business."[50]

For a few weeks, however, "his business" would be forgotten as Custer boarded a train for Monroe. Five months ago, he had left there a brevet captain, and now he would be returning a brigadier general. The engine could not have steamed west fast enough for him. George Custer had some unfinished business of his own at line's end.

Chapter 7

"MY OWN BRIGHT PARTICULAR *STAR*"

■ The July 23, 1863, issue of the *Monroe Commercial* confirmed what had been rumored in the city for some time. "Upon the first appearance of the report that Captain Custer had been made a Brigadier General of the Cavalry," the newspaper stated, "we were in some doubt as to its genuineness; but it proved to be a bona-fide appointment." Custer had earned the promotion and "will no doubt prove fully capable and efficient," it concluded.[1]

Since that date, Monroe residents had read additional stories about the brigadier in Eastern newspapers. By summer's end, Custer had become a hero among the city folk, and when he arrived on September 16, numerous individuals sought his company. The *Commercial* and the *Monroe Monitor* noted his return and briefly sketched the circumstances of his being wounded. A delegation of young men planned a party in his honor. It was a touch of the fame and public approbation he had sought for so long, and he undoubtedly savored it.[2]

The homecoming was even warmer at the home of his sister and brother-in-law, Ann and David Reed. Ann had always been special to Autie, and he had written to her whenever he could, describing his exploits and assuring her of his safety. If he had not learned it earlier in a recent letter from her, she now informed him that their parents had bought the house of a Dr. Stephens on the corner of Cass and Third streets in Monroe. Both Ann and Autie had been trying for months to persuade Emanuel and Maria to sell their farm in Ohio and relocate in Monroe. They finally relented, but as Ann told her brother, they would need financial assistance to furnish the home. Only Autie, with his income as a general, could provide them with help. "It all depends on you," Ann said. Their parents would not settle affairs in Ohio, however, before he returned to the army.[3]

But Custer's immediate interest centered upon Libbie Bacon. He had not seen her in five months, nor had he corresponded directly with her. He had kept in contact with Fannie Fifield—a fact that Libbie knew—and suitors continued to call at the Bacon residence, a circumstance he must have surmised. His ardor and love for her had not abated, but neither had her parents' resistance to the relationship. But if a captain could not offer a young woman an acceptable future, perhaps a brigadier general could.

During his service with the army, strands of a web connected them to each other. Libbie did not violate Judge Bacon's stricture that his daughter could not write to Custer or receive letters from him. But before he returned to duty in April, she and Autie conspired with Nettie Humphrey to circumvent the judge's wishes. Autie would correspond with Nettie, who would share the contents with Libbie, and when Nettie replied, she would include Libbie's thoughts. The arrangement allowed Libbie to convince herself that she was a dutiful daughter while assuring Autie that he would not be forgotten.[4]

When Custer returned to Monroe on September 16, he intended to resume the "attack," as Libbie described it months earlier. He was not a man easily broken, even bent. But Libbie's feelings toward him seemed as confounding as ever. Nettie's letters contained mixed signals, indications both of irreconcilable difficulties and of a willingness to continue the relationship. When Custer called, as Libbie told it later, she "saw him at once, because I could not avoid him. I tried to, but I did not succeed." In fact, her resistance to him had all but ceased. She was in love with him and had been for longer than she wanted to admit.[5]

Weeks earlier, David Reed, Custer's brother-in-law, had called at the Bacon residence. He had come, he said to Libbie, at Autie's request to share with her a drawing of him by Alfred Waud in *Harper's Weekly* and a letter that described the scene. During their conversation, which must have been awkward at times, Reed indicated that it was Libbie, not, as Libbie supposed, Fanny Fifield whom Custer loved. That night, in her journal, she enthused: "I love him still. I know it is love from fancy with no foundation, but I love him still and theory vanishes when practice comes in to play. There is no similarity of tastes between us and I will never think of it, but *I love him*. His career is much to me."[6]

She still enjoyed the attention of several young men, suffered from doubts about her feelings toward Autie, and worried about her parents' objection to him. As an obedient daughter, she should have rejected Autie, but he was unlike any man she knew. She called it "my violent fancy for C," believing that "I am under the influence of it *now*." Such emotions may pass within a year, she wrote in mid-August, but "it seems as if devoted love for me influenced me even at this distance. If it were possible I should say his spirit influenced and partly controlled mine tho' miles separated us."[7]

A month later, they were brought together again, and although Libbie contended that she wished to avoid him, she had anticipated the moment for a long time. Autie strolled with her, sat in a nearby pew in church, and escorted her to the masquerade party given in his honor on the night of September 28. He attended the dance as Louis XVI; she, as a gypsy girl with a tambourine. Together, they danced into the early hours of the morning. Finally, in the garden of the Bacon residence, he proposed once more, and she accepted. There could be no announced engagement or planned wedding, Libbie said, until her parents consented. He would have to approach her father, and until then, they must continue to exchange letters through Nettie Humphrey. Autie agreed to the terms. "I never *even thought of marrying him,*" she asserted later to her cousin. "Indeed I did not know I loved him so until he left Monroe in the spring."[8]

Custer's leave ended on October 5. Libbie, her father, Nettie, and some friends accompanied him to the railroad station. Judge Bacon had recently returned from a business trip—he allegedly departed Monroe when he heard that Custer wished to speak with him about Libbie— and at the station spoke briefly to Custer about military matters. Custer replied that he had wanted to discuss with him another concern but would write instead. "Very well," responded Bacon, and Custer boarded the train after the farewells. That night Libbie confided in the journal: "The last few leaves will bear a name I love—Dear C—try as I did to suppress the 'fancy' for six months it did no good. The *fancy* I know was more, it was *love*. I do love him and have all the time. He is *dear,*

dear. I *tried* so hard to think it was an idle, passing fancy. But I love him. I believe I shall marry him sometime." [9]

The brigadier took a steamer from Toledo to Cleveland, where he boarded a train for Baltimore, arriving in the city early on the seventh. While waiting for a train to Washington, he wrote to Nettie: "I have thought much of my intended letter to Libbie's father, my mind alternating between hope and fear—fear that I may suffer from some unfounded prejudice. . . . I feel that her father, valuing her happiness, would not refuse were he to learn from her own lips our real relation to one another." That evening, he attended a theater in the capital, losing his wallet with seventy dollars in it. On the eighth, he sat for "a magnificent photograph" that cost thirty dollars and would be ready within a few months. That evening, he arrived at the Michigan Brigade's camp, located southwest of Culpeper Court House, along the Robertson River. The troopers gave him three cheers, and the brigade band played "Hail to the Chief." He thought that even Eliza seemed pleased with his return. [10]

Since the engagement at Culpeper on September 13, elements of the Union army had pushed south of the Rappahannock River toward the Rapidan and Robertson rivers. Beyond the Rapidan, the Confederates were posted, and contact between the opponents came at fords. The fighting was infrequent, and for most of the time, the Federal cavalrymen had little to do except picket duty. In Kilpatrick's camps, the men amused themselves with horse races. When Custer arrived on the eighth, the troopers had enjoyed over ten days of quiet. [11]

The routine ended on October 9, when Federal scouts reported the advance of Confederate forces across the Rapidan toward Madison Court House. General Lee had decided to undertake an offensive around the Union army's right flank, forcing General Meade to give battle. With Jeb Stuart's cavalrymen in the van, the infantry and artillery units marched toward the Robertson River and Judson Kilpatrick's mounted division beyond the stream. If Lee's troops could shove aside the Union horsemen and infantry supports, the Southerners would have a clear route to the Rappahannock and Meade's right flank. [12]

During the day, Kilpatrick directed Custer to be prepared to move at once and to instruct his pickets to maintain the "greatest vigilance." Later, scouts informed Custer that Southerners were moving "in heavy column toward my right." His men cooked rations, filled bags with forage, and saddled their mounts. "Often I think of the vast responsibility resting on me," he wrote to Nettie Humphrey, "of the many lives entrusted to my keeping, of the happiness of so many households depending on my discretion and judgment—and to think that I am just leaving my boyhood makes the responsibility appear greater." It was not from "egotism, self-conceit" that he spoke, but from the recognition of "my duty to my country, my command." " 'First be sure you're right, then go ahead!' I ask myself, 'Is it right?' Satisfied that it is so, I let nothing swerve me from my purpose." If a general "adopts public opinion as guide," he concluded, he "cannot entertain one purpose long, for what pleases one will displeasure another."[13]

His responsibility increased rapidly on the tenth, as the enemy crossed the Robertson River, driving toward Culpeper Court House. Kilpatrick withdrew the division to James City, a village of a half dozen dwellings located between Madison Court House and Culpeper. Stuart's horsemen approached in the afternoon, and a skirmish ensued north and east of the town. Artillery batteries supported the opposing troopers, with neither side securing an advantage. Stuart retired after a few hours, but to the west Confederate infantry were passing beyond Kilpatrick's flank. The Yankees bivouacked on the ground. During the night, Kilpatrick received orders from Pleasonton to retreat across the Rappahannock, covering Union infantry.[14]

The division started out at seven o'clock, pursued closely by Stuart with two brigades. While passing through Culpeper, Kilpatrick's rear guard tumbled back upon the main Union body, forcing Custer to deploy the Michigan Brigade on the ridge north of town from which the Yankees had attacked on September 13. Stuart, however, shifted units beyond Custer's flank, and Kilpatrick ordered the march resumed. The Northerners followed the tracks of the Orange & Alexandria Railroad—Custer's brigade on the left; Brigadier General Henry Davies's, on the right. "All moving in column (solid), each brigade, regt. and battery with its distinct battle flag forming an imposing display," asserted one of Kilpatrick's staff officers.[15]

It was a race to the Rappahannock River, with Stuart's troopers gnawing at the flank and rear. Suddenly, as the Yankees reached Auburn, the mansion of John Minor Botts outside of Brandy Station, they reined up. To their right and front, on a parallel road, moved an entire Confederate cavalry division, three brigades of Major General Fitzhugh Lee.

Stuart had been pushing the Federals into a trap, and it was closing. A Vermonter thought that the situation "was sufficiently exciting." [16]

While Lee aligned his division across the railroad tracks in front of Brandy Station, Stuart attacked the enemy rear guard—the Second New York and Seventh Michigan—across Botts's farmland. The Federals repulsed the thrust, and Kilpatrick ordered the Second New York to counterattack. The New Yorkers galloped over the crest of a ridge, smashing into the columns of the Fourth and Fifth North Carolina and routing the regiments. The Eighteenth Pennsylvania then plowed into another Southern regiment, stabilizing the Union left flank and rear. But from the east came several regiments of Lee's division in a mounted charge. Pleasonton, who was accompanying Kilpatrick, deployed the division's two batteries in line, and the artillerists gouged holes in the enemy ranks, sending them rearward. [17]

At Brandy Station, meanwhile, Brigadier General John Buford's cavalry division had engaged one of Fitz Lee's brigades. Lee had been pursuing Buford's command from Stevensburg when he sighted Kilpatrick's columns along the railroad tracks. While Buford halted at Brandy Station, Lee wheeled two brigades to confront Kilpatrick and posted the other one toward Buford. When Lee attacked Kilpatrick, Buford charged Lee's rear. It was a battle along three parallel lines, with two opposing divisions caught between enemy lines. At times, war defied reason. [18]

Pleasonton, Kilpatrick, and Custer conferred, with Custer proposing that they "cut an opening to the River." Pleasonton approved, and Custer rode to his brigade. With Stuart still poised on the flank, Custer detached the Sixth and Seventh Michigan to guard it, and formed the First and Fifth Michigan in a column of squadrons. Across the railroad bed, Davies aligned his Union regiments in a similar formation. [19]

Custer spurred to the front of the First and Fifth and shouted, "Draw sabers!" The clang of metal upon metal rolled back along the stacked squadrons. "I told them of the situation frankly," as he described his words, "of the great responsibility resting on them, and how confident I was that they would respond nobly to the trust reposed in them." A trooper in the First recorded the general's words in his diary to the effect that he "says there is good ground over there & he thinks we can learn the Rebs a lesson." A member of the Fifth recalled them as, "Men of Michigan, there are some people between us and where we want to go. I'm going, and want you to go with me. Come on, you Wolverines."[20]

The troopers' versions were probably closer to the truth, but whatever he said, the men responded with three cheers. Custer turned to the brigade's band—he had organized it during July or August, most likely from members of the Seventh Michigan's band. The musicians struck up "Yankee Doodle," and Custer shouted, "Forward!" The regiments started at a trot, with the general, his staff, orderlies, and a new battle flag in the lead. As they rode, Custer turned in the saddle, watching the forest of drawn sabers "advance in the sunlight." "I never expect to see a prettier sight," he avowed. As he described it in his report, the enthusiasm of men made each one "feel as if he was a host in himself." An onlooking officer called it "a magnificent charge."[21]

They closed to within forty rods of Lee's line when Custer shouted, "Charge!" Bugles echoed the command; the men yelled a "battle cry" and, as one of them put it, plunged into the Southern ranks "like a mad bull." The Rebels scattered, only to wheel around and counterattack. It was a frightful melee. Custer had two horses shot from under him within fifteen minutes, while Lieutenant Edward Granger, a staff officer, and Sergeant Michael Bellior, the color bearer, had their mounts slain. The new battle flag was saved, and both men remounted.[22]

The combat surged—the Yankees trying to clear a path, the Rebels trying to seal it. At one point, Kilpatrick galloped up to Colonel Russell Alger of the Fifth and yelled, "Alger, you charge and give them hell, and I'll give them heller." To the rear, Stuart charged with his men, knifing into Kilpatrick's wagons and ambulances. The Sixth and Seventh Michigan drove them back long enough for the teamsters to escape with most of the train. But Custer's and Davies's men had sliced through, opening a route to Brandy Station. Before Stuart could close from the rear and Lee could try to shut the breach, the Federals joined Buford at the station.[23]

When Stuart united with Lee, the Confederates attacked the Federals, were repulsed, and charged again. Pleasonton's orders were to cross the Rappahannock, so he withdrew in successive lines, one division pulling back as the other unit covered the retreat. The Southerners chewed at the Yankees until darkness. The final contingent of Union cavalry crossed the pontoon bridge at Rappahannock Station at eight o'clock. It had been a long day, and as trooper Charlie Osburn of the

Fifth Michigan rode over the bridge, he turned to his messmate, John Bigelow, and remarked, "John, it's your turn to cook coffee tonight."[24]

The Union cavalrymen returned to the saddle early on October 12. Lee's offensive had unhinged Meade's line, and the Federals were in retreat, following the tracks of the Orange & Alexandria Railroad. From the twelfth to the fifteenth, it was a race, as Meade's units marched north while Lee's command tried to punish the retreating enemy. The major engagement of the operations occurred at Bristoe Station, on the fourteenth, giving its name to the campaign. The Federals repulsed the Confederate attacks at Bristoe, inflicting heavy casualties on the troops from two Southern corps. By the fifteenth, Meade's corps had crossed Bull Run and deployed behind the stream. It was raining as Stuart's horsemen probed toward Bull Run to confirm that the Federals had eluded Lee's grasp.[25]

Pleasonton's cavalry corps had shielded the infantry and artillery during the withdrawal. By the afternoon of the fifteenth, Kilpatrick's division had passed Bull Run, camping on the old battlefield, picketing the fords. On the sixteenth and seventeenth, detachments from Custer's and Davies's brigades conducted reconnaissances south to Manassas Junction and Gainesville. With Meade positioned in a defensive line, Lee had abandoned the offensive, beginning his withdrawal after wrecking sections of the railroad that had served as Meade's main supply line.[26]

By Sunday, October 18, Meade had received reports that indicated a Confederate retirement. He wanted confirmation, and Kilpatrick's division advanced on Warrenton Turnpike. Stuart's troopers still screened Lee's rear, and the clash ignited at Gainesville. The First Vermont Cavalry spearheaded Custer's thrust, clearing the village of Rebels. Kilpatrick encamped for the night. Orders from Meade, through Pleasonton, arrived later, directing a reconnaissance toward Warrenton at first light the next morning. The division would march without support from other units of the army.[27]

During the night, Stuart withdrew Major General Wade Hampton's division, which he personally commanded in the officer's absence, to a position behind a flooded Broad Run at Buckland Mills, three miles west of Gainesville on the turnpike. Stuart strung sharpshooters along the stream's west bank, backed by horse artillery and a brigade. Shortly after daylight, the van of Custer's brigade approached on the turnpike. The First Vermont swatted aside the enemy pickets, who crossed Broad

Run at a stone bridge on the pike. With the front cleared of friends, Stuart's sharpshooters laced the Federal column. Custer and his staff spurred forward, halting on the road. The cluster of horsemen brought an immediate response from the Rebel gun crews, with one shell bursting above the party. No one was harmed, and Custer brought forward the Fifth, Sixth, and Seventh Michigan, deploying them dismounted on both sides of the turnpike.[28]

Confederate resistance held firm throughout the cold, rainy morning. Custer sent an orderly to Kilpatrick, asking for support from Davies's brigade, and shifted the Seventh Michigan downstream to locate a crossing point. Before noon, however, the Southerners pulled back, disappearing behind a ridge to the west. The Federals filed across on the stone bridge and halted in some fields south of the pike. The sudden withdrawal of Stuart's veterans bothered Custer—it seemed as if the Confederate commander wanted the Yankees to follow him. In fact, Stuart was setting a trap, hoping to draw the enemy west while Fitz Lee's division, approaching from Auburn to the east, would hit the Federals on the flank, with Stuart wheeling about to strike the front. Stuart needed Kilpatrick to accept the bait.[29]

Kilpatrick, Davies's troopers, and the division's wagons joined Custer after midday. The division commander was looking for a fight, and after Custer explained the situation, Kilpatrick ordered Custer to mount the brigade and follow Davies as they pursued. Custer objected, saying that neither his men nor their horses had eaten since the previous night and he would not move until they had a meal and the mounts fodder. Kilpatrick agreed and then spurred after Davies's men.[30]

The Michiganders, Vermonters, and Pennington's artillerymen relaxed in the fields, enjoying the rest and food. Custer posted pickets and sent the Seventh Michigan on a scout to Greenwich, roughly four miles to the south. About midafternoon, he directed the First and Fifth Michigan, First Vermont, and Pennington's battery to prepare to follow Davies. He ordered Major James Kidd, commanding the Sixth Michigan, to cover the march by holding a swath of trees, approximately six hundred yards to the south, until the command had moved and then to file in rear of the column. Custer warned Kidd to be cautious as the Seventh Michigan should be returning from the scout.[31]

Kidd mounted the regiment and led it across the fields, while Custer started west on the pike. As the Sixth approached a fence that divided the fields, a lone horseman emerged from the woods. Captain Don G. Lovell pointed out the rider to Kidd, who remarked, "The General said we might expect some mounted men of the Seventh from that direction."

"But that vidette is a rebel; he is dressed in grey," piped Lovell.

"It can't be possible," Kidd replied.

The major hesitated—he had been in temporary command of the regiment for only a week—but then waved the column forward. The horseman began circling. "Look at that," exclaimed Lovell, "that is a rebel signal; our men don't do that." Suddenly, the solitary cavalryman reined in, shouldered a carbine, and shot one of the horses in the front set of fours of the regiment. "There, ———," Lovell cursed. "Now you know it is a rebel, don't you." Kidd shouted to the men to dismount and form a line behind the fence. He then sent an aide to alert Custer.[32]

Kidd waited no longer, instructing his men to open fire with their Spencer rifles. The woods flashed in reply. The dismounted Confederates belonged to Colonel Thomas Owen's Virginia brigade, the lead unit of Lee's division, which had ridden from Auburn on a road west of Greenwich, thus avoiding the Seventh Michigan. When Custer heard the explosion of gunfire to the rear, he immediately turned the column around, hurrying the regiments down the turnpike. He filed the units into the field south of the road, dismounting the Fifth Michigan on Kidd's right, directing Pennington to unlimber the battery, posting the First Vermont on the left on horseback, and keeping the First Michigan mounted and in reserve. When the Seventh Michigan, bypassing Lee's Rebels, returned from the scout, Custer shifted it in line beside the Fifth.[33]

By now, Lee, one of Custer's former academy instructors, had his entire division up and pressed the attack. In the center of the Federal line, Pennington's gunners worked the cannon. Amid the pieces, a member held the battery's new flag, a beautiful banner made for the command by Tiffany's in New York, at a cost of $125. It was made of red satin, edged in heavy gold bullion, with chenille crossed cannon and "M" and "U.S." stitched in needlework. The unit had been in service since Bull Run, and the flag listed the engagements. It would be bloody work for Lee's men before they captured this flag.[34]

But the Southerners were game—"a desperate effort was made to capture my battery," reported Custer. The Sixth Michigan retired before the assault, and at points the Rebels came within twenty yards of the Union line. With the Confederates reaching the turnpike on Custer's right, he ordered a withdrawal across Broad Run. His men executed it with skill and valor. While the battery and other regiments raced over the stone bridge, the First Michigan held back the enemy and then spurred over the narrow span. Unfortunately for the brigade, a battalion of the Fifth Michigan, posted in the woods near the pike, was cut off from its mounts and was bagged by the Southerners. Custer asserted in a letter that a staff officer of Kilpatrick's had placed the men there without his knowledge and was responsible for their capture. Kidd's subsequent account supported Custer's version as to where the battalion was surrounded.[35]

While a portion of Lee's command pursued to Gainesville, Stuart closed the vise on Davies's brigade. Davies had passed through New Baltimore, four miles west of Buckland Mills, when a courier informed Kilpatrick that the enemy held the turnpike to the rear. Kilpatrick sent the wagons and two regiments on an alternate route from New Baltimore, while the Second New York and First West Virginia Cavalry engaged the Rebels. The New Yorkers and West Virginians fought well, but with the Southerners in overwhelming numbers, Davies ordered every man to try to escape on his own. The regiments dissolved as the men galloped for Broad Run. Most of the Federals, including Kilpatrick and Davies, eluded the pursuers, but it was an embarrassing debacle that Stuart's veterans dubbed the "Buckland Races." After dark, the division reunited at Gainesville, with most of the wagons secured.[36]

"Under very distressing circumstances I turn to you and *her* for consolation," Custer wrote to Nettie Humphrey on the day after Buckland. "It is for others I feel. Yesterday, October 19th, was the most disastrous this Division ever passed through." The Confederates had captured his headquarters wagon, with the loss of Jacob Greene's desk that contained his Gettysburg report and monthly returns for the brigade. He blamed Kilpatrick for the interference with his command that resulted in the capture of the battalion of the Fifth Michigan. He regretted the loss of the men, but he was not responsible for it. "So yesterday," he concluded, "was not a gala day for me."[37]

In fact, Buckland and the entire Bristoe Campaign elicited uncharacteristic criticism from Custer. Custer's dissatisfaction with Kilpatrick became evident. While officers and men of the division had written of their concern and disgust with the commander's rashness at Hunterstown, Gettysburg, and Falling Waters, Custer had remained silent, at least in his correspondence. But the near rout of his brigade on the nineteenth changed his attitude toward his superior officer and his willingness to complain about him in his private writings. Within a fortnight of his letter of the twentieth to Nettie Humphrey, he wrote two more, both filled with disdain for and resentment of Kilpatrick.[38]

The brigadier's disgruntlement extended to army headquarters. "It is felt by every officer and private in the Cavalry Corps from Gen. Pleasonton down," Custer disclosed to Isaac Christiancy in a letter of October 29, that "the movements of this army for the past three or four weeks have been a complete farce." Major General Gouverneur K. Warren, commander of the Second Corps, groused that retreating before Lee's advance was a "d———d humbug and a disgrace," according to Custer. "I am equally well satisfied," he added, "that this army could have attacked Lee at any time during the past month." But Meade failed to exploit his numerical superiority, and allowed Lee to seize the initiative. "I have written to you more freely than I would to my own father or to any person living," Custer stated to Christiancy, asking the latter to keep the views confidential.[39]

In part, the dark interpretation of the campaign resulted from the conditions in his brigade. Between October 11 and 19, he had lost 214 men either killed, wounded, or missing. The ranks had been so reduced that he expected hundreds of Michigan conscripts to be sent to the command. Within the regiments, the troopers were dressed in "rags," and hundreds of mounts needed to be replaced. Furthermore, he had only two staff officers available for duty—two were ill; a third was under arrest, and Jacob Greene and James Christiancy were in Monroe, on leave. The responsibilities of command that he had written about on October 9 had drained—at least temporarily—Custer's ebullient spirit.[40]

While the army had been posted behind Bull Run, Custer sat down and wrote the promised letter to Judge Bacon, dated October 16. "I had hoped for a personal interview," he stated, but circumstances precluded that when he was in Monroe. He asked permission to marry Libbie, and then, addressing what he knew to be concerns of the judge, he admitted, "It is true that I have often committed errors of judgment, but as I grew older I learned the necessity of propriety. I am aware of your fear of intemperance, but surely my conduct for the past two years

—during which I have not violated the solemn promise I made my sister, with God to witness, should dispel that fear." As for his conduct toward Libbie during the past winter, he had avoided visits with her "to prevent gossip." "I left home when but sixteen," he concluded, "and have been surrounded with temptation, but I have always had a purpose in life."[41]

The letter arrived at the Bacon residence on October 21. Judge Bacon and his wife read it several times. Rhoda, Libbie's stepmother, had shared her husband's misgivings, and Daniel's brother, Albert Bacon, who had deep affection for his niece, had voiced vehement opposition to the prospective union. But Judge Bacon knew Libbie's feelings toward Autie, and his concerns had to be weighed against his daughter's happiness. He replied the next day, stating at the outset that Custer's request would require "weeks or even months before I can feel to give you a definite answer." Custer must understand, the judge noted, that since the death of Libbie's mother, he had had the major responsibility for his daughter's welfare. Fortunately, Sophia had been a good mother to her, and "you will not therefore be surprised that we have had a watchful care over her and have guarded her reputation with intense parental solicitude."

"Your ability, energy and force of character I have always admired," the judge professed at the end of the letter, "and no one can feel more gratified than myself at your well-earned reputation and your high and honorable position." On the evening of October 5, the day Custer left Monroe, he "had a full and free interview" with Libbie and "shall talk with her more upon this important subject which she is at full liberty to communicate to you."[42]

Three days later, Sunday, October 25, father and daughter sat together by the fireplace and discussed "this important subject." The conversation was "intimate," in Libbie's word, lasting until the fire burned down into embers. Judge Bacon was frank, "kind and considerate," granting Libbie permission to correspond with Custer. His acquiescence and honesty surprised and pleased Libbie, but the prospects of a marriage ceremony in a little more than three months frightened her. She thought it might be another two years before the union was consummated. Nevertheless, her father's acceptance of Autie had made it possible. "What a great soul he has," Libbie wrote of her father afterward.[43]

Libbie retired to her bedroom, and her emotions flowed into the journal. She thought of the nearly three weeks she and Autie had had together, remembering that "I never was kissed so much before. I thought he would eat me. My forehead and my eyelids and cheeks and lips bear testimony—and his star scratched my face. I have so much to write." Her spirit was with him tonight, and she yearned to "feel his strong arms around me and his dear lips to mine." The doubts she had about her love for him "seem to be vanishing like the morning dew." "Yes, I love him devotedly. Every other man seems so ordinary beside my own bright particular *star*." She then went to bed, wrapped, as she had just written, in "love's young dream." [44]

"My more than friend—at last—Am I a little glad to write you some of the thoughts I cannot control?" Libbie began her first letter to Autie, two days later, on the twenty-seventh. "I have enjoyed your letters to Nettie, but am delighted to possess some of my own." She then informed him of her conversation with her father. "As for my dignified and peculiar mother," Libbie asserted, "she is becoming reconciled. But it is not resignation I want, but whole-hearted consent. I love her dearly and respect her opinions, but not her prejudices." Rhoda objected to a "speedy union," and he must be patient. "Ah, dear man, if I am worth having am I not worth waiting for? The very thought of marriage makes me tremble. Girls have so much fun." The idea of leaving home would be "painful," and she implored him "not even to mention it for at least a year." Father, she ended it, "is so proud of you." [45]

In Virginia, meanwhile, Custer attended to the duties of command and waited anxiously for the mail. On the night of Sunday, November 1, Jacob Greene and James Christiancy, escorted into camp by guards, returned from Monroe. Custer welcomed them warmly, and together they sat by the fire, chatting and singing songs until five o'clock the next morning. While they sang "Then You'll Remember Me," Custer thought of Libbie, who had promised to sing it for him when they met again. Perhaps, spirits did "commune" as she believed, for in Monroe that night, she entered into the journal: "I love you Armstrong Custer. I love *you*. I love my love and my love loves me—and I am happy." [46]

MARRIAGE

■ Autumn settles over Virginia's Piedmont like the visit of an old friend each year. The heat and humidity of summer subside into warm days and cool nights. On the region's western flank rise the Blue Ridge Mountains, the forested sides a quilt of golds, browns, and reds. Nature charms before the passage into winter. It is a time and a place where a traveler can find peace. In the autumn of 1863, however, war returned with the old friend to the land at the foot of the mountain.

With the rout of Union cavalry in the "Buckland Races," the Bristoe Campaign concluded. Before long, the operations resumed the pattern of activity before the campaign, with the armies of Robert E. Lee and George G. Meade divided by the Rappahannock and Rapidan rivers. Opposing mounted units rimmed the armies' fronts, posted at the numerous fords. Behind them, infantry and artillery units covered the approaches from the shallows. It was familiar warfare for the men in each army.

In the Michigan Brigade, the routine of the first three weeks of November was noted by members in their diaries. Entries varied little: "camp," "picket," "nothing," "saber drill," "quiet," "some skirmishing," and "camp moved." Regiments in the brigade alternated duty at the fords. Twice during the weeks, the brigade crossed the Rapidan River on reconnaissances that resulted in minor clashes with the Confederates. Morale remained high in the command, which Judson Kilpatrick had termed "that Brigade of Mich devils." Like their commander, many of the troopers now wore red neckties as a brigade badge. "No troops get credit of doing anything but those from Mich.," bragged a cavalryman of the Seventh Michigan in a letter.[1]

The rhythm of activity likewise slowed at brigade headquarters. For George Custer, however, the suspension of campaigning was a mixed blessing. Inaction rubbed at him. Energetic and untiring, he preferred

field operations to camp routine. His visits to picket posts and super-
vision of drills reflected both his responsibilities as a commander and
his natural restiveness. The men of the brigade attributed Custer's fortune in being spared from serious injury or death in combat to the
fact, as one officer put it, that "he never was still, he was always on the
move." He even spoke rapidly, whether he was roaming along a battle
line or sitting by a campfire. In a whirlwind, Custer would have been
at home.[2]

But duties required attention. The major problem Custer grappled
with was the quality of new mounts for the men. When he complained
to Alfred Pleasonton about the matter, the letter was forwarded to
Major General George Stoneman, chief of cavalry, who shot back that
the bureau had sufficient horses for the brigade, and as Stoneman understood it, "Custer's brigade are great horse killers."[3]

Ironically, one of the pleasures Custer enjoyed most during the interlude was horse races. Several times officers and men gathered to wager
on the horseflesh. Custer, Pleasonton, and Kilpatrick joined others in
placing bets. Custer explained to Libbie that his fondness for races and
poker games was for no "other purpose but to kill time." He promised
her that "I have made the resolution to abstain in future from both"
because he knew that "they were wrong in principle" and that "you
would not like to have me engage in them." It was a pledge that he
found more difficult to honor than the one to his sister about abstaining
from alcoholic beverages.[4]

The gambling was symptomatic of Custer's spendthrift habits. As
noted previously, money appealed to him from an early age—it became
one of the justifications for attending West Point. But as he explained
in a letter of November 6 to Ann Reed, "Between you and me I could
keep a family with the money I spend needlessly." He described himself
as "extravagant in many ways," and that concerned him now with his
obligation to his parents, who had secured a house in Monroe and were
dissatisfied with the cost of living in the city. David Reed had loaned
them $200 toward the purchase, but as Emanuel Custer grumbled,
"Greenbacks do not go far" in Monroe, and he had not sold his farm
in Ohio. Custer was assisting his parents with expenses, and with his
habits, his general's pay of $124 a month seemed to be inadequate,
especially as he planned for a marriage and his and Libbie's needs. He
hinted to his sister about the latter, asserting that "I am going to make

a great change some of these days, a change for the better. I think you will approve of it, when you know more about it." [5]

In fact, Libbie, her parents, and marriage were probably never far from Custer's thoughts during these November weeks. When he wrote to Ann, he most likely had received Judge Bacon's and Libbie's letters. Both of them indicated that the proposed union was months, possibly years, in the future. Custer did not accept that timetable. He desired Libbie and wanted the ceremony as soon as possible, preferably during the winter of 1864, when the cessation of field operations would almost insure him a furlough. On November 22, he wrote a lengthy letter to Libbie about the subject. [6]

"I am sorry that I cannot accede to almost the first *written* request my little Gypsie has made," Custer stated, "but such unfortunately is the case. You bid me maintain strict silence upon a certain subject until next winter and then we are to discuss the subject of your becoming Mrs. ———— and arrive at a conclusion the following winter. This like all other bargains requires two to complete it. Now had you presented a single, good reason why the course you make out should be adopted, I might have yielded assent, but you have not done so." [7]

He would wait for her reply, noting in the letter, however, that he expected the army to advance against the enemy within days. Libbie should read the newspapers for accounts of the operation. He would write to her twice a week, as she had decided to do, but the campaign could limit his opportunities. [8]

As Custer predicted, the Federals undertook an offensive thrust across the Rappahannock and Rapidan rivers before the advent of winter. Since the Bristoe Campaign, the administration in Washington had been prodding George Meade to initiate such a movement. Meade had 85,000 troops to Lee's 48,000, and the Union commander hoped to force his opponent to retire toward Richmond by turning the Confederate right flank. On November 26, the Union army crossed the Rapidan River in what would be called the Mine Run Campaign. [9]

Like Bristoe, the campaign became one of maneuver. When Lee learned of the Union movement, he shifted his units into a strong defensive position behind Mine Run. Meade probed for a weak sector for several days before abandoning the attempt on December 1. During the week-long operation, Custer commanded the Third Cavalry Division in the absence of Kilpatrick, who had learned on the twenty-fourth of the death of his wife the day before and secured a furlough. Custer's brigades held Morton's Ford on the Rapidan, skirmishing with the Rebels. He withdrew on December 2, after covering the retirement of infantry and artillery units. Both armies soon returned to their camps.[10]

Mine Run concluded field operations in Virginia for the year. Since the fearful carnage of Gettysburg, neither side had been willing to renew the bloodletting, preferring maneuver to battle. While it spared lives, this pattern of warfare yielded limited results. But like an alluring siren, war always beckoned, down another road to a new place at a later time. For the present, both armies began preparations to settle into winter camps. As they had for months, the Rappahannock and Rapidan rivers provided the barrier between the two opposing forces.

The Third Cavalry Division established its winter quarters in the vicinity of Stevensburg, near Brandy Station and Culpeper Court House. The construction of huts for the officers and men did not commence until a few days before Christmas. Members of the Michigan Brigade used six-mule teams to drag trees, which the men fashioned into logs. They secured additional lumber, nails, and bricks from old, abandoned houses that crews of men leveled. The huts measured roughly twelve feet square and were aligned along company streets in each regiment. With fireplaces and windows, the crude dwellings sufficed during the cold weather months.[11]

While details worked at the construction of huts, their comrades performed the routine duties of an army in the field. Regiments rotated picket posts along the Rapidan River every three days. Inspections of equipment, of firearms, and of horses, dress parades, a divisional review, pay musters, and guard mounts comprised the schedule during December. On Christmas Eve, officers at Michigan Brigade headquarters held a dance, with the staff members and orderlies enjoying each other as partners. Duty was suspended on Christmas as the men endeavored to prepare special meals. By year's end, the campsite had been finished—a village of neat, defined lines, inhabited by homesick men.[12]

Custer commanded the division until December 21, when Kilpatrick returned to duty. Except for the Mine Run operations, the burdens of the four-week assignment had been modest. His concerns focused on family matters and the response from Monroe about the marriage ceremony. In November, he had stated to his sister that he had "made arrangements" to secure his brother Tom an officer's commission and an appointment to his staff. Six weeks later, on December 19, he inquired of Colonel Russell A. Alger of the Fifth Michigan Cavalry, who was home on leave, "Have you done anything toward procuring that appointment for that brother of mine?" Evidently, Custer's "arrangements" relied upon Alger using the latter's influence in the state capital. If Alger tried, he failed.[13]

Custer's efforts to persuade Libbie to agree to a winter marriage intensified in December. As Libbie remarked later, his proposal "was as much a cavalry charge as any he ever took in the field," and his insistence on an early wedding rivaled the earlier assault in its relentlessness. He enlisted Nettie Humphrey in the effort, asking the latter, "Cannot you *threaten* her, or use your influence to induce her to do as she *ought?*" With the Bacon family, he took the direct approach with a series of letters.[14]

On December 7, Custer wrote to Judge Bacon, informing the latter that he would be sending a package with a large, colored photograph of himself for Libbie. It was a Christmas present for her, and he requested that the judge place it in her room as a surprise. Four days later, he wrote a second letter to his future father-in-law, assuring him that "I plainly recognize the weight of the responsibility resting upon me, when you consent to entrust me with the future happiness and welfare of one who is united to you by the strongest ties of affection and relationship." He promised that as her husband his future conduct would be "guided and activated by the principles of right," and that "an aim of my life" would be "to make myself deserving of the high and sacred trust you have reposed in me."[15]

On December 12, Daniel Bacon replied to Custer's letter of the seventh. Addressing his letter "My Young Friend," the judge agreed to "carry out your wishes by placing in Libbies room the great object of her love and affection." As for the wedding, Bacon was frank:

> You cannot at your age in life realize the feelings of a parent when called upon to give up and give away an only offspring. I feel that I have kept you in suspense quite too long, and yet when you consider my affection and desire for her happiness you will pardon me for this unreasonable delay. I feel too that I have no right to impose terms on my daughter requiring her to remain single, to marry and settle near me that I may enjoy the closeness of her company the little time left me or to make choice for her. I have too much regard for her present and future happiness, for which I have lived.

Continuing, he affirmed that "you are the object of my choice." The judge thought that he would "perhaps be more gratified if you were a professor of the christian religion, but it would ill become me to require such of your hands." He was pleased "as a Mich. man" about Custer's "well earned military reputation" and "in view of our relations I am more than gratified." Finally, Bacon, a practical man, believed it necessary to inform his future son-in-law that "I am not a wealthy man," with most of his assets in real estate. He had saved "a few hundred dollars" for Libbie, but that money "will be mainly absorbed in her outfit as the wife of a General." Upon his death, Libbie could not expect to inherit an estate that would exceed $10,000. "May God in his kind Providence favor the union," Bacon stated at the end of the letter.[16]

Judge Bacon had acquiesced to his daughter's wishes, and Custer could have been only pleased when he read the words. More important, on December 17, he received a letter from Libbie, dated the fourteenth, in which she yielded to his importuning and agreed to a winter wedding date. "I am so supremely happy," Autie exclaimed that same day, "that I can scarcely write, my thoughts go wandering from one subject to another so rapidly that it is with difficulty that I return [to] one long enough to transfer it to paper. Am I not dreaming? Surely such unalloyed pleasure never before was enjoyed by mortal man."

"My heartfelt joy" could not be expressed in writing, he went on. "I will wait until I see you, for then I can make up in action what language fails to make clear. In one full loving embrace I can testify more clearly than in words the ecstasy I feel at this moment." He recognized that many details must be resolved, but he was certain he could secure a thirty-day leave and his staff could accompany him. Where was Conway Noble? Should he get wedding cards in Washington? Libbie's choices as bridesmaids were "the very persons I would have desired." "Pardon the brevity of this letter, it is unavoidable," he concluded. "Good night *my little wife*. I will soon come to you. Armstrong."[17]

He shared his joy with Ann Reed and Isaac Christiancy within a few days. To his sister, he was forthright. "I am coming home in February to be married to Libbie Bacon. . . . I know you approve my choice." He asked her to have his shirts cleaned, and "tell Pop I forgot to get his consent." To Christiancy, he confided that "I will entrust you with a secret which I have communicated to no one except my own family and desire you to retain it." He was returning to Monroe to marry, and "Libbie Bacon is the fortunate or unfortunate person, whichever it will be, who will unite her destinies with mine." Custer hoped that Christiancy and his family could attend the ceremony.[18]

In Monroe, meanwhile, Libbie busied herself with preparations for the wedding. She had agreed to be married in February, but no date could be set nor invitations delivered until Autie secured a furlough. The ceremony would be held in the First Presbyterian Church, with the reception at the Bacon residence. For her gown and trousseau, she turned to seamstresses outside of Monroe, ordering dresses and underclothes from Detroit and silks from New York City. For the next several weeks, activity in the Bacon household was hectic.[19]

Like Autie, however, Libbie could not conceal her happiness at the prospects of an early marriage. Nettie Humphrey described her friend's feelings toward Autie as "blissful love." On December 23, after her parents placed the photograph of Autie in her room, she gushed to him in a letter, "My dear 'Beloved Star'—you could not have given me anything on earth that so delighted me—except yourself." She importuned him to save his "golden curls," so that "when I'm old I'll have a wig made from them." "If loveing with one's whole soul is insanity," she ended it, "I am ripe for an insane asylum." Three more letters followed within eight days.[20]

On New Year's Eve, Libbie attended a party at the seminary and was escorted home by a young man, who kissed her on the cheek when he departed. She was flattered, but her stepmother warned her that Autie might not approve. "She quite frightened me," Libbie told him as she related the evening events the next day. "But, dearest, you must trust me, as I trust you."[21]

As January progressed, however, Libbie's mood fluctuated and her patience frayed with the demands of planning a wedding and with the realization that soon she would assume new burdens. Her stepmother was grumbling about the hurried marriage. Laura Noble's mother cautioned Libbie about a wife's responsibility for the "development" of her husband's character—"it is a solemn thought to become a wife," Libbie wrote to Autie. Then when Autie lectured her about her attire in a letter, her spunk and willfulness boiled over. "It is useless to tell me what Mrs. Alger wears," Libbie lashed back. "She is not a bride. And you are not marrying a girl *entirely* unknown in this State and elsewhere." "I have changed my mind about not wanting ostentation," Libbie informed him. "If we begin by regulating our actions by the opinions of others we shall never have any of our own. I want to be married in the evening, in the church."[22]

Custer evidently offered no other advice to Libbie on fashionable clothing and submitted to her wedding plans. While she attended to the mounting details in Monroe, he unexpectedly became embroiled in a controversy about the confirmation of his brigadiership by the Senate. About January 5 or 6, Alfred Pleasonton confided to Custer that he had heard a rumor that Republican Senator Jacob M. Howard of Michigan, a member of the Military Affairs Committee, opposed the nomination because of Custer's "youth" and of the fact that he was not "a *Michigan Man.*" According to Custer, Pleasonton was "perfectly shocked" by the information, telling his subordinate that "it would be a lasting disgrace on the part of the government to allow such injustice." The cavalry commander remarked that if Custer had any influence in the state, he had "to bring it to bear."[23]

That night, Custer wrote to senators Howard and Zachariah Chandler, and Congressman F. W. Kellogg, all of Michigan, asking them "to look after my interests." Following Pleasonton's advice, he wrote three letters to Isaac Christiancy, one undated and the other two on January 7. In them, Custer related what he had been told by Pleasonton and then blamed Governor Austin Blair and Brigadier General Joseph Copeland, who had commanded the Michigan Brigade until Custer's appointment, as the ones "at the bottom of this attempt." Custer had been led to believe that Howard and Chandler supported his confirmation until Pleasonton spoke to him. "I have addressed this letter to you," Custer stated to his friend, "with the hope that you could and would bring influence to bear with both Howard and Chandler which would carry their votes in my favor. If my confirmation was placed in the hands of the army I would not expect a single opposing vote."[24]

Christiancy replied on the fourteenth, assuring Custer that he would correspond with the senators, but intimating that the opposition to the nomination resulted more from politics than from Custer's age or birthplace. Like Emanuel Custer, his son was a Democrat, and more significantly, a former member of George McClellan's staff, an association that roused the ire of Republicans in Washington. As the war hardened, so too had the political climate in the capital. A general's political views, particularly on the question of slavery and the Emancipation Proclamation, were as important as his battlefield prowess. Radical Republicans demanded acceptance of the party's prosecution of the war, and despite Custer's fine record, his confirmation could be jeopardized by his views.[25]

By the time Christiancy's letter reached Virginia, Custer had heard in writing from Senator Howard. As Christiancy surmised, Howard wanted to know if the brigadier was a "McClellan man" and/or a Copperhead, as it had been *"hinted"* in the capital. The senator requested that Custer respond "at once." "It was just the opportunity I desired," Custer informed Christiancy later, to present "a full exposition of my views regarding the war policy of the administration."[26]

"As Commander in Chief of the Army and as my Superior officer," Custer affirmed to Howard, President Lincoln "cannot issue any decree or order which will not receive my unqualified *support*. . . . But I do *not* stop here. . . . All his acts, proclamations and decisions embraced in his war policy have received not only my support, but my most hearty, earnest and cordial *approval*." As for Lincoln's Emancipation Proclamation, Custer's friends *"can* testify that I have insisted that so long as a single slave was held in bondage, I for one, was opposed to peace on any terms." He believed that he had "liberated more slaves" than any other general in the army. "I would *offer* no compromise," Custer concluded, "except that which is offered at the point of the bayonet."[27]

On the face of it, the statement was a remarkable one. Custer had worshiped McClellan, undoubtedly had shared the general's view as to the conduct of the war, and had blamed the machinations of Lincoln and Secretary of War Edwin Stanton for his hero's dismissal. But since January 1, 1863, when the proclamation went into effect, Custer had not criticized it in surviving correspondence, and his record as a combat officer indicated nothing but a soldier committed to the cause. The war altered the opinions and beliefs of many individuals, military and civilian, and Custer appears to have changed with the conflict's course. As a good soldier, duty required that he obey the policy, and Custer would not waver in his commitment to Union victory and all that it meant. Before the war's end, he would repeat more than once the views he expressed to Howard.[28]

The letter satisfied Howard, who shared it with colleagues. The Senate confirmed Custer as brigadier general, but the experience enlightened him. He had in the past relied on influential supporters and friends in Michigan and Ohio, but now it was necessary to curry the favor of powerful men in Washington. The Army of the Potomac had been cursed with politics since its creation, and while advancement was earned on a battlefield, it had to be secured in the capital. He surely knew it before, but the episode reaffirmed it. If ambition required sponsors, Custer was amenable. Furthermore, as he noted to Judge Bacon, he would not forget those individuals who had "labored to injure and defame me." [29]

With the matter resolved and a furlough granted, Custer, Jacob Greene, James Christiancy, and George Yates boarded a train at six o'clock on the morning of January 27, 1864, for the trip to Monroe. Before they departed, brigade officers gathered to congratulate the groom, who joked, "Thank you gentlemen. I'm going out to the Department of the West to get a command, or a new commander, and I don't know which." The train rattled through Washington, Baltimore, Harrisburg, Pittsburgh, and into Ohio, where Custer paused a few days to visit old friends. [30]

Upon the four officers' arrival in Monroe, the Custer family welcomed them with a party. It had been difficult for the general's parents to accept the prospect of his marriage. Although Emanuel and Maria believed that Libbie was a fine choice for a wife, they depended on Autie for financial assistance. It worried them, but they had become reconciled to the fact. It would be another eighteen months until Emanuel could sell the farm in Ohio and net a profit of a thousand dollars. [31]

Libbie had set the wedding date for Tuesday, February 9, the day before the beginning of Lent. During the days prior to the ceremony, she and Autie were feted by Monroe society at various teas and receptions. On Friday evening, the fifth, the activities culminated in a large party for invited guests at the Humphrey House. Monroe embraced its most famous adopted son and the daughter of one of its most respected citizens. [32]

The First Presbyterian Church—which still stands—"was filled almost to suffocation," in the words of a newspaper reporter, by 6 P.M. on February 9. Friends, acquaintances, and the curious, including members of the Seventh Michigan Infantry who nudged their way into the church before boarding a train for the army, filled the pews and vestibule, and stood along the aisles. Minutes after six o'clock, as the church glowed with a warm light, the groom, Jacob Greene, and two longtime Monroe friends, John Bulkley and Conway Noble, entered, walking down the west aisle to the front. Next, in the east aisle, came Libbie's close friends Nettie Humphrey, Anna Darrah, and Marie Miller, the bride, and her father.[33]

The couple united before the altar—Custer in dress uniform, with his hair trimmed; Libbie in a gown that her cousin described as "a rich white rep silk with deep points and extensive trail, bertha of point lace; veil floated back from a bunch of orange blossoms fixed above the brow." Reverend Erasmus J. Boyd, Libbie's friend and mentor, performed the traditional ceremony, assisted by Reverend D. C. Mattoon. When the couple exchanged vows, Libbie, at her father's request, used her given name of Elizabeth. "It was said," a proud Judge Bacon boasted two days later, "to be the most splendid wedding ever seen in the State."[34]

General and Mrs. Custer greeted an estimated three hundred invited attendees to the reception in the parlor of the Bacon home. Rebecca Richmond, Libbie's cousin, had never met Autie and was struck by his attention to the bride; it seemed as if he never left her side throughout the time. "Not one of us was prepossessed in his favor," Rebecca informed her sister afterward, "but in no time everyone pronounced him 'a trump,' a 'right bower.' . . . I was most agreeably disappointed after the reports I heard. Mary, he isn't one bit foppish or conceited. He does not put on airs. He is a simple, frank, manly fellow. And he fairly idolizes Libbie. I am sure he will make her a true, noble husband."[35]

The guests filed past the wedding gifts in an adjoining room. The couple received a silver dinner service, engraved with "Custer," from the First Vermont Cavalry; a seven-piece silver tea set from the Seventh Michigan Cavalry; a silver card case; a card receiver; sugar and berry spoons; syrup cup; gold-lined thimble; two white silk fans; a book of Elizabeth Browning's poems; books for brides; a mosaic chess stand of Grand Rapids marble; and knit breakfast shawls. The Bacons gave Libbie a gold watch, a "handsome" Bible, and a white parasol with black lace.[36]

When the reception—"a very brilliant affair," to a reporter—ended at ten o'clock, Libbie and the bridesmaids retired upstairs to dress for travel. Libbie's trousseau "was rich and in fine taste," consisting mainly of dark browns and greens. The families accompanied the wedding party to the railroad station, where they boarded a midnight train to Cleveland. The farewells were difficult—they always were for Autie and his mother—but as Judge Bacon stated later, "I did not act the babe as I had feared I might at parting, for I had schooled myself beforehand."[37]

The Bacons returned to their home, staying awake all night from fear of burglars until they placed the silver sets in the bank the next morning. Weeks later, the judge declared to his sister that "I never engaged in an enterprise with more cheerfulness, and yet a good deal was useless and largely extravagant. I had as you know but the one, and that one had fully met my expectation." In the end, he admitted, he had yielded to Libbie and her choice of a husband, knowing now that "it is not common for a couple to come together whose highest aspirations are fully gratified." His concerns for her remained, however, for "what awaits Custer no one can say. Libbie may be a widow or have a maimed husband."[38]

The four couples of the wedding party arrived at 9 A.M., on the tenth, in Cleveland, where Charles Noble, a friend of the Custers, hosted them at his home for an afternoon reception and for "a brilliant party" in the evening. Autie and Libbie departed the next morning for Buffalo and then on to Rochester, New York. Here they enjoyed a performance of *Uncle Tom's Cabin* before traveling to Onondaga, the hometown of Libbie's aunt and uncle, Charity and Oren Smith. They enjoyed the hospitality of Judge Bacon's sister and her husband until the fifteenth, when they left for Howlett Hill, the home of Denison and Eliza Bacon Sabin. The Sabins held a reception for the couple, inviting Libbie's numerous relatives in the area.[39]

From Howlett Hill, they journeyed down the Hudson River to West Point. If she had not known it already, Libbie soon learned of Autie's fondness for the academy, its traditions, and his memories of the place. "I never dreamed there was so lovely a place in the United States," Libbie wrote upon seeing it. "Everyone was delighted to see Autie. Even the dogs welcomed him." While he visited with instructors, cadets escorted Libbie across the grounds, including a stroll along Lovers' Walk. One of the faculty members boasted that he had the pleasure of kissing the bride.[40]

On the train from West Point to New York City, Autie fumed with jealousy. "I was amazed," Libbie wrote in a letter, "to see my blithe bridegroom turned into an incarnated thundercloud." The professor's kiss and the cadets' attention to her infuriated Autie, and his anger reduced Libbie to tears. He refused to listen to her explanation, and as she related, "I quite expected to be sent home to my parents." Finally, Libbie blurted out, "Well, you left me with them, Autie!" There was steel under her beauty and softness, and he retreated. By the time they reached the city, they had reconciled.[41]

The Custers rented a room at the Metropolitan Hotel, but their stay was brief, barely long enough for Autie to visit a phrenologist at the request of his father-in-law, who believed in the practice of studying the character and mental capacity of an individual by the conformation of the skull. The phrenologist did not know Autie's identity and cautioned him to "avoid overdoing." While in the city, he received telegrams from the army that inquired when he would return to the brigade. From New York, they journeyed to Washington, D.C.[42]

The capital, thought Libbie, "was bewildering and delightful to me." They found a room at a boardinghouse, attended church, and enjoyed several dinners with members of the Michigan congressional delegation and other dignitaries. Autie took her to a theater to view the melodramatic play *East Lynn*. Libbie noted later that her husband "laughed at the fun and cried at the pathos in the theatres with all the abandon of a boy unconscious of surroundings." But the pleasures of the honeymoon and the city ended with an order for Autie to report immediately for duty.[43]

"I was supremely happy," Autie told his sister subsequently about the honeymoon. Except for his outburst of jealousy, he and Libbie had enjoyed the pleasures of relatives, friends, important persons, sightseeing, and of each other. The physical consummation of their love began during these weeks and revealed, at least to Libbie for the first time, the sexual gratification between a man and a woman. Autie had discovered earlier the mystery that enticed youth, but in Libbie, he found fulfillment he probably had never known. For her, the veil lifted, and together, they indulged. Their private correspondence—the surviving letters of Autie—contain a frankness about their mutual desire for each other that attests to the passion and sensuality of their relationship. Their love burned—emotionally and physically.[44]

When the orders to report to the army reached Custer in the capital, he and Libbie boarded a train as soon as possible, traveling across the

Virginia countryside that had borne so much of the conflict for three years. The general's staff met them at the station and escorted the couple to brigade headquarters, with Libbie riding in an ambulance, "a very sad sort of vehicle to me," she remembered. Custer brought her to Clover Hill, the residence of John S. "Jack" Barbour, president of the Orange & Alexandria Railroad, and his family near Stevensburg. The Barbours had relocated when Custer selected the house as winter head-quarters. The lower floor held brigade offices, while the upper level, with several rooms, served as quarters. The room reserved for the Cus-ters, recalled Libbie, had a barren floor and walls, "rough furniture," and a four-poster bed that wives of Michigan troopers who were in camp kindly decorated with calico curtains—"it looked very homey" to Libbie.[45]

The swiftness of the departure from Washington and the scene at Stevensburg—a sea of huts, wagons, men, cannon, and horses—over-whelmed Libbie. "I found myself in a few hours," she wrote, "on the extreme wing of the Army of the Potomac, in an isolated Virginia farm-house, finishing my honeymoon alone." Much of what she wit-nessed she initially could not comprehend. To her, an army functioned in mysterious ways. "All the new life was in the way of surprise," she asserted. "If I had been transported to Mars it could not have been greater."[46]

Libbie was struck particularly by the deference and respect given to her husband by staff members and subordinate officers. Military proto-col required such behavior, but she admitted later that she had possessed no idea of "the position or power of a General." Once when she inquired of Autie if junior officers always saluted him, he replied, "You better believe they do or discipline would remind them." Writing many years later, Libbie stated: "All this saluting, addressing in the third per-son, never speaking unless spoken to, and so many observances that go to enhance that dignity that hinges around a King seem now so tremendously like some play being acted. It is not in the least real to me now."[47]

As the bride of the general, Libbie enjoyed special attention. Staff members catered to her, with Chief of Staff Jacob Greene insuring that her needs were met. At headquarters, however, no one welcomed her more than Eliza. The servant now had more than men to cook and to care for, and she relished it. In her soft voice and gentle manner, Eliza soon governed Libbie as skillfully as she did "the Ginnel." "You felt just as she wanted you to feel," Libbie explained, "as if you were a child and had a nurse."[48]

From the outset, Autie told Libbie that as his wife he did not want her to be cleaning or cooking; those were Eliza's tasks. Consequently, as Libbie noted, "it was not necessary for me to learn to be a house-keeper." Eliza had "sole control" of the chores, assisted by a young white lad, Johnnie Cisco, who had attached himself to the general. Cisco laundered Autie's shirts, held extra horses in battle, and waited tables at headquarters. Libbie called him "Eliza's special henchman about the kitchen," but all of them liked the waif who had suddenly appeared at headquarters. Where Cisco came from, no one knew, and he did not explain.[49]

The Custers joined the army as the cavalry camps stirred with prepa-rations for an operation. It had been a quiet winter along the Rappa-hannock and Rapidan rivers, with the routine interrupted by visits from politicians, family members and friends from home, reviews, horse races, dances, and horseback rides. In Custer's brigade, the entire com-plement of the First Michigan had been granted a thirty-day furlough to recruit and to reorganize in the state. Along the sections of the Rapidan picketed by the Michiganders and Vermonters, they had nego-tiated a truce with the Confederates. A member of the Fifth Michigan wrote his father that the men "have the finest times, in the world talking with the 'Rebs.' We trade spurs and coffee and all such things. They are good friends now but when they come to fight they are as bad as ever." Even the weather was mild and pleasant throughout most of the season.[50]

Judson Kilpatrick ended the winter interlude with a plan for a mounted raid on Richmond. In mid-February, at Abraham Lincoln's request, Kilpatrick journeyed to Washington and discussed with the president and Secretary of War Edwin Stanton his idea of a cavalry thrust into the Confederate capital to free Federal prisoners confined in Libby Prison and on Belle Isle in the James River. Lincoln sanctioned the audacious operation, asking George Meade for his views. Meade sought the opinion of cavalry commander Alfred Pleasonton, who ob-jected to it. But the president desired it, and Meade approved the raid. Colonel Ulric Dahlgren, son of Admiral John Dahlgren and a former member of Meade's staff who had lost his right leg below the knee from a wound during the Gettysburg Campaign, came from Washington and volunteered. Kilpatrick welcomed Dahlgren, whose name would be subsequently attached to the operation.[51]

Kilpatrick culled the ranks of his division for the best mounted troopers to comprise his command of approximately 4,000 men. A large detachment of the Michigan Brigade was assigned to the raiding force. To draw the enemy's attention away from Kilpatrick, Meade ordered a diversion toward Charlottesville, with Custer appointed as the commander. The purpose of the feint was "to facilitate other operations of this army," and if circumstances permitted, Custer should destroy the railroad bridge over the Rivanna River and sever the telegraph lines between Lynchburg and Gordonsville. His force consisted of the First and Fifth United States Cavalry, Sixth Ohio and Sixth Pennsylvania Cavalry, and a battery of horse artillery. Elements of Major General John Sedgwick's Sixth Corps were directed to Madison Court House as support for the cavalrymen.[52]

Custer left headquarters on Sunday, February 28, for the rendezvous of the units at Madison Court House. For Libbie, it was the first of countless farewells as a soldier's wife. At such times, Eliza doted upon her, and as Libbie described it, "treated me like an infant, coddling, crooning over me, 'He'll come back Miss Libbie. He always does you know. Didn't he tell you he'd come back to you!'"[53]

At Madison Court House, while the cavalrymen filed into bivouacs before the march, Custer conferred with Sedgwick, telling the corps commander that if he (Custer) did not return in three days, his force had been cut off by the Rebels and he would take an alternate route. As instructed, he would communicate with Sedgwick during the raid. Earlier, Custer had briefed the officers of the command on the plan, and at 1 A.M. on the twenty-ninth, reveille sounded. An hour later, the Federal horsemen clattered out of the town.[54]

About daylight, the Federals crossed the Rapidan River at Bank's Mills Ford, after scattering enemy pickets at Wolf Town. The column proceeded to Stanardsville, chasing away additional gray-clad videttes as the townsfolk lined the street, watching the horsemen pass. Scouts from the Sixth Pennsylvania Cavalry prowled ahead of the main body and, about two o'clock in the afternoon, collided with a group of Rebels about a mile and a half north of the Rivanna River. The Pennsylvanians drove them south, and Custer led his men across the river at the Rio

Bridge, a long wooden span. Just beyond the river, the Northerners discovered a camp of Stuart's horse artillery, composed of four batteries under Captain Marcellus N. Moorman.[55]

Custer halted the column, sending two detachments of Regulars forward in a reconnaissance. Captain Joseph P. Ash and 60-odd men of the Fifth United States Cavalry moved downstream, and before the Confederate artillerists had evacuated the camp, Ash's men charged, scattering the Southerners and capturing six caissons and two forges. Moorman's gunners extricated all of the cannon and deployed four on a ridge. While Ash's troopers burned the camp, Custer approached with the main body, and according to the Rebels, mistakenly exchanged gunfire with Ash's detachment. Moorman's men remained on horseback in support of the artillery pieces, with Custer mistaking them for enemy cavalry. When he received an erroneous report of the approach of infantry, he ordered a withdrawal.[56]

The raiders recrossed the Rio Bridge, burning it and the nearby Rio Mills, which contained corn and meal. Custer halted to feed and rest the horses about eight miles southwest of Stanardsville. Rain began falling heavily, and the night was "intensely dark." When the march resumed, Colonel William Stedman and a 500-man detachment, riding in the van, became separated from the column "through a misunderstanding," in Custer's words. The rain had changed to sleet, and Custer ordered the men to bivouac for the night. Alfred Waud of *Harper's Weekly* accompanied the Federals and wrote afterward, "The night was rainy, and all had to lie upon the ground and get wet through. It was difficult to get fires to burn, and the rain began to freeze upon the limbs of the trees, so that by morning everything appeared to be cased in crystal."[57]

The Yankees slogged through Stanardsville toward the Rapidan River on the morning of March 1. North of the town the road forked—one branch to Burton's Ford, the other to Bank's Mills Ford. Here on a ridge beyond the intersection, the Virginia cavalry brigade of Brigadier General Williams C. Wickham covered the Burton's Ford Road, while a smaller contingent guarded Bank's Mills Ford. The Virginians had marched after Custer's attack on the camp and now were posted between the Federals and the river.[58]

When Wickham's men drove in the van of the Union column, Custer placed the main body in a ravine, deployed a section of artillery on a ridge, and counterattacked with a detachment of Regulars. The Federals scattered the Rebels, capturing about twenty of them. The gunfire, however, had drawn the Virginians at Bank's Mills Ford toward the action. Feinting an advance against the Confederate brigade, Custer directed his troopers down the road to Bank's Mills. Although the Northerners were slowed by hundreds of runaway slaves, they eluded the Virginians and crossed the river, burning the two mills as they passed. Stedman's cavalrymen met them en route to Madison Court House, having remarched when they heard the sounds of combat. The command reached Madison Court House about 6 P.M., with Custer reporting the capture of 500 horses and a Virginia state flag, without the loss of a single man.[59]

Pleasonton and Meade praised Custer, with the latter describing the raid as "perfectly successful." The March 19 issue of *Harper's Weekly* featured Waud's drawing of Custer leading a charge on its cover. But its design as a diversionary operation to assist Kilpatrick failed to have an effect on the Confederates. While Kilpatrick tried in his report to conceal the magnitude of his losses and the raid's complete failure, the division commander had in truth lost 340 men, over 500 horses and arms, and uncounted quantities of equipment. Among the dead was Ulric Dahlgren, killed in an ambush as his command tried to elude pursuers. At army headquarters, universal disdain for Kilpatrick percolated when Meade learned of the details. A staff member described "Kill-Cavalry" as "a frothy braggart without brains and not overstocked with desire to fall on the field." He predicted that "Kill has rather dished himself." [60]

Custer rejoined Libbie at Clover Hill on March 2. In the aftermath of the raids, the routine of winter resumed. Custer had minimal duties, so he and Libbie dined with various generals, including Pleasonton, who had a six-course meal prepared. On pleasant, sunny days, the couple enjoyed carriage rides together, escorted by several troopers. On March 14, while they were returning to camp from a ride, the carriage team was frightened and suddenly bolted, throwing Custer from the vehicle. Libbie was unharmed because the horses broke loose from the carriage before the animals could topple it—"Everybody seems to think it is a miracle I was not killed," she informed her parents. Custer suffered a concussion.[61]

About a week after the accident, Pleasonton approached Kilpatrick and Custer about a potentially embarrassing matter for the pair of generals. On March 13, authorities in Washington had arrested a twenty-year-old woman named Anna E. Jones, familiarly called Annie, on charges of espionage. The next day, Miss Jones dictated a statement to a notary public, claiming that in the summer of 1863 she had been with the army "as the friend and companion of Genl. Custer." The brigadier's attention to her, she added, angered Kilpatrick, who reported her to army headquarters, alleging that she was a Confederate spy. She was arrested and confined in Old Capitol Prison in Washington for three months.[62]

At the request of Washington authorities, Pleasonton asked for an explanation from each of the implicated generals. Kilpatrick did not prepare a statement, but Custer replied on March 22. According to Custer, he first met Annie Jones when she appeared at his headquarters seeking a position as a nurse at one of the field hospitals. She stayed a week, while Custer queried surgeons whether they needed another nurse. Unsuccessful, Custer ordered her to leave, and "I informed her that she must never visit my command again."[63]

Several weeks later, Annie reappeared at Custer's camp, arriving in an ambulance escorted by soldiers assigned by Major General Gouverneur Warren. Custer refused initially to speak with her, but relented, granting her permission to spend the night. When she departed the next morning, he warned her that should she return, a guard would escort her away. "Her whole object and purpose in being with the army seemed to be to distinguish herself by some deed or daring," Custer wrote. "In this respect alone, she seemed to be insane." "So far as her statement in relation to Gen. Kilpatrick and myself goes," he concluded, "it is simply untrue. I do not believe she is or ever was a spy. This part of her reputation has been genuine by her information."[64]

With the submission of his statement, Custer was finished officially with Annie Jones. As a recently married man, Custer surely wished that his name had not been linked to her. When the alleged liaison occurred, Custer was not engaged to Libbie, but they were corresponding through Nettie Humphrey. It was only weeks later, however, that Custer returned to Monroe on leave and renewed his proposal of marriage.

As for Annie Jones, she admitted in her statement that she had been a companion of various officers and generals since she had journeyed from her home in Massachusetts in August 1861. Although she was arrested a number of times for espionage, there is no evidence of her being a spy for the Confederacy. She appears to have been a young woman enamored of military officers and who enjoyed the attention accorded a general's "companion." In the end, she proved to be an annoying embarrassment to them and other officials. Eventually, she obtained her parole and disappeared from the record.[65]

The credibility of her allegations toward Kilpatrick and Custer cannot be verified. Within the army, Kilpatrick had a notorious reputation as a womanizer. If a compliant, apparently attractive Annie Jones entered his camp, Kilpatrick would probably have welcomed her. Whether Custer induced her away from his superior officer, as she maintained, is speculative. He denied it unequivocally, but to do otherwise at the time could have caused him problems in his marriage. Miss Jones was desperate to prove her innocence when she made the statement and implicated a number of officers. Too often, history moves within shadows, and with Custer and Annie Jones, the truth eludes.[66]

Two days after Custer responded to Pleasonton's inquiry, on March 24, he secured a ten-day leave of absence that was extended to twenty days because of the concussion. He had not rested after the accident, and his condition worsened. He and Libbie used the furlough to resume their honeymoon, visiting Baltimore and Washington. In the capital, they were feted by senators and congressmen, and met President Lincoln. When the leave expired, Libbie remained behind in a boarding-house in Washington. Spring brought a renewal of the war, and with the Federals, it brought change.[67]

Chapter 9

"WHERE IN HELL IS THE REAR?"

■ When George and Libbie Custer boarded a train on March 24, 1864, to begin his twenty-day furlough, she was the only woman in the railroad car. She received courteous attention from the officers, who enjoyed the presence of an attractive young woman. For her part, Libbie closely studied one of the generals, and four days later described him in a letter to her parents: "Sandy hair and mustache; eyes greenish-blue. Short, and, Mother, not 'tasty' but very ordinary-looking. No show-off but quite unassuming, talked all the time and was funny." [1]

It seemed to be that way with Ulysses S. Grant. As his reputation rose during the conflict, expectations of the man preceded the general. Invariably, those individuals who met him for the first time chose similar words as Libbie's: "very ordinary-looking," "unassuming." A man of modest height and of a reserved manner, he eschewed fancy uniforms and military pomp. But Grant wore well—a fact that President Abraham Lincoln appreciated as the Civil War entered its fourth year.

Sam Grant, as his friends in the Regular Army called him, was forty-one years old when Lincoln appointed him general-in-chief of the armies of the United States, asking the Senate to reinstate the rank of lieutenant general and to confirm the officer. Since the winter of 1862, Grant had fashioned an unrivaled string of victories in the West —Forts Henry and Donelson, Shiloh, Vicksburg, and Chattanooga. As Lincoln remarked, the general could not be spared, because he fought, and the president rewarded the fighter with authority no American soldier had held since George Washington.[2]

Grant saw warfare in unvarnished terms. He was a relentless opponent, a general who understood and accepted that fighting meant killing. He possessed unbending determination and the moral courage to order men to their deaths. One of George Meade's staff officers assessed the new commander as well as anyone when he saw him in the spring of 1864, writing, "Grant is a man of a good deal of rough dignity; rather taciturn; quick and decided in speech. He habitually wears an expression as if he had determined to drive his head through a brick wall, and was about to do it. I have much confidence in him."[3]

Whether Grant merited such confidence would have to wait until Virginia's roads dried, armies marched, and he confronted Robert E. Lee. Before then, however, the general-in-chief's accession to command meant changes in the Army of the Potomac. On March 25, Meade, who retained command of the army at Grant's insistence, reorganized the infantry, eliminating the First and Third corps, parceling their units into the Second, Fifth, and Sixth corps. Meade believed that with fewer corps he could maintain better tactical control of the army's major units.[4]

On the same day, Major General Alfred Pleasonton was relieved as commander of the Cavalry Corps. While Pleasonton had not been a brilliant commander, he had rejuvenated the mounted arm. But he also had aroused the antagonism of Meade and of authorities in Washington. He had complained often and stridently about the Cavalry Bureau and its remount program. Most recently, he had opposed the Kilpatrick-Dahlgren raid, and although correct in his judgment, the operation had had Meade's approval. Finally, Grant had his own ideas about the cavalry, wanting a commander of his choosing for the corps. In the end, Pleasonton was gone from the eastern army, exiled to the Department of the Missouri.[5]

Grant selected Major General Philip H. Sheridan as Pleasonton's replacement, summoning the thirty-three-year-old officer from the western theater, where he commanded an infantry division. A West Pointer, Sheridan had led cavalry at the regimental level and infantry at the brigade and divisional levels. Grant had known little about Sheridan until Chattanooga, when the latter's troops scaled Missionary Ridge, wrenching it from its Southern defenders. Sheridan was a fiery, aggressive combat officer, the type Grant admired, and it was this spirit the general-in-chief desired in a cavalry commander.[6]

Like Grant, Sheridan did not impress physically. An Irishman, he was, according to an officer, "a small, broad-shouldered, squat man, with black hair and a square head." He possessed a barrel chest, but he had inordinately short legs. After Lincoln met him, he wryly described the general as "a brown, chunky little chap, with a long body, short legs, not enough neck to hang him, and such long arms that if his ankles itch he can scratch them without stooping." To the troops, he was "Little Phil."[7]

But Sheridan's stature as a warrior could not be measured in inches. "In making an estimate of the man," argued an officer, "it was the ensemble of his qualities that had to be considered. He had to be taken 'all in all.' " He was brusque, profane, demanding, tireless, patriotic, a man who evaded neither command nor responsibility. Within him, fires burned. Naturally impulsive and eager, Sheridan was transformed upon a battlefield. "His eyes fairly blazed and the whole man seemed to expand mentally and physically," in the opinion of a staff officer. Confident, unforgiving to those who accepted failure, Sheridan infused his combativeness, "like an electric shock," into the souls of his men. Unlike any who came before him, he would unsheathe the sword.[8]

To the horse soldiers of the cavalry corps, however, Sheridan's qualities as a commander could only be a topic of speculation for the present. Uncertainty, fed by rumor, swept through the camps. "Gen Grant is tearing down and building," remarked Major James H. Kidd of the Sixth Michigan Cavalry, "whether for good or bad remains to be seen." Among the Michiganders, the story circulated that their commander, George Custer, might be transferred. " 'Bad luck' to those who are instrumental in removing him," Major Kidd groused to his father about the prospects of losing Custer. "We swear by him. His move is our battle cry. He can get twice the fight out of this brigade than any other man can possibly do."[9]

The conjecture about Custer resulted, in part, from the other changes implemented under Sheridan. While some in the corps believed that Wesley Merritt might receive permanent command of John Buford's First Division, that post went to Brigadier General Alfred T. A. Torbert, a thirty-year-old Delawarean who had commanded infantry troops for the past three years. A quiet, handsome man, Torbert had no experience with the mounted arm, and his appointment stirred comment. Merritt had performed capably as Buford's temporary replacement, but he may have been viewed as one of the deposed Pleasonton's favorites.[10]

Like Pleasonton, Judson Kilpatrick's days with the army were numbered with the arrival of Grant and Sheridan. Although Kilpatrick was "very much offended" by Pleasonton's dismissal, he must have suspected that his command of the Third Division was in jeopardy. His report on the Richmond raid fooled few, if any, in higher authority, and in mid-April he was relieved of duty and assigned to the West. His successor, picked by Grant, was Brigadier General James H. Wilson, a former member of the commander's staff and, at the time, chief of the Cavalry Bureau. Wilson was twenty-six years old, a classmate of Merritt's at West Point, and an engineer officer by experience.[11]

Custer rejoined the army from his leave amid the command upheaval, arriving on April 14. His chief of staff, Jacob Greene, had written him during the furlough, reporting that "we are blue as a whole whetstone." As would be expected, the removal of Pleasonton troubled Custer. He owed his brigadiership to Pleasonton, and during the past eleven months the pair had become close friends. During the previous fall, Custer related to Libbie that Pleasonton usually greeted him upon his return from a raid or action with, "Well, boy, I am glad to see you back. I was *anxious about you*." Custer added that "I do not believe a father could love his son more than Genl. Pleasonton loves me."[12]

It was more than just his affection for Pleasonton, however, that motivated Custer in his reaction to his friend's transfer to "an obscure command." Custer believed that he deserved promotion to divisional command, but with Pleasonton gone, he would not secure it. He refused to contact "my numerous friends in Washington" to intercede on his behalf, probably knowing that his political allies could not persuade Lincoln to countermand Grant's selections. A new wind, coming from the West, was blowing across Virginia, and the Union army and Custer could do nothing but bend with it.[13]

Two other factors compounded his disgruntlement. Upon his return, Custer heard rumors similar to the ones recounted by Kidd that he would be transferred from the Michigan Brigade, "by far the best Cavalry brigade in the United States army," he asserted. Custer blamed some of "Grant's favorites" for wanting him removed, and he threatened to resign his commission if assigned to another unit. With the reports persisting, he went directly to Meade and Sheridan, who assured the brigadier that he would retain the Michigan Brigade.[14]

Furthermore, the appointment of Wilson to the Third Division galled Custer. Not only did Custer believe that the post should have been his—Kilpatrick told him that he merited it—but Wilson was junior in rank to Custer, Merritt, and Henry Davies. Since Wilson could not command senior officers, Grant and Sheridan assigned Davies to a brigade in David Gregg's Second Division and transferred Custer and the Michiganders to Torbert's First Division. The order pleased Custer because he had known Torbert and described him as "an old and intimate friend of mine and a very worthy gentleman." As for Wilson, Custer resented and disliked him from the beginning, writing to his sister several days after the reassignment that the new division commander "has made himself ridiculous by the ignorance he displays in regard to cavalry." His opinion of Wilson would not improve with time.[15]

Sheridan, meanwhile, prepared the corps for spring operations with drills, inspections, and reviews. The mounted command numbered slightly over 12,000 effectives, divided into the three divisions. The first Vermont Cavalry had been transferred from the Michigan Brigade, so Custer now had his original complement of four regiments—First, Fifth, Sixth, and Seventh Michigan, commanded respectively by Lieutenant Colonel Peter Stagg, Colonel Russell A. Alger, Major James H. Kidd, and Major Henry W. Granger.[16]

Before the army advanced, however, Sheridan and Torbert sent Custer to Washington on official duty, granting him forty-eight hours in the capital. The trip allowed him time with Libbie, and as she recounted it to her parents, when Autie arrived at the boardinghouse, "the door burst open. He rushed upstairs so fast the people thought the house was on fire." He had written twice to her since he left her in the city a fortnight before, expressing in both letters how much he loved her and missed her, "whose lips were ever ready to attest for heartfelt devotion to me."[17]

Undoubtedly, Libbie related to Autie the details of a reception she had attended at the White House. President Lincoln, whom Libbie described in a letter home as "the gloomiest, most painfully careworn looking man I ever saw," and Mrs. Mary Lincoln, "short, squatty, and plain," in Libbie's words, hosted the event. When Libbie reached the president in the receiving line, Lincoln said to her, "So this is the young woman whose husband goes into a charge with a whoop and a shout. Well, I'm told he won't do so any more." Libbie politely disagreed with the president, who joked, "Oh, then you want to be a widow, I see." [18]

Custer returned to the army after the two-day interlude, as activity quickened. In the camp of the Michigan Brigade outside of Culpeper, Custer ordered saber and dismounted skirmish drills, inspected arms, and held a review and a dress parade. The regiments received new Spencer carbines and rifles, and Companies I and M of the Sixth Michigan rejoined their comrades after a year's detached duty in Maryland and West Virginia. [19]

The brigade may not have been the best cavalry unit in the army, as Custer affirmed, but the troopers were veterans, well armed and well mounted, confident in themselves and their commander, whom they now called "Old Curley." "Gen. Custer still commands us. He is a dashing fellow—nothing less," wrote a trooper. Another Michigander argued that "we have our Brigadier General Custar one of the Best Generals there is in the Army." "I believe," stated a member of the Fifth Michigan of his commander, "that he is the best cavalry officer left in the Army of the Potomac." To an officer of the Sixth Michigan, one reason for the men's devotion to, and respect for, Custer could be attributed to the fact "that his men were always at the front, and were always on the best of terms with him. A private could talk to him as freely as an officer. If he had any complaint to make, Custer was always ready to listen." [20]

As for himself, Custer welcomed the resumption of field operations. He had recovered from the concussion, although Chief of Staff Jacob Greene probably continued to scold him about taking care of himself, reminding the general that "you are only flesh and blood & can break down like any other man." Despite his disappointment about promotion and command changes, Custer had accepted Sheridan, writing to his sister that "Gen Sheridan from what I learn and see is an able and good Commander and I like him very much." If Sheridan fulfilled expectations, the Cavalry Corps could be a formidable weapon, and Custer and the Michiganders wanted to be a part of it, or as James Kidd predicted earlier in a letter to his father, when the campaign begins, it "will come with a smash." [21]

The anticipation ended on May 4, when the Army of the Potomac

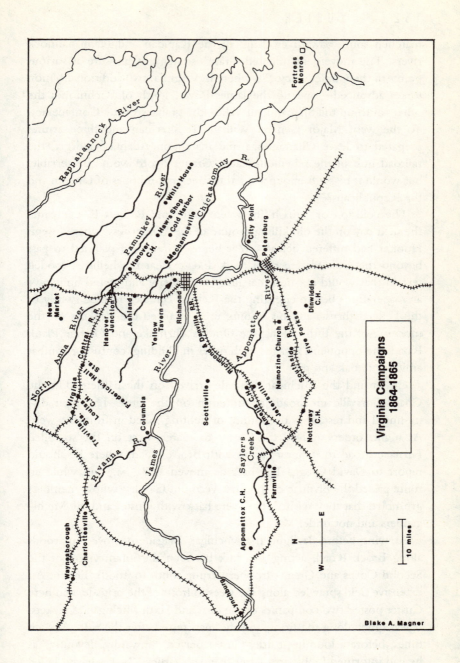

Virginia Campaigns
1864-1865

Fortress Monroe

Rappahannock River

Pamunkey River

Haw's Shop
White House
Cold Harbor
Mechanicsville

Chickahominy R.

City Point
Petersburg

Hanover C.H.

Ashland

Richmond

Yellow
Tavern

Appomattox River

Dinwiddie
C.H.

New
Market

North Anna River

Virginia Central R.R.

Hanover
Junction

Richmond & Danville R.R.

Namozine Church

Five Forks

Southside R.R.

Louisa
C.H.

Frederick's Hall
Sta.

Trevilian
Sta.

Columbia

James River

Scottsville

Amelia C.H.

Jetersville

Nottoway
C.H.

Rivanna R.

Sayler's
Creek

Farmville

Waynesborough

Charlottesville

Appomattox C.H.

N
E
W
S

10 miles

Lynchburg

Blake A. Magner

marched south toward crossings of the Rapidan and Rappahannock rivers. The movement initiated Grant's strategy of pressure at various points in the Confederacy. Elsewhere in Virginia, two additional Union forces advanced—one up the James River, south of Richmond; the other south up the Shenandoah Valley, the granary of the Confederacy. To the west, Major General William T. Sherman and three armies prepared to leave Chattanooga and march on Atlanta, Georgia, the railroad hub of the rebellious states. Grant's sword would be terrible, but would it be swift enough to aid the reelection hopes of Lincoln and the Republicans? [22]

The collision or "smash" between Grant and Robert E. Lee came the next day on the old killing ground of the Wilderness, where Joseph Hooker had suffered defeat a year before. Grant had planned to pass beyond the Confederate right flank and to clear the hellish, wooded terrain that would negate his artillery superiority and would limit cavalry operations before engaging the Rebels. But Lee reacted swiftly to the Federal thrust, and his leading units attacked the Yankees on the morning of the fifth. Along the Orange Turnpike and Orange Plank Road, the opponents ravaged each other in blinding, confusing combat amid scrub oak and pine. [23]

Custer and the Michigan Brigade arrived on the battlefield at the Chancellorsville crossroads about noon on the fifth. The men dismounted and rested, as the sounds of fighting rolled in from the west. At night, orders arrived for Custer to march west on the so-called Furnace Road to its intersection with Brock Road, where he should report to David Gregg. The brigade moved at 2 A.M., and while en route passed the bivouac of the First Vermont Cavalry, whose members grumbled that they wished they were back with Custer and the Michiganders and not under Wilson. [24]

Arriving before daylight, the Michigan Brigade deployed in woods along Brock Road, acting as a link between the infantrymen of the Second Corps and Gregg's troopers strung south to Todd's Tavern. An extensive field sprawled along the trees in front of the brigade, and here Custer posted two companies of the First and Sixth Michigan as pickets. It was quiet along the front, and the men rested after the ride. At such times, before a looming battle, Custer prayed, "inwardly, devoutly," as he had informed Libbie in a letter five days earlier. "Never have I failed to command myself to God's keeping," he wrote, "asking Him to forgive my past sins, and to watch over me while in danger . . . and to receive me if I fell. . . . After having done so all anxiety for myself, here or hereafter, is dispelled. I feel that my destiny is in the hands of the Almighty. This belief, more than any other fact or reason, makes me brave and fearless as I am." [25]

Suddenly, about nine o'clock, a mounted regiment of Confederate cavalry charged the Michigan picket line. When Custer heard the gun-fire, he rode to the front of the brigade and signaled to the band, which was positioned between the two front regiments, to play "Yankee Doodle." By now, every member of the brigade knew the meaning of the song's notes, or as an officer put it, "every man's hand went to his sabre. It was always the signal for a charge." Custer wheeled in his saddle, raised his sword, and shouted: "Forward, by divisions!" [26]

The First and Sixth Michigan burst from the woods, surging across the field. They galloped to a ravine that bisected the field, dismounted, and raked the Southerners with their Spencers. The Confederates, the so-called "Comanches" of the Thirty-fifth Virginia Cavalry, peeled back upon their support. Custer did not know it yet, but the gray-clad troopers belonged to Brigadier General Thomas Rosser, his best friend at West Point. Neither man had time on this morning to recall that winter's day in 1861 when they stood at the barracks windows, cheering the songs played by the academy band and contemplating their country's future. That was before the storm they now found themselves in, on opposite sides in a nameless field cleared for killing. [27]

Rosser shoved his men on foot into the field, the combat escalating. Custer rode behind the Michiganders in the ravine. He was a conspicuous target, but it did not matter to him. "Custer was always on horse-back," stated James Kidd. "He never was seen on foot in battle, even when every other officer and man in his command was dismounted. And he rode close to the very front line, fearless and resolute." When a second Confederate brigade bolstered Rosser's line and overlapped the Federal right flank, Custer added the Fifth Michigan to that section of the line and placed the Seventh Michigan beside the First. Neither side could gain an advantage until Colonel Thomas Devin's Union brigade arrived, and Custer attacked with the Fifth and Sixth Michigan and Seventeenth Pennsylvania, lashing the Rebel left flank. In the center, the First and Seventh Michigan charged out of the ravine, and the enemy fled in disorder. In his report, Custer described the action as "an obstinate fight." [28]

To the north of the cavalry, the two armies concluded the fearful slaughter begun the day before. The Federals clung to Brock Road, repulsing Confederate attacks. Lee had caught Grant in the Wilderness and exacted a terrible price. Unlike his predecessors, however, Grant accepted the costs, and on May 7 issued orders for the march. It would not be rearward to the rivers, but south, toward the crossroads of Spotsylvania Court House. The war in Virginia had taken a new course.[29]

On May 7 and 8, the Union horsemen prowled along the army's left flank, skirmishing with Jeb Stuart's troopers. During the eighth, Wilson's men occupied Spotsylvania Court House, the target of Grant's march, but were ordered to retire. Conflicting instructions from Meade's and Sheridan's headquarters hampered operations. Believing the cavalry was delaying the march of the infantry, Meade summoned Sheridan to headquarters on the morning of the eighth. Both men had combustible tempers, and when they met, it was an explosive exchange, spiced with curses. Finally, Sheridan growled that he "could whip Stuart" if Meade would give him the opportunity. When the army commander reported the encounter to Grant, noting Sheridan's assertion about Stuart, the general-in-chief remarked: "Did Sheridan say that? Well, he generally knows what he is talking about. Let him start right out and do it." Meade issued orders at 10 P.M. for Sheridan to "proceed against the enemy's cavalry."[30]

Before daylight on May 9, the Union cavalrymen, 10,000 in number, filed into a column of fours that stretched for thirteen miles in length. To onlookers, it was an impressive array—a huge lance in blue that heralded the ascendancy of Federal cavalry in Virginia. On this day, the Michigan Brigade led the march, with the Sixth Michigan in the van. Custer and his staff rode behind the regiment as it paced the movement south toward the Confederate capital. At Beaver Dam Station on the Virginia Central Railroad, his men seized two locomotives, a large amount of commissary and medical stores, and released over 300 Northern prisoners. After destroying a section of the track and burning the stores they could not carry away, they bivouacked south of the North Anna River.[31]

The Yankees stirred early on the tenth, but the pace of the march was more leisurely than on the previous day. Sheridan framed the column with flankers, anticipating the presence of Stuart's horsemen. The Northerners covered eighteen miles and crossed the South Anna River before camping near Ground Squirrel Bridge on Mountain Road. Sheridan had impressed most of the command with his conduct of the march.[32]

Sheridan had his men in the saddle by one o'clock on the morning of May 11. Once again, the pace of the march was methodical, with the First Cavalry Division, temporarily under Wesley Merritt, in the lead on Mountain Road. At daylight, a Confederate cavalry brigade struck the rear of the Union column, forcing Sheridan to detach units. The Rebels had followed the Yankees for two days, skirmishing with them but not impeding their march. It was the same once more in the early morning's light. Merritt's division proceeded on the road, reaching its intersection with Telegraph Road at Yellow Tavern, two miles north of Richmond's outer defenses, about eleven o'clock. Here, at last, Sheridan found Stuart deployed to give battle.[33]

Stuart and the brigades of Brigadier Generals Williams C. Wickham and Lunsford Lomax, roughly 3,000 Virginians in seven regiments, had arrived at Yellow Tavern barely an hour before the enemy. Stuart had raced on a circuitous route to interdict the Federals, exhausting horses and men. He posted Wickham's four regiments west of Telegraph Road on a ridge parallel to Mountain Road and faced it south. Lomax's three regiments deployed on a ridge behind a fringe of trees east of Telegraph Road, forming an obtuse angle with Wickham's brigade on its right. Several cannon of the horse artillery supported the dismounted troopers. The Southerners held a good defensive position, but there were not enough of them.[34]

Merritt initiated the action by pushing forward two brigades against Wickham's men, while holding Custer's Michiganders in reserve. Before long, the Fifteenth Virginia, Lomax's right regiment that connected with Wickham's left, opened fire from the woods beneath the ridge. Custer ordered the Fifth and Sixth Michigan to advance on foot. The Fifth went in first, spilling into a field. The Confederate line exploded in gunfire. "Words cannot picture the scene that followed out there in that level field," remembered Sergeant E. L. Tripp. "We were trying to return the fire, shooting in three directions." Suddenly, Custer galloped into the Fifth's ranks, shouting, "Lie down, men—lie down! We'll fix them!" Behind him came the Sixth, which covered the Fifth's left flank, and together they surged toward the woods, driving the Virginians up the slope. The Yankees halted in a swale, lying there for nearly two hours, exchanging carbine fire with the enemy.[35]

While the combat subsided during midafternoon, Custer surveyed Lomax's position, convinced that an attack could capture three Confederate cannon. Merritt approved, and Custer secured the First Vermont as support for the assault. The Vermonters and the Seventh Michigan deployed on foot, while the First Michigan formed in a column of squadrons on horseback. Custer took "his place at the head of the regiment as usual," noted a member of the First Michigan, instructed the men to draw their sabers, and signaled to the band to strike up "Yankee Doodle." [36]

The First Michigan emerged from the woods at a walk, and the Southern artillerists reacted with shellfire and canister. Custer increased the pace to a trot as outriders leveled fences in the regiment's path. Descending into a ravine, the troopers veered right and emerged on the Rebel flank. Custer ordered the charge, and "with such fury," in the words of one of them, the Yankees plowed into Lomax's ranks, scattering the enemy and overrunning two cannon. Behind them, their Michigan and Vermont comrades charged dismounted. Stuart led a counterattack with elements of the First Virginia, but the Federals shattered it, and one of the Michiganders shot the famous Confederate commander in the abdomen with a pistol. Stuart died the next day in Richmond. [37]

The entire Confederate line dissolved as Merritt hit Wickham with his other two brigades. The Yankees cheered their decisive victory over the vaunted horsemen of Jeb Stuart. Although the mortally wounded Confederate had only a third of his corps on the field, the Federals had won a decisive victory and, with Stuart's death on May 12, inflicted an irreparable loss upon the Southern mounted arm. Custer's "brilliant charge" had earned the victory. [38]

Sheridan allowed little time for celebration as the cavalry marched south toward Richmond. In the darkness, the guide, a Southern sympathizer, led Wilson's division into the city's outer defensive works, and it came under fire from infantry and Home Guards. The Federals halted for the night, but at daylight on May 12, Confederate cavalry attacked the rear of Sheridan's column, and the city's defenders resumed their pounding of Wilson's men. Sheridan instructed Custer to secure the railroad bridge over the Chickahominy River at Meadow Bridge. The Fifth Michigan spearheaded the assault on foot, supported by the Sixth. A Rebel shell burst near Custer, splattering him with mud, but once a

detail laid planks over the tracks, he led a mounted charge. The Southerners broke, and the Yankees swarmed over two cannon. With a passage opened, Sheridan followed with the corps, camping for the night
at Mechanicsville, where the horsemen found "an immense quantity of
corn on the ear," enough to feed the entire command. Rain began
falling as the men slept.[39]

The Federals marched east down the Peninsula on the thirteenth and
fourteenth, finally halting along the James River near Malvern Hill.
Here Sheridan sent the wounded downriver to Fortress Monroe and
rested and refitted the command until the seventeenth. While in camp,
Custer wrote three letters to Libbie. It was the first opportunity he had
had since the campaign began. In Washington, newspapers had reported
his death in the Wilderness fighting, and Libbie was frantic until Congressman John Bingham came to her with confirmation from the War
Department that Autie was fine.[40]

"We have passed through days of carnage and have lost heavily," Autie
began his initial letter to Libbie. "The Michigan Brigade," he added,
"has covered itself with undying glory." Merritt had praised the unit,
and Sheridan sent a staff officer to congratulate Custer at Yellow Tavern.
As for Wilson, he "proved himself an imbecile and nearly ruined the
corps by his blunders." He had to "rescue" Wilson, Custer wrote, and
members of the First Vermont jokingly tried to obtain "a pair of Custer's old boots" to command them, instead of Wilson. "Your Boy," he
boasted to Libbie, "was never before the object of such attention, and
has succeeded beyond his highest expectations." He cautioned her,
however, that this information was only for her and her parents.[41]

In the third letter, dated May 17, Autie turned to personal matters.
"I never loved my Gipsie as I do now," he assured Libbie. He was
"homesick" and thought of her constantly. "Little did I dream that my
existence my entire being my whole future life would be so completely
wrapt up in you." His love has increased in "intensity," and if they
were together now, he "would almost overpower" her with "kisses and
embraces."[42]

Later on the seventeenth, the Cavalry Corps broke camp and started
the return march to the army. Uncertain as to the location of either
Grant's or Lee's forces, Sheridan moved cautiously north. In all, it took
a week, until May 24, before the horsemen clattered in from their raid.
Throughout the march, shortages of subsistence and forage plagued the

column, and when the troopers rejoined the army north of the Pamun-key River near Hanover Court House, they were exhausted and hungry.[43]

Since the cavalrymen had departed on the raid on May 9, the two main armies had bloodied each other in a series of engagements at Spotsylvania Court House, until May 21, when Grant shifted Meade's army south once again, hoping to interpose it between Lee's forces and Richmond. Operating on interior lines, Lee raced ahead of the Federals and placed his veterans in a strong defensive position south of the North Anna River. Grant pushed three of the army's four corps across the river to engage the Confederates. By the twenty-fourth, when the cavalry returned, the opponents were stalemated along the river. Al-though ill, Lee had frustrated another of Grant's sidles to the south.[44]

Grant, however, would not relinquish his grip nor the strategic initia-tive. After dark on May 26, the Union infantry and artillery withdrew to the north bank of the North Anna River and started south toward the Pamunkey River. During the day, the First and Second Cavalry divisions feinted crossings of the Pamunkey River at Hanover Court House, before marching downstream to Dabney's Ferry, opposite Han-overtown, Grant's designated crossing point. At daylight on the twenty-seventh, the First Michigan Cavalry splashed across the Pamunkey, securing the site. Custer hurried his other regiments forward, and while the Sixth Michigan probed ahead for the Rebel units, Custer and the First Michigan began laying a pontoon bridge. While Custer oversaw the work, his horse faltered in the current, and he jumped off, swim-ming to shore "amid the cheers of the boys."[45]

On Saturday, May 28, while the Federal infantry corps filed over the pontoon, Sheridan protected the crossing by advancing west from Hanovertown. David Gregg's division led the movement, colliding with two divisions of Stuart's cavalry, temporarily under Major General Wade Hampton, at Haw's Shop, named for a large blacksmith shop, three miles from Hanovertown. The Southerners manned a strong position among trees and behind a swamp, supported by horse artillery. Gregg deployed his brigades in woods, and by late afternoon, when Sheridan ordered Custer's brigade forward, Gregg's troopers were clinging to the wood line.[46]

Custer formed the Michiganders into two lines on foot, and ad-vanced them to the edge of the woods. A wind of Confederate artillery

shells rattled the branches of the trees, while the rifle fire of the Southerners sounded "like that of hot flames crackling through dry timber."
Michiganders fell under the storm. Custer and his staff rode along the
line, exhorting the men and receiving three cheers. When one of the
enemy brigades began withdrawing, Custer ordered a charge. The Yankees burst from the trees "into that sanguinary hell of fire," with the
general and his staff in the forefront. A bullet killed James Christiancy's
horse and another smashed into his thigh. Near him, Jacob Greene
toppled to the ground, stunned by a spent rifle ball that hit him in the
head.[47]

"This fight was terrific," proclaimed Major James Kidd, but the
Michiganders routed the Confederates, grabbing a number of the
enemy. The engagement cost the brigade 41 killed, but as another
Federal noted, Custer's men delivered "one of the most gallant charges
of the war." For his bravery, Christiancy would eventually be awarded
the Medal of Honor. In Kidd's opinion, credit for the brigade's performance belonged to Custer. Six days after Haw's Shop, the major wrote
to his parents: "For all that this Brigade has accomplished all praise is
due to Gen Custer. So brave a man I never saw and as competent as
brave." "Under him," Kidd continued, "a man is ashamed to be cow-
ardly. Under *him* our men can achieve wonders."[48]

The Federals tended to their wounded comrades and buried those
for whom the war had ended. After nightfall, the cavalrymen marched
to Old Church, five miles to the southeast, and camped, resting
throughout the twenty-ninth. With the armies on the move, Cold
Harbor, a crossroads six miles beyond Old Church, became a vital
junction for both the Northerners and the Southerners. With Cold
Harbor in Union hands, Grant's new supply base at White House on
the Pamunkey River could be secured. Sheridan understood this, and
pushed videttes toward the village on the twenty-ninth. The fight for
Cold Harbor began the next day.[49]

Colonel Thomas Devin's brigade of the First Cavalry Division engaged the Rebels along Matadequin Creek on May 30. Merritt's and
Custer's brigades supported Devin's in the afternoon, with the Michiganders repulsing an enemy assault with their Spencers—"repeating
carbines are edge," one of them jotted in his diary. On the afternoon of
the thirty-first, Sheridan pushed toward Cold Harbor with Torbert's
division. On contact, Confederate artillery pounded the Federals. "I

was never in a hotter place in my life," remembered a Michigander, as the shells severed tree limbs. Southern infantry and cavalry fought stubbornly, but a mounted charge by a battalion of the First Michigan secured Cold Harbor. With only Torbert's division and some horse artillery at hand and with the bulk of Lee's army at Mechanicsville, less than six miles away, Sheridan pulled out after dark. But orders from Meade "to hold the place at all hazards" stopped the withdrawal, and the troopers strengthened their fieldworks through the night and waited.[50]

The Confederates came at daylight on June 1, an infantry division, backed by artillery. When the Rebels cleared some woods, the Federals unleashed a withering fire with their Spencers. The infantrymen staggered, retired, and then charged with the grit of veterans. The doors of the furnace opened again, blasting apart the attackers' line. In the midst of the fury, Custer rode along the works, shouting encouragement, the only mounted man along the Union line. About noon, troops of the Federal Sixth Corps relieved the cavalrymen. "Never did the uniform and arms of the infantry look better," asserted James Kidd. Custer had the brigade band play "Hail Columbia." While the infantrymen filed into the works, Sheridan mounted his men, marching them to White House, where they encamped. Cold Harbor belonged to the Army of the Potomac for another bloody rendezvous.[51]

For the next ten days, Grant and Lee confronted each other at Cold Harbor, a battleground in June 1862, east of Richmond. Lee's veterans manned one of the finest defensive positions they ever held, and on June 3, when Grant ordered a frontal assault, the Confederates destroyed it in less than an hour, inflicting roughly 7,000 casualties. Grant did not repeat the mistake, and the combat settled into a deadly monotony. While the infantry and artillery bore the battle, Sheridan's horsemen guarded flanks and recouped their strength.[52]

During this period of time, Custer visited Clover Lea, the home of the Basset family, whose daughter was Ella More Basset Washington, stepmother of James B. Washington, whom Custer had befriended on the Peninsula in May 1862. Clover Lea was located south of Dabney's Ferry, where the Federals had crossed the Pamunkey on May 28. Ella Washington had sent two notes to Custer on the twenty-ninth after Yankee foragers raided the homestead. He visited her the next day, arrested some men who were there, and promised to post guards.[53]

Custer returned two more times to Clover Lea, walking under the trees and conversing with Ella, who was twenty-nine years old, much younger than her husband. In her diary, she described the Union general as " 'among them but not of them.' " At one point, he joked that if he stayed longer he would become a Confederate. "How I wish he was one," she confided, "and then I could esteem and admire him as I do our own gallant leaders." When he left, Custer had a photograph of himself and one of him and Libbie sent to her.[54]

On June 6, the date of his final visit to Clover Lea, Custer wrote to Libbie. She had been "frantic" awaiting news from him, unable to resist crying for hours at a time. Around her, each day, she saw the war's cost as wagons stacked with coffins and ambulances filled with the wounded passed her boardinghouse. "This is the saddest city," she thought. She fretted about the prices—"money simply melts away here," she complained to her parents. While she attended a few social events, Libbie spent many hours with Custer's aide, James Christiancy, whom she nursed as he healed from his wound at Haw's Shop.[55]

Her husband's letter was most welcome, but his words offered little reassurance about his safety. The cavalry was to march tomorrow, June 7, on another raid, he wrote, and then added, "Need I repeat to my darling that while living she is my all, and if Destiny wills me to die, wills that my country needs my death, my last prayer will be for her, my last breath will speak her name and that Heaven will not be Heaven till we are joined." He ended it with, "Yours through time and eternity, Autie." In "the saddest city," Libbie probably cried again.[56]

As Custer stated to his wife, Sheridan and the divisions of Torbert and Gregg headed west on the seventh. With the opposing armies locked in place at Cold Harbor, Grant ordered Sheridan to seize Charlottesville, seventy miles to the west, to wreck the Virginia Central Railroad and the James River Canal, and if possible, to join Major General David Hunter's Union army as it advanced on the railroad center of Lynchburg. It was a daunting task, certain to bring a response from Lee's horsemen. With three days' rations and two days' forage in saddlebags, Sheridan's troopers rode away from Cold Harbor.[57]

As the men had come to expect, the pace of the march was unhurried, steady, conserving the strength of the riders and the mounts. The troopers had confidence in Sheridan; he was, according to one of them, "something tangible, something we saw and knew . . . a part of us, as

well as our leader." By nightfall on June 10, the Federals were bivouacked at Clayton's Store. Three miles to the south lay Trevilian Station and the tracks of the Virginia Central Railroad, Sheridan's initial
target. Union scouting parties reported the presence of enemy cavalrymen toward the railroad depot. Sheridan had learned from prisoners on
the ninth that Confederate horsemen were en route to Gordonsville,
and if the reports were valid, the Rebels encountered by the scouts must
be this force. Sheridan issued instructions for an advance, expecting a
fight.[58]

At Trevilian Station, Sheridan's counterpart, Wade Hampton, also
anticipated a battle on the tenth. He had a division of three brigades,
and six miles to the east at Louisa Court House, the two-brigade division of Fitzhugh Lee. In all, Hampton had roughly 5,000 men and three
batteries of a dozen cannon to oppose Sheridan's 6,000 troopers and
three batteries of horse artillery. Hampton planned to attack the Federals
from two directions—his division moving directly north to Clayton's
Store and Lee's division moving from Louisa Court House against Sheridan's flank.[59]

Hampton's scheme was predicated on the belief that the Northerners
would remain at Clayton's Store, but that was not Sheridan's method of
warfare. With the enemy at hand, the aggressive Union general intended to strike. When Hampton's two leading brigades advanced toward Clayton's Store, they encountered Merritt's and Devin's brigades
on the road to Trevilian Station. Within minutes, flashes of carbines and
rifles rippled along the lines. It had the look of Haw's Shop a fortnight
earlier, as the dismounted opponents pounded each other from opposite
stands of timber.[60]

To the east, on the road to Louisa Court House, the First and Seventh
Michigan collided with the van of Lee's division. Custer's duty was to
protect the flank, and when the Confederates retired, he turned down
a woodcutter's road that lay west of the Clayton's Store–Louisa Court
House Road. The Fifth Michigan led the brigade's march, striking the
railroad about a mile east of the station. As the Yankees swung west,
they saw before them Hampton's wagon train and a horse artillery
battery parked opposite the station, south of the Gordonsville-Louisa
Court House Road. It was a prize beyond expectations, and Custer
hurriedly deployed two cannon of Lieutenant Alexander Pennington's
Battery M, Second United States Cavalry, and ordered the Fifth Michigan to charge.[61]

The Michiganders plowed into the wagons, grabbing teamsters and overrunning the artillery pieces. In their excitement, however, the members of the Fifth Michigan pursued beyond the station. Suddenly, from the north, a Confederate regiment appeared in the rear of the Fifth. Pennington's gunners, Custer, and his staff began firing on the Rebels as the Sixth Michigan arrived. "Custer never lost his nerve under any circumstances," averred Major James Kidd, commander of the Sixth. "He was, however, unmistakably excited. 'Charge them' was his laconic command; and it was repeated with emphasis." Drawing sabers, two squadrons of Kidd's veterans surged forward, splintering into pieces the Southern regiment.[62]

Before Kidd could regroup his men, however, the Fifth Michigan came tumbling back from the west, driven by Brigadier General Thomas Rosser's Confederate brigade. The Virginians charged to the station, scattering Kidd's troopers and capturing numbers of them, including the major. Custer counterattacked with four companies of the Sixth Michigan. Rosser's men reeled under the charge, and Kidd and his Michiganders escaped. The First and Seventh Michigan, with the brigade's wagons, arrived at Trevilian, and Custer had a rail barricade placed across the road in front of Rosser. The wagons rolled into a field southwest of the station while the regiments dismounted, with the men grabbing their carbines.[63]

The Michigan Brigade had been in difficult places before, but nothing in their experience compared to Trevilian Station. From the east, Fitz Lee's two brigades of Virginians attacked; from the west, Rosser's men rallied and came on; and from the north, Hampton turned around regiments and advanced. In the words of a Federal, they suddenly discovered "that our brigade is surrounded by whole rebel Cavalry Corps." Lee's charge overran the Yankees' wagons, seizing Custer's headquarters wagon with desk, papers, letters from Libbie, dress uniform, and general's commission. One of the vehicles seized was Eliza's "antique ruin of a family carriage." Eliza herself was also grabbed, but she escaped hours later.[64]

Custer's Wolverines, as he called them by now, were trapped, caught "on the inside of a living triangle," as one eyewitness described their position. "It is the most mixed up fight I ever saw," a Michigander recorded in his diary after it was finished. For the next three hours, the "living triangle" flamed as the Federals repulsed one Confederate thrust after another. "Never has the brigade fought so long or so desperately,"

Custer wrote to Libbie afterward. The Yankees fought in small detachments as the combat lapped and receded at various points along the triangle. When the Rebels breached a section of a line, the Northerners resealed it. Valor was a common commodity on both sides at Trevilian Station.[65]

Custer's performance was remarkable. "Custer was everywhere present giving directions to his subordinate commanders," remembered Kidd. The Sixth Michigan's major now understood why Custer wore "so singular a uniform." "It individualized him," believed Kidd. "Wherever seen, it was recognized. There was but one Custer, and by his unique appearance and heroic bearing he was readily distinguished from all others." Perhaps never before did his identifiable presence mean more to his Wolverines than during these three hours.[66]

When Pennington ran to Custer and reported that the enemy had captured a cannon, Custer exclaimed, "No! I'll be damned if they have! Come on!" and led thirty men in a counterattack. Repulsed, he gathered horse holders, and they retook the gun in hand-to-hand combat. When a trooper of the Fifth Michigan fell wounded and began moaning, Custer raced to his assistance, placed the trooper over his shoulder, and carried him to safety, although momentarily stunned by a ricocheted bullet. When the brigade's color bearer collapsed with a mortal wound, the general ripped the flag from its staff, draping it across his shoulder.[67]

As Kidd asserted, Custer, with Private Joseph Fought blowing on his bugle at his side, appeared to be everywhere amid the fury and carnage. He had three horses shot from under him. At one point, a confused officer confronted the general, asking if they should move horses and equipment to the rear. "Yes, by all means," Custer responded. "Where in hell is the rear?"[68]

Finally, Sheridan, with Merritt's and Devin's brigades, punched an avenue through Hampton's line north of the station and relieved the Michiganders. The Confederates withdrew south and west of the battlefield, and the Federals encamped in the fields around Trevilian, with surgeons working in field hospitals. Neither side had had enough.[69]

Torbert's division did not march west on Gordonsville Road until midafternoon on June 12. Two miles west of Trevilian Station, the Federals found the Rebels in and along a large stand of trees south of the railroad. Sheridan deployed Merritt's and Custer's brigades across the tracks in woods. The fighting swirled across the intervening fields for several hours, as the Yankees undertook seven dismounted assaults on the Southern position and were repulsed each time. Casualties mounted until Sheridan disengaged at ten o'clock. Convinced that Hampton had been reinforced and that he could not join Hunter's army, Sheridan withdrew across the North Anna River during the night and bivouacked. Burdened with hundreds of prisoners and wounded comrades, the Northerners faced a slow, circuitous march until they rejoined the army.[70]

The two-day Battle of Trevilian Station cost Sheridan a reported 1,007 killed, wounded, and captured. Of that total, the Michigan Brigade incurred 416 casualties, the most of any of the Union brigades. Three hundred nine of the Michiganders had been captured, including Major Jacob Greene, Custer's chief of staff. Greene faced months in a Confederate prison, but for his "distinguished gallantry" on June 11, he would receive promotion to brevet lieutenant colonel. Although Southern losses are imprecise, it would appear that Hampton lost slightly more men than Sheridan. For the numbers engaged, the toll had been dear, particularly in prisoners.[71]

For Custer, his losses had been both personally painful and embarrassing. Besides Greene, young Johnnie Cisco had been nabbed by the Rebels while he guarded the general's extra horses. Custer lost all of his personal belongings, including a pair of field glasses with his name inscribed on them. But the letters from Libbie, whom he chided later —"Somebody must be more careful hereafter in the use of *double entendre*"—were published in a Richmond newspaper for the enjoyment of its readers.[72]

Trevilian Station marked the conclusion of forty days of almost relentless campaigning by the Union cavalry. During this period of time, Sheridan and his troopers established themselves as a fighting force unmatched by previous mounted commands in the army. Arguably, no general or unit equaled Custer and the Michigan Brigade in their performance. The War Department rewarded him with promotion to full captain and then to brevet lieutenant colonel in the Regular Army. "Custer," wrote one of Sheridan's staff officers, "was a man of boundless confidence in himself and great faith in his lucky star." Yellow Tavern, Haw's Shop, Cold Harbor, and Trevilian Station earned him that.[73]

"DAUGHTER OF THE STARS"

■ The presidential steamer *River Queen* docked at a wharf at City Point, Virginia, on Friday, July 8, 1864. Located at the confluence of the Appomattox and James rivers, eight miles northeast of Petersburg, City Point had been converted from a nondescript village into a huge depot for Union armies during the past three weeks. In an unending flow, ships were off-loaded by gangs of contraband workers who hauled the mounds of matériel to warehouses. The stream of food, medicines, arms, ammunition, ordnance, and equipment testified to the agricultural and industrial might of the North. City Point held the stores for Confederate defeat.[1]

Union General-in-Chief Ulysses S. Grant had brought the war to City Point. Stopped by General Robert E. Lee's Confederates at Cold Harbor, Grant decided to shift the main thrust of his campaign to south of the James River, against Petersburg, a railroad center Lee had to hold if he was to defend Richmond, twenty miles north of the so-called Cockade City. Lee narrowly secured Petersburg in mid-June, and when the *River Queen* tied up with a congressional delegation on board, extensive fieldworks scarred the countryside, portending a long, costly siege.[2]

Aboard the *River Queen* was Libbie Custer, a guest of the official party. She had charmed an invitation from Congressman F. W. Kellogg of Michigan—"Any lady can get that man to do anything," she told her husband—for the brief, two-day excursion. Libbie and Autie had not seen each other for over two months, and she needed to escape Washington. Her anxiety for Autie's safety had deepened as the newspapers reported the fearful carnage of May and June. To an aunt, she had confided that "I never dreamed I could spend such unhappy hours as I have while they were fighting." She had tried to comfort herself with the thought that "I believe if ever God sends men into the world for a special purpose Armstrong was born to be a soldier." [3]

Libbie had passed the days nursing Jim Christiancy, writing letters to Autie and to family members, sewing her clothes, attending occasional social functions, and visiting hospitals where members of the Michigan Brigade were patients. She had been reluctant to go to the hospitals, as if trying to shield herself from war's reality, until she learned of the Michiganders. But the wagonloads of coffins, the "army" of widows in black, and the hospitals, "a sad cordon of suffering," daily affected her. "Washington," she recalled years later, "belonged to everyone and no people in particular" in the summer of 1864. [4]

In the letters to Autie, Libbie could not hide her concern for his safety but promised to "learn to be brave." She described the parties, repeated comments made about him, and relayed gossip. She wished for peace, she wrote, for a time when they could begin a family, even enclosing in one letter a drawing she had done of a child in her dreams. When she expressed her longing for him, he reminded her about "the need for more prudence in writing" because of the letters seized by Confederates at Trevilian Station. She replied that "I shall not again offend my dear boy's sense of nicety by departing from that delicate propriety which, I believe, was born in me." [5]

The trip to City Point became a reprieve for Libbie, and Autie was there to greet her. The cavalry had rejoined the army from the Trevilian Raid on June 28, and were resting nearby. As a welcome for the politicians and their guests, Philip Sheridan brought a band on board the steamer that evening, and the group enjoyed a dance. "You should have seen Genl. Sheridan dance," Libbie wrote to a friend, "it was too funny. He had never danced until this summer and he enters into it with his whole soul. He is short and so bright." Autie accompanied Libbie back to Washington on July 9, staying the night at the boardinghouse at 471 6th Street, before taking a steamer on Sunday to City Point. [6]

The next day, July 11, Custer requested a twenty-day furlough because of illness, "remittent fever and diarrhoea," and it was granted. He left for Washington on the thirteenth, moving James Kidd to write home that "I could not imagine a greater disaster to our brigade if he does not return before we take the field again." Gathering up Libbie and luggage, the couple entrained for Michigan, spending the next two weeks with family in Monroe and Traverse City. They were back in the capital by the twenty-ninth, and Custer reported for duty on the thirtieth. Kidd's fears of a movement before his return had been alleviated.[7]

On the day of Custer's return, however, two events transpired that would reshape the military situation in Virginia for the summer and fall. At Petersburg, the Federals detonated a mine filled with gunpowder under the Confederate lines. The explosion created a huge crater in the works, but the resultant attack ended in a bloody debacle for the Northerners. The campaign at Petersburg now would settle into a siege. To the north, meanwhile, Confederate cavalrymen burned the community of Chambersburg, Pennsylvania, destroying over 400 buildings, including 274 residences.[8]

The smoldering ruin of Chambersburg was the culmination of six weeks of Union embarrassment and defeat in northern Virginia, Maryland, and the Shenandoah Valley. While at Cold Harbor, on June 12, Robert E. Lee decided to seize the strategic initiative in Virginia and ordered Lieutenant General Jubal A. Early and the army's Second Corps west to secure Lynchburg from the advance of Major General David Hunter's Union forces. Early's veterans raced to the railroad center, confronted Hunter's troops, and drove them into the Allegheny Mountains. With the Shenandoah Valley cleared of the enemy, Early, in accordance with Lee's instructions, marched into Maryland, defeating an amalgam of Federal units at Monocacy before threatening the defenses of Washington on July 11–12. The gray-clad raiders withdrew to Virginia, and at the Battle of Second Kernstown, on the twenty-fourth, routed their pursuers. Six days later, Early's horsemen torched Chambersburg.[9]

Newspapers in the North railed about Confederate troops at the doorstep of the capital, with the *New York Times* editorializing that it was "the old story again. The back door, by way of the Shenandoah Valley, has been left invitingly opened." If President Lincoln expected to win reelection, the "back door" needed to be shut. During the last week of July, he and Grant exchanged messages about the situation

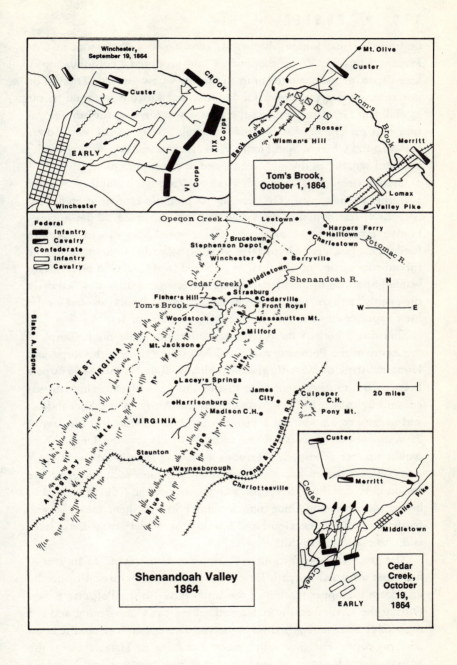

Winchester, September 19, 1864

CROOK

Custer

XIX Corps

VI Corps

EARLY

Winchester

Tom's Brook, October 1, 1864

Mt. Olive

Custer

Tom's Brook

Back Road

Rosser

Wisman's Hill

Merritt

Lomax

Valley Pike

Federal
- Infantry
- Cavalry

Confederate
- Infantry
- Cavalry

Opeqon Creek

Leetown

Harpers Ferry

Halltown

Charlestown

Potomac R.

Brucetown

Stephenson Depot

Winchester

Berryville

Cedar Creek

Middletown

Shenandoah R.

Fisher's Hill

Strasburg

Cedarville

Tom's Brook

Front Royal

Woodstock

Massanutten Mt.

Milford

Mt. Jackson

Mts.

Lacey's Springs

James City

Culpeper C.H.

Harrisonburg

Madison C.H.

Pony Mt.

WEST VIRGINIA

VIRGINIA

Blake A. Magner

Staunton

Waynesborough

Charlottesville

Orange & Alexandria R.R.

ALLEGHENY Mts.

BLUE Ridge

N

W   E

S

20 miles

Shenandoah Valley 1864

Custer

Merritt

Cedar Creek

Valley Pike

Middletown

EARLY

Cedar Creek, October 19, 1864

beyond the Blue Ridge Mountains, agreeing to a conference at City Point, on July 31. When they met, Grant proposed a consolidation of four departments into one command under a new general. They could not agree on a replacement for Hunter, and Lincoln returned to the capital. But Grant telegraphed the next day, informing the administration that his choice was Sheridan. Lincoln, Secretary of War Edwin Stanton, and Chief of Staff Henry Halleck expressed concerns about his youthful age, but in the end, acquiesced to the appointment.[10]

Grant ordered Sheridan and his staff to Washington and then boarded a steamer to the capital. The general-in-chief met Hunter at Frederick, Maryland, learning that the latter had lost "all trace of the enemy." Hunter asked to be relieved, and Grant wired Sheridan to report to Frederick. The generals met on August 6, with Grant handing the subordinate a copy of instructions prepared for Hunter. In brief, Grant wanted Sheridan to advance south up the Shenandoah Valley, "to drive the enemy" and to "take all provisions, forage, and stock wanted for the use of your command; such as cannot be consumed, destroy."[11]

Sheridan inherited three separate commands—the Sixth Corps of the Army of the Potomac, two divisions of the Nineteenth Corps, and Hunter's Army of West Virginia—which he found outside of Harpers Ferry at the northern entrance to the Valley, as the Shenandoah was commonly called. He designated them the Army of the Shenandoah and began preparations for a march south when he arrived on August 7. Within two weeks, with the addition of cavalry, the Union force would number almost 50,000 troops, including the garrison at Harpers Ferry. Never before had the government assigned such forces to the region in which the Yankees had known only defeat. "There seemed to be for our arms something akin to fatality in the Shenandoah Valley," recalled a staff officer. Grant and Sheridan were determined, as Grant said, "to put a stop to this."[12]

The great Valley of Virginia—"Daughter of the Stars" to Indians— had been a natural warpath for centuries, slanting southwest to northeast, from the upper reaches of the James River to the Potomac River. During the Civil War, the rich farmland fed the Confederacy, and the region's craftsmen supplied other needs. Twice, Lee had used it as an invasion route. For fifty miles, from Strasburg to Harrisonburg, the Massanutten Mountain divided the Valley into two sections. The Valley's terrain favored warriors, particularly mounted commands, which could operate on the good roads and fight on the cultivated fields.[13]

Consequently, Grant released the First and Third Cavalry divisions from the Petersburg front, assigning them to Sheridan. Alfred Torbert's division departed on transports from City Point, on August 3 and 4, with Custer and the Michigan Brigade embarking on the latter day. Unloading at the capital, the horsemen passed through the city in contingents, marching west toward Frederick. By August 9, the division had joined Sheridan outside of Harpers Ferry. Sheridan appointed Torbert chief of cavalry for the army, with Wesley Merritt assuming command of the division.[14]

Since Alfred Pleasonton had jumped Merritt and Custer to brigadiers in June 1863, the pair had been friendly rivals within the Cavalry Corps. Five years older than Custer, Merritt had graduated from West Point in 1860, serving as a staff officer and as temporary commander of the Reserve Brigade during George Stoneman's cavalry raid in April–May 1863. He had been a solid, capable brigade commander, but lacked Custer's aggressiveness and flair. James Kidd regarded him as a modest, charming gentleman, who was reliable in combat. To one of Sheridan's staff members, Merritt was "tall, slender, and intellectual-looking. He had a constitution of iron, and underneath a rather passive demeanor concealed a fiery ambition."[15]

With the arrival of the First Cavalry Division, Sheridan started the army's advance south up the Valley on August 10. "My object," he stated afterward in his campaign report, was "to destroy, to the best of my ability, that which was truly the Confederacy—its armies," adding that "every officer and man was made to understand that when a victory was gained, it was not more than their duty, nor less than their country expected from her gallant sons."[16]

Accompanying the Army of the Shenandoah was James Taylor, special artist for *Frank Leslie's Illustrated Newspaper*. As the cavalry clattered south, Taylor saw Custer for the first time. "A picturesque presence was the debonair" general, Taylor wrote. Mounted on a "coal-black charger" named Bess, Custer "was tall and sinewy without an ounce of superfluous flesh. His features were clear cut, his cheek-bones prominent, while his eye was steel gray with the sharpness of an eagle's glance." He had "straw-colored spiral locks" and an "enormous 'Adam's apple.' " Custer's uniform remained the black velvet, with the wide-collared blue shirt, broad-brimmed black felt hat, and high cavalry boots. Taylor sketched the general as he moved with the troops.[17]

As Sheridan expected, Jubal Early's outnumbered army—it counted perhaps 17,000—retired from the Winchester area before the Federal advance. By nightfall on August 12, the Rebels had filed on to Fisher's Hill, a formidable defensive position, south of Strasburg, while the Yankees halted at Cedar Creek, four miles north of the eminence, just beyond Middletown. Despite his aggressive nature, Sheridan acted cautiously, having been counseled earlier in Washington by Stanton and Halleck that the administration could not afford another defeat in the Valley. He tested the Confederate works with a reconnaissance in force on the thirteenth, but settled for minor skirmishing. The next day, he received reports of an enemy force approaching the region via Front Royal, which lay beyond the Massanutten Mountain and Sheridan's left flank. He dispatched Colonel Thomas Devin's brigade to Cedarville, a few miles north of Front Royal.[18]

Confirmation of another Rebel force in the region reached Sheridan on the fifteenth, and he ordered a withdrawal after dark. The infantry and artillery of the Nineteenth Corps began the march in a rainstorm at eleven o'clock. The next morning, Sheridan kept his remaining units in line along Cedar Creek, but sent Merritt and his two other brigades to Cedarville. The Michigan Brigade had engaged Early's horsemen on the eleventh, but had not been in action at Cedar Creek. On the thirteenth, a detail from the brigade captured an alleged Confederate spy. He was hanged the next day in Middletown—"it was a hard looken sight," a Michigander recorded in his diary.[19]

Custer and his men located Devin's brigade less than four miles north of Front Royal across the road to Winchester about 2 P.M. Custer assigned pickets to relieve Devin's troopers, while the rest of the Michiganders unsaddled their mounts and relaxed. Before long, gunfire erupted toward the front, and an orderly soon reined up, reporting that Rebels were advancing in force. The Confederates belonged to the infantry division of Major General Joseph Kershaw and the cavalry division of Major General Fitzhugh Lee, under the overall command of Lieutenant General Richard H. Anderson. They had left Petersburg over ten days ago, a counterstroke by Lee to Grant's action in the Valley. Front Royal lay at the confluence of the North and South forks of the Shenandoah River, and on this day, Anderson needed to secure the fords if he were to advance on Sheridan's flank.[20]

The oncoming Southerners were a Georgia infantry brigade and a Virginia cavalry brigade. When the orderly reported the attack, Custer had the bugler blow "To horse," borrowed an aide's mount, and rode to the crest of a ridge. The Georgians were splashing across the ford, while the Virginians were closing on a bridge over Crooked Run. As the Michiganders arrived on the ridge, Custer deployed each regiment, posting Captain Dunbar Ransom's Battery C, Third United States Artillery, in the center. When the Georgians crossed the crest of Guard Hill, Ransom's Regulars blasted them with canister. On Custer's right, one of Devin's regiments charged the Virginians at the bridge.[21]

The fighting escalated rapidly as the Rebels held Guard Hill and the Federals attacked. The Fifth Michigan charged dismounted, supported by a mounted battalion of the First Michigan. In Custer's word, the combat was "severe." As was his habit, he rode along the brigade's line "to encourage the men," according to a sergeant of the First Michigan. A bullet grazed his head, clipping off some hair; an inch to the right and he would have been killed. Custer sent the Seventh Michigan forward, and its assault routed the Southerners, who fled toward the ford. First Lieutenant Edward Granger of his staff joined the Seventh and was mortally wounded and captured by the fleeing Confederates.[22]

Kershaw pushed a second infantry brigade across the ford, ending the Union pursuit. According to a newspaper story, the Yankees bagged about 150 prisoners. Custer and Devin retired to their position, encamping for the night. As Custer rode to the rear, Ransom's artillerists removed their caps in salute and gave him three cheers. "It is the first time I ever knew of such a demonstration except in the case of General McClellan," Custer boasted to Libbie in a letter. "I certainly felt highly flattered."[23]

Custer deserved the cheers of the Regulars. Once again, he demonstrated his consummate ability as a combat officer. "He loved war," a biographer of him has avowed. "It nourished and energized him. It triggered those complex mechanisms of intellect and instinct that made his tactical decisions nearly flawless." Combat was "the catalyst," and in its terrible confines, he flourished, reaping the glory he coveted. After the engagement, when asked by an officer in the brigade if the odds against him or the situation made a difference in how he fought, Custer replied that neither one mattered because "he knew that his men were going to follow him, and that gave him confidence to do things which he would not have done if he had not known what his men would do." The Michigan Brigade "had made his reputation."[24]

On August 17, the entire Union army marched north down the Valley, with the infantry and artillery following the macadamized Valley Pike, the region's main transportation artery. Early's army pursued, and clashes flared between the opposing mounted units. Brigadier General James Wilson's Third Cavalry Division joined Sheridan's forces on this day, entering the Valley through a gap in the Blue Ridge. The cavalry rimmed the rear and began implementing Grant's orders to destroy crops and barns. "The day had been an unpleasant one," remembered a Pennsylvania cavalryman, "the weather was hot and the roads very dusty, and the grief of the inhabitants, as they saw their harvests disappearing in flame and smoke, and their flock being driven off, was a sad sight. It was a phase of warfare we had not seen before, and though we admitted its necessity, we could not but sympathize with the sufferers." [25]

Custer and the Michigan Brigade halted in the Berryville area, east of Winchester, remaining in the vicinity until August 21. On the nineteenth, detachments of the Fifth Michigan roamed across the countryside, torching haystacks and barns filled with grain. Thirty of the Michiganders rode to the Benjamin Morgan farm, east of Berryville, and were preparing to fire the barn when Confederate horsemen attacked. The Yankees not gunned down in the charge were captured and shoved into a line along the Morgan lane and shot. The Southerners spurred away, leaving the bodies where they lay. But one of the Michiganders, Private Samuel K. Davis, Company L, feigning death after being shot in the face, crawled away and hid. Soon a pair of Rebels returned, examining each body to be sure the Yankees were dead, and finding one alive, shot him in the head. When some of his comrades arrived at the lane, Davis signaled them and recounted the gruesome story. [26]

Custer reacted furiously when informed about the incident. He ordered Colonel Russell Alger to take the Fifth and Sixth Michigan and to burn houses, barns, and outbuildings on four farms. Cautioning the colonel about ambushes, Custer directed that the men should be "very careful that no loyal man is molested" and that all victims should be told the reasons for destruction. Later in the day, Custer extended the order, including the residences of ten "of the most prominent secessionists" in the vicinity of the "attack and murder." By nightfall, Alger had executed Custer's instructions. [27]

The flames that glowed in the Virginia darkness burned more than the homes and livelihoods of fourteen families. As the Pennsylvanian had stated, "a phase of warfare we had not seen before" had been carried by horsemen with torches into the Valley of Virginia. Grant's orders marked a passage in the nature of the conflict. While Union general David Hunter's incendiarism in the Upper Valley in June and the destruction of Chambersburg signaled revengeful actions, Grant planned to destroy the sinews that sustained the Confederate armies in the field. To the general-in-chief, military necessity dictated the policy with Southern civilians paying a price for their allegiance to the Confederate cause. These few days of fire in the Valley were only a harbinger.

In turn, the implementation of Grant's policy caused a backlash from Southerners that resulted in the brutality found in Morgan's lane. The Confederate attackers at Morgan's belonged to the Forty-third Battalion of Virginia Cavalry, or Mosby's Rangers. Created by John Singleton Mosby, the Rangers had operated from a base in the counties of Fauquier and Loudoun in the Virginia Piedmont, waging guerrilla warfare against Union wagon trains, railroads, outposts, and detachments since January 1863. A remarkable warrior, Mosby had molded his young partisans into a superb force that ruled their section of the Old Dominion known as "Mosby's Confederacy." The nature of Ranger warfare engendered hatred among their enemies, but the elusive Rangers had defied Federal countermeasures.[28]

When Sheridan's army entered the Valley, Mosby shifted the focus of his operations across the Blue Ridge Mountains. Each day, contingents of Rangers, wreathed by outriders and scouts, rode from their base, searching for Federal units or moving toward a predetermined target. On August 13, nearly 300 Rangers struck Sheridan's wagon train at the edge of Berryville, capturing a hundred vehicles, which they looted before burning. The wagons belonged to Sheridan's cavalry. Then, on the nineteenth, the Rebels killed the Michiganders at Morgan's farm. Within the broad confines of the campaign between Sheridan and Early, a smaller, deadly, and unforgiving struggle would simmer.[29]

The Union withdrawal down the Valley ended on August 22, when the Northerners entered their fieldworks at Halltown, outside of Harpers Ferry. Early's and Anderson's forces combined and, trailing the enemy, halted at Charlestown and constructed works. Neither commander would risk an assault on the other's lines, and the operations stalled—Early maintaining a bold front, Sheridan acting cautiously under instructions from Washington. On August 25, Early feinted an invasion toward Maryland with part of his infantry and Fitzhugh Lee's cavalry division. Sheridan, meanwhile, sent Torbert with Merritt's and Wilson's divisions on a reconnaissance upriver toward Williamsport, Maryland.[30]

Torbert's horsemen collided with Confederate infantry at Leetown —"a complete surprise to both parties," according to Major James Kidd of the Sixth Michigan. Torbert wanted nothing to do with Rebel foot soldiers and ordered a retreat, assigning Custer's brigade as a rear guard. The Michiganders stalled the enemy advance, halting south of Shepherdstown for a brief rest. Suddenly, Confederate cavalry opened fire, and as the First and Seventh Michigan prepared to charge, a gray-clad infantry brigade triggered a volley. Instead of attacking, the Southerners swung around Custer's flank, moving toward a ford on the Potomac River in the Yankees' rear. The horse artillery battery with the Michiganders blasted the enemy, slowing the advance. Custer's men retired toward the river, firing as they pulled back, with their line bending into the shape of a horseshoe as more Confederate units appeared in front and on each flank.[31]

The gunfire alerted Torbert, who sent Devin's brigade against the enemy. Parts of the First New York Dragoons and Seventeenth Pennsylvania were cut off from their comrades in the assault and joined the beleaguered Michiganders. A Pennsylvanian wrote that they "found his [Custer's] little band fighting like tigers, as they always fought. I don't think there was a man in his command but what loved him, for they were never in a tight place but what he was there to lead them and share the dangers with them." With Devin's attack repulsed, Custer extricated the brigade, crossing the river one regiment at a time. "That it escaped," asserted a disgruntled James Kidd, "no thanks were due to General Torbert." The brigade rejoined the army at Halltown on the twenty-seventh.[32]

Two days after the clash at Shepherdstown, "Old Jube," as the Confederates dubbed Early, withdrew from Charlestown toward Winchester. Sheridan probed the enemy lines, and then occupied Charlestown. Three weeks of "backward and forward and forward and backward again," as Kidd phrased the operations, brought both armies into positions similar to those they had held on August 10. Another Union officer grumbled that it was "mimic war." On September 3, Sheridan sidled the army south to Berryville, with the Federals building field-works from there to Summit Point, a distance of eight miles. Early tested the new line before falling back to Winchester, seven miles west of Berryville. Opequon Creek served as a divide between the opponents, and for the next fortnight, soldiers on both sides enjoyed the interlude.[33]

Like a majority of the army, Custer welcomed the respite. He wrote to his father that the Valley was "fine country," with good water, climate, and campsites. The transfer from Petersburg "is well liked throughout the command." A staff officer of Sheridan's described the evenings' activities at Custer's headquarters as "jolly." An added pleasure was Libbie's decision to come from Washington to be as near to him as she could. She found a room in a house at Sandy Hook, Maryland, a mile downriver from Harpers Ferry. Here Custer visited her twice during the two weeks, jokingly calling her "my dear little Army Crow." "Libbie," he told his father, "is a true soldier's wife."[34]

In his letter to his father, Custer mentioned that during the final week of August, Torbert summoned him to headquarters and asked if Custer would take command of Brigadier General Alfred Duffié's cavalry division, stationed at Cumberland, Maryland. If he accepted, Torbert promised that the Michigan Brigade could join him. "I of course assented," Custer wrote, but Sheridan delayed the transfer until field operations ceased, when Custer would have time to rectify the division's "present disorganized state." Sheridan also argued that it would be asking Custer to risk his reputation if assigned at this time. The condition of Duffié's unit "would have but little influence with me," Custer declared. "I would rather for my own reputation take hold and reorganize and discipline such a command." Sheridan's insistence, however, ended the matter.[35]

Custer's version of his promotion and transfer poses some intriguing questions. Had Torbert offered the assignment without conferring with Sheridan? Was the cavalry chief trying to placate Custer, who may have been privately voicing dissatisfaction with Merritt's, instead of his, appointment to divisional command? Were Sheridan's stated objections specious? Would he have been willing to part with his best brigade commander and best cavalry brigade? Had Custer's desire for higher rank and more responsibility so affected his judgment that he seized any opportunity for promotion, even if it were in the war's backwater?

For the present, then, Custer stayed in command of the brigade. As the letter indicated, his ambition burned as intensely as ever. He deserved promotion, and as Sheridan evidently alluded, he possessed a reputation, both within and outside of the army, that few, if any, brigadiers could equal. From the time of Gettysburg, Custer enjoyed favorable newspaper coverage. He was, to be sure, a compelling figure, whose attire, flamboyance, and combat record attracted reporters. Custer embodied the age's beau ideal of a cavalryman. In turn, Custer cultivated the press, sitting for numerous interviews, recounting operations. He fascinated a nation, a fearless "Boy General," dressed in velvet and touched with "luck," at the forefront of a charge. The image was true —Custer stood alone as a cavalry brigade commander.

A correspondent for the *New York Tribune* filed a typical description of the "Boy General" that appeared in the newspaper on August 22, 1864. "Gen. Custer is as gallant a cavalier as one would wish to see," the reporter asserted. "No officer in the ranks of the Union army entertains for his rebel enemy a more sincere contempt than Gen. C. and probably no cavalry officer in our army is better known or feared by the foe. . . . Always circumspect, never rash, and viewing the circumstances under which he is placed as coolly as a chess player."[36]

While Custer coveted such public acclaim, his reputation brought with it scrutiny. Politics had seeped into the Union army since its inception. As noted previously, Custer had had to answer allegations about his views on the war's conduct and his association with George McClellan. The charge that he was a "McClellan man" reemerged when the Democratic Party nominated the former general as its presidential candidate on a peace platform at the end of August. If he hoped to secure promotion, Custer could not be viewed as a supporter of his hero.

Whether of his own volition or at the request of Isaac Christiancy, Custer addressed the issue in a letter to his friend on September 16:

> I am a "Peace Man" in favor of an "Armistice" and of sending "Peace Commissioners." I desire an honorable and lasting peace; such a peace can only be secured by the acknowledgement of one government supreme and entire; it must embrace all the states and must possess self sustaining power, in other words the decisions of the general government as affecting individual states must be supreme and admitting of no appeal. The Peace Commissioners I am in favor of are those sent from the cannon's mouth. The only armistice I would yield to would be that forced by the points of our bayonets.

In his view, he continued, the Confederates' "last man is in the field." "To me it seems like madness to think of *proposing* an armistice particularly at the present time when success is everywhere attending our armies and the rebel conspiracy is about to crumble to pieces." If the government sought an armistice, it would lose the respect of the citizenry. He concluded: "Let the public sentiment be the echo of that which is found in the heart of every soldier in the army, that we are fighting for human rights and liberty, for the preservation of a free people, a free government and having secured these privileges to our selves we desire and intend to transmit them unsullied and untarnished to those who come after us in all time to come."[37]

The carefully worded statement was a forthright expression of the Lincoln administration's and the Republican Party's position, and as Custer surely knew, Christiancy shared it with others. At the Custer home in Monroe, however, the words agitated Emanuel Custer. Earlier, Emanuel had written to his son that "if I had it in my power I would give him [McClellan] evry vote in the army. . . . I hope that Mc will be elected it would be nothing against you it would be in your favor." But when the old Jacksonian Democrat learned the contents of Autie's letter, he was "upset" and informed his son that it "puts me in a tight place." Emanuel could not believe that Autie did not support McClellan, who had done so much for him. His father reminded Autie that in 1862, when Emanuel criticized the army commander, Autie had threatened to cease writing letters to his parents. Emanuel was uncompromising in his devotion to the Democratic Party; Autie, uncompromising in his devotion to the Union cause.[38]

When Custer wrote to Christiancy, Lincoln's reelection campaign had been revitalized with the capture of Atlanta, Georgia, on September 2, by William Sherman's forces. "Atlanta is ours, and fairly won," the general wired the War Department, and the Northern populace celebrated the news. Sherman's accomplishment had shattered the military stalemate, and among the citizenry the belief emerged that the horrific sacrifices of three years had not been in vain. If additional successes could be achieved, Lincoln's election would be assured and his war policy sustained. The fall of the Georgia rail center heralded an end.[39]

For Grant, the seizure of Atlanta with its military and political implications offered the opportunity for a strike in Virginia. For weeks, he had been frustrated with the cautionary policy imposed upon Sheridan by the administration in the Shenandoah Valley. The time had come for

Sheridan to assail Early's army and lay waste to the Confederacy's granary. Grant telegraphed his subordinate that he would travel to the Valley for a conference. The pair met at the residence of Thomas Rutherford in Charlestown, on September 16. In his pocket, Grant had plans for an operation, but Sheridan outlined a proposal and said that he could "whip them." From a Quaker teacher in Winchester, Sheridan had learned that one infantry division was en route to Richmond to rejoin Lee, reducing Early's infantry strength by one-fourth. Grant asked if the army could advance by the twentieth, with Sheridan replying that he could move on the nineteenth. "Go in," said Grant.[40]

The Federals stirred from the camps after midnight on Monday, September 19, cooking coffee, securing arms and equipment. By two o'clock, cavalry units marched west from the Berryville area toward the Opequon Creek crossings. Confederate pickets covered the shallows, with Early's army encamped at Winchester and along the Valley Pike north of the town. James Wilson's cavalry division led Sheridan's infantry and artillery units on the Berryville-Winchester Road, due west, directly toward the Rebels, while Wesley Merritt's horsemen angled northwest to lower fords on the Opequon. Cavalry chief Torbert had been blunt in his instructions to subordinates: "The move means fight."[41]

Custer and the Michigan Brigade marched across country to Locke's, or Wadesville, Ford, roughly three-fourths of a mile downstream from Siever's, or Ridgway, Ford, where Thomas Devin's and Colonel Charles Lowell's brigades were assigned. Arriving at daylight, Custer dismounted the Sixth Michigan in a ravine and sent them up a slope to the crest of a ridge that overlooked the ford. Colonel James Kidd's troopers deployed on the ridge, north of the farmhouse and outbuildings of Josiah and Rebecca Locke, the family for whom the crossing was named. Across the creek, concealed in woods, Confederate cavalrymen fired upon Kidd's men as they formed their lines. The Michiganders answered with their Spencer carbines, and Custer rode back to order a mounted charge.[42]

The road to the ford passed around the southern nose of the ridge, below the farmhouse, before turning north parallel to the creek, then bending west into the shallows. Custer formed the Twenty-fifth New York Cavalry, temporarily attached to the brigade, into a column of fours on the road behind the ridge, supported by the Seventh Michigan. At his command, the New Yorkers spurred ahead around the end of the ridge toward the ford. The Rebels blasted the column, and the New Yorkers veered away, circling past Kidd's troopers, who were raking the Southern position with gunfire. The Seventh Michigan followed the lead regiment, and Custer's initial thrust was repulsed.[43]

Convinced that he confronted infantry, Custer brought up the First Michigan on foot, and with the Sixth, prepared to attack dismounted, with the Seventh in support on horseback. But the Rebels, only dismounted cavalry, began withdrawing when they learned that Lowell's brigade was advancing on their flank. Seeing the enemy retiring, Kidd charged with his regiment, splashing across the creek and securing the ford. Custer regrouped his regiments and rode west.[44]

The advance of Merritt's division soon stalled when the Federals encountered Confederate infantry that belonged to the division of Brigadier General Gabriel C. Wharton. For roughly four hours, neither Merritt nor Torbert, who accompanied the division, pressed the Southern position. Finally, about eleven o'clock, Custer attacked the enemy behind fieldworks near Brucetown and was repulsed. Wharton's soldiers, meanwhile, had been ordered to Winchester by Early as Sheridan's infantry and artillery commands assaulted the Confederate army east of the town. Early required every musket he had and sent for the infantry division. The Confederate commander would have to depend upon his outmatched cavalry to hold the army's flank north of Winchester.[45]

The Union horsemen closed on their mounted opponents at Stephenson's Depot, five miles north of Winchester, about 1:30 P.M., coming from two directions—Merritt's division from the east; Brevet Major General William Averell's two brigades from the north. Averell's men had fought the Rebels throughout the morning along the Valley Pike, and when they and Merritt's veterans linked up, the Yankees attacked. The Confederates, under Fitzhugh Lee, held an open stand of pines along the pike, watching the Northerners advance "in a compact mass and powerful in numbers," according to one of them. Lee did not wait, however, for the gale in Union blue to blow in but ordered a charge. The Southerners burst from the trees and were met by Custer's men. Using sabers, the Yankees shredded the enemy ranks, driving them into the woods. Lee plunged into the splinters to rally his troopers, had a horse killed under him, and suffered a wound. The gray-jacketed horsemen fled toward Winchester, with Custer's regiments in pursuit.[46]

The Michigan Brigade galloped south until Confederate batteries and an infantry brigade lashed the Federals with shellfire and musketry. Custer withdrew, and the Union cavalry paused. The divisions aligned themselves astride the Pike, with Averell on the west of the road, Merritt on the east. It was three o'clock on a beautiful September day, and in the words of Merritt, "the field was open for cavalry operations such as the war had not seen."[47]

To the south, the Third Battle of Winchester was accelerating toward a climax. Sheridan's offensive had bogged down all morning as he shuttled his entire army through the narrow, confining, two-mile-long Berryville Canyon. It was a mistake, allowing Early time to regroup his infantry divisions on a plateau east of the town. When the Union assault finally rolled forward at 11:40 A.M., the Confederates met it with fierce counterattacks. Early threw every reserve he had on the field into the combat and nearly wrecked Sheridan's army until the Federal commander sealed the gap in his lines with a counterthrust that brought a temporary cessation to the fury. But at three o'clock, Brevet Major General George Crook's two divisions attacked from the north and east, pressing the Confederate line into an inverted L-shape on a ridge north and east of Winchester. An hour later, Sheridan advanced the Sixth and Nineteenth corps against Early's position and sent orders for the cavalry to charge.[48]

The instructions reached Torbert as the cauldron of hell at Winchester boiled. Sheridan's instructions filtered down, with officers adjusting ranks and offering final advice and encouragement. Since he had taken command of the cavalry in the spring, Sheridan had wanted it to be the army's thunderbolt, and its time had come to fulfill the general's expectations. Bands played music as the line of horsemen moved forward. "A more enlivening and imposing spectacle never was seen," contended Kidd. "Guidons fluttered and sabers glistened. Officers vied with their men in gallantry and in zeal." "I never saw such a sight in my life as that of the tremendous force," recalled an onlooking Virginian, with the "flying banners" and "flashing sabers."[49]

From a walk, to a trot, to a gallop, the thunder rolled. "The horror of a cavalry charge is indescribable," confessed a Pennsylvanian in the ranks. On the plateau, Confederate gunners and infantrymen braced themselves. The Rebels unleashed shellfire and musketry into the Federals, but Sheridan's lance kept coming. "No man ever saw a more thrilling sight than that cavalry charge," claimed a Union infantryman.

The cavalrymen crashed over the works into the enemy ranks. "Every man's saber was waving above his head," remembered a New York trooper, "and with a savage yell, we swept down upon the trembling wretches like a besom of destruction. Then ensued a scene which may well be called the 'carnival of death.'" [50]

Caught in a closing vise of Union infantry and cavalry, the Confederates, members of Stonewall Jackson's famous "foot cavalry," ran toward Winchester. Federal horsemen chased the fugitives, pleading with the Rebels, "Men, for God's sake surrender—don't force us to cut you down and kill you." Pockets of Southerners resisted, slowing the Union rush. Custer was in the midst of the carnage and was nearly killed by an enemy infantrymen who fired at him at close range. The general, however, reared his horse just before the shot, and the bullet grazed his leg. "He was perfectly reckless in his contempt of danger," growled a staff officer, "and seemed to take infinite pleasure in exposing himself in the most unnecessary manner." [51]

"I shall never forget it," a Union officer wrote his mother afterward. "We rode completely over the Rebel infantry." Troopers grabbed battle flags and herded together prisoners. The gunfire still continued, and Peter Boehm, Custer's orderly and bugler, had his arm shattered. But the Southerners were finished, and only the stubborn valor of some units, and nightfall, saved Early's army. When it was finished, Custer slapped Major Charles Deane of the Sixth Michigan on the shoulder and laughed, "Major, this is the bulliest day since Christ was born." In the words of Sheridan's chief of staff, they sent Old Jube's army 'whirling through Winchester.' " But a member of the Michigan Brigade, who was less effusive than his commander, scribbled in his diary, "it was the hardest days fight i ever saw." [52]

Third Winchester, or Opequon, was a decisive victory for the Federals, the first major battle won by Union arms in the Shenandoah Valley. The men in the ranks attributed it to Sheridan; he "is a trump," thought one of them. "We may have had a blinder faith in McClellan," argued another, "but no such intelligent trust as we now had in Sheridan." "They simply believed he was going to win," wrote a staff officer of the troops, "and every man apparently was determined to be on hand and see him do it." The president rewarded him with promotion to brigadier general in the Regular Army. [53]

In the cavalry bivouacs that night, the praise for Sheridan and the satisfaction with the day's outcome were probably the most deeply expressed in the army. "For the first time during the war," an Ohioan asserted, "the Federal cavalry was really raised to the dignity of a third arm of the service, and given its full share in the hard fighting." In James Kidd's opinion, Sheridan "was the only general of that war who knew how to make cavalry and infantry supplement each other in battle." A Confederate officer admitted that Third Winchester was "the first time that I have ever seen cavalry very effective in a general engagement." In his report, Custer boasted that the cavalry charge "stands unequaled, valued according to its daring and success, in the history of this war." His sentiment was shared by many fellow officers and troopers.[54]

The Confederates had halted the retreat on Fisher's Hill, south of Strasburg, and here the Federals found them on the afternoon of September 20. The Rebels called the four-mile bluff "their Gibraltar," while a Northerner described it as "the bugbear of the Valley." From its crest, Early had stopped Sheridan in mid-August, but it was a month later, and Early did not have the numbers to defend it. This time, Sheridan had no restraints on his operations. During the evening, Sheridan and his senior officers agreed to a flank assault against the western flank of the Confederate line. The operation required nearly two days to execute, but on the afternoon of the twenty-second, Crook's divisions plunged down Little North Mountain, perpendicular to Early's works, caving in the flank. Units of the Sixth and Nineteenth corps charged up the face of Fisher's Hill, and for the second time in three days, the Southern army was routed. The riches of the Upper Valley, a critical objective of Grant's strategy, lay open to the Yankees.[55]

While Sheridan planned the assault on Fisher's Hill, he dispatched Torbert with Wilson's division and two of Merritt's brigades, including Custer's, to the Luray Valley, across the Massanutten Mountain from the main valley. Sheridan ordered Torbert to march south, cross the Massanutten at New Market Gap, and seal the Confederate escape route. If Torbert succeeded, Early's army would be crushed between a hammer of Union infantry and an anvil of Union cavalry. But, on the twenty-second, Torbert refused to attack a Confederate cavalry division posted in a strong defensive position behind Overall's Run at Milford. Instead, Torbert turned around, marching back toward Front Royal at the northern end of the Luray Valley.[56]

The cavalry's wagon train led the march of the Union column on the morning of September 23. As the wagons rolled into Front Royal, a detachment of Mosby's Rangers attacked, its commander believing that the train had few guards. The guerrillas surged into the column, but behind the wagons came Charles Lowell's Reserve Brigade, whose members spurred forward. The Federals, claimed an eyewitness, "came up like a flock of birds when a stone is cast into it." The Rangers scattered toward the mountains to the east, pursued by the Yankees. In the wild race and swirling action, Lieutenant Charles McMaster of the Second United States Cavalry was wounded in the head, telling his comrades that the Rebels had shot him after he had surrendered. The Regulars had captured six of Mosby's men, and when the news spread about McMaster, they demanded revenge.[57]

Torbert, Merritt, and Custer entered Front Royal as the anger of the men boiled. The Federals' hatred of Mosby's guerrillas had festered since the destruction of their wagons at Berryville and the execution of members of the Fifth Michigan at Benjamin Morgan's. It did not matter whether McMaster was telling the truth or not—the evidence indicates that his version is reliable—a burning wound needed to be seared shut. The captors took four of the prisoners and executed them in a lot behind a church, under an elm tree, and in a farmer's field. One of the victims was Henry Rhodes, a seventeen-year-old from Front Royal, who had ridden with the Rangers on a borrowed horse that morning. Members of the Fifth Michigan shot him as his widowed mother screamed and begged for mercy. The final two captives were hanged from a walnut tree after refusing to reveal the location of Mosby's headquarters. On the body of one of them a Northerner tied a placard with the words on it, "This will be the fate of Mosby and all his men."[58]

When John Mosby learned of the men's fate, he interviewed towns-folk and concluded that Custer was to blame for the executions. In fact, Torbert and/or Merritt gave the orders. Custer was present and undoubtedly concurred with the decision. There is no evidence, how-ever, that he issued a direct order for the execution of any of the prisoners. Numbers of Federal officers and enlisted men were disturbed by the slayings, with a Massachusetts officer admitting, "I am glad to say that my Regt. had nothing to do with this." It would seem that Torbert and Merritt acceded to the will of a majority of Lowell's men and perhaps a majority of the Michigan Brigade. But in the wake of the incident, Mosby was convinced that Custer had been the man responsi-ble, a view from which the partisan commander never wavered.[59]

The Federals rode away from Front Royal later in the day, rejoining the army on the twenty-fourth. When Sheridan learned of the results of Torbert's mission, he was furious, subsequently criticizing the cavalry chief in his report, and never forgiving him for the "feeble effort" and "failure." Sheridan believed that he had the destruction of Early's army in his grasp, but Torbert and Averell denied him the opportunity. The commanding general accused Averell of a lackluster pursuit from Fisher's Hill, and on the night of the twenty-third, removed him from divisional command, assigning Colonel William Powell to the post. Sheridan could be merciless if he thought a subordinate was derelict in his duty, but it seems that Averell's major flaw was that he was an outsider, not a member of the Cavalry Corps of the Army of the Potomac.[60]

Three days after the removal of Averell, on September 26, James Wilson, commander of the Third Cavalry Division, was ordered to Georgia to assume command of Sherman's cavalry. Grant had telegraphed Sheridan, requesting either Torbert or Wilson for the assignment, and Sheridan selected Wilson. Since his appointment in April, Wilson had not been a popular officer with the division, and his record had been less than distinguished. An Ohio trooper claimed later that most of the men had only "contempt for a man who persisted in holding a position over thousands, of whom hundreds were his superiors in ability and courage." James Kidd, a fair-minded officer, contended that Wilson "had Kilpatrick's fatuity for getting into scrapes, but lacked his skill in getting out." For Wilson, however, the transfer would be a blessing as he demonstrated in the conflict's final weeks his ability as a commander of mounted units.[61]

Sheridan chose Custer as Wilson's successor, appointing the brigadier on the twenty-sixth. From the time of the reorganization of the Cavalry Corps in the spring, Custer believed that he deserved divisional command. He disliked and resented Wilson from the latter's arrival, describing Grant's former staff officer as "the upstart and imbecile Wilson" and as "this Court favorite," whose performance he termed a "disgrace." Now Sheridan had rewarded his services—the War Department would promote him to brevet colonel in the Regular Army for Third Winchester—with command of Wilson's division, and Custer surely savored it. He probably told himself that he would show the "Court favorite" how a cavalry division should be led. Ironically, Wilson, who disliked Custer, recommended his successor for promotion to major general in October.[62]

The news of Custer's promotion hit the Michigan Brigade like a well-aimed volley. Under his leadership, the Wolverines had become the most renowned cavalry unit in the army. He had earned their loyalty and devotion at Gettysburg, and they had never wavered in their feelings toward him. Service under Custer had meant fighting and casualties, but he never took them into combat unless he rode with them. To be sure, the costs had mounted, with nearly 350 men killed or mortally wounded, and another 1,275 or so wounded, captured, or missing. No other mounted brigade had incurred such losses, but as James Kidd affirmed, Custer was "not regardless of human life." His brand of warfare carried a price, but it brought victories and reputation. The red neckties that they wore attested to their pride as members of Custer's Michigan Brigade, and long after the war had ceased, former members of the Michigan Brigade would continue to wear their uniforms proudly at reunions and Memorial Day parades.[63]

The brigade's initial reaction, however, was a mix of anger and despair. Colonel Peter Stagg of the First Michigan declared in his report that on September 26 the brigade "suffered the most severe loss of the campaign, General Custer being relieved." Trooper J. W. Monaghan of the Seventh wrote in his diary that "i reckon our Brig will go to the divle now, for the want of a commander." Custer tried to reassure the officers by telling them that he had spoken with Sheridan and Torbert, who promised that the Michiganders would be transferred to the Third Cavalry Division when the cavalry command was reorganized after the campaign. Custer informed Libbie: "You would be surprised at the feeling shown. Some of the officers said they would resign if the exchange were not made." Several officers cried at his departure, and members of the band threatened "to break their horns."[64]

To the members of the Third Cavalry Division, the news elicited approval. A Pennsylvanian claimed that the men were "elated" with Custer's appointment, while a New Yorker stated that "the boys liked General Custer, there was some get up and get to him." A regimental commander wrote to his parents that the command was "very much pleased at the change. Think you will hear better accounts of us now as we have a gallant leader." A Vermonter, who had served earlier under Custer, asserted that his comrades "welcomed the change, though they knew it meant mounted charges, instead of dismounted skirmishing, and a foremost place in every fight."[65]

Custer joined his new command as Sheridan's army was encamped around Harrisonburg. With the rout at Fisher's Hill, Early retreated up the Valley, turned east, and halted at Brown's Gap in the shadow of the Blue Ridge. "The rebels are scarce in the Shenandoah Valley just now," boasted a Pennsylvanian in his diary, and the Federals stopped at Harrisonburg, in the heart of the Upper Valley, roughly sixty miles south of Winchester. Here the Federals remained until October 6, implementing Grant's instructions by "devastating crops and devouring cattle," in the words of a Union officer. "The heavens are aglow with the flames from burning barns," a soldier noted in his diary one night. Sheridan intended to make the region "a barren waste" before his army departed.[66]

On October 3, Lieutenant John R. Meigs of Sheridan's staff was killed by some Confederates near the village of Dayton while returning to army headquarters after delivering dispatches to Custer. The son of Union Quartermaster General Montgomery Meigs and an 1863 West Point graduate, ranking first in the class, Meigs was a favorite of Sheridan's. When the army commander learned of the lieutenant's death, he reacted with stunned fury, attributing the killing to Rebel guerrillas. Determined "to teach to these abettors of the foul deed—a lesson they would never forget," Sheridan ordered Custer to burn all dwellings in Dayton and in a five-mile area around the town. Custer allegedly told Sheridan to "look out for smoke" when he received the instructions.[67]

The Third Cavalry Division began the incendiary work with the farms outside of Dayton on the fourth. "This was the most heart-sickening duty we had ever performed," remembered a New Yorker. "Splendid mansions in great number, in the vicinity, were laid in ashes." In all, the Federals destroyed seventeen houses, five barns, and several outbuildings, most of which were owned by pacifist Mennonites. Before the horsemen entered Dayton, Sheridan's wrath abated, and he canceled the order. For years, the residents referred to the section as the "Burnt District."[68]

Unfortunately for the Valley folk, the destruction in the Harrisonburg area was only a harbinger of the storm of flame about to descend upon the region. For nearly a fortnight Sheridan and Grant had exchanged telegrams on future operations, with the latter arguing that Sheridan's army should cross the Blue Ridge and march on Gordonsville and Charlottesville. But Sheridan convinced his superior that he could not sustain his army in such a movement, rebutting that the best policy "will be to let the burning of the crops of the Valley be the end of this campaign and let some of this army go somewhere else." Reluctantly, Grant acquiesced, and during the night of October 5, the Federals began a retrograde march north, down the Valley.[69]

While the Union infantry and artillery units followed the Valley Pike, the cavalry roamed across the countryside from the Alleghenies to the Blue Ridge, torching barns, mills, haystacks, and grain fields, and herding or slaughtering livestock. The destruction—systematic and purposeful—ravaged the region, an unnatural, infernal tempest of fire and smoke. Soldiers in both armies left graphic descriptions of the three days, October 6–8, of devastation. "The very air," declared a Confederate diarist, "is impregnated with the smell of burning property." At night, the horizon appeared as "one bright sheet of flame." The property damage has been calculated at twenty million dollars in depreciated Confederate currency in 1864. "When this is completed," Sheridan wired Grant during the march, "the Valley, from Winchester up to Staunton, ninety-two miles, will have but little in it for man or beast." The victims would remember it as "the Burning." Grant's sword, unsheathed by Sheridan in the Shenandoah Valley and later by Sherman in Georgia and the Carolinas, was indeed terrible.[70]

The Confederate army trailed the Federals, with Early directing his mounted units "to pursue the enemy, to harass him and to ascertain his purposes." The scenes of destruction infuriated the Rebels, who were "eager to get them [the Northerners] within sword range," according to one of the Southerners. On the Valley Pike, Major General Lunsford Lomax's division harried Merritt's troopers, while on the Back Road, west of the pike, Brigadier General Thomas Rosser's division engaged his old friend's command. The Rebels were aggressive, igniting skirmishes and rearguard actions. Merritt's and Custer's men repulsed each sortie, but the constant work slowed the march and limited the burning. By the night of October 8, the Yankees had crossed Tom's Brook near Woodstock, with the Confederates encamping south of the small stream.[71]

The boldness of the enemy cavalry angered Sheridan, particularly after he learned that Rosser was being called the "Savior of the Valley." "I deemed it best to make this delay of one day here and settle this new cavalry general," Sheridan explained to Grant from Strasburg. He summoned Torbert to headquarters during the night, and in Sheridan's words, told the cavalry chief to "finish this 'Savior of the Valley.'" Torbert reported his commander's words as "start out at daylight and whip the rebel cavalry or get whipped myself." Merritt would attack Lomax along the Valley Pike; Custer would hit Rosser along the Back Road.[72]

Reveille sounded early in the camps of the Third Cavalry Division on the cold morning of October 9—"this was the beginning point of the glorious record of the old 3rd Div.," wrote an Ohio trooper afterward. Custer led the column south toward Tom's Brook, brushing aside enemy videttes at Mt. Olive, a small village just north of the stream. Halting on a ridge above Tom's Brook, Custer examined Rosser's position, the center of which lay on Wisman's Hill, as the local folks called it, that overlooked a farm owned by the Wisman family, next to the brook's ford. "This position was well adapted for defense," Custer stated in his report.[73]

Dismounted Union skirmishers descended toward the stream, engaging Rosser's sharpshooters. Before long, two batteries of the Second U.S. Horse Artillery opened fire on Wisman's Hill, but defective ammunition caused little damage to the Confederates, whose horse artillerists responded with shellfire. Custer deployed his lead brigade into line under Colonel Alexander Pennington, the Michigan Brigade's former battery commander, during the artillery duel. Reluctant to undertake a frontal attack, Custer waited, testing Rosser's line with mounted skirmishers. He described the enemy resistance as "stubborn." At one point in the action, recognizing Rosser on the distant hill, Custer rode in front of the line and removed his sombrero-style hat from his head, sweeping it down to his knee in a salute to his academy friend. Pointing to the Union general, Rosser allegedly told some officers: "That's General Custer, the Yanks are so proud of, and I intend to give him the best whipping to-day that he ever got. See if I don't."[74]

The stalemate lasted through midmorning, when Custer decided to outflank the Confederate left. Ordering three regiments to turn the position, he brought up a second brigade for the attack. When a Virginia colonel detected the Union maneuver, he warned Rosser, who dismissed it, replying that "I'll drive them into Strasburg by ten o'clock." It was a hollow vow, as a short time later the New Yorkers and Pennsylvanians crashed into Rosser's left flank. When Custer saw the attack, he ordered bugles sounded, and with Sergeant John Buckley, color bearer of the Fifth New York, by his side, led the charge down the Back Road.

He was a "terrible demon" in combat, thought a New Yorker of his new commander.[75]

The Yankees splashed across Tom's Brook, urging their mounts up the slope of the hill. Rosser's line dissolved under the combined assaults, fleeing south. The Federals overran two cannon, pursued for two miles, and shattered a second patchwork line. Confederate resistance evaporated, and it became a race to safety for the Southerners. They were, in Custer's words, an "affrighted herd," and his men seized prisoners, four more cannon, and numerous wagons, including Rosser's headquarters wagon. The Rebels "lost more in that one fight than we had ever done before, in all our fights together," grumbled Thomas Munford, the Virginian who had alerted Rosser to the flank attack.[76]

On the Valley Pike, Merritt's troopers crushed Lomax's line, precipitating a rout similar to Custer's. The Union pursuit covered twenty miles. Custer said, "Never since the opening of this war had there been witnessed such a complete and decisive overthrow of the enemy's cavalry." When a Confederate artilleryman saw his mounted comrades after the debacle, he remarked that there were "some without arms, some without hats, some without jackets, and some without sensibility." The Yankees dubbed the Battle of Tom's Brook the "Woodstock Races."[77]

The entire Union army celebrated the victory. "When the trophies began to come in," a Pennsylvania infantry captain informed his wife, "it caused a regular laugh for it was the most fantastic parade I ever saw in military style." Sheridan claimed it was "beyond my power to describe." Torbert termed the rout "the most decisive the country had ever witnessed," while Merritt asserted that "never has there been, in the history of this war, a more complete victory." A Michigander jotted in his diary, "it was one of the worst whipens that the reb Cav ever got."[78]

Probably no one in the Union camps celebrated more than Custer. October 9, he boasted to Libbie, "was a glorious day for your Boy." He had marked his succession to his new command by a brilliant victory. From the captured wagons, he recovered Libbie's ambrotype that he had lost at Trevilian Station. His men also secured Rosser's uniform coat, and on the tenth, Custer, who was shorter and much thinner than his friend, strutted through the camps while wearing it. The veterans cheered him, and he richly enjoyed the joke.[79]

An officer in the Third Cavalry Division admitted in his journal that his commander was "a picturesque figure" in the Confederate general's coat, but then added: "With Custer as leader we are all heroes and hankering for a fight. We always have the band playing on the front in an advance, and tooting defiantly in the rear on retreat." After Tom's Brook, avowed an Ohio trooper, "we never began but we felt sure of victory. Custar always used to say that he could tell in 20 minutes after opening a fight if we could beat the enemy." He had given them confidence, both in him and in themselves. They would need it before long.[80]

First known photograph of George A. Custer, age seventeen, June 1857. *(Courtesy of Little Big Horn Battlefield National Monument Archives)*

G. A. Custer in cadet uniform, U.S.M.A., summer 1859, taken while on leave. *(From the author's collection)*

(Below) Captain G. A. Custer and Brigadier General Alfred Pleasonton, Falmouth, Virginia, June 1863. As cavalry commander, Pleasonton recommended Custer for a brigadiership three weeks later. *(Courtesy of United States Army Military History Institute)*

Libbie and Brigadier General G. A. Custer
shortly after their marriage in February 1864.
(Courtesy of United States Army Military History Institute)

Major General Judson Kilpatrick, Custer's first
division commander, known in the army as
"Kil-cavalry" for his rashness in battle. *(Courtesy of
United States Army Military History Institute)*

Lieutenant General Ulysses S. Grant, general-in-chief of the union armies and future president, with whom Custer clashed in the spring of 1876. *(Courtesy of United States Army Military History Institute)*

Major General James H. Wilson, Custer's division commander and rival in 1864. *(Courtesy of United States Army Military History Institute)*

Left to right: Major General Philip Sheridan, Lieutenant Colonel James Forsyth, Major General Wesley Merritt, Brigadier General Thomas Devin, and Major General G. A. Custer, January 1865, before their Charlottesville raid. *(Courtesy of United States Army Military History Institute)*

Major General G. A. Custer, January 1865. *(Courtesy of United States Army Military History Institute)*

(Below) Major General G. A. Custer, family members, and staff on the porch of Elmwood, the home of George W. Ward, Winchester, Virginia, February 26, 1865. G. A. Custer stands in the center, to his right is Libbie Custer, and behind him are Daniel and Rhoda Bacon and Rebecca Richmond. Orderly Joseph Fought is behind the flag on the left and Lieutenant Tom Custer is seated first on the step. Lieutenant James Christiancy is seated under the pillar at the right of the group. *(Courtesy of Little Big Horn Battlefield National Monument Archives)*

Major General G. A. Custer, Tom Custer, and Libbie Custer, spring 1865. *(Courtesy of United States Army Military History Institute)*

(Below right) Eliza Brown, Custer's servant for six years, and Libbie and Major General G. A. Custer, April 1865. *(Courtesy of Little Big Horn Battlefield National Monument Archives)*

Libbie Bacon Custer after her marriage, February 1864. *(Courtesy of United States Army Military History Institute)*

Brigadier General G. A. Custer in black velvet uniform as sketched by James Taylor in Harpers Ferry, Virginia, August 1864. *(Courtesy of United States Army Military History Institute)*

Major General G. A. Custer, May 1865, with his trademark red necktie and wide-collared shirt with a silver star. *(Courtesy of United States Army Military History Institute)*

Brigadier General G. A. Custer and staff of the Michigan Brigade at Stevensburg, Virginia, February 1864. Captain Jacob Greene and Eliza Brown are seated on the steps in front of Custer. In the rear of the group on the porch, Sergeant Michael Bellior holds the general's flag. *(Courtesy of United States Army Military History Institute)*

Custer's Demand, a painting by Charles C. Schreyvogel, depicting Custer's meeting with Kiowa, December 1868. With Custer are Lieutenant Tom Custer and Lieutenant Schuyler Crosby. The scout and interpreter was supposedly Abner "Sharp" Grover, who was not actually present. *(Courtesy of Little Big Horn Battlefield National Monument Archives)*

How, Kola, a painting by Charles C. Schreyvogel depicting a cavalry charge on the plains. *(Courtesy of Little Big Horn Battlefield National Monument Archives)*

G. A. Custer in buckskins, c. 1872. A renowned hunter and sportsman, he escorted numerous groups on buffalo hunts. *(Courtesy of United States Army Military History Institute)*

A cavalry platoon in skirmish formation on the plains, 1886. *(Courtesy of United States Army Military History Institute)*

The Custers' quarters, Fort Abraham Lincoln, Dakota Territory, November 1873. Lieutenant Colonel G. A. Custer stands third from left, and next to him on his left is Libbie Custer. Agnes Bates, guest of the Custers, is seated to Libbie's left. Captain George Yates is seated in the center, with Margaret Custer Calhoun seated behind and to the left of Yates. Captain Tom Custer stands second from the top on the right, and to his right is Mrs. Annie Yates. *(Courtesy of Little Big Horn Battlefied National Monument Archives)*

Margaret Custer and Libbie Bacon Custer. The only daughter of Emanuel and Maria Custer, Margaret would lose three brothers and her husband, Lieutenant James Calhoun, at Little Big Horn. *(Courtesy of United States Army Military History Institute)*

G. A. Custer in civilian attire before the Black Hills expedition, June 1874. *(Courtesy of United States Army Military History Institute)*

Lieutenant Colonel G. A. Custer in dress uniform, three months before his death, March 1876. *(Courtesy of United States Army Military History Institute)*

"Lonesome" Charley Reynolds, guide for Custer, 1873–1876. Killed at Little Big Horn. *(Courtesy of United States Army Military History Institute)*

Major Marcus Reno, Seventh Cavalry, photographed as a brevet brigadier general during the Civil War. His performance at Little Big Horn resulted in a court of inquiry. *(Courtesy of United States Army Military History Institute)*

Captain George Yates, Seventh Cavalry, commander of Company F, the "Band Box Troop," and good friend of Custer, with whom he died at Little Big Horn. *(Courtesy of United States Army Military History Institute)*

Officers of the Seventh Cavalry. Seated left to right: Lieutenant Charles Varnum, chief of scouts at Little Big Horn; Captain Frederick Benteen, whose hatred of Custer divided the regiment and shaped its history; Lieutenant Benjamin Hodgson, one of the regiment's most popular officers, who was killed at Little Big Horn. Standing: a Lieutenant Bronson. *(Courtesy of Little Big Horn Battlefield National Monument Archives)*

Brigadier General Alfred H. Terry, commander of the expedition against the Sioux in the summer of 1876. *(Courtesy of Little Big Horn Battlefield National Monument Archives)*

Gall, Hunkpapa Lakota chief, who fought the Seventh Cavalry in 1873 and 1874, and at Little Big Horn. *(Courtesy of United States Army Military History Institute)*

Lakota family in a village, late 1800s. *(Courtesy of United States Army Military History Institute)*

tting Bull, Hunkpapa Lakota holy man, whose defiance of the U.S. government contributed to the Sioux war of 1876. *(Courtesy of United States Army Military History Institute)*

Curley, Crow scout for the army at Little Big Horn, who watched the battle from a distance and left an important account of the action. *(Courtesy of United States Army Military History Institute)*

Little Big Horn River, looking east, toward Major Marcus Reno's command retreat from the valley floor to the ridges beyond. *(Courtesy of United States Army Military History Institute)*

(Left, center) View looking west into Little Big Horn Valley and the village site from the crest of Reno Hill. Surviving troops of the Seventh Cavalry defended this ground until the morning of June 27, 1876. *(Courtesy of United States Army Military History Institute)*

(Above) Custer Ridge, looking east from the valley floor. The Sioux and Cheyenne warriors swarmed across the terrain in the foreground, attacking toward Custer Hill (B), and Calhoun Hill (C). Members of Captain Myles Keogh's Company I fell in the area on the east side of the ridge, where the arrow points. *(Courtesy of United States Army Military History Institute)*

The so-called Keogh Sector on the east side of Custer Ridge, looking north-northwest from Calhoun Hill. On this ground, troopers of Companies C, I, and L were trapped and killed as they fled toward Custer Hill on the horizon, far left. *(Courtesy of Little Big Horn Battlefield National Monument Archives)*

The southwestern slope of Custer Hill, viewed from the crest, looking west toward the deep ravine, Little Big Horn River, and the site of the village. Stones mark the positions of slain troopers. *(Courtesy of United States Army Military History Institute)*

Close-up view of Custer Hill and stone markers. Here were found the bodies of George and Thomas Custer. *(Courtesy of Little Big Horn Battlefield National Monument Archives)*

Custer Ridge, viewed from near the present-day park museum, looking east. Custer Hill is at left, marked by a monument, fence, and stone markers. *(Courtesy of United States Army Military History Institute)*

11

MAJOR

GENERAL

■ "Mail call!" echoed through the camps of the Army of the Shenandoah on Tuesday, October 18, 1864. Soldiers scrambled to hear their names called. It was such a beautiful autumn day that a man wanted to reach out, grab, and hold it. The weather brightened the already ebullient spirits of the men. Since Tom's Brook, the war seemed distant, except for drills and a skirmish with the enemy five days earlier. The consensus among the Yankees was that "Old Jube" Early's Rebels were, as one of them expressed it, "thoroughly and permanently broken, dispirited, and disposed of." Speculation had it that the army would be leaving the Valley and "Little Phil" Sheridan was in Washington for that purpose. If not, the fields north of Cedar Creek, outside of Middletown, provided good campsites. Life and death framed a soldier's experience, and this day affirmed life.[1]

But the whisper of death was not far away. While the Northerners relaxed, shared letters, and cooked meals, four miles south of Cedar Creek, on Fisher's Hill, Early and his senior generals plotted an audacious attack. Major General John B. Gordon and others had examined the Union position from Massanutten Mountain and were convinced that the Federals' left flank lay exposed to an assault. Prodded by Robert E. Lee to assume the offensive, Early agreed to Gordon's proposal of a night march around the vulnerable flank. The movement demanded timeliness, coordination, and luck, but if successful, it offered redemption to Early and his veterans. At 8 P.M. on the eighteenth, the Confederates marched.[2]

A heavy fog had settled in along Cedar Creek during the night, wrapping itself around the rows of Union tents. As Gordon had promised Early, the Southerners were ready when dawn creased the morning sky. Screaming their "Rebel yell," the Confederates charged from out of the mists. Before some of the Federal units could offer resistance, the attackers were over the fieldworks and among the tents. Three Union divisions collapsed under the onslaught, fleeing in a panic-stricken rout. Generals sacrificed regiments and brigades to delay the gray-clad surge, but the Rebels blasted apart the units, driving two more divisions from the field. A pocket of resistance formed by three Sixth Corps brigades in the Middletown cemetery stemmed the Southern attack for an hour, giving their comrades time to regroup on a ridge north of Middletown. By eleven o'clock, the Army of the Shenandoah had been swept from their camps by one of the war's most brilliantly conceived and executed offensives. As he rode into Middletown, Jubal Early thought of Napoleon Bonaparte's victory at Austerlitz.[3]

George Custer and the Third Cavalry Division protected the army's right flank about two miles west of the main bivouac area along the Valley Pike. About 4 A.M., Custer sounded "Boots and Saddles" when his picket post on Cedar Creek opened fire on Confederate cavalry. One regiment rode to support of the videttes, and the remaining units unsaddled and prepared breakfast. But the explosion of gunfire to the east that announced the enemy assault caused Custer to order his trains to the rear and the mounts resaddled. Along the creek, Thomas Rosser's gray-clad cavalry pushed across, backed by horse artillery. Custer countered with a brigade and cannon, which stopped Rosser, who did not press the attack. About 8:30 A.M., Alfred Torbert instructed Custer to move toward Middletown with one brigade.[4]

As the troopers marched across the fields north of Middletown, they encountered a "stream of stragglers." The panic among the infantrymen and artillerists had subsided, but the horsemen witnessed the magnitude of the disaster. Major General Horatio G. Wright, acting army commander, posted Custer's brigade and Wesley Merritt's division east of the turnpike. From Middletown, Confederate infantry soon emerged, advancing on the Union cavalry. The Yankees repulsed the sortie with their repeating firearms, and Early's offensive had reached its zenith. The Southern commander fashioned a battle line at the village's edge and halted.[5]

In time, Early's decision to halt generated controversy, but his men were exhausted and hungry, with hundreds of them absent from the ranks, pillaging the abandoned camps. The morning's victory had been staggering, evident by the park of captured cannon, men, and matériel. Once the Confederates failed to seize the Valley Pike north of town, however, the offensive crested. With the Union cavalry overlapping his flanks, Early abandoned the attack for the present. Conditions on the field guided his judgment.[6]

Philip Sheridan reached the Cedar Creek battlefield at approximately 10:30 A.M. He had come from Winchester, nearly eleven miles to the north, riding through the wreckage of his army. When he arrived at the ridge where Wright rallied the units, he met with his generals, learning the details of the fighting. When Custer saw him, according to one of Sheridan's aides, the brigadier hugged and kissed the short Irishman, who pulled away, embarrassed, grumbling, "We had not time to lose." A corps commander reported that his men could cover a retreat to Winchester, but Sheridan barked, "Retreat—Hell! We'll be back in our camps tonight." A staff officer suggested that he ride along the army's front so that the men could see him. With hat in hand—he had an odd-shaped, unmistakable head—Sheridan rode the length of the line, greeted by thunderous cheers, cursing and assuring the men that they would sleep in their campsites tonight.[7]

About one o'clock, Early tested the Federal line on the wooded ridge with three infantry divisions. The advance amounted to a reconnaissance in force, and when the Yankees unleashed a few volleys, the Confederates retired to a position midway between the town and the ridge, with the divisions deploying behind stone walls. The tactical initiative now shifted to Sheridan, who prepared for a counterstroke. Earlier he had directed Custer to the right flank, granting the subordinate discretion to use his judgment once the assault began. An erroneous report about enemy infantry at Winchester delayed the attack, but finally at four o'clock scores of bugles blared the charge. The struggle for the Shenandoah Valley would be settled.[8]

The Yankees cleared the tree line, and the Confederate line exploded. But it was a day for redemption, and the Federals leaned into the cauldron. Across the fields, the opponents pounded each other. Early's veterans stood—clusters of proud men around shredded battle flags. But time had run out for these Southern warriors as Custer's horsemen charged from the west. When two infantry brigades advanced simultaneously, the Confederate left flank collapsed. "Regiment after regiment, brigade after brigade, in rapid succession was crushed," recounted Confederate general John Gordon, "and, like hard clods of clay under a pelting rain, the superb commands crumbled to pieces."[9]

Except for a few islands of resistance, Early's army disintegrated into a "stampede" for Cedar Creek. Custer reacted at once to the rout, redirecting his regiments toward the stream west of the pike. Dressed in his velvet uniform—"his fighting trim," to the men—he led the First Vermont and Fifth New York Cavalry across Hottle's Ford. "It seemed like Custer was bent on capturing the whole of Early's army," asserted a trooper.[10]

The roadbed was jammed with wagons, cannon, ambulances, and soldiers. The Yankees knifed into the column, and "the slaughter was fearful," claimed one of them. According to a cavalryman, Custer "appeared to forget his position. He was giving orders to the teamsters to get off their mules." Hundreds of Rebels surrendered, only to escape into the darkness. "Night alone prevented the capture of Early and his entire army," Custer grumbled afterward.[11]

The booty amounted to forty-five cannon, five flags, dozens of vehicles, and scores of prisoners. "Aside from the joy I feel at the general result of the engagement," Custer wrote a friend, "I feel particularly elated at the success of my Division." Colonel William Wells, commander of a brigade, described the affair as "the greatest thing on record," adding in the letter that the men "had made Genl *Custer a Brevet Major General.* he commands our Div. and a Gallant Officer he is too." A trooper contended that "had the Third Division been commanded by a man of less prowess than Custer" the enemy would have eluded capture.[12]

With the booty and captives secured, Custer hurried to army headquarters, located at Belle Grove, a limestone mansion south of Middletown. A large fire blazed in the yard, and "the excitement was intense" when Custer reined up. Dismounting, he strode across the yard to Sheridan, lifted the diminutive commander into the air, whirled him around, and exclaimed, "By God, Phil, we've cleaned them out of their guns and got ours back!" Sheridan was probably embarrassed, but as he had told his staff, Custer "was as boyish as he was brave."[13]

Custer's celebration was tempered when he learned that an old academy friend, Confederate Major General Stephen Dodson Ramseur, was inside Belle Grove, grievously wounded. A North Carolinian, Ramseur had fallen during the rout while trying to rally his troops and, after being placed in an ambulance, was captured by Custer's men south of Cedar Creek. The Southerner had learned recently of the birth of his child and had worn a flower on his uniform in its honor. When Custer saw his friend, who lay on a bed, he greeted him "in his bluff, hearty manner," but the wounded man "scarcely responded." Custer may have talked of the party at Benny Havens's in the spring of 1860, when none of those present could have thought of such a rendezvous. Other academy friends of Ramseur visited, but the wound drained away life. A devout man, Ramseur died quietly on the morning of October 20. West Point had given another of its own.[14]

Cedar Creek "practically ended the campaign in the Shenandoah Valley," declared Sheridan in his report. The granary of the Confederacy had been conquered and devastated. No longer did the region stand as an invincible symbol for Southern arms. Third Winchester, Fisher's Hill, Tom's Brook, and Cedar Creek were a drumroll of Union victories that insured Lincoln's reelection and made Sheridan one of the North's foremost heroes. "The little man who rode so large a horse," as a soldier described Sheridan, fused an amalgam of commands into an army, led it to victory over a formidable, but outnumbered, opponent, and guaranteed himself a place among the conflict's front rank of generals. A grateful government promoted him to major general in the Regular Army, and poet T. Buchanan Read enshrined him in Northerners' imagination with "Sheridan's Ride."[15]

Instrumental to Union success in the campaign was Sheridan's use of the cavalry. During the operations, according to an historian of the mounted units, "the Union cavalry in the East truly came into its own." Writing after Third Winchester, a Confederate general attested to the dominance of Sheridan's horsemen, stating, "That Yankee cavalry is a formidable force. The country is favorable for their operations, and we have no cavalry to confront them." The disparity worsened, however, as the Union cavalry served as the instruments of destruction, vanquished their opponents at Tom's Brook, and proved to be the decisive edge at Cedar Creek. After the final battle, the Southerners, in the words of a Massachusetts officer, "think our cavalry is the best in the world." Credit for this belonged primarily to Sheridan.[16]

For Custer, the campaign demonstrated, once again, his prowess as a cavalry officer. As a brigade commander, he had no equal in the army, and when promoted to divisional command, he handled the additional units with consummate skill. If he had a weakness as a divisional leader, it was his penchant for riding at the forefront in a charge. As he showed at Tom's Brook, Custer was neither rash nor careless, but an officer who acted with deliberateness until a weakness in an opponent's position could be located and exploited. He possessed an instinct for combat, a feel for the right moment to assail the enemy. As he had with the Michigan Brigade, he then led the Third Division at the front in a charge. Confederate prisoners likened him and his troopers to "flying devils," a fitting designation.[17]

On October 21, Sheridan recommended to Ulysses Grant the promotion of George Getty of the Sixth Corps and "the brave boys Merritt and Custer" to brevet major generals. As an additional honor to Custer, Sheridan directed him to carry the captured Confederate battle flags to Washington and to present them to Secretary of War Edwin Stanton. Departing from the Valley by special train the next day, Custer and his detail arrived in the capital, where he and his men rode up Pennsylvania Avenue in an omnibus, with the flags flying from the windows, to the accompaniment of "a storm of cheers." Soldiers in the city hugged their comrades, and a few, according to Libbie Custer, kissed her husband's hand.[18]

Stanton postponed the ceremony until Tuesday, October 25, because of illness. Custer seized the opportunity to travel to Newark, New Jersey, where Libbie was visiting her stepmother's relatives, the William Russell family. Arriving on Sunday, the brigadier was greeted by the Russell children, who raced upstairs with the news. Libbie was in her bedroom, crying, after reading in the morning paper that Autie was in Washington. The surprise gladdened Libbie at once, and the next morning the couple boarded a train for the capital.[19]

Standing by her husband's side, Libbie watched as the men presented the captured standards to the secretary of war in his office on the morning of the twenty-fifth. One trooper remarked to Stanton that "the 3rd Division wouldn't be worth a cent if it wasn't for" its general. The secretary told Custer that "the history of war does not produce the parallel" of his and the division's achievements in the campaign. Stanton then announced to the gathering that Custer had been brevetted a major general and, shaking his hand said, "General, a gallant officer always makes gallant soldiers." The new rank dated from October 19.[20]

Major General Custer rejoined the army on October 28. Following Cedar Creek, Early's command had retired south up the Valley, with the Federals pursuing briefly before returning to their camps along the stream. During the next few weeks, "Jubal occasionally came up to the front and barked, but there was no more bite in him," in the words of a Northerner. In mid-November, Sheridan transferred units to Petersburg and to Maryland, retaining the two divisions of the Nineteenth Corps and Merritt's and Custer's mounted commands. In response, Robert E. Lee ordered the Second Corps to Petersburg, leaving Early with an infantry division and some cavalry units. The Confederates marched to Staunton and settled in for the winter.[21]

Sheridan, meanwhile, relocated to Winchester, where his men prepared quarters, designating them Camp Russell in honor of Brigadier General David Russell, who had been killed at Third Winchester. Custer's Third Division encamped south and west of Winchester toward Kernstown. For the present, tents served as shelter. Drills, inspections, picket duty, and occasional reconnaissances marked the duty, but an Ohio sergeant remembered the weeks as "exceedingly pleasant & agreeable."[22]

Custer brought Libbie from Washington, meeting her at the railroad station in Martinsburg on November 6. Escorted by 150 men, they arrived the next day at his headquarters—three tents, with barn doors for floors, pitched in "an enclosure of evergreens." It was temporary lodging, and within a week, Custer moved Libbie into Long Meadow, the residence of Robert and Sarah Glass, located four miles south of Winchester. The Glass family welcomed the general and his wife, knowing that their property would be protected, and here the Custers boarded for the next two months.[23]

Long Meadow—which still stands as a private residence—was a "large, roomy, Virginia mansion," in Libbie's description. A limestone house, with an attached log wing, the Glass home had two large rooms downstairs and two bedrooms upstairs. Five fireplaces, two of which were graced with step mantels, known as "Winchester mantels," heated the rooms. The Custers used two of the rooms, with the staff and Eliza in outbuildings. They had their meals in the log summer kitchen, which was the original structure on the site, having served once as a fort. The Glasses, whom Libbie described as "such nice people," were evidently Quakers.[24]

The weeks together at Long Meadow were probably the happiest of the war for the Custers. "Remember," Libbie had written to Autie before she joined him, "I cannot love as I do without my life blending with yours. I would not lose my individuality, but would be, as a wife should be, part of her husband, a life within a life. I was never an admirer of a submissive wife, but I wish to look to my husband as superior in judgment and experience and to be guided by him in all things." Desiring to be a "model wife," Libbie needed to be with him as much as he needed her, and the time at Long Meadow fulfilled their needs.[25]

Since their marriage, Libbie had learned to accept Autie's habit of not speaking, of "long silences," as she called them. She attributed them to the many hours of guard duty he had been required to walk as a cadet at West Point. If she were not the cause, "I was content to submit to these periods of silence." Autie's brooding quietness evidently strained the intimacy of their relationship at times, but Libbie bowed to his will, living with the hours when he preferred to be alone.[26]

"My life is one of constant variety," Libbie wrote her parents soon after her arrival at Long Meadow. For a while, she was the only officer's wife with the army and received plentiful attention. Sheridan visited her—"He is so mild and unassuming in his manner," she thought—and together they chatted, undoubtedly at times about her husband, whom Sheridan liked to call "youngster." During the day, she and Autie frequently rode horses across the countryside. On one occasion, correspondent and artist James Taylor saw the couple, and described Libbie as a "handsome little woman," with a "wealth of brown hair, all free to the breeze, about her shoulders in loving play." She wore a "tight-fitting jacket of velvet" as part of a long, black riding habit. In the evenings, they entertained staff and guests in the sitting room of Long Meadow, and on Sundays attended Christ Episcopal Church on Boscawen Street in Winchester.[27]

Shortly after Libbie joined her husband, Tom Custer arrived. Autie's months of effort to secure a position for his brother on the staff had succeeded when Colonel James Kidd of the Sixth Michigan Cavalry commissioned him a second lieutenant in the regiment. Tom received a discharge from the Twenty-first Ohio, the unit he had enlisted in in September 1861, and journeyed to Virginia. Autie requested a transfer to his staff, and Sheridan willingly granted it.[28]

The reunion elated the brothers. Since their childhood, when Tom tagged along with Autie, sniffing for mischief, perpetrating practical jokes, the brothers shared a bond of deep, abiding affection for each other. Autie felt responsible for his younger brother, and Tom worshipped Autie. Whenever they met, according to Libbie, both of them emitted "a great whoop and yell, such as was peculiar to the Custers." Like Autie, Tom was thin, but shorter, with blue eyes and sandy-colored hair, and with a nature brimming with life.[29]

"We could not help spoiling him owing to his charm and our deep affection," Libbie wrote of her and Autie's treatment of Tom. Frequently, after official duty ended for the day, the brothers scuffled with each other, and were embarrassed occasionally when another staff officer walked in on them. On duty, however, Autie demanded much from Tom, who complained to Libbie that "that old galoot" growled at him for "every little darned thing just because I happen to be his brother." To a fellow staff member, Tom grumbled, "If anyone thinks it is a soft thing to be a commanding officer's brother, he misses his guess."[30]

Tom rode with Autie on their first operation together at the end of November, marching west into the Allegheny Mountains to intercept Confederate raiders who had burned buildings and wrecked the railroad at New Creek, West Virginia. It was a difficult task because of the mountainous terrain and cold weather, with the Southerners, under Thomas Rosser, eluding the pursuers. The Federals were struck with the "wild and magnificent" scenery of the region, but returned weary and saddlesore after five days. Autie galloped ahead of the division when it was five miles from Winchester to embrace Libbie.[31]

Three weeks later, at the urging of Grant, Sheridan ordered Alfred Torbert and the cavalry on a raid to Gordonsville to destroy the Orange & Alexandria Railroad. The cavalry left Winchester on December 19—Merritt's division, accompanied by Torbert, headed east through the Blue Ridge; Custer's two brigades, south toward Staunton. Custer followed the Valley Pike, camping the first night at Woodstock. On the twentieth, "a most delightful day," the Yankees passed through Mt. Jackson and halted south of the town in an expanse of flat land known locally as Meem's Bottom. Here Custer formed the division into a square and, standing on a cannon in the center, announced the Union victory at Nashville, Tennessee, repeated a rumor that Jefferson Davis had tried to commit suicide, and warned the men not to waste ammunition if they encountered the enemy. The troopers cheered three times, re-formed into a column, and proceeded south to New Market, where some citizens warned them that Confederate cavalry was approaching. At sundown, Custer halted the command at Lacey's Springs, nine miles north of Harrisonburg.[32]

Sleet began falling as the Yankees bivouacked. Custer posted Colonel Alexander Pennington's brigade east of the pike, south of an inn, or "mansion," that served as headquarters, and Brigadier General George Chapman's brigade and the wagons north of the inn and across the pike. He ordered pickets from five regiments to cover the roads in the vicinity and designated 4 A.M. for reveille. The men were hungry and, despite the weather, foraged for food at nearby homesteads. Without tents, they lay on the ground, covered only with blankets. During the night, the temperature plunged, changing the sleet to snow, which accumulated to nearly five inches.[33]

The "air was full of flying snow" when the Yankees rolled from their blankets. In some regiments, men began to cook breakfast and saddle the horses. Suddenly, from the north and west, Chapman's troopers heard "sharp, short, fierce, bark like yells" followed by "a dull thundering sound" as Confederate cavalry charged into the wagons and bivouac sites. The Southerners belonged to Rosser's division and had ridden through the wretched night to reach the Union camp, after being alerted by a signal station of the enemy's march during the day. Eluding the picket posts, the Rebels attacked without bugle calls or shouts and now were among the Northerners.[34]

The surprise assault scattered three of Chapman's regiments and, as he reported, caused "great confusion for a short time." Forming the First Vermont and Twenty-second New York Cavalry, Chapman led a counterattack that blunted the force of the thrust. The darkness and the snow created a blinding action; "you could not tell friend from foe," asserted a Federal. When Custer heard the gunfire, he sprinted from the inn, without a coat, hat, or boots, grabbed a band member's unsaddled horse, mounted, and rode to the Second Ohio Cavalry, shouting at the men to charge down the pike. "BUSINESS WAS LIVELY for a short time," wrote an Ohioan. "But we soon got them turned, and started back down the hill." Union casualties amounted to fewer than one hundred, with Custer estimating his friend's losses as above that number.[35]

Rosser's boldness, however, ended the Union raid. The Federals departed Lacey's Springs later in the day, riding north through the fields because of the pike's slippery surface. A cold wind blasted the column for the next two days, moving one trooper to assert that it "was the coldest march I ever made." The men, he added, "could ride but a little while at a time, then dismount and walk to get warm. Some of the men froze their feet." They arrived at Camp Russell on the twenty-third and received orders to begin the construction of permanent winter quarters. Like Custer, Merritt encountered Confederate cavalry and returned to Winchester.[36]

The Custers had planned to travel to Monroe for Christmas, but the raid prevented a furlough. Instead, they enjoyed the holidays at Long Meadow with Tom who, Autie admitted to Libbie's father, "with a little more experience will make a valuable and most efficient aide." From December 30 to January 13, 1865, Custer served on a court-martial board. With the duty finished, he requested a twenty-day furlough, and Sheridan approved it. Before he and Libbie departed for Michigan, the army commander hosted a surprise party for the couple—"We learned of it in time to be prepared," wrote Libbie. The walls of the house were decorated with crossed sabers, regimental flags, and boughs of ever-green, and a Winchester baker prepared a turkey, cake, biscuits, candy, and coffee for the festivities. The Custers appreciated Sheridan's kind-ness.[37]

Autie and Libbie divided the furlough between their families in Monroe and relatives and friends in Grand Rapids. A fellow passenger on the train to Grand Rapids sketched the general in his diary and recorded a description of him. "Genl Custar," he wrote, "reminded me of Tennysons description of King Arthur, he is tall straight with light complexion, clear blue eyes, golden hair which hangs in curls on his shoulders has fine nose." While in Grand Rapids, the couple stayed with the William Richmond family, Libbie's kinfolk. There was "a good deal of ceremony & display at the Rapids and on the way," according to Daniel Bacon, with Autie meeting numerous families of men in the Michigan Brigade. Because of the activities, he requested and was granted a five-day extension of his leave.[38]

On Sunday evening, February 5, the Custers attended a Week of Prayer service at the Monroe Presbyterian Church. While Custer knelt in prayer, as he stated afterward, he accepted Jesus Christ as his Savior. When he returned to the army, he wrote to the minister, describing his conversion, and concluded the letter with: "I feel somewhat like the pilot of a vessel who has been steering his ship upon familiar and safe waters but has been called upon to make a voyage fraught with danger. Having in safety and with success completed one voyage, he is imbued with confidence and renewed courage, and the second voyage is robbed of half its terror. So it is with me." [39]

The next morning, February 6, Autie, Libbie, Tom, Rhoda Bacon, Rebecca Richmond, and several of the general's staff officers boarded a train for Virginia. Libbie's stepmother and cousin planned to spend some time with the couple in Winchester, with Daniel Bacon following in a few weeks. Libbie's evident happiness during the leave so pleased her father that he wrote Custer a brief letter after their departure. He thanked God for her felicity and then acknowledged to his son-in-law, "I do myself only partial justice when I say in all sincerity, that I am made happy in thought, that you are all I could desire or wish, and I am not without pride, at your well earned, and fully appreciated reputation." [40]

The party arrived in Washington at midnight on the ninth. In the morning, Autie and Libbie escorted Rhoda and Rebecca to the Capitol, introducing them to a number of senators and representatives. They attended the theater in the evening, then left for Virginia early on the tenth. The train carried them to Stephenson's Depot, north of Winchester, where several officers and an escort met them. Autie, Libbie, Rhoda, and Rebecca rode to headquarters in a "mammoth ancient green sleigh," as Rebecca described it, while the staff members rode on horseback. During his absence, the staff had relocated headquarters from Long Meadow to Elmwood, the residence of George W. Ward, a member of the Virginia House of Delegates. [41]

Located on Romney Pike west of Winchester, Elmwood was a spacious, white-painted brick house that contained five rooms downstairs and an equal number upstairs. Autie and Libbie occupied a front room, across the main hall from his office on the first floor, with Mrs. Bacon and Rebecca Richmond sharing a room on the same level, and the staff members and Mr. and Mrs. Ward in second-story rooms. The Custers and their guests dined in one room while the general's officers had a mess room adjacent to their bedrooms. Elmwood provided them with ample space, more than at Long Meadow. [42]

As February neared an end, however, war's reality returned. From

City Point, Grant had reiterated his concern about the railroads that supplied Lee's army at Petersburg, proposing to Sheridan a cavalry raid upon the Virginia Central Railroad and the James River Canal. Sheridan concurred with the plan, assuring the general-in-chief that he was "very certain" the railroad and canal could be destroyed, but he would have to wait until the weather abated and the snow melted. By the twenty-fifth, the snow was gone, and Sheridan issued detailed instructions to his subordinate officers about ammunition, forage, and number of wagons. He ordered that preparations be completed by 6 A.M., February 27.[43]

To augment Custer's division, Sheridan assigned Colonel Henry Capehart's brigade of the Second Division to the Third Division. Custer welcomed the four veteran regiments, but there was irony in the transfer of the brigade. Since November, the Michigan Brigade had sought reassignment to Custer's command, with officers of the regiments endorsing letters to Wesley Merritt, requesting to be "with our old well tried and favorite commander." In January, rumors circulated in the camps that they would be placed under Custer. "We are all glad of it," stated a member of the brigade, "for the Michigan men think he is the best general there is." But Sheridan never actually ordered the transfer, probably because of Merritt's understandable objection to losing a solid, experienced command. When the cavalry marched, however, Merritt no longer commanded the division, having been appointed acting cavalry chief in Alfred Torbert's absence on leave. Thomas Devin, a fine, reliable brigadier, led the First Division.[44]

During breakfast at Elmwood on Sunday, February 26, Custer informed Libbie's parents—Daniel Bacon had recently joined them—and Rebecca Richmond that the army would march the next morning at six o'clock and that they should prepare to leave by train for Washington as soon as the cavalry departed. Later that morning, Custer held a review of Pennington's and Colonel John J. Coppinger's brigade and, when it was concluded, told his officers of the movement. Returning to Elmwood, Custer gathered Libbie, their guests, and staff officers for a photograph that was taken while they stood on the steps of Elmwood's porch.[45]

Nearly 10,000 cavalrymen and horse artillerists, with cannon, wagons, and ambulances, filed into column on the morning of February 27. It was an imposing display of power, this Army of the Shenandoah on the march. Sheridan had informed Grant earlier that "the cavalry officers say the cavalry was never in such good condition," and they knew of what they spoke. In armament, horseflesh, experience, prowess, and leadership, the horsemen were a matchless command; no mounted unit on either side could equal them. A Winchester woman watched them pass on this morning and noted, "I witnessed one of the grandest spectacles that can be imagined as they were leaving—10,000 cavalry passing our house four abreast, thoroughly equipped in every detail." The mounts' coats glistened, the accoutrements "shone like gold." "It was a grand sight, requiring hours in passing."[46]

"Uncle Tommy" Devin's First Division led the march, trailed by Custer's Third Division and the wagon train. Before he departed, Custer made his farewells to Libbie, her parents, and Rebecca. Neither he nor Libbie knew how long this separation would last, but she was returning to her former boardinghouse, owned by a Mrs. Hyatt, in the capital, and there she would wait, with her fears, as a good soldier's wife. She believed that he would be in less danger now that he commanded a division.[47]

The Federals bivouacked for the night at Woodstock. Custer's division rode in the advance on the twenty-eighth, with the march slowed by a difficult crossing of the North Fork of the Shenandoah River south of Mt. Jackson that resulted in the drowning of one man. Rain fell heavily on March 1, and the column crawled through mud that was fetlock deep on the horses. Late in the afternoon, beyond Harrisonburg, Coppinger's brigade encountered dismounted Confederate cavalry on the south bank of the North River. When the Yankees appeared, the Rebels torched a covered bridge over the stream, but Coppinger's men charged on horseback, routing the enemy and saving the structure. The entire command bedded down four miles north of Staunton.[48]

The mud-splattered Northerners entered Staunton on March 2. Here Sheridan learned that Jubal Early and a patchwork force held Waynesborough, several miles to the east on the road through Rockfish Gap in the Blue Ridge to Charlottesville. Grant had wanted Sheridan to capture Lynchburg, due south of Staunton, to wreck the canal and railroads there, and then to proceed into North Carolina and join William Sherman's forces. In Staunton, however, Sheridan decided to march east and engage Early. He offered various explanations later for the decision, but as one historian has argued, he probably never intended to march to Lynchburg or into North Carolina.[49]

While details destroyed quartermaster and commissary stores, Sheridan conferred with Custer, ordering the latter to "ascertain something definite in regard to the position, movements, and strength of the enemy, and, if possible, destroy the railroad bridge over the South River at that point." Promising Sheridan that he would find Early, Custer mounted his division, leading it toward Waynesborough. Rain and sleet pelted the riders as they slogged through the mud. The Yankees halted before the Rebel position about two o'clock, and Custer surveyed Early's line. The redoubtable Confederate warrior had two brigades of infantry, a dozen cannon, and a handful of cavalry, roughly 2,000 men in total, on a ridge east of the river and town. Early meant to fight, but he had his back to a swollen river and both flanks unsecured.[50]

Custer's reconnaissance detected a gap between the river and Early's left flank. While the Second Brigade, commanded by Colonel William Wells, skirmished with the Confederates, Custer sent Lieutenant Colonel Edward W. Whitaker with the Second Ohio, Third New Jersey, and First Connecticut, all armed with Spencers, into woods opposite the gap with orders to attack, dismounted, at a signal. Whitaker had been serving as Custer's chief of staff less than a month, but the Connecticut officer was capable, with a distinguished record as a cavalryman. The three regiments filed into the trees, formed into a battle line, and waited. Along the road, Custer aligned the Eighth New York on horseback for a mounted charge.[51]

At Custer's signal, bugler Joseph Fought sounded the attack. The New Yorkers urged their mounts forward through the muddy road, and Whitaker's command broke from the trees, firing the Spencers and ascending the ridge. "So sudden was our attack and so great was the enemy's surprise," reported Custer, "that but little time was offered for resistance." Early's line disintegrated upon contact—so much had been drained from his veterans from Winchester to Cedar Creek that they had nothing left to give. A Confederate officer admitted subsequently that it was "one of the most terrible panics and stampedes" he had witnessed in the war. Custer added two mounted regiments to the assault, and the Federals rode down and captured hundreds of Rebels, many of whom simply threw down their arms, waiting for their captors. Early eluded the pursuers, a beaten man, riding alone from his final battlefield.[52]

"I never saw men in better humor than these Yankees were," asserted a Rebel prisoner. Their mood was understandable as they looked around at the haul they had seized. Over 1,200 captives, 11 cannon, 17 battle flags, and approximately 150 wagons, including Early's headquarters wagon, from which Custer was presented the Confederate general's chess set. As the Federals corralled the captives and vehicles, Captain George B. Sanford of Sheridan's staff rode into Waynesborough and met Custer, who asked if Sheridan was nearby. When Sanford replied that he was en route, Custer reported the number of prisoners, flags, and cannon seized. The aide turned to find Sheridan, to whom he repeated the general's figures. Minutes later, as Sanford recounted it, "up came Custer himself with his following, and in the hands of his orderlies, one to each, were the seventeen battle flags streaming in the wind. It was a great spectacle and the sort of thing which Custer thoroughly enjoyed."[53]

Union casualties amounted to nine killed and wounded in the engagement that Sheridan described as "this brilliant fight." The Northerners encamped in the Staunton-Waynesborough area. Before he slept, Custer invited Chaplain Theodore J. Holmes of the First Connecticut Cavalry to his tent. They prayed and read a chapter from the Bible together. "He and I alone with God," Custer wrote to Libbie, "gave thanks for the victory."[54]

Chapter

12

"THE BEST

CAVALRY GENERAL

IN THE ARMY"

■ The grave of Thomas Jefferson lay below the crest of his beloved little mountain, on his estate called Monticello outside of Charlottesville, Virginia. Along with James Madison and other of the Founding Fathers, Jefferson had provided the intellectual underpinnings for the states'-rights doctrine. In time, their fellow Southerners advanced the idea, advocating it as a defense of their property and as a rationale for the dissolution of the Union. But on the afternoon of March 3, 1865, Jefferson's neighbors beheld the consequences of that principle.

Throughout that rainy, cold Friday, the rumor skittered through Charlottesville of the approach of Union cavalry. Mayor Christopher L. Fowler and members of the city council conferred while the faculty of the University of Virginia gathered to plead for the protection of the institution's buildings. Stories of the destruction of dwellings and outbuildings across the Blue Ridge Mountains in the Shenandoah Valley fueled the anxieties. Finally, at three o'clock, on Ivy Road, a column of blue-clad riders appeared—dark figures, at first, the vanguard perhaps of a terrible ordeal. Mayor Fowler and the councilmen met the Union commander, Brevet Major General George Custer, who accepted the town's surrender and assured the delegation that personal property would not be vandalized.[1]

The Yankees had been on the march since early morning from across the mountains, slowed by the burning of railroad bridges and military stores, and, in a trooper's words, "awful roads." When the meeting ended with the civilian officials, Custer led his division through the beautiful community as the residents watched in silence. "The male population of the town," remarked an Ohio private, "seemed to be made up of one-armed and one-legged Rebels." Chief of Staff Edward Whitaker posted guards at each intersection and on the university's grounds. The troopers scattered a contingent of Confederate cavalry before bivouacking near Monticello, which soon attracted crowds of curious Northerners. Behind Custer's men came Philip Sheridan, the First Cavalry Division, and the wagons. The home of the third president of the United States belonged to the Union once again.[2]

The cavalry occupied Charlottesville until March 6. While the Federals spared the town, they destroyed miles of railroad north and south of Charlottesville, burning ties, twisting rails into incongruous shapes, leveling bridges, and wrecking culverts. March 6 dawned clear and warm, and with bands playing national songs and with regimental colors unfurled, Sheridan's horsemen marched away from Charlottesville, cantering south toward Lynchburg. "The roads [are] still in a horrible condition," reported a newspaperman with the column, but by the eighth, the Yankees reached the James River at New Market, roughly thirty miles northeast, or downstream, from Lynchburg.[3]

Once at New Market, Sheridan had planned to cross the James at either of two bridges in the region, move overland to the Appomattox River, destroy the Southside Railroad that supplied Lee's army at Petersburg, and unite with Grant's forces at the Cockade City. Confederate troops, however, had burned both spans, and Union scouts reported the presence of enemy infantry and a cavalry division in Lynchburg. When a pontoon bridge, laid by his engineers, reached only the midpoint of the swollen stream, Sheridan abandoned his designs. He was, as he stated, "master of all the country north of the James River," and decided to join Grant by marching east along the river, inflicting as much damage as he could to the canal and the Virginia Central Railroad. This section of Virginia had been spared from the fist of Union power until now.[4]

From March 9 to March 18, through Scottsville, Columbia, Frederick's Hall Station, Ashland to White House on the Pamunkey River, northeast of Richmond, the Federals carried war's wrath. "Continuous rain" churned roads into quagmires, hampered the burning of railroad

ties, buildings, and bridges, and produced miserable conditions in campsites. As they neared Richmond's defenses, they clashed with groups of
Confederates. In a skirmish at Ashland on the fifteenth, Custer's mount
tripped in a hole, turning a complete somersault and pinning the general beneath it. If the horse had struggled to rise, it would have crushed
Custer under its weight, but his staff members calmed the animal and
rolled him off their commander. On March 18, the sun rose in a clear
sky, and the spirits of the men soared when they reached the Pamunkey
River, where gunboats and transports were anchored. Rations were
issued, and the next morning the cavalrymen filed across a replanked
railroad bridge, settling into camp for a deserved rest. In the evening
some bands played "Auld Lang Syne" and "Home, Sweet Home."[5]

The *New York Times* correspondent who accompanied the troopers
declared at raid's end that "the command to-day is as ready for field
service as it was when it first marched out of Winchester." In his report,
Wesley Merritt was effusive in his praise, describing it as "a campaign
which, for brilliancy of conception and perfect success in execution,
has never been equaled in the operations of cavalry in this or any other
country." Years later, Sheridan stated in his memoirs that "the hardships
of this march far exceeded those of any previous campaigns by the
cavalry." In Sheridan's view, the men overcame incessant rains, flooded
streams, and bottomless roads, destroyed a Confederate force at Waynesborough and inflicted incalculable damage to the Confederate war
effort.[6]

While in camp at White House, Custer wrote to Libbie. They had
been apart nearly a month, and he had had few opportunities to write
to her during the raid. Among a collection of Custer correspondence
are two fragments of letters, neither of which retain their dates. It would
appear that one or both of them could have been written during the
expedition. If not, Custer's words reveal, nevertheless, his sexual
yearning for Libbie and his frankness in expressing it. The authenticity
of each fragment is unquestionable, while the contents provide a
glimpse into their physical relationship during the initial years of marriage.

"I am longing and anxiously hoping for the time to come when I
can be with my darling little one again," he confided to her. "It seems
so long since I saw her and had 'Just one.' I do not think the squirrel
you sent me can satisfy the want and cravings of 'our mutual friend.'

What would I not give Just for one kiss from those dear lips." And at another time, written on a Sunday, he confessed, "Oh I do want one so badly. I know *where* I would kiss somebody if I was with her tonight." [7]

Custer was fond also of boasting of his accomplishments to Libbie, undoubtedly to impress his young wife. On March 18, as the cavalry bivouacked across the river from White House, he recounted the expedition. "Our raid has been a chain of successes, and the 3rd Division has done all the fighting," he wrote. "I wish you could see your boy's headquarters now. My flag is floating over the gate, and near it, ranged along the fences, are 16 battle-flags, captured by the 3rd Division. Neither was Genl. Sheridan nor Genl. Merritt within 10 miles when these captures were made. Nor did they know what I was doing. . . . The 3rd stands higher than ever, in advance all the time."

He estimated that his men had captured 3,000 Rebels, with a loss of fewer than 30 Federals. "Never have I witnessed such enthusiasm. . . . I thought they—men and officers—would throw themselves under my horse's feet. Genl. Sheridan said 'Old Custer is a trump.' And 'Custer, that command is just crazy at being with, etc., etc.' Oh, my angel, I have the most glorious Division. They behaved splendidly. I am more than repaid for the trouble I took last winter. Genl. Sheridan and others speak of the difference between it and others." [8]

Within a few days, Custer penned another letter to Libbie, enclosing with it a letter he had received from Theodore J. Holmes, the chaplain with whom Custer prayed on the night after Waynesborough. Holmes was leaving the service and wanted to offer his gratitude for, as he stated, "the privilege of the relation to you afforded by the past weeks." The time "has enabled me to know you better," Holmes wrote, "and has made me respect you even more heartily than before. I cannot express my gratefulness to the Almighty that He should have made you such a General and such a man. I rejoice with the 3rd Division, with the army, with the whole country in the splendid military genius that has your name glorious in the history of the War. But even more I rejoice in the position you have taken deliberately, and, I believe, finally, in regard to a moral and religious life." Proud of Holmes's gracious words, Custer asked Libbie to share the letter with family and friends in Monroe. [9]

In Washington, meanwhile, Libbie enjoyed the company of Rebecca Richmond, attended inaugural activities, and fretted about Autie's safety. On March 4, she and Rebecca stood near President Abraham Lincoln as he took the oath for a second term and delivered his eloquent address. Two days later, they went to the inaugural ball at the Patent Office, escorted by Senator Zachariah Chandler, with whom Libbie danced "simply out of etiquette." While the Union cavalry marched from Winchester to White House, Libbie and Rebecca traced the route on a map that they had in their room. In one of Libbie's letters to Autie, she admonished him: "Don't expose yourself so much in battle. Just do your duty, and don't rush out so daringly. Oh, Autie, we must die together." [10]

When the cavalry arrived at White House, Sheridan forwarded the seventeen captured battle flags, carried by the troopers who seized them, to Washington, where the men presented each one in a ceremony at Secretary of War Edwin Stanton's office. Libbie attended and was introduced by Stanton as "the wife of the gallant General." "Oh, what a happy day that was—the proudest of my life," she exclaimed to Autie. As the individual troopers stepped forward with a flag, an official read, "Brevet Major-General Custer commanding." "I could hardly keep from crying out my praise of my boy," she wrote to him. "But I knew it was a conspicuous place, so tried to behave as quiet and unassuming as I could." When she prepared to leave, Libbie remarked to Stanton that she was waiting for a letter from her husband. "General Custer is writing lasting letters in the pages of his country's history," the Secretary responded. [11]

Sheridan's command stayed at White House a week, recuperating, gleaning disabled horses from the ranks, and sending dismounted troopers to remount depots. On March 25, the Federals started south, crossing the James River on a pontoon bridge the next day. On the twenty-seventh, they rejoined the army, filing over the Appomattox River to City Point. Confederate artillerists spotted the column and greeted the Yankees with "their great camp kettle shells" that inflicted few casualties. They camped in the army's rear, foraged, and welcomed paymasters. [12]

At City Point, as the cavalry rode in, Grant conferred with William Sherman, who had journeyed to headquarters from North Carolina. Determined to finish Lee and his army as soon as possible, the general-in-chief had summoned his friend, whose campaign during the previous four months had been a giant swath of destruction through Georgia and South Carolina, to coordinate future movements. Sherman stated that his armies could begin marching through North Carolina by April 10, modifying the direction of the movement according to circumstances at Petersburg. If Grant forced Lee to abandon the city, Sherman would endeavor to intercept the Rebels; if Lee repulsed Grant's offensive, Sherman would unite his command with the commanding general's. Grant approved, and Sherman boarded a steamer for North Carolina.[13]

Grant, however, would not wait until Sherman could advance. If he could stretch Lee's lines far enough, they might snap, and Petersburg and Richmond would be doomed. Consequently, on March 28, Grant ordered another westward sidle against the Confederate right front, utilizing the Second and Fifth infantry corps and Sheridan's cavalry. The general-in-chief targeted the crossroads of Dinwiddie Court House and the Southside Railroad beyond for the horsemen, instructing Sheridan to hit the enemy with every unit he had if the Southerners came out from behind their fieldworks. Grant expected and desired a counterstrike by Lee, but if the Confederate general chose to defend the works, he gave Sheridan discretionary orders.[14]

Sheridan's 9,000 officers and men marched at 5 A.M. on the twenty-ninth, along roads and across country, halting for the night beyond Rowanty's Creek. Grant had added the Second Cavalry Division, under Sheridan's old friend and Valley comrade, George Crook, to the strike force, and Crook's men paced the movement, with Custer's division trailing Thomas Devin's, guarding the wagon train. During the night, a heavy rainstorm blew in, continuing in torrents throughout the hours of darkness. Custer slept on two rails, with a stick for a pillow, covered by a poncho. When he awoke on the morning of the thirtieth, he met Eliza, remarking that he had thought of Libbie as soon as he arose. "Oh of course you would think of Miss Libbie the first thing," the servant grumbled, "and I expect you wanted her there with you . . . and she just as willing, she'd have said 'Oh, isn't this nice!' "[15]

"Never did I see harder rain in my life," remembered an Ohio sergeant of the downpours on the thirtieth. Custer's men struggled all day with the wagons, inching the vehicles forward. "Wagons in the mud up to the Hubs," recounted a trooper, "and men with Rails or poles lifting the wheels out only to be repeated a few feet farther on. The men in mud up to their knees, and the atmosphere blue with the Curses issuing from men and officers alike." By nightfall, Custer had halted the column six miles from Dinwiddie Court House, where Sheridan had encountered Confederate infantry north of the village toward Five Forks.[16]

Peter Boehm overtook Custer's division as it bivouacked in the mud. Recovered from his wound, Custer's former bugler was now a second lieutenant and was reporting for duty as an aide. Boehm had traveled from Washington, and when he met Custer, he presented the general with a new headquarters flag, sewn by Libbie. The guidon was of red and blue silk, with white crossed sabers on both sides and edged with white cord. "What renders it infinitely dear to me is that it is the work of my darling's hands," Custer wrote to Libbie.[17]

Before Boehm had arrived, Custer found a dry place and wrote a letter to Libbie, relating to her the incident with Eliza and the day's march. At the end, he responded to one of her recent letters, the contents of which can be surmised by his reply:

> I am glad to hear that there is a safe place upon Somebodys carpet because as that lady remarked in reference to piercing ears etc there are a great many ways of *doing things,* some of which I believe are not generally known. I know a certain young lady who had never worn ear rings and when the piercing was about to be performed was quite nervous both as to the time and manner of *doing* such *things.* How I smile sometimes when riding along as I think of the simplicity with which certain queries were proposed by an anxious search after information. I hope to test the truth of Somebodys statement relative to the condition of the carpet in Somebodys room.[18]

Rain began falling again before sunrise on March 31. At Dinwiddie Court House, Sheridan pushed brigades from Devin's and Crook's divisions north and west toward Five Forks. As Grant had foreseen, Lee had decided to give battle along the Confederate right flank, shifting infantry and cavalry units to Five Forks. If the intersection, located six miles north of Dinwiddie Court House, fell to the Federals, Lee's entire front at Petersburg and the Southside Railroad, his main supply line, would be in danger. The collision came on the afternoon of the thirty-first, when Southern infantry and cavalry assailed Sheridan's horsemen. The Rebels shoved the Yankees south toward Dinwiddie Court House, and Sheridan called on Custer for two brigades as support.[19]

Custer and his staff rode ahead of the regiments, met Sheridan in town, and received orders to deploy along the road to Five Forks. When his units arrived, Custer posted Henry Capehart's brigade on a ridge to the left of the road and Alexander Pennington's on the right in advance of Capehart's line. To the front, one of Crook's brigades was retiring before Major General George Pickett's gray-clad infantrymen. Peter Boehm of Custer's staff spurred forward, carrying the new headquarters flag, and tried to rally Crook's men. Rebel bullets tore the silk banner, with one of them clipping off Libbie's name, which she had sewn on it. The retreating Federals halted on the ridge to the right and rear of Pennington, and for his bravery, Boehm would be awarded the Medal of Honor thirty years later.[20]

Sheridan joined Custer about this time and, according to a staff officer, stated loudly, "General! General! You understand? I want you to *give* it to them." Custer reacted impatiently and replied, "Yes, yes, I'll give it to them." But before Custer could attack, Pickett's Virginians charged, driving back Pennington's men. The Northerners halted on the ridge beside Capehart's brigade and began piling up rails for a barricade. The Confederates had paused, but it was only momentarily. As they advanced toward the ridge, Custer, Sheridan, Wesley Merritt, and staff officers rode along the line, encouraging the troopers, who cheered. A Union battery opened fire, and the dismounted horsemen triggered a volley. The Virginians reeled, pulled back, regrouped, and came on a second time. The Yankees lashed the ranks with carbine fire, and Pickett ordered a withdrawal. Custer counterattacked, but the fighting soon ended as darkness settled in. In his report, Sheridan cited Merritt and the three division commanders for their "courage and ability."[21]

Shortly after the combat drained away, Colonel Horace Porter of Grant's staff met Sheridan behind Custer's line. Porter had been sent by the general-in-chief to ascertain the situation on the army's left flank. The day's action may not have gone as Sheridan wanted, but he saw opportunity for his command. "This force," the Irishman contended, pointing toward the Rebels, "is in more danger than I am—if I am cut off from the Army of the Potomac, it is cut off from Lee's army, and not a man in it should ever be allowed to get back to Lee. We at last have drawn the enemy's infantry out of its fortifications and this is our chance to attack it." He asked for an infantry corps, and Porter responded that Major General Gouverneur Warren's Fifth Corps could be brought up. With that settled, Porter returned to headquarters, describing his conversation with Sheridan to Grant, who issued the orders through George Meade to Warren.[22]

Warren's 12,000 men marched that night on Boydton Plank Road toward Five Forks. Delayed by the necessity of rebuilding a bridge over a stream, the van of the Union infantry approached the Confederate position at seven o'clock on April 1. Pickett, meanwhile, had learned of Warren's advance and withdrew his men into the fieldworks along White Oak Road at the crossroads. The Virginian had five brigades of infantry, three divisions of cavalry, and ten cannon, roughly 10,000 men, with orders from Lee to hold Five Forks "at all hazards."[23]

From Dinwiddie Court House, Custer's division led the cavalry, nudging Pickett's rear guard into the works. Halting in woods several hundred yards south of White Oak Road, Custer strung out a skirmish line and deployed his brigades in line west of the road from the courthouse. The dismounted Yankees probed forward, igniting musketry from the Southerners. "The enemy had evidently resolved to oppose our farther advance with the greatest determination," he reported. Devin's two brigades soon filed into position on Custer's right, connecting with the Fifth Corps. The horse soldiers gnawed at the Rebel works throughout the afternoon, waiting to hear the sounds of Warren's assault.[24]

Phil Sheridan possessed a short fuse, and it had been clipped to a nub with the delays along Warren's front. During the afternoon, he visited the corps commander, prodded Warren to hurry the deployment, and ordered Ranald Mackenzie's cavalry division to support the infantry's right flank. He instructed Warren to hit the Rebels with the entire corps. Finally, at 4:15 P.M., the Fifth Corps rolled forward, and the woods around Five Forks exploded in fury.[25]

When Wesley Merritt heard the gunfire, he directed Pennington's brigade to charge. Custer had planned to use the brigade as support for his attack against the Confederate right flank, but Merritt's orders precluded the movement. Twice Pennington's troopers attacked on foot, blasted back each time by what an Ohioan thought was "the most infernal fire it was ever my lot to be under." Regrouping, the veterans plunged into the woods a third time. By now, however, Warren's soldiers had caved in the Confederate left, unraveling the Southern line from east to west. With Devin's brigades on their right, Pennington's troopers poured over the works, grabbing clumps of prisoners and silencing a pair of cannon.[26]

On the Union left, meanwhile, Custer mounted the brigades of William Wells and Henry Capehart, leading them forward at a trot. Clearing the woods, Custer's men swung toward the Confederate right flank along White Oak Road. Before them were cleared fields that extended to the enemy line in woods. The division commander rode to Wells's brigade, ordering the Eighth and Fifteenth New York Cavalry to charge three Rebel cannon. As the New Yorkers spurred forward, Custer shouted to them, "Yell like hell." Southern infantry and cannon, however, repulsed the thrust. The horsemen tried a second time with similar results.[27]

Custer now shifted Capehart's brigade farther to the west, aligning it on Wells's left flank. With the troopers came the unit's band, which Custer placed on a knoll within range of Confederate fire. The musicians struck up "Hail Columbia," the signal for the attack. "A perfect sheet of lead" poured from the enemy line, with most of the bullets whizzing over the Federals' heads. Two of the bandsmen, however, were wounded by the volley, and as their leader informed Custer that night, "General, we were playing 'Hail Columbia' when suddenly turning around I saw that all except three of my men left, and accordingly we followed them."[28]

As the notes faded to the rear, the Northerners charged into a "withering fire." Custer rode in the forefront with several of his staff. Peter Boehm, whose courage had rallied the men the day before, was severely wounded by a bullet in the right elbow. The Yankees closed on the works until a Confederate cavalry division advanced against Capehart's left flank. In a hand-to-hand melee, the Rebels stopped the Federals, and as Custer reported, "for some time success was varied and uncertain." On their right, however, Union infantry and cavalry had seized the enemy barricades, scouring the line westward. The Southern horsemen withdrew, and Custer's men pursued for six miles. Pickett's position at Five Forks had been crushed under an onslaught promised by Phil Sheridan.[29]

During the fighting, Sheridan had followed the infantry, shouting to them, "See the Sons of Bitches run! Give them Hell, boys!" The Yankees complied, shredding to pieces Pickett's ranks, capturing at least

4,500 men, 13 battle flags, and 6 cannon. Despite the magnitude of the victory, Sheridan was furious at Warren, relieving the veteran general of command. It would be fourteen years until a court of inquiry exonerated Warren. For the present, however, Sheridan appointed a new corps commander and began preparations for a morning march. Custer joined Sheridan at headquarters along White Oak Road, lying on the ground and covering his face with his long hair. Sleep was a welcome companion.[30]

For nearly ten months, Lee's Army of Northern Virginia had defended Petersburg and Richmond, walking daily in the trenches with death and maiming. The Confederates had been since the summer of 1862 the finest army in the country, but the siege had reduced the ranks to shadows, and when the Federals came on April 2, Lee's men gave what they could a final time. Individual units fought with a valor that had been the army's soul, buying time for Lee to abandon Petersburg and save enough of the army for a retreat. Shielded by the darkness— perhaps the blackest of nights in the army's history—the Southerners fled, crossing the Appomattox River and turning west to escape their victorious opponent. The next day, the Yankees occupied Petersburg and Richmond, a city ravaged by a conflagration. If Lee's army could be brought to bay, the Confederacy was finished.

Grant extended the fist of Union power on April 3. To intercept the Rebels, Grant turned to Sheridan and the cavalry—the four divisions of Devin, Crook, Custer, and Mackenzie—approximately 12,000 officers and men. They were, as Wesley Merritt asserted, "as good cavalry as the world ever saw," a weapon Lee could no longer match. Already, they were in pursuit, pushing north and west from Five Forks on the second, hounding the rearguard units south of the Appomattox River. Sheridan had forged them for such an operation, and now Grant sounded the call.[31]

Custer's division led the pursuit on April 3, overtaking the Rebels at Namozine Church, a few miles south of the river. On the second, Custer and Merritt had exchanged words when the latter asked Custer to relieve Devin's division and to engage the enemy. Custer told Merritt to "finish your own work." On this day, however, the work belonged to Custer, and his men, spearheaded by Wells's brigade, routed an outnumbered brigade of North Carolina cavalry, capturing 350 men, a cannon, and the flag of the Second North Carolina Cavalry. In the action, Tom Custer leaped his horse over the works and forced about a dozen Southerners to surrender with the colors, an act that earned him a Medal of Honor.[32]

While the Confederate units marched northwest toward Amelia Court House to join Lee's main army on the fourth, the Union cavalry rode west toward Jetersville along the Richmond & Danville Railroad. The Federal horsemen moved slowly as their column met the Second Corps, resulting in a jammed roadway. Camping for rest and food in the evening, the cavalry remounted at 11 P.M., riding all night and arriving at Jetersville at 8 A.M. on the fifth. Sheridan began preparations for an attack on some Confederate units, but George Meade countermanded the order until the infantry arrived. By nightfall, the bulk of the Union army was bivouacked around Jetersville.[33]

With Grant at Jetersville, Lee redirected the retreat toward Farmville, where he hoped to secure supplies and recross to the north side of the Appomattox River at High Bridge. On roughly parallel routes, the opponents moved on April 6. The roads were a "sea of mud," but by late afternoon, Sheridan's cavalry and the Sixth Corps had overtaken the troops of Confederate generals Richard S. Ewell and Richard H. Anderson in bottomlands along Sayler's Creek. Ewell's and Anderson's commands had become separated from the rest of the army and were caught in a vise of Union infantry and cavalry, including Custer's division. The Rebels fought fiercely but were overwhelmed, with approximately 8,000 surrendering. "Yelling like Indians," the Yankees grabbed scores of wagons, more than a dozen cannon, stands of colors, and six generals. When Lee witnessed the debacle, he exclaimed, "My God! Has the army dissolved?"[34]

For a second time in three days, Tom Custer plunged into the combat. Urging his mount over the works, Tom spurred toward a Confederate color bearer and, grabbing the flag, ordered the soldier to surrender. But the Rebel fired his rifle, with the bullet grazing Tom's cheek and neck. Tom killed the man with his pistol and rode away with the flag. For the action, he was awarded a second Medal of Honor.[35]

Days later, Custer recounted his brother's exploits in a letter to Libbie's father. "You might infer that Tom lacks caution, judgment," Autie stated. "On the contrary he possesses both in an unusual degree. His excellent judgment tells him when to press the enemy, and when to be moderate. Of all my staff officers he is quickest in perceiving at a glance the exact state of things. This trait frequently excites comment." Continuing, the older brother admitted that he had had concerns about Tom's conduct in battle and his personal habits. "But now I am as proud of him as I can be, as soldier, brother," affirmed Autie. "He has quit the use of tobacco, is moderate in drink, is respected and admired by officers and all who come in contact with him." [36]

On the night of April 6, at his campsite, Custer entertained an academy classmate, Frank Huger, an artillery colonel, and Major General Joseph Kershaw, an infantry division commander. Custer shared a meal and blankets with the two Confederate officers. Kershaw described his host as "a spare, lithe and sinewy figure, about medium height, bright, dark blue eyes, even restless," and with "a quick, nervous, energetic movement, and an air of hauteur, telling of the habit of command." After breakfast on the seventh, when Custer prepared to leave his guests, thirty troopers, each carrying a captured battle flag and one of them with two, appeared at the bivouac. When Kershaw inquired about them, Custer replied: "That is my escort for the day. It is my custom after a battle to select for my escort a sort of *garde de honeur* those men of each regiment who most distinguish themselves in action, bearing for the time, the trophies which they have taken from the enemy. These men are selected as the captors of the flags which they bear." With that, Custer shook Kershaw's hand and rode away, trailed by a cluster of star-crossed red flags. [37]

While Custer formed the division for the day's march, a long column of Confederate prisoners filed past the cavalrymen. The war had ended for them at Sayler's Creek, and as they plodded east, Custer ordered the band to play "Yankee Doodle," "Hail Columbia," and "Dixie." When the Southerners heard the final tune, "this called out rousing cheers from them," according to a Federal. "That is as near cheers as they ever come, but still it had a sharpness about it, reminding us of the rebel yell & causing us to clutch our carbines with nervous grasp." "It was impossible not to accord them respect as brave men," concluded the trooper. [38]

For their comrades still in the ranks with Lee, April 7 and 8 brought more miles of retreat in an effort to save what was beyond salvation. Like a dying giant, the army dragged itself west, crossing the Appomattox River beyond Farmville en route to Lynchburg, Lee's new destination. Two Union infantry corps trailed the Confederates north of the river while Sheridan's cavalry and the remaining infantry marched south of the stream. Sensing the mortal wound inflicted on the enemy at Sayler's Creek, Grant wrote Lee on the seventh, asking his opponent to surrender to avoid "any further effusion of blood." When Lee replied with a request for terms, Grant answered on the eighth, that "the men and officers surrendered shall be disqualified from taking up arms again" until exchanged.[39]

Late on the afternoon of April 8, Custer's division approached Appomattox Station on the Southside Railroad. The command had been on the march all day, leading the Union cavalry. By now, the strain of the past week showed on the faces of the men, including the tireless Custer. They sustained themselves with the belief that "the Confederate army was in its last throes." But they pushed toward the station, having learned from two of Sheridan's scouts that three trainloads of supplies were waiting at the depot for Lee's men.[40]

When the trains and station came into view, Custer rushed Pennington's brigade forward, directing the colonel of the Second New York to "go in, old fellow, don't let anything stop you," while sending the Second Ohio and Third New Jersey at a gallop around the station to prevent the escape of the trains toward Lynchburg. Obeying the orders, the New Yorkers went in, routing a handful of guards and seizing the engines. Volunteers clambered on board, stoked the furnaces, and started the trains down the tracks toward Farmville. From the prisoners, the Yankees learned that an enemy force lay northeast of the station.[41]

Custer, meanwhile, trailed the attack force until stopped by the screams of two women who were running down the road, claiming that soldiers were robbing their home. Jumping from his horse, Custer ran into the house, owned by a George Abbitt, grabbed one of the culprits, flattened him with a punch to the face, and then finding a second man, threw an ax that hit the thief on the head. The general had the pair arrested and ordered guards posted at the residence. Receiving the women's gratitude, Custer remounted, riding for the station.[42]

The seizure of the trains alerted the Confederates beyond the depot, and before long they shelled the tracks with artillery. The Southerners were Lee's surplus artillery, approximately one hundred cannon, under Brigadier General R. Lindsay Walker, a small brigade of cavalry, and a wagon train, posted on a ridge a half-mile from the station. Woods screened the opponents from each other before giving way to cleared fields directly in front of the Southern line. When Custer saw the artillery pieces and wagons before him, he decided to attack at once with Pennington's men, not waiting for his two other brigades to arrive.[43]

Pennington's New Yorkers and Ohioans went in first, through the woods and into a gale of artillery fire that blew them back. The Third New Jersey followed with similar results. Sobered by the repulses, Custer ceased the attack until Wells's and Capehart's regiments came up and deployed. It was dark, between eight and nine o'clock, when the Federals were ready. Custer spurred along the ranks, shouting, "Boys, the 3rd Div. must have those guns. I'm going to charge if I go alone." [44]

At a signal, the Yankees advanced in column of regiments into the woods. Walker's gunners unleashed charges of canister, the "most terrible" one officer believed he ever encountered. The cannon flashes outlined the oncoming horsemen. As usual, Custer rode in the forefront, with his men convinced that he would be killed in such an exposed position. But the artillery fire and carbine fire of the Rebels could not stop the assault by the entire division. Within minutes, the Yankees were among the gun crews and wagons, shooting or sabering those who would not surrender. Earlier, Walker had withdrawn most of the artillery pieces, but the troopers seized at least 24 cannon, 5 battle flags, nearly 200 wagons, and 1,000 prisoners. Some of the cavalry pursued the Rebels to Appomattox Court House, where they encountered Lee's infantry and were stopped. Devin's division reached the station and, with Custer's brigades, encamped. Lee's route to Lynchburg had been cut off.[45]

Phil Sheridan arrived at Appomattox Station as Custer's men gathered the captures. He ordered the cavalry posted toward the courthouse and then scribbled a dispatch to Grant, stating that if the infantry "can get up tonight we will perhaps finish the job in the morning. I do not think Lee means to surrender until compelled to do so." He forbade campfires, and the troopers slept on the ground with the reins of their mounts in their hands.[46]

At daybreak on April 9, Palm Sunday, Confederate infantry, backed by thirty cannon, advanced against the Federals. As Sheridan had predicted to Grant, Lee intended to open a gap in the Union line through which his army might escape. The Southerners came on for one more time, but it was not to be. The infantry that Sheridan wanted had arrived and, replacing the cavalry, stopped the Rebels. Proud, defiant to the end, the Army of Northern Virginia now belonged to history.[47]

Custer had brought his division forward about eight o'clock. The twenty-five-year-old general rode at the front of the column, trailed by his honor guard with the captured enemy battle flags. Halting on a ridge that overlooked the Confederate position, Custer prepared to attack according to Sheridan's instructions. Rifle and artillery fire indicated that the Southerners may have not accepted the inevitable, and Sheridan was determined to settle it.[48]

Before Custer finished his deployment, however, Major Robert Sims, a Confederate staff officer, carrying a white towel on a stick, was escorted by a Federal officer to Custer. Sims stated that General Lee requested a suspension of hostilities. Custer offered his compliments to Lee, but replied that he was not the commander on the field and could not halt the attack unless Lee announced an unconditional surrender. Turning to Chief of Staff Edward Whitaker, Custer directed the lieutenant colonel to return with Sims to the enemy lines and to wait for a response.[49]

Sims led Whitaker to Generals James Longstreet and John Gordon, who informed the Federal officer that Lee had ridden to the rear to send a message to Grant for a truce and a meeting. According to Whitaker, both of the generals "assured me of an absolute surrender," and although Custer's chief of staff remained suspicious "of their good faith," he returned to the Union lines, met infantry officers, and announced the surrender. As Whitaker rode to find Custer, the news raced along the line, greeted by cheering. Reaching the cavalry division, Whitaker learned that Custer had entered the Confederate lines.[50]

Custer, meanwhile, had suspended the attack, and instead of waiting for Whitaker to return, rode forward with an orderly. His motivations for his action cannot be ascertained with certainty—he may have been concerned about Whitaker, but it would appear that ambition and a craving for glory led him into the enemy ranks. Meeting Major William H. Gibbes, a Confederate artillery officer who knew the general from the academy, Custer was escorted to Longstreet. The conversation between the cavalry commander and Lee's senior lieutenant resulted in a subsequent controversy. While Custer's defenders have dismissed the story as false, Confederate accounts of the meeting provide a version that seems creditable, supported by ample documentation.[51]

An eyewitness to the meeting between Custer and Longstreet described the conversation as "animated." According to Longstreet, Custer declared when they met, "In the name of General Sheridan I demand the unconditional surrender of this army."

"I am not the commander of this army," replied Longstreet, "and if I were would not surrender it to General Sheridan."

Custer repeated his demand, and now visibly irritated, Longstreet shot back that they were not whipped, and if Custer were not satisfied, he could attack. Longstreet then ordered him out of their lines, with Custer asking for protection during the return ride. Gibbes volunteered, escorting the Union general to the Federal position. A Confederate staff officer who was present asserted later that "if I ever saw a man with his tail between his legs it was Custer." [52]

Most likely, Custer wanted to be the officer who received the surrender of the Confederate army, but Longstreet possessed neither the authority nor the willingness to comply. In turn, Custer was embarrassed by the incident. Nevertheless, stillness came to the field, and during the afternoon, Lee met Grant in the home of Wilmer McLean and accepted the generous terms of surrender. Some accounts place Custer in the parlor during the negotiations, but he was not present, probably close at hand to the house, visiting with friends in the Confederate army. [53]

Sheridan was in the McLean residence, and when Lee and Grant departed, he took the oval-shaped pine table used by Grant, reportedly paying the owner $20 for it. The next day, Sheridan presented it to Custer as a gift for Libbie, enclosing a note, "My Dear Madam, I respectfully present to you the small writing table on which the conditions for the surrender of the Army of Northern Virginia were written by Lt. General Grant—and permit me to say, Madam, that there is scarcely an individual in our service who has contributed more to bring about this desirable result than your gallant husband." Libbie cherished the gift, and today it is among the collections of the Smithsonian Institution. [54]

The reconciliation of the sections began in the McLean home. For those with former friends in the opposing armies, the end offered an opportunity for a renewal. In particular, Custer sought academy classmates and acquaintances, welcoming them to his campsite. "He was always a boy," a Union officer wrote of Custer, "and absolutely free from harboring a spirit of malice, hatred or revenge." He told Libbie afterward that seven Confederate officers slept in his tent that night. [55]

Before he retired, Custer prepared a congratulatory letter to his men. "With profound gratitude toward the God of battles," he began, "by whose blessings our enemies have been humbled and our arms rendered triumphant, your commanding general avails himself of this his first opportunity to express to you his admiration of the heroic manner in which you have passed through the series of battles which to-day resulted in the surrender of the enemy's entire army. The record established by your indomitable courage is unparalleled in the annals of the war." Then, after recounting their accomplishments during the past six months and expressing a wish to return home, Custer concluded, "And now, speaking for myself alone, when the war is ended and the task of the historian begins; when those deeds of daring which have rendered the name and fame of the Third Cavalry Division imperishable, are inscribed upon the bright pages of our country's history, I only ask that my name be written as that of the commander of the Third Cavalry Division." [56]

Wesley Merritt praised Custer for his performance during the Appomattox Campaign, describing it in his report as "the gallant, daring, and rapid execution of the brave commander of the Third Division." Sheridan recommended Custer for promotion to brevet major general in the Regular Army, citing him for "personal gallantry and high ability" since the cavalry's departure from Winchester in February. The War Department concurred, and Custer received the brevet ranks of brigadier and major general. Congressman John A. Bingham, meanwhile, had urged Secretary of War Edwin Stanton to make Custer a full major general of volunteers. Stanton approved, but it was not confirmed by the Senate until February 23, 1866, to date from April 15, 1865. [57]

On April 12, the Confederates formally surrendered their arms and cannon in a ceremony at Appomattox Court House. By then, Sheridan's cavalry was en route to Petersburg, having started on the tenth. The horsemen retraced their route of the previous week, marching at a leisurely pace. On April 16, they learned of the assassination of President Abraham Lincoln on the fourteenth by John Wilkes Booth. The mood of the men darkened at the news, and rumblings of revenge stalked the camp. Two days later, they arrived at Petersburg and encamped. [58]

At Nottoway Court House, west of Petersburg, Libbie met Custer, having journeyed from Washington. During the two-day march that brought them to Petersburg, Libbie rode in a spring wagon beside her husband at the head of the column. Custer also welcomed back Captain Jacob Greene, who had been exchanged from a Confederate prison before the surrender. For Custer and his men, the six-day halt in the city was a necessity. Probably speaking for the entire corps, he wrote Ann Reed, "I never needed rest so much as I do now."[59]

While at Petersburg, Custer wrote to Judge Isaac Christiancy. Dated April 21, the letter was written as the government searched Virginia and Maryland for Lincoln's assassin and his fellow conspirators, and as the North clamored for all those that could be possibly linked to the plot, including officials of the fleeing Confederate government. Custer granted Christiancy permission to have the letter published, so when he composed it, he worded it for a national audience. After noting that the "deepest gloom" pervaded the army over Lincoln's death, he praised the martyred president, declaring that "I have been a firm and unconditional supporter of the President, and believe there is no man in the nation who could have brought us through the war to the present time so successfully and satisfactorily as Abraham Lincoln."

Custer endorsed President Andrew Johnson's policy "that treason is the blackest of crimes and that the traitors must be punished." He affirmed, "I believe I express the universal opinion of the army," continuing, "Extermination is the only true policy we can adopt toward the political leaders of the rebellion, and at the same time do justice to ourselves and to our posterity. All members of the rebellious government, editors of newspapers, and other outspoken supporters of the traitorous cause must face retribution. Our free government and free institutions shall be purged from every disloyal traitor."[60]

Radical Republicans in Congress and throughout the North surely welcomed the statement from one of the army's most renowned generals. With Jefferson Davis and his cabinet still uncaught, with Booth still free, and with General Joseph E. Johnston's Confederate army still in the field against Sherman in North Carolina, Custer's views reflected the sentiments of the military and civilian populace. No evidence exists that Custer believed otherwise, but such a public declaration could only receive approbation—a fact Custer understood. If doubts persisted about his acceptance of the administration's prosecution of the war, his words reinforced his combat record.

The situation in North Carolina compelled Grant to order Sheridan's

cavalry in that direction. On April 24, the horsemen marched southwest
out of Petersburg, but four days later Sheridan received confirmation of
Johnston's surrender. Returning to the Cockade City, the command
remained there until May 10. Authorities in Washington had decided
to honor the Union soldiers with a Grand Review through the city on
May 23 and 24. On May 21, the cavalry of the Army of the Potomac
passed through the capital, camping on the outskirts. The men cleaned
equipment, shined weapons, and endured a final inspection the next
day.[61]

Tuesday, May 23, belonged to the Army of the Potomac, George
Meade's army, the men who had endured the carnage of Antietam, the
hellfire of Fredericksburg, the ferocity of Gettysburg, and the slaughter
of the war's final year. From the Capitol, with its now finished dome,
to the reviewing stand in front of the White House, they marched
down Pennsylvania Avenue in serried ranks. Crowds thronged the side-
walks: "It really looked as if the whole North had emptied itself into
Washington for the purpose of honoring *us*," remembered a veteran. It
was a passing earned by those who marched.[62]

The cavalry was at its post, in the van, leading its comrades toward a
destination. Wesley Merritt rode at the forefront—Sheridan had been
ordered to Louisiana—and behind the commander came Custer and
the Third Division, with each member wearing a red necktie, the
command's adopted badge, in honor of its general. As they passed, the
onlookers shouted, "Cedar Creek! Winchester! Cedar Creek!" They
rode with a pride and self-assurance, believing, arguably with justification, that they belonged to the finest combat unit in the army.[63]

Custer sat on Don Juan, one of his favorite mounts, and as horse and
rider approached the reviewing stand, a woman stepped forward from
the crowd—accounts conflict—and tossed a wreath of evergreens and
flowers toward the famous general. Frightened by the wreath, Don Juan
bolted toward the dignitaries on the stand. Custer reined in Don Juan,
but dropped his sword and lost his hat. The crowd cheered and ap-
plauded his horsemanship, with some grumbling that the incident was
typical of the flamboyant cavalryman.[64]

When the Third Cavalry Division had passed in review, the command returned to its camp, where, as one member stated, the men
"took final leave of its beloved commander." Custer and Libbie rode
along the entire length of the division, receiving cheer after cheer. "The

scene was an affecting one," recalled a trooper, "and one long to be remembered." Custer spoke a few words, bade them a farewell, and spurred away. Already, he had orders to join Sheridan—the army would be his life for at least a while. For his men, disbandment and home awaited.[65]

In time, membership in either the Michigan Brigade or the Third Cavalry Division became the proudest association of the veterans' lives. Frayed red neckties, worn at reunions, symbolized a bond between the general and his men that future events and controversies never severed. Almost to a man, they believed that Custer was "the best Cavalry General in the Army," as one former officer declared. "He never asked his men to go where he would not lead them," an old trooper asserted about Custer, and to them, that mattered above all else.[66]

When they saw him for the last time as their commander, he was twenty-five years old, a major general who had attained that rank at an age younger than any other man in the army. Whatever doubts officers and men may have harbored about him when he was promoted to brigadier before Gettysburg, Custer had removed them with a combat prowess and a command leadership that was nearly, if not entirely, unequaled among brigade and division commanders in the cavalry corps. To be sure, Custer and fellow cavalry leaders rose to prominence against a foe that could no longer match the Federals in horseflesh and armament. But the dominance of the Union mounted units in the war's final eighteen months resulted from both the organization of the cavalry and the officers and men who filled its ranks. A measure of a warrior is the ability to exploit enemy weaknesses, and in this, Custer had few peers.

Combat fitted Custer as well as his distinctive uniform. Universally, the rank and file under him testified to his bravery, aggressiveness, calm demeanor, and instinctiveness in the fluid conditions of a battle. He learned early at Hunterstown the value of deliberateness, of reconnaissance, of preparation before an attack, and those attributes marked his generalship on most fields. But when the right time came to strike, Custer seized it, or as Jacob Greene, who rode beside him many times, perceptively noted, "When he set out to destroy an enemy, he laid hand on him as soon as possible, and never took it off. He knew the whole art of war."[67]

In Custer, the warrior magnified the man. His zest for life, his flamboyance, his affinity for gallantry and pageantry, his ambition, and his fearlessness were not only elements of the man but of the soldier. He was perhaps the war's last knight. "If there ever was any poetry or romance in war," Sheridan contended about Custer, "he could develop it." A soldier's duty merged with a personal quest for glory that made Custer a superb cavalry commander and a dashing, unmistakable hero. He accepted battle's terribleness because it was always, to him, a clarion call. When he shouted at Gettysburg, "Come on, you Wolverines," it was not an order, but an answer to a summons.[68]

A knight's quest required a cause, however. When Custer received the crowd's adulation at the Grand Review, peace had replaced war. The country was reuniting, and with peace, Americans resumed their historic mission, the progress defined as the conquest of a continent. Custer would travel west, into a land inhabited by a native population whose ways of life had defied understanding and had unsettled American consciences. Without a cause, George Custer traveled toward a sunset.

Chapter

13

RECONSTRUCTION

SOLDIER

■ "We were like children let out of school, and everything interested us," Libbie Custer wrote later of her and her husband's enjoyment of a steamboat trip down the Mississippi River at the end of May 1865. Neither of them had ever been on the river, and they were fascinated by the scenery and sights. When they arrived at New Orleans, the couple rented a room at the St. Charles Hotel, indulging themselves in the city's famous cuisine. Libbie admitted that she *"stuffed"* herself at a French restaurant. New Orleans was different, she thought, "everything has an air parisienne, and yet is very Southern in its architecture. To be cool is the one affect studied till it is reduced to a science." [1]

A block from the St. Charles in "an elegant mansion" was the head-quarters of Major General Philip Sheridan, and here George Custer reported upon his arrival. Sheridan had been ordered to New Orleans by General-in-Chief Ulysses S. Grant to eliminate Confederate units still operating in Texas—"the whole state should be scoured," as Grant put it—and if necessary, to be prepared for a campaign along the Rio Grande. For two years, thousands of French troops had occupied Mexico, overthrowing the government of Benito Juárez and installing Arch-duke Ferdinand Maximilian as emperor of Mexico. The French had come on the pretext of collecting debts owed to them by the Mexicans, but the real purpose was Louis Napoleon's designs to create a French empire in the Americas. While the Civil War raged, the Federal government objected officially to the French, but with peace in the United States, military intervention to remove Maximilian became an option. [2]

Grant entrusted the operation to Sheridan, who chose Custer and

Wesley Merritt as cavalry commanders. Custer had not expected the assignment, but when Sheridan asked "Would you like to go with me" in a confidential dispatch, he agreed. By the time Custer came to New Orleans, Sheridan had been designating units for the campaign. In mid-June, Sheridan telegraphed Grant that he had ordered Custer with 4,000 cavalry to Houston; Merritt with 4,000 cavalry to San Antonio; the Twenty-fifth Corps, numbering about 16,000 infantry and artillery, to Brownsville, across the Rio Grande from Matamoros; and 7,000 men of the Fourth Corps to Galveston and Houston.[3]

During the third week of June, the Custers, Eliza, and the general's staff left New Orleans by steamboat for Alexandria, Louisiana, on the Red River, the rendezvous site for the command. Located 120 miles downriver from Shreveport, Alexandria had been occupied by Union forces during the so-called Red River Campaign in the spring of 1864. The town and its residents had suffered under the occupation, with a number of houses either damaged or burned. A year later, the scars remained evident, and in Libbie's words, "we found everything a hundred years behind the times." The general selected a large, one-story, deserted house for headquarters and residence. It had a long, wide main hall, with spacious rooms and numerous windows and doors that "admit every bit of air stirring."[4]

The first contingent of troops arrived on June 23, with the remaining units filtering in during the next fortnight. The command consisted of five veteran volunteer regiments—First Iowa, Second Wisconsin, Seventh Indiana, Fifth and Twelfth Illinois Cavalry—which Custer organized into two brigades under Brigadier General James W. Forsyth, Sheridan's former chief of staff, and Colonel William Thompson. The length of service among the regiments varied from less than two years for the Seventh Indiana to nearly four years for the First Iowa.[5]

With the regiments, however, came a smoldering resentment. To the members, the Confederacy was finished, the war was over, and they deserved to be mustered out like other units in the army. Instead, they found themselves in the sweltering, mosquito-infested heat of Louisiana, with the possibility of a campaign into Texas and even Mexico. While at Memphis, the troopers of the Second Wisconsin had submitted a petition to be disbanded. When the cavalrymen arrived at Alexandria, they were in no mood for discipline, training, or restrictive orders. They had fought the battle, and now they wanted to go home.[6]

A confrontation with Custer occurred within twenty-four hours of the first companies' disembarkation at Alexandria. Local citizens complained to him on June 24 of the theft of property. He reacted by issuing an order that forbade foraging, unless authorized by his headquarters. "Every violation of this order will receive prompt and severe punishment," the general declared. "Owing to the delays of courts martial, and their impracticability when the command is unsettled, it is hereby ordered that any enlisted man violating the above order, or committing depredations upon the persons or property of citizens, will have his head shaved, and in addition will receive twenty-five lashes upon his back, well laid on." If any officer failed to report violations, he would be arrested and dishonorably dismissed from service.[7]

Determined to impose his will and authority from the outset, Custer had issued an arbitrary, inflammatory, and illegal order. The Articles of War of the United States Army required that any officer or enlisted man charged with the violations specified by Custer should be tried before a general court-martial or before a civil magistrate. Furthermore, the punishment of flogging had been abolished by an act of Congress in August 1861. With this action, Custer exceeded his authority and ignited a test of wills between himself and the rank and file of the regiments.[8]

In Custer's defense, he had received instructions from Sheridan to be conciliatory in the treatment of civilians and to enforce "rigid discipline among the troops, and to prevent outrages on private persons and property." Compounding his difficulties were a lack of rations and the noncooperation of many of the regimental officers. As a result, according to Custer in his report, which was supported by a statement of James Forsyth, "bands of soldiers" roamed the countryside, stealing from and threatening the inhabitants. "No citizen was safe in his own home, either during the day or night," Forsyth avowed. When he appealed to regimental commanders to punish those apprehended, the officers defended the men's actions, arguing that they should be allowed "a little liberty." "In no instance," he contended, "did my efforts in this direction succeed."[9]

When Custer acted, he incurred the wrath of the men. While at Alexandria, he had a deserter executed, but at the last moment spared the life of Lieutenant L. L. Lancaster, who was convicted by a court-martial of mutiny against the commander of the Second Wisconsin.

Had he not relented, members of the regiment threatened to kill the general, although Custer probably knew nothing about it. Lancaster was dishonorably discharged and sentenced to three years of hard labor at Dry Tortugas Prison. Sheridan, however, commuted the sentence, ordering his release in February 1866.[10]

After the incident, the men's hatred of Custer deepened, as rations remained scarce and of poor quality. By contrast, Libbie wrote to her parents that they had ample supply of fruits and vegetables, purchased cheaply, for headquarters. In fact, Libbie enjoyed the weeks at Alexandria, taking daily horseback rides with Autie and visiting former slaves with Eliza. But she noticed her husband's difficulties with the troops and wrote subsequently that "they hated us, I suppose. That is the penalty the commanding officer generally pays for what still seems to me the questionable privilege of rank and power."[11]

Although inadequately supplied and mounted, the command left Alexandria for Texas on August 8. The day before, Custer issued orders for the conduct of the march, directing in part that the column be closed up at all times, that no enlisted man could leave it on horseback, that no foraging parties were permitted, and that no fences could be used for firewood. If a soldier violated the orders, he would be dismounted and assigned to the "foot battalion" of unmounted men. The purpose of the strict march requirements, Custer informed the officers and men, was "to cultivate the most friendly feelings" of the inhabitants of the region through which they would pass.[12]

The march of 240 miles took nineteen days, much of it through country one trooper thought seemed "as if even God himself had abandoned it." During the initial leg, the column passed through vast pine forests, where the water was scarce and foul. Custer had the command move in the cool of the mornings and evenings, with drill after they encamped for the day. An Iowan claimed later that nothing during the war compared in hardship to this march to Hempstead, Texas, northwest of Houston. There were daily desertions. Unable to forage without risk of punishment, the men were frequently hungry because of the inadequate rations. Libbie Custer and Eliza endured it all, with a spring wagon specially fitted for the general's wife.[13]

Once they crossed the Trinity River, the country opened into broad, flat lowlands with better water. The cavalry reached Hempstead on the Houston & Texas Central Railroad on August 26, and established camp at Liendo, the plantation of Leonard Groce that had been used as a Confederate prison site during the war. The Groces occupied the house while the Custers and the regiments pitched tents along the stream. Later, when Libbie became ill, the Groces brought her into the house to be nursed until she recovered.[14]

On the twenty-eighth, the commissary issued hardtack and hog jowls to the men. The rations were not fit to eat, and numbers of the troopers foraged in the vicinity, including a group from the Seventh Indiana that killed a calf. When the owner protested to Custer, he investigated, arrested several, and had three of them flogged and their heads shaved. Two weeks later, a similar incident occurred, and two privates received twenty-five lashes. The anger of the men boiled toward Custer, with the lieutenant colonel of the First Iowa swearing that the general would not touch another member of the regiment. Eventually, the governor and legislature of Iowa condemned Custer officially for his actions.[15]

These whippings were the last recorded punishments of this kind. The rank and file of the regiments never forgave Custer, and their later writings indicated the depth of hatred toward him. They blamed him for "incompetence or criminal negligence" in not securing adequate supplies and described his orders as "inconsistent and tyrannical." One of them offered an explanation for Custer's actions: "He was only twenty-five years of age, and had the usual egotism and self-importance of a young man. He was a regular army officer, and had bred in him the tyranny of the regular army. He did not distinguish between a regular soldier and a volunteer. . . . He had no sympathy in common with the private soldiers, but regarded them simply as machines created for the special purpose of obeying his imperial will." It was a damning indictment of a commanding officer, and one in stark contrast to the views of members of the Michigan Brigade and Third Cavalry Division.[16]

But nothing in Custer's experience had prepared him for the situation he encountered at Alexandria. During the war, he had known only loyalty and devotion from the officers and men of his commands. Bound in a common cause, he led and they followed, with few discipline problems and with an officer corps of merit. He attended to their welfare, but to be sure, the government met the needs of the Union soldiers in the field. In Louisiana and Texas, however, Custer encountered a rank and file whose sense of betrayal by the government fostered ill discipline and strident resentment. While it would appear that any general would have had difficulty with the regiment, Custer reacted with illegal punishments and unbending discipline. Had he not imposed his authority—endorsed by Sheridan—the men could have become marauders throughout the region. He deserved credit for preventing this, but his methods, in violation of the Articles of War, cannot be justified.

The command remained at Hempstead for over two months. While there, the news arrived that Louis Napoleon had ordered a withdrawal of French forces from Mexico, and the duty now became that of an occupation force. Detachments patrolled the countryside, welcomed by law-abiding citizens. On September 7, the Fifth Illinois mustered out and left for home. Discipline and supply problems still plagued the command, and about a dozen troopers died of disease. The cooler autumn weather brought relief from the smothering heat and humidity.[17]

Except for Libbie's unspecified illness, the Custers' stay in Hempstead was more pleasurable than their time in Alexandria. Shortly after their arrival, Nettie Humphrey, now Mrs. Jacob Greene, and Emanuel Custer joined them from Monroe. Autie had secured for his father an appointment as forage agent, a job with "little to do and fine pay," in Libbie's words. Nepotism was a common practice in the army, and Autie was never adverse to having a family member benefit from it.[18]

The reunion with Autie and Tom seemed to reinvigorate Emanuel. Within a few weeks, Autie wrote to his sister and brother-in-law that "I have not seen Pap look so well as he does now for years, he is much fleshier [than] when he came and is always in the best of spirits." Frequently, the father joined Autie and Libbie on evening rides and hunted with his sons. While at Alexandria, his sons had hunted game every morning and evening when duty permitted. The sport became a passion for the brothers that further service in the West only intensified. Autie had always liked dogs, gathering a stray here and there, and when he began hunting, he started collecting a pack of dogs of various types. Soon, whenever he rode forth, a cloud of mongrel animals, barking and yelping, scurried after him.[19]

The Custers often accepted the hospitality of local planters. Since his West Point years, Custer had been fascinated with the ideal of Southern life and had counted among his closest friends cadets from the region.

Despite his war record, the Texans found a sympathetic, if not kindred, fellow in him. Although the conflict reduced their wealth—and bankrupted many of them—the planters retained influence and status that appealed to Custer. His rank and fame accorded him access to the powerful, and increasingly he exploited and enjoyed the advantage.[20]

While Custer empathized with the planters' difficulties with the reality of freedman labor, he saw the peculiar institution for what it was. "If the War has attained nothing else," he wrote his father-in-law about slavery, "it has placed America under a debt of gratitude for all time, for removal of this evil." While in Louisiana, he, Libbie, and Eliza had attended black prayer meetings, and there and elsewhere, he saw the scars from whippings on ex-slaves' backs, convincing him that the institution was worse in the lower South than in Virginia. Although he opposed suffrage for freedmen, he stated that "I am in favor of elevating the negro to the extent of his capacity and intelligence, and of our doing everything in our power to advance the race morally and mentally as well as physically, also socially."[21]

The region around Hempstead had been spared destruction during the war, but the planters were not spared from the new economic reality with the abolition of the antebellum labor system. Plantations once worth over $50,000 were now worth less than $10,000. For individuals with money, the opportunities beckoned. Custer thought about buying property for speculation and advised his father-in-law to purchase acreage. But as Libbie noted in a letter to her parents, Autie believed "that so long as the government needs his services he should not invest."[22]

In late October, orders came for the command to relocate to Austin. Custer was to assume the post as chief of cavalry of the Department of Texas, with headquarters in the capital. Once again, Libbie regretted leaving, writing home: "We shall never forget their kindness to us. No country in the world can equal the South for hospitality." Except for the Twelfth Illinois, which was sent to Houston, the cavalry departed Hempstead on October 30, arriving in Austin on November 4, after a march of 124 miles.[23]

At the request of Provisional Governor Andrew Jackson Hamilton, Custer occupied the Blind Asylum as headquarters and posted the regiments in various camps outside the city. The Sixth United States Cavalry, Lieutenant Colonel Samuel D. Sturgis commanding, occupied Austin and was added to Custer's force. The capital had been flooded with reports of lawlessness throughout the state and with stories of marauding Indians. Texans professing loyalty to the federal government risked their lives. Alleged secret organizations existed to undermine the government's authority. It was these conditions that brought Custer and the cavalry to Austin, and for the next three months detachments from the capital patrolled sections of the state, enforcing the law.[24]

During this time, Custer remained at headquarters in the city. Located on Austin's eastern edge, the Blind Asylum was a large, two-story stone building that had been closed during the war. It provided ample room for the general, his wife and staff members, with a long front parlor that served as the office and smaller rooms for quarters. The Custers used the room above the parlor as their own. The building stands today as a part of the University of Texas campus.[25]

Discipline and morale problems still plagued the regiments that came with Custer from Hempstead. One of the worst regiments, the Second Wisconsin, mustered out on November 15, and left Austin two days later. In one instance, a captain in the First Iowa wrote a letter home that detailed the conditions of the march from Alexandria to Hempstead, blaming Custer. It was published in a newspaper, and when Custer learned of it, he confronted the officer, who admitted to it and refused to retract it. Furious, the general grabbed a horsewhip, and the captain reached for his sword. Fortunately, Major Jacob Greene stepped into the office, and the general backed down without receiving the officer's admission of wrongdoing.[26]

"Austin is a pretty place," Libbie wrote two weeks after their arrival, "and has not so much of a dilapidated air as so many Southern towns have." As they had at Alexandria and Hempstead, the couple socialized with the local elite. The city was noted for its swift horses, and almost daily, races were held between the military and the civilians, with purses to the winners and betting among the spectators. Custer also hunted as often as he could, using at times a new sporting rifle presented to him by the Spencer Company. He and Libbie continued their horseback rides together, and at Christmas, they hosted a party at the Blind Asylum, with Autie serving as Santa Claus. At one time during their stay, Libbie exclaimed, "Oh, I am enjoying life so thoroughly."[27]

In Washington, meanwhile, on December 28, the War Department mustered out over a score of generals, including Alfred Pleasonton, George Crook, Wesley Merritt, and Custer, and granted each officer a thirty-day leave. For Custer, the order meant that he reverted to the rank of captain in the Fifth United States Cavalry. In January, Daniel Bacon corresponded with Senator Zachariah Chandler of Michigan, interceding on behalf of his son-in-law for a promotion. Nothing came of it for the present, and on January 31, 1866, he relinquished command.[28]

By horseback and wagon, the Custers left Austin on February 4. With them were Eliza and his staff, who, like Custer, had been mustered out. Most of them had been with him for two years, rode at his side in combat, laughed and joked together around campfires, and would remain loyal to him until life's end. Except for Tom Custer, they were all Michiganders, either the general's friend or a member of the Michigan Brigade. For Jacob Greene, James Christiancy, Fred Nims, L. W. Barnhart, Farnham Lyon, George Lee, and Edward Earle, the journey from Austin marked a passage. They had supported and executed his disciplinary measures during the previous months, and if they were disturbed by them, they kept silent, unless in the privacy of a meeting with the general. The bond between them went deep.[29]

The party retraced the route to Hempstead, and then went on to Galveston, where they boarded a coastal ship for New Orleans. A gulf storm brought anxious moments, but they arrived safely in the city that Libbie so much enjoyed, spending a few days shopping, and dining at French restaurants. A steamboat carried them up the Mississippi to Cairo, Illinois, where they boarded a train to Detroit and Monroe. Here Custer and Libbie boarded with her parents. He had been ordered to Washington to testify before the Joint Committee on Reconstruction, and when he left Monroe, she remained at home, to save on expenses.[30]

Custer appeared before the committee on March 10, providing a lengthy description of affairs in Texas and concluding that "the government should maintain its present control of the States lately in rebellion until satisfied that they may, without detriment, be intrusted with their former rights and privileges." While in the capital, he attended a dinner party at Chief Justice Salmon Chase's and met with Secretary of War Edwin Stanton, who greeted the officer with "Custer, stand up. I want to see you all over once more. It does me good to look at you again!" Custer had come to the War Department to request Regular Army commissions for his brother and George Yates, which Stanton promised to approve. In a letter to Libbie, he wrote that "I am *so* lonesome," and that he had refused to attend the theater or opera without her.[31]

By April 1, he was in New York City. Uncertain whether to remain in the army—he had rejected the idea of diplomatic service—he came to the financial center to explore business opportunities for himself. His fame assured him entry into circles of wealthy individuals, who feted the war hero and spoke of the possibilities, particularly in railroads and mining. Already the age was being stamped with the glorification of money and the men who acquired it. To Libbie, he confided, "For you and you alone I long to become wealthy, not for wealth alone but for the power it brings. I am willing to make any honorable sacrifice." [32]

In the end, however, the renowned soldier neither invested money nor accepted a position with a firm, if one was offered. While his words to Libbie indicated his desire for financial wealth and status, he may have concluded that he was ill suited for a business career. He certainly enjoyed the attention and attended numerous dinners, shows, and parties. He saw former West Point friends, and with them "went out on an expedition of fun" to shooting galleries. "We also had considerable sport with females we met on the street—'Nymphes du Pave' they are called," he informed Libbie. "Sport alone was our object. At no time did I forget you." In another letter, he mentioned that he had been sitting beside a baroness in a low-cut gown at a party, and teased that "I have not seen such sights since I was weaned." [33]

A telegram from Monroe ended Custer's stay in New York City, with the news that Daniel Bacon had died on May 18. A victim of cholera, the judge "knew of his approaching end, and was prepared." "He seemed triumphantly happy, so near Heaven, so contented in regard to me," Libbie wrote to an aunt afterward. Before the end, he told his daughter that "Armstrong was born a soldier and it is better even if you sorrow your life long that he die as he would wish, a soldier." The judge was buried beside Libbie's mother, Sophia, in Woodland Cemetery. [34]

"Our house is not the same," Libbie confessed soon after the funeral. She understood her father's death better than her mother's when she was a child, but for weeks she had watched him succumb to the disease. She was forced to endure the grief without her husband, whose letters mentioned gala parties and attractive women. Her religious faith reaffirmed the promise of salvation, and it comforted her. In the darkness of night, alone in bed before sleep denied the present, Libbie Bacon Custer surely cried. [35]

When Autie returned, he took her to Detroit and Toledo to visit friends and on carriage rides into the country, away from the memories locked in the Bacon home. The judge's will designated her as his heir, with the stipulation that $5,000 should be invested, with its annual interest to provide for Rhoda Bacon, Libbie's stepmother, as long as she lived. She and Custer sold some of her father's real estate and, for a time, thought that the home would have to be relinquished. The couple had some time, as Rhoda moved to Tecumseh to live with a nephew. Custer's future, however, was now a more pressing concern.[36]

While in New York, Custer had contacted Don Matías Romero, a Mexican diplomat, about the minister's search for an adjutant general of the Mexican army. In turn, Romero sought Ulysses S. Grant's opinion of Custer, and the general-in-chief replied:

> This will introduce to your acquaintance Gen. Custer, who rendered such distinguished service as a cavalry officer during the war. There was no officer in that branch of service who had the confidence of Gen. Sheridan to a greater degree than Gen. Custer, and there is no officer in whose judgment I have greater faith than in Sheridan's. Please understand then that I mean by this to endorse Gen. Custer in a high degree.[37]

Grant added in the letter that he would support Custer's request for a year's leave of absence. With this, the Mexican government offered Custer the position and $10,000 in gold. But Libbie vehemently opposed the idea, and Sheridan counseled against it. Both Grant and Secretary Stanton endorsed his request for a leave, but Secretary of State William Seward interceded and denied permission, not wanting a United States army officer directing troops against French soldiers. If Custer wanted the command, he would have to resign from the army, an action he refused to take.[38]

In the country, meanwhile, the Reconstruction policies of President Andrew Johnson polarized the parties and the sections. A native Tennessean, Johnson had promoted lenient measures that pardoned ex-Confederates and reestablished state governments in the Southern states. He cooperated with Southern planters, whose efforts to reimpose some form of labor system on the freedmen clashed with Radical Republicans' determination to protect the rights of former slaves. In April 1866, Johnson vetoed the Civil Rights Act, only to have it overridden by Congress. A month later, Memphis exploded in three days of racial violence, followed by similar incidents elsewhere in the South. On July 30, whites killed blacks in what Sheridan described as "an absolute massacre" in New Orleans. By then, most Northerners had rejected the president's course of action.[39]

With the events of New Orleans in newspapers, the National Union Convention opened its sessions in Philadelphia. A coalition of moderates and conservatives, its purpose was to establish a third political party that endorsed Johnson's Reconstruction program. One of the elected delegates was George Custer. While his testimony before the congressional committee in March reflected Radical Republican viewpoints on the continual need for military force in the South, he was a moderate, who had described Johnson earlier "as firm and upright as a tombstone" in defense of the Constitution. Convinced that if the Radicals were permitted to impose their will on the former Confederate states the country would be convulsed in another war, he agreed to participate in the convention. Libbie opposed the idea, and her instincts were correct.[40]

The delegates failed to organize a party, settling for a platform that supported congressional candidates who favored Johnson's policies. Custer returned to Monroe for several days before traveling to New York City to join the president, cabinet members, politicians, and other military officers in the so-called "swing around the circle." The campaign tour resulted in a political fiasco for Johnson as individuals in the crowds taunted him and his supporters. In Harrison County, Ohio, Custer's home, the opponents of the president were so outspoken that Custer became furious and publicly stated he was "ashamed" of them. Pro-Republican newspapers spared no member of Johnson's group in their criticism, with the *Monroe Commercial* flailing its local hero for his presence on platforms with Johnson, even alleging that the president would reward him with a colonelcy.[41]

Custer was back in Monroe by the final week in September. His political experience had been embarrassing, although he adhered to his convictions about the country's future course toward the South. It also cured him of any inclination to enter elective politics—much to Libbie's relief. Earlier, when friends approached him about accepting a nomination as a candidate for Michigan's First Congressional District, he felt compelled to write a letter to the *Detroit Free Press,* declaring: "I wish it to be understood that I am not a candidate for any office, and cannot consistently accept any nomination if tendered me. I do not deem it important or requisite that I should state the reasons inducing me to adopt this course."[42]

The public turmoil contrasted with the private happiness of the couple. Libbie recovered slowly from her father's death, but despite the whirlwind he found himself in, Autie was particularly solicitous of her needs and comforts. "He is growing so much dearer and dearer every day," Libbie confided to Rebecca Richmond about him, "I am at loss to know how he can get any better. He is so indulgent and far more devoted than when we first were married."[43]

Most important, the months of uncertainty about their future had been resolved—Custer had accepted the lieutenant colonelcy of the Seventh Cavalry. In July, Congress had authorized the creation of four additional cavalry regiments, the Seventh through Tenth. Custer was appointed on August 3, to rank from July 28. He would have preferred a colonelcy and command of the regiment, but he took the commission. Now with his leave expiring on September 24, orders arrived for him to report for duty in Kansas, and the couple packed for the trip.[44]

Chapter

14

COURT-MARTIAL

■ Fort Riley sprawled across the Kansas plain 116 miles west of Fort Leavenworth, near the confluence of the Republican and Smoky Hill rivers. Although no walls enclosed the fort, it had the look of permanence, with its buildings of locally quarried sandstone. Six two-story barracks and six double houses for officers edged the four sides of a parade ground, while five long stables, mess houses, chapel and chaplain's residence, sutler's store, post office, and various other structures gave "the post the appearance of a little city." Outside the garrison, the tracks of the Kansas Pacific Railroad, a branch of the Union Pacific Railroad, linked Riley to the eastern settlements, while construction crews spiked rails into ties to the west.[1]

The fort was one of several posts the army had established in Kansas to guard settlements and a route west to Denver, Colorado. White settlers had followed the Smoky Hill River into Colorado, and by the fall of 1866 a stage line, with over twenty-five stations, tied the Colorado goldfields to the end of the tracks. Forts Harker, Hays, and Wallace were located on or near the stage route, while Forts Larned and Dodge lay to the south of the Smoky Hill on the Arkansas River. With Leavenworth, the six posts comprised the army's presence in the state.[2]

In the summer of 1866, Fort Riley had been designated as the organizational site for the Seventh Cavalry, and here George and Libbie Custer came, arriving on October 16. Accompanied by Eliza and Anna Darrah, one of Libbie's bridesmaids, they had traveled leisurely from Monroe, visiting friends in Detroit and seeing the sights of St. Louis. "We had an elegant time" in the Mississippi River city, wrote Libbie. They toured the botanical gardens and a fair, attended a hotel ball, and saw the play *Rosedale* at a theater.[3]

One of the members of the cast was Lawrence Barrett, a twenty-eight-year-old former officer in the Union army. After the performance, Custer invited the actor to their hotel room, beginning, in Barrett's words, "the most genuine friendship." A reserved man, Barrett found in Custer a personal opposite. But Custer's humor, joyousness, and zest for life appealed to the actor. He later described his friend as "the sunny affectionate Custer" who "seemed in private to become as gentle as a woman." The friendship became a bond that only death would sever.[4]

From St. Louis, the couple completed the trip to the fort. Upon arrival, they moved into one half of a double house for officers. The quarters were spacious, with an ample number of rooms and a wide veranda. Libbie soon had lace curtains on the windows that reminded her of home. "Our house is so comfortable and cheery," she informed her cousin, "for we have sunlight in the parlor all day." Carpet on the bedroom floor, a private dressing room, and a large parlor for entertainment added to its appeal.[5]

Libbie was so pleased with the accommodations and with Fort Riley that in the same letter to Rebecca Richmond she exclaimed: "We are living almost in luxury. It does not seem *life* in the army for you know I have had mostly a rough time." She shopped at a market in Junction City, four miles away, went on rides in the evening with Autie, attended dinners and dances, and witnessed her first buffalo hunt when a Russian prince visited. Her major complaint was the wind which, she said later, "blew unceasingly all the five years we were in Kansas."[6]

Custer reported for duty on November 1 and assumed temporary command of the regiment. But the War Department had instituted examinations for officers in the new regiments, and on the ninth he departed for Washington, not returning until December 16. By then, Colonel Andrew J. Smith had arrived at the fort to take command of the Seventh. Smith was graduated from West Point a year before Custer was born, led dragoons on the frontier until 1861, and served at the divisional and corps levels during the conflict, attaining the rank of major general. A competent officer, Smith was rewarded for his service with the colonelcy of the Seventh. But his association with the regiment was nominal. On February 27, 1867, he assumed command of the District of the Upper Arkansas, relinquishing direction of the regiment to Custer.[7]

The recruitment of enlisted personnel and officers for the Seventh Cavalry had begun in August under the command of Major John W.

Davidson of the Second Cavalry. Organized into a regiment on September 10, the Seventh received recruits and officers incrementally throughout the autumn. As officers were commissioned and arrived at Fort Riley, Davidson formed companies and began parceling them out to the other posts in Kansas. When Smith replaced Davidson at the end of November, only regimental headquarters and four companies remained at Riley. By year's end, 15 officers and 963 enlisted men had joined the Seventh, but of that latter figure, 12 had died of wounds or disease, and 80 had deserted.[8]

The desertion rate was symptomatic of the caliber of recruits and the harshness of military life in the postwar army. No longer did men enter the ranks who were motivated by the desire to save the Union or to end human bondage as they were during the Civil War. Instead, volunteers enlisted either to secure employment, to flee a past, or to seek adventure. Consequently, in the words of a historian, "the postwar regular ranks filled with recruits of a lower order of intelligence, physical fitness, and motivation." Recent immigrants comprised a disproportionate percentage of troops, with the records indicating that between 1865 and 1874 one-half of the enlisted personnel was foreign-born. Of this figure, natives of Ireland and Germany accounted for the majority. While the volunteers reflected the country's diverse social and economic classes, the bulk of them were unskilled laborers, particularly from cities where the army had most of its recruiting stations.[9]

If assigned to a regiment on the frontier, such as the Seventh Cavalry, the recruits soon encountered the reality of life on an isolated post in an unforgiving land. Earning $13 a month as privates, the troops endured monotony, boredom, rigid rules, inferior food and quarters, disease, and occasional danger. The weather, the land, and the army's routine broke hundreds of men, who fled the ranks in staggering numbers. Each year during the postwar decades, the army lost on average about one-fourth of its personnel to desertion. When the replacements arrived, the cycle renewed itself. But despite the hardships, many men served for years, constituting a nucleus of veterans amid the turnover of troops in each regiment.[10]

Critical to the training and discipline of the enlisted men was the quality of noncommissioned and commissioned officers in the regiments. During the immediate years after 1865, Civil War veterans wore the stripes of corporals and sergeants or the shoulder straps of lieutenants, captains, and majors. With regiments segmented and dispersed, companies became the units of identification, of shared experience, and of loyalty for the rank and file. Regimental commanders relied heavily upon subordinates to drill and to discipline the men. Some commanders, like Custer, succeeded in stamping an individual identity upon their regiments that fostered unit pride at that level.[11]

Of the officers who reported for duty with the Seventh Cavalry during the summer and autumn of 1866 and the winter of 1867, a number of them would become an integral part of the regiment's record and history. All of them were Civil War veterans, with solid, if not distinguished, records in most cases. A Kentuckian, Wyckliffe Cooper was the ranking major. A capable officer, Cooper drank too much alcohol—a common curse in the army—and ended his own life in June 1867. By then, Major Joel H. Elliott, a young, dynamic former school superintendent, had joined the regiment.[12]

The captains included Louis M. Hamilton, Albert Barnitz, Myles Keogh, Robert M. West, and Frederick W. Benteen. A grandson of Alexander Hamilton, Louis Hamilton was at twenty-two years old the youngest captain in the army. Albert Barnitz had served under Custer in the Third Cavalry Division, but his good opinion of the general would soon change. An Irishman, twenty-four-year-old Myles Keogh had been a lieutenant in the Papal Guards until emigrating to the United States, where he earned a brevet lieutenant colonelcy in the war. Like Cooper and others, Keogh enjoyed the bottle.[13]

Robert M. West had received a brevet brigadier generalcy during the Civil War, temporarily commanding a cavalry division during the conflict's final weeks. While West would serve with the Seventh for less than three years, he was a disruptive officer. Evidently, he hated Custer from the first day they met.[14]

But of all the captains, no one was more destined to shape the internal dynamics of the regiment and history's verdict of it and Custer than Frederick W. Benteen. A native Virginian, Benteen rose from lieutenant to lieutenant colonel in the war, serving at the end under Custer's rival, James H. Wilson, during the so-called Selma Raid. His bravery and capability as an officer were unquestioned, but while he had a backbone of steel, he possessed a soul of vinegar. Taciturn and cynical, Benteen was the antithesis of Custer. He claimed later that he had sized up Custer as a boisterous braggart after their first meeting when the latter read his congratulatory order to the Third Cavalry Division to Benteen, and as a "demi-semi quaver" after an all-night poker game. His opinion of him only worsened over time.[15]

Among the lieutenants, however, Custer found a group of loyal supporters. Tom Custer joined the regiment through his brother's intervention, transferring from the Second Infantry. Like Tom Custer, Myles Moylan owed his commission in the regiment to the senior Custer. A cavalryman since 1857, Moylan had a checkered Civil War record, including a dismissal from service for unauthorized leave in Washington. Reenlisting under the name of Charles Thomas, he rose to the rank of captain, with the brevet of major. He joined the Seventh as sergeant major but was promoted to first lieutenant in December 1866.[16]

Another lieutenant, who would be in time the regiment's adjutant, was a giant Canadian, William W. Cooke. Twenty years old, Cooke came from a wealthy physician's family in Ontario, and after he allegedly fathered an illegitimate child at sixteen, his family sent him to the United States, where he enlisted in the army. He suffered a wound and served with distinction in a New York cavalry regiment. Within the Seventh, he was regarded as the best shot and one of the most handsome officers, with his long dundreary whiskers. Eventually, Custer placed so much trust in Cooke that he gave the subordinate orders to kill Libbie if she were to be captured by Indians.[17]

A fourth loyal lieutenant was Algernon E. Smith. Dubbed "Fresh" by fellow officers and men to distinguish him from another Smith, he was a New Yorker who had commanded an infantry company in the war, suffering a severe wound in the assault on Fort Fisher at Wilmington, North Carolina. His wife, Nettie, became one of Libbie Custer's closest friends among the officers' wives.[18]

Finally, Thomas B. Weir was an Ohioan, like the Custers, who had served in a Michigan regiment during the war. A graduate of the University of Michigan, Weir was a handsome, twenty-eight-year-old bachelor, whom women, including Libbie, found appealing, despite his problems with alcohol. Like the others, Weir would prove to be a solid, reliable officer.[19]

Factionalism among officers infested every regiment. Within the army's caste system, in which promotion could be measured in decades now that the conflict had ended, and within the intimacy of post life, human frailties of pettiness, jealousy, and resentment festered. Favoritism by a regimental commander could mean assignment to better companies, favorable recommendations, and increased opportunities for advancement. In a profession that measured authority, status, and pay by defined ranks, perceived or real preference ignited internal disputes that caused divisions among members. The effects of such internecine turmoil could weaken morale and the combat prowess of units.[20]

The extent, and the effects, of factionalism within the Seventh Cavalry have been the subject of considerable historical inquiry. Because of the command's rendezvous with death at Little Big Horn, nearly every facet of the Seventh's history has undergone scrutiny. Undoubtedly, groups of officers coalesced into pro-and anti-Custer cliques. He was a strong personality, a galvanizing individual whose character traits, fame, and methods of command elicited reactions. But were such divisions deeper, more crippling in the Seventh than in other regiments, or has the wealth of writings articulated its troubles more clearly than those of other units? With Custer, numerous matters appear larger than they were, but the internal dissension in the regiment cannot be dismissed.

It began during the regiment's early days. Libbie Custer commented later on her husband's difficulties with the "medley of incongruous elements." When she spoke to him of "the inharmonious feeling" that she saw, he cautioned her to have patience, advising that she "must neither look for fidelity or friendship, in its best sense, until the whole of them had been in a fight together; that it was on the battle-field, when all faced death together, where the truest affection was formed among soldiers." For the Seventh Cavalry, however, it would never be as he predicted.[21]

The Seventh's and other frontier regiments' personnel and organizational problems were compounded, even magnified, by the army's mission during the postwar years. While some units of the military enforced congressional Reconstruction in the South, other commands served as the advance guard in the rush of American civilization across the Great Plains, the vast, flat, treeless sea of prairie grass between the Mississippi River and the Rocky Mountains. Here stretched an endless, untapped expanse of land. While the Civil War had stayed the inevitable for four years, peace brought a renewal of the movement.[22]

From its inception, the United States was as much an idea as a country. For those who were here and for those who would come, it offered the opportunity for betterment. America rewarded hard work and ambition. To Americans, progress—individual and collective—characterized the human saga, and in America it meant the conquest of a wilderness. The settlers paddled against currents, carved roads, shouldered wagons, felled trees, built homes, and plotted towns. Their struggles seeped into the nation's character.[23]

From the beginning, however, American progress exacted a price. Conquest of the wilderness meant the subjugation of Indians, or Native Americans, who inhabited the unmarked regions. Unrelenting, in numbers that seemed greater than the forests, the whites came, wresting the land from the natives, banishing the tribes from the course of American society. At the end of the Civil War, the Great Plains remained the largest final homeland of the Indians, and here white Americans sought further expansion of civilization and progress.[24]

By government estimates, 270,000 Indians in 125 groups dwelled in the country in 1866. Of that population, 100,000 could oppose the army and white settlers, with most of them in the nomadic tribes of the Great Plains—Sioux, Cheyenne, Arapaho, Kiowa, and Comanche. Proud, independent, they roamed the land, following the uncounted herds of buffalo, relying on the beast for food, clothing, shelter, and tools. Their religions and cultures revered nature; their societies honored warriors. Unlike the tribes east of the Mississippi River, Plains warriors were superb horsemen and masters of guerrilla warfare. While tribalism and intertribal animosities weakened Indian resistance to the whites, they were formidable opponents, mounted fighters who when seen in single file on a horizon's edge portended a fearful resolution between cultures divided by a chasm of blindness and misunderstanding.[25]

In the decade before the Civil War, officials from Washington negotiated treaties that reserved land drained by the North and South Platte rivers and the Arkansas River for the Southern Cheyenne, Arapaho, Comanche, Kiowa, and Kiowa-Apache. But during the four years of conflict between the North and the South, white incursions were met with Indian raids in Colorado, Kansas, and Nebraska. The killings mounted, climaxing in the Sand Creek Massacre of Southern Cheyenne by Colorado cavalrymen in November 1864. The Cheyenne lashed back until some bands signed a treaty of peace in October 1865. But the summer heat of 1866 brought a renewal, particularly from the Sioux, who resisted the opening of the Bozeman Trail into the Montana goldfields. The Sioux waged war into the winter, killing every member of an 81-man force under Captain William Fetterman, near Fort Phil Kearny, on December 21.[26]

By the end of 1866, the army stood at the center of white America's confusion and guilt over its relationship with the Indians. From the west, legislatures, citizens, and railroad companies clamored for protection; from the east, politicians, bureaucrats, religious organizations, and humanitarian individuals proposed peaceful solutions. Congress mirrored its divided constituents—members of the House of Representatives supported the use of force, if inexpensive, while senators argued for negotiation with the tribes. Ultimately, the policy followed the worn road of treaties that placed tribes on reservations, with the government responsible for the welfare of the Native Americans. For the bands or tribes that accepted reservation life, the government classified them as "friendly Indians," and for those that refused, they were designated "hostiles." Replete with ambiguities and contradictions, the policy guaranteed war.[27]

Despite the country's muddled thoughts, the army saw its role in starker terms. When Major General William T. Sherman, commander of the Military Division of the Missouri, whose authority embraced the Great Plains, learned of the "Fetterman Massacre," he asserted, "We must act with vindictive earnestness against the Sioux, even to their extermination, men, women, and children." Unfortunately for the army, neither Sherman nor other ranking officers had a strategy for the conquest of the tribes. Instead, bowing to demands of western interests, the army built forts—*wa-cee-chee,* or "bad fighters tepees," to Indians— to protect settlers and towns. But the posts, many of which Sherman later described as "abominable habitations" for the troops, were inadequately manned. When the army assumed the offensive, detachments from the forts concentrated for the operation.[28]

The cavalry bore the burden of the campaigns because of the vastness of the Great Plains and the elusiveness of the enemy. The columns of cavalry, however, were restricted in their mobility by slow-moving wagons filled with food and forage. One mounted officer compared cavalry on the march to a dog on a chain, arguing that it was "within the length of chain, irresistible, beyond it powerless." Against the Plains warriors, for whom the rank and file had minimal respect as opponents, the cavalry was a tethered giant, but a giant, nonetheless, supported by organization, technology, railroads, and settlers.[29]

The army's initial campaign against the tribes of the central and

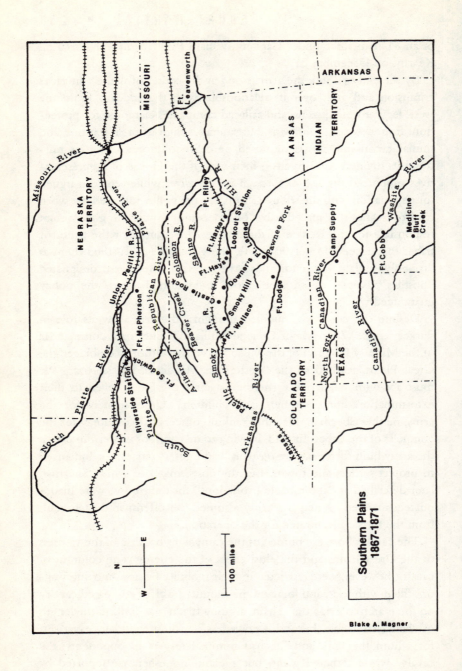

Southern Plains
1867-1871

100 miles

Blake A. Magner

southern plains came with the warmth of spring in 1867. Following a tour of the region during the previous year and responding to the arguments of government officials, railroad executives, and the citizenry, Sherman had proposed to army commander Lieutenant General Ulysses S. Grant that the Southern Cheyenne, Arapaho, Kiowa, and others be settled south of the Arkansas River, and the Sioux be moved north of the Platte River. With the relocation of the tribes, a wide swath of Nebraska and Kansas would be opened to the railroad and to white homesteaders. With Grant's approval, Sherman ordered two forces into the field. While the operation against the Sioux was stalled by a delegation sent from Washington to negotiate, the second prong advanced into the area between the Smoky Hill and Arkansas rivers in late March 1867.[30]

Sherman assigned the campaign against the southern tribes to Major General Winfield Scott Hancock, commander of the Department of the Missouri, a subdivision of the Military Division of the Missouri. In his instructions, Sherman directed Hancock "to confer with them to ascertain if they want to fight, in which case he will indulge them." Tall and handsome, Hancock had been one of the Union's finest generals during the war, but had no experience with Indians. Determined to impress the tribes with the military's power, he gathered a force of 1,400 troops, the largest force yet arrayed against Plains warriors, comprising eleven companies of the Seventh Cavalry, seven companies of the Thirty-seventh Infantry, and an artillery battery. Departing Fort Riley at the end of March, the command arrived on April 7 at Fort Larned, where Hancock expected to meet with tribal chiefs.[31]

Fort Larned was located on Pawnee Fork, on the southern fringe of the traditional buffalo range of the Southern Cheyenne and Arapaho. Various bands of Indians had spent the winter in the region, and by the time Hancock reached the fort, a large village of Cheyenne, Arapaho, Kiowa, and Southern Brulé and Oglala Sioux lay thirty-five miles upstream from Larned. With the army were two Indian agents, Edward W. Wynkoop and Jesse H. Leavenworth, both of whom assured Hancock that the chiefs sought peace, although factions—primarily younger warriors—opposed concessions to the whites. Division within the tribes was as fractious as it was within the councils of their enemies.[32]

On April 12, after a delay caused by a snowstorm and a buffalo hunt, a delegation of about a dozen chiefs met with Hancock and other officers, including Custer, at the fort. After preliminaries, Hancock spoke of peace, asserting that Indian raids against railroad construction crews, settler cabins, and stagecoach stations must cease, or the chiefs would be responsible for war. Disappointed about the number of chiefs who had come to the fort, he then announced that he would march to the village for a council. The chiefs departed, after consenting to the passage of the army through their land. Wynkoop warned Hancock that such a force would frighten the Indians, whose memories of Sand Creek remained fresh.[33]

The troops left Larned on the morning of the thirteenth, marching twenty-one miles upstream before encamping. White Horse of the Cheyenne and Pawnee Killer of the Sioux visited the campsite, and Hancock agreed to meet the next morning with all the chiefs. When the leaders did not appear on the fourteenth, the general ordered a march to the village. Proceeding a few miles, the column stopped before a line of Cheyenne and Sioux warriors on the crest of a ridge. To Custer, the sight was "one of the finest and most imposing military displays, prepared according to the Indian art of war, which it has ever been my lot to behold. It was nothing more nor less than an Indian line of battle drawn directly across our line of march; as if to say, Thus far and no further. Most of the Indians were mounted; all were bedecked in their brightest colors, their heads crowned with the brilliant war bonnet, their lances bearing the crimson pennant, bows strung, and quivers full of barbed arrows."[34]

Before either side made a tragic mistake, Wynkoop spurred ahead and assured the Indians of their safety. Consenting to a meeting with Hancock, several chiefs rode to a point midway between the groups, spoke with the general, and agreed to allow the troops to bivouac near the village. Hancock's men trailed the warriors to the site, where the chiefs soon reported that the women and children had fled upon the army's approach. More negotiations ensued, ending with a promise that the women and children would return to the camp. After dark, however, Edward Guerrier, an interpreter, informed Hancock that the Indian men were preparing to leave. The general ordered Custer to surround the village with cavalry. While the troopers moved into position, Custer, Guerrier, and a few others crawled forward to a lodge, discovering the entire village was deserted, with suppers simmering in kettles. They found only an elderly Sioux man and a young, mixed-blood girl, about ten years old, who allegedly had been raped and abandoned.[35]

Furious at what he believed was Indian treachery, Hancock ordered Custer with eight companies of the Seventh and scouts in pursuit. Starting on the morning of the fifteenth, the cavalry marched north-west, following the trail. Throughout the day, however, the size of the track narrowed as bands of Indians, like eddies from a stream, dispersed from the main body. It was a common native tactic, and one Custer remembered. The next day, as the companies rode toward the Smoky Hill River, Custer left the march to hunt buffalo, accompanied only by his dogs. While chasing a beast, he accidentally discharged his pistol when the buffalo turned toward him, killing his mount, Custis Lee, Libbie's favorite horse. It was foolish of him to ride out without an escort, but he soon met a squad of men, who retrieved his saddle and brought him back to the column.[36]

Custer pushed ahead during the night of the sixteenth–seventeenth. Before the cavalry marched, he wrote a message to Hancock: "The hasty flight of the Indians, and their abandonment of, to them, valuable property, convinces me that they are influenced by fear alone, and it is my impression that no council can be held with them in the presence of a large military force."[37]

The troopers forded the Smoky Hill River about 4 A.M. on the seventeenth, and encamped. A detachment scouted ahead for the stage line, followed hours later by the main force. In a mixture of cold rain and sleet, they plodded east on the eighteenth, reaching the ruins of Lookout Station that had been burned by a party of Indians. They found the charred remains of three men and buried them. Custer could not identify the attackers or locate their trail and, without forage for the mounts, marched to Fort Hays to the east, having covered roughly 150 miles in four days, exhausting men and horses. Hancock, meanwhile, despite the protests of Wynkoop, burned the village of 251 lodges on Pawnee Fork. The flames ignited a bloody summer.[38]

The Seventh established a camp along Big Creek about a half-mile from Fort Hays. Custer found neither adequate forage nor the supplies that he had expected. Within days of the command's arrival, men began deserting, ten of them fleeing with horses and arms during a single night. As conditions worsened, with surgeons reporting numerous cases of scurvy, dozens more disappeared. By the end of May, ninety had fled. While Custer requested additional rations and sent parties out to kill buffalo, shortages persisted. As he had in Louisiana and Texas, he reacted with harsh discipline, on one occasion shaving the heads of six men who had left camp to buy canned fruit from a sutler. Although they were away less than an hour and missed no duty or roll calls, he imposed the punishment, which Captain Albert Barnitz described as "atrocious" because all the men were "perfectly crazy" for fruits and vegetables.[39]

In letters to his wife, Barnitz wrote a scorching description of his commander while at Big Creek. On May 6, Barnitz asserted that "General Custer has become 'billious' notwithstanding. He appears to be mad about something, and is very much on his dignity. . . . He is really quite 'obstreperous.'" Nine days later, following his arrest for not feeding horses and discarding forage, the indignant captain fumed about Custer: "I am thoroughly *disgusted* with him! He is the most complete example of a petty tyrant that I have ever seen. . . . If General Custer is to remain long in command of the regiment, as now appears probable, I don't know how matters will result." Barnitz then predicted in another letter that he would lose "whatever little influence for good he may have once possessed in the Regiment" by "his tyrannical conduct."[40]

Barnitz was not alone in noting Custer's temperament during these weeks. Theodore Davis, a correspondent-artist for *Harper's Weekly,* visited Fort Hays and described the cavalry officer as "depressed" and "of somber mien." Davis stated also that he had never seen him "so moody." Custer had been duped by the enemy, knew it, and allowed it to gnaw at him. In his first independent operation with the Seventh Cavalry, he had lost the quarry—a Civil War hero outwitted by Indians. The experience sobered him and depressed him. The conditions at Fort Hays only exacerbated his mood, and when discipline infractions and desertions mounted, he reacted severely, if Barnitz is to be believed.[41]

Compounding his professional difficulties were his private yearnings. He had been away from Libbie for nearly two months and missed her deeply. On May 7, he wrote to her: "You remember how eager I was to have you for my little wife? I was not as impatient then as now. I almost feel tempted to desert and fly to you. I would come if the cars were running, this far." Two days later, he asked Libbie to bring butter, lard, vegetables, fruit, and a croquet set when she came to Fort Hays, and then added: "I know *something* much, very much better and be sure you bring *it* along. *I am entirely out at present,* and have been for so long as to almost forget how it tastes. . . . Remember, every moment gone can never be reclaimed."[42]

A week after Custer wrote the second letter, traveling in an ambulance with an escort, Libbie, Anna Darrah, and Eliza arrived at the Big Creek camp. Custer had prepared a large tent with a wooden floor, given to him by Colonel Andrew Smith, for them. Additional tents were erected nearby for Anna and Eliza, the site placed a few hundred yards from the troops for privacy. They would be together for a fortnight.[43]

In an early letter from Hays, Custer informed his wife that he had voiced in writing "strong" opposition to "an Indian War, depicting as strongly as possible as I could the serious results that would follow." But whether or not the army wanted a war, the Kansas-Nebraska frontier had a minor one in the wake of Hancock's destruction of the village. Parties of Sioux, Cheyenne, and Arapaho warriors attacked railroad construction crews and stagecoach stations and killed settlers. Reports of marauding Indians—many false—inundated the forts, and at Hays, Custer assigned handfuls of men to the stations and sent out patrols, with instructions to kill every Indian encountered, regardless of age or sex, if they were not judged to be "friendly." Hancock and Smith visited with him to confer about countermeasures, but by the end of May the prairie belonged to the natives.[44]

Sherman, meanwhile, had sent messengers to friendly bands of Sioux with word either to camp at forts along the Platte River or to move their villages north of the stream. Consequently, the division commander ordered the Seventh to patrol the region south of the Platte and along the Republican River, with instructions "to hunt out and chastise the Cheyennes and that portion of the Sioux who are their allies between the Smoky Hill and the Platte."[45]

Custer and six companies of the Seventh, approximately 350 officers and men, departed Fort Hays on June 1. Libbie, Anna Darrah, and Eliza remained in the camp at Big Creek, with plans to return east to Fort Riley as soon as possible. Colonel Smith, however, forbade them to attempt the trip until the route was safer. On the nights of June 6 and 7, violent thunderstorms swept into the area, turning Big Creek into a torrent of water that drowned several troopers. Captain Barnitz and his wife Jennie joined Libbie, Anna, and Eliza in Libbie's tent, and endured the frightful storms, hearing the screams of those men pulled into the flooded creek, until the ninth, when the waters subsided. Shortly afterward, Libbie's party traveled to Fort Harker and then to Riley, where she waited to hear from Autie.[46]

By the time Big Creek returned to its banks, Custer was approaching Fort McPherson on the Platte River in Nebraska. William "Medicine Bill" Comstock served as guide for the column. A grandnephew of James Fenimore Cooper, Comstock was, in Myles Keogh's opinion, "an eccentric genius and ardent admirer of everything reckless and daring," who had received his nickname from the Arapaho after he severed the finger of a snake-bitten man to save his life. A native of Michigan, Comstock had apparently lived with Indians for two years and knew the country between Hays and McPherson as well as any white man. He guided Custer across the 220 miles without difficulty, arriving on June 10. On the seventh, the cavalry had encountered about 100 warriors, who moved away without incident. The only tragedy on the march had been Major Wyckliffe Cooper's suicide, which Custer attributed to alcohol.[47]

At McPherson, Custer met with Pawnee Killer and several other Sioux chiefs whose band was along the river. In Custer's words, he tried "to induce" them "to bring their lodges into the vicinity of the fort, and remain at peace with the whites." The chiefs rejected the proposal but assured him of their peaceful intentions. Sherman arrived at the fort on the following day, and when Custer related his discussions with the Sioux, the general scoffed at their desire for peace. Instead, Sherman directed the subordinate officer to search for the Sioux by scouring the region along the forks of the Republican River and the South Platte west of Fort Sedgwick in Colorado. If he overtook any Indians, Sherman granted Custer permission to pursue in any direction.[48]

During their conversations, Sherman mentioned that Custer could be retained along the Platte and the tracks of the Union Pacific Railroad into the autumn. If Libbie wanted to join her husband, Sherman said he could arrange for railroad passes, but she should wait until she heard from her husband at Sedgwick. Custer recounted Sherman's words in a letter, dated June 17, but suggested to her that if she could travel to Fort Wallace on the Smoky Hill route, "I will send a squadron there to meet you." "I am on a roving commission," he noted near the end, "going nowhere in particular, but where I please."[49]

The six companies started from McPherson on the same day he wrote to Libbie. The cavalry covered the 107 miles to the fork in the Republican River, encamping on the twenty-first. Here Custer decided that he would secure supplies from Wallace, instead of Sedgwick as Sherman directed, both being roughly seventy-five miles from his campsite. On June 22, he detached Lieutenant Samuel M. Robbins and Company D, with twelve wagons, to Wallace, and ordered Captain Robert West and Company K on a scout on Beaver Creek, south of the Republican. If Libbie were at Wallace, Robbins was instructed to return with her. On the following day, he sent Major Joel Elliott to Sedgwick with a report and to secure additional orders.[50]

At the Republican campsite, the remaining troopers spent the twenty-fourth repulsing an attempt by Sioux to scatter their horses, parleying with Pawnee Killer, pursuing the Indians, and fending off an attack. The Sioux's aggressiveness convinced Custer to send Captain Edward Myers and Company E to Beaver Creek, to locate West's company, and together, to escort the supply train from Wallace. It was a wise decision, because the two companies overtook the wagons on the twenty-sixth, while under attack by an estimated 300 Cheyenne and Sioux under Roman Nose. The appearance of the additional troopers ended the fighting, and the companies and supplies joined Custer the next day. Libbie had not been at the fort, but he learned that the Indians were raiding along the Smoky Hill stage line and had attacked Wallace's garrison six days earlier.[51]

Custer had encountered Indians, and under Sherman's original instructions, he was authorized to use his judgment. When Elliott's party returned on the twenty-eighth without new orders but with a suggestion from Colonel Christopher C. Augur to operate on the Smoky Hill line, the Seventh's commander had sufficient evidence to indicate that the raiding bands were targeting the forts and stations on that route. Instead, complying with Sherman's orders, he marched west along the South Fork of the Republican River before turning north toward the Platte. In the sweltering summer heat, across a tract of waterless terrain, he pushed the companies. His concern for Libbie's whereabouts and welfare had increased—"I never was so anxious in my life," he wrote to her on the twenty-second—and he may have led his command toward the Platte hoping that she had gone to Sedgwick instead of Wallace.[52]

The cavalry reached Riverside Station on the Union Pacific Railroad west of Fort Sedgwick on July 5. The final sixty miles had been a grueling march, and when they arrived, thirty men deserted during the night. Custer wired Sedgwick for orders and learned that Lieutenant Lyman Kidder and a detachment of the Second Cavalry had been sent with instructions toward the Republican River. The commandant at Sedgwick repeated the orders carried by Kidder, which directed Custer to Fort Wallace, where the Indians had attacked a second time on June 26. Along the Smoky Hill route, the conditions had worsened, and Sherman was under pressure to punish the warriors. The district commander needed and wanted Custer's companies.[53]

Although short of supplies, Custer started for Wallace the next day. His urgency, in part, he attributed later to the "great anxiety" about the fate of Kidder's party. Consequently, he drove his command in a forced march, and after a noon halt, thirteen men rode away in an effort to desert. Outraged, he ordered Major Elliott, several officers and troopers, to bring them back, either dead or alive. "I felt that severe and summary measures must be taken," he wrote subsequently. When Elliott's detachment overtook the deserters, one of them fired at the major. Elliott and others responded, mortally wounding trooper Charles Johnson and wounding two more. Upon their return to camp, Custer loudly told surgeon I. T. Coates not to treat the men, although privately informing the doctor to care for them. "The effect was all that could be desired," he asserted in his notes. "There was not another desertion as long as I remained with the command."[54]

The march resumed at daylight, and after four punishing days, the companies found the remains of Kidder and eleven men south of the Republican River. They had been dead about ten days, their bodies burned and mutilated, with skulls crushed and body parts severed. It was a sight that paled the hardest of men, and a burial detail dug graves. From there, they continued south, arriving at Wallace on the thirteenth, having covered 181 miles in a week.[55]

Expecting orders and possible news about Libbie at Wallace, Custer found neither. Assigning Elliott to command, he instructed company commanders to select a dozen men with the best mounts from each of the six companies for a detail. On the evening of the fifteenth, with three officers and seventy-two men, Custer left Wallace, riding east on the Smoky Hill route. It was the beginning of a journey into controversy.[56]

In his memoirs, *My Life on the Plains,* Custer argued that he under-took the trip to secure supplies at Fort Harker because the "reserve of stores" at Wallace "was well-nigh exhausted," to obtain new orders, to gather additional horses, and to forward medical supplies to treat cholera victims. Except for the remark about orders, the reasons cited by him were not true. In fact, Myles Keogh, who was at Wallace, asserted that he had a month's supply of stores at the fort, and cholera had not struck yet at Wallace. Instead, Custer offered rationalizations for his conduct that he came to believe. The truth he chose to hide.[57]

Upon his arrival at Wallace, his apprehension about Libbie reached a breaking point. The fears for her overrode his judgment. Since he had left her at Fort Hays on June 1, he had allowed his desire to be with her to affect his conduct of operations. No other explanation of his risking the lives of men in a dangerous ride from Wallace seems credible. It was conduct that cannot be justified and was deserving of the subsequent court-martial proceedings.[58]

Some historians have charged that Custer had ridden from Wallace in a jealous rage. In their version, he had learned in a letter from an officer that Eliza was urging him to hurry to Fort Riley to "look after his wife a little closer." Allegedly, Lieutenant Thomas Weir and Libbie had been together too often for Eliza. The source for this information, however, was Frederick Benteen, who hated Custer. Undoubtedly, Lib-bie found Weir to be an attractive man, but no evidence exists that she did more than flirt with him.[59]

Weir's attention to her may have been enough to ignite Custer's fury, but documentation is lacking. If her husband suspected Weir of im-proper conduct, his subsequent relationship with the officer belies any smoldering resentment or anger. Finally, the alleged letter from the officer has never been located. With Custer, speculation, based upon suspect evidence, darkens numerous aspects of his life. While his deci-sion to return to her indicates irrational behavior, he may have been only a husband consumed with a desire to be with his wife.[60]

Relentlessly, Custer pushed the detachment across the Kansas plains. En route, he met Benteen and wagons with forage and two mail stages that he searched through for letters from Libbie. East of Castle Rock Station, a trooper deserted with his spare horse, and Custer ordered Sergeant James Connelly with a detail of six men after the culprit. Capturing the trooper at the station, the party started back for the main party, but were attacked by Indians, who killed one man and wounded another. Connelly overtook Custer at Downer's Station and reported the incident. Upon learning of it, the men clamored to find their comrades, but Custer refused, although Captain Louis Hamilton interceded twice, asking for permission and warning that the men threatened mutiny. Unswayed, the commander led the column east, arguing later that he believed both men were dead and that the warriors were gone. In fact, an infantry detail located the victims and found the wounded man to be alive.[61]

Early on the morning of the eighteenth, the exhausted officers and men reined up at Fort Hays, nearly 150 miles east of Wallace. In an almost unending march, they had covered the distance in roughly fifty-seven hours. At Hays, Custer left the detachment with Louis Hamilton, ordering him to continue to Fort Harker after a rest. During the night, twenty men deserted. Custer, meanwhile, with Tom Custer, William Cooke, reporter Theodore Davis, and an orderly left Hays in two ambulances. About nine o'clock that night, the party met a supply train, which had orders for Custer to remain at Wallace and operate between the Platte and Arkansas rivers. "The cavalry should be kept constantly employed," the instructions stated.[62]

The ambulances rolled into Harker before 2:30 A.M. on the nineteenth, and immediately Custer awoke Colonel Andrew J. Smith, district commander, spoke with the officer, and then boarded a train for Riley at three o'clock. Later that morning, he was reunited with Libbie. Back at Harker, meanwhile, a clear-headed Smith learned the details of the ride from Wallace and telegraphed his subordinate to return to Wallace at once, unless ordered otherwise. Custer sent a telegram, requesting a delay, but Smith denied it. It was not until the twenty-first before the couple could secure a train from Riley, and when Custer reported that day, Smith placed him under arrest for leaving his command without permission. Department commander Winfield Hancock wired Smith the next day, asserting that Custer "should have been arrested as his action was without warrant and highly injurious to the service, especially under the circumstances."[63]

On August 27, Lieutenant General Ulysses Grant ordered a general court-martial of the lieutenant colonel to convene at Fort Leavenworth on September 17. Smith had charged Custer with "absence without leave from his command," with one specification, or instance, and with "conduct to the prejudice of good order and military discipline," with three specifications. In the latter charge, Smith specified that he "did seriously prejudice the public interest by overmarching and damaging the horses," used the ambulances without authority, and neglected his duty by not trying to "recover or bury" the bodies of the two troopers. Additionally, Captain Robert West of the Seventh filed a charge that accused Custer of ordering that deserters *"be shot down"* without trial and of denying the wounded men medical treatment.[64]

Custer pleaded not guilty and spent the weeks before the trial preparing a defense with the assistance of his counsel, Captain Charles C. Parsons of the Fourth Artillery, a former academy classmate of his. In time, Custer became convinced of his innocence, and if Libbie is to be believed, they regarded the trial as "nothing but a plan of persecution for Autie," blaming Hancock for it "to cover up the failure of the Indian expedition."[65]

The court convened two days ahead of schedule, on September 15, at Fort Leavenworth, adjourning within thirty minutes because of the absence of a member. On the sixteenth, Parsons objected to Colonel John W. Davidson being on the court, alleging that the officer had expressed publicly "an opinion prejudicial to the accused." When Davidson admitted that he had said "he did not see 'how General Custer expected to get out of these charges,' " the court dismissed him. Testimony began on the seventeenth, with the trial lasting until October 11. Parsons's conduct of the defense pleased Custer, and on the trial's final day, the counselor read a lengthy statement of the defendant that answered each charge and specification in detail and concluded with a plea for acquittal.[66]

The court found Custer guilty of all three charges but cleared him of criminality in regard to the ambulances and the treatment of the deserters. The members ruled that he should be "suspended from rank and command for one year, and forfeit his pay for the same time." On November 18, Sherman stated officially that Grant had approved the findings and sentence, noting that "the levity of the sentence, considering the nature of the offenses of Brvt. Major General Custer if found guilty, is to be remarked on."

The Custers reacted with indignation at the verdict and sentence. The couple had persuaded themselves that the court had been prejudicial and improperly constituted. "The sentence is unjust as possible,"

Libbie asserted in a letter. Autie wrote to a former Third Cavalry Division officer, denying the accusations and criticizing the court. The officer gave the letter to an Ohio newspaper, which printed it. When court members read Custer's words—published by other newspapers— they asked Grant to take action, but the commanding general allowed the furor to subside.[67]

Custer was not finished, however. He charged West with drunkenness on duty, and in the subsequent trial, which divided the officers of the regiment, the captain was found guilty and suspended from rank and pay for two months. In turn, West accused Custer and William Cooke of the murder of trooper Charles Johnson in a civil court. After listening to the testimony, the local magistrate dismissed the charge.[68]

During the trial, Libbie had written that "we are quite determined not to live apart again, even if he leaves the army otherwise so delightful to us." But months later, as 1867 ended, their future in the army remained uncertain. The Kansas and Nebraska frontier and its native inhabitants had defeated Custer. Seemingly, he had been intimidated by his opponents, the weather, supply problems, and terrain. His actions had resulted in desertions and the deaths of men. He had allowed his concern for his wife to affect his judgment adversely. When confronted officially with the consequences, he deluded himself into believing that he had been unjustly accused and treated. In their quarters at Fort Leavenworth, as winter settled over Kansas, the Custers were together, united in their beliefs.[69]

15

WINTER

WAR

■ Major General Philip H. Sheridan leaned into the winds. When the Civil War ended, the hero of the Shenandoah Valley and Appomattox campaigns assumed direction of Reconstruction in Louisiana and Texas. For nearly two years, his administration angered white Southerners and exasperated President Andrew Johnson, whose policies the general opposed. A dispute with the governor of Texas resulted, at last, in Sheridan's removal from command in the summer of 1867, and after a six-month leave, he reported to Fort Leavenworth, Kansas, on March 2, 1868, as commander of the Department of the Missouri. On the Kansas plains, the wind was ceaseless.[1]

The department comprised four military districts, with 6,000 troops and twenty-seven forts and camps. The military's duty had not changed since the previous summer when Sheridan's predecessor, Winfield S. Hancock, was charged with protecting the region between the Platte and Arkansas rivers. Hancock's failed campaign led to his relief from command and spurred debate over Indian policy. In July, Congress created a peace commission whose purposes were to secure the area between the rivers for white settlement and to concentrate tribes on reservations. If the Indians—"misguided creatures" to reformers and peace advocates—could be placed on designated lands, they could be Christianized and taught to be farmers. By its title, the commission reflected optimistic assumptions—misunderstandings—that would encounter a different reality on the frontier.[2]

Commissioner of Indian Affairs Nathaniel G. Taylor led the delegation of three senators and three generals to a wooded valley along

Medicine Lodge Creek in southern Kansas in October 1867. Chiefs from the Kiowa, Comanche, Cheyenne, and Arapaho met with the commissioners, signing a treaty that ceded their traditional hunting grounds between the Platte and the Arkansas and accepted reservations in Indian Territory, present-day Oklahoma. In return, the commissioners promised annuities for thirty years. Months later, at Fort Laramie, Wyoming, the Sioux agreed to relocation on a huge reservation, which included nearly all of present South Dakota west of the Missouri River. The treaty also granted the Sioux hunting rights in Nebraska and Wyoming north of the Platte River and designated as "unceded Indian territory" the Powder River country of present Montana, barring all white incursion without consent of the tribe.[3]

Words on paper could not bridge the cultural chasm between whites and natives, however. Captain Albert Barnitz of the Seventh Cavalry was present at Medicine Lodge Creek and wrote in his journal that the tribes *"have no idea that* they are giving up, or that they have ever given up the country which they claim as their own, the country north of the Arkansas. The treaty all amounts to nothing." He believed that war was inevitable because of the Indians' misinterpretation.[4]

In July 1868, the Southern Cheyenne reported to Fort Larned to receive promised supplies, arms, and ammunition. When the superintendent refused because of a Cheyenne raid on a Kaw Indian settlement the previous month, the Indians were angered. After much discussion, the superintendent relented, but on their return journey, the Cheyenne attacked white homesteads on the Saline and Solomon rivers, burning the cabins, stealing the livestock, killing fifteen men, and raping five women. The citizenry of Kansas howled for action from the army.[5]

Phil Sheridan had few illusions about the efforts of the peace commissioners. While he agreed with the necessity of reservations, he believed that only coercion could force the tribes onto the restricted lands. Like most military officers, Sheridan argued for the transfer of Indian policy from the Department of the Interior's Indian Bureau to the War Department. To him, such a change would save money and bring a resolution. A pragmatic man who seldom questioned the correctness of his views, Sheridan believed that the army was the instrument that would ultimately insure white conquest of the frontier.[6]

He understood, however, the country's ambivalence toward, and division over, the army's role in the West. Writing in 1870, the general contended: "We cannot avoid being abused by one side or the other. If we allow the defenseless people on the frontier to be scalped and ravished, we are burnt in effigy and execrated as soulless monsters, insensible to the sufferings of humanity. If the Indian is punished to give security to these people, we are the same soulless monsters from the other side."[7]

But in Kansas, in the summer of 1868, Sheridan confronted irate settlers, businessmen, and politicians who demanded the punishment of the marauding warriors. The slayings on the Saline and Solomon rivers ignited weeks of fury in the state. Sheridan's primary concern was the protection of the Kansas Pacific Railroad and the settlements. He transferred his headquarters to Fort Hays and sent out the Seventh Cavalry and the black "buffalo soldiers" of the Tenth Cavalry in counterstrikes that brought few results.[8]

In August, he created an elite force of scouts, composed of frontiersmen, under Major George "Sandy" Forsyth. When the scouts discovered a village on the north fork of the Arikara in eastern Colorado, on September 17, the Sioux, Cheyenne, and Arapaho attacked. For nine days on an island, Forsyth's men repulsed Indian sorties with Spencer repeaters, but in the so-called Battle of Beecher's Island—named for Lieutenant Frederick Beecher, who was slain—they suffered casualties that amounted to half the command.[9]

By mid-September, Sheridan's frustrations with the army's failures to subdue the Indians had boiled over. Nowhere on the Kansas frontier were settlers safe, with scores of them dead and with hundreds of livestock driven off by the raiding parties. "I now regard the Cheyennes and Arapahoes at war," Sheridan wrote on September 19, "and that it will be impossible for our troops to discriminate between the well-disposed and the warlike parts of those bands, unless an absolute separation be made." He directed Colonel William Hazen at Fort Cobb in Indian Territory to order all friendly bands to use the post as their agency. For the Indians who refused to comply, the commander proposed retribution.[10]

Sheridan had concluded also that he required the services of an officer who could bring energy and aggressiveness to the operations. When Lieutenant Colonel Alfred Sully returned after only one week in the field with a force of infantry and cavalry, Sheridan dispatched a telegram to George Custer in Monroe, Michigan. Dated September 24, the message read: "Generals Sherman, Sully, and myself, and nearly all the officers of your regiment have asked for you, and I hope the application can be successful. Can you come at once?"[11]

Since April, Sheridan had tried to have Custer reinstated. When the court had found Custer guilty and sentenced him to suspension from rank and pay for a year, Sheridan voiced publicly his disagreement with the verdict. He allowed the Custers to use his quarters at Fort Leavenworth during the winter while he was on leave. Then, six weeks after he assumed departmental command, he wrote to Grant's chief of staff, John A. Rawlins, asking if Grant would pardon Custer and return him to duty. "There was no one with me [during the war] whom I more highly appreciated than General Custer," Sheridan asserted. "He never failed me, and if his late misdeeds could be forgotten, or overlooked on account of his gallantry and faithfulness in the past, it would be gratifying to him and to myself, and a benefit to the service."[12]

Despite his respect and affection for Sheridan, Grant did not pardon Custer, most likely because of the officer's letter that had appeared in the newspapers condemning the court's verdict and its members. By September, however, Custer had been out of the army for ten months, and when Sheridan requested his services, the War Department wired Custer on the twenty-fifth: "The remainder of your sentence has been remitted by the Secretary of War. Report in person without delay [to] General Sheridan, for duty."[13]

Custer boarded a train for Kansas immediately following the receipt of the telegrams. During his suspension, he and Libbie had been living as civilians for only three months, having spent the winter and spring at Fort Leavenworth. They enjoyed the post's social activities, and he busied himself writing installments of a memoir for Harper & Brothers. The couple considered a trip to Europe, but when he could not secure a position with a business firm, they abandoned the idea. Moving back to Monroe in June, they lived in the Bacon residence and visited with family and friends. Custer hunted and fished, waiting until he could rejoin the regiment. When Sheridan's unexpected message and subsequent orders arrived, he rushed to comply, although it meant an indefinite separation from Libbie, who remained in Monroe with Eliza. The army had summoned, and their desire "not to live apart again" bowed to the reality of a soldier's life.[14]

The lieutenant colonel arrived at Fort Leavenworth on September

30. Pleased with the reception by fellow officers, he wrote to Libbie two days later: "Don't tell Mother but I was overjoyed to get back to the post again and the big house never seemed so welcome. I experienced a home feeling here in the garrison that I cannot find in civil life." From the post, he traveled to Fort Hays, where he met Sheridan. At a breakfast together, Sheridan told his trusted subordinate, "Custer, I rely on you in everything, and shall send you on this expedition without orders, leaving you to act entirely on your own judgment." Departing from Hays with an escort on October 5, Custer rode south to the campsite of the Seventh Cavalry on Cavalry Creek, forty-two miles south of Fort Dodge, arriving on the eleventh.[15]

"With hair cut short, and a perfect menagerie of Scotch fox hounds," according to Albert Barnitz, Custer appeared at the camp. Although the men had been satisfied with Major Joel Elliott's leadership, a trooper recalled that when Custer arrived, "we were all very glad to see him again, as he was the only man capable of taking charge of the regiment." The change of command was evident at once, or as an officer remarked, "we had unconsciously fallen into a state of inertia, and appeared to be leading an aimless sort of existence, but with his coming, action, purpose, energy and general strengthening of the loose joints was the order of the day."[16]

While Custer galvanized the Seventh for field operations, supply shortages forced the regiment to return to Fort Dodge, where he welcomed hundreds of recruits, ordered drills, organized a body of sharpshooters, and assigned horses of a similar color to each company. The Sixth Michigan Cavalry had each company similarly mounted during the war, and he undoubtedly adopted the idea to give the companies of the Seventh a distinctive appearance and to promote morale. Initially, however, officers and men grumbled about the order that required numbers of them to swap trained mounts for new ones. Captain Barnitz predicted that the plan "will result in numerous desertions," arguing that Custer should have waited until the campaign's conclusion.[17]

Custer's letters during these weeks reflected his exuberance over the prospects of the forthcoming operation. "Some of the officers think this may be a campaign on paper," he noted to Libbie, "but I know Genl. Sheridan better. We are going to the heart of the Indian country where white troops have never been before." To a friend, he contended that "we are going on what is likely to prove a pretty hard campaign, both on men and horses. We may be out a month or even two months," but he was confident that they would do "all the harm we can to the Indians." Finally, in another letter to his wife, he cautioned her that she might not hear from him for an extended period of time, for he expected that "we will be on the wing all winter." "The Indians have grown up in the belief," he added, "that soldiers cannot and dare not follow them" into their country.[18]

At Fort Hays, meanwhile, Sheridan had formulated campaign plans. With William T. Sherman's approval, Sheridan proposed a winter operation against the tribes. Two summers of chasing elusive specters across the Kansas–Nebraska prairie had convinced both generals that to inflict punishment on the Indians the army would have to assail them when their mobility was restricted. The perils of a campaign on the plains in the winter were evident; in fact so much so that when veteran frontiersman Jim Bridger heard of Sheridan's proposal, he came to Fort Hays and told the general, "You can't hunt Indians on the plains in the winter for blizzards don't respect man or beast."[19]

Sherman and Sheridan were men not bent by difficulties. They had been the architects of "total warfare" in Georgia and the Shenandoah Valley, respectively, during the Civil War, and were determined to visit upon the hostile tribes a similar fate. "These Indians require to be soundly whipped," Sherman asserted, "and the ringleaders in the present trouble hung, their ponies killed, and such destruction of their property as will make them very poor." To Sheridan, the division commander declared that "if it results in the utter annihilation of these Indians, it is but the result of what they have been warned again and again."[20]

Sheridan ordered into the field contingents of troops from Colorado and New Mexico, but the main strike component was to be a combined force of infantry and cavalry under Alfred Sully and Custer against a reported winter encampment in the Washita River valley in western Indian Territory. To augment the latter command, Sheridan received authorization to organize a regiment of volunteer Kansas cavalry for six months and, on October 9, asked Governor Samuel J. Crawford to raise the companies. Four days later, a party of warriors attacked cabins in Ottawa County, killing four men, raping two young girls, and carrying off a woman. The raid incensed Kansans, and within three weeks, volunteers filled the ranks of the Nineteenth Kansas Cavalry. A former

Civil War general, Crawford resigned as governor to accept command of the regiment. On November 1, Sheridan ordered Sully and Custer south to establish a supply base on the North Canadian River, ninety miles south of Fort Dodge.[21]

Earlier, Custer had informed Sheridan that "I can move on the proposed campaign and in *good* condition in half an hour's notice," but when the directive arrived to advance, supply shortages still plagued the command. It was not until November 12 that enough food and forage could be amassed for the troops to march from Fort Dodge. En route, the column crossed the trail of an estimated 100 warriors, and Custer wanted to pursue them. But Sully refused the request, unwilling to move against the Indians until Crawford's regiment joined them. On the seventeenth, they reached the designated site of the supply base, with construction of the stockaded Camp Supply beginning the next day.[22]

Sheridan and his staff rode into Camp Supply on November 21. The department commander's presence at the base indicated the importance that he attached to the campaign. Upon arrival, Sheridan resolved a disagreement over seniority between the two subordinates. As district commander, Sully had authority over Custer, but Camp Supply lay beyond the boundaries of the district. By brevet rank, Custer was senior officer, and army regulations specified that when regulars and volunteers served together—upon the Kansans' arrival—brevet rank denoted precedence. Sheridan settled the matter swiftly, however, by ordering Sully back to Fort Harker to command the district.[23]

That evening, Custer invited officers to an informal reception for Sheridan. Sitting around a large campfire, the commander greeted them "in his good, genial way." "Like Grant," thought Captain Barnitz, "Sheridan is a man of few words, but he always *looks* very animated, and although he really does not say much, you came away with the impression that you have had quite a prolonged and interesting conversation with him!" When he spoke, Sheridan talked briefly about the prospective movement, expressing little disappointment that they had not yet encountered Indians.[24]

Unwilling to wait on the Kansans, the general instructed Custer to be prepared to march with the eleven companies of the Seventh Cavalry and the contingent of scouts. He issued the orders on the twenty-second, directing the cavalry to "proceed South in the direction of the

Antelope Hills, thence toward the Washita River, the supposed Winter seat of the hostile tribes; to destroy their villages and ponies, to kill or hang all warriors, and bring back all women and children."[25]

To locate the target, Sheridan had provided Custer with four experienced frontier scouts and a dozen Osage guides, whom Custer described as "a splendid looking set of warriors" and "superb horsemen." The frontiersmen were Ben Clark, Moses E. "California Joe" Milner, Raphael Romero, and Jack Corbin. Clark served as chief of scouts, having the complete confidence of Sheridan, who regarded him in time as the finest that he ever knew. The most picturesque and most popular with the officers and men was Milner, a loquacious man in his forties, with a "luxuriant crop of long, almost black hair" to his shoulders, black eyes and beard, and a ubiquitous briarwood pipe in his mouth. Each scout knew his business and could be relied upon by Custer.[26]

The members of the Seventh Cavalry stirred at 3 A.M. on November 23, and were met with a blizzard that had covered the ground during the night with twelve inches of snow. Even if the snow remained on the ground for a week, Custer vowed to Sheridan, they would find the foe. At daylight, after a breakfast of corn mush and coffee, and to the accompaniment of the band playing "The Girl I Left Behind Me," between 800 and 900 cavalrymen, with wagons, marched south, disappearing into the storm. Custer rode in the van, using a compass as a guide. Nothing seemed to affect his confidence, believing, as he boasted to Nettie Humphrey Greene in an earlier letter, that "we are as certain to find Indians as you are to find ducks in the Monroe marsh."[27]

Custer halted the march at two o'clock in the afternoon to allow the wagon train to come up. On the twenty-fourth, under clear skies and a warm sun, the column covered eighteen miles before encamping in woods. Custer killed numerous buffalo, and the men had meat for supper. The scouts led them south all day on the twenty-fifth, using the Antelope Hills as a marker. After marching thirty-five miles, the command bivouacked on the north bank of the South Canadian River, roughly seventy miles from Camp Supply and twenty-odd miles from the Washita River valley.[28]

The Seventh had penetrated deeply into Indian country without discovering fresh trails or other signs of native presence. Consequently, Custer sent Major Elliott with three companies and a guide on a scout up the north bank of the river at daylight on the twenty-sixth. While

Elliott conducted the reconnaissance, the main body crossed the swollen stream at a ford located by Milner. It was arduous work in the bitterly cold weather, necessitating the double-teaming of the wagons. Before the entire command had crossed, Jack Corbin rode in, reporting that Elliott had found a day-old trail of an estimated 150 warriors that led to the southeast. Custer ordered the major to follow it as he moved the command in that direction.[29]

Gathering the officers for a meeting, Custer informed them of Elliott's message and issued instructions: each man to carry 100 rounds of ammunition; 7 wagons, with good teams, to be selected to carry light supplies and extra ammunition; 80 troopers with worn mounts to guard the main wagon train; and preparations for the march completed. Captain Louis Hamilton, who was officer of the day, was assigned to the wagons, but he wanted to be with his company and asked his fellow officers if one of them would assume his duty. Lieutenant Edward Mathey suffered from snow blindness and agreed, with Custer's approval.[30]

The eight companies rode southeast, and about sunset, intercepted Elliott's trail. Custer hurried a courier ahead with orders for the major to halt, build fires, and feed his men and horses with rations and forage that would be sent. About nine o'clock, the main column joined Elliott, and the troopers had an hour to make coffee and have supper. Before the march resumed, each company commander received word that there should be no conversation above a whisper and no matches struck. In column of fours, with Custer and the scouts a half-mile in front, the Seventh moved through the darkness, their horses' hooves cracking the snow crust. At midnight they reached the Washita River and turned downstream, following the stream's course. An hour later, Little Beaver, leader of the Osage scouts, smelled smoke, and the command halted. Little Beaver crawled to the crest of a ridge, where he could view the valley, and upon his return was asked by Custer, "What is it?" "Heap Injuns down there," exclaimed the Osage.[31]

The village discovered by the Osage was nestled in a wooded bend on the south side of the Washita River. Consisting of forty-nine lodges, the village belonged to Black Kettle's band of Cheyenne, the surviving victims of the Sand Creek Massacre four years earlier. During the preceding weeks, various groups of Cheyenne, Arapaho, Kiowa, and Comanche had journeyed to Fort Cobb to seek sanctuary. Colonel Hazen offered the Kiowa and Comanche protection and supplies, but denied them to the Cheyenne and Arapaho because of their raids into Kansas. He warned the latter tribes that if they desired peace they would have to surrender to Sheridan. Otherwise, the general would search for them and attack their villages. The tribal councils divided over war or peace, and the tribes withdrew into the Washita Valley, one hundred miles northwest of Fort Cobb.[32]

Ironically, Black Kettle had returned from the post on November 26. When a Kiowa war party rode in and reported a trail of cavalry in the direction of the river valley, the elders met but dismissed the idea of white men on the march in winter. Black Kettle renewed his argument for peace, the memory of Sand Creek haunting the chief. The council decided to send emissaries to Sheridan and, as a precaution, to move the village farther downstream among other bands the next day. It was too late for the voices of peace.[33]

On a ridge north of the river, meanwhile, Custer had brought his officers together to view the target. Speaking quietly, the lieutenant colonel outlined the attack plan: Major Elliott and Companies G, H, and M would pass behind the hills to the east, swing around, and charge upstream from the northeast; Captain William Thompson and Companies B and F would recross the river, move behind bluffs, and come in from the south; Captain Edward Myers and Companies E and I would follow Thompson and deploy in woods west of the village; and Custer with the sharpshooters, scouts, and Companies A, D, C, and K would attack from the north, directly onto the village. The assault would be at daybreak, unless they were discovered, then immediately. The band would be on the ridge with Custer, and it would signal the charge by playing a song.[34]

Custer "particularly enjoined" them that "all were to go in *with a rush*." He asked for questions, and Captain Thompson remarked, "General, suppose we find more Indians there than we can handle?"

"Huh," rebutted Custer, "all I am afraid of is we won't find half enough. There are not Indians enough in the country to whip the Seventh Cavalry."[35]

When the officers returned to the companies, the men discarded overcoats and haversacks, mounted, and rode through the cold darkness of a winter's morning. Delays occurred, with Thompson's and Myers's contingents losing their way. At daybreak, unaware of the two detachments' difficulties, Custer turned in his saddle and readied the band when a rifle shot rang out from the village. Trumpeters sounded "Charge," and band members struck up "Garry Owen," an Irish tune that would become the regimental battle song from this morning on. The musicians managed only a few notes before their instruments froze. It did not matter, for the cheers of the cavalrymen signaled the coming fury.[36]

In the village, Cheyenne warriors scrambled from tepees with weapons in hand and sprinted to the riverbank, while women and children either huddled in the lodges or ran, screaming, across the snow-covered ground. The sharpshooters on foot and Custer's four mounted companies struck the defenders first at the river. Custer plunged through the warriors, shooting down one of them, and with his horse, bowling over another. Galloping to a knoll south of the village, he halted to direct the action.[37]

"There was never a more complete surprise," he reported. But the Cheyenne resisted fiercely, desperate men trying to save their families. Captain Louis Hamilton, who had wanted to be in the attack, tumbled from his saddle in the initial charge, dying on the ground. A bullet ripped into the abdomen of Captain Albert Barnitz, wounding him so severely that his comrades despaired for his life. Barnitz would recover, however, as the bullet missed vital organs. Within ten minutes, the cavalry secured the village and began herding women and children into a large tepee and hunting down warriors who fought from ravines and the woods. Among the Cheyenne dead was Black Kettle, whose body lay in the river.[38]

The delay in the attack by Myers's and Thompson's companies created a gap between them and Elliott's command through which many Indians fled. Elliott gathered together the regiment's sergeant major and eighteen enlisted men, all volunteers, and pursued the villagers. As he spurred away, the major shouted to a fellow officer, "Here goes for a brevet or a coffin." The detachment galloped downstream to the east, trying to shoot or capture the fugitives, who had scattered across the prairie. Suddenly, beyond a tributary of the river, Elliott and his men encountered a swarm of Indians on horseback. Unknown to the Seventh, a large encampment of Cheyenne, Arapaho, and Kiowa lay several miles downriver from Black Kettle's village. When gunfire exploded in the morning's stillness, scores of warriors mounted and raced west, meeting the oncoming band of cavalrymen.[39]

Outnumbered, Elliott dismounted the troopers, who lay down in high grass, forming a circle. The Indians scorched the ground with bullets and arrows. An Arapaho, Tobacco, rode among the defenders, striking three of them before being blasted from his horse, dead. Other warriors crept closer, and in one final rush, killed all the cavalrymen, stripping them of their uniforms and mutilating their corpses. Elliott's bravado and rashness had earned for himself and nineteen men their coffins.[40]

Upriver, meanwhile, the Seventh Cavalry flushed out pockets of Black Kettle's warriors, searched tepees, and corralled hundreds of ponies. Custer, who knew nothing of Elliott's vainglorious pursuit, stopped the Osage from killing women and children, and when Ben Clark told him that Myers's troopers were firing on the defenseless fugitives, he ordered it ceased. Carbine shots punctuated the clamor in the village as a handful of Cheyenne still resisted among the ravines.[41]

Lieutenant Edward Godfrey soon reported to Custer. Chasing some ponies and Indians, Godfrey had crossed to the north side of the river with a platoon and had ridden downstream. Two sergeants cautioned the lieutenant against moving too far away from the village. Halting, Godfrey dismounted and crawled to the crest of a rise, where as he recounted it, "I was amazed to find that as far as I could see down the well wooded, tortuous valley there were tepees—tepees. Not only could I see tepees, but mounted warriors scurrying in our direction." The platoon hurried toward the village, exchanging gunfire with their pursuers.[42]

When Godfrey found Custer, he related what he had discovered. Initially, the commander scoffed at the report, putting the lieutenant "through a lot of rapid fire questions." Godfrey rode away but soon returned at Custer's direction. For a second time, the superior interrogated the subaltern, who added that he had heard firing farther down the valley and believed it could have been from Elliott's detachment. Custer rebutted that Myers's companies had ridden in that direction but had reported no sounds of fighting. Minutes later, Romero, an interpreter, brought to Custer a Cheyenne woman, who confirmed the presence of other villages in the valley.[43]

Custer ordered company commanders to dismount the men and form a defensive perimeter around the village, while details leveled the lodges and piled them on to bonfires. Officers allowed the captives to secure some of their possessions before the troopers threw the rest of the items into the flames. Before long, the hills around the village darkened with warriors from downriver. They surrounded the cavalry-men but kept their distance as the troopers fired their Spencer carbines whenever some of the braver individuals sortied forward. When the details began slaughtering the nearly 900 ponies, the Indians wailed, and a party of them advanced only to be scattered by a counterattack by two companies under Frederick Benteen. The thrust by Benteen was, in the words of a trooper, "the prettiest sight I had ever wit-nessed."[44]

Although the tribesmen recoiled temporarily, difficulties mounted for the Seventh. Quartermaster James Bell ran a gauntlet of fire to bring in the reserve ammunition, and the squad assigned to the haversacks and overcoats followed, reporting that the enemy had seized them. If the Indians discovered either the seven wagons or the main supply train, the men and horses would be without food or forage for the return march. Underlying these concerns was the voiced speculation about Elliott's detachment. In response, Custer sent Captain Myers and troops on a scout downriver. Myers reported back that they had traveled two miles and saw no signs of the missing personnel. Custer had few options, except to abandon the hunt and to extricate the command. The safety of an entire regiment overrode the fate of twenty men, who may have escaped and were lost.[45]

The wounded troopers were prepared for a march, prisoners were herded together, companies were formed into columns, and the band played music as Custer led the Seventh Cavalry east, downstream toward the other villages. The display of power was a decoy, and it succeeded as the warriors rushed toward their lodges. At nightfall, the Seventh wheeled around, marching out of the Washita River valley. Custer pushed the exhausted, cold men until 2 A.M. on the twenty-eighth, when they halted and rested for a few hours. Scouts rode ahead to locate the wagon train, which the regiment reached at ten o'clock. The men cooked breakfasts, and Custer jotted a note for Sheridan to be carried by a courier: "We have cleaned Black Kettle and his band out so thoroughly that they can neither fight, dress, sleep, eat or ride without sponging upon their friends. It was a regular Indian 'Sailor's Creek' "— a reference to the Confederate defeat before Appomattox.[46]

On December 2, the Seventh Cavalry marched triumphantly into Camp Supply. Alerted to the regiment's approach, Sheridan, officers, the infantry companies, and the Nineteenth Kansas, which had arrived on November 28, formed ranks to welcome the victors. Custer was a master of such moments, his soul infused by the pageantry accorded the brotherhood of soldiers. With painted faces, the Osage scouts led, chanting war songs and firing their guns. Behind them came Ben Clark's band of frontiersmen, followed by the captive Cheyenne. At the head of the regiment, the bandsmen marched, announcing their arrival with the strains of "Garry Owen." Lieutenant William Cooke's sharp-shooters trailed the musicians, and farther back, rode Custer, dressed in buckskins, and the eleven companies, aligned in sets of fours. As the cavalrymen passed Sheridan, the officers saluted the general with their sabers. The short, barrel–chested Irishman lifted his cap in response, and it was finished.[47]

Custer conferred with Sheridan, reporting casualties as 1 officer killed, Louis Hamilton, 14 officers and men wounded, and Elliott and 19 troopers missing. From the tabulations of company commanders, Custer stated that 103 Indians had been killed, a figure that had to include women and children. Subsequently, the Cheyenne claimed that only 14 warriors had been slain, and 17 women and children. While no accurate number will ever be known, Custer's count was probably closer to the truth. He had interceded to prevent a purposeful killing of the women and children, but in the dim light of morning and the confusion in the village, most likely dozens of them were shot or sabered. Their deaths, however, ignited a firestorm of protest from critics of the army.[48]

The fate of Elliott's party clouded the celebration at Camp Supply. Custer contended to Sheridan that he believed that Elliott had become lost and would eventually reach Camp Supply. Sheridan thought other-wise but knew that nothing could be done for the present. When the truth became known, an unspecified number of officers in the regiment blamed Custer. At the center of the critics stood Benteen, whom Elliott had served under in the Civil War. Two months later, Benteen wrote a letter that was published in the *St. Louis Democrat* without his name attached, accusing Custer of abandoning Elliott and the enlisted men. When Custer learned of the letter, he summoned officers to headquar-ters and threatened to horsewhip the man responsible for it if he learned his identity. Stepping forward with his hand on his pistol, Benteen admitted to the authorship, and Custer ended the matter.[49]

The response to the deaths of Elliott and his men within the Seventh

Cavalry has been part of the history of that regiment. According to the standard and accepted accounts, the dissension within the regiment deepened the split between the pro- and anti-Custer factions that ultimately contributed to the harvest of death on the Little Big Horn nearly eight years later. Once again, Benteen's and a few others' statements form the crux of the evidence. There are contrary views that dispute the fact that many in the regiment held Custer accountable. A member of the detail that buried the men contended years later, "I never heard a word of criticism of General Custer for returning to Camp Supply without recovering the bodies at the time of the fight."[50]

Had the majority of the Seventh believed that Custer had left men behind who may have been alive? Did he desert them as he had the two troopers in Kansas during his dash to meet Libbie in the summer of 1867? It would seem that most of the rank and file believed before they left the battlefield that Elliott's group had been killed. Once Myers's detachment returned without evidence of their fate, nothing was left for the command to do in the presence of hundreds of warriors except to retire in safety. For this successful withdrawal, according to a trooper, the men praised Custer. Custer acted judiciously under the conditions on the field.[51]

But while Custer deserves praise for his judicious escape, he deserves criticism for his tactical leadership at Washita. In the words of a biographer, he "violated a fundamental military precept: he attacked an enemy of unknown strength on a battlefield of unknown terrain." If he had conducted further reconnaissances downriver, however, he risked discovery of the command and the loss of the advantage of surprise. Custer accomplished what other field commanders had failed to do in two summers on the plains—he had located a hostile village. To achieve surprise, he gambled that it was an isolated village. In fact, he would have won a victory virtually without loss had not Elliott ridden for glory. By attacking when he did, Custer had the psychological edge over his stunned opponents. Washita taught Custer lessons he would remember, brought him national fame now as an Indian fighter, and inflicted a punishing defeat on the Cheyenne that drove other tribal bands to seek security at Fort Cobb.[52]

Voices arose in the East, excoriating the military, and Custer and Sheridan in particular. Peace advocates and Indian sympathizers charged "massacre" and likened the two officers to "savages." But in the collective mind of many Americans, Custer and the Seventh Cavalry became identified with victory on the frontier. It was an image that would not be dispelled. Since Appomattox, Custer's renown and reputation had been tarnished, but on a winter's morning, along an unknown river, he refurbished both. Washita would echo along the columns of the Seventh Cavalry for years until there was another village beside another unknown river.[53]

To Phil Sheridan, however, Washita was a beginning. Ignoring the criticism, he declared that "the victory was complete, and the punishment just." He, Sherman, and Secretary of War John M. Schofield praised Custer and the regiment officially. In Sheridan's view, the winter war was not finished until the remaining hostile tribes were compelled to surrender. On December 7, the Seventh Cavalry and the Nineteenth Kansas, 1,700 men, marched south from Camp Supply. Sheridan accompanied the troops, assigning Custer to immediate field command.[54]

Following the Seventh's route to Washita, the units reached the battlefield on the tenth. Sheridan, Custer, and a detail searched the area the next day, finally solving the Elliott mystery. When Sheridan viewed the mutilated remains, he growled that it was "animalistic behavior of devilish savages." On the site of the encampment downstream, some men found the body of Clara Blinn and her two-year-old son, Willie, who had been captured in early October. The boy's skull had been crushed, and she had been shot in the head. From the campsites, trails led in three directions, one of them to the east, toward Fort Cobb. Sheridan decided to follow the latter trail, and in a snowstorm, the troopers marched on the twelfth. They struggled through "almost impassable country," and approached the fort on the morning of the seventeenth.[55]

About 10 A.M. that morning, a small party of warriors with a flag of truce met the column, delivering a message from Colonel William Hazen at the fort. "I send this to day," the note read, "that all the camps this side of the point reported to have been friendly, and have not been on the war path this season." Hazen suggested that Sheridan negotiate with Satanta or Black Eagle, Kiowa chiefs, to learn the location of the Cheyenne and Arapaho camps.[56]

The general was furious, terming the message "a pretty good joke." He and Custer had brought with them three Washita captives, including Black Kettle's sister, Mah-wis-sa. When they had discovered the body of Clara Blinn, Mah-wis-sa said that she had been a prisoner of the

Kiowa, under Satanta and Lone Wolf. The Cheyenne woman was lying, however, to protect her people and the Arapaho, who had taken Mrs. Blinn and her son. Sheridan would never learn the truth; in his mind, the evidence condemned the Kiowa, and now Hazen expected him to negotiate with the "devilish savages." Compounding Sheridan's wrath was the news that Satanta and Lone Wolf were about a mile ahead, wanting a parley and holding a courier as a hostage.[57]

Like Sheridan, Custer derided the idea of the Kiowa's innocence and requested permission to attack. But Sheridan hesitated, reluctant to ignore the statement of Hazen, who had been appointed by Sherman. Instead, he sent Custer, his aide-de-camp, Lieutenant Schuyler Crosby, newspaper reporter Randolph Keim, interpreters, several officers, and fifty Indian scouts to meet with the Kiowa chiefs, who waited for them in the valley. The interpreters spoke with Satanta and Lone Wolf, and then waved Custer, Crosby, and Keim forward. Each man was armed with a rifle, prepared to use it.[58]

Satanta was a proud, even arrogant man, whom a trooper described as "quite large and very strongly built, much more noble looking than the others." He spoke for the Kiowa, insisting that he desired peace with the white man, while the warriors prepared to attack Custer's group to cover the flight of the village. But the appearance of Sheridan with the main column deterred them. Custer stated that the army would honor Hazen's letter if the village would come to the fort. Satanta and Lone Wolf accepted, consenting to accompany the soldiers. The village would have to follow at a slower pace because of their ponies' weakened condition, the chiefs said, and Custer agreed. Accompanied by the chiefs and a number of warriors, Custer returned to Sheridan.[59]

The cavalry entered Cobb on the night of December 18. Hazen soon realized that he could not dissuade either Sheridan or Custer about the guilt of the tribe. Accusing Satanta and Little Wolf of "untold murders and outrages," Sheridan directed Custer to give them an ultimatum that if their village did not come to the fort as they had promised by sunset on the twentieth, he would hang them. Custer delivered the message to Satanta and Lone Wolf. Stoically, they listened to the words, and after speaking together, Lone Wolf, the head tribal chief, sent Satanta's son to the village. Sheridan would have executed the chief, in all likelihood, but the threat worked, with the Kiowa coming in the next evening. "I will always regret, however," affirmed Sheridan in his report, "that I did not hang these Indians; they had deserved it many times; and I shall also regret that I do not punish the whole tribe when I first met them." [60]

During the next fortnight, messengers departed from Cobb, bearing offers of peace from Sheridan to the tribes who remained away from the reservation. With their people destitute and hungry, several chiefs accepted, swelling the population around the post. Even a delegation from the Cheyenne and Arapaho came in, seeking a letter of protection until their villages could move to the installation. Sheridan agreed, but warned them that with the spring they could not "commence killing white people," or he would "make war on them winter and summer as long as I live, or until they are wiped out." It would take some time for their people to reach the fort, the Indians stated, but as an act of good faith, two chiefs consented to remain at the fort. It was New Year's Day, 1869, and Sheridan "considered the campaign ended." [61]

While at Fort Cobb, Custer received a dozen letters from Libbie. They had been separated for three months, each celebrating Christmas and New Year's hundreds of miles from one another. He had been needling Sheridan for a leave as soon as operations permitted it. Hazen hosted a party, and Sheridan a banquet on Christmas, and although he wanted to see her, Custer wrote, the "job here must be finished." [62]

On January 6, 1869, the Seventh and Nineteenth Cavalry marched from Fort Cobb. Since his arrival, Sheridan had been seeking a site for a new post to alleviate supply and forage shortages at Cobb, with its burgeoning native population. When Colonel Benjamin Grierson of the Tenth Cavalry found an excellent location on Medicine Bluff Creek at the eastern foot of the Wichita Mountains, thirty miles south of Cobb, Sheridan moved Custer's command there. The black cavalrymen of the Tenth were assigned to the construction duty, and upon completion, Sheridan named it Fort Sill, in honor of his academy classmate and friend, Brigadier General Joshua Sill, who had been killed in the Civil War. The Indians at Fort Cobb soon followed the troops to Medicine Bluff Creek. [63]

Missing from the native camps outside of Fort Sill were the Cheyenne and Arapaho, whose chiefs had promised their surrender on New Year's Day. Custer proposed to Sheridan that he take forty men and accompany Little Robe and Yellow Bear to their villages to urge the natives to comply. Reluctantly, Sheridan consented, but then refused to order the mission, believing that only volunteers should undertake such dangerous work. Custer found the volunteers—mostly from Cooke's sharpshooters—and on January 22, started west on the best mounts that they gleaned from the herd. Before he departed, an officer handed him a derringer to be used on himself.[64]

Passing west of the Wichita Mountains, Custer found the camp of Little Raven's Arapaho on the twenty-sixth, and succeeded in convincing the tribal leaders to move to Fort Sill. From the Arapaho, he learned that the Cheyenne had fled into Texas, and then granted permission to Little Robe to join his people. Custer encamped near the village and waited until Lieutenant Cooke arrived with supplies, a dozen men, and California Joe Milner. Sheridan had sent a note along, cautioning his subordinate to "keep close watch" on the Indians to prevent them "from getting the advantage of you." Custer responded with braggadocio, asserting that he and his men were ready to "clean out the whole institution" if the Cheyenne and Arapaho were disrespectful.[65]

Following Little Robe's trail, the cavalrymen and scouts rode west, but within days, lost it. With provisions exhausted, Custer turned back, reaching Fort Sill on February 8. They had ridden four hundred miles, surviving on horseflesh and parched corn the final days. Sheridan was disappointed with the failure to track down the Cheyenne, but he approved of Custer's decision to abandon the search.[66]

The next day, February 9, the fifth anniversary of the Custers' wedding, Autie wrote a twenty-nine-page letter to Libbie. Most of it recounted the scout and other military matters, but he told her, "To-day is our wedding anniversary. I am sorry we cannot spend it together, but I shall celebrate it in my heart." The officers and men wanted to go "home" to Fort Leavenworth, but "none of us feel that we could or ought to leave here until the Indian matter is settled." Their reunion would have to wait.[67]

By the time Custer returned to the fort, the men had been living "on quarter rations of bread for ten days." "Genl. Sheridan," he noted to Libbie, "has been worried almost to distraction," cursing the quartermasters. Unfortunately, the shortages worsened during the month, as the officers and men had to bake bread, "unwholesome stuff," on shovels over fires. The stock of candles was depleted, and forage supplies became critical. On February 23, Sheridan left Fort Sill, to expedite the flow of supplies to the garrisons in Indian Territory and to establish a supply depot at the mouth of Salt Creek on the north fork of the Red River. Before he departed, Sheridan ordered Custer with the Seventh and Nineteenth Kansas into the field against the Cheyenne, expecting to join Custer at Salt Creek.[68]

Sheridan's plans changed when he reached Camp Supply, with receipt of a telegram from President-elect Ulysses Grant asking the general to come to Washington at once. The general wrote to Custer on March 2, informing the latter that supplies would be forwarded to the Washita River crossing and suggesting that the Kansas regiment be disbanded. "Should you be able to strike the rascals on your way up, so much the better," continued Sheridan. "But, should you not, it will only hasten their final surrender here or at Medicine Bluff. At all events I do not anticipate further trouble." Concluding, Sheridan wrote, "I will push your claims on the subject of promotion as soon as I get to Washington, and, if anything can be done, *you may rely on me* to look out for your interests."[69]

Custer left Fort Sill on the day Sheridan sent the letter. He had selected the fittest horses from both regiments, distributed them to the Seventh, and had the Kansans march on foot. On March 5, they reached the North Fork of the Red River, despite struggling through rain and mud for two days. When scouts found an Indian trail, Custer decided to divide the command, sending back men from both regiments to the Washita and keeping 800 with mounts. If he were to find the Cheyenne, he needed mobility.[70]

The Osage scouts dogged the trail until it narrowed to the track of a single lodge. The Cheyenne had scattered, eluding Custer as had Pawnee Killer's Sioux two springs before in Kansas. Unbowed, with provisions nearly expended, he followed the solitary tepee. On March 13, however, the trail swelled from the marks of hundreds of lodge poles, and on the afternoon of the fifteenth, the Osage sighted two villages of 260 lodges on Sweetwater Creek in the Texas Panhandle. With Lieutenant Cooke and some scouts, Custer rode into the Cheyenne village of Chief Medicine Arrows.[71]

Escorted into the chief's tepee, seated among the tribal leaders, the officer smoked a large ceremonial clay pipe and talked of peace. The Cheyenne listened, for the winter treks had weakened their people and the ponies. When Custer asked where he could camp his men, Medicine Arrows agreed to show him a favorable site. Before Custer stood, a holy man tamped the ashes from the pipe on one of Custer's boots, and in his language, exclaimed that if the white leader were treacherous with the Cheyenne, all of the soldiers would die.[72]

By this time, the command had deployed about a mile away. For months, the Kansans had been away from home, enduring miserable rations and worse weather, searching for these Indians, whom they believed had killed, raped, and burned in Kansas. At last, the murderers had been found, and the volunteers wanted vengeance. "It looked, at one time, like they could not be restrained," recalled a Kansan about his comrades. "The line officers argued, begged and cursed. The accidental discharge of a carbine, or the shout of a reckless soldier, would have precipitated a killing that could not have been stopped." But Custer sent Cooke with orders against firing. He had learned that the Indians held two captive white women. To a Kansan, however, Custer was "a coward and traitor to our regiment."[73]

The foes negotiated for three days about the release of the captives and the surrender of the villages. When the Indians tried to sneak away, Custer took three chiefs as prisoners and threatened to hang them unless the white women were freed. Boldly, he had ropes hung across a willow tree limb and the chiefs placed nearby. The Cheyenne relented, freeing Mrs. Anna Morgan and twelve-year-old Sarah Catherine White. Anna Morgan's brother, Daniel Brewster, was with the troops, hired by Custer as a paid scout while he searched for her. The chiefs promised to report to Camp Supply as soon as their ponies could make the journey. Hi-es-tzie, or "Long Hair," as the Cheyenne now called Custer, accepted their words. He pledged to free the women and children captured at Washita and kept the three chiefs as hostages until the Cheyenne came to Camp Supply.[74]

The cavalry marched east on the twenty-second. With food stores depleted, the troopers slaughtered mules. On the evening of March 28, they all but crawled into Camp Supply. In a letter to Libbie, her husband boasted: "I have been successful in my campaign against the Cheyennes. I outmarched them, outwitted them at their own game." A few days after their arrival, a newspaper quoted him as saying: "I now hold the captive Cheyenne chiefs as hostages for the good behavior of their tribe and for the fulfillment of the promise of the latter to come in and conform to the demands of the government. This I consider, is the end of the Indian war."[75]

16

NORTH TO

DAKOTA

■ Libbie Custer greeted her husband at Fort Leavenworth, Kansas, on April 9, 1869. It was a joyous reunion because they had not been together for nearly six months. Despite her vow after the court-martial that they would not "live apart again," she had accepted the separation when the army summoned Autie to duty. She would bear the sacrifices, for love and from a sense of duty. She recognized that his rank and, more important, his national fame accorded them privileges and a standing other army wives could only envy. But now they planned to be together indefinitely, and after enjoying the social life at the post for nearly three weeks, the Custers traveled to Fort Hays, where the Seventh Cavalry had come after the campaign against the Cheyenne.[1]

The campsite of the regiment lay in a northern bend of Big Creek, two miles east of Fort Hays, which had been relocated and rebuilt since a terrible flood in June 1867. The cavalrymen's tents rimmed a large, flat ground, and beyond it, in a cluster of tents, the Custers would spend the summer and fall. The quarters provided them with privacy, sufficient room, and accommodations for Eliza and guests. A front and a back porch graced their tents, which Libbie decorated by draping Indian blankets and animal skins over the crude furniture. In her memoirs, Libbie recalled the canvas home fondly, noting that in the evenings she, Autie, and Tom Custer sat on the back porch, imagining "Big Creek to be the Hudson, and the cotton-wood, whose foliage is anything but thick, to be a graceful maple or a stately, branching elm."[2]

Of immediate interest, even fascination, to Libbie were the Cheyenne captives, who were held in a stockade at Fort Hays. Her husband visited them frequently, meeting with the three hostage chiefs from Medicine Arrows's village. Once she overcame her initial fear of them, Libbie sometimes went to the stockade without him, and in her memoirs of these years devoted numerous pages to the Cheyenne. Like most whites, she never bridged the cultural divide between the races, but her portrait was generally sympathetic.[3]

The captive that Libbie most wanted to meet was a woman about twenty years old named Me-o-tzi, or Mo-nah-se-tah, as the whites called her. In Cheyenne, her name meant "Young Grass That Shoots in Spring," and she was the daughter of Chief Little Rock, who had been slain at Washita. Autie had written to Libbie about the birth of Mo-nah-se-tah's child in January 1869, and of her value to him as an interpreter. She had accompanied him to the camp of Medicine Arrows and had been the one who confirmed the presence of the two white women in the village. When the cavalry returned to Fort Hays, she joined the others in the stockade.[4]

Accounts agree that Mo-nah-se-tah was a physically striking woman, with raven hair and "bright, laughing eyes." Libbie called her "the acknowledged belle among all other Indian maidens," and in Custer's words, she was "an enchanting comely squaw." Mo-nah-se-tah was also alleged to have become Custer's mistress, sharing his bed during February and March, and bearing him a son, named Yellow Swallow or Yellow Tail. No definitive proof of such a relationship exists—there is not even documentation that she gave birth to a second child at the end of 1869. The charge of Custer's infidelity is woven from three strands: the venomous writings of Benteen, the memories of scout Ben Clark, and Cheyenne oral tradition.[5]

Benteen's and Clark's assertions are both suspect—Benteen's hatred of Custer seemingly nourished that officer's soul in later years, and Clark blamed Custer for his subsequent dismissal as an army scout. Cheyenne accounts are not tainted by personal animosity and have more credibility. Most likely, though, Custer could not have fathered a child. As noted previously, his infection with gonorrhea at West Point probably made him sterile. Ironically, by 1868, Libbie and Autie had accepted that their marriage would be childless, with Autie writing to her about it, trying to comfort her. Later, Libbie stated that she had had two regrets in her life—his death, and having had no children.[6]

Not surprisingly, historians divide over the issue. But the truth defies historical inquiry without the discovery of new information. Mo-nah-se-tah may have been Custer's mistress; she may have borne a child to a fair-haired white man, and if so, it may have been to Tom Custer, not Autie Custer; and she may have been at Little Big Horn and may have spared the older brother's body from mutilation as her cousin, Kate Big Head, later contended. History intrigues especially when the truth eludes, but what seems to be overlooked in the allegations about Custer and other women, and for which a rich store of documentation exists —the letters of the Custers—is the relationship between Autie and Libbie Custer, one of the era's great romances.[7]

The months of captivity for the Cheyenne resulted ultimately in tragedy. Angered by delays and conditions in the stockade, the chiefs and several squaws attacked guards with knives. In the struggle, the troopers killed or mortally wounded Big Head and Dull Knife, two of the chiefs. When news of the incident reached the tribes outside the reservation, warriors raided settlements and attacked railroad construction crews. The army chased the raiders, but the forays continued until the remaining Cheyenne in the stockade were released. While Philip Sheridan and Custer may have believed that their winter campaigns had ended the Indian wars in Kansas and the Indian Territory, numerous bands of tribes refused to settle on the reservation and to abandon their nomadic life.[8]

In Washington, meanwhile, the new administration of Ulysses Grant instituted a "peace policy" toward the Plains tribes. "The proper treatment of the original occupants of this land—the Indians—is one deserving of careful study," stated Grant in his inaugural speech. "I will favor any course towards them which tends to their civilization and ultimate citizenship." In time, the government hired members of churches, mostly Quakers, as agents on reservations and tried to provide the native peoples with quality goods and supplies. For the tribes who refused to accept reservation life, Grant ordered "a sharp and severe war policy." The program removed army officers, like Colonel William Hazen, as agents and assigned to the military the burden of punishing the "hostiles." Despite its intentions and goals, the "peace policy" neither eliminated corruption on the reservation nor secured peace.[9]

The summer of 1869 in Kansas proved to be less bloody than either of the previous ones. The companies of the Seventh Cavalry were parceled out to the various posts along the Kansas Pacific Railroad, with detachments patrolling the prairie. In June, Colonel Samuel D. Sturgis assumed command of the regiment, with headquarters at Fort Leavenworth. He succeeded Colonel Andrew J. Smith, who had retired in January after over three decades in the army. Called "Old Buckskins" by the enlisted men, Sturgis would command the Seventh for over a dozen years, frequently serving on detached duty, giving Custer direction of the regiment.[10]

Most likely, Custer hoped that the colonelcy of the Seventh would be his after Washita. When Sheridan promised to "push your claims on the subject of promotion" in the capital, the general may have meant the vacancy that arose with Smith's retirement. At the time, Custer had planned to attend Grant's inaugural, saying to Libbie: "I dare not trust it to paper what is planned but if everything works favorably Custer luck is going to surpass all former experience, and you will be as greatly surprised as my greatest enemy. There are but two persons besides Gen Sheridan and myself who know what is contemplated." But his aspirations—and they were far higher than a colonelcy—met opposition from someone in Washington. Undoubtedly, Sheridan pressed his friend's case, telling the subordinate later, "Custer, you are the only man that never failed me."[11]

With Sturgis's appointment to the Seventh, Custer applied for the position of commandant of cadets at West Point. Since his initial days as a plebe at the academy, the institution had been a special place to Custer. The position he now sought offered prestige in the military and stability for a number of years. Sturgis endorsed the application, but the appointment went to Lieutenant Colonel Emory Upton, a distinguished Civil War officer whose writings would reshape America's military doctrines.[12]

For Custer, however, duty at Fort Hays provided him with a quiet interlude. He dispatched patrols, occasionally riding with units, and attended to the constant disciplinary problems. Like other frontier posts, Fort Hays induced civilians to establish a town nearby, and in the fall of 1867, a ramshackle collection of shanties and canvas-covered crude buildings had sprouted up outside the post, dubbed Hays City. By May 1869, according to a newspaper, the town was a wretched place— "officers, soldiers, citizens, blacklegs, gamblers, pimps, nymphs du pave, and all mingle here." Gunfire was so constant that Libbie likened the noise to a continual Fourth of July. Frequently, the bullets found a mark, and Hays City boasted the first "Boot Hill" in the West. When troopers caused trouble in the town or broke military rules, Custer incarcerated them in a twenty-foot circular hole, twenty feet deep, with a roof of logs and a ladder, that he had had dug in the camp. The men resented the pit, and it probably increased desertions.[13]

It was "such a pleasant summer," Libbie exclaimed to a friend, describing "this wild jolly life" as "perfectly fascinating." She and her husband resumed their evening horseback rides together, with Custer often on a horse he had purchased during the previous winter and had named Dandy. Brother Tom was a constant companion, and when he and Autie did something with which Libbie disagreed, Tom referred to her jokingly as the "Old Lady." Like his brother, Tom collected a menagerie of pets, including rattlesnakes, which he kept in a box, opening it for curious spectators. Tom's bulldog was, recalled Libbie, "always a terror to me."[14]

Custer had acquired some notoriety as a buffalo hunter, and he received nearly two hundred requests from individuals for him to lead them on a hunt. His reputation as a sportsman and hunter resulted in part from magazine articles he had written for *Turf, Field and Farm,* a sportsman's journal. Using the pseudonym Nomad, he submitted his first piece in 1867. Readers knew that Custer was Nomad, and buffalo hunting—a "magnificent sport" to Libbie—had captured the fancy of wealthy individuals. During the summer and fall, Custer escorted visiting wealthy Englishmen, showman P. T. Barnum, and a group of friends from Michigan, led by Detroit mayor K. C. Barker, on separate hunts. Libbie joined in a few of the excursions and entertained the guests at the camp.[15]

One member of the Custer household at Big Creek who did not enjoy the summer was Eliza. As the weeks passed, her unhappiness became evident to Libbie, who inquired about it. "Miss Libbie," replied the servant, "you's always got the ginnel, but I hain't got nobody, and there ain't no picnics nor church socials nor no buyings out here." When Eliza "got on a spree & was insolent," in Libbie's words, the couple dismissed her. She had been an integral part of their lives for six years, issuing orders in her soft voice and grumbling, "No matter whether it's right or wrong, Miss Libbie's sho' to side with Ginnel." She would marry a man named Denison, and years later, would visit Libbie in New York City.[16]

In mid-October, the Custers left Fort Hays for Fort Leavenworth. He had requested assignment to regimental headquarters at the larger installation for the winter, and it was approved. Before they departed from Fort Hays, the couple purchased two tracts of land in the state— 120 acres in Morris County for $1,700 dollars, and 18 acres from the Kansas Pacific Railroad for $109. Once at Leavenworth, Custer asked for a twenty-day leave to attend to personal matters in the East, and leaving Libbie at the fort and accompanied by Tom Custer and William Cooke, he boarded a Chicago-bound train on November 10.[17]

Custer visited with Sheridan in Chicago, with Mayor Barker and friends in Detroit, and with Cooke's family in Hamilton, Ontario. While in Detroit, he wrote to Libbie that although she was not with him, it was "the nicest time I ever had on leave." "But I do want my bunkey," he assured her. "I cannot get used to sleeping alone." He secured an extension of the leave until January 10, 1870, so he spent Christmas with the family in Monroe. For New Year's, he resolved, as he told Libbie, to cease playing poker for money "so long as I am a married man." "He did love to gamble," asserted an officer in the Seventh, "not for the money, but for the thrill of the game." In time, he frequently watched games and sat in, playing other individuals' hands.[18]

While in Monroe, Custer wrote an intriguing letter to Libbie. Evidently, he committed some transgression before he left Kansas or while on furlough of which Libbie had learned. "You may perhaps think of me when I return," he stated, "that spark of distrust which I alone am responsible for first placing in your mind but which others have fanned into a flame, will be rekindled and bitter burning words will be the result. But they will not come from me, at least I hope they may not." Although most men "in my situation, feeling that the greatest disappointment of their lives have overtaken them, that the love of the one person whose love alone was desirable was surely but slowing departing from them," would "drown their troubles in drink and dissipation." He would not and "will live such a life that I at least may have no further reproach to answer for."

Continuing, he avowed: "My love for you is as unquenchable as my life and if my belief in a future state is true, my love will survive my life and accompany me to that future. You may doubt my love but that does not disprove its existence. I love you purely unselfishly and simply, no woman has nor ever can share my love with you." Only Libbie dwelled in his heart: "It has been so. It is and will be." She was the "one single object of love." [19]

He rejoined his wife at Leavenworth by January 10, and if "bitter burning words" were exchanged, it remains unknown. It would be the last time he wrote such a letter to her. Upon his return, they enjoyed the social activities at the post, attending dances, a "Grand ball" on Washington's birthday, dinners, parlor games and hosting a masquerade ball in their quarters. Visiting with them were Margaret, or Maggie, Custer, Autie's eighteen-year-old sister, and Rebecca Richmond, Libbie's cousin. Finally, in April, the War Department ordered Custer and five companies back to Fort Hays. [20]

It was another bloody summer in western Kansas and eastern Colorado in 1870. Native warriors raided on both sides of the border and along the upper reaches of the Saline, Solomon, and Republican rivers. Custer commanded the Seventh's companies at Forts Hays and Harker, sending out patrols and warning officers to be alert. At Hays, he and Libbie lived again among the troopers in Camp Sturgis, named for the regimental commander. While recruits reported for duty throughout the summer, deserters continued to drain away the Seventh's strength. As Indian attacks mounted, Custer shifted companies from one post to another, and in mid-July he personally led a detachment into the region along the Saline River. But the scouts, patrols, and counteroperations failed to deter the raids. [21]

When at Camp Sturgis, the couple entertained friends, guests, ranking military officers, and dignitaries. Once more, many of them came to Kansas to participate in a buffalo hunt. During one excursion on the plains, a party of Indians appeared and exchanged gunshots with Custer and Lieutenant Cooke. Libbie and other women were nearby, and she screamed, "Autie will be killed." Soon, however, her husband and Cooke rode up, telling them it had been a joke as the Indians were army scouts. Lieutenant Colonel Wesley Merritt, Custer's friend and rival, had been with the frightened women and reacted furiously, although he had seen numerous examples of Custer's brand of humor. [22]

One of the guests at Fort Hays who spent much time with the Custers was Annie Gibson Roberts, the twenty-one-year-old niece of Major George Gibson of the Fifth Infantry. Gibson and his wife, Fannie, had invited Annie to stay with them at the post. The daughter of a renowned civil engineer, Annie had lived in Brazil, was fluent in several languages, could ride a horse and shoot a rifle, and when she killed a buffalo, she earned Custer's respect. Bright and pleasant, she attracted suitors among officers of the Seventh. Captain George Yates won her love, and in February 1872, they would be married.[23]

Annie's marriage to Yates brought her into the life of the Seventh Cavalry and into close association with the Custers. At some time, she placed on paper in a series of notes a physical description and a characterization of George Custer. She remembered him as a man of about 165 pounds, with "no spare flesh, well-knit—strong muscles lean & lithe." She thought that he appeared in photographs to be "much older looking" during the Civil War than when she knew him in the 1870s. His eyes were "a piercing blue; keen, thoughtful, observant & very *quick* in glancing at any object & sizing it up." His hair was "a real gold in color," and his fair complexion had been "bronzed by outdoors life." When he spoke, his voice was "pleasant in tone but quick and energetic with sometimes a slight hesitation as if words rolled out rapidly but not fast enough for the thought which preceded them. A nervous forceful manner in speaking." To Annie, "all his motions were rapid—he ate rapidly & etc."

Custer's "manner was calculated to inspire one with confidence," contended Annie, "it was kindly, but sometimes coolly critical. Nothing escaped him & this was sometimes no doubt disturbing to a stranger." Like Libbie, Annie remarked about his moodiness and periods of silence, at times, but he "usually possessed high animal spirits and was humorous, and very appreciative of that quality in those around him." She considered him to be "magnanimous & forgiving by nature—he rose above the little jealousies of military life." "He has been known," she added in explanation, "to give a good detail to a man he knew was not his friend."[24]

In the autumn, the Custers returned to Fort Leavenworth. After a trip to Washington, D.C., for an appearance before an examining board, Custer began a sixty-day furlough on January 11, 1871, that was eventually extended to September 3. He headed east while Libbie visited with a cousin in Topeka, before continuing on to Monroe. He had requested the leave to pursue business prospects.[25]

The allure of acquiring wealth had enticed the Custers since the end of the war. He had thought seriously of a career on Wall Street in 1866, attracted to the lifestyle, prestige, and power of monied men, but decided to remain in the army. He and Libbie never abandoned their dreams of money and status, and with the anticipated reassignment of the Seventh Cavalry to Reconstruction duty in the South, he decided to exploit his fame in a mining enterprise in Colorado. With a Michigan friend, he sought investors for the so-called Stevens Lode outside of Georgetown, Colorado.[26]

Throughout the spring and summer, he traveled to New York City from Monroe, spending weeks at a time with some of the city's wealthiest capitalists. Early in his efforts, he intimated to Libbie, "Can it be that my little Standby and I who have long wished to possess a small fortune, are about to have our hopes and wishes realized? If I succeed in this operation as now seems certain, it is to be but the stepping stone to large and more profitable undertakings." He and his partner floated two thousand shares of stock at $50 a share. Although he did not have the money, he subscribed $35,000 and obtained $15,000 from August Belmont, $10,000 from John Jacob Astor, and thousands more from others. But the certainty of the Custers' "stepping stone" was never realized, and despite several years of assaying and mining, the investment failed.[27]

While in New York, Custer moved among the city's most fashionable circles, attending the theater, and dinners in fine restaurants, private clubs, and elegant mansions. Attired in suits from Brooks Brothers, he mingled socially with the tycoons, dined with newspapermen Horace Greeley and Whitelaw Reid, escorted ladies to the opera and plays, visited the training camp of Joe Coburn, a famous prizefighter of the era, and greeted Sheridan, who had returned from Europe as an observer during the Franco-Prussian War. He kept Libbie informed through letters, describing the season's clothing styles and teasing her about the attention he was receiving from young women. "Married life in New York does not seem married life to me," he stated to Libbie, adding in another letter that "few wealthy people seem to enjoy their married life. . . . I have yet to find husband and wife here who enjoy life as we do."[28]

The dream of wealth from the Colorado silver mine beckoned still when Custer reported for duty at Louisville, Kentucky, on September 3. By then, the Seventh Cavalry had been transferred from the Kansas frontier to the South, with its companies distributed in nine states. Regimental headquarters were established in Louisville, and Custer and

Company A were assigned to Elizabethtown, Kentucky, roughly forty miles south of the Ohio River city. The War Department, however, had appointed him to temporary service on a board that inspected and purchased horses for the cavalry, and within a week he returned to Monroe for Libbie. While in Michigan, they concluded the purchase with his brother Nevin and Nevin's wife of a farm of 116 acres outside of Monroe for $5,280. After Little Big Horn, Libbie sold their share in the farm to Nevin for $1.[29]

Neither of the Custers welcomed the new assignment. Autie had written to Libbie earlier that "duty in the South has somewhat of a political aspect, which I always seek to avoid." Once she settled into rooms in an "old hotel," she described Elizabethtown as "the stillest, dullest place. No sound to be heard but the Sheriff in the Court House calling 'Hear ye,' three times as each case comes up. This part of Kentucky is very poor, the people low and uneducated." To keep busy, Libbie sewed on a new machine that Autie had purchased for her—"I make it fly," she told an aunt.[30]

Elizabethtown was home to the Custers, however, until the spring of 1873. While Kentucky remained relatively peaceful, the states of the former Confederacy had exploded in violence with the ratification of the Fifteenth Amendment, which granted African Americans suffrage in 1870. The Ku Klux Klan and the Knights of the White Camelia terrorized black officeholders, white scalawags and carpetbaggers, teachers of freedmen's children, and pro-Republican newspaper editors. The white organizations dragged black prisoners from jails and lynched them, killed the livestock of black farmers, burned homes and schoolhouses, and intimidated white supporters of freedmen's rights. In Washington, Grant reacted by pulling military units, like the Seventh Cavalry, from other duties to assist federal marshals in the enforcement of laws. But it was not until 1872 that the army succeeded in breaking the power of the Ku Klux Klan and forcing it underground.[31]

A trooper of the Seventh remembered the months in the South as "pretty dull soldiering." Weeks passed without incidents, with routine and boredom marking most days. In Elizabethtown, Custer chafed at the official inactivity, spending afternoons riding into the countryside or playing chess in the office of a local judge. Whenever he and Libbie could escape, they visited Lexington, Louisville, Cincinnati, or Monroe. In January 1872, he joined Sheridan on a buffalo hunt arranged for

Russian Grand Duke Alexis Romanov, who was on a visit to the United States. With Buffalo Bill Cody as a guide and a hundred Sioux warriors from a reservation, the party hunted in Kansas and Colorado, before the duke took the Custers with him to New Orleans. Newspapers covered the excursion extensively, enhancing Custer's reputation as a sportsman. Upon their return, the Custers traveled to Monroe for the marriage of Margaret Custer to Lieutenant James Calhoun of the Seventh Cavalry, whom she had met on one of her visits to her brothers.[32]

While at Elizabethtown, Custer wrote a series of magazine articles for *Galaxy,* a fortnightly publication. An editor had approached him about a series of articles on his experiences on the plains, offering $100 for each installment. The opportunity "opened to him a world of interest," recalled Libbie about her husband's literary career. "I think he had no idea when it was first suggested to him, that he could write." *Galaxy* offered him a wider audience than his submissions to *Turf, Field and Farm,* and he "dashed off" pages, with his first article appearing in May 1872. He proved to be a skillful writer. In 1874, Sheldon & Company, owners of *Galaxy,* published the articles in a book, *My Life on the Plains,* which remains in print today.[33]

Final escape from Elizabethtown came in February 1873, with orders for the Seventh Cavalry to report to Dakota Territory. At the request of the Northern Pacific Railroad, the War Department had agreed to provide military protection for an engineering party to be sent into the Yellowstone region of Montana and Wyoming. Since 1866, the military had argued that railroads would, as Sherman expressed it, "help to bring the Indian problem to a final solution." With Grant in the White House, the railroads had a powerful ally, with the president convinced similarly that the tracks "will go far to a permanent settlement of our Indian difficulties." When the department approved the operation, Sherman warned Sheridan that the "Northern Pacific Railroad is going to give you a great deal of trouble." In turn, Sheridan requested the Seventh Cavalry.[34]

With the companies of the Seventh scattered throughout the South, the authorities designated Louisville and Memphis, Tennessee, as rendezvous points, assigning Custer to the latter. By the end of March, seven companies had arrived at Memphis, and within a few days began boarding steamers in increments for the trip to Cairo, Illinois, where the companies from Louisville would unite with them. Custer left the city aboard the *Grand Tower* with the final contingent on April 6. At Cairo—"the forlornest place," to English novelist Charles Dickens—the troopers piled into railroad freight cars, with Companies B and C, the last group, departing with the Custers on the seventh, for Yankton, Dakota Territory. Two companies went with Colonel Sturgis to Minnesota to escort surveyors along the Canadian border. On April 8, Autie and Libbie celebrated her thirty-first birthday on the train.[35]

Captain George Yates and Company F arrived at rail's end in Yankton, the territorial capital, on April 9. Yates, who had his wife and infant son with him, prepared a campsite east of the town for the trailing companies that arrived on the tenth and eleventh. When Custer came, he moved the tents a half-mile to the west, confined officers to the camp, and sent their wives to the St. Charles Hotel, "the slovenly outrage they call a hotel," in a lieutenant's opinion. He and Libbie moved into a log cabin within the confines of the camp, which he designated Camp Sturgis.[36]

Sunday, April 13, was warm, with a heavy rain falling by nightfall. While the cavalrymen and townsfolk slept, the wind shifted to the northwest, plummeting temperatures and changing the rain to snow. By Monday morning, a foot of snow lay on the ground, and a plains blizzard raged. Custer ordered the men and mounts into Yankton, while wives of enlisted personnel stayed behind in tents. He was so ill that a surgeon ordered him to bed. With two servants and the doctor, the Custers rode out the savage storm in the cabin.[37]

The blizzard worsened during the night of the fourteenth-fifteenth. At the storm's zenith, six troopers stumbled into the cabin, joining the Custers until it abated. Someone from the women's tents came for the surgeon, and in the fury, the doctor delivered a baby boy. With the morning's light, a rescue party from town piled the women onto a makeshift sled and brought them into Yankton. Tom Custer came to the cabin for his brother and Libbie. Autie was too weak to leave, but he persuaded her to return with Tom. The blizzard had paralyzed the region for forty-eight hours, a landmark event in Yankton's history that townsfolk referred to years afterward as "the Custer storm of 1873."[38]

It required four days of digging out and warming weather for normal activity to resume. During the blizzard, numerous troopers risked their lives to desert, and when the weather abated, more slipped away. The companies of the Seventh had not been together as a regiment for two years. To Custer, the command needed discipline, a return to the routine of a unit in the field. He instituted drills twice daily, bugle calls, inspections, and issued specific orders for officers. Years earlier while in Kansas, he told a captain that "I always have known that my course when on duty was not calculated to make me popular with my subordinates, that I never expected to be a popular commander in times of peace. That while I was on duty and exercising command, I intended to carry out my own views according to my best judgment, even if I knew I would be opposed by the entire command." He preferred to "have the approval and good will of all men," but he intended "to follow what I think the best course whether I make friends or enemies."[39]

If Second Lieutenant Charles Larned is to be believed, Custer's orders and demands caused dissension among the rank and file. "Custer is not making himself at all agreeable to the officers of his command," Larned wrote on April 19. "He keeps himself aloof and spends his time in excogitating annoying, vexatious, and useless orders which visit us like the swarm of evils from Pandora's box, small, numberless, and disagreeable." Eleven days later, the lieutenant complained that Custer was wearing out the men "by ceaseless and unnecessary labor." The commander, continued Larned, "is not belying his reputation—which is that of a man selfishly indifferent to others, and ruthlessly determined to make himself conspicuous at all hazards."[40]

Colonel Samuel Sturgis arrived at Yankton on May 1, to assume command of the regiment. He had been ordered there, in Larned's opinion, because of "Custer's nonsense" that was causing desertions and of alleged discrepancies in the quartermaster's office. It appears that a number of disgruntled officers contacted Sturgis, and the department commander, Brigadier General Alfred H. Terry, sent Sturgis without investigating the substance of the officers' charges. When the colonel joined the Seventh, he perhaps conferred with the officers, but he took no action against Custer, who retained direct command over the companies.[41]

On May 7, the Seventh Cavalry rode out of Yankton in a column of fours, with Custer and the band in front. They were heading to Fort Rice, which lay nearly four hundred miles up the Missouri River from Yankton. It would take the regiment over a month to reach its destination. (Colonel Sturgis made the trip by river steamer.) En route, the troopers passed through several Indian agencies. At the Yankton Sioux reservation, dogs attacked the horses, and when Custer ordered the animals shot, several men, women, and children were killed as they tried to save the dogs. News of the incident raced upriver, and other bands avoided the cavalry. A trooper remembered the march as "a wonderful trip." "It was wonderful to be young," he declared, "and to be riding into Indian country as part of the finest regiment of cavalry in the world. We were all mighty proud of the Seventh. It just didn't seem like anything could ever happen to it." [42]

Custer's difficulties with the officers persisted, including a confrontation with Captain Frederick Benteen. When the regiment arrived at Fort Sully on May 22, a court-martial was ordered by Terry. Unwilling to have the Seventh's internal problems aired in the fort, Custer directed that the proceedings be held in camp. Initially, he confined all officers within the camp's limits, but ultimately relented, allowing the court to meet in the fort. According to Larned, who served as judge advocate, Custer continued to "hector and annoy" members of the court until a dozen officers protested to General Terry. The lieutenant colonel was, argued Larned, "making himself utterly detested by every line officer." [43]

The depth of discontent among the rank and file is difficult to assess. One evening on the trail, however, a group of officers gathered around First Lieutenant Edward S. Godfrey's campfire, chatting and smoking pipes. When Custer walked up and sat down, the officers began to filter away, singly, excusing themselves. Embarrassed, Godfrey stayed for hours, while Custer talked endlessly. [44]

Departing Fort Sully on May 30, the regiment completed the final segment of the march on June 9, halting across the Missouri from Fort Rice. A steamer began ferrying the companies across the stream. Within two weeks, the troopers would head west. "We'd just like to see the bunch of Indians that would dare fight the Seventh Cavalry," avowed Private Charles Windolph. "All we knew or cared about was that we were going into the last of the real Indian country." [45]

17

LAKOTA

GOLD

■ They were "the People," the Lakota, in their language. Comprised of seven divisions, or tribes, the Lakota were the westernmost of three branches—Nakota, Dakota, and Lakota—that white men, in a corruption of an Indian word, called the "Sioux," which meant "enemies" or "serpents." By 1873, the Lakota Sioux had dominated the northern Great Plains for a century. Independent, adaptive, and aggressive, they had wrested vast swaths of land from the Arikara, Cheyenne, and Crow, ruling present-day western North and South Dakota and eastern Montana, from the Missouri River west to the valley of the Yellowstone River. They offered no concessions to their numerous enemies and sought few alliances.[1]

Among their lodges, the People honored bravery, generosity, truthfulness, fortitude, and wisdom. Linked by family hunting groups, they lived a nomadic existence that followed the herds of buffalo. Wakontanka, or Great Spirit or Great Mystery, and a host of lesser deities ruled their spiritual and natural world, the truth of which the Lakota found in dreams and visions. It was a patriarchal, clannish society governed by councils of elders, shamans, and warriors. Each summer, the seven divisions of the Lakota gathered for a grand council. Their lives blended kinship, religion, and nature into an ordered harmony.[2]

The Lakota revered bravery above all virtues in a man. "It is better to die on the battlefield than to live to be old," the Lakota believed. Bravery was, in the words of a tribal historian, "a way of being, of acting, of doing." Their society encouraged warfare, teaching young males the path of the warrior. Of all the Plains tribes, none were more admired and feared than the Lakota. They were magnificent fighters who had come from the east, taken by blood what they wanted, and guarded it with fierceness against all interlopers.[3]

By the 1860s, the Lakota, or Teton, Sioux numbered upward of 30,000 when from the east, like themselves, came their most formidable enemy, the *wasichus*—their term for white people, which meant "you can't get rid of them." When the *wasichus* built forts and began to open the Bozeman Trail into Montana, the Sioux resisted, killing them and shutting down their inroads. In 1868, at Fort Laramie, bands of Teton and Yankton Sioux negotiated from the U.S. government an agreement to abandon the forts along the Bozeman Trail and accepted the so-called "Great Sioux Reservation" that encompassed all of future South Dakota west of the Missouri River. The treaty also designated an "unceded territory" from the reservation's western boundary to the Big Horn Mountains, embracing the valleys of the Powder, Tongue, and Big Horn rivers, in which the Sioux hunted buffalo. But thousands of Teton Sioux and Cheyenne never accepted the terms, desiring only to be left alone, and were regarded by the government as "nontreaties."[4]

The distinction between the Indians who accepted the treaty and the nontreaties was an impossible one. While thousands of Sioux and Cheyenne spent the fall and winter months at the five agencies on the reservation, they joined the nontreaties during the summer, hunting buffalo and roaming their lands. In turn, the nontreaties received supplies and fomented trouble at the agencies, remaining uncompromising in refusing to relinquish their freedom. The latter heard the truth from Sitting Bull, a *wichashu wakan,* or a man who could reveal the will of the Great Mystery. "I never taught my people to trust Americans," Sitting Bull stated. "I have told them the truth—that the Americans are great liars. I have never dealt with the Americans. Why should I? The land belonged to my people. I say never dealt with them—I mean I never treated with them in a way to surrender my people's rights."[5]

While the land belonged to the Lakota, as Sitting Bull argued, the treaty permitted the construction of railroads through the reservation and "unceded territory." The proposed route of the Northern Pacific Railroad, however, cut through the heart of the Lakota's traditional buffalo range along the Yellowstone River and its tributaries. In 1871 and 1872, survey crews, escorted by the military, explored the region, preparatory to the larger enterprise planned for the summer of 1873.

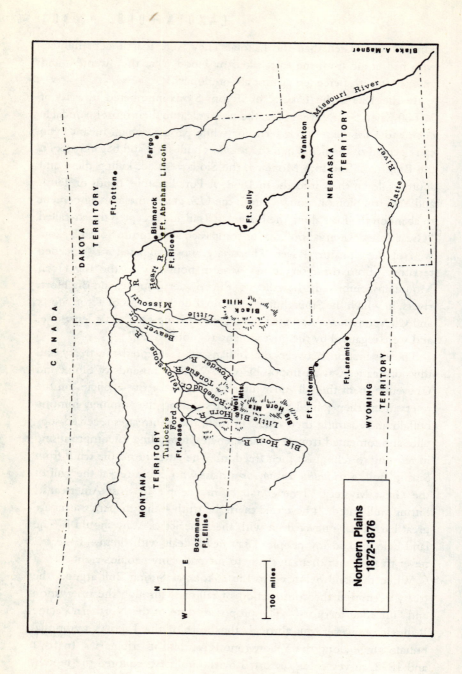

**Northern Plains
1872-1876**

N
W — E
S

100 miles

CANADA

DAKOTA TERRITORY

MONTANA TERRITORY

WYOMING TERRITORY

NEBRASKA TERRITORY

Missouri River

Platte River

Ft. Totten

Fargo

Bismarck
Ft. Abraham Lincoln

Heart R.

Ft. Rice

Missouri

Little C. R.

Beaver C.

Ft. Sully

Yankton

Black Hills

Yellowstone R.

Powder R.

Tongue R.

Rosebud Cr.

Little Big Horn R.

Big Horn R.

Wolf Mts.

Big Horn Mts.

Tullock's Ford

Ft. Pease

Bozeman

Ft. Ellis

Ft. Fetterman

Ft. Laramie

Blake A. Magner

To the Lakota, particularly the nontreaties, the construction of a railroad through Yellowstone Valley could not be tolerated, and if the crews came, there would be *wasichus* blood on Lakota land.[6]

The expedition that rendezvoused at Fort Rice, Dakota Territory, in June 1873 consisted of nineteen companies of infantry, two cannon, and ten companies of the Seventh Cavalry under George Custer. In all there were seventy-nine officers and 1,451 men, commanded by Colonel David S. Stanley. With the military were 353 civilians, comprising the engineering and scientific parties and the teamsters. Nearly 300 wagons carried the equipment and supplies, with 450 head of beef on the hoof. Much attention and care marked the preparations, moving one participant to remark that the civilians' "train of wagons was most admirably fitted for their use and were wonders of labor-saving and space."[7]

With a swarm of Indian scouts and the Seventh Cavalry in the van, the expedition marched out of Fort Rice on June 20. "Now began the summer of my discontent," recalled Libbie Custer. Unable to remain at the post because of the lack of quarters, she and Autie had decided that she would return to Monroe and reside with his parents. For Libbie, the weeks would pass slowly, her happiness measured by the arrival of a letter from Autie.[8]

Except for the separation from Libbie, Custer welcomed the prospect of weeks in the field. It had been three years since he had led the regiment in a march across the plains. Like a spirited horse, he bucked on a tether of inactivity. Restless and energetic, he was, said an officer, "never more in his element than when mounted on Dandy, his favorite horse, and riding at the head of the regiment." With limitless miles of wilderness before him, Custer spurred away from Fort Rice.[9]

Almost every day while on the march, Custer roamed ahead of the column either scouting for a route—"a service for which he always volunteered," reported Stanley—or hunting for game with a detail. "It seemed that the man was so full of nervous energy," remarked a private, "that it was impossible for him to move along patiently." He disappeared for hours at a time, relaying messages to Stanley when he believed it necessary. An excellent scout, Custer performed valuable duty for Stanley, but it appeared that the cavalry officer preferred to be away from the commander's authority, testing the extent of Stanley's reach.[10]

It seems, likewise, that Stanley anticipated difficulties with Custer from the outset. Stanley was forty-five years old, an academy graduate who had served as an infantry division commander during the Civil War. He was also, in the words of a historian, "a squat, humorless, peevish alcoholic . . . the antithesis of Custer." Eight days out of Fort Rice, he was writing to his wife, "I have had no trouble with Custer, and will try to avoid having any; but I have seen enough of him to convince me that he is a cold-blooded, untruthful and unprincipled man." The cavalry officer had irritated Stanley during the initial week by bringing along a black servant, Mary Adams, a cast iron cooking stove, and a sutler for the troops, although Stanley had given the latter permission to accompany them. Nevertheless, the colonel complained, concluding his letter, "As I said I will try, but am not sure I can avoid trouble with him." [11]

The initial clash between the two officers came on July 1, three days after Stanley forewarned his wife and following a miserable week of rain that slowed the wagons and flooded streams. "The winds have been terrible, and the whole prairie has become a swamp," grumbled Stanley, adding that "I never saw such weather in my life." By the first, the column had reached an overflowing Muddy Creek. While infantrymen labored all day to fashion a makeshift pontoon bridge from wagons and empty water kegs, Custer marched the cavalry miles into the country, sending a courier back to Stanley with a request for food and forage. Stanley had not ordered the movement, expecting Custer to assist with the crossing, and when the message arrived, he reacted furiously. He directed Custer to halt at once, return his wagons for the supplies, and "never to presume to make another movement without orders." [12]

The commander described the incident to his wife as "a little flurry with Custer." "I knew from the start it had to be done," he asserted, "and I am glad to have so good a chance, when there could be no doubt who was right. He was just gradually assuming command, and now he knows he has a commanding officer who will not tolerate his arrogance." [13]

Stanley's accounts of events and assessments of Custer's character and actions were clouded by the officer's alcoholism. A week after the incident at Muddy Creek, a drunken Stanley confronted Custer about the use of a government mount by a civilian, Fred Calhoun, a brother of Lieutenant James Calhoun, Custer's brother-in-law. When the colonel asked why Custer allowed Calhoun to ride the horse, Custer shot back that it was by the same authority that Stanley permitted a *New York Times* reporter the benefit of a mount. Stanley ordered Custer under arrest, assigning him to the rear of the column during the next day's march.[14]

On July 9, while the command marched fifteen miles, Custer "led the pelican with becoming grace today riding in the rear," Lieutenant Calhoun jotted in his dairy, using an army expression for an officer under arrest. While Custer refused "to retract anything," according to Calhoun, "Stanley is beginning to sober up and sees he has done a very foolish action." On the tenth, a clear-headed Stanley released the lieutenant colonel from arrest, and that night visited him and apologized. Afterward, Custer wrote to Libbie: "I banished the affair from my mind. . . . Genl. Stanley, when not possessed by the fiend of intemperance, is one of the kindest, most agreeable and considerate officers I ever served under."[15]

Overt disagreement between the officers ended with the incident. Custer declared subsequently to Libbie that "since my arrest complete harmony exists between Genl. Stanley and myself. He frequently drops in at my headquarters, and adopts every suggestion I make." Similarly, albeit from a different perspective, Stanley confided to his wife, "Custer . . . has behaved very well, since he agreed to do so." In fact, Custer assumed more command responsibilities as Stanley's continuous inebriation disrupted march schedules and caused dissatisfaction among the officers and men.[16]

On the day Stanley released Custer from arrest, the expedition entered the Badlands. When Alfred Sully first saw the region in 1864, he likened it to "hell with the fires out." The passage through was difficult. Custer marveled at the scenery, telling Libbie that "each step was a kaleidoscopic shifting of views, sublime beyond description." On July 14, they sighted the Yellowstone River, and on the following day found the steamer *Far West* at the mouth of Glendive Creek. Details transferred supplies from the boat to a supply depot that Stanley established eight miles above the creek's confluence with the river. Here the command encamped for over a week.[17]

It had been a month since they had left Fort Rice, and except for the problems with Stanley, Custer had enjoyed the trip. "I have so much to write of this," he exclaimed to Libbie while in camp, "I scarcely know where to begin, where to leave off, what to put down or what to omit."

He thought that the region "seemed almost like a new world," terming it "the Wonderland." He had hunted frequently, and bragged to his wife about his marksmanship. Each night upon his return to a campsite, Mary Adams, an excellent cook, had prepared a fine meal. A former slave, Mary "is a great favorite with all and never complains although she has had some rough experience already," he stated.[18]

In this "perfect wilderness," the men gathered each night around campfires. Poker games flourished, but Custer assured Libbie, "I never feel tempted to take a hand." At his headquarters, his brother Tom, the Calhouns, Myles Moylan, and several civilians passed the evenings. With the railroad party were Fred Nims, a former officer on Custer's staff, and President Ulysses S. Grant's son, Fred, whom Custer described as "most congenial, so modest and unassuming." But a constant companion with Custer was his old friend and former Confederate rival, Thomas Rosser. Serving as chief engineer on the project, Rosser had provided Stanley and Custer each with a sixteen-foot-square tent, and in the latter's, the two friends spent many evenings reminiscing and conversing. "Rosser regards Custer as the best cavalry officer of his rank in the army," stated a geologist on the expedition, "and Custer seems to regard his former antagonist with the esteem of a brother."[19]

The march resumed on July 24, with the *Far West* ferrying the men and wagons to the west bank of the Yellowstone River. During the next week, they moved west and south, slowed by "rugged terrain." The companies of the Seventh rode ahead, searching for wagon routes. When he could, Custer hunted and collected petrified wood and fossils. He had learned taxidermy, and at night prepared animal hides and heads for mounting. On July 31, the cavalry met the steamboat *Josephine* on the Yellowstone, receiving supplies and mail. By the night of August 3, the expedition was bivouacked several miles downstream from the Tongue River in the heart of Lakota land.[20]

The next morning, with Tom Custer, Myles Moylan, James Calhoun, Second Lieutenant Charles Varnum, and Companies A and B, consisting of 86 enlisted men, Custer scouted upriver. En route, Arikara scout Bloody Knife discovered an Indian trail, estimating the number of warriors at less than 20 and predicting the command would be in a fight either on this day or the next. Before ten o'clock, the cavalrymen arrived opposite the mouth of the Tongue River and halted in a grove of cottonwood trees to rest. It was scorching hot, with temperatures reaching 110 degrees in the afternoon. About noon, pickets shouted, "Indians! Indians!" A handful of Sioux were trying to scatter the horses, but rifle shots repulsed them.[21]

Custer mounted twenty men, and with Tom and Calhoun, chased the Sioux, directing Moylan to follow with the main body. Riding two miles in pursuit up a valley, Custer halted the detachment. He suspected a trap, and taking an orderly with him, he spurred forward, circling his horse in the Plains tribes' sign of a parley. Suddenly, from a stand of timber, approximately 300 Sioux, "stripped almost naked," charged, their war whoops echoing across the valley. The officer and the orderly "rode as only a man rides whose life is the prize." Tom Custer shouted to the troopers to dismount and to form a line. When the pair of riders cleared the men, they triggered three volleys that scattered the Sioux, who dismounted and opened fire. Moylan arrived within minutes with the remainder of the squadron.[22]

Caught in the open, with Indians edging closer through the tall grass, Custer ordered a withdrawal on foot to the cottonwoods. The cavalrymen executed the movement with skill and, once the horses were secure among the trees, deployed behind the bank of an old, dry streambed. Custer put every man he could on the line, leaving a handful to control the mounts. The Sioux, in his words, "displayed unusual boldness, frequently charging up to our line and firing with great deliberation and accuracy." But the soldiers repulsed each sortie. Finally, the Indians fired the grass, advancing behind the smoke, only to be driven back again.[23]

For three hours, the men clung to the embankment in the punishing heat, shooting at the movement of grass or at figures darting through the smoke. With the ammunition nearly expended, Custer mounted the squadron and counterattacked. The bold maneuver surprised the Sioux, who ran to their ponies and fled on horseback. Moylan and the companies pursued for three miles before returning to the grove. Not since Washita had Custer faced so many Indians in an engagement, but he proved that he still knew how to fight them. The affair demonstrated also how a unit of cavalry, with discipline, firepower, and leadership, could oppose a larger force of Plains warriors.[24]

During the combat, downriver from the cottonwoods site, a group of approximately thirty Sioux killed Dr. John Honsinger, regimental veterinarian, Augustus Baliran, the sutler, and Private John H. Ball. The trio had ridden ahead of the main body to join Custer, but were over-taken by the Indians and slain. They were buried the next day.[25]

On August 5, the entire command pushed up the Yellowstone. The cavalry patrolled to the front, discovering four separate Indian trails on the seventh. When the horsemen crossed the track of a large village the next day, Stanley instructed Custer to follow it. Seven companies rode out that night, keeping in the saddle until late on the ninth, when they reached the Yellowstone, near the mouth of the Big Horn River. The tracks had dispersed at the stream's edge, but Bloody Knife swam the river and found the trail on the south side. The cavalry spent the tenth trying to cross the swift current, but failed. The men bivouacked in a ravine for the night.[26]

At daybreak on the eleventh, the elusive Sioux opened fire on the cavalry from a bluff across the river. The troopers scrambled into a line and responded with carbine fire. While the cavalry had failed to cross the stream, hundreds of Sioux swam their ponies through the current and charged both flanks of the cavalrymen's position. Custer shifted companies to meet the onslaught, riding along the length of the line, trailed by an orderly with a guidon. Bullets and arrows snipped the air, but as a newspaperman reported later, Custer "seemed to lead a charmed life. Fear was not an element in his nature. He exposed himself freely and recklessly."[27]

Adopting the tactics he had used the week before, Custer ordered a counterattack. He had brought the band with him, and from the ravine, the musicians played "Garry Owen," signaling the charge. The cavalry-men surged toward the Sioux and broke their momentum. Custer tumbled to the ground when his horse was killed under him. The Indians scattered before the counterthrust, fleeing across the river. "It was a small affair," in the opinion of an officer, that cost the cavalry one man killed and three wounded. Custer estimated Sioux dead in the two engagements at forty.[28]

The valley of the Yellowstone belonged to the Lakota, and they would resist white incursions with ferocity. Custer admitted that in the attack of August 4 the Sioux "displayed unusual boldness." In his subsequent report, Stanley declared that "until the Sioux are quelled, nothing can be done to ever test the capabilities of the country when it is settled." The army must, in the colonel's opinion, "overawe or destroy the hostile Sioux." Before that occurred, however, they would have to be found amid the valleys of the Yellowstone and its tributaries. While seven companies of cavalry could not manage passage of a river, an entire Sioux village, including women and children, crossed it. The Lakota were a formidable opponent.[29]

From the engagement site, the expedition marched west, reaching on August 15 Pompey's Pillar, an irregular bluff of sandstone that towered several hundred feet above the valley floor and had been named by Meriwether Lewis and William Clark. After a day's rest, the column turned east, beginning the journey back to Dakota Territory. Difficult miles of march remained, and on a number of days Custer pushed the cavalry across the terrain. He seldom felt fatigue, and disregarded the condition of men and mounts. The men began calling him "Hard Ass," because of his seeming tirelessness in the saddle. On September 4, they arrived at the supply depot, dubbed Stanley's Stockade, near Glendive Creek. Here the cavalry waited until the main body with Stanley came in. Custer and six companies left on the twelfth, escorting the railroad engineers on the final leg.[30]

Throughout the expedition, Custer had described the country, recounted incidents, boasted of his hunting exploits, and wrote of his love for Libbie in a series of letters, including one that was forty-two pages long. But as he marched east toward a reunion, the anticipation increased his yearning for her. In a veiled but obvious reference to his sexual desire for her, he teased: "John says it is an awful long time between drinks in Betseytown. I wonder if you remember him or have you entirely forgotten that there is such a person. He certainly retains a vivid recollection of you and does not hesitate to remind me that you are not forgotten."[31]

Later, in a similar manner, he wrote: "It has reached a late hour of the night and I must get to my oh so lonely couch. But 'there's a better day a commin boys' and following the better day will be a better night 'Don't it Isaac?' I will try and add a P.S. tomorrow as we may not move until noon the crossing not being completed until tomorrow. So goodnight." He finished it the next day with, "Good morning my Rosebud. John has been making constant and earnest inquiries for his bunkey for a long time and this morning he seems more persistent than ever probably due to the fact that he knows he is homeward bound."[32]

At sundown, on September 21, the companies rode into Fort Abraham Lincoln, Dakota Territory. It would be several days before Stanley, the infantry, and wagon trains sighted the post on the west bank of the Missouri River. In Stanley's estimation, the expedition had covered 935 miles in ninety-five days. The commander prepared a lengthy report, describing the Yellowstone River as "the most beautiful one in the world," but if the railroad wanted to lay tracks and sell land to home-steaders, the company confronted the hostility of the Sioux and "the yearly prairie-fire." The immediate prospects of construction and settle-ment ended, however, on the day Custer reached the fort, when the New York Stock Exchange and numerous banks closed after the col-lapse of Jay Cooke & Company, a financial firm, plunging the country into the Panic of 1873. The Northern Pacific Railroad declared bank-ruptcy.[33]

To the government, the railroad company, and the public, the expedi-tion was a success. General Sherman telegraphed Custer, "Welcome Home." Newspapers printed summaries of the trip, with one of them calling Custer "Glorious Boy." The editor of *Galaxy* magazine re-quested additional articles. Northern Pacific officials praised him, mov-ing Custer to exclaim to Libbie, "My girl never saw people more enthusiastic over her Bo than these railroad representatives."[34]

Upon his return, Custer received orders from the War Department that assigned him to command at Fort Abraham Lincoln. Established in 1872, five miles south of Bismarck, the fort had been laid out originally as Fort McKeen for infantry on a bluff above the river, but Philip Sheridan convinced the department to relocate it to the plain below the crest in the summer of 1873. When the Seventh Cavalry arrived, the barracks and other buildings were still under construction. Once com-pleted, the pine barracks housed six companies of cavalry, with three companies of infantry in quarters on the bluff. The other six companies of the Seventh were posted at Fort Rice, twenty-five miles downriver, and Fort Totten to the northeast. Custer and the servant, Mary Adams, prepared his quarters before he boarded a train for Monroe, and Libbie.[35]

He spent nearly a month in Monroe, returning with his wife on November 16. Tom Custer escorted them to the post, where the band welcomed the couple with "Home, Sweet Home," and "Garry Owen." Mary awaited with "a grand supper ready," and the Custers settled into their quarters. They had lived in finer houses, but the walls were plas-tered and provided them with ample room. With cold weather, the entire garrison found it difficult to keep the quarters and barracks warm because as the unseasoned lumber dried, it created cracks in the walls.[36]

The couple reigned over a vibrant social life at the fort during the winter months. "Reception hops" on Friday nights, monthly company balls, drama performances, hunts, sleigh rides, card games, and nightly gatherings for conversation and charades comprised the social calendar. When in their quarters, Autie read books, and Libbie painted and sewed. With no school at the post, he enjoyed teaching several children in their home. Their "daily life was very simple," in her words. Occasionally, they visited Bismarck's stores. The enlisted men and bachelor officers frequented Pleasant Point—"Whiskey Point" to the troopers— directly across the river from the fort. Libbie grumbled that the place was "a wretched little collection of huts, occupied by outlaws." But here whiskey flowed and prostitutes beckoned.[37]

On the night of February 6, 1874, the chimney in the Custers' quarters ignited insulation made of petroleum-based paper in the attic, causing an explosion and fire that swiftly engulfed the roof of the home. Libbie and a guest, Agnes Bates, fled in blankets to the Calhouns next door. Men scrambled from barracks, forming a bucket brigade, but the flames spread rapidly, destroying the house. If the wind had been blowing, the fire could have leveled a number of buildings. Libbie and Agnes lost their wardrobes, but Custer saved his uniforms. Their lives had been spared, and he was sanguine about the losses, writing to his mother three days later, "It is better that we should have been burned out than that the calamity should have fallen upon others here."[38]

Carpenters built new quarters for the Custers, with Libbie requesting and getting a bay window in the parlor. The two-story dwelling had a library, dining room, kitchen, parlor, a dressing room, billiards room, servant's quarters, and several bedrooms, but "no modern improvements." Custer jammed the library with "trophies of the chase," including antlers, animal heads, pelts, a sandhill crane, an eagle, two foxes, and a white owl. He hung his saber and equipment on deer antlers and draped beaver and mountain lion skins over chairs. A stand of arms filled a corner. Over his desk he placed a photograph of Libbie in her wedding dress, and on the walls hung photographs of George McClellan, Sheridan, and Lawrence Barrett, his actor friend. Cluttered with the collections of a soldier and a huntsman, the library mirrored the man.[39]

During the reconstruction of the quarters, Custer became embroiled in a public dispute with Colonel William Hazen. He and Hazen had known each other since their academy days. It was Lieutenant Hazen who had arrested Custer in June 1861, in connection with a fistfight between two cadets. Their paths crossed again in 1868 and 1869 in Indian Territory during the Washita Campaign and its aftermath. Neither officer liked the other, and when Hazen, who had been assigned by Sheridan to remote Fort Buford in northwest Dakota in 1872, read the promotional literature about the agricultural possibilities of land in Dakota and Montana, he prepared a response that was published in the *New York Tribune* on February 7. Hazen argued that the land from Texas to Canada, between the Missouri River and the Rockies, was not worth "a penny an acre." [40]

The officer's assertions created a furor among executives of railroads with vast landholdings in the region, army officers, and other vested interests. Tom Rosser of the Northern Pacific Railroad contacted his old friend, for a rebuttal to Hazen. Using his Yellowstone report and material supplied by the company, Custer wrote a lengthy letter that was as overly optimistic about the land's natural wealth and prospects as Hazen's was darkly pessimistic. The *Minneapolis Tribune* printed Custer's rejoinder on April 17, and the letter went on to receive wide circulation. Hazen relished a controversy, and eventually he answered with another article and a book, entitled *Our Barren Lands.* The colonel even reopened an old wound, publishing privately, "Some Corrections of 'My Life on the Plains' " a pamphlet that criticized Custer's, and indirectly Sheridan's, version of events during the winter of 1868–1869. [41]

Custer ignored Hazen's subsequent writings; he had fulfilled Rosser's request, and the Northern Pacific was grateful. Like most army officers, Custer believed that the interests of the railroads served the interests of the nation. The military and the federal government gave financial aid for the construction of the transcontinental railroads, convinced that with the laying of each mile of track, the country took one more step in the conquest of the continent. The companies reciprocated with free passes for politicians, officers, and their spouses, and with other favors. Within the ethical standards of the era, the relationship between private businessmen and public officials, civilian and military, was accepted. Custer moved within the standards of those times. [42]

Other business interests, besides railroads, demanded the army's assistance. By the spring of 1874, no area of the West glistened brighter in the country's imagination with the allure of hidden wealth than the Black Hills of Dakota. For over half a century, rumors had abounded about Black Hills gold. Mysterious, unexplored, the region enticed whites, and as settlers entered Dakota, the pressure increased for the government to open the area for miners and lumbermen. The Black Hills bewitched.[43]

To the Lakota, however, Paha Sapa, "Hills That Are Black," were sacred, a place where spirits dwelled. The pine-forested hills were central to Lakota traditions and religion. When the Lakota entered Paha Sapa, they came usually in small bands or family groups. The hills' mysteries nourished Lakota souls and gave meaning to dreams and visions. Under terms of the Fort Laramie Treaty of 1868, the Black Hills formed the western border of the reservation, and whites were forbidden "to pass over, settle upon, or reside" in the 4,500 square miles that comprised the region. The words on paper were clear, and the Lakota would never compromise over Paha Sapa.[44]

From the headquarters of the Division of the Missouri in Chicago, Philip Sheridan had little, if any, concern for Lakota spirits. He viewed the Black Hills as the bastion of Sioux power, and if the Indian raids were to be ended and the tribe subdued, the army had to control the region. Consequently, on May 1, Sheridan requested authorization from William Sherman for an expedition that would explore the Black Hills for the establishment of a post in the region. Sherman approved, and a month later, Sheridan assigned Custer to command, stating that he was the officer "whom I thought especially fitted for such an undertaking." The division commander instructed Custer to compile a detailed and complete description of the area. To emphasize the importance of the operation to Sheridan, the general appointed his trusted staff officer, Major George "Sandy" Forsyth, with orders to maintain a daily diary, and Lieutenant Colonel Fred Grant, the president's son, to Custer's command.[45]

Sheridan designated Fort Abraham Lincoln as the rendezvous point, and here during June the elements gathered. In its size, the command rivaled the Yellowstone force in 1873, consisting of ten companies of the Seventh Cavalry, two infantry companies, Gatling guns, a cannon, and seventy-five Indian scouts. An engineering detachment, two geologists, two prospectors, three newspaper correspondents, a photographer, teamsters, and civilian employees, including Autie and Tom's twenty-five-year-old brother, Boston, who was hired as a forage master, accompanied the soldiers. In all, the expedition numbered 951.[46]

The War Department issued to the rank and file of the Seventh the new model 1873 breech-loading or "trapdoor" Springfield carbine. Weighing seven pounds, the weapon had an effective range of one thousand yards but was considered accurate only to three hundred yards. The carbine used a copper .45-.55-caliber cartridge, which, as the men learned, did not eject properly at times. The troopers began carrying knives to pry out jammed cases.[47]

Custer oversaw the preparations. Unlike on the Yellowstone expedition, he was senior commander, and he wanted the operation to bear his imprint. The newspapermen promised that it would receive wide circulation with his name linked prominently to its success or failure. He had been enthusiastic about the plan from the inception, endeavoring to convince Lawrence Barrett to forgo the stage for the summer and join him. "It would do more to renew and strengthen your energies physical and mental than anything you might do," he contended to the actor. "You would return a new man and feel as if you had really been drinking the true elixir of life." Although he anticipated opposition from the Sioux, he asserted that "the trip will be deeply interesting from many courses. We expect to discover a rich and valuable country."[48]

"It is a delightful morning," Lieutenant James Calhoun recorded in his diary of July 2, 1874. "The air is serene and the sun is shining in all its glory. . . . Nature seems to smile on our movement. Everything seems to encourage us onward." At 8 A.M., by sets of fours, ten companies of the Seventh Cavalry wheeled into column, and as officers rode along the ranks, the men cheered. The regimental band, all sixteen members mounted on white horses, played "Garry Owen." At the front, the Indian scouts added splashes of color to the blue of the cavalry. Finally, at a signal, George Custer, with his hair cut short, led the Black Hills expedition out of Fort Abraham Lincoln. The *New York Times* editorialized three days later that "those who ought to know affirm that this is the best equipped expedition that was ever fitted out for service on the plains."[49]

The command would be gone for sixty days and would, by one calculation, march 883 miles. For most of the members, it was a summer trip not to be forgotten. They passed through the heart of the Black

Hills, marveling at the narrow valleys and looming hills, which a private likened to "a great castle, surrounded by high walls that seemed to have no gates in them. It was as if the Almighty had set this place aside, and put a sign on it that read: 'No white men wanted here!'"[50]

On march days, Custer had a fixed schedule for reveille, breakfast, and "To saddle." In the evenings, he scouted ahead for the next day's route and possible campsites. The commander was, in a private's opinion, "a good plainsmen. He had an eye for it." After a march, or while in bivouac, the men climbed the hills, searched through "Indian" caves, hunted, fished, played the first baseball game in the Black Hills, and listened to band concerts. Calhoun filled his diary with comments such as, "a magnificent country," and "elegant valley," and "the whole command is in excellent spirits." But the "burning heat," long marches on some days, alkaline water, difficult stream crossings, and steep terrain exacted a toll from the men. Accidents injured a few; bad water caused dysentery in many, and Indian alarms denied sleep to all.[51]

Custer was effusive in his descriptions of the expedition in his letters to his wife. "Everybody pronounces this the best trip ever had," he avowed to her at one point. While he was tired often, he enjoyed the work and assured her that "I ride at the head of the cavalry and *keep inside the lines all the time.*" When he scouted, he always rode forth with a detachment of seventy or eighty men and a number of Indian scouts. Like the men, he climbed the hills, explored the caves, and hunted, killing his first grizzly bear on August 7. He also informed Libbie that "I am gradually forming my menagerie; Rattlesnakes, jack rabbits, eagle, owl."[52]

Various officers and civilians visited Custer's headquarters, a large hospital tent, each evening. Tom and Boston were constant companions, while Sandy Forsyth, Fred Grant, and Captain William Ludlow, one of the cadets involved in the scrape that resulted in Custer's court-martial at West Point and now chief engineering officer, were frequent guests. A favorite of Custer was "Lonesome" Charley Reynolds, who had served with Custer as a scout the year before. Darkly handsome, Reynolds rarely spoke, but in a trooper's opinion, "he was all nerve, afraid of nothing, and he had a good head on his shoulders." He acted as the expedition's guide.[53]

After entering the Black Hills, Custer always surrounded the camps with pickets, expecting trouble from the Sioux. Scouts discovered signs of their presence, but it was not until July 26, in Castle Creek Valley, that the whites encountered a village, which consisted of only five lodges and twenty-seven Indians. Custer smoked a peace pipe with sixty-three-year-old Chief One Stab and invited the Sioux to his camp the next day for presents of coffee, sugar, and bacon. When One Stab's band appeared, the Arikara scouts wanted Custer to allow them to kill their enemies. The frightened Sioux scattered into the hills, all of them escaping except One Stab, whom Custer retained as a guide.[54]

Three days later, on July 30, the prospectors, William McKay and Horatio Nelson Ross, discovered flecks of gold in the upper reaches of French Creek in a narrow valley that had been named Custer Park. Whenever the expedition reached a stream, McKay and Ross panned for the metal but had been unsuccessful until that day. Two days of work produced an estimated seventy-five dollars' worth of gold that caused a frenzy of prospecting from the troopers. "The gold fever is like taking dope," asserted a private. "You're helpless when it strikes you." For a day or two, his comrades "had it bad."[55]

Custer, meanwhile, prepared a report of the expedition's progress to date and, with stories from the correspondents, sent it with Charley Reynolds to Fort Laramie. Detachments explored other sections of the region for several days, and then on August 7, Custer started north for Fort Abraham Lincoln. Clearing the Black Hills a week later, he marched the column an average of over twenty miles a day. On August 30, following a halt to clean uniforms and equipment, he led the command into the fort to the accompaniment of "Garry Owen" by the band. It was, as trumpeter Theodore Ewert groused in his diary, a "Grrrrrand Entree."[56]

By now, the news of gold in the Black Hills had raced across the country. The reports by Custer and the correspondents delivered by Reynolds had unloosed the speculation. In his report, the expedition's commander stated that "almost every earth produced gold in small yet paying quantities," but cautioned that "until further examination is made regarding the richness of gold, no opinion should be formed." The newspapermen, however, glowed in their descriptions of the finds, igniting gold mania, particularly in the West. When Professor Newton H. Winchell, a geologist with the scientific team, stated publicly that he had seen no gold, Western newspapers reviled him. In frontier towns, miners formed companies, and by fall, groups had entered Paha Sapa and were prepared to spend the winter.[57]

The controversy extended into the next year, with Custer answering Winchell's claims in the press. In the spring of 1875, the government outfitted a second expedition that spent much of the summer analyzing the streams and ground for gold. When it reported that the Black Hills held deposits of the metal that would require capital and workers to extract, the furor was renewed. In September, a commission negotiated with the Sioux for the purchase of the region. The chiefs refused—they had been threatened by tribal members with death if they conceded. By year's end, an estimated 15,000 miners were in the Black Hills.[58]

But back in the early summer of 1874, before the command left Fort Abraham Lincoln, Lakota chiefs had warned the army of the consequences if they violated the sacred land of the Black Hills. When the expedition returned to the post and when miners followed, the Lakota called Custer's route the "Thieves' Road." The *wasichus* had no honor; they were liars as Sitting Bull said. Pehin Hanska, "Long Hair" Custer, had led them into the dwelling place of spirits. In Lakota councils, the leaders talked of war.[59]

C h a p t e r

18

TOWARD

LITTLE BIG HORN

■ George Armstrong Custer celebrated his thirty-fifth birthday on December 5, 1874, at Fort Abraham Lincoln, Dakota Territory. Whether he took time for reflection during the day is unknown. Most likely, he did not. He preferred not to measure life but to ride it like a spirited thoroughbred. As a man, he had resisted maturity, retaining a youthful exuberance for life that had endeared him to friends and had damned him to enemies. He had chosen a soldier's calling, and it had rewarded him richly with the fame he coveted. Although childless, his marriage had given him shared love and fulfillment. Perhaps if he chose not to remember, not to give thanks, he should have. Unknown to him, time had quickened.

Since his return from the Black Hills on August 30, he and Libbie had lived at the post, except for a six-week leave during which they had visited family and friends in Michigan, and had attended the wedding of Fred Grant and Ida Marie Honore. Despite the furor over gold in the Black Hills, the expedition had been as successful as he had hoped and as the army intended. It had recorded the region's topography, mapped the courses of streams, verified the presence of mineral deposits, and analyzed soil fertility, water resources, and timber reserves. With its completion, the War Department assigned companies of the Seventh Cavalry to various posts, and Custer reassumed command at Lincoln.[1]

The Custers' second winter at the fort was, as Libbie recalled, "very much the same as the first." Autie attended to routine administrative duties, ordered drills when the weather permitted, and met with Sioux chiefs from the reservation, listening to their complaints of being cheated by government agents. Although the campaign into the Black Hills had infuriated the tribe, the winter months passed in relative peace.[2]

The only serious incident occurred before Christmas with the arrest of a Sioux warrior named Rain-in-the-Face. Scout Charley Reynolds had overheard him as he bragged about killing three white men on the Yellowstone River two summers ago. Under orders from Custer, George Yates, Tom Custer, and a detail seized him at a trading post and brought him to Fort Lincoln. The Lakota confessed to leading the party that had slain Dr. John Honsinger, sutler Augustus Baliran, and Trooper John Ball on August 4, 1873. But after four months in the guardhouse, while the army wrestled with the legal questions of trying an Indian in a white man's court, Rain-in-the-Face joined two civilian prisoners in an escape.[3]

A week after the warrior's flight, Custer boarded a train for the East. He met with Philip Sheridan for a few days in Chicago, and then continued on to New York City, where he sought additional investors for the Stevens Mine in Colorado. He remained in the city about a month, failing to procure more funds. While there, he learned that his friend Detroit mayor K. C. Barker had drowned in a yacht accident. Following a visit to his parents in Monroe, he returned to the fort on June 3.[4]

Sheridan had assigned the 1875 Black Hills expedition to another officer, so Custer and the Seventh had a routine summer in the Dakota. Gold miners flooded into Sioux lands, but the influx brought no serious reprisals by the tribe. On September 24, Autie, Libbie, Tom, and Lieutenant William Cooke departed Fort Lincoln on a leave which for Autie would extend into the winter of 1876.[5]

While Libbie stopped in Michigan for a visit, the three men proceeded to New York City. As bachelors, Tom Custer and Cooke eagerly sought the city's pleasures before their furloughs expired at the end of November. Custer, meanwhile, renewed his pursuit of financial opportunities. His and his wife's burning desire for wealth caused him to be drawn into schemes and investments of questionable ethics and legality.[6]

Before he left Fort Lincoln, Custer received a letter from Colonel Rufus Ingalls, acting chief quartermaster general of the army. Ingalls had served in the Army of the Potomac with distinction as its quartermaster general and had known Custer since 1862. In his post, Ingalls had developed a close association with one of the era's most colorful businessman, Ben Holladay, whose stagecoaches and steamboats dominated transportation in the West. Holladay had prospered within the Gilded Age's pliant business standards and ethics.[7]

In the letter to his friend, Ingalls informed Custer that Holladay had secured a "promise" of a slice of the Indian trade from the Department of the Interior. "We want to do a big thing in the Black Hills," confided Ingalls. "Ben wants to put in Stages and be Sutler to new Posts." Holladay wanted Custer's thoughts on the plan, with Ingalls asking, "Now, what should he do to be in right *place* at right *time?*"[8]

Furthermore, the quartermaster general desired Custer's advice about the army's adopting Goodenough horseshoes for the mounted regiments. "If I can have control over the whole subject of horse shoes & c," stated Ingalls, "I mean to ask a Board with yourself as President." But Ingalls had concerns about the quality of the shoes and asked, "What think you?"[9]

Whether Custer responded to Ingalls's inquiries remains unknown—no letter has been discovered, nor is there evidence that the two officers met personally while Custer was on leave. What is known is that Holladay cosigned a promissory note in February 1876, when Custer's plunge into Wall Street railroad stock speculation resulted in a loss of $8,500. Various investors were involved in a transaction of nearly $400,000 that in subsequent litigation a court described as a "pretended sale." Custer had not invested any money, and when the scheme collapsed, he covered his debt to the brokerage firm Justh & Company by signing a six-month note at 7 percent interest. Seven years later, the court noted, "It seems to us impossible to read these papers without being impressed with the idea that they refer to an illicit business, with which Custer was rather ashamed to be connected."[10]

Was Holladay's generosity linked to Custer's assistance or advice on the tycoon's Black Hills dealings? The answer eludes without evidence. A post tradership could be lucrative, but it was often steeped in corruption, a practice Custer had condemned. If Custer considered a partnership with Holladay, it would have been brazen hypocrisy on his part.

The extent of Custer's involvement in suspicious business schemes may never be resolved. His craving for wealth cannot be doubted, and led him into risky speculations in the Stevens Mine and in railroad stocks. He received no known financial gain from the former and lost a considerable sum of money, for him, in the latter. He and his wife never seemed to have enough funds for their lifestyle and were enamored of the glamour and power of the monied elite. There is no proof of malfeasance by Custer in the form of accepting kickbacks from sutlers and traders as alleged later by Captain Frederick Benteen or of entanglement in a Black Hills tradership. Ingalls's letter asked only for advice, and Custer's reply is unknown. Suspicions persist, but without new documentation, they remain only suspicions. Custer achieved national renown that never brought the wealth he coveted.[11]

Although his financial deals failed, Custer enjoyed the four months in New York City. Libbie joined him in a few weeks, and together they attended dinners, theaters, and receptions. Admirers stopped them on the streets and offered invitations to social functions. Lawrence Barrett and his wife were in the city, and the two couples spent much time with each other. "The happiest hours of my association with him were passed [there]" remembered the actor. When their money tightened, the Custers moved to a room across the street from the Hotel Brunswick. For Christmas, Autie gave Libbie black silk for a dress, and she presented him with a set of solid silver tablespoons and teaspoons.[12]

After New Year's, an agent from the Redpath Lyceum Bureau in Boston approached Custer with a proposal. The firm scheduled nationwide lecture tours for prominent individuals and offered the famous soldier a contract for a series of lectures, five nights a week for four or five months, at $200 per presentation. Although a financially attractive proposition, he declined for the present, explaining that he required time for the preparation of the lectures. Perhaps next autumn, after the conclusion of summer operations, he might accept. He expected, as he wrote to Tom shortly afterward, "to be in the field, in the summer, with the 7th, and think there will be lively work before us. I think the 7th Cavalry may have its greatest campaign ahead."[13]

During the second week of February, the Custers departed for Dakota Territory. When they arrived at St. Paul, Minnesota, they learned that the trains had ceased running to Bismarck because of the snow. Custer spoke with officials of the Northern Pacific Railroad, for which he had rendered valuable service in the past, and the company agreed to outfit a special train with three engines, two snow plows, freight and cattle cars, and forty employees to remove snowdrifts.[14]

"At first everything went smoothly," recounted Libbie. Beyond Fargo, however, the trains stalled in a blizzard—"there seemed to be a perfect wall of ice," in her description. Workers toiled for hours, but an engine had become wedged in a drift. The snow intensified, and they were stranded. "The days seemed to stretch on endlessly," she thought.[15]

Finally, a passenger who knew telegraphy tapped into the line and sent messages to Fargo and Fort Lincoln. From the fort, Tom Custer replied, "Shall I come out for you? You say nothing about the old lady; is she with you?" Autie wired back not to attempt to rescue them, but he should have known his brother. In a mule-drawn sleigh, Tom covered the sixty-five miles, found the train, loaded Autie, the "old lady," and three hounds into the vehicle, and brought them safely to the fort, arriving on March 12. It would be another week before the snow thawed enough for the train to complete the journey.[16]

The couple had barely settled into the warmth of their quarters when a telegram arrived from Washington summoning Custer to the capital. Sent by Representative Heister Clymer, the message requested that the officer appear before the House Committee on Expenditures. Custer hesitated initially to comply, sought the advice of his department commander, Brigadier General Alfred H. Terry, about whether legally he had to testify, but in the end, decided to make the trip. He left the fort by sleigh on March 21, arriving in Washington a week later.[17]

Politics fueled the capital's agenda in the presidential election year. Grant harbored designs on a third term while Democrats in the House probed for scandals in the executive branch. For months, Clymer's committee had been investigating charges of the sale of post traderships by Secretary of War William W. Belknap, who as a young man, ironically, had been the chairman's roommate at Princeton University. When the evidence mounted of his guilt regarding the tradership at Fort Sill, Belknap, a large hulk of a man, met with Grant on March 2, and tearfully submitted his resignation. The president accepted, hoping that the secretary's removal would end impeachment proceedings.[18]

Belknap and his two wives—after his first wife died in 1870, he married her sister—had collected an estimated $20,000 from the trader. The Democratic House voted to impeach him for "malfeasance in office," but Clymer wanted to broaden the investigation to ensnare as many Grant appointees as he could, so he called additional witnesses who might possess threads of evidence. The telegram to Custer followed.[19]

Custer had been an outspoken critic of the system, and perhaps more important to the committee, had public ties to leading Democratic supporters in New York. For two years, he had written the *Galaxy* articles under a nom de plume and had supplied material on the Republican administration in Washington to James Gordon Bennett's *New York Herald,* and to the *New York World,* both anti-Grant journals. Disagreeing with the president's Reconstruction policies, Custer hoped for a Democratic victory in the fall. With his fame, his political leanings, and his knowledge of affairs at army posts, he was an appealing witness to the committee.[20]

Custer should have remembered his wife's advice of a decade earlier to avoid politics. "Do not be anxious," he wrote to her at one point. "I seek to follow a moderate and prudent course, avoiding prominence." But, in fact, he was neither moderate nor prudent. He lunched with Clymer and other leading Democrats, and in his testimony before the committee, he gave more hearsay than factual evidence, implicating Orvil Grant, the president's brother, in the schemes. On April 18, he testified before Representative Henry B. Banning's Committee on Military Affairs, presenting again hearsay statements against Major Lewis Merrill of the Seventh Cavalry for alleged bribe-taking while on duty in South Carolina. The pro-Republican *New York Times* observed that Custer "is full of information as an egg is of meat, but somehow it is only hearsay and gossip, and no witnesses appear to corroborate it. If this sort of thing goes too far, the Democrats, if they should have control of the next Administration, may not, after all, make him a Brigadier-General."[21]

Leaving the capital on April 20, Custer visited the exhibits at the Centennial Exposition in Philadelphia before traveling on to New York City. While in Philadelphia, a telegram overtook him, calling him back to Washington to appear before the Senate if needed. But that body had no need for Custer's testimony, and he soon sought permission to return to Dakota Territory. He met with General-in-Chief William Sherman and the new secretary of war, Alphonso Taft, who agreed to write to the Senate and request the lieutenant colonel's release. The next day at a cabinet meeting, however, Grant, furious with Custer over the testimony and public lunches with Democrats, directed Taft not to write the letter and to assign another commander to the troops at Fort Lincoln.[22]

Evidence indicates that Custer did not know that the president had removed him from command. When the Senate granted him permission to leave on the twenty-ninth, he met with Sherman, who suggested that Custer delay his departure until Monday, May 1, to call upon Grant. Twice during the month, Custer had gone to the White House, but the president refused to receive him. On the first, Custer waited five hours in an anteroom before Grant sent word he would not see him. Before he departed, Custer scribbled a note to his former commander stating that he had come not to solicit a favor but to refute "certain unjust impressions concerning myself which I have reason to believe are entertained against *me*. I desired this opportunity simply as a matter of justice and I regret that the President has declined to give me an opportunity to submit to him a brief statement which justice to him as well as to me demanded." [23]

From the White House, Custer walked to the War Department, inquired whether General Sherman was in his office, and, learning that he had not returned from New York, received permission from the adjutant and inspector generals to rejoin his command. Boarding a train that evening, he headed west, stopping briefly in Monroe to visit his parents, arriving at Chicago on May 4. At the railroad station as he prepared to depart for St. Paul, one of Philip Sheridan's staff officers handed him a telegram from Sherman. It read: "I am at this moment advised that General Custer started last night for St. Paul and Fort Abraham Lincoln. He was not justified in leaving without seeing the President and myself. Please intercept him and await further orders; meantime let the expedition proceed without him." [24]

The embarrassed and shocked Custer wired Sherman and explained the circumstances of his departure. Sherman sympathized with Custer because his order had been dictated at Grant's insistence, so he relented and sent a telegram that night, granting Custer authority to proceed to departmental headquarters at St. Paul. [25]

At the Minnesota city, Alfred Terry, commander of the Department of Dakota, welcomed his subordinate, whom the general confided later to friends "with tears in his eyes, begged my aid." Terry offered his assistance. Since the War Department had designated him field commander for the summer campaign a week earlier, Terry had tried to persuade superiors that he required Custer's experience and spirit for the operation. Consequently, when the cavalryman arrived, the pair of them prepared a message for the president. "I appeal to you as a soldier," the telegram read under Custer's name, "to spare me the humiliation of seeing my regiment march to meet the enemy and I not share its dangers." Terry endorsed it and sent it to headquarters in Chicago. [26]

His longtime friend's activities in Washington before Congress had infuriated Phil Sheridan. The division commander believed that Custer had acted unwisely, even discrediting the army. But Sheridan knew also that the controversial officer was the best man to command the planned expedition against the Sioux. In words critical of the subordinate, the general endorsed the request for clemency.[27]

In Washington, meanwhile, opponents of the administration had been castigating the president for his treatment of the officer. With Sherman, Sheridan, and Terry supporting Custer's reinstatement, Grant acquiesced, but gave him command only of the Seventh Cavalry. Terry was directed into the field as overall commander. On May 8, Grant's decision reached Terry's headquarters. The news elated Custer. Reportedly, a short time later he met Captain William Ludlow on the street, exclaiming to the engineer officer that he intended to "cut loose from Gen. Terry during the summer" as he had from David Stanley in 1873. Two days later, Terry and Custer boarded a train for Fort Lincoln.[28]

The campaign toward which the two men traveled had been stillborn for several months. Its genesis lay in a White House meeting on November 3, 1875, attended by President Grant, Secretary Belknap, Secretary of the Interior Zachariah Chandler, Benjamin R. Cowen, Chandler's assistant secretary, Lieutenant General Sheridan, and Brigadier General George Crook, commander of the Department of the Platte and Sheridan's former Civil War subordinate. The Lakotas' adamant refusal to sell the Black Hills prompted the meeting at the White House. It had been less than a month since the commission sent to negotiate the purchase of the Black Hills from the Sioux had returned and reported to Congress that a price for the region should be established, given to the tribe "as a finality," and if rejected, their annuities and rations ceased. The commissioners also believed that the Lakota would never accept unless compelled by the military. Such a scenario suited the president.[29]

At the White House meeting, the participants, in the word of a historian, "contrived" a war against the Sioux. They decided that the army would not stem the flood of miners into the region, and if the "hostile" or nontreaty bands remained away from the reservation, the army would move against them. There would be no more negotiations with the tribe—the power of the military would be the messenger.[30]

During the next few weeks, the administration prepared the documentation for the justification of a war against the Sioux. On December 6, at the direction of Secretary Chandler, Indian Commissioner E. P. Smith instructed his agents on the reservation to inform tribal leaders that the nonreservation bands must report to the agencies before January 31, 1876, or the army would force them onto the reservation. Runners carried the ultimatum to the winter camps. Some complied; most did not. On February 1, before some of the groups could have learned of the deadline, Chandler apprised Belknap that Sioux were now a War Department concern.[31]

Belknap forwarded authority to Sheridan to commence a winter campaign against the "hostiles" on the seventh. The division commander planned a three-pronged strike into the Yellowstone River valley and its tributaries. From Fort Lincoln, Custer and the Seventh Cavalry would march upriver; from Montana forts, Colonel John Gibbon, with infantry and cavalry, would descend the Yellowstone; and from Fort Fetterman, Wyoming, Crook and a combined force would move north into the Powder River region. It was an operation similar to the one directed by Sheridan in the winter of 1868.[32]

The campaign sputtered, stalled, and eventually failed. Winter weather locked in the Seventh at Fort Lincoln. In Wyoming, Crook marched on March 1, plowed through snow and bitter temperatures, and on the sixteenth a detachment of the command surprised and seized a large village of Sioux and Cheyenne on the Powder River. A battle ensued after the warriors recovered, until Colonel J. J. Reynolds unaccountably withdrew without destroying the tepees or their contents. Convinced that he could not expect to surprise other villages, Crook abandoned the operation, returning to Fort Fetterman.[33]

In Montana, Gibbon had been unable to unite the components of his so-called Montana Column until after Crook turned south toward Wyoming. It was not until the beginning of April before the units marched east from Fort Ellis, a rectangular compound on the Gallatin River, three miles east of present-day Bozeman, Montana. From there, they pushed along the north bank of the Yellowstone, reaching Fort Pease, a stockade built in 1875 and located on the site of Custer's fight with the Sioux below the mouth of the Big Horn River on August 11, 1873. When Terry and Custer left St. Paul on May 10, Gibbon was marching toward a campsite six miles above the mouth of Rosebud Creek.[34]

Consequently, by mid-May, Sheridan's campaign had been reshaped —Gibbon's troopers would combine with Custer's Dakota Column, both under Terry, while Crook returned to the field. Neither the district commander nor the two department commanders knew where the "hostiles" were or the number of warriors with the bands. It would be a search across an area of perhaps 100,000 square miles. Sheridan could not direct it from Chicago, so as he informed Sherman later, "I have given no instructions to Generals Crook or Terry as I think it would be unwise to make any combinations in such country as they will have to operate in. Each column will be able to take care of itself."[35]

Preparations were nearing completion at Fort Lincoln when Terry and Custer arrived on May 14. Eager to be back, the Seventh's commander plunged into the work, and in the words of a private, "was as happy as a boy with a new red sled. He put a lot of zip into us." Forty-three-year-old Mark Kellogg of the *Bismarck Tribune* and the *New York Herald,* who had permission to accompany the column, saw him at the post and wrote:

> Gen. George A. Custer, dressed in a dashing suit of buckskin, is prominent everywhere. Here, there, flitting to and fro, in his quick eager way, taking in everything connected with his command, as well as generally, with the keen, incisive manner for which he is so well known. The General is full of perfect readiness for a fray with the hostile red devils, and woe to the body of scalp-lifters that comes within reach of himself and brave companions in arms.[36]

The Dakota Column consisted of the entire complement of the Seventh Cavalry, including four companies that had returned recently from occupation duty in the South, three companies of infantry, and a detachment with three Gatling guns. A contingent of Arikara scouts, teamsters, and civilian employees completed the force. In the latter group were Boston Custer, hired as a forage master, and Harry Armstrong "Autie" Reed, eighteen-year-old son of David and Ann Reed. Young Reed had come west on vacation, and his uncle Autie took him along as a herder. By the night of the sixteenth, all was readied. Custer spoke with Terry, assuring the general that despite rumors he might have heard, he wanted to serve under him.[37]

The members of the Dakota Column awoke to a heavy fog and a

raw chill on the morning of May 17. By seven o'clock, the column had formed in its campsite outside of Fort Lincoln, stretching for two miles. To the accompaniment of "Garry Owen," the cavalrymen, infantrymen, wagons, and beef herd marched. Libbie Custer and Maggie Custer Calhoun accompanied their husbands for the day. In the post's "Returns," under the Seventh Cavalry, a clerk recorded, "Operations in the field against Hostile Indians." [38]

The command covered thirteen miles that day, bivouacking along the Heart River. Paymasters distributed pay to the troopers, who resented the fact that Custer had waited until they were beyond the enticements of Bismarck. Reveille sounded before daybreak on the eighteenth, and the men forded the river, heading due west for the Little Missouri River, where reports placed bands of Sioux. From a bluff above the Heart River crossing, Libbie and Maggie watched them fade beyond the horizon. Libbie had tearfully clung to Autie before he mounted, knowing that the separation could be long. It would be immeasurable. [39]

"Lonesome" Charley Reynolds guided the column, relying on his memory of the route followed by Stanley's expedition three years earlier. The march was slow, at times difficult with the crossing of streams on pontoon bridges. Custer kept his wife posted in letters, obeying her wishes by writing: "I have been extremely prudent—sufficiently so to satisfy you. I go nowhere without taking an escort." By the twenty-ninth, they reached the Little Missouri and bivouacked, roughly 165 miles from Fort Lincoln. Terry ordered Custer and four companies of the Seventh on a scout upriver the next day. They rode twenty-five miles, crossing the crooked stream thirty-four times, but discovered no signs of Indian encampments. "Bloody Knife looks on in wonder at me because I never get tired," Custer wrote to Libbie, "and says no other man could ride all night and never sleep." [40]

The men and wagons crossed the river on May 31. During the day's march, the three Custer brothers rode away from the column without authority. Terry rebuked the lieutenant colonel for it, and Custer promised in writing to "remain with, and exercise command of, the main portion of my regiment." A spring blizzard on June 1 halted the march for a day and a half. Two days later, they reached Beaver Creek, about thirty-five miles east of Glendive Depot on the Yellowstone River. Here scouts from Gibbon located them with a message from the colonel. Gibbon reported that the "hostiles" were apparently in large numbers

discovered five abandoned campsites, estimating the size at between 350 and 400 lodges. Terry knew as much from Gibbon, but by traveling thirty miles up the Rosebud, the major determined that the natives were not on the creek's lower section. Terry now needed to reformulate his plans.[49]

Terry, Custer, Gibbon, and Major James Brisbin, commander of companies of the Second Cavalry, met on the *Far West* during the afternoon of June 21. For two hours, the officers discussed the details of an offensive movement. Gibbon's and Reno's information indicated that there were probably 800 warriors in the village, but how many bands from the reservation had joined the so-called winter roamers was difficult to know. They surmised that the Indians were encamped either on the upper Rosebud or in the valleys of the Big Horn or Little Big Horn rivers. To find the quarry and then trap them, the commands would operate separately. They knew that the natives would be harder to overtake and capture than to defeat in an engagement.[50]

Consequently, uncertainty and flexibility characterized the operational plan. Custer and the Seventh Cavalry would advance up the Rosebud to its headwaters, and if the trail turned toward the Little Big Horn, as expected, the cavalry would descend the stream, scouting to the left to preclude a flight of the natives to the south or southeast. Gibbon, meanwhile, and the infantry and Brisbin's mounted companies would proceed up the Yellowstone to the mouth of the Big Horn, and from there to the confluence of that stream and the Little Big Horn. The two commands should join on or about June 26, but circumstances in the field could affect the timetable. If either force encountered the warriors before they reunited, the officers believed that each contingent possessed sufficient numbers and firepower to overcome them. Terry would accompany Gibbon and give Custer written orders the next morning.[51]

That night, Terry came to Custer's tent. The general undoubtedly wanted to clarify the instructions and to listen to Custer's views while they were alone together. Terry had interceded with superiors and the president to secure Custer's services and trusted him. He recognized that there were a number of variables in the plan and that the orders had to be followed at Custer's discretion. During the conversation—the evidence is convincing—Terry said, "Use your own judgment and do what you think best if you strike the trail."[52]

Campfire talk that night centered around the next day's movement.

Veteran troopers knew that with Custer they would have hours of hard riding in the saddle. Few expected that the Sioux would stand and fight. For years, the Seventh had chased specters across the plains in the heat of summers and seldom exchanged gunfire with them, except on the Yellowstone in 1873. Most soldiers probably bedded down early, anticipating that sleep might be precious during the next several days.[53]

The announcement of the offensive electrified Boston Custer and Autie Reed. Both wrote letters home that night, with the older man stating that they were marching "with the full hope and belief of overhauling" the Indians. "They will be much entertained," he thought. The nephew was more excited, however, exclaiming to his parents that "business is now going to commence in earnest." Like others, the teenager expected "some tall riding," but if they caught the Sioux, "Boss and I are going to cabbage some good ponies and robes. When I get back I will write a long letter telling you about our scout."[54]

The mood in the camps might have darkened had the men known of recent events to the south. Since Crook's attack on a village in March 1876, the bands had gathered into a large village, and tribal leaders and warriors were determined to resist further incursions. They had wintered along the Tongue and Powder rivers, shifting locations as the spring grass matured. When Gibbon's scouts had discovered them on the Tongue and then Rosebud Creek, the Lakota and Cheyenne had been in the region for months.[55]

About the beginning of June, they moved up the Rosebud, holding on the sixth the most sacred Lakota ceremony, the Sun Dance. Participants danced around a "pole of suffering," with their arms pierced and without food or water, seeking a vision. Sitting Bull had strips of skin cut from each arm, endured the agony, and saw the future with dead soldiers "falling right into our camp." Their enemies, he said, "do not possess ears. They are supposed to die, but you are not supposed to take their spoils." His words thrilled the Lakota.[56]

From the ceremonial site, they ascended the Rosebud until hunters reported the approach of soldiers from the south. Following Davis Creek, they crossed the divide into the valley of Greasy Grass, or the Little Big Horn, camping on a tributary, Great Medicine Dance Creek. On June 17, the warriors attacked near the headwaters of the Rosebud. The soldiers belonged to Crook, who had returned to the field at the end of May. It was a fierce action at points, but Crook's men held their position at nightfall. The aggressiveness of the enemy surprised Crook, and on the eighteenth he retreated south, away from the village that the army had been seeking for months.[57]

The Lakota, remembered a warrior named He Dog, "wished to be let alone" to gather buffalo meat after the Battle of the Rosebud. As Crook withdrew, the natives moved their village to the east bank of the Little Big Horn. Throughout the preceding weeks, lodges of reservation Lakota and Cheyenne had joined the village, which by June 22 had grown to 1,000 tepees, with perhaps 7,000 people, of whom 2,000 were warriors. On June 24, they crossed the river and camped on a broad level plain. That night, the Cheyenne held a social dance for young men and women. "The People" and their allies had come together in the largest village any elder could remember. Here they would stay for a few days. Black Elk, a Lakota holy man, said that the land the *wasichus* promised "would be ours as long as grass should grow and water flow."[58]

But the soldiers had no ears and were coming. At the mouth of the Rosebud on the morning of June 22, the Seventh Cavalry prepared to march, off-loading supplies from the *Far West,* packing the mules, and checking arms and equipment. To complement the Arikara scouts, Terry had assigned six Crow and several guides and interpreters to the command. The Crow called Custer "Son of the Morning Star" and were as he wrote Libbie, "magnificent-looking men, so much handsomer and more Indian-like than any we have ever seen, and so jolly and sportive." They had reluctantly joined the "Light Eyes," as they termed whites, although the Lakota and the Cheyenne were longtime enemies. One trooper thought that "they were half scared to death of the Sioux."[59]

The guides and interpreters were experienced frontiersmen. Quiet and handsome Charley Reynolds had Custer's trust but was unfamiliar with the territory. To guide them, Gibbon gave the regiment Mitch Bouyer, or Boyer, of mixed French and Sioux ancestry. The colonel regarded him, except for Jim Bridger, "the best guide in the country." He had led Reno on his scout, and the Indians called him "the man with the calf-skin vest." Forty-six-year-old Frederic Gerard, who sold chickens to officers' wives at Fort Lincoln, served as interpreter for the Arikara. An interpreter for the Dakota Sioux scouts was Isaiah Dorman, an African American married to a Santee Sioux woman. Finally, as a courier and scout, Terry assigned George Herendeen, a reticent, unassuming man, like Reynolds.[60]

By noon, the command was ready to march. Before he left, Custer wrote a brief letter to Libbie. "Do not be anxious about me," he requested. "You would be surprised how closely I obey your instructions about keeping with the column. I hope to have a good report to send you by the next mail." In Fort Lincoln, that same day, Libbie wrote, "My own darling—I dreamed of you as I knew I should." There were rumors of an attack on the post, but she cautioned him not to be concerned. At the end, she confided: "Your safety is ever in my mind. My thoughts, my dreams, my prayers, are all for you. God bless and keep my darling. Ever your own Libbie." [61]

When he wrote to his wife, Custer had a copy of Terry's written orders, which specified what had been discussed at the conference and in Custer's tent. The orders read:

Camp at Mouth of Rosebud River, Montana Ter'y, June 22, 1876.
Lieut. Col Custer, 7th Cav'y.
Colonel:

The Brig. Gen'l Commanding directs that, as soon as your regiment can be made ready for the march, you will proceed up the Rosebud in pursuit of the Indians whose trail was discovered by Major Reno a few days since. It is, of course, impossible to give you any definite instructions in regard to this movement, and were it not impossible to do so the Dept. Commander places too much confidence in your zeal, energy, and ability to wish to impose upon you precise orders which might hamper your action when nearly in contact with the enemy. He will, however, indicate to you his own views of what your action should be, and he desires that you should conform to them unless you shall see sufficient reason for departing from them. He thinks that you should proceed up the Rosebud until you ascertain definitely the direction in which the trail above spoken of leads. Should it be found (as it appears almost certain that it will be found) to turn towards the Little Horn, he thinks that you should still proceed southward, perhaps as far as the headwaters of the Tongue, and then turn towards the Little Horn, feeling constantly, however, to your left, so as to preclude the possibility of the escape of the Indians to the South or Southeast by passing around your left flank. The column of Colonel Gibbon is now in motion for the mouth of the Big Horn. As soon as it reaches that point it will cross the Yellowstone and move up at least as far as the forks of the Big and Little Horns. Of course its future movements, must be controlled by circumstances as they arise, but it is hoped that the Indians, if upon the Little Horn, may be so nearly inclosed by the two columns that their escape will be impossible.

The Department Commander desires that on your way up the Rosebud you should thoroughly examine the upper part of Tulloch's Creek, and that you should endeavor to send a scout through to Colonel Gibbon's column, with information of the result of your examination. The lower part of this creek will be examined by a detachment from Col. Gibbon's command. The supply steamer will be pushed up the Big Horn as far as the forks if the river is found to be navigable for that distance, and the Dept. Commander, who will accompany the column of Colonel Gibbon, desires you to report to him there not later than the time for which your troops are rationed, unless in the meantime you receive further orders.

> Very respectfully
> Your obedient servant
> (Signed) E. W. Smith
> Captain 18th Infantry
> Act'g Asst. Adj't General [62]

At midday, the Seventh Cavalry wheeled into column to pass in review for Terry, Gibbon, and staff officers. "Probably never had a more eager command started for hostile Indians," claimed Lieutenant Winfield Scott Edgerly. The members believed "that nothing but the rapid flight of the Indians could save them from fight or surrender." The regiment numbered 31 officers and 566 men. The scouts, guides, civilian employees, and Mark Kellogg brought the total to 647. The packtrain consisted of 175 mules. [63]

The Seventh had the look of men who knew their work. They wore dark-blue flannel blouses and sky-blue kersey pants, with the seats and upper legs reinforced with white canvas. Nearly all wore either a gray slouch or wide-brimmed regulation black felt hat. They carried their 1873 Springfield carbines on slings, and their 1872 .45-caliber Colt revolvers in holsters. They sat in McClellan saddles and carried one blanket and one haversack. As individual men, they averaged five feet seven inches in height and 140 pounds in weight. Thirty percent of them were Irish and German immigrants, and a fifth were recruits with limited or no experience. Their commander believed in them, and most of them in him. They bore his imprint, and if factionalism among officers crippled their efficiency, it was not evident on the surface. The Seventh was special, or as a veteran officer of another command asserted, "when on Indian campaign, Custer's men rode into action with something of the pomp and panoply of war that distinguished them around their camps."[64]

At last, the signal was given to march. Custer and his adjutant, William Cooke, both clad in buckskin suits, rode along the length of the column. Earlier, the commander had rejected the offer of Brisbin's four companies of cavalry and the Gatling guns. He probably believed that he did not need the additional men and that Gibbon could use them, and knew that the heavy weapons would slow his march as the one gun with Reno had done. Before he left, Gibbon joked to him, "Now, Custer, don't be greedy but wait for us." He responded, "No, I will not." He then went to the front and led the Seventh up the Rosebud. Lieutenant James Bradley, chief of scouts for Gibbon, later jotted in his diary: "Though it is General Terry's expectation that we will arrive in the neighborhood of the Sioux village about the same time and assist each other in the attack, it is understood that if Custer arrives first he is at liberty to attack it at once, if he deems prudent."[65]

The Seventh followed the east bank of the Rosebud, with the pace slowed by packs falling off the mules. Custer halted at four o'clock after covering only a dozen miles. He summoned Lieutenant Edward G. Mathey, a native of France who had served in the Union army, to headquarters and assigned him to command of the packtrain, admonishing the subordinate to report after each day's march. After supper, he ordered the officers to a conference at headquarters.[66]

The officers gathered about eight o'clock, sitting or squatting on the ground. The commander was in a "serious mood" and specified rules for the conduct of marches—no trumpet calls except in emergencies; movements at 5 A.M.; and twenty-five to thirty miles each day. He cautioned them to remind the men about the need not to waste rations and to spare horseflesh. "He took particular pains to impress upon the officers his reliance upon their judgment, discretion, and loyalty," recalled Lieutenant Edward S. Godfrey. From government reports and intelligence, he thought that they could encounter 1,000 warriors, perhaps even 1,500, but he and Terry were confident the Seventh could whip them. He welcomed suggestions from any of them, but he wanted no grumbling, and strict obedience of orders. Major Reno interjected a few remarks, and after all of them checked watches, Custer bade them good night.[67]

"Everybody was in excellent spirits," stated Lieutenant Edgerly, "and we all felt that the worst that could happen would be the getting away of the Indians." Lieutenant Godfrey remembered the meeting well years later, commenting:

> This "talk" of his, as we called it, was considered at the time as something extraordinary for General Custer, for it was not his habit to unbosom himself to others. In it he showed concession and a reliance on others; there was an indefinable something that was *not* Custer. His manner and tone, usually brusque and aggressive, or somewhat curt, was on this occasion conciliatory and subdued. There was something akin to an appeal, as if depressed, that made a deep impression on all present.[68]

The Seventh returned to the saddle at five o'clock on the morning of June 23. The Crow and Arikara rode in the front and on the flanks. The ascent was methodical and tiring, necessitating several crossings of the Rosebud. They passed three old campsites, and halted on the stream's west bank at 4:30 P.M., having covered thirty-three miles. Problems with the packtrain still hampered the column. During the day, they discovered two trails that eventually converged.[69]

Custer had appointed Lieutenant Charles Varnum as chief of scouts, impressing upon the capable, twenty-seven-year-old West Pointer the need for vigilance by the scouts. No trail can be missed, the commander stated, because it could be that of a separate band or could lead to the village. Consequently, the pace of the march on the twenty-fourth was governed by the activity of the scouts.[70]

Varnum's scouts preceded the cavalry from the night's bivouac and roamed miles from the main route up the creek. Throughout the sunny, hot day, they brought in reports of fresher trails that merged into the older tracks. Custer halted the column at various points, initially at the site of the Sun Dance camp for an hour and then at the mouth of East Muddy Creek for four hours until Varnum and the Arikaras could follow a trail that seemingly diverged, as George Herendeen reported, farther back at Lame Deer Creek. Custer was "rather angry" when he thought that a trail had been missed. After a two-hour ride, Varnum confirmed that it had led into the others.[71]

About 4 P.M., a Crow rode in with the news of a fresh campsite below the forks of Davis Creek and Rosebud Creek. Custer remounted the command, leading it up the Rosebud an hour later. The Arikara scoured the country for divergent trails. About 7:45 P.M., the regiment halted two miles below the forks in a bend of Rosebud Creek at present-day Busby, Montana. "The trail was now fresh and the whole valley scratched up by trailing lodgepoles," stated Lieutenant George Wallace. They would have to wait until the scouts had determined whether the village had gone south up Rosebud Creek, west up Davis Creek across the divide to the Little Big Horn, north down Tullock's Fork, or scattered on any of the routes.[72]

The Crow returned about nine o'clock. With Bouyer interpreting, they reported that the trail followed Davis Creek across the divide—the *Cha Tish,* or Wolf Mountains—to the Little Big Horn. They had ridden to the crest of Cha Tish, but could not discern a village in the afternoon haze. There was a place, a squat double-peaked ridge, the Crow's Nest, from which they could see into the valley in the clear air of morning, they stated. The Crow wanted a white man to go with them, and Custer summoned Varnum. Custer explained the situation to the lieutenant, admitting that "it was a tough mean job." It had been a long day for Varnum, but as he said, "that means me" when the scouts asked for a Light Eyes. With Bouyer, Reynolds, the Crow, and a handful of Arikara, the chief of scouts rode west.[73]

For Custer, the information demanded a decision. Much has been written since about his disobedience of Terry's orders that recommended a movement to the headwaters of the Tongue before turning west, and a scout down Tullock's Fork. The general prepared the instructions, however, uncertain about the village's location and believing it to be, most likely, on the upper Little Big Horn, not on the lower section of the river as the Crow had discovered. Although Custer had intended to scout the Tullock's Fork region, the evidence indicated no lodges had moved down the stream. Confronted with the new information, he concluded to follow "a hot trail," in Herendeen's words. Except for Crook's command, of which Custer knew nothing, the Indians had eluded the army for months, and now he had them within grasp. He chose to use the discretion that Terry had given him.[74]

After Varnum departed, Custer met with his officers and recounted the intelligence. He planned to cross the divide before daylight, conceal the regiment during the twenty-fifth, and attack at daylight the next day, he explained. He then ordered them to be prepared to move at 11:30 P.M. But delays ensued, and it was not until after midnight that they marched into a night as "dark as pitch." The column ascended Davis Creek, halting after seven miles, minutes after three o'clock. The troopers bedded down for an hour's sleep before cooking breakfast.[75]

The men were seated around the campfires when Arikara couriers delivered a note from Varnum. The Crow had detected the village and its pony herd, the lieutenant had written. Deciding to see for himself, Custer rode out with Gerard and Bloody Knife. Before they left, Bloody Knife told his friend, through Gerard, that "we'll find enough Sioux to keep us fighting two or three days." Smiling, Custer replied, "I guess we'll get through them in one day."[76]

Custer joined Varnum's party on the Crow's Nest about an hour later. The chief of scouts admitted that he had not seen the ponies or the lodges, but the Crow had been adamant. Borrowing the lieutenant's spyglasses, Custer gazed to the west and, after a few minutes, grumbled, "Well I've got about as good eyes as anybody and I can't see any village, Indians or anything else."

"Well, General," rebutted Bouyer, "if you don't find more Indians in that valley than you ever saw together, you can hang me."

Jumping up, frustration evident, Custer shot back, "It would do a damned sight of good to hang you, wouldn't it."[77]

Varnum had more information, however. The scouts had seen a pair of Indians about a mile away and six or seven warriors along the crest of a ridge—"they were outlined against the sky, and looked like giants on immense horses," remembered Varnum. The Crow were convinced that, like them, the enemy had seen the smoke from the Seventh's breakfast campfires. Furious at the white men's stupidity, the scouts believed that the village would be alerted to the regiment's approach.[78]

Custer descended the Crow's Nest. His scouts had found the quarry at last. Although he had not seen the village, he believed them that it was probably the greatest concentration of Indians he had ever confronted. He had planned to conceal and rest his men during the day and to strike at daybreak—as he had at Washita—on the twenty-sixth. The command might have been detected, but he would wait until tomorrow to cross the divide—toward the Little Big Horn.

■ To the Lakota, it was another day in the Moon of the Ripe Juneberries. To the *wasichus,* it was June 25, 1876. If any members of the Seventh Cavalry thought of it, they might have recalled that it was a Sabbath day. And on both sides of the Wolf Mountains in Montana Territory, men waited.[1]

When Lieutenant Colonel George Custer climbed down the Crow's Nest, he saw his brother, Captain Tom Custer, and Adjutant William Cooke approaching, with his regiment not far behind them. The pair of officers reported that a sergeant had left behind a bag at their camp on Davis Creek, and upon his return with a squad to retrieve it, fired upon some Indians at the site. The natives fled and probably were en route to the village.[2]

Custer ordered an officers' call, and when they had gathered, he summarized the situation. While neither he nor Lieutenant Charles Varnum could discern the village, the Crows and Mitch Bouyer assured them that it lay in the valley of the Little Big Horn. But the scouts had seen several Sioux and were certain that the enemy knew of their presence. Now the news of the incident on the trail made it more likely that the tribesmen had been alerted. Before the Sioux could scatter, the Seventh had to advance at once. Check the men's equipment and arms and detail seven of them from each company for the packtrain, he concluded. The order of march would be assigned as each company reported in. Some discussion ensued, but it was brief. They hurried to the companies—a sense of urgency was evident in Custer's remarks.[3]

While the company officers attended to the instructions, Mitch Bouyer approached Custer and said, "General, I have been with these Indians for thirty years, and this is the largest village I have ever heard of." Whether Custer responded is unknown, but the enemy's strength was not the pressing concern at that time. Although he believed that the

1000066639-L3P0B4-BR01

HELLO! Canada
PO BOX 919 STN MAIN
MARKHAM ON L3P 9Z9

SAVE BIG!

HELLO! CANADA

OTHERS PAY

$5.99
NEWSSTAND COVER PRICE

YOU PAY

$1.99
AN ISSUE

We'll pay the tax!

☐ **53 ISSUES (1 year)** for
$1.99 an issue – **Save 67%** *
– **we'll pay the tax!**
☐ Bill me later in full

☐ **26 ISSUES** for $2.29
an issue – **Save 62%** *
– plus taxes.
☐ Bill me later in 4 easy instalments

NAME

ADDRESS

CITY _____ PROVINCE _____ POSTAL CODE

EMAIL

hellomagazine.ca/deal1

*Plus taxes, savings off newsstand cover price. Offer valid only in Canada. Not valid with any other offer. *HELLO! Canada* is published weekly except for occasional combined, expanded or premium issues. GST/HST 89552 5954, QST 1090169528. Other organizations may ask to mail offers to subscribers; if you do not wish to receive these offers, check here ☐. ©2018 Rogers Media.

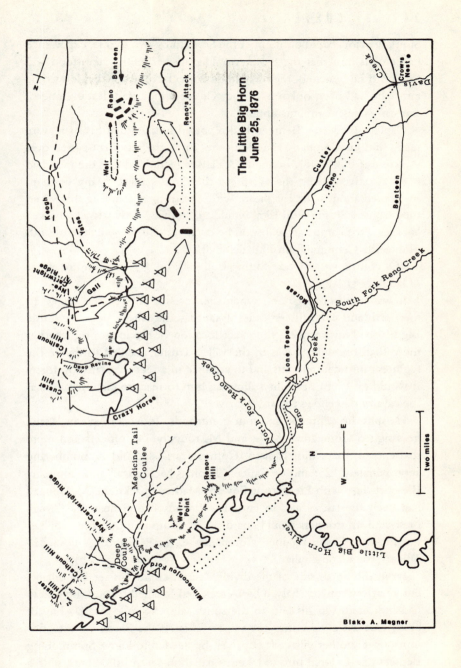

**The Little Big Horn
June 25, 1876**

Benteen

Reno

Weir

Reno's Attack

Keogh

Yates

Nye-Cartwright Ridge

Gall

Calhoun Hill

Deep Ravine

Custer Hill

Crazy Horse

Medicine Tail Coulee

North Fork Reno Creek

Crow's Nest

Davis

Custer

Reno

Benteen

South Fork Reno Creek

Morass

Lone Tepee

Reno Creek

Nye-Cartwright Ridge

Deep Coulee

Calhoun Hill

Custer Hill

Minneconjou Ford

Weir's Point

Reno's Hill

Little Big Horn River

N
E
W
S

two miles

Blake A. Magner

Sioux warriors could outnumber the Seventh by two to one, experience had taught him that the Sioux would disperse before they stood and fought. If he hesitated, they would be gone. Beyond the divide was the target he had been ordered to find. Custer remounted, leading one of the army's best regiments uphill.[4]

Captain Frederick Benteen had reported initially that his men were ready, and his Company H rode in the van as the regiment passed over the crest of the Wolf Mountains. A private recounted that the men had been talkative during the ascent to the Crow's Nest. Many of them speculated about what lay ahead, with one trooper claiming that when they bagged Sitting Bull they would go home. "If that is all," barked another, "the campaign will soon be over, and Custer will take us with him to the Centennial [in Philadelphia]."

"Of course, we will take Sitting Bull with us," joked a third to a roar of laughter.[5]

It was minutes past noon when the Seventh entered the valley. To the north and west, fifteen miles distant lay the village along the Little Big Horn. Not knowing the exact location of the lodges or whether more than one village was in the valley, Custer decided to divide the regiment into components and to advance in a reconnaissance in force. It would give him flexibility, allowing him to react to circumstances as the cavalry descended toward the river.[6]

He split the regiment into four commands. To Major Marcus Reno, he assigned Companies A, G, and M, roughly 140 officers and men; to Benteen, the senior captain, Companies D, H, and K, numbering approximately 125; and to Captain Thomas McDougall and Company B escort duty with Lieutenant Edward Mathey's packtrain. McDougall had been the last officer to complete the inspection near the Crow's Nest, and his troopers would guard the extra ammunition and supplies. For himself, Custer retained Companies C, E, F, I, and L, about 220 officers, men, and civilians.[7]

From the north side of the divide, Custer could not see the village, but a narrow canyon, halved by a creek, led in the direction the Crows had indicated. On his left, to the south, about a mile away, a line of bluffs blocked a view into the upper valley. If the Sioux were to flee south or if another village lay upriver, he needed to know. Summoning Benteen, he ordered him to take his battalion toward the bluffs, send a reconnaissance party, under an officer, to the crest, and return to the trail through the canyon if nothing were found. Before long, however, as he rode down into the valley, Custer saw two additional ridges beyond the first series of bluffs and twice dispatched couriers to the captain to push on to the intervening hills.[8]

The Seventh began the descent at 12:15 P.M., with Benteen veering to the south. A summer's sun heated the day through cloudless skies. Custer's and Reno's battalions marched through the defile on opposite sides of Great Medicine Dance Creek, or Reno Creek.★ About eight miles from the divide, Custer signaled for Reno to join his companies on the north bank. The battalions then halted at a lodge site that contained the remains of a Sioux warrior. Here the cavalrymen met the scouts with Varnum and Lieutenant Luther Hare.[9]

The two officers, Bouyer, George Herendeen, the Crow, and the Arikara had preceded the battalions and from a bluff above the tepee had watched a group of Indians who were fleeing down Reno Creek. The scouts mistook them for members of the main village, but the natives, perhaps numbering forty, had remained encamped along the creek when the Sioux and Cheyenne relocated the lodges to the west side of Little Big Horn the day before, and now were hurrying toward the river. Hare reported the news to Custer, who saw the clouds of dust stirred by the group. The commander, probably through Cooke, directed Reno to take his battalion and the scouts and pursue the Sioux. The other five companies would follow.[10]

The Arikaras refused to go forward ahead of the cavalry, however. They had read the signs, and to them, there were too many Sioux in the valley. Custer accused them of being cowards, threatening to seize their horses and weapons. Frank Gerard interceded with the scouts, and they relented. Some evidence indicates that at this time Bouyer and the Crow repeated their concern to Custer about the enemy's strength. But Son of the Morning Star, recounted a Crow, "was like a feather borne by the wind and had to go."[11]

Reno's companies spurred ahead; Custer's battalion trailed but before long overtook the lead battalion at a flat about a half-mile above the confluence of the North Fork of Reno Creek and the main channel of the Little Big Horn. Reno had reined up when the Crow saw two warriors circling their horses on a distant hill. The river was a mile and

★ For clarity, modern designations of terrain sites are used.

a quarter ahead, and in the valley beyond, dust rolled up. When Custer arrived, Half Yellow Face, a Crow, said, "The Sioux must be running away." Minutes later, from a nearby bluff, Gerard waved his hat, shouting, "Here are your Indians, running like devils!"[12]

The time approached three o'clock. For nearly seven hours Custer had been operating on the belief that his command had been detected and on the assumption that the Sioux would disperse and flee. Now on the flat, his supposition appeared to be confirmed. He had not viewed the village, learning its size and location, had discounted the scouts' concern about the number of enemies, and had not heard a word from Benteen, who was leading one-fourth of the companies. He must have thought that Benteen's battalion could not be far behind, but if he waited for it to arrive, the enemy probably would be in full flight. Prudence demanded caution—terrain, opponent's strength, and opponent's position were unknown. But Custer had always been an aggressive fighter, an officer who seized the edge on battlefields. Relying upon experience, the information at hand, and his superb combat instincts, Custer issued an order to attack.

Cooke delivered the verbal command to Reno. While the adjutant's exact words have been a matter of dispute, Lieutenant George Wallace heard Cooke and recounted them as, "The Indians are about two miles and a half ahead, on the jump, follow them as fast as you can and charge them wherever you find them and we will support you." The battalion advanced toward the river, moving at a "fast trot," according to Reno. Hare, Gerard, and the Arikara rode ahead of the companies.[13]

As Reno departed, Varnum joined Custer. The chief of scouts had been well in advance of the column, seeking a view of the village. When he reined up, he asked where Reno was going. "To begin the attack," replied Custer, who then inquired, "What can you see?"

"The whole valley in front is full of Indians and you can see them when you take that rise," the lieutenant reported, pointing to a hill to the north.[14]

Custer ordered Varnum to join Reno, and the lieutenant rode forward, overtaking the battalion's van as it crossed the river. Reno had struck the stream at a natural ford. He allowed the men to water their horses, and the files became strung out as it required about fifteen minutes for the passage. Reforming in a strip of woods, the companies then advanced in three columns at a trot. Reno soon shifted Companies

A and M into a battle line, with G behind in reserve. The troopers urged their mounts to a gallop on the level ground. On their left the Arikara rode. Twenty yards in front, Marcus Reno led troops in his first engagement against Plains warriors.[15]

Lakota and Cheyenne accounts agreed that Reno's charge surprised them. While some had known of the approach of *wasichu* soldiers for several hours, apparently they expected an attack at daybreak on the twenty-sixth. When outriders warned them of the oncoming cavalry-men, "all through that great camp was the confusion of complete surprise," asserted White Bull, nephew of Sitting Bull. Other tribesmen claimed that women began leveling the tepees. Whatever the extent of disorder, surprise, and terror in the village, the warriors rallied quickly to confront the attackers.[16]

As the cavalry's scouts had warned, the village was massive, extending from the site of the present railroad station at Garryowen, Montana, about three miles north to the area of Minneconjou Ford on the river. It consisted of seven large circles—six Sioux and one Cheyenne—placed among the river's bends, and scattered smaller encampments of unmarried men. Estimates of its population have varied—in some instances, widely—but it contained probably 7,000 men, women, and children, of which as many as 2,000 were warriors.[17]

Numbers alone did not describe the strength of the Lakota and Cheyenne on this day. "Never before or after were the northern Plains tribes better prepared for war," historian Robert M. Utley has percep-tively noted. "They were numerous, united, confident, superbly led, emotionally charged to defend their homeland and freedom." When the battalion of cavalry appeared, they swarmed to meet the *wasichus*.[18]

Marcus Reno's conduct on this day resulted in an eventual court of inquiry and has produced reams of disputatious writings. His defenders are few; his opponents, many. At best, he saved most of his command from certain annihilation; at worst, he was either a coward or was drunk on the battlefield. Whether because of discretion, misjudgment, or the rumored "yellow streak," his conduct during the battle's first hour shaped events across the river where Custer's battalion rode to its ren-dezvous.[19]

When the warriors advanced to meet the attack, Reno halted the charge, dismounting some of the men into a skirmish line. For roughly twenty minutes, the troopers held the ground, until the enemy overlapped their left flank and rear, and Reno ordered a withdrawal into a grove of cottonwoods and underbrush. The combat raged—"lead was coming so fast that it was knocking the dust in our eyes," remembered a private, "but no one seemed to be hit." [20]

The Sioux dashed forward, fired, and darted back in increasing numbers. Reno was on horseback near Bloody Knife when a bullet from an enemy volley, discharged at fifty feet, smashed into the scout's head and splattered blood and pieces of brains over the major's face and uniform. Reno lost his composure and most likely his nerve. He shouted to the men to mount and follow him. "All was confusion," averred Gerard, and a dozen or more men never heard the order as it was passed down. While Reno later contended that it was a charge, it was in fact a retreat that rapidly degenerated into a rout. Instead of being at the rear where duty required him to be, Reno raced from the woods in the lead. [21]

It was in mounting panic that the troopers followed the major out of the shelter of the woods and on to the open prairie. "Every man seemed to be running on his own hook," testified acting assistant surgeon Henry Porter. The Lakota surged forward for the kill. They blasted troopers from the saddle with gunfire at short range or dragged them to the ground, slaying with hatchets and war clubs. Charley Reynolds died early in the retreat, surrounded by warriors. Interpreter Isaiah Dorman, who was married to a Lakota woman, was slain, and his body terribly mutilated. Lieutenants Donald McIntosh and Benjamin Hodgson, 2 sergeants, 4 corporals, 9 privates, a farrier, 2 scouts, and 11 unidentified men never made it to the river or just beyond. The heads of Bloody Knife and four troopers were allegedly placed on poles in the village. [22]

The survivors scrambled up precipitous bluffs to what was subsequently called Reno Hill. Some of those left behind in the woods escaped detection and eventually joined their comrades on the elevation. In all, the battalion had lost 35 killed—1 on the skirmish line, 3 in the timber, 31 during the retreat—and 11 wounded. Five scouts were slain and 2 wounded. The discipline and cohesion of Reno's command was yet another casualty of the battle. The triumphant shouts of the Lakota rolled up the slope. [23]

Within minutes, however, Benteen's battalion climbed up the rise. Like Reno's, Benteen's performance has generated intense and contentious historical scrutiny. He has been accused of deliberate slowness during his approach to the field when the prospect of an engagement and a subsequent order from Custer to "be quick" demanded celerity. In his actions, some see the poison of his hatred for his commander. Although his motivations cannot be documented, his record can.[24]

In retrospect, judged by the rigors of duty, the standards of conduct, orders, and the situation, Benteen failed Custer and the regiment. As directed, he conducted his reconnaissance to the south, saw that no villages lay upriver, and followed a tributary of Reno Creek to its mouth, where he struck the two battalions' trail. He traveled only a mile farther than the other companies to reach this point, although his march passed over more rugged terrain. From here, he descended Reno Creek, halting twice to water the horses—once at a "morass" and once near the Sioux burial lodge, perhaps consuming thirty minutes. He had not sent a courier to inform Custer of the reconnaissance's results or of his progress to rejoin the command.[25]

At the second watering stop, the battalion heard gunfire toward the valley. Impatient at the delay, Captain Thomas Weir, commander of Company D and the man that Benteen later said was the officer whose attentions to Libbie Custer caused her husband to ride across Kansas, led his men forward, followed by the other two companies. Before long, Sergeant Daniel Kanipe met them, carrying orders from Custer for Captain McDougall to hurry the packtrain to the front and for Benteen "to come quick." When Benteen inquired about the situation, the sergeant exclaimed that "they are licking the stuffing out of them."[26]

The companies proceeded—the gait varying between a walk and a trot—to the flat where Reno and Custer had separated. Coming upstream, Trumpeter John Martin met Benteen and handed him a note from Custer's adjutant: "Benteen, Come on—big village—be quick—bring packs. W. W. Cooke, P.S. Bring pacs." Scribbled in haste, with its brevity confusing about the packtrain, the message was clear in its intent. Cooke knew that the packtrain was not far behind because its van reached the lone tepee as the troopers departed. Benteen quickened the pace, came to the North Fork of Reno Creek, and turning right, followed Custer's trail to the hill where Reno's men had fled. Ironically, when Benteen had first struck the main trail miles up Reno Creek, Boston Custer had passed them, riding to the front to join his brothers. He arrived in time.[27]

Benteen's men found "utter confusion" on the crest of Reno Hill. Many of the survivors of the valley fight seemed gripped with "terror," while officers—some weeping—shouted orders, urging soldiers to rally and to descend the slope for their wounded comrades. Reno "was in an excited condition," recalled a lieutenant. Benteen asked the major about Custer's location, but Reno did not know. Showing the senior officer the message brought by Martin, Benteen suggested that the combined units "make a junction with him as soon as possible." Duty now compelled Reno as senior officer to obey Custer's order. But when he learned that his adjutant, Benny Hodgson, had been shot down near the river, he led a detail down the hill to retrieve the body, absenting himself for twenty or more minutes.[28]

Soon after the union of the two battalions, the officers and men heard "heavy firing by volleys down the creek," avowed Lieutenant Winfield Scott Edgerly. The sound was "perfectly distinct" and "was heard by everybody about me." In time, Reno and Benteen denied that they heard gunfire, but the evidence from others on the hill is overwhelming. Finally, for a second time, Captain Weir seized the initiative, leading his company to the north. Halting at a rise, the present Weir Point, the troopers could see dust and chaos to the north and soon encountered some Sioux and Cheyenne resistance. Reno and Benteen followed eventually with the other companies, but the mounting number of warriors, who "looked as thick as grasshoppers in a harvest field," contended a private, forced a disjointed withdrawal to Reno Hill. The cavalrymen formed a defensive arc on the crest and engaged the enemy. All of them either said aloud or thought, where was Custer? The answer would haunt a nation.[29]

When Reno's men advanced to the attack, Custer trailed with his five companies, sending ahead Adjutant Cooke and Captain Myles Keogh to report back on developments with the major's battalion. Bringing his command to the South Fork of Reno Creek, Custer halted, giving the men time to water their mounts. He soon learned, probably from Keogh, that Reno had crossed the river and was moving to charge the Sioux. Moments later, Cooke rode up and stated that Fred Gerard had returned to the ford, exclaiming that the enemy was not fleeing, but riding forth to give battle. Two couriers from Reno then arrived and confirmed the news.[30]

Custer reacted swiftly to the information. For reasons that will never be known, he turned the column to the north across the creek's main channel and ascended the bluffs east of the river. Instead of supporting Reno from the rear, he decided to move on the warriors' flank. He may have thought that the native opposition was a rear-guard action while the main body of warriors escaped, or that if they were not breaking camp, he could support Reno by an envelopment of the village. The decision was his, and five companies of cavalry followed.[31]

As the column climbed the slope, Mitch Bouyer and four Crow scouts met it and led it onto the crest. From the heights, Custer and his men viewed the village for the first time. As he had guessed, Sioux and Cheyenne women and children were fleeing to the north and west. Turning in the saddle and waving his hat, he shouted, "We've caught them napping." The troopers cheered. From the heights they saw Reno's engagement on the valley floor, and members of the latter's battalion later recalled spying their comrades on the bluffs. At this point, Custer dispatched Sergeant Kanipe to the packtrain.[32]

At last, the Seventh's commander had the target in sight, not the hundreds of lodges, but the women and children whose capture would end warrior resistance. He and his men advanced downstream behind the bluffs at a fast trot, filing into a cedar-lined coulee and turning west for the river. Here Cooke scribbled the note to Benteen and handed it to Trumpeter Martin. Galloping to the rear, Martin passed Boston Custer, who soon joined his brothers and undoubtedly reported that Benteen was en route. The horsemen proceeded down a large ravine, South Medicine Tail Coulee, that debouched at the river about a mile and a half to the north and west.[33]

The terrain east of the river differed starkly from the broad, level prairie on the west side. Beneath a carpet of buffalo grass and sagebrush, gullies and ravines scarred the slopes of narrow, sharp ridges. The elevations followed no general direction but looked as though some prehistoric giant had tossed them haphazardly aside. The network of rises and depressions favored an opponent who fought with guerrilla and infiltration tactics.[34]

In Medicine Tail Coulee, Custer separated the battalion into two squadrons, or wings. Companies C, I, and L went to the senior captain, Keogh. Keogh had served in the Civil War and then joined the regiment in November 1866. Respected by Custer, Keogh was a solid, fearless officer, who at times drank too much whiskey. A fellow Civil War officer once asserted that there was too much "style" to the Irishman for him to be well liked, adding that "his uniform was spotless and fitted him like the skin on a sausage."[35]

The second wing went to Custer's old friend Captain George Yates, second in rank to Keogh, and was comprised of his own Company F, known within the regiment as the "Band Box Troop" because it was regarded as the model unit, and First Lieutenant Algernon "Fresh" Smith's Company E, whose members rode distinctive gray mounts. Tall, handsome, blond, loyal to his commander, Yates was one of the Seventh's most popular officers. He was, in the words of a trooper, "an example of a kind and indulgent officer."[36]

At this time, Bouyer and Curley returned from Weir Point, reporting that Reno's men were abandoning the valley. As he had earlier, with the three Crow, Custer released the pair of scouts from further service —their duty did not require fighting—but Bouyer chose to stay as Curley rode away.[37]

Although the truth can never be established with certainty, it would appear that Custer shaped his movements by his commitment to the offensive and the anticipated approach of Benteen. He may have decided even before the scouts returned to push Yates's wing down Medicine Tail Coulee on a reconnaissance, while moving Keogh's squadron to present-day Luce Ridge to the north and east. From the elevation, Keogh's three companies could await Benteen and cover Yates's rear. He may also have sent a detail of troopers to scout farther to the north and east.[38]

The movement consumed perhaps thirty minutes. Yates encountered some resistance at Minneconjou Ford at the mouth of Medicine Tail Coulee, forcing him to dismount part of Smith's company. On Luce Ridge, Keogh's men engaged parties of warriors with skirmish fire. In all likelihood, since the battalion had scaled the bluffs east of the river, a number of Sioux and Cheyenne had sniped at the column, their strength increasing as the cavalrymen proceeded. The warriors posed no serious danger to the five companies as yet.[39]

With flankers rimming the two companies, Yates retired from the ford, passing up a broad ravine, the present-day Deep, or North Medicine Tail, Coulee. From Luce Ridge, Keogh moved north to the present Nye-Cartwright Ridge, where the men fired some rounds at the gathering enemy. From there, Keogh's wing reunited with Yates's command on what is now called Calhoun Hill, the southern terminus of a sharp-crested hogback, now Custer Ridge, that extended north for a mile to a knoll, today's Custer Hill.[40]

The battalion had incurred minor casualties, mostly in Yates's wing.

The enemy appeared bolder and more numerous, but Custer must not have been overly concerned. Committed to the offensive, he left Keogh's companies on Calhoun Hill to establish a position that could protect the rear and combine with Benteen, whose arrival he must have thought imminent.[41]

Custer rode north on the east of Custer Ridge with the regimental staff and Yates's Companies E and F. It was a reconnaissance operation, and passing around the ridge's north end, the column moved northwest toward the river, searching for a ford to cross and hoping to snare the fleeing tribesmen. When they located a shallows, the cavalrymen withdrew to near the present Cemetery Ridge near the visitors' center. Here Company E deployed on foot, with the Band Box Troop in reserve. Clusters of warriors charged the troopers' line, trying to steal horses. Smith's men held, but young Lakota warriors raced forward and scattered some of the mounts. The companies reunited above present-day Deep Ravine and withdrew before the enemy fire toward Custer Hill. Lives now were to be measured in minutes.[42]

After the defeat of Reno in the valley and the rapid spread of the alarm of more *wasichus* on the ridges east of the river, the Lakota and Cheyenne poured across the stream. They were inflamed by the victory, and many were well armed with repeater rifles and other firearms. They came, stated a Lakota, "without discipline, like bees swarming out of a hive," filling the ravines and coulees and seizing the crests of ridges. Crazy Horse, an Oglala Lakota with a reputation for bravery and fierceness in combat, led a group across Custer Ridge, passing between the cavalry wings when Yates's men were near the river to the north. He turned south toward the *wasichus* on Calhoun Hill.[43]

The combat at Calhoun Hill escalated rapidly to a fearful climax. From nearby ridges and ravines, working ever closer on foot, the warriors raked the cavalrymen with arrows and rifle fire. Concealed by the tall grass, hundreds of tribesmen infiltrated closer to the troopers' position. When bolder ones pressed forward to present-day Greasy Grass Ridge, Company C advanced down the slope to present-day Calhoun Coulee to counter the threat. Lame White Man, a Cheyenne, led a surge up the coulee against the company, whose members broke and withdrew toward their comrades in Company L. "The Indians kept coming like an increasing flood which could not be checked," said Red Hawk, a Lakota.[44]

From a distance, the Crow scout Curley saw the dust and heard the gunfire. It was a continuous roll, he thought, "like the snapping of the threads in the tearing of a blanket." In the midst of the fury, chiefs cried, "Hi-yi-yi," the command to follow, and the Lakota shouted, *"Hokahey! Hokahey!"*—"A Good day to die! A Good day to die!" From the south and east, Gall, a Lakota chief, attacked with hundreds of warriors. The two companies had stood well until the collapse of Company C, but now against these combined onslaughts, they disintegrated.[45]

On the slopes and crest of Calhoun Hill, death walked. Maggie Custer Calhoun's husband fell, his body identified later by the fillings in his teeth. With their horses stampeded, and gripped by terror, the troopers ran, spilling the panic into the ranks of Company I in a hollow to the north. Keogh's men had been in reserve, engaged with Crazy Horse's band. The fury blew over them from three directions. The warriors closed, and as one Lakota recounted, made "short work of killing them." The troopers not killed instantly died from hatchet blows across their foreheads or eyes.[46]

It became "a moving fight," according to a Lakota. Some of the cavalrymen gathered in clusters and died together. In one group lay Myles Keogh, a trumpeter, and three sergeants. The warriors stripped Keogh's body of everything except a gold chain with an Agnus Dei emblem. But most of the troopers were so frightened that their enemies said they acted like drunken men, an accurate analogy for individuals overwhelmed by the horror they faced. "They did not seem to know enough to shoot," recalled a native. To a Lakota woman who watched, "the Indians acted just like they were driving buffalo to a good place where they could be easily slaughtered."[47]

A few troopers of Keogh's wing escaped, reaching their comrades on Custer Hill. "We rode straight for Custer," declared White Bull of the warriors from Calhoun Hill. The addition of hundreds more finished the beleaguered companies on Custer Hill. There were probably about 102 officers and men on the knoll and slopes originally, but the enemy's fire had reduced that number by the time the fugitives from Keogh's squadron came in.[48]

Most of the cavalrymen were deployed on the southwest slope of the heights, but on the crest, a perimeter defense had been established. In it stood Custer, dressed in buckskin pants and a blue blouse, with his hair cut short. Around him were troopers of Companies E and F, and the regimental staff, including Tom Custer, who evidently had been attached to it and not in command of his Company C. Adjutant William Cooke, Color Sergeant Henry Vickory, and Chief Trumpeter Henry Voss were at hand. Nearby, perhaps on the slope, were Boston Custer, who rode miles to be at his brothers' sides, and Autie Reed, Ann's son, who had attached himself to his uncles.[49]

They made a stand worthy of brave men. The Lakota told the truth in their cry, but it was not a good day to die for members of the Seventh Cavalry. Caught within a ring of arrows and bullets, the cavalrymen fell, singly, perhaps in pairs at once. The Lakota and Cheyenne edged nearer through the buffalo grass, dashing forward to count coup (touch a live enemy), a warrior's highest act of courage, and killing at a closer range.[50]

Precisely when individual officers and men died on the hill, history cannot determine, but there were few left when about forty men of Company E rushed off the hill toward the river. They formed a skirmish line on the slope for a few minutes, but then Hunkpapa Lakota attacked. Twenty-eight troopers broke through and sought shelter in Deep Ravine. "We were right on top of the soldiers," a warrior stated, "and there was no use in their hiding from us." The soldiers were finished. On the hill other warriors killed the *wasichus* who were still alive, using knives and hatchets. Although they did not know whom they had slain, in time the Lakota remembered the day as Pehin Hanska Ktepi, the day "they killed long Hair."[51]

More than men died on and along that Montana ridge. With the complete destruction of the five cavalry companies, accounts can only be partial. Archaeology and Lakota and Cheyenne accounts can establish tactical patterns, offer insights into the conduct of the troopers and the warriors, frame the sequence of events, and provide information for analysis and judgment. What cannot be known are the motivations and thoughts of George Custer. To him have been ascribed internal furies that blinded him to the dangers in the valley and impelled him to cross the divide. He thirsted, relentlessly, for glory; he sought redemption from the humiliation in Washington; and he dreamed of a presidential nomination. All of these motivations have been posited as explanations. Although they have been predicated upon a few strands of evidence and upon a presumed understanding of the man's character, they remain only speculations.

History should be unsparing—it seeks the truth. Analyses of Little

Big Horn have been unending and will probably never cease, for at the center lies a mystery. Studies of the battle have listed factors that contributed to the outcome, have identified individuals whose conduct merited censure, and have enriched our understanding with details. But two singular facts stand amid the controversy. The decisions of George Custer—justified or unjustified, from whatever motives—resulted in a tragedy for himself and over 250 members of the Seventh Cavalry, and he bears primary responsibility. Second, in the plain words of Black Elk, a Lakota, "Those *wasichus* had come to kill our fathers and mothers and us, and it was our country." Or, as Two Moons, a Cheyenne, said, "We wanted our revenge, and it came with Custer." [52]

The battle at Little Big Horn did not end at Custer Hill. With the defeat of Custer's battalion, the warriors swarmed back to Reno Hill, where seven companies and the packtrain were trapped. Until nightfall of the twenty-fifth, and through much of the afternoon of the twenty-sixth, the warriors assailed the defenders. "The bullets fell like a perfect shower of hail" during the final day, remembered Lieutenant Francis Gibson. Benteen demonstrated his steel as he assumed unofficial command because of Reno's evident unfitness. The senior captain walked behind the horseshoe-shaped line throughout both days, reminding the men that "it is a groundhog case; it is live or die with us. We must fight it out with them." Late on the afternoon of June 26, the Lakota and Cheyenne disappeared, and silence came at last. [53]

Relief arrived from the north on the twenty-seventh with the approach of Gibbon's Montana Column. The second contingent of General Terry's command had camped only nine miles from Reno Hill the night before. Warriors had appeared in their front and then withdrew. Three Crow scouts rode in, reporting that Custer's regiment had attacked a large village. On the morning of the twenty-seventh, Gibbon's men advanced cautiously up the valley, discovered the carnage—"the stench from the dead bodies and dead horses was something terrible," recorded an officer in his journal—and carried the awful news to the Seventh's survivors. [54]

The work of burying their comrades belonged to members of the regiment. The magnitude of the defeat—five entire companies wiped out—and the mutilations of the bodies stunned the men. "It was the most horrible sight my eyes rested on," admitted Lieutenant Gibson. Near the river lay Mark Kellogg, the newspaperman who had promised readers he would be with Custer at "the death"—he kept his word. Up the slope were Mitch Bouyer, Boston Custer, and Autie Reed. On the crest, the mutilated remains of Tom Custer rested near his older brother.[55]

Lieutenant Colonel George A. Custer had died amid a knot of slain men and horses at the southwest base of the present monument on Custer Hill. He had been struck with a bullet near his temple and another in his ribs below the heart. After death, his left thigh had been slashed to the bone, a finger had been severed, and an arrow shaft had been shoved into his penis. When Frederick Benteen saw his body, the captain allegedly growled, "There he is, God damn him, he will never fight anymore."[56]

A member of the detail remembered the work as "hard digging," while another confessed that the burials "were simply a respectful gesture." Officers counted bodies at certain locations—42 on Custer Hill; 28 in the Deep Ravine; and a large group around Keogh. In all, 263 officers, men, scouts, and civilians had been slain. Of that number, 210 fell in Custer's battalion. Lakota and Cheyenne casualties have been disputed, but their killed and wounded, including perhaps 10 dead women and children, had to approach 75 or more. Before the troopers departed, they recognized Comanche, Myles Keogh's claybank gelding, near the stream. The men tended to the animal's numerous wounds and brought him with them as the command abandoned the valley of the Little Big Horn.[57]

The news of the disaster preceded the return of Terry's command. To the country in the midst of a centennial celebration of its independence, the deaths of Custer and over two hundred officers and men were staggering. In white America's imagination, the Seventh Cavalry and its famous commander embodied the frontier army. Newspapers editorialized about the battle, ascribing blame to Custer, the army, and/or the president, and demanding revenge against the victors. In Chicago, Lieutenant General Philip Sheridan attributed the defeat to the imprudence of the regiment's commander, the officer whom he had said never failed him. In Washington, President Grant stated publicly, "I regard Custer's massacre as a sacrifice of troops, brought on by Custer himself, that was wholly unnecessary—wholly unnecessary." In Monroe, Michigan, "a great silence came over" the city, with bells tolling every hour and residents gathering on streets, speaking in hushed voices.

In the homes of Emanuel and Maria Custer and David and Ann Reed, the grief never departed.[58]

July 5, 1876, was a "beautiful day" at Fort Abraham Lincoln, Dakota Territory. Early in the morning, a message from General Terry arrived at the fort. Captain William S. McCaskey of the Twentieth Infantry read the contents, and with the post surgeon and a lieutenant went to the quarters of Lieutenant Colonel Custer. Libbie Custer, Maggie Calhoun, and Emma Reed, older sister of Autie Reed, greeted them in the parlor. The captain gave them the awful news. Maggie sobbed, asking, "Is there no message for me?" Writing later, Libbie said, "I wanted to die." But Autie had impressed upon her the responsibilities of a commander's wife, and, composing herself, she walked through the doorway to comfort others. The battle widowed twenty-six women at the fort. Of her husband's death, she confessed afterward, "To lose him would be to close the windows of life that let in the sunshine."[59]

The army returned to the battlefield at Little Big Horn in July 1877. A detachment had been sent to exhume the remains of the officers. They located the graves of eleven officers and of Boston Custer and removed what was left of the men. The caskets of Tom Custer, George Yates, James Calhoun, Algernon Smith, and Donald McIntosh were shipped to Fort Leavenworth for reburial in the national cemetery. Eventually, McIntosh's remains were relocated to Arlington National Cemetery. Others went home—William Cooke to Hamilton, Ontario; Myles Keogh to Auburn, New York; Benny Hodgson to Philadelphia; and Boston Custer to Monroe. What were believed to be the remains of George Custer were collected and shipped east.[60]

"General Custer asked me to lay him at West Point," his widow wrote the academy superintendent in the summer of 1877, "and I would like to carry out his request." Autie had told her often that he loved the place on the bluffs above the Hudson River better than any other on earth. "Its traditions were dear to him," Libbie wrote, and he returned with military honors on October 10, 1877. The flag of Captain Louis Hamilton, who had been slain at Washita, covered the casket. Custer's wife, father, and sister attended. Within two years, the academy erected a statue to him, but Libbie hated it so much that authorities removed it in 1884. Finally, in 1905, the pedestal was placed at the gravesite, mounted with a shaft. The original statue was lost and never found.[61]

More than half a century passed before Libbie joined him at West Point. She never remarried, devoting herself, as she said, into making her husband a hero to America's youth. She watched with interest the proceedings of the Reno Court of Inquiry in Chicago during the winter of 1879. But the army and some of the Seventh Cavalry's officers preferred to bury the controversy, and the board ruled that "there was nothing in his [Reno's] conduct which requires the animadversion from this Court." Libbie wanted to tell her husband's story in the West and produced three books—*Boots and Saddles* (1885), *Tenting on the Plains* (1887), and *Following the Guidon* (1890).[62] She resided in New York during her final decades, enjoying winters in Florida and periodic trips to Europe. She maintained contacts with former members of her husband's commands and admirers, retaining letters from them. She cherished one note from President Theodore Roosevelt, who wrote, "Your husband is one of my heroes as you so well know." She lived comfortably, leaving an estate valued at slightly over $100,000. She suffered a heart attack on Sunday, April 2, 1933, and died on Tuesday, the fourth. She would have been ninety-one years old on April 8, the day she was placed beside her "own bright particular *star.*"[63]

Libbie's devotion to her husband's memory attracted supporters. Within six months of Little Big Horn, Frederick Whittaker's *A Complete Life of Gen. George A. Custer* appeared. It was a lengthy biography that portrayed the subject as a dashing cavalier and planted that image in the country's memory. Since then, that portrait of George Custer has been tarnished, buffed, and tarnished again. Artists, authors, Hollywood, and political activists have depicted the man as a vainglorious fool, a fearless soldier, a butcherer of Native Americans, and a superb cavalryman. He has become the singular symbol of the nation's guilt over its sad history of continental conquest. The loser at Little Big Horn has overshadowed the excellent Civil War general. He sometimes seems to be only a symbol in America's mind, a man drained of substance.[64]

In life, he coveted fame, embraced the glory that could be achieved on a battlefield, and strove to fashion an image of himself. Much of what he aspired for, he achieved, earning it in the fury of combat when the nation's future was still being shaped. But from this distance in time, he remains a man of contradictions, a figure whose compelling characteristic was a zest for life with wise and poor judgment mixed together.[65]

In 1867, Custer offered an assessment of himself and of his aspirations. "In years long numbered with the past, when I was merging upon manhood," he stated, "my every thought was ambitious—not to be wealthy, not to be learned, but to be great. I desired to link my name with acts and men, and in such manner as to be a mark of honor, not only to the present but to future generations."[66]

He has perhaps been denied greatness, but not immortality. It came to him on a day in the Moon of the Ripe Juneberries on a nondescript hill in Montana. But the winds that fill the coulees and ravines and lap over the ridges along the Little Big Horn River eventually blow east to Gettysburg, Haw's Shop, Trevilian Station, Winchester, Cedar Creek, Waynesborough, and Appomattox. It is in all those places, the hallowed grounds of Montana, but also of Pennsylvania and of Virginia, that the measure of George Armstrong Custer must be taken.

NOTES

Works cited by author and short titles will be found in full in the Bibliography. The following abbreviations are used in the footnotes:

B&G	*Blue & Gray*
B&L	*Battles and Leaders*
BHCL	*Burton Historical Collection Leaflet*
BL	Babcock Library
CBHMA	Custer Battlefield Historical and Museum Association
CMU	Central Michigan University
CHS	Cincinnati Historical Society
CR	Compiled Records
CSR	Compiled Service Records
CV	*Confederate Veteran*
CWH	*Civil War History*
CWTI	*Civil War Times Illustrated*
DC	Dartmouth College
DU	Duke University
EB/EBC	Elizabeth Bacon/Custer
EU	Emory University
GAC	George Armstrong Custer
GG	*Greasy Grass*
GNMP	Gettysburg National Military Park
HL	Huntington Library
KHQ	*Kansas Historical Quarterly*
LBBNM	Little Big Horn Battlefield National Monument
LC	Library of Congress
MCHMA	Monroe County Historical and Museum Association
MCLS	Monroe County Library System
MH	*Military History*
MHS	Massachusetts Historical Society
MOLLUS	Military Order Loyal Legion of the United States
MTHS	Montana Historical Society
MSR/GAC	Military Service Record/George A. Custer
NA	National Archives
NHHS	New Hampshire Historical Society
NLBHA	*Newsletter, Little Big Horn Associates*

NYPL	New York Public Library
OH	*Ohio History*
OR	*The War of the Rebellion: A Compilation of the Official Records of the Union and Confederate Armies*
RPL	Rochester Public Library
RR	*Research Review*
SHSP	*Southern Historical Society Papers*
TFCHQ	*The Filson Club History Quarterly*
UM	University of Michigan
UNC	University of North Carolina
USAGR	United States Adjutant General Records
USAMHI	United States Army Military History Institute
USMAA	United States Military Academy Archives
USMAL	United States Military Academy Library
UVA	University of Virginia
UVM	University of Vermont
VMHB	*Virginia Magazine of History and Biography*
WMU	Western Michigan University
YU	Yale University

Chapter 1: "YELLOW-HAIRED LADDIE"

1. Schmitt, *General George Crook,* p. 137; Calkins, *Battles,* pp. 28–37, 57, 58, 74.

2. Carroll and Horn, *Custer Geneaologies,* n.p.

3. Ibid.; "Geneaological Information from Emanuel Custer Bible," GAC Papers, MCHMA; Ronsheim, *Life,* p. 1.

4. Carroll and Horn, *Custer Geneaologies,* n.p.; Wallace, *Custer's Ohio Boyhood,* p. 6.

5. Carroll, *General Custer and New Rumley,* pp. 2, 5; Wallace, *Custer's Ohio Boyhood,* p. 5; Monaghan, *Custer,* pp. 3, 6.

6. Wallace, *Custer's Ohio Boyhood,* p. 6; Carroll, *General Custer and New Rumley,* pp. 2, 3; *New York Times,* October 4, 1906.

7. Wallace, *Custer's Ohio Boyhood,* pp. 6, 7, 33; Carroll and Horn, *Custer Geneaologies,* n.p.

8. Wallace, *Custer's Ohio Boyhood,* pp. 5, 6; Bell, *Ancestry,* pp. 1, 2; Custer and Horn, *Custer Geneaologies,* n.p.

9. Wallace, *Custer's Ohio Boyhood,* pp. 6, 7; Carroll, *General Custer and New Rumley,* p. 3; *Monroe Democrat,* July 6, 1906.

10. Carroll and Horn, *Custer Geneaologies,* n.p.; Wallace, *Custer's Ohio Boyhood,* pp. 7, 34; Hurless, "Where," MCLS.

11. Wallace, *Custer's Ohio Boyhood,* pp. 7, 9; Carroll and Horn, *Custer Geneaologies,* n.p.

12. Wallace, *Custer's Ohio Boyhood,* p. 43; *New York Times,* October 4, 1906.

13. Wallace, *Custer's Ohio Boyhood*, p. 7; *New York Times,* October 4, 1906; Monaghan, *Custer,* p. 5.

14. Monaghan, *Custer,* p. 4; Wallace, *Custer's Ohio Boyhood,* pp. 9, 35; "Geneaological Information from Emanuel Custer Bible," GAC Papers, MCHMA.

15. Carroll and Horn, *Custer Geneaologies,* n.p.; Wallace, *Custer's Ohio Boyhood,* p. 9.

16. Custer, *Tenting,* p. 1; Ambrose, *Crazy Horse,* p. 87; Monaghan, *Custer,* p. 5.

17. Ambrose, *Crazy Horse,* p. 87.

18. Carroll, *General Custer and New Rumley,* p. 3; S. R. Grabill to Gentlemen, January 3, 1914, Camp Papers, LBBNM; Wallace, *Custer's Ohio Boyhood,* pp. 12, 13; Day, "If You Want," *GG* 9: 7.

19. Frost, *Custer Legends,* pp. 12, 102; Custer, *Tenting,* p. 289; Wallace, *Custer's Ohio Boyhood,* p. 12.

20. Frost, *Custer Legends,* p. 101; Hunt, "Custer," p. 2, UM; Wallace, *Custer's Ohio Boyhood,* pp. 9, 11.

21. Frost, *Custer Legends,* p. 101; a slightly different version in Ambrose, *Crazy Horse,* p. 88.

22. Wallace, *Custer's Ohio Boyhood,* p. 11; Hunt, "Custer," p. 3, UM; Ronsheim, *Life,* p. 2; S. R. Grabill to Gentlemen, January 3, 1914, Camp Papers, LBBNM.

23. Wallace, *Custer's Ohio Boyhood,* pp. 13, 14, 15; Carroll, *General Custer and New Rumley,* pp. 3, 4; Ronsheim, *Life,* p. 2.

24. Frost, *General Custer's Libbie,* p. 27n; Frost, *Custer Legends,* p. 8; Wallace, *Custer's Ohio Boyhood,* pp. 11, 37; *Monroe Democrat,* July 6, 1906.

25. Utley, *Cavalier,* p. 13.

26. Frost, *General Custer's Libbie,* pp. 13, 14, 19, 22; O'Neil and O'Neil, *Custers,* p. 19.

27. Frost, *General Custer's Libbie,* pp. 27n, 44, 114; O'Neil and O'Neil, *Custers,* p. 1; Frost, *Custer Legends,* pp. 12, 15.

28. Wallace, *Custer's Ohio Boyhood,* pp. 15, 16, 18; Ronsheim, *Life,* pp. 3, 5.

29. Wallace, *Custer's Ohio Boyhood,* p. 17; GAC to Father and Mother, October 5, 1865, Merington Papers, NYPL; Ambrose, *Crazy Horse,* p. 85; A. T. O'Neil, "Custer Recollections," p. 27; Utley, *Cavalier,* p. 14; Ronsheim, *Life,* pp. 3, 4.

30. Wallace, *Custer's Ohio Boyhood,* pp. 18, 21, 23; Ronsheim, *Life,* p. 4; *Cadiz Republican,* September 17, 1953.

31. Monaghan, *Custer,* p. 10, 11; Wallace, *Custer's Ohio Boyhood,* p. 23; *Cadiz Republican,* September 17, 1953.

32. Wallace, *Custer's Ohio Boyhood,* p. 24; Monaghan, *Custer,* p. 10.

33. Monaghan, *Custer,* p. 11.

34. Ibid., p. 11; Utley, *Cavalier,* p. 14; Wallace, *Custer's Ohio Boyhood,* p. 23; T. E. O'Neil, "Two Men," *RR* 8 (1): 11.

35. Wallace, *Custer's Ohio Boyhood*, p. 23; *Cadiz Republican*, September 17, 1953; Katz, *Custer*, p. 2.

36. Wallace, *Custer's Ohio Boyhood*, p. 19; Monaghan, *Custer*, p. 11; Utley, *Cavalier*, p. 15.

37. T. E. O'Neil, "Two Men," *RR* 8 (1): 10; *New York Times*, October 4, 1906.

38. Beauregard, "General," *B&G* 6 (1): 33; there is an undated fragment of letter—which appears to be in the hand of the editor—that purports to be another letter from GAC to Bingham; its validity is questionable. Merington Papers, NYPL.

39. Beauregard, "General," *B&G* 6 (1): 33.

40. Ibid., pp. 33, 34; Kidd, *Historical*, n.p.; *New York Times*, October 4, 1906; Merington, *Custer Story*, p. 7.

41. T. E. O'Neil, "Two Men," *RR* 8 (1): 11; Wallace, *Custer's Ohio Boyhood*, pp. 23, 24; Utley, *Cavalier*, p. 15; John A. Bingham to Jefferson Davis, November 18, 1856, MSR/GAC, NA.

42. John A. Bingham to Jefferson Davis, January 17, 1857, GAC to Jefferson Davis, January 29, 1857, MSR/GAC, NA; Wallace, *Custer's Ohio Boyhood*, p. 24; Reynolds, *Civil War*, p. 13; Monaghan, *Custer*, p. 12; fragment of an undated letter of John A. Bingham, Merington Papers, NYPL.

43. Wallace, *Custer's Ohio Boyhood*, p. 24; Monaghan, *Custer*, pp. 12, 13; Custer, *Boots*, p. 84.

Chapter 2: WEST POINT

1. John A. Bingham to Jefferson Davis, November 18, 1856, MSR/GAC, NA; Post Orders, No. 5, p. 55, USMAA; Monaghan, *Custer*, pp. 13, 20, 21, 22; sources conflict as to the number of members of the class, placing it at sixty-eight, see Register of Merit, 1853 to 1865, No. 3, p. 104, USMAA; Monaghan, *Custer*, p. 22; Carroll, *Four on Custer*, p. 10. Post Orders, No. 5, however, cites sixty-five members.

2. Sergent, *They Lie*, pp. 12, 13, 15, 200; Brown, *Cushing*, p. 31; Schaff, *Spirit*, pp. 15, 16.

3. Horn, *"Skinned,"* passim; Wert, *General James Longstreet*, p. 28.

4. Wert, *General James Longstreet*, pp. 28, 29; Crary, *Dear Belle*, pp. 17–19.

5. Sergent, *They Lie*, pp. 27, 200.

6. Crary, *Dear Belle*, p. 17–20.

7. GAC to Minnie St. John, August 7, 1857; Frost, *Custer Legends*, p. 45.

8. Register of Delinquencies, 1856–1861, p. 192, USMAA; Horn, *"Skinned,"* pp. 1, 2; Frost, *Custer Legends*, p. 45.

9. Sergent, *They Lie*, pp. 23, 24, 55; Brown, *Cushing*, p. 31.

10. Sergent, *They Lie*, p. 55; Morrison, "Struggle," *CWH* 19 (2): 141, 142.

11. Monaghan, *Custer*, pp. 18, 31, 33; Carroll, *Custer and His Times*,

p. 9; Schaff, *Spirit,* p. 133; Hutton, *Custer Reader,* p. 203; Sergent, *They Lie,* p. 9; "Members of Class That Graduated on May 6, 1861—Resigned on Account of Secession of their States," typescript, GAC Collection, MCLS; Carroll, *Four on Custer,* pp. 26–28.

12. Sergent, *They Lie,* pp. 115, 128, 149, 183, 189; Monaghan, *Custer,* pp. 22, 25; Carroll, *Four on Custer,* pp. 26–28.

13. Schaff, *Spirit,* pp. 86, 194; A. T. O'Neil, "Custer Recollections," p. 25.

14. A. T. O'Neil, "Custer Recollections," p. 25; Horn, *"Skinned,"* passim; Carroll, *Custer in the Civil War,* p. 87; Register of Delinquencies, 1856–1861, p. 192, USMAA.

15. Crary, *Dear Belle,* p. 42; Frost, *Custer Legends,* p. 136; Hutton, *Custer Reader,* p. 9.

16. Frost, *Custer Legends,* p. 137; Reynolds, *Civil War,* p. 20.

17. Schaff, *Spirit,* pp. 26, 193–195; Reynolds, *Civil War,* pp. 36, 40; Frost, *Custer Legends,* p. 137; Sergent, *They Lie,* p. 44.

18. Sergent, *They Lie,* p. 38.

19. *Regulations for the U.S. Military Academy,* p. 12.

20. Hutton, *Custer Reader,* p. 9; Connell, *Son,* p. 108.

21. Register of Merit, 1853 to 1865, No. 3, pp. 104, 108, 113; *Official Register,* p. 14; Post Orders, No. 5, pp. 84, 88, 104, all in USMAA; GAC to Brother and Sister, June 30, 1858, GAC Papers, MCLS.

22. Register of Delinquencies, 1856–1861, p. 192; Post Orders, No. 5, p. 106, USMAA; Horn, *"Skinned,"* pp. iii, 103.

23. Post Orders, No. 5, p. 122; Register of Delinquencies, 1856–1861, p. 193, USMAA; Horn, *"Skinned,"* pp. 3–6.

24. GAC to Brother and Sister, June 30, 1858, GAC Collection, MCLS.

25. Monaghan, *Custer,* p. 29; "The Red Man," GAC Collection, MCLS; Urwin and Fagan, *Custer,* pp. 122, 130; Ambrose, *Crazy Horse,* p. 111.

26. *Official Register,* p. 13, Record of Delinquencies, 1856–1861, p. 342; Register of Merit, 1853 to 1865, No. 3, pp. 117, 123, USMAA; Horn, *"Skinned,"* pp. 7–10; GAC to Mollie, November 13, 1858, Letters to Dear Mollie, GAC Papers, YU.

27. Post Orders, No. 5, p. 254, USMAA; Brown, *Cushing,* p. 41.

28. GAC to Mollie, November 13, 1858, Letters to Dear Mollie, GAC Papers, YU.

29. GAC to Mollie, January 1, 1859, Letters to Dear Mollie, GAC Papers. YU.

30. Ibid.

31. T. E. O'Neil, "Custer's First Romance," *NLBHA* 28 (2): 7; *Cadiz Republican,* September 17, 1953.

32. GAC to Brother, August 11, 1859, Merington Papers, NYPL; Post Orders, No. 5, p. 254, USMAA.

33. Sergent, *They Lie,* p. 75; Field Records of Hospitals, Entry 544, NA; Lowry, *Story,* p. 102; Andrews, interview with author, December 14, 1994.

34. Lowry, *Story,* pp. 102, 104, 105; Andrews, interview with author, December 14, 1994.

35. GAC to Brother and Sister, October 2, 1859, GAC Collection, MCLS; GAC to Augusta Ward, December 13, 1859, typescript, GAC Letters, RPL; Andrews, interview with author, December 14, 1994.

36. GAC to Augusta Ward, December 13, 1859, typescript, GAC Letters, RPL; Register of Merit, 1853 to 1865, No. 3, pp. 133, 139, 146, USMAA.

37. Post Orders, No. 5, pp. 306, 326, 364; Record of Delinquencies, 1856–1861, p. 343; *Official Register,* p. 12, USMAA; Horn, *"Skinned,"* pp. 11–14.

38. Crary, *Dear Belle,* pp. 37, 38, 53, 54, 55; Sergent, *They Lie,* p. 86; Brown, *Cushing,* pp. 45, 46.

39. Carroll, *Custer in the Civil War,* pp. 79, 80.

40. GAC to Sister, November 10, 1860, GAC Collection, MCLS.

41. Carroll, *Custer in the Civil War,* pp. 83, 84; Sergent, *They Lie,* pp. 89, 90; "Members of Class That Graduated on May 6, 1861—Resigned on Account of Secession of their States," typescript, GAC Collection, MCLS.

42. Sergent, *They Lie,* pp. 90–95.

43. Crary, *Dear Belle,* pp. 42–44.

44. Ibid., pp. 42, 43; Register of Merit, 1853 to 1865, No. 3, p. 150, USMAA.

45. Brown, *Cushing,* p. 48; Schaff, *Spirit,* p. 208.

46. GAC to Sister, April 10, 1861, GAC Collection, MCLS.

47. GAC to Sister, April 22, 1861, GAC Collection, MCLS.

48. Ibid.

49. Sergent, *They Lie,* pp. 100–101; Brown, *Cushing,* p. 32; GAC to [Brother and Sister], May 31, 1861, GAC Collection, MCLS.

50. Brown, *Cushing,* p. 32; Dunphy, "West Point," *RR* 7 (1): 24; Register of Merit, 1853 to 1865, No. 3, pp. 150, 151, 158; *Official Register,* p. 12; Record of Delinquencies, 1856–1861, pp. 448, 449, USMAA; Horn, *"Skinned,"* p. iii.

51. Hutton, *Custer and His Times,* pp. 68, 70; Carroll, *Custer in the Civil War,* pp. 87, 88; Special Orders, No. 21, p. 8, USMAA.

52. Special Orders, No. 21, p. 8, USMAA; MSR/GAC, NA; Frost, *Custer Legends,* p. 76.

53. Special Orders, No. 21, pp. 8, 9, USMAA; MSR/GAC, NA; Frost, *Custer Legends,* pp. 76, 77.

54. Beauregard, "General," *B&G* 6 (1): 34; Reynolds, *Civil War,* p. 35; Carroll, *Custer in the Civil War,* p. 89.

55. Carroll, *Custer in the Civil War,* p. 89; Monaghan, *Custer,* pp. 41, 43, 44; Katz, *Custer,* p. 4.

Chapter 3: A Beginning

1. Warner, *Generals in Blue,* pp. 429–30.

2. Carroll, *Custer in the Civil War,* pp. 89, 90.

3. Ibid., pp. 90, 91.

4. Ibid., pp. 92–94; Monaghan, *Custer,* pp. 47–50; Merington, *Custer Story,* p. 12.

5. Carroll, *Custer in the Civil War,* p. 96.

6. Ibid., pp. 101, 102.

7. Ibid., pp. 103, 105; Urwin, *Custer Victorious,* p. 46; Crary, *Dear Belle,* pp. 103–6.

8. Warner, *Generals in Blue,* pp. 290–91.

9. Ibid., p. 291; Sears, *George B. McClellan,* pp. 95–101, 110, 111.

10. Starr, *Union Cavalry,* 1:58–59; MSR/GAC, NA; Carroll, *Custer in the Civil War,* p. 114.

11. Carroll, *Custer in the Civil War,* pp. 114, 115, 118; Warner, *Generals in Blue,* pp. 258–59.

12. MSR/GAC, NA; Charles R. Greenleaf to GAC, October 1, 1861, Frost Collection, MCHMA; Crary, *Dear Belle,* p. 107.

13. *Toledo Blade,* December 26, 1981; Wallace, *Custer's Ohio Boyhood,* pp. 25, 27; Carroll, *They Rode,* p. 66.

14. GAC to My Darling Sister, February 27, 1862, GAC Collection, MCLS; Utley, *Cavalier,* p. 18.

15. Sears, *George B. McClellan,* pp. 108–16, 338.

16. Ibid., pp. 113–14; Starr, *Union Cavalry,* 1:234–38.

17. GAC to My Darling Sister, February 27, 1862, GAC Collection, MCLS; Merington, *Custer Story,* p. 26.

18. Wert, *General James Longstreet,* pp. 97–99.

19. GAC to Parents, March 17, 1862, GAC Collection, MCLS; Carroll, *Custer in the Civil War,* p. 129.

20. GAC to Parents, March 17, 1862, GAC Collection, MCLS; Merington, *Custer Story,* p. 27; Carroll, *Custer in the Civil War,* pp. 129, 130.

21. GAC to Parents, March 13, 1862, GAC Collection, MCLS.

22. Wert, *General James Longstreet,* p. 100; *OR* 11 (1): 5, 8; Sears, *George B. McClellan,* pp. 167–68.

23. Sears, *George B. McClellan,* p. 168; GAC to Parents, March 26, 1862, GAC to Sister, March 28, 1862, GAC Collection, MCLS.

24. Wert, *General James Longstreet,* pp. 100–103.

25. GAC to My Dear Sister, April 11, 1862, GAC Collection, MCLS; Merington, *Custer Story,* p. 29.

26. E. H. Custer to GAC, April 18, 1862, typescript, Frost Collection, MCHMA; T. E. O'Neil, "Sister's Letter," *NLBHA* 27 (2): 6–7.

27. GAC to Sister, April 19, 1862, GAC Collection, MCLS.

28. The confusion with Custer's staff assignment is not clarified by the records. MSR/GAC, NA; *OR,* 11, pt. 1:152, 153; Carroll, *Custer in the Civil War,* p. 143.

29. Carroll, *Custer in the Civil War,* pp. 146, 147; Sears, *To the Gates,* pp. 41, 54.

30. Carroll, *Custer in the Civil War,* pp. 146, 147, 149; GAC to Sister, May 15, 1862, GAC Collection, MCLS.

31. *OR,* 11, pt. 1:526; Wert, *General James Longstreet,* pp. 103, 104.

32. *OR,* 11, pt. 1:535; Sears, *To the Gates,* pp. 70–73; *Civil War,* MOLLUS, Nebr., 1:155.

33. Sears, *To the Gates,* pp. 73, 74; *OR,* 11, pt. 1:535.

34. *Civil War,* MOLLUS, Nebr., 1:155–56; GAC to Sister, May 15, 1862, GAC Collection, MCLS; *OR,* 11, pt. 1:535, 536.

35. *OR,* 11, pt. 1:536, 543, 608–13; GAC to Sister, May 15, 1862, GAC Collection, MCLS; Hutton, *Custer Reader,* p. 10; Sears, *To the Gates,* pp. 78–81.

36. GAC to Sister, May 15, 1862, GAC Collection, MCLS; Starr, *Union Cavalry,* 1:268.

37. Wert, *General James Longstreet,* pp. 107, 108.

38. *OR,* 11, pt. 1:111, 651; *National Tribune,* May 7, 1903.

39. *OR,* 11, pt. 1:651, 652; Barrett, *Reminiscences,* p. 13; *National Tribune,* May 7, 1903.

40. *OR,* 11, pt. 1:652, 653, 654; *National Tribune,* May 7, 1903; Barrett, *Reminiscences,* p. 13; Pohanka, "George Yates," *GG* 8: 12; Reynolds, *Civil War,* p. 75.

41. *OR,* 11, pt. 1:651; McClellan, *McClellan's Own Story,* p. 364; Merington, *Custer Story,* p. 31.

42. MSR/GAC, NA; Reynolds, *Civil War,* p. 74; McClellan, *McClellan's Own Story,* p. 365.

43. Sears, *To the Gates,* pp. 103–10.

44. Ibid., pp. 103, 104, 110, 111, 112.

45. Ibid., chap. 6; Wert, *General James Longstreet,* chap. 6.

46. Shillinburg, "More," *RR* 8 (2): 3, 4; A. T. O'Neil, "Custer Recollections," p. 31; Reynolds, *Civil War,* p. 25; Monaghan, *Custer,* p. 83.

47. Wert, *General James Longstreet,* pp. 127–36; Sears, *To the Gates,* pp. 146–56.

48. Wert, *General James Longstreet,* chap. 7; Sears, *To the Gates,* chap. 8–12.

49. *OR,* 11, pt. 1:117; pt. 2:75; Sears, *Civil War Papers,* p. 320; GAC to Brother and Sister, July 13, 1862, GAC Collection, MCLS.

50. GAC to Brother and Sister, July 13, 1862, GAC Collection, MCLS; Merington, *Custer Story,* p. 27.

51. GAC to Brother and Sister, July 13, 1862, GAC Collection, MCLS; GAC to Augusta Ward, July 26, 1862, typescript, GAC Letters, RPL; Sears, *For Country,* p. 263; Sears, *George B. McClellan,* chap. 10.

52. *OR,* 11, pt. 2:954, 955; MSR/GAC, NA; Merington, *Custer Story,* pp. 32, 33.

53. Sears, *George B. McClellan,* pp. 240–45.

54. Ibid., pp. 245–47; Merington, *Custer Story,* pp. 34, 35.

55. Sears, *George B. McClellan,* pp. 247, 260–62; Wert, *General James Longstreet,* chap. 8; Meyer, *Civil War,* p. 20; Long, *Civil War,* pp. 260, 261.

56. The best account of the Antietam Campaign is Sears, *Landscape Turned Red,* passim; Long, *Civil War,* pp. 264–67; *OR,* 19, pt. 1:210; Sears, *Civil War Papers,* p. 463; USAGR, NA; Furst, Diary, USAMHI.

57. Long, *Civil War,* pp. 268–70; Emanuel Custer's views on abolition are stated in a letter, Emanuel H. Custer to GAC, March 2, 1862, typescript, Frost Collection, MCHMA.

58. Sears, *George B. McClellan,* pp. 330–33; Long, *Civil War,* pp. 268–81; GAC to Augusta Ward, October 3, 1862, typescript, GAC Letters, RPL.

59. GAC to Sister, September 27, 1862, GAC Collection, MCLS; Merington, *Custer Story,* p. 35; GAC to Augusta Ward, October 3, 1862, typescript, GAC Letters, RPL.

60. GAC to Augusta Ward, October 3, 1862, typescript, GAC Letters, RPL.

61. Sears, *George B. McClellan,* pp. 340–44; Long, *Civil War,* pp. 284–87.

62. Reynolds, *Civil War,* p. 74; Carroll, *Custer in the Civil War,* p. 112; Sears, *George B. McClellan,* pp. 110, 111; Henry Christiancy Diary, typescript, p. 12, Christiancy-Pickett Papers, USAMHI.

Chapter 4: LIBBIE

1. Leckie, *Elizabeth Bacon Custer,* p. 6; T. E. O'Neil, *Garry Owen,* 8:2.

2. Frost, *General Custer's Libbie,* pp. 14, 15; Leckie, *Elizabeth Bacon Custer,* p. 3.

3. Frost, *General Custer's Libbie,* pp. 14–17; Leckie, *Elizabeth Bacon Custer,* pp. 4, 5; GAC to Augusta Ward, August 19, 1875, typescript, GAC Letters, RPL.

4. Frost, *General Custer's Libbie,* pp. 17, 18; Leckie, *Elizabeth Bacon Custer,* pp. 5–7; O'Neil and O'Neil, *Custers,* p. 4.

5. Leckie, *Elizabeth Bacon Custer,* p. 7; EBC, Journal, YU.

6. Leckie, *Elizabeth Bacon Custer,* pp. 8, 9; EBC, Journal, YU.

7. EBC, Journal, YU; Frost, *General Custer's Libbie,* p. 25.

8. EBC, Journal, YU; Merington, *Custer Story,* p. 41.

9. Leckie, *Elizabeth Bacon Custer,* p. 10; Frost, *General Custer's Libbie,* p. 25; O'Neil and O'Neil, *Custers,* pp. 8, 9.

10. EBC, Journal, YU; Leckie, *Elizabeth Bacon Custer,* pp. 10, 11; Frost, *General Custer's Libbie,* p. 25; Merington, *Custer Story,* p. 38.

11. Leckie, *Elizabeth Bacon Custer,* pp. 11–14; Frost, *General Custer's Libbie,* pp. 28–30.

12. EBC, Journal, YU; Frost, *General Custer's Libbie,* pp. 29–31; Leckie, *Elizabeth Bacon Custer,* pp. 15, 16.

13. Frost, *General Custer's Libbie,* pp. 29, 31, 32; Leckie, *Elizabeth Bacon Custer,* p. 16.

14. Frost, *General Custer's Libbie,* pp. 31, 32; Leckie, *Elizabeth Bacon Custer,* p. 16.

15. Frost, *General Custer's Libbie,* pp. 32, 33; Merington, *Custer Story,* pp. 42, 43; Daniel S. Bacon to Sister, December 26, 1864, typescript, Frost Collection, MCHMA.

16. Frost, *General Custer's Libbie,* pp. 32, 33.

17. Merington, *Custer Story,* pp. 42, 43; Frost, *General Custer's Libbie,* pp. 33, 34; Leckie, *Elizabeth Bacon Custer,* p. 22.

18. Frost, *General Custer's Libbie,* pp. 29, 33, 34, 39, 58; Leckie, *Elizabeth Bacon Custer,* pp. 18–22.

19. Leckie, *Elizabeth Bacon Custer,* pp. 21, 22; Merington, *Custer Story,* p. 48.

20. Merington, *Custer Story,* pp. 46, 47; "Some Monroe Memories," *BHCL,* pp. 9, 10.

21. Merington, *Custer Story,* pp. 47, 48, 50, 51.

22. Ibid., p. 47; Leckie, *Elizabeth Bacon Custer,* p. 24.

23. T. E. O'Neil, "Two Men," *RR* 8 (1): 12; Urwin, *Custer Victorious,* p. 51; Henry Christiancy Diary, typescript, p. 12, Christiancy-Pickett Papers, USAMHI.

24. T. E. O'Neil, "Two Men," *RR* 8 (1): 12.

25. GAC to I. P. Christiancy, November 21, 1862, GAC Letters, USMAL.

26. Ibid., Henry Christiancy Diary, typescript, p. 12, Christiancy-Pickett papers, USAMHI; *OR* 21:433.

27. Merington, *Custer Story,* pp. 48, 49; Leckie, *Elizabeth Bacon Custer,* p. 24.

28. Merington, *Custer Story,* p. 50; Leckie, *Elizabeth Bacon Custer,* p. 25; Frost, *General Custer's Libbie,* p. 58.

29. Merington, *Custer Story,* p. 50; Frost, *General Custer's Libbie,* pp. 16, 58, 59.

30. Frost, *General Custer's Libbie,* p. 59; Merington, *Custer Story,* p. 50.

31. Merington, *Custer Story,* pp. 50–51.

32. Frost, *General Custer's Libbie,* pp. 59, 60; Leckie, *Elizabeth Bacon Custer,* p. 25.

33. Frost, *General Custer's Libbie,* p. 60.

34. Ibid., pp. 33, 60, 61.

35. Ibid., pp. 62, 63; GAC to Sister, April 13, 1863, GAC Collection, MCLS.

36. GAC to Sister, April 13, 1863, GAC Collection, MCLS.

37. Ibid; Special Orders, No. 174, copy, GAC Collection, MCLS; MSR/GAC, NA; Monaghan, *Custer,* p. 115.

Chapter 5: "COME ON, YOU WOLVERINES"

1. Furgurson, *Chancellorsville,* pp. 111, 339; Long, *Civil War,* pp. 342–51.

2. Furgurson, *Chancellorsville,* chaps. 1 and 2.

3. MSR/GAC, NA; Furgurson, *Chancellorsville,* p. 333; Pleasonton file, USAGR, NA.

4. Furgurson, *Chancellorsville,* p. 333.

5. GAC to Sister, May 17, 1863, GAC Collection, MCLS.

6. Starr, *Union Cavalry,* 1:58, 59, 60, 66, 67, 153, 154, 157, 172, 235–37, 339.

7. Ibid., pp. 23, 214.

8. Ibid., p. 339; Long, *Civil War,* p. 329; Furgurson, *Chancellorsville,* pp. 280–83, 323–24; Edward A. Thayer to Brother, January 20, 1863, Thayer Papers, NHHS.

9. Starr, *Union Cavalry,* 1:363, 367; Furgurson, *Chancellorsville,* pp. 162, 208; *OR,* 25, pt. 2:513.

10. Warner, *Generals in Blue,* p. 373; Starr, *Union Cavalry,* 1:313.

11. Longacre, *Cavalry,* p. 48; O'Neill, *Cavalry Battles,* p. 11.

12. Longacre, *Cavalry,* pp. 48, 49; Alexander, "Gettysburg," *B&G* 6 (1): 9; *OR,* 25, pt. 1:773, 775; Starr, *Union Cavalry,* 1:314.

13. Starr, *Union Cavalry,* 1:314n, 315; Longacre, *Cavalry,* pp. 48, 49.

14. Longacre, *Cavalry,* p. 49; Alexander, "Gettysburg," *B&G* 6 (1): 9.

15. *OR,* 25, pt. 2:574; Longacre, *Cavalry,* pp. 50–54; Nevins, *Diary,* p. 309.

16. GAC to Hon. I. P. Christiancy, May 17, 1863, typescript, Christiancy-Pickett Papers, USAMHI; *OR,* 27, pt. 1:1046; Pohanka, "George Yates," *GG* 8: 11, 12; Pleasonton file, USAGR, NA.

17. *OR,* 25, pt. 1:1116: Merington, *Custer Story,* pp. 53, 54; GAC to Sister, May 27, 1863, GAC Collection, MCLS.

18. GAC to Hon. I. P. Christiancy, May 17, 1863, typescript, Christiancy-Pickett Papers, USAMHI; GAC to Judge Christiancy, May 31, 1863, GAC Letters, USMAL; I. P. Christiancy to GAC, February 10, 1875, Merington Papers, NYPL.

19. A. Pleasonton to Austin Blair, May 30, 1863; GAC to Judge Christiancy, May 31, 1863, GAC Letters, USMAL.

20. Harris, *Personal Reminiscences,* pp. 17, 23; Urwin, *Custer Victorious,* pp. 53, 66; *OR,* 25, pt. 2:588.

21. Longacre, *Cavalry,* pp. 35–37.

22. Ibid., p. 62; *OR,* 27, pt. 3:27.

23. Longacre, *Cavalry,* p. 63; Clark B. Hall to author, February 14, 1994, author's collection; GAC to Sister, June 8, 1863, GAC Collection, MCLS.

24. Longacre, *Cavalry,* pp. 51, 66, 67; *OR,* 27, pt. 1:1046; Merington, *Custer Story,* pp. 58, 59; Clark B. Hall to author, February 14, 1994, author's collection.

25. Monaghan, *Custer,* p. 127; Urwin, *Custer Victorious,* p. 53; Thomas

C. Devin's Report, Hooker Papers, HL; Merington, *Custer Story,* pp. 58, 59; Clark B. Hall to author, February 14, 1994, author's collection; *OR,* 27, pt. 1:1046.

26. Longacre, *Cavalry,* chap. 3; Nevins, *Diary,* p. 221.

27. Long, *Civil War,* pp. 364–67.

28. Ibid., pp. 367–69; O'Neill, *Cavalry Battles,* passim.

29. O'Neill, *Cavalry Battles,* p. 39; Meyer, *Civil War,* pp. 33, 34.

30. Merington, *Custer Story,* pp. 55, 56, 58; O'Neill, *Cavalry Battles,* pp. 60, 182n; *New York Times,* June 20, 1863.

31. Long, *Civil War,* pp. 369–71; Alfred Pleasonton to John F. Farnsworth, June 23, 1863, Pleasonton Papers, LC; Warner, *Generals in Blue,* p. 469.

32. Alfred Pleasonton to John F. Farnsworth, June 23, 1863, Pleasonton Papers, LC.

33. Pleasonton to Farnsworth, second letter, dated June 23, 1863, Pleasonton Papers, LC.

34. Hutton, *Custer Reader,* p. 15; *OR,* 27, pt. 3:369, 376; Warner, *Generals in Blue,* pp. 315–16. ·

35. *OR,* 27, pt. 1:61; Coddington, *Gettysburg Campaign,* pp. 217–18.

36. Coddington, *Gettysburg Campaign,* pp. 219–21; *OR,* 27, pt. 1:61; pt. 3:373, 376; MSR/GAC, NA.

37. GAC to Judge Christiancy, July 26, 1863, Christiancy-Pickett Papers, USAMHI; Whittaker, *Complete Life,* pp. 161–63; Monaghan, *Custer,* pp. 132–33; Urwin, *Custer Victorious,* p. 43.

38. GAC to Judge Christiancy, July 26, 1863, Christiancy-Pickett Papers, USAMHI.

39. Merington, *Custer Story,* pp. 36, 59, 60; EBC to W. M. Shilling, July 5, 1919, EBC Collection, MCLS.

40. Merington, *Custer Story,* pp. 59, 60; EBC to Mrs. Alexander, August 11, [1926], EBC Collection, MCLS.

41. Frost, *Custer Legends,* p. 47; Meyer, *Civil War,* pp. 48, 49; Kidd, *Personal Recollections,* pp. 129, 130.

42. Kidd, *Personal Recollections,* pp. 128, 129.

43. *OR,* 27, pt. 3:373, 376; Longacre, *Cavalry,* pp. 18–20, 166; GAC to Judge Christiancy, July 26, 1863, Christiancy-Pickett Papers, USAMHI.

44. *OR,* 27, pt. 3:375, 376, 377; Longacre, *Cavalry,* chap. 8.

45. Kidd, *Personal Recollections,* pp. 120, 121, 124; Harris, *Michigan Brigade,* pp. 5, 7.

46. May, *Michigan,* pp. 15, 32, 33, 37, 41; Urwin, *Custer Victorious,* pp. 66–68; Lee, *Personal,* pp. iii, iv.

47. GAC to Sister, July 26, 1863, GAC Collection, MCLS.

48. Hyde, "Custer in Virginia," *The Frontier,* p. 7; Macomber, Diary, CMU; Harrington, Diary, WMU.

49. *OR,* 27, pt. 1:991, 992; pt. 3:400; Special Orders No. 99, MCS/

GAC, NA; Macomber, Diary, CMU; Harrington, Diary, WMU; Barbour, Diary, UM; Kidd, *Personal Recollections,* pp. 124, 125.

50. *OR,* 27, pt. 1:992; Harrington, Diary, WMU; *Encounter,* pp. 43, 47.

51. Kidd, *Personal Recollections,* pp. 125–26; Rodenbough, Potter, and Seal, *History,* p. 15; Alexander, "Gettysburg," *B&G* 6 (1): 25; Longacre, *Cavalry,* p. 175.

52. *Encounter,* pp. 47, 48; Rodenbough, Potter, and Seal, *History,* pp. 15, 16; Longacre, *Cavalry,* pp. 175, 176.

53. *OR,* 27, pt. 1:992; Alexander, "Gettysburg," *B&G* 6 (1): 26; Schultz, "Cavalry Fight," *CWTI* 23 (10): 15; Meyer, *Civil War,* p. 97.

54. *OR,* 27, pt. 1:992, 1000; Alexander, "Gettysburg," *B&G* 6 (1): 26, 27; *Encounter,* pp. 55, 234.

55. Barbour, Diary, UM; Haven, "In the Steps," p. 76; Kidd, *Personal Recollections,* pp. 125–27; *OR,* 27, pt. 1:999.

56. Barbour, Diary, UM; Kidd, *Personal Recollections,* pp. 127, 128; Haven, "In the Steps," p. 76; Wayne C. Mann to Author, March 9, 1994, author's collection; Sloan, "Goodbye," *CWTI* 23 (3): 31–33.

57. Kidd, *Personal Recollections,* pp. 127, 128; *OR,* 27, pt. 1:1000; Macomber, Diary, CMU; Alexander, "Gettysburg," *B&G* 6 (1): 26, 27; Busey and Martin, *Regimental Strengths,* p. 108.

58. Alexander, "Gettysburg,"*B&G* 6 (1): 27; *Encounter,* p. 55; Longacre, *Cavalry,* pp. 177, 178.

59. Longacre, *Cavalry,* pp. 178, 179; Macomber, Diary, CMU; Barbour, Diary, UM.

60. Shevchuk, "Battle," *Gettysburg* 1: 98; Macomber, Diary, CMU; Barbour, Diary, UM; *OR,* 27, pt. 1:992.

61. Shevchuk, "Battle," *Gettysburg* 1: 96, 98; *OR,* 27, pt. 1:992; Kidd, *Personal Recollections,* p. 134.

62. Alexander, "Gettysburg," *B&G* 6 (1): 30; Shevchuk, "Battle," *Gettysburg* 1: 98, 99; James Kidd to Father and Mother, July 9, 1863, Kidd Papers, UM; Baird, "Reminiscences," p. 32, UM; *New York Times,* July 21, 1863.

63. *OR,* 27, pt. 1:992; Shevchuk, "Battle," *Gettysburg* 1: 99; Carroll, *Custer in the Civil War,* p. 82.

64. *OR,* 27, pt. 1:992, 999; CR, Sixth Michigan Cavalry, NA; Shevchuk, "Battle," *Gettysburg* 1: 99, 100.

65. *OR,* 27, pt. 1:992; Kidd, *Personal Recollections,* p. 135; *New York Times,* July 21, 1863; Urwin, *Custer Victorious,* pp. 70, 72; Shevchuk, "Battle," *Gettysburg* 1: 102, 103; Baird, "Reminiscences," p. 33, UM.

66. *OR,* 27, pt. 1:992; Kidd, *Personal Recollections,* p. 135; the best one-volume work on Gettysburg remains Coddington, *Gettysburg Campaign.*

67. Krolick, "Forgotten Field," *Gettysburg* 4: 78, 80; Harris, *Michigan Brigade,* p. 8.

68. Alexander, "Gettysburg," *B&G* 6 (1): 37; *Annals,* p. 475; Rawle, *History,* pp. 274, 275.

69. Krolick, "Forgotten Field," *Gettysburg* 4: 82; Baird, "Reminiscences," p. 33, UM; Harris, *Michigan Brigade,* p. 9; Kidd, *Personal Recollections,* p. 141; George G. Briggs to J. B. Bachelder, March 26, April 24, 1886, Seventh Michigan Cavalry File, GNMP; Robertson, *Michigan,* p. 404; Wayne C. Mann to author, March 9, 1994, author's collection.

70. Alexander, "Gettysburg," *B&G* 6 (1): 32; Longacre, *Cavalry,* p. 225; Robertson, *Michigan,* p. 409; *OR,* 27, pt. 1:956; Rawle, *History,* p. 273.

71. *OR,* 27, pt. 1:956; Rawle, *History,* p. 273; Alexander, "Gettysburg," *B&G* 6 (1): 32; A. E. Mathews to John B. Bachelder, June 11, 1887, First Michigan Cavalry File, GNMP.

72. Rawle, *History,* pp. 273, 275; Krolick, "Forgotten Field," *Gettysburg* 4: 84; Harris, *Michigan Brigade,* pp. 9, 10; Alexander, "Gettysburg," *B&G* 6 (1): 36.

73. Longacre, *Cavalry,* pp. 229, 230; Kidd, *Personal Recollections,* p. 148; Rawle, *History,* p. 276; *B&L* 3: 404.

74. Harris, *Michigan Brigade,* p. 13; Rawle, *History,* p. 276; Krolick, "Forgotten Field," *Gettysburg* 4: 84; J. A. Clark to My Dear Friend, July 30, 1863, Clark Papers, UM; Kidd, *Personal Recollections,* pp. 148, 149; Lee, *Personal,* p. 155; L. S. Trowbridge to R. A. Alger, February 19, 1886, Fifth Michigan Cavalry File, GNMP.

75. Lee, *Personal,* p. 155; Urwin, *Custer Victorious,* p. 78; J. A. Clark to My Dear Friend, July 30, 1863, Clark Papers, UM.

76. Lee, *Personal,* pp. 155–58; Urwin, *Custer Victorious,* pp. 77, 78; Rawle, *History,* p. 276; Kidd, *Personal Recollections,* p. 150; Alexander, "Gettysburg," *B&G* 6 (1): 36.

77. Longacre, *Cavalry,* p. 231; R. A. Alger to John B. Bachelder, January 1, 1886, L. S. Trowbridge to Wife, [July 1863], Fifth Michigan Cavalry File, GNMP.

78. Longacre, *Cavalry,* pp. 237–38; Rawle, *History,* p. 277; *Annals,* p. 481; Kidd, *Personal Recollections,* p. 153.

79. Rawle, *History,* pp. 277, 278; Kidd, *Personal Recollections,* p. 153; James H. Kidd to Father and Mother, July 9, 1863, Kidd Papers, UM.

80. Kidd, *Personal Recollections,* p. 154; A. E. Mathews to John B. Bachelder, June 11, 1887, C. M. Norton to A. E. Mathews, July 3, 1886, First Michigan Cavalry File, GNMP; Rawle, *History,* p. 278; Robertson, *Michigan,* p. 410; Meyer, *Civil War,* p. 52.

81. A. E. Mathews to John B. Bachelder, June 11, 1887, First Michigan Cavalry File, GNMP; Rawle, *History,* pp. 279, 280, 301; *B&L* 3: 404; Harris, *Michigan Brigade,* pp. 13, 14.

82. Robertson, *Michigan,* p. 410; *OR,* 27, pt. 1: 155, 958; GAC to Sister, July 26, 1863, GAC Collection, MCLS; Thomas, *Bold Dragoon,* p. 249; Longacre, *Cavalry,* p. 244; Sylvia, "Custer," *North South Trader* 3 (4): 22.

83. Macomber, Diary, CMU; Barbour, Diary, UM; Andrew Newton Buck to Brother and Sisters, July 9, 1863, Buck Family Papers, UM; Edward Corselius to Mother, July 4, 1863, Corselius Papers, UM.

84. James H. Kidd to Father and Mother, July 9, 1863, Kidd Papers, UM.

Chapter 6: ''FIGHTING WAS HIS BUSINESS''

1. *National Tribune,* October 10, 1887.

2. Macomber, Diary, CMU; Longacre, *Cavalry,* pp. 241–44; Rodenbough, Potter, and Seal, *History,* p. 17.

3. *OR,* 27, pt. 1:993; USAGR, Kilpatrick File, NA; Longacre, *Cavalry,* pp. 247, 248.

4. *OR,* 27, pt. 1:993, 994; Macomber, Diary, CMU; Kidd, *Personal Recollections,* p. 166; Conrad and Alexander, *When War Passed,* pp. 394, 395.

5. Conrad and Alexander, *When War Passed,* p. 395; *OR,* 27, pt. 1:998; Macomber, Diary, CMU.

6. *OR,* 27, pt. 1:994, 998, 999; Conrad and Alexander, *When War Passed,* pp. 395–97; Kidd, *Personal Recollections,* p. 168; James H. Kidd to Father and Mother, July 9, 1863, Kidd Papers, UM.

7. Kidd, *Personal Recollections,* pp. 169, 170; Starr, *Union Cavalry,* 1:448; *OR,* 27, pt. 1:994; Russell A. Alger to L. G. Estes, February 12, 1897, Russell A. Alger to S. L. Gillespie, April 27, 1899, Alger Papers, UM; *National Tribune,* November 10, 1887.

8. *OR,* 27, pt. 1:994, 1000, 1019; Kidd, *Personal Recollections,* pp. 170, 171; Macomber, Diary, CMU; USAGR, Kilpatrick File, NA; James H. Kidd to Father and Mother, July 9, 1863, Kidd Papers, UM.

9. Coddington, *Gettysburg Campaign,* pp. 535–52.

10. *OR,* 27, pt. 1:995, 998–1000; USAGR, Kilpatrick File, NA; Macomber, Diary, CMU; Edward W. Whitaker to Sister Mary, August 6, 1863, typescript, Whitaker Papers, BL.

11. Coddington, *Gettysburg Campaign,* pp. 564–70; Longacre, *Cavalry,* pp. 262–67.

12. USAGR, Kilpatrick File, NA; Morey, Diary, UM; Macomber, Diary, CMU; Longacre, *Cavalry,* pp. 265–67.

13. USAGR, Kilpatrick File, NA; Kidd, *Personal Recollections,* pp. 183, 184; *OR,* 27, pt. 1:990.

14. Kidd, *Personal Recollections,* p. 184; Taylor, *Sketchbook,* p. 305; *OR,* 27, pt. 1:990; Edward W. Whitaker to Sister Mary, August 6, 1863, typescript, Whitaker Papers, BL.

15. Haven, "In the Steps," p. 78; *New York Times,* July 29, 1863; Kidd, *Personal Recollections,* pp. 185, 186; CR, Sixth Michigan Cavalry, NA; Coddington, *Gettysburg Campaign,* p. 571; Addison Ray Stone to Nellie, July 16, 1863, Stone Papers, UM.

16. Bush, "Sixth Michigan," *Gettysburg* 9: 114; *New York Times,* August 6, 1863; *National Tribune,* December 23, 1915; Macomber, Diary, CMU;

Millbrook, *Study,* pp. 31, 32; *OR,* 27, pt. 1:990, 1000; Morey, Diary, UM; Victor Comte to Elise, July 16, 1863, Comte Papers, UM.

17. *OR,* 27, pt. 1:929, 990, 1000; Coddington, *Gettysburg Campaign,* p. 571; Nevins, *Diary,* p. 265; Macomber, Diary, CMU; Morey, Diary, UM.

18. Harrington, Diary, WMU; USAGR, Kilpatrick File, NA; Pohanka, "Letters," *B&G* 6 (3): 6.

19. Kidd, *Personal Recollections,* pp. 164, 165.

20. Hutton, *Custer Reader,* p. 17; Andrew Newton Buck to Brother and Sister, July 9, 1863, Seventh Michigan Cavalry File, GNMP; Hunt, "Custer," p. 27, UM; Urwin, *Custer Victorious,* pp. 59, 82.

21. *OR,* 27, pt. 1:918, 992–96; Urwin, *Custer Victorious,* p. 278; MSR/GAC, NA.

22. Kidd, *Personal Recollections,* pp. 130, 131; Wert, *From Winchester,* p. 190.

23. Kidd, *Personal Recollections,* p. 131, 132; Urwin, *Custer Victorious,* p. 270.

24. Kidd, *Personal Recollections,* pp. 131, 132.

25. *OR,* 27, pt. 1:148, 1004; Macomber, Diary, CMU; Harrington, Diary, WMU; GAC to Sister, July 26, 1863, GAC Collection, MCLS.

26. Coddington, *Gettysburg Campaign,* pp. 572, 573; Long, *Civil War,* pp. 385–89.

27. Long, *Civil War,* pp. 390–93; *OR,* 27, pt. 1:1002, 1003, 1004; pt. 3:792; Macomber, Diary, CMU; Harrington, Diary, WMU.

28. Henderson, *Road,* pp. 4, 5, 15.

29. GAC to Sister, July 26, 1863, GAC Collection, MCLS; Hunt, "Custer," p. 66, UM; Reynolds, *Civil War,* p. 57; *OR,* 29, pt. 2:63; GAC to J. H. Kilpatrick, August 13, 1863, Forsyth Papers, UM.

30. Crary, *Dear Belle,* pp. 146, 214–15.

31. Frost, *Custer Legends,* pp. 69, 71n; Merington, *Custer Story,* p. 63.

32. Merington, *Custer Story,* p. 63.

33. CSR, Christiancy File, NA; Henry Christiancy Diary, Christiancy-Pickett Papers, USAMHI; Frost, *General Custer's Libbie,* p. 88; Reynolds, *Civil War,* p. 70.

34. GAC to Sister, July 26, 1863, GAC Collection, MCLS; CSR, Granger File, NA; O'Neil and O'Neil, *Custer,* p. 20; Gustavus Lange to Michigan Military Agent, April 15, 1865, GAC, Correspondence and Orders, LBBNM; Urwin, *Custer Victorious,* p. 118; Victor Comte to Elise, July 16, 1863, Comte Papers, UM.

35. Frost, *General Custer's Libbie,* p. 95; Custer, *Tenting,* p. 41; Carroll, *Custer and His Times,* p. 155; *Billings Gazette,* May 27, 1961.

36. Custer, *Tenting,* pp. 40, 41.

37. Reynolds, *Civil War,* p. 70; Frost, *General Custer's Libbie,* p. 95; *B&L* 4: 234.

38. F. W. Benteen to D. F. Barry, September 28, 1895, Barry Papers, LBBNM.

39. Ibid.; Custer, *Tenting*, p. 42.

40. Harrington, Diary, WMU; Barbour, Diary, UM; USAGR, Davies File, NA; Benedict, *Vermont*, 2:533, 610; *OR*, 29, pt. 2:128.

41. *OR*, 29, pt. 1:78; Harrington, Diary, WMU; James Christiancy to D. S. Bacon, August 27, 1863, GAC Collection, MCLS.

42. James Christiancy to D. S. Bacon, August 27, 1863, GAC Collection, MCLS.

43. Harrington, Diary, WMU; *OR*, 29, pt. 1:111, 112; Henderson, *Road*, pp. 32, 33; *New York Times*, September 17, 1863.

44. *OR*, 29, pt. 1:118, 119; Henderson, *Road*, pp. 36, 38; *New York Times*, September 28, October 21, 1863.

45. Henderson, *Road*, pp. 38, 39; *New York Times*, September 28, 1863; *OR*, 29, pt. 1:119.

46. *New York Times*, September 17, 28, 1863; *OR*, 29, pt. 1:118, 128; Henderson, *Road*, p. 39.

47. Henderson, *Road*, p. 40; *New York Times*, September 17, 28, 1863; Hunt, "Custer," p. 28, UM; Benedict, *Vermont*, 2:613; Glazier, *Three Years*, p. 322.

48. Agassiz, *Meade's Headquarters*, p. 17; MSR/GAC, NA; *OR*, 29, pt. 1:99.

49. Agassiz, *Meade's Headquarters*, p. 17.

50. Frost, *General Custer's Libbie*, p. 70; Haven, "In the Steps," p. 102.

Chapter 7: "My Own Bright Particular *Star*"

1. Urwin, *Custer Victorious*, p. 55.

2. Frost, *General Custer's Libbie*, p. 75.

3. Lydia Reed to GAC, September 4, 1863, typescript, Frost Collection, MCHMA; O'Neil and O'Neil, *Custers*, pp. 7, 8.

4. Frost, *General Custer's Libbie*, p. 64.

5. Merington, *Custer Story*, p. 64; Frost, *General Custer's Libbie*, p. 75.

6. Ibid., p. 74; Leckie, *Elizabeth Bacon Custer*, p. 31.

7. Frost, *General Custer's Libbie*, p. 75.

8. Ibid., p. 75; Merington, *Custer Story*, p. 64.

9. Merington, *Custer Story*, p. 64; Frost, *General Custer's Libbie*, pp. 75, 76.

10. Merington, *Custer Story*, p. 65; Frost, *General Custer's Libbie*, p. 76; GAC to Sister, October 25, 1863, GAC Collection, MCLS; Harrington, Diary, WMU; Henderson, *Road*, p. 73.

11. Henderson, *Road*, pp. 72, 73; Harrington, Diary, WMU; Morey, Diary, UM.

12. Henderson, *Road*, pp. 70, 71, 72; *OR*, 29, pt. 1:389.

13. *OR*, 29, pt. 1:389; pt. 2:270; Merington, *Custer Story*, p. 65.

14. *OR*, 29, pt. 1:230, 374, 381, 389, 390; Henderson, *Road*, pp. 78–81, 84, 86; *National Tribune*, July 24, 1919; Macomber, Diary, CMU.

15. *OR*, 29, pt. 1:381, 390; Macomber, Diary, CMU; Henderson,

Road, pp. 94, 95; Edward W. Whitaker to Sister Ada, October 17–18, 1863, typescript, Whitaker Papers, BL.

16. Henderson, *Road,* pp. 96, 99; USAGR, Kilpatrick File, NA; *OR,* 29, pt. 1:381, 390, 394; Benedict, *Vermont,* 2:617.

17. Henderson, *Road,* pp. 96, 100; *OR,* 29, pt. 1:381, 390.

18. Henderson, *Road,* pp. 99, 100; *OR,* 29, pt. 1:381, 394.

19. *OR,* 29, pt. 1:390; USAGR, Kilpatrick File, NA; Merington, *Custer Story,* p. 66.

20. *OR,* 29, pt. 1:390; Merington, *Custer Story,* p. 66; Macomber, Diary, CMU; *National Tribune,* July 24, 1919.

21. *OR,* 29, pt. 1:390, 394; Merington, *Custer Story,* p. 66; *National Tribune,* July 24, 1919; Urwin, *Custer Victorious,* p. 68; Robertson, "Fifth Cavalry," pp. 3, 4, UM.

22. *OR,* 29, pt. 1:390; *National Tribune,* July 24, 1919; Macomber, Diary, CMU; GAC to Sister, October 25, 1863, GAC Collection, MCLS; GAC to My Dear Friend, October 29, 1863, Christiancy-Pickett Papers, USAMHI.

23. *OR,* 29, pt. 1:387, 390; *National Tribune,* July 24, 1919; Merington, *Custer Story,* p. 66; Henderson, *Road,* pp. 102, 103.

24. Henderson, *Road,* pp. 102, 103; Merington, *Custer Story,* pp. 66, 67; *OR,* 29, pt. 1:381, 391; Macomber, Diary, CMU; *New York Times,* October 14, 1863; *National Tribune,* July 24, 1919.

25. Macomber, Diary, CMU; Henderson, *Road,* chap. 9–13.

26. *OR,* 29, pt. 1:237, 391; Macomber, Diary, CMU; Merington, *Custer Story,* p. 67; Henderson, *Road,* pp. 196–199.

27. *OR,* 29, pt. 1:391; Edward W. Whitaker to Sister Ada, October 17–18, 1863, typescript, Whitaker Papers, BL; Henderson, *Road,* pp. 201, 202.

28. *OR,* 29, pt. 1:391, 397; Harrington, Diary, WMU; Merington, *Custer Story,* p. 68; Kidd, *Personal Recollections,* pp. 213, 214.

29. *OR,* 29, pt. 1:391; Kidd, *Personal Recollections,* pp. 214, 215; Henderson, *Road,* pp. 202, 203.

30. *OR,* 29, pt. 1:382, 391; Kidd, *Personal Recollections,* pp. 216, 217.

31. Kidd, *Personal Recollections,* pp. 217, 218; *OR,* 29, pt. 1:391; Merington, *Custer Story,* p. 68.

32. Kidd, *Personal Recollections,* pp. 218–20.

33. Ibid., p. 221; *OR,* 29, pt. 1:391; Henderson, *Road,* pp. 203, 204.

34. *OR,* 29, pt. 1:391; Henderson, *Road,* p. 204; *New York Times,* October 26, 1863.

35. *OR,* 29, pt. 1:391, 392; Kidd, *Personal Recollections,* pp. 221–23; Merington, *Custer Story,* pp. 68, 69; *New York Times,* October 22, 1863.

36. *OR,* 29, pt. 1:382, 392; Harrington, Diary, WMU; Macomber, Diary, CMU; Henderson, *Road,* pp. 204, 205; *New York Times,* October 23, 1863.

37. Merington, *Custer Story,* pp. 68–69.

38. Ibid., pp. 69, 71, 72; GAC to My Dear Friend, October 29, 1863, Christiancy-Pickett Papers, USAMHI.

39. GAC to My Dear Friend, October 29, 1863, Christiancy-Pickett Papers, USAMHI; [GAC to I. P. Christiancy], fragment of letter, October 29, 1863, GAC Papers, USMAL.

40. GAC to My Dear Friend, October 29, 1863, Christiancy-Pickett Papers, USAMHI; [GAC to I. P. Christiancy], fragment of letter, October 29, 1863, GAC Papers, USMAL.

41. Frost, *General Custer's Libbie,* p. 77; Merington, *Custer Story,* p. 67.

42. Frost, *General Custer's Libbie,* pp. 78, 79.

43. Ibid., p. 80; Merington, *Custer Story,* pp. 73, 74.

44. Frost, *General Custer's Libbie,* p. 80.

45. Merington, *Custer Story,* pp. 73–74.

46. Ibid., pp. 71, 72; Frost, *General Custer's Libbie,* p. 81.

Chapter 8: MARRIAGE

1. Harrington, Diary, WMU; Macomber, Diary, CMU; *OR,* 29, pt. 1:655; pt. 2:462, 475; EBC to Mrs. Alexander, August 11, [1926], EBC Collection, MCLS; John R. Morey to Cousin William, September 6, 1863, Morey Papers, UM; Andrew Newton Buck to Brother and Sisters, November 9, 1863, Buck Papers, UM.

2. Utley, *Cavalier,* pp. 33–34; Reynolds, *Civil War,* p. 60.

3. *OR,* 29, pt. 2:448.

4. Harrington, Diary, WMU; Macomber, Diary, CMU; Frost, *General Custer's Libbie,* pp. 84, 85.

5. GAC to Sister, November 6, 1863, GAC Collection, MCLS; *Monroe Evening News,* October 28, 1965; Frost, *General Custer's Libbie,* p. 92.

6. Frost, *General Custer's Libbie,* pp. 83–85.

7. Ibid., p. 84.

8. Ibid., pp. 83, 85.

9. *OR,* 29, pt. 1:811; Long, *Civil War,* p. 439.

10. *OR,* 29, pt. 1:811–13; Harrington, Diary, WMU; Macomber, Diary, CMU; Edward W. Whitaker to Sister Ada, November 24, 1863, typescript, Whitaker Papers, BL; Long, *Civil War,* pp. 439–42.

11. James H. Kidd to Father, December 24, 1863, Kidd Papers, UM; *OR,* 29, pt. 2:555.

12. James H. Kidd to Father, December 24, 1863, Kidd Papers, UM; Harrington, Diary, WMU; Macomber, Diary, CMU; GAC to Sister, December 7, 1863, GAC Collection, MCLS.

13. Harrington, Diary, WMU; GAC to Sister, November 6, 1863, GAC Collection, MCLS; GAC to R. A. Alger, December 19, 1863; G. L. Osburne to R. A. Alger, December 21, 1863, Alger Papers, UM.

14. Reynolds, *Civil War,* p. 6; Frost, *General Custer's Libbie,* pp. 85, 86.

15. Merington, *Custer Story*, p. 76; Frost, *General Custer's Libbie*, p. 86; GAC to D. S. Bacon, December 11, 1863, Merington Papers, NYPL; D. S. Bacon to My Young Friend, December 12, 1863, typescript, Frost Collection, MCHMA.

16. D. S. Bacon to My Young Friend, December 12, 1863, typescript, Frost Collection, MCHMA; Frost, *General Custer's Libbie*, p. 86.

17. Frost, *General Custer's Libbie*, p. 87.

18. GAC to Sister, December 22, 1863, GAC Collection, MCLS; GAC to My Dear Friend, December 19, 1863, GAC Papers, USMAL.

19. Merington, *Custer Story*, p. 79; O'Neil and O'Neil, *Custers*, pp. 6, 7.

20. Nettie Humphrey to My Darling Girl, December 31, 1863, typescript, Frost Collection, MCHMA; Merington, *Custer Story*, pp. 74–77.

21. Ibid., p. 77.

22. Ibid., pp. 78, 79.

23. GAC to My Dear Friend, n.d. [January 7, 1864], GAC Papers, USMAL; Hutton, *Custer Reader*, p. 18.

24. GAC to My Dear Friend, n.d. [two letters of January 7, 1864], GAC Papers, USMAL.

25. GAC to My dear Friend, January 20, 1864, GAC Papers, USMAL; GAC to D. S. Bacon, January 19, 1864, Merington Papers, NYPL.

26. GAC to My Dear Friend, January 19, 1864, GAC Papers, USMAL; Carroll, *Custer in the Civil War*, p. 173.

27. Hutton, *Custer Reader*, pp. 18–19.

28. Ibid., p. 29n.

29. Merington, *Custer Story*, p. 80; GAC to D. S. Bacon, January 19, 1864, Merington Papers, NYPL; GAC to My Dear Friend, January 20, 1864, GAC Papers, USMAL.

30. Kidd, Diary, Kidd Papers, UM; Reynolds, *Civil War*, p. 8; Frost, *General Custer's Libbie*, pp. 90, 91.

31. Frost, *General Custer's Libbie*, p. 92.

32. Ibid., p. 92; Merington, *Custer Story*, p. 80.

33. *Monroe Commerical*, February 11, 1864; *Detroit Advertiser and Tribune*, February 11, 1864; Wayne C. Mann to author, February 9, 1994, author's collection; Frost, *General Custer's Libbie*, pp. 92, 93; O'Neil and O'Neil, *A Custer Time Line*, pp. 6, 7.

34. *Detroit Advertiser and Tribune*, February 11, 1864; *Monroe Commercial*, February 11, 1864; Merington, *Custer Story*, p. 81; Frost, *General Custer's Libbie*, pp. 92, 93.

35. *Detroit Advertiser and Tribune*, February 11, 1864; *Monroe Commercial*, February 11, 1864; reception card, GAC Collection, MCHMA; Merington, *Custer Story*, pp. 81–82.

36. Merington, *Custer Story*, pp. 82, 83; *Detroit Advertiser and Tribune*, February 11, 1864; Frost, *General Custer's Libbie*, p. 92.

37. Merington, *Custer Story*, pp. 81, 82, 83; *Monroe Commercial*, Febru-

ary 11, 1864; *Detroit Advertiser and Tribune*, February 11, 1864; Custer, *Boots*, p. 84.

38. Merington, *Custer Story*, p. 81; Daniel S. Bacon to Sister, April 13, 1864, typescript, Frost Collection, MCHMA.

39. Merington, *Custer Story*, pp. 82–84; Frost, *General Custer's Libbie*, pp. 92, 93.

40. Frost, *General Custer's Libbie*, p. 94; Merington, *Custer Story*, p. 84.

41. Merington, *Custer Story*, pp. 84, 85.

42. Frost, *General Custer's Libbie*, p. 94.

43. Ibid., p. 94; GAC to Sister, April 23, 1864, GAC Collection, MCLS.

44. GAC to Sister, April 23, 1864, GAC Collection, MCLS; fragments of letters, GAC to EBC, n.d. [c. March 1865], Merington Papers, NYPL.

45. Custer, *Boots*, p. 1; Reynolds, *Civil War*, pp. 44, 45; Hall, "Season," *B&G* 8 (4): 15, 48; Clark B. Hall to author, February 14, 1994, author's collection.

46. Custer, *Boots*, pp. 1–2; Reynolds, *Civil War*, p. 56.

47. Reynolds, *Civil War*, pp. 53, 54, 58.

48. Ibid., pp. 45, 54; Frost, *General Custer's Libbie*, p. 96.

49. Reynolds, *Civil War*, p. 50; Hutton, *Custer Reader*, p. 53; Frost, *General Custer's Libbie*, p. 96.

50. Morey, Diary; John R. Morey to Cousin William, January 18, 1864, Morey Papers, UM; Kidd, *Personal Recollections*, pp. 228, 229, 232, 233, 234; Urwin, *Custer Victorious*, p. 113; Benedict, *Vermont*, 2:626; Rodenbough, Potter, and Seal, *History*, pp. 46, 47; CR, First Michigan, NA; Edward W. Whitaker to Sister Ada, February 26, 1864, typescript, Whitaker Papers, BL; William Ball to Father, February 5, 1864, Ball Papers, WMU.

51. Starr, *Union Cavalry*, 2:57–61.

52. Ibid., p. 60; *OR*, 33:598, 599, 620, 783; O'Neil, *Custer Chronicles*, 1:2.

53. *OR*, 33:162; Custer, *Boots*, p. 2; Reynolds, *Civil War*, pp. 46, 48.

54. *OR*, 33:164, 615, 616; Moore, "Custer's Raid," *VMHB* 79 (3): 340, 342; Pohanka, "George Yates," *GG* 8: 13; *New York Times*, March 3, 1864.

55. *OR*, 33:162; Moore, "Custer's Raid," *VMHB* 79 (3): 166, 167, 342, 344; T. E. O'Neil, *Custer Chronicles*, 1:2, 4; *New York Times*, March 3, 1864.

56. *OR*, 33:162, 164; Moore, "Custer's Raid," *VMHB*, 79, 3: 344, 345; *New York Times*, March 3, 1864.

57. *OR*, 33:162, 164, 165; Moore, "Custer's Raid," *VMHB* 79 (3): 345, 346; *New York Times*, March 3, 1864; T. E. O'Neil, *Custer Chronicles*, 1:4; Urwin, *Custer Victorious*, p. 121.

58. *OR*, 33:162, 165; Moore, "Custer's Raid," *VMHB* 79 (3): 346, 347; *New York Times*, March 3, 1864.

59. *OR*, 33:162, 163, 165, 166; *New York Times*, March 3, 1864; Moore, "Custer's Raid," *VMHB* 79 (3): 347, 348.

60. *OR*, 33:163, 171; Frost, *General Custer's Libbie*, p. 103; Starr, *Union Cavalry*, 2:66, 67; Agassiz, *Meade's Headquarters*, p. 79.

61. Meringhton, *Custer Story*, pp. 86, 87; Daniel S. Bacon to Sister, April 13, 1864, typescript, Frost Collection, MCHMA; EBC to Parents, March 20, 1864, Meringhton Papers, NYPL; MSR/GAC, NA.

62. McCann, "Anna E. Jones," *Incidents* 2 (1): 16, 18, 20; Frost, *Custer Legends*, pp. 70, 71.

63. McCann, "Anna E. Jones," *Incidents* 2 (1): 18–19; Frost, *Custer Legends*, p. 71; *Toledo Blade*, December 13, 1957.

64. McCann, "Anna E. Jones," *Incidents* 2 (1): 19–20.

65. Ibid., pp. 16–23.

66. Ibid., p. 20. McCann accepts Annie Jones's allegations as accurate, dismissing both Kilpatrick and Custer as womanizers, although he offers nothing to substantiate his charges toward Custer.

67. MSR/GAC, NA; EBC to Father and Mother, April 3, 1864, typescript, Meringhton Papers, NYPL; Meringhton, *Custer Story*, pp. 87, 88, 89.

Chapter 9: "WHERE IN HELL IS THE REAR?"

1. Meringhton, *Custer Story*, p. 87.

2. Wert, *From Winchester*, pp. 3, 4.

3. Agassiz, *Meade's Headquarters*, p. 81.

4. Arner, *Mutiny*, pp. 41–43.

5. Starr, *Union Cavalry*, 2:73, 74; Morris, *Sheridan*, p. 155; Nevins, *Diary*, p. 341; Warner, *Generals in Blue*, pp. 373–74.

6. Wert, *From Winchester*, pp. 16, 17.

7. Ibid., p. 17; Agassiz, *Meade's Headquarters*, p. 82; Morris, *Sheridan*, p. 1.

8. Kidd, *Personal Recollections*, p. 299; Morris, *Sheridan*, p. 3; DuPont, *Campaign*, p. 134; Hagemann, *Fighting*, pp. 222, 223; *War Papers*, MOLLUS, Wis., 1:371; Wert, *From Winchester*, pp. 17, 18.

9. J. H. Kidd to Father, April 11, 1864, Kidd Papers, UM.

10. Starr, *Union Cavalry*, 2:77; Hagemann, *Fighting*, p. 224; Warner, *Generals in Blue*, p. 508.

11. Jacob Greene to GAC, March 30, 1864, Meringhton Papers, NYPL; Starr, *Union Cavalry*, 2:75; *OR*, 33: 893; Warner, *Generals in Blue*, pp. 566–67.

12. Jacob Greene to GAC, March 30, 1864, Meringhton Papers, NYPL; GAC to Sister, April 23, 1864, GAC Collection, MCLS; Meringhton, *Custer Story*, p. 69.

13. GAC to Sister, April 23, 1864, GAC Collection, MCLS.

14. Ibid.

15. Ibid.; GAC to EBC, April 16, 1864, Meringhton Papers, NYPL; F. W. Kellogg to GAC, April 17, 1864, GAC Correspondence, LBBNM; Starr, *Union Cavalry*, 2:75, 76.

16. *OR,* 33:1033, 1043; Kidd, *Personal Recollections,* p. 263; Merington, *Custer Story,* pp. 92, 93; *B&L* 4: 188; Macomber, Diary, CMU.

17. Merington, *Custer Story,* pp. 92, 94; GAC to EBC, April 16, 1864, Merington Papers, NYPL.

18. Merington, *Custer Story,* p. 91.

19. Macomber, Diary, CMU; George Gray to James H. Kidd, April 28, 1864, Kidd Papers, UM; William Ball to Father and Mother, Brother and Sister, May 2, 1864, Ball Papers, WMU; CR, Sixth Michigan Cavalry, NA.

20. Merington, *Custer Story,* p. 94; Andrew Newton Buck to Brother and Sister, May 3, 1864, Buck Papers, UM; Joseph Douglass to Friend, April 20, 1864, Douglass-Nellis Papers, UM; Edward Corselius to Brother, April 21, 1864, Corselius Papers, UM; Urwin, *Custer Victorious,* pp. 277–78.

21. GAC to EBC, April 16, 1864; Jacob Greene to GAC, March 30, 1864, Merington Papers, NYPL; GAC to Sister, April 23, 1864, GAC Collection, MCLS; James H. Kidd to Father, April 11, 1864, Kidd Papers, UM.

22. Wert, *From Winchester,* p. 5; Long, *Civil War,* p. 492.

23. Long, *Civil War,* pp. 492, 493.

24. *OR,* 36, pt. 2:429; Macomber, Diary, CMU; *War Papers,* MOLLUS, Wis., 1:232; Kidd, *Personal Recollections,* p. 264.

25. *OR,* 36, pt. 2:466; *War Papers,* MOLLUS, Wis., 1:232, 233; Kidd, *Personal Recollections,* pp. 265, 266; Macomber, Diary, CMU; Merington, *Custer Story,* p. 95.

26. *OR,* 36, pt. 2:466; Kidd, *Personal Recollections,* pp. 265, 266; Macomber, Diary, CMU; Steere, *Wilderness,* pp. 379, 381; Urwin, *Custer Victorious,* p. 95.

27. *OR,* 36, pt. 2:466; Kidd, *Personal Recollections,* p. 267, 268; Steere, *Wilderness,* p. 381.

28. *OR,* 36, pt. 2:466, 467; *War Papers,* MOLLUS, Wis., 1:235–37; Kidd, *Personal Recollections,* pp. 268–70; Myers, *Comanches,* p. 268; Kidd, *Historical Sketches,* n.p.; Steere, *Wilderness,* pp. 381–83.

29. Steere, *Wilderness,* chaps. 19–26.

30. *OR,* 36, pt. 2:494, 514, 516; Macomber, Diary, CMU; Allen, *Down,* pp. 273, 274; Starr, *Union Cavalry,* 2:93–96.

31. Kidd, *Personal Recollections,* pp. 288–93; Macomber, Diary, CMU; Athearn, "Civil War Diary," *VMHB* 62: 101; Rodenbough, Potter, and Seal, *History,* p. 50.

32. Kidd, *Personal Recollections,* pp. 294, 295; Rodenbough, Potter, and Seal, *History,* p. 50; Macomber, Diary, CMU; Starr, *Union Cavalry,* 2:99, 100.

33. Macomber, Diary, CMU; Kidd, *Personal Recollections,* p. 295; Cheney, *History,* p. 165; Starr, *Union Cavalry,* 2:100–103.

34. Starr, *Union Cavalry,* 2:102–4; Thomas, *Bold Dragoon,* p. 290; Kidd, *Personal Recollections,* p. 296.

35. Cheney, *History,* p. 165; Urwin, *Custer Victorious,* pp. 139, 140; Kidd, *Personal Recollections,* pp. 301–3.

36. *OR,* 36, pt. 1:817, 818; Kidd, *Personal Recollections,* pp. 304, 305; Benedict, *Vermont,* 2:637; Urwin, *Custer Victorious,* pp. 140, 141; Macomber, Diary, CMU.

37. Macomber, Diary, CMU; *OR,* 36, pt. 1:818; Benedict, *Vermont,* 2:638; Urwin, *Custer Victorious,* pp. 142–44; *National Tribune,* June 23, 1887; Starr, *Union Cavalry,* 2:105–7; Thomas, *Bold Dragoon,* p. 292.

38. Starr, *Union Cavalry,* 2:107–9; Moyer, *History,* p. 75; Isham, *Historical Sketch,* pp. 50, 51; Lee, *Personal,* pp. 125, 126.

39. Kidd, *Personal Recollections,* pp. 307–13; Macomber, Diary, CMU; Viola, *Memoirs,* p. 40; Urwin, *Custer Victorious,* pp. 145–47.

40. Kidd, *Personal Recollections,* pp. 313, 314; Macomber, Diary, CMU; Merington, *Custer Story,* pp. 97, 98, 109.

41. Merington, *Custer Story,* pp. 97, 98.

42. GAC to EBC, May 17, 1864, Merington Papers, NYPL.

43. Kidd, *Personal Recollections,* pp. 314–17; Macomber, Diary, CMU; *OR,* 36, pt. 3:98, 99, 117; Rowe, "Camp Tales," p. 70, UM; Cheney, *History,* pp. 171, 172; Tarbell Papers, USAMHI.

44. Long, *Civil War,* pp. 506–9.

45. Kidd, *Personal Recollections,* pp. 318, 319; *War Papers,* MOLLUS, Wis., 1:225, 226; Rowe, "Camp Tales," p. 72, UM; Macomber, Diary, CMU; Kidd, Diary, Kidd Papers, UM; Page, *Letters,* p. 84.

46. Starr, *Union Cavalry,* 2:117, 118; Williams, "Haw's Shop," *CWTI* 9 (9): 14, 18; Kidd, *Personal Recollections,* pp. 322, 323; Macomber, Diary, CMU.

47. James H. Kidd to Father and Mother, June 3, 1864, Kidd Papers, UM; Macomber, Diary, CMU; Williams, "Haw's Shop," *CWTI* 9 (9): 18; Kidd, *Personal Recollections,* pp. 325, 326; CSR, James Christiancy File, NA; Merington, *Custer Story,* pp. 99, 100; Millbrook Study, pp. 63, 64; Kidd, *Historical Sketch,* n.p.

48. James H. Kidd to Father and Mother, June 3, 1864, Kidd Papers, UM; F. M. Wright to Friend, July 4, 1864, Ball Papers, WMU; Williams, "Haw's Shop," *CWTI* 9 (9): 18; Lloyd, *History,* p. 96; Kidd, *Personal Recollections,* p. 327; Millbrook, *Study,* p. 64; CSR, James Christiancy File, NA.

49. Kidd, *Personal Recollections,* p. 329; Macomber, Diary, CMU; Starr, *Union Cavalry,* 2:119, 120.

50. Macomber, Diary, CMU; Kidd, *Personal Recollections,* pp. 329–32; Rowe, "Camp Tales," pp. 74, 75, 76, UM; Starr, *Union Cavalry,* 2:119, 120.

51. James H. Kidd to Father and Mother, June 3, 1864, Kidd Papers, UM; Kidd, *Personal Recollections,* pp. 333, 335, 336; Macomber, Diary, CMU; Baltz, *Battle,* p. 84; Starr, *Union Cavalry,* 2:121–23.

52. Baltz, *Battle,* passim; Starr, *Union Cavalry,* 2:125, 126; Macomber, Diary, CMU.

53. Hall, "'Army of Devils,'" *CWTI* 16 (10): 19–23; Shillinburg, "More," *RR* 8 (2): 2–6.

54. Hall, "'Army of Devils,'" *CWTI* 16 (10): 21, 23, 24; Schillinburg, "More," *RR* 8 (2): 6–9.

55. Merington, *Custer Story,* pp. 98, 101, 106, 108, 202.

56. Ibid., p. 103.

57. Morris, "Sweltering," *MH* 9 (6): 42; Kidd, *Personal Recollections,* p. 342; Macomber, Diary, CMU.

58. James H. Kidd to Father and Mother, June 21, 1864, Kidd Papers, UM; Macomber, Diary, CMU; *Personal Narratives,* MOLLUS, R.I., 6:196; Starr, *Union Cavalry,* 2:134–36.

59. Starr, *Union Cavalry,* 2:136, 137; Swank, *Battle,* pp. 6, 7.

60. Kidd, *Personal Recollections,* p. 347; Hutton, *Custer Reader,* pp. 57, 58; Morris, "Sweltering," *MH* 9 (6): 46.

61. Kidd, *Personal Recollections,* pp. 348–50; Morris, "Sweltering," *MH* 9 (6): 46; Swank, *Battle,* pp. 13, 14, 16, 62.

62. Kidd, *Personal Recollections,* pp. 351–53; Isham, *Historical Sketch,* p. 58.

63. Kidd, *Personal Recollections,* pp. 355, 357; Isham, *Historical Sketch,* p. 58; Swank, *Battle,* pp. 9, 10, 17; James H. Kidd to Father and Mother, June 21, 1864, Kidd Papers, UM.

64. Macomber, Diary, CMU; Merington, *Custer Story,* pp. 104, 105; Lee, *Personal,* p. 53; Kidd, *Personal Recollections,* pp. 357, 359, 360; *B&L* 4: 234.

65. Urwin, *Custer Reader,* pp. 163, 273; Morris, "Sweltering," *MH* 9 (6): 48; Macomber, Diary, CMU; Kidd, *Personal Recollections,* p. 360.

66. Kidd, *Personal Recollections,* p. 360; Kidd, *Historical Sketch,* n.p.

67. Merington, *Custer Story,* p. 105; Lee, *Personal,* p. 231; Pyne, *History,* p. 263; Macomber, Diary, CMU.

68. Merington, *Custer Story,* p. 105; Urwin, *Custer Victorious,* pp. 38n, 162; Lee, *Personal,* p. 230.

69. Kidd, *Personal Recollections,* pp. 360, 361; Swank, *Battle,* pp. 22, 23.

70. Swank, *Battle,* pp. 19–25; Kidd, *Personal Recollections,* pp. 362–64; Morris, *Sheridan,* pp. 175–76.

71. Swank, *Battle,* pp. 27, 31, 32; Kidd, *Personal Recollections,* p. 365; Merington, *Custer Story,* p. 104; CSR, Jacob Greene File, NA.

72. Merington, *Custer Story,* pp. 104, 105; Frost, *General Custer's Libbie,* p. 108; I. P. Christiancy to EBC, December 17, 1876, typescript, Frost Collection, MCHMA.

73. MSR/GAC, NA; Hagemann, *Fighting,* p. 226.

Chapter 10: "DAUGHTER OF THE STARS"

1. Trudeau, *Last Citadel,* pp. 131, 132; Frost, *General Custer's Libbie,* p. 111.

2. Trudeau, *Last Citadel,* chap. 1–2; Frost, *General Custer's Libbie,* p. 111.

3. Frost, *General Custer's Libbie,* p. 111; Reynolds, *Civil War,* pp. 89, 97, 98.

4. Reynolds, *Civil War,* pp. 89–91, 93–94.

5. Merington, *Custer Story,* pp. 102, 105, 107, 112.

6. Ibid., pp. 112–14; Frost, *General Custer's Libbie,* p. 111; James H. Kidd to Father, July 12, 1864, Kidd Papers, UM; EBC to Aunt Eliza, July 3, 1864, GAC Collection, MCLS.

7. MSR/GAC, NA; Frost, *General Custer's Libbie,* p. 111; James H. Kidd to Father, July 12, 1864, Kidd Papers, UM; Edward W. Whitaker to Sister Ada, July 29, 1864, typescript, GAC Collection, MCHMA.

8. Wert, *From Winchester,* pp. 8–10.

9. Ibid., pp. 7–8.

10. Ibid., pp. 10–12.

11. Ibid., pp. 12, 13; *OR,* 43, pt. 1:698.

12. Wert, *From Winchester,* pp. 15–16, 22; Crowninshield, "Sheridan," *Atlantic Monthly* 42; p. 684; Grant, *Personal Memoirs,* 2:317.

13. Wert, *From Winchester,* pp. 26–28.

14. Barbour, Diary, UM; Monaghan, Diary, typescript, p. 3, Monaghan Family Papers, UM; Kidd, *Personal Recollections,* p. 373; Moyer, *History,* p. 94; CR, First Michigan Cavalry File, NA.

15. Warner, *Generals in Blue,* p. 321; Hagemann, *Fighting,* pp. 22, 225; Kidd, *Personal Recollections,* pp. 237, 238.

16. Wert, *From Winchester,* pp. 30, 31; *OR,* 43, pt. 1:54.

17. Taylor, *Sketchbook,* pp. 1, 35, 534.

18. Wert, *From Wichester,* pp. 29–32.

19. Ibid., p. 32; Monaghan, Diary, typescript, p. 4, Monaghan Family Papers, UM; *New York Times,* August 20, 21, 1864; Barbour, Diary, UM; Lee, *Personal,* p. 210; GAC to Peter Milton Shafor, October 29, 1864, Forsyth Papers, UM.

20. Monaghan, Diary, typescript, p. 4, Monaghan Family Papers, UM; *New York Times,* August 25, 1864; Wert, *From Winchester,* pp. 33, 34; Ferguson, "Memoranda," DU; *SHSP,* 7:507, 508.

21. *New York Times,* August 25, 1864; Kidd, *Personal Recollections,* pp. 375, 376; *SHSP,* 7:508; Ferguson, "Memoranda," DU.

22. *New York Times,* August 25, 1864; Merington, *Custer Story,* p. 114; Rowe, "Camp Tales," pp. 79, 80, UM; *SHSP,* 7:508; Ferguson, "Memoranda," DU; CSR, Edward Granger File, NA.

23. Ferguson, "Memoranda," DU; *SHSP,* 7:508; Monaghan, Diary, typescript, p. 4, Monaghan Family Papers, UM; Simon, *Papers,* 12, p. 13n; Merington, *Custer Story,* p. 115.

24. Utley, *Cavalier,* p. 36; Urwin, *Custer Victorious,* p. 276.

25. Wert, *From Winchester,* pp. 32, 33; Boudrye, *Historic Records,* pp. 164, 165; Pickerill, *History,* pp. 157, 158; Carr, Diary, typescript, p. 27, USAMHI; Gracey, *Annals,* p. 286–87.

26. Monaghan, Diary, typescript, p. 4, Monaghan Family Papers, UM; Barbour, Diary, UM; *New York Times,* August 25, 1864; CSR, Samuel K. Davis File, Fifth Michigan Cavalry, NA; Wert, *Mosby's Rangers,* pp. 195–96.

27. GAC to R. A. Alger, two orders, August 19, 1864, Alger Papers, UM; *New York Times,* August 25, 1864.

28. Wert, *Mosby's Rangers,* passim.

29. Ibid., pp. 187–97.

30. Wert, *From Winchester,* p. 38; *SHSP,* 7:508, 509; Kidd, *Personal Recollections,* p. 378.

31. Kidd, *Personal Recollections,* pp. 379–80; Barbour, Diary, UM.

32. Bowen, *Regimental History,* pp. 217–19; Cheney, *History,* pp. 213–14; Hall, *History,* pp. 217, 218; Moyer, *History,* p. 345; Barbour, Diary, UM; Kidd, *Personal Recollections,* pp. 380–81.

33. Wert, *From Winchester,* pp. 38–39; James H. Kidd to Father and Mother, September 9, 1864, Kidd Papers, UM.

34. GAC to Father, September 2, 1864; GAC to Sister, September 17, 1864, GAC Collection, MCLS; James H. Kidd to Father and Mother, September 9, 1864, Kidd Papers, UM; Merington, *Custer Story,* p. 119; Hagemann, *Fighting,* p. 301.

35. GAC to Father, September 2, 1864, GAC Collection, MCLS.

36. Urwin, *Custer Victorious,* p. 36; other accounts of his exploits in the valley in August can be found in *New York Times,* August 25, 29, September 5, 1864.

37. GAC to My Dear Friend, September 16, 1864, GAC Papers, USMAL.

38. E. H. Custer to GAC, September 6, 22, 1864, typescripts, Frost Collection, MCHMA.

39. Wert, *From Winchester,* p. 39.

40. Ibid., pp. 40–43; Taylor, *Sketchbook,* p. 353.

41. Wert, *From Winchester,* pp. 47–52, 71.

42. Ibid., pp. 71–73; *OR,* 43, pt. 2:104; Barbour, Diary, UM; Kern, interview with author, July 24, 1994; Elliott and Burleson, interview with author, July 24, 1994; Kidd, *Personal Recollections,* pp. 385–86.

43. Kidd, *Personal Recollections,* pp. 386, 387; Elliott and Burleson, interview with author, July 24, 1864; Kern, interview with author, July 24, 1994.

44. Kidd, *Personal Recollections,* pp. 387–89; *OR,* 43, pt. 1:454, 455; Wert, *From Winchester,* pp. 72–75.

45. Wert, *From Winchester,* pp. 76, 77; *OR,* 43, pt. 1:443, 455, 555.

46. Wert, *From Winchester,* pp. 78, 79; Isham, *Historical Sketch,* p. 70; Cheney, *History,* pp. 219, 220; *OR,* 43, pt. 1:443, 455, 482.

47. Wert, *From Winchester*, pp. 79, 80; *OR,* 43, pt. 1:427, 456; Farrar, *Twenty-Second Pennsylvania*, p. 371n.

48. Wert, *From Winchester*, chap. 4–5.

49. *OR,* 43, pt. 1:456; Kidd, *Personal Recollections*, pp. 390, 391; *SHSP,* 37:234.

50. Kidd, *Personal Recollections*, pp. 392, 393; Wert, *From Winchester*, pp. 95–96; Slease, *Fourteenth Pennsylvania*, p. 186; Benedict, *Vermont*, 2:150; Bowen, *Regimental History*, p. 232.

51. Bowen, *Regimental History*, p. 232; Wert, *From Winchester*, pp. 95, 96; Urwin, *Custer Victorious*, p. 187; Taylor, *Sketchbook*, p. 366; Hagemann, *Fighting*, p. 226; Harris, *Autobiography*, p. 98.

52. *OR,* 43, pt. 1:427, 428, 457, 550; Wert, *From Winchester*, pp. 96–99; Caspar Crowninshield to My Dear Mommy, October 5, 1864, Crowninshield Papers, MHS; Urwin, *Custer Victorious*, p. 188; Robertson, *Michigan,* pp. 433, 434; Merington, *Custer Story*, p. 61; Monaghan, Diary, typescript, p. 7, Monaghan Family Papers, UM.

53. Wert, *From Winchester*, pp. 103, 104; Hagemann, *Fighting*, p. 223; Morris, *Sheridan*, p. 202.

54. Wert, *From Winchester*, pp. 105, 106; Kidd, *Personal Recollections*, p. 394; *SHSP,* 27:7; *OR,* 43, pt. 1:458.

55. Wert, *From Winchester*, chap. 6–7.

56. Ibid., pp. 112–13, 130–31.

57. Wert, *Mosby's Rangers*, pp. 211–14.

58. Ibid., pp. 214–18.

59. Ibid., pp. 217, 218; Monaghan, Diary, typescript, p. 8, Monaghan Family Papers, UM; Thompson, Diary, Thompson Papers, DU.

60. Wert, *From Winchester*, pp. 132, 133; *OR,* 43, pt. 1:48.

61. *OR,* 43, pt. 1:508; pt. 2:170; Gause, *Four Years*, p. 321; *War Papers,* MOLLUS, Mo., 2:232; Wert, *From Winchester*, p. 144.

62. Special Orders, No. 42, September 26, 1864, GAC Collection, MCLS; MSR/GAC, NA; Merington, *Custer Story*, pp. 110, 111; *OR,* 39, pt. 3:444.

63. Robertson, *Michigan,* pp. 392, 394, 396, 398; Hutton, *Custer Reader,* p. 7; *OR,* 43, pt. 1:136; Kidd, *Personal Recollections*, p. 131.

64. *OR,* 43, pt. 1:463; Monaghan, Diary, typescript, p. 8, Monaghan Family Papers; GAC to J. H. Kidd, October 3, 1864, Kidd Papers, UM; Merington, *Custer Story*, p. 120.

65. Rodenbough, Potter, and Seal, *History*, p. 59; Norton, *Deeds*, p. 93; William Wells to Parents, October 4, 1864, Wells Papers, UVM; Benedict, *Vermont,* 2:661.

66. Wert, *From Winchester*, pp. 133–34, 143–45; Keiser, Diary, USAMHI, DeForest, *Volunteers Adventures*, p. 197; Murphy, Papers, DU; *OR,* 43, pt. 2:288, 289.

67. Wert, *From Winchester*, p. 145; Taylor, *Sketchbook*, pp. 434, 435; Hagemann, *Fighting*, p. 302.

68. Boudrye, *Historic Records,* pp. 176, 177; Hannaford, "Reminiscences," pp. 178-2, 179-3, 179-4, CHS; Horst, *Mennonites,* pp. 101, 102; Wayland, *Virginia,* pp. 189, 194.

69. Wert, *From Winchester,* pp. 157, 158.

70. Ibid., pp. 157–60.

71. Ibid., pp. 160–61; McDonald, *History,* p. 303; Hannaford, "Reminiscences," pp. 180-3–87-4, CHS; Thompson, Papers, p. 6, DU.

72. *OR,* 43, pt. 1:31, 431.

73. Ibid., p. 520; Hannaford, "Reminiscences," 187–4, 188–1, CHS; Tischler, interview with author, August 19, 1994; Allan L. Tischler to author, August 23, 1994; Richard L. Thornton to Allan L. Tischler, October 12, 1994, original in author's collection; Klease, *Shenandoah County,* p. 91; Murphy, Papers, DU.

74. *OR,* 43, pt. 1:520, 521; Benedict, *Vermont,* 2:663; Urwin, *Custer Victorious,* p. 199; Merington, *Custer Story,* p. 249; Hunt, "Custer," p. 43, UM.

75. *OR,* 43, pt. 1:521; Bushong and Bushong, *Fightin' Tom Rosser,* pp. 119–20; Boudrye, *Historic Records,* pp. 178, 180.

76. *OR,* 43, pt. 1:521; Wert, *From Winchester,* pp. 162–63; GAC to Peter Milton Shafor, October 29, 1864, Forsyth Papers, UM; *SHSP,* 12:453.

77. *OR,* 43, pt. 1:521; Wert, *From Winchester,* pp. 163, 164; Humphrey, Diary, UVA.

78. *OR,* 43, pt. 2:339, 431, 448; John Suter to Wife, October 13, 1864, Suter Papers, USAMHI; Monaghan, Diary, typescript, p. 10, Monaghan Papers, UM.

79. Merington, *Custer Story,* p. 122; Rodenbough, Potter, and Seal, *History,* p. 60.

80. Rodenbough, Potter, and Seal, *History,* p. 60; Hannaford, "Reminiscences," pp. 317-4, 318-1, CHS.

Chapter 11: MAJOR GENERAL

1. Wert, *From Winchester,* pp. 165, 166, 168–69, 174.

2. Ibid., pp. 173–76.

3. Ibid., chaps. 11 and 12.

4. Ibid., pp. 213–15; Hannaford, "Reminiscences," pp. 196-1, 196-2, 196-3, 197-1, CHS; *National Tribune,* May 26, 1887, and March 1, 1894.

5. Wert, *From Winchester,* pp. 215–19.

6. Ibid., pp. 217–19.

7. Ibid., pp. 221–25; Greiner, *General,* p. 358.

8. Wert, *From Winchester,* pp. 226–30; *New York Times,* October 27, 1864.

9. Hatton, "Just a Little Bit," *OH* 84 (3): 123; GAC to Peter Milton Shafor, October 29, 1864, Forsyth Papers, UM; Hannaford, "Reminiscenses," p. 201-1, CHS; Wert, *From Winchester,* pp. 230–34.

10. Wert, *From Winchester,* pp. 234–35; Pickerill, *History,* pp. 168, 169; Hannaford, "Reminiscences," p. 214-4, CHS; *New York Times,* October 27, 1864; *OR,* 43, pt. 1: p. 53.

11. Benedict, *Vermont* 2:667; Woodbury, Papers, DC; Gause, *Four Years,* p. 337; GAC to My Dear Friend, October 29, 1864, GAC Papers, UM.

12. William Wells to Anna Richardson, October 27, 1864, Wells Papers, UVM; Woodbury, Papers, DC; Benedict, *Vermont,* 2:667; GAC to Peter Milton Shafor, October 29, 1864, Forsyth Papers, UM; Gause, *Four Years,* p. 339.

13. Hagemann, *Fighting,* pp. 295, 296; Quarles, *Some,* pp. 125, 126; Taylor, *Sketchbook,* pp. 117, 520; *National Tribune,* September 13, 1883; Greiner, *General,* p. 358.

14. Hagemann, *Fighting,* p. 296; DuPont, *Campaign,* pp. 172–74; Wert, *From Winchester,* pp. 209, 237–38.

15. Wert, *From Winchester,* chap. 14; Clark, *One Hundred and Sixteenth Regiment,* p. 207.

16. Wert, *From Winchester,* p. 249; Starr, *Union Cavalry,* 2:256, 258; Caspar Crowninshield to My Dear Mommy, October 21, 1864, Crownin-shield Papers, MHS.

17. Urwin, *Custer Victorious,* p. 35; Kidd, *Personal Recollections,* p. 131; Hagemann, *Fighting,* p. 316; Joseph Jessup to Brother, September 27, 1864, Jessup Papers, UM.

18. Simon, *Papers,* 12, p. 335n; William Wells to Parents, October 21, 1864, Wells Papers, UVM; MSR/GAC, NA; Merington, *Custer Story,* p. 126.

19. Merington, *Custer Story,* pp. 124, 126; Frost, *General Custer's Libbie,* pp. 118, 119; Leckie, *Elizabeth Bacon Custer,* p. 59.

20. Merington, *Custer Story,* pp. 126, 127; Simon, *Papers,* 12:352; GAC to Peter Milton Shafor, October 29, 1864, Forsyth Papers, UM; Taylor, *Sketchbook,* p. 535; Utley, *Cavalier,* p. 30; MSR/GAC, NA.

21. Wert, *From Winchester,* p. 250; Merington, *Custer Story,* p. 128.

22. Hannaford, "Reminiscences," pp. 211-3–20-1, 233-4, 234-4, CHS; William Wells to Anna Richardson, November 16, 1864, Wells Papers, UVM; J. L. Sperry to Sister, November 17, 1864, Sperry Papers, DU; Quarles, *Some,* pp. 47, 48; Rhodes, *All,* p. 197; MSR/GAC, NA.

23. Merington, *Custer Story,* pp. 131, 132; Pickerill, *History,* p. 170; Delauter, *Winchester,* p. 85.

24. Merington, *Custer Story,* p. 132; GAC to Father [D. S. Bacon], November 20, 1864, Merington Papers, NYPL; Pell and Pell, interview with author, July 23, 1994; Quarles, *Some,* pp. 103–5; Reynolds, *Civil War,* p. 123.

25. Merington, *Custer Story,* p. 121; Leckie, *Elizabeth Bacon Custer,* pp. xix, xx.

26. Reynolds, *Civil War,* p. 38.

27. Ibid., p. 103; EBC to Father and Mother, November 20, 1864, Merington Papers, NYPL; Taylor, *Sketchbook,* p. 540; Allan Tischler to Author, June 29, 1994, author's collection; Delauter, *Winchester,* p. 94.

28. Frost, *General Custer's Libbie,* pp. 121, 122; Day, "If You Want," *GG* 9: 4.

29. Custer, *Boots,* p. 245; Day, "If You Want," *GG* 9: 4.

30. Frost, *General Custer's Libbie,* p. 122; Reynolds, *Civil War,* pp. 126, 127; Day, "If You Want," *GG* 9: 4.

31. Hannaford, "Reminiscences," pp. 224-1–32-1, CHS; Hatton, "Just a Little Bit," *OH* 84(3): 125; Merington, *Custer Story,* p. 134.

32. Sheridan, *Personal Memoirs,* 2:102; *OR,* 43, pt. 1:675; Hannaford, "Reminiscences," pp. 235-1–36-2, CHS; Gause, *Four Years,* p. 344; Starr, *Union Cavalry,* 2:339.

33. Hannaford, "Reminiscences," p. 236-3, CHS; Gause, *Four Years,* p. 344; *OR,* 43, pt. 1:675; Norton, *Red Neck Ties,* p. 60; Hunt, "Custer," p. 47, UM; Hatton, "Just a Little Bit," *OH* 84 (3): 125.

34. Eri Woodbury to A. J., December 24, 1864, Woodbury Papers, DC; Hannaford, "Reminiscences," p. 237-1, CHS; McDonald, *History,* pp. 331–33.

35. USAGR, George Chapman File, NA; Eri Woodbury to A. J., December 24, 1864, Woodbury Papers, DC; Hunt, "Custer," pp. 47, 48, UM; Gause, *Four Years,* pp. 344, 345; Norton, *Red Neck Ties,* p. 60; Hatton, "Just a Little Bit," *OH* 84 (3): 125, 126; *OR,* 43, pt. 1:676.

36. Eri Woodbury to A. J., December 24, 1864, Woodbury Papers, DC; Hannaford, "Reminiscences," pp. 240-4, 241-1, 243-4, 244-4, CHS; Gause, *Four Years,* pp. 347, 348; Sheridan, *Personal Memoirs,* 2:102, 104.

37. Daniel S. Bacon to Sister, December 26, 1864, typescript, Frost Collection, MCHMA; Merington, *Custer Story,* pp. 133, 135; USAGR, George Chapman File, NA.

38. Ives, Papers, DC; Daniel S. Bacon to Sister, February 17, 1865, typescript, Frost Collection, MCHMA; GAC, Correspondence and Orders, LBBNM; Father to James H. Kidd, January 30, 1865, Kidd Papers, UM.

39. Frost, *General Custer's Libbie,* p. 124; D. S. Bacon to GAC, February 8, 1865, typescript, Frost Collection, MCHMA.

40. Rebecca L. Richmond to Mother and Sister, February 12, 1865, Richmond Papers, USAMHI; D. S. Bacon to GAC, February 8, 1865, typescript, Frost Collection, MCHMA.

41. Rebecca L. Richmond to Mother and Sister, February 12, 1865, Richmond Papers, USAMHI; William Wells to Anna Richardson, February 12, 1865, Wells Papers, UVM; *Winchester Star,* July 18, 1990.

42. A diagram of Elmwood, its rooms, and occupants is contained in Rebecca L. Richmond to Father, February 19, 1865, Richmond Papers, USAMHI; *Winchester Star,* July 18, 1990.

43. *OR,* 46, pt. 2:495, 496, 553, 619, 620, 701, 702, 703; Starr, *Union Cavalry,* 2:365.

44. Letters of Michigan Brigade officers in GAC, Correspondence and Orders, LBBNM; *OR,* 46, pt. 1:725; Haven, "In the Steps," p. 221; Starr, *Union Cavalry,* 2:365, 366.

45. Rebecca L. Richmond to Dear Ones at Home, February 28, 1865, Richmond Papers, USAMHI; Norton, *Deeds,* p. 108; William Wells to Brother Henry, February 26, 1865, Wells Papers, UVM; Katz, *Custer,* p. 35, which misidentifies the house and Rebecca Richmond.

46. Gardiner, *Operations,* p. 7; Starr, *Union Cavalry,* 2:367; Wert, "Old Jubilee's Last Battle," *CWTI* 16 (5): 23–24.

47. *OR,* 46, pt. 1:501; *New York Times,* March 21, 1865; Rebecca L. Richmond to Dear Ones at Home, February 28, 1865; Rebecca L. Richmond to Father, March 12, 1865, Richmond Papers, USAMHI; Daniel S. Bacon to Sister, February 17, 1865, typescript, Frost Collection, MCHMA.

48. *OR,* 46, pt. 1:501, 504, 505; *New York Times,* March 13, 21, 1865; Hannaford, "Reminiscences," pp. 265-1–68-1, CHS; Sutton, *History,* pp. 189–92; Wells, Diary, Wells Papers, UVM.

49. *OR,* 46, pt. 1:475, 477, 502; Starr, *Union Cavalry,* 2:370–71.

50. *OR,* 46, pt. 1:476, 502; Starr, *Union Cavalry,* 2:371, 372; Hannaford, "Reminiscences," p. 268-3, CHS; Sutton, *History,* p. 192.

51. *OR,* 46, pt. 1:502; Hutton, *Custer Reader,* p. 74; "Military Record of Edward W. Whitaker," typescript, Edward W. Whitaker to Sister, February 13, 1865, typescript, Whitaker Papers, BL.

52. *OR,* 46, pt. 1:502; *New York Times,* March 21, 1865; Hutton, *Custer Reader,* pp. 74, 75; Hannaford, "Reminiscences," pp. 269-1, 269-2, CHS; Starr, *Union Cavalry,* 2:372–73.

53. Wert, "Old Jubilee's Last Battle," *CWTI* 16 (5): 27; *OR,* 46, pt. 1:127, 503, 509, 792, 794; Wells, Diary, Wells Papers, UVM; Hagemann, *Fighting,* p. 316.

54. *OR,* 46, pt. 1:476, 503; Merington, *Custer Story,* p. 141.

Chapter 12: ''THE BEST CAVALRY GENERAL IN THE ARMY''

1. Hannaford, "Reminiscences," pp. 272-4, 273-1, CHS; *Charlottesville Daily Progress,* June 30, 1943; *New York Times,* March 21, 1865; *OR,* 46, pt. 1:503; Tenney, *War Diary,* p. 146.

2. *OR,* 46, pt. 1:503; *New York Times,* March 21, 1865; Sutton, *History,* pp. 198, 199; Hatton, "Just a Little Bit," *OH* 84 (4): 223.

3. *OR,* 46, pt. 1:818, 833, 834, 848; Sutton, *History,* pp. 199, 200; Wells, Diary, Wells Papers, UVM; Tenney, *War Diary,* p. 146; *New York Times,* March 21, 1865.

4. *OR,* 46, pt. 1:478; Sheridan, *Personal Memoirs,* 2:119.

5. The daily route of Sheridan's cavalry can be followed in *OR,* 46, pt.

1:479, 503, 506, 507, 918, 919, 931, 940–42, 892, 909, 981–82, 994; pt. 3:15; Sutton, *History,* pp. 202–4; Tenney, *War Diary,* pp. 147–48; Hannaford, "Reminiscences," pp. 278-3–86-3, CHS; Merington, *Custer Story,* p. 141; *New York Times,* March 21, 1865.

6. *New York Times,* March 20, 1865; *OR,* 46, pt. 1:488; Sheridan, *Personal Memoirs,* 2:123.

7. Fragments of two letters, c. 1864 or 1865, Merington Papers, NYPL. Merington, editor of Custer's and Libbie's letters, deleted portions of the letters before publication, unwilling to present to the world their sexual expressions.

8. Merington, *Custer Story,* pp. 140–41.

9. Ibid., p. 143.

10. Ibid., pp. 136, 144; Rebecca L. Richmond to Father, March 12, 1865, Richmond Papers, USAMHI; Reynolds, *Civil War,* p. 131.

11. Millbrook, *Study,* pp. 18–20; Merington, *Custer Story,* p. 145.

12. *OR,* 46, pt. 3:68, 80, 106, 166, 191; Sutton, *History,* p. 207; Hannaford, "Reminiscences," pp. 289-4–92-3, CHS.

13. Bearss and Calkins, *Battle,* p. 1.

14. Ibid., pp. 2–3.

15. Ibid., pp. 14, 16; *OR,* 46, pt. 1:113, 1101; pt. 3:234, 235; Sutton, *History,* pp. 208, 209; Hannaford, "Reminiscences," pp. 292-4, 293-1, 293-2, 293-3, CHS; GAC to EBC, March 30, 1865, Merington Papers, NYPL; Merington, *Custer Story,* p. 146, CSR, Peter Boehm File, NA.

16. Hannaford, "Reminiscences," pp. 293-3, 293-4, 294-1, CHS; Sutton, *History,* p. 209; Tremain, *Last Hours,* pp. 21, 23, 30; Bearss and Calkins, *Battle,* pp. 30–31; *OR,* 46, pt. 3:326; Hunt, "Custer," pp. 54–55, UM.

17. Merington, *Custer Story,* p. 147.

18. GAC to EBC, March 30, 1865, Merington Papers, NYPL.

19. Bearss and Calkins, *Battle,* pp. 29, 30, 32, 34, 35, 37–41, 44; *OR,* 46, pt. 1:1130.

20. *OR,* 46, pt. 1:1130; Bearss and Calkins, *Battle,* pp. 44, 45; Hannaford, "Reminiscences," pp. 295-1, 295-2, CHS; CSR, Peter Boehm File, NA.

21. Tremain, *Last Hours,* p. 54; *OR,* 46, pt. 1:1103, 1130; Hannaford, "Reminiscences," pp. 295-3, 295-4, CHS; CSR, Peter Boehm File, NA; Sheridan, *Personal Memoirs,* 2:153; Merington, *Custer Story,* p. 148; Bearss and Calkins, *Battle,* pp. 44–46.

22. *B&L* 4: 711; Bearss and Calkins, *Battle,* p. 73.

23. Bearss and Calkins, *Battle,* pp. 74–77.

24. Ibid., pp. 83–85; *OR,* 46, pt. 1:1130; Hannaford, "Reminiscences," pp. 297-2–98-2, CHS.

25. Bearss and Calkins, *Battle,* pp. 86, 87, 90, 92.

26. Ibid., pp. 105–7; Hannaford, "Reminiscences," pp. 298-2, 298-4, CHS; *OR,* 46, pt. 1:1117, 1131, 1135, 1136; GAC to E. W. Whitaker,

October 15, 1867, typescript, Merington Papers, NYPL; Hatton, "Just a Little Bit," *OH* 84 (4): 225, 226.

27. *OR,* 46, pt. 1:1130, 1131; Bearss and Calkins, *Battle,* p. 107; Calkins, "Battle of Five Forks," *B&G* 9 (4): 20, 46; Wells, Diary, Wells Papers, UVM; Benedict, *Vermont,* 2:679; Sutton, *History,* p. 212; Hunt, "Custer," pp. 56, 57, UM.

28. *OR,* 46, pt. 1:1131; Sutton, *History,* p. 213; *New York Times,* April 3, 14, 1865; Benedict, *Vermont,* 2:680.

29. *OR,* 46, pt. 1:1131; Wells, Diary, Wells Papers, UVM; Chauncey, *Red Neck Ties,* p. 70; Bearss and Calkins, *Battle,* pp. 108, 109.

30. Bearss and Calkins, *Battle,* pp. 110, 113; Townsend, *Rustics,* p. 261.

31. *OR,* 46, pt. 1:1131; pt. 3:489, 490; *War Papers,* MOLLUS, Mo., 1:110; Calkins, "With Shouts," *B&G* 7 (6): 32–33; Sutton, *History,* p. 218.

32. *OR,* 46, pt. 1:1131; pt. 3:529, 530; Woodbury, Papers, DC; Hannaford, "Reminiscences," pp. 304-4-5-4, CHS; Calkins, "With Shouts," *B&G* 7 (6): 33–36; Day, "If You Want," *GG* 9: 4, 5; *New York Times,* April 7, 14, 1865.

33. *OR,* 46, pt. 1:1132; pt. 3:551; Wells, Diary, Wells Papers, UVM; Tenney, *War Diary,* p. 154; Woodbury, Papers, DC; Sutton, *History,* pp. 219–20; Long, *Civil War,* pp. 666–67.

34. *OR,* 46, pt. 1:1125, 1132, 1136; pt. 3:610; Gallagher, *Fighting,* p. 524; Preston, *History,* p. 251; Sutton, *History,* pp. 220–21; Stevenson, *Boots,* p. 345; Hannaford, "Reminiscences," p. 309-1, CHS; Long, *Civil War,* pp. 667–68.

35. Merington, *Custer Story,* pp. 150, 151; Charles A. Sanford to Goodrich, April 18, 1865, Sanford Papers, DU; Millbrook, *Study,* p. 21; Horn, "Tom Custer's Civil War Wounds Considered," *NLBHA* 24, no. 3 (1995): 6.

36. Merington, *Custer Story,* p. 151.

37. Frost, *General Custer's Libbie,* pp. 127–28; Schaff, *Sunset,* pp. 110, 114.

38. Hannaford, "Reminiscences," p. 316-4, CHS.

39. Long, *Civil War,* pp. 608, 609; Calkins, *Battles,* pp. 3, 6, 7, 10, 12, 19, 20.

40. Calkins, *Battles,* p. 28; Sutton, *History,* p. 8; Reynolds, *Civil War,* pp. 142, 143; Schmitt, *General George Crook,* p. 137; Bakeless, "Mystery," *CWTI* 9 (3): 19, 28.

41. Calkins, *Battles,* pp. 29–30; Sutton, *History,* pp. 223, 224; Hannaford, "Reminiscences," pp. 318-2, 318-3, 318-4, CHS; *New York Times,* April 20, 1865.

42. Hunt, "Custer," pp. 61–62, UM; Calkins, *Battles,* p. 29.

43. Calkins, *Battles,* pp. 30, 32, 33; Urwin, *Custer Victorious,* p. 251; Sutton, *History,* p. 223.

44. Calkins, *Battles,* pp. 33–35; Schaff, *Sunset,* p. 176; Tenney, *War Diary,* p. 158.

45. Merington, *Custer Story,* p. 162; Calkins, *Battles,* pp. 36–37, 40;

Sutton, *History,* pp. 223–24; Schorn, Papers, USAMHI; Woodbury, Papers, DC; Benedict, *Vermont,* 2:683; *OR,* 46, pt. 1:1132.

46. Schaff, *Sunset,* p. 197; *OR,* 46, pt. 3:653, 654; Reynolds, *Civil War,* pp. 142–43.

47. Calkins, *Battle,* pp. 57–58, 66, 73, 80, 88, 90.

48. Ibid., p. 74; Sheridan, *Personal Memoirs,* 2:193–94; Edward W. Whitaker to J. L. Chamberlain, April 29, 1901, typescript, Whitaker Papers, BL; Benedict, *Vermont,* 2:684; *National Tribune,* June 25, 1896.

49. Edward W. Whitaker to J. L. Chamberlain, April 29, 1901, typescript, Whitaker Papers, BL; *National Tribune,* June 25, 1896; *OR,* 46, pt. 1:1132, 1133; *Detroit Free Press,* June 14, 1896; William Wells to Anna Richardson, April 11, 1865, Wells Papers, UVM; *New York Times,* April 10, 1865; *CV* 7:398; Colt, *Defend,* p. 371.

50. Edward W. Whitaker to J. L. Chamberlain, April 29, 1901, typescript, Whitaker Papers, BL; *National Tribune,* June 25, 1896; *Detroit Free Press,* June 14, 1896.

51. Edward W. Whitaker to J. L. Chamberlain, April 29, 1901, typescript, Whitaker Papers, BL; William H. Gibbes to E. P. Alexander, undated, Alexander Papers, UNC; *New York Times,* April 20, 1865; Cauble, *Surrender,* p. 35; Monaghan, *Custer,* pp. 243–44; Urwin, *Custer Victorious,* p. 255.

52. Confederate accounts of the meeting are numerous: William H. Gibbes to E. P. Alexander, n.d. [October 10, 1890]; J. S. Dorsey Cullen to E. P. Alexander, n.d. [1887 or 1888]; John B. Gordon to E. P. Alexander, March 27, 1888; John C. Haskell to E. P. Alexander, October 10, 1902; Joseph Packard to E. P. Alexander, October 31, 1902; Frederick Colston to E. P. Alexander, October 31, 1902; James M. Garnett to Frederick Colston, November 1, 1902; all in Alexander Papers, UNC; E. P. Alexander to James Longstreet, October 26, 1902, Longstreet Papers, EU; Haskell, "Memoirs," pp. 64–65, DU; Goree, *Letters,* pp. 301–2, 327.

53. Cauble, *Surrender,* p. 56; Schaff, *Spirit,* pp. 169, 170; Monaghan, *Custer,* p. 245; Urwin, *Custer Victorious,* pp. 256, 257.

54. Urwin, *Custer Victorious,* p. 257; Cauble, *Surrender,* pp. 112, 113; Merington, *Custer Story,* p. 165.

55. Merington, *Custer Story,* pp. 159, 160; Lee, *Personal,* p. 68; Devin, "Fierce Resistance," *CWTI* 17 (8): 39; Frost, *General Custer's Libbie,* p. 128; Reynolds, *Civil War,* p. 143; Schaff, *Sunset,* p. 177.

56. Urwin, *Custer Victorious,* pp. 257–60.

57. *OR,* 46, pt. 1:1112, 1121; MSR/GAC, NA.

58. *OR,* 46, pt. 1:941; pt. 3:676, 694, 709, 733, 812, 1048; Hannaford, "Reminiscences," pp. 328-1–30-4, CHS; Merington, *Custer Story,* p. 165.

59. Merington, *Custer Story,* pp. 163–65; *OR,* 46, pt. 2:549; Reynolds, *Civil War,* p. 55; GAC to J. L. Greene, April 19, 1865, Merington Papers, NYPL; GAC to My Dear Sister, April 21, 1865, GAC Collection, MCLS.

60. *New York Times,* May 7, 1865; Frost, *General Custer's Libbie,* p. 133.

61. *OR,* 46, pt. 3:908, 909, 947, 948, 961, 1120; Hannaford, "Reminiscences," pp. 331-3–41-4, CHS; Tremain, *Last Hours,* p. 312; Frost, *General Custer's Libbie,* p. 133.

62. *OR,* 46, pt. 3:1191; Nevins, *Diary,* p. 527; Hannaford, "Reminiscences," p. 342-3, CHS.

63. Hannaford, "Reminiscences," p. 342-3, CHS; Hein, *Memories,* p. 37; Benedict, *Vermont,* 2:686; Hatton, "Just a Little Bit," *OH* 84 (4): 231–32; Crozier, *Yankee Reporters,* p. 420.

64. Frost, *Custer Legends,* pp. 124–25; Reynolds, *Civil War,* pp. 161–62; Hein, *Memories,* pp. 37, 38; *National Tribune,* May 27, August 26, 1915.

65. Merington, *Custer Story,* p. 167; Hannaford, "Reminiscences," pp. 342-4, 343-1, CHS; Custer, *Tenting,* pp. 28, 29; Sutton, *History,* pp. 238, 239; Chauncey, *Red Neck Ties,* pp. 81–82; *OR,* 46, pt. 3:1195.

66. Urwin, *Custer Victorious,* p. 35; Schaff, *Sunset,* p. 181; *National Tribune,* September 22, October 13, 1892.

67. duBois, *Kick the Dead Lion,* pp. 97n–98n; Urwin, *Custer Victorious,* p. 35; A. T. O'Neil, "Custer Recollections," pp. 15, 18; Frost, *Custer Legends,* p. 194; Kidd, *Personal Recollections,* p. 131; Hagemann, *Fighting,* p. 316.

68. Greiner, *General,* p. 357.

Chapter 13: RECONSTRUCTION SOLDIER

1. Custer, *Tenting,* pp. 53, 56–59, 61–67; EBC to Rebecca, June 29, 1865, EBC Collection, MCLS.

2. EBC to Rebecca, June 29, 1865, EBC Collection, MCLS; Carroll, *Custer in Texas,* pp. 6–7.

3. Carroll, *Custer in Texas,* pp. 6–8; Philip H. Sheridan to GAC, May 7, 17, 1865, GAC, Correspondence and Orders, 1856–1876, LBBNM; Custer, *Tenting,* p. 31; Sheridan, *Personal Memoirs,* 2:211, 213.

4. GAC to Brother and Sister, June 23, 1865, GAC Collection, MCLS; Custer, *Tenting,* pp. 72, 74; EBC to Rebecca, June 29, 1865, EBC Collection, MCLS.

5. Special Orders, No. 13, June 18, 1865, MSR/GAC, NA; Carroll, *Custer in Texas,* pp. 8, 30, 247.

6. Carroll, *Custer in Texas,* pp. 32, 33, 259, 260.

7. Ibid., p. 30.

8. *Revised Regulations,* pp. 504–5, 507, 512n-13n.

9. Carroll, *Custer in Texas,* pp. 31, 217–19, 268–69.

10. Ibid., pp. 33, 50, 51, 269; Utley, *Cavalier,* p. 37.

11. Merington, *Custer Story,* pp. 168, 169; EBC to Rebecca, June 29, 1865, EBC Collection, MCLS; GAC to Father and Mother, July 9, 1865, GAC Collection, MCLS; Custer, *Tenting,* pp. 78, 80, 82, 93, 95, 98, 114, 116.

12. Carroll, *Custer in Texas,* pp. 58–60, 72; *National Tribune,* April 28, 1892.

13. Carroll, *Custer in Texas,* pp. 72–73, 80–83; Custer, *Tenting,* pp. 126, 131, 133, 135, 138, 141; Merington, *Custer Story,* pp. 167–68; EBC to Aunt Eliza, September 3, 1865, Merington Papers, NYPL; *National Tribune,* April 28, 1892.

14. Carroll, *Custer in Texas,* p. 73; Carroll, *Custer's Cavalry,* pp. 15, 16, 18; Custer, *Tenting,* p. 151.

15. *National Tribune,* August 2, 1900; Lothrop, *History,* pp. 231, 232, 233–37; Carroll, *Custer in Texas,* pp. 104–5, 205–37.

16. *National Tribune,* April 28, 1892, August 2, 1900; Lothrop, *History,* p. 235; Carroll, *Custer in Texas,* pp. 205–37; Utley, *Cavalier,* p. 38.

17. Utley, *Cavalier,* p. 38; Monaghan, *Custer,* pp. 260–61; Lothrop, *History,* p. 237; Carroll, *Custer's Cavalry,* p. 18.

18. Frost, *General Custer's Libbie,* p. 142; EBC to Father and Mother, August 6, 1865, Merington Papers, NYPL; GAC to Brother and Sister, October 15, 1865, GAC Collection, MCLS.

19. GAC to Brother and Sister, October 15, 1865, GAC Collection, MCLS; Custer, *Tenting,* pp. 161, 164; Monaghan, *Custer,* pp. 260, 261.

20. Carroll, *Custer in Texas,* p. 121; Custer, *Tenting,* p. 161; Monaghan, *Custer,* p. 262.

21. Merington, *Custer Story,* p. 168; Custer, *Tenting,* p. 80; Carroll, *Custer in Texas,* p. 121.

22. GAC to Brother and Sister, October 15, 1865, GAC Collection, MCLS; Merington, *Custer Story,* pp. 167–70.

23. MSR/GAC, NA; Carroll, *Custer's Cavalry,* p. 18; Carroll, *Custer in Texas,* p. 138; Custer, *Tenting,* pp. 210–11.

24. Carroll, *Custer's Cavalry,* pp. 20, 22; Custer's report on conditions in Texas is in Carroll, *Custer in Texas,* pp. 272–78.

25. Custer, *Tenting,* p. 216; Shannon, "Custer's Texas Home," *Texas Highways* 33 (2): 42–47; EBC to Rebecca, November 17, 1865, EBC Collection, MCLS.

26. Carroll, *Custer's Cavalry,* p. 24; Merington, *Custer Story,* p. 171; *National Tribune,* April 28, 1892.

27. EBC to Rebecca, November 17, 1865, EBC Collection, MCLS; Custer, *Tenting,* pp. 221–23, 230, 241, 243, 245, 246; Lothrop, *History,* pp. 240–41; Viola, *Memoirs,* p. 74; Carroll, *Custer's Cavalry,* p. 22; GAC to Crosby, October 28, 1868, GAC Papers, YU; Carroll, *Custer in Texas,* pp. 158, 161.

28. Carroll, *Custer in Texas,* pp. 178–80; MSR/GAC, NA; D. S. Bacon to GAC, January 20, 1866, typescript, Frost Collection, MCHMA.

29. Frost, *General Custer's Libbie,* p. 137; Carroll, *Custer's Cavalry,* p. 24; CSR, Jacob Greene File, NA.

30. Custer, *Tenting,* pp. 266–83; Monaghan, *Custer,* pp. 265–66.

31. Carroll, *Custer in Texas,* pp. 271–78; Merington, *Custer Story,* pp. 177–80.

32. Merington, *Custer Story,* pp. 180–82; Utley, *Cavalier,* p. 39.

33. Merington, *Custer Story,* pp. 180–82; Utley, *Cavalier,* pp. 38, 39; Monaghan, *Custer,* pp. 268, 269.

34. Frost, *General Custer's Libbie,* pp. 150, 151, 260; Merington, *Custer Story,* p. 182; O'Neil and O'Neil, *Custers,* p. 5; Leckie, *Elizabeth Bacon Custer,* p. 86.

35. Merington, *Custer Story,* p. 183.

36. Ibid., p. 183; EBC to R. A. Alger, July 15 [186?], Alger Papers, UM; Frost, *General Custer's Libbie,* pp. 151, 260; Leckie, *Elizabeth Bacon Custer,* pp. 86, 87.

37. Frost, *General Custer's Libbie,* p. 150; duBois, *Kick the Dead Lion,* p. 97n; Merington, *Custer Story,* p. 183.

38. Merington, *Custer Story,* pp. 183–84; Frost, *General Custer's Libbie,* pp. 151, 152.

39. Foner, *Reconstruction,* pp. 187, 189, 190, 191, 251, 261–63.

40. Ibid., p. 264; Merington, *Custer Story,* pp. 179, 187, 188; Beauregard, "General," *B&G* 6 (1): 35.

41. Foner, *Reconstruction,* p. 264; Beauregard, "General," *B&G* 6 (1): 35; Merington, *Custer Story,* pp. 188–90; T. E. O'Neil, "Hero," *NLBHA* 28 (6): 5–7; Wallace, *Custer's Ohio Boyhood,* p. 29.

42. EBC to Rebecca, August 29, 1866, EBC Collection, MCLS; O'Neil, "Custer and Politics," *NLBHA* 28 (4): 5; Stanton, "Letter," *NLBHA* 27 (3): 7.

43. Leckie, *Elizabeth Bacon Custer,* p. 88; EBC to Rebecca, August 29, 1866, EBC Collection, MCLS.

44. MSR/GAC, NA; Chandler, *Garry Owen,* p. 2.

Chapter 14: COURT-MARTIAL

1. EBC to Rebecca, December 6, 1866, EBC Collection, MCLS; Ryan, "Ten Years," LBBNM; Grinnell, *Fighting Cheyennes,* p. 257.

2. Frost, *Court-Martial,* p. 72; Grinnell, *Fighting Cheyennes,* pp. 256–57.

3. Custer, *Tenting,* pp. 334, 336, 340, 343; EBC to Rebecca, December 6, 1866, EBC Collection, MCLS; Millbrook, "Mrs. General Custer," *KHQ* 40 (1): 63–65.

4. Custer, *Tenting,* p. 343; A. T. O'Neil, *Actor,* pp. 7, 8, 10, 11, 12, 15.

5. EBC to Rebecca, December 6, 1866, EBC Collection, MCLS; Millbrook, "Mrs. General Custer," *KHQ* 40 (1): 66–67.

6. EBC to Rebecca, December 6, 1866; EBC Collection, MCLS; Custer, *Tenting,* pp. 374, 404.

7. Millbrook, "Mrs. General Custer," *KHQ* 40 (1): 63, 76; Warner, *Generals in Blue,* pp. 454–55; Utley, *Cavalier,* p. 45.

8. Chandler, *Garry Owen,* pp. 2, 3; Millbrook, "Custer's," *KHQ* 39 (1): 75, 76; Michno, *Mystery,* p. 1.

9. Utley, *Frontier Regulars,* pp. 21–22.

10. Ibid., pp. 21–22; Hutton, *Custer and His Times,* pp. 127–29.

11. Hutton, *Custer and His Times,* p. 127; Utley, *Frontier Regulars,* pp. 22, 23, 25, 26.

12. Dustin, *Custer Tragedy,* pp. 223, 224; Monaghan, *Custer,* pp. 281, 282; Utley, *Cavalier,* pp. 45, 46; Leckie, *Elizabeth Bacon Custer,* p. 90.

13. Dustin, *Custer Tragedy,* pp. 223, 224; Monaghan, *Custer,* p. 282; Utley, *Cavalier,* p. 46; Carroll, *They Rode,* pp. 136–37.

14. Monaghan, *Custer,* p. 282; *OR* 46, pt. 1:929; Chandler, *Garry Owen,* p. 3; Utley, *Cavalier,* p. 46.

15. Carroll, *They Rode,* pp. 27–28; Carroll, *Camp Talk,* pp. x–xii; Hunt, *I Fought,* pp. 2, 3; F. W. Benteen to D. F. Barry, September 28, 1895, Barry Papers, LBBNM; Carroll, *Benteen-Goldin,* p. 247; Monaghan, *Custer,* p. 282.

16. Chandler, *Garry Owen,* p. 3; Dustin, *Custer Tragedy,* pp. 223, 224; Day, "If You Want," *GG* 9: 7; Carroll, *They Rode,* pp. 66–67, 181–82.

17. Carroll, *They Rode,* p. 58; Rosevear and Rosevear, *Canadians,* pp. 3–4; Hutton, *Custer and His Times,* p. 160.

18. Carroll, *They Rode,* p. 230; Leckie, *Elizabeth Bacon Custer,* p. 91.

19. Carroll, *They Rode,* pp. 260–61; Leckie, *Elizabeth Bacon Custer,* p. 91.

20. Utley, *Frontier Regulars,* pp. 19–21.

21. Custer, *Tenting,* p. 433; Utley, *Cavalier,* pp. 46–47; Monaghan, *Custer,* pp. 282–83.

22. Ambrose, *Crazy Horse,* pp. 3, 4; Utley, *Indian Frontier,* p. 33.

23. Ambrose, *Crazy Horse,* p. 33; Utley, *Indian Frontier,* p. 33.

24. Utley, *Indian Frontier,* p. 33; Ambrose, *Crazy Horse,* pp. 30, 33.

25. Utley, *Frontier Regulars,* pp. 4–6; Utley, *Indian Frontier,* pp. xix, 4, 169, 170; Berthong, *Southern Cheyennes,* pp. 32, 33; Hardoff, *Hokahey!,* p. 13; Ryan, "Ten Years," LBBNM.

26. Berthong, *Southern Cheyennes,* pp. 121, 123, 149–51, 217, 245, 266; Utley, *Frontier Regulars,* pp. 108–9.

27. Utley, *Indian Frontier,* pp. 101–3, 164, 165; Plainfeather, "Role," *CBHMA,* 1990, pp. 37–38.

28. Utley, *Indian Frontier,* pp. 105, 166, 167; Utley, *Frontier Regulars,* pp. 47–49, 85; *New York Herald,* May 10, 1921.

29. Utley, *Indian Frontier,* pp. 105, 166, 167; Hutton, *Phil Sheridan,* p. 145; Utley, *Frontier Regulars,* pp. 49, 51, 61.

30. Berthong, *Southern Cheyennes,* pp. 266–68, 270–71; Wooster, *Military,* p. 124; Utley, *Frontier Regulars,* pp. 117, 118.

31. Berthong, *Southern Cheyennes,* pp. 272, 273; Millbrook, "Custer's," *KHQ* 39 (1): 76–78; Utley, *Frontier Regulars,* pp. 118–20; Grinnell, *Fighting Cheyennes,* p. 249.

32. Jones, *Treaty,* p. 8; Utley, *Frontier Regulars,* pp. 118, 119; Berthong, *Southern Cheyennes,* p. 273.

33. Berthong, *Southern Cheyennes,* p. 274; Utley, *Frontier Regulars,* p. 120; Millbrook, "Custer's," *KHQ* 39 (1): 78; Custer, *My Life,* pp. 30–31.

34. Millbrook, "Custer's," *KHQ* 39 (1): 78, 79; Berthong, *Southern Cheyennes,* pp. 274, 275; Custer, *My Life,* pp. 32–33.

35. Custer, *My Life,* pp. 34–42; Millbrook, "Custer's," *KHQ* 39 (1): 80–82; Utley, *Life,* pp. 31–35.

36. Custer, *My Life,* pp. 46–51; Millbrook, "Custer's," *KHQ* 39 (1): 83–87; Utley, *Life,* p. 35.

37. Millbrook, "Custer's," *KHQ* 39 (1): 89, 90.

38. Ibid., pp. 90–94; Utley, *Life,* pp. 36, 37; Hutton, *Custer Reader,* p. 104; Ryan, "Ten Years," LBBNM; Custer, *Tenting,* pp. 551–62.

39. Utley, *Life,* pp. 43, 44, 51; Hutton, *Custer Reader,* pp. 119–22; Burkey, *Custer,* pp. 8, 17; Ryan, "Ten Years," LBBNM.

40. Utley, *Life,* pp. 46, 49, 50, 51, 52.

41. Utley, *Cavalier,* p. 50; Burkey, *Custer,* pp. 6, 19; Ryan, "Ten Years," LBBNM.

42. Merington, *Custer Story,* p. 202; Frost, *General Custer's Libbie,* p. 163.

43. Utley, *Life,* pp. 52, 53; Merington, *Custer Story,* p. 201; Custer, *Tenting,* pp. 601, 606, 607, 609, 630, 631.

44. Merington, *Custer Story,* pp. 196, 199, 202, 203; Burkey, *Custer,* pp. 10, 14.

45. Hutton, *Custer Reader,* p. 123; Custer, *My Life,* p. 66; T. B. Weir to GAC, May 31, 1867, GAC, Correspondence and Orders, LBBNM.

46. Custer, *Tenting,* pp. 643–44, 656, 670; Utley, *Life,* pp. 56–57; Merington, *Custer Story,* p. 204.

47. Burkey, *Custer,* pp. 20, 21n; Frost, *Court-Martial,* pp. 41–42, 45; Hutton, *Custer and His Times,* pp. 186–87, 194; Merington, *Custer Story,* p. 204; Hutton, *Custer Reader,* p. 124.

48. Custer, *My Life,* pp. 75–76; Hutton, *Custer Reader,* pp. 124, 125.

49. Custer, *Tenting,* pp. 581–82.

50. Hutton, *Custer Reader,* pp. 125, 126; Custer, *My Life,* pp. 77–78; Berthong, *Southern Cheyennes,* p. 285.

51. Custer, *My Life,* pp. 79–89; Burkey, *Custer,* p. 29; Hutton, *Custer Reader,* pp. 126–29; Berthong, *Southern Cheyennes,* pp. 282, 285, 286; Ryan, "Ten Years," LBBNM.

52. Hutton, *Custer Reader,* p. 129; Custer, *My Life,* pp. 98–100; Merington, *Custer Story,* p. 207; Utley, *Cavalier,* p. 52; Custer, *Tenting,* p. 583.

53. Hutton, *Custer Reader,* pp. 129–34; Merington, *Custer Story,* p. 207; Custer, *My Life,* pp. 100–101.

54. Merington, *Custer Story,* pp. 205–6; Hutton, *Custer Reader,* p. 134; Custer, *My Life,* pp. 104–5.

55. Frost, *Court-Martial,* pp. 14, 68, 69, 76; Michno, *Mystery,* p. 6; Brininstool, *Troopers,* p. 326, 329; Hutton, *Custer Reader,* pp. 135, 136; Burkey, *Custer,* p. 29; Custer, *My Life,* pp. 106–12.

56. Hutton, *Custer Reader,* pp. 137, 138.

57. Ibid., pp. 137, 138; Custer, *My Life*, p. 114.

58. Burkey, *Custer*, p. 32; Utley, *Life*, p. 86; Merington, *Custer Story*, p. 212.

59. Utley, *Cavalier*, pp. 107, 108; Leckie, *Elizabeth Bacon Custer*, p. 102, 103.

60. Utley, *Cavalier*, pp. 107, 108; Leckie, *Elizabeth Bacon Custer*, pp. 107, 108.

61. Hutton, *Custer Reader*, pp. 139–41; Custer, *My Life*, pp. 114–18; Merington, *Custer Story*, p. 209.

62. Hutton, *Custer Reader*, pp. 141–42; Merington, *Custer Story*, p. 209; Grinnell, *Fighting Cheyennes*, p. 256.

63. Hutton, *Custer Reader*, pp. 141, 142; Merington, *Custer Story*, pp. 209, 210; Frost, *Court-Martial*, pp. 85, 99.

64. Frost, *Court-Martial*, pp. 86, 99–102.

65. Ibid., pp. 92, 102; Merington, *Custer Story*, pp. 211, 213.

66. The entire court-martial proceedings are printed in Frost, *Court-Martial*, pp. 96–246; Merington, *Custer Story*, p. 212.

67. Frost, *Court-Martial*, pp. 245–47; T. E. O'Neil, *Custer Chronicles*, 1:14, 15; Merington, *Custer Story*, p. 214; *New York Times*, December 31, 1867.

68. Frost, *Court-Martial*, pp. 261–64; Hutton, *Custer Reader*, pp. 147, 148, 158n.

69. Merington, *Custer Story*, p. 212; Hutton, *Custer Reader*, p. 148; Utley, *Cavalier*, p. 54.

Chapter 15: WINTER WAR

1. Hutton, *Phil Sheridan*, pp. 22–25, 27, 28; Morris, *Sheridan*, chap. 8.

2. Hutton, *Phil Sheridan*, pp. 28, 29; Wooster, *Military*, pp. 42, 43; Utley, *Life*, p. 107; Jones, *Treaty*, p. vii; Levine, "Indian Fighters," *CWH* 31 (4): 334.

3. Utley, *Life*, pp. 107, 108, 111, 115, 116; Utley, *Indian Frontier*, pp. 109, 114, 118, 120, 178; Duncan and Smith, "Captives," *RR* 7 (2): 3; Jones, *Treaty*, p. vii; Utley, *Frontier Regulars*, p. 140.

4. Utley, *Life*, p. 115.

5. Utley, *Indian Frontier*, pp. 122, 123.

6. Hutton, *Phil Sheridan*, pp. xiv, 181–83; Levine, "Indian Fighters," *CWH* 31 (4): 334, 335, 339, 349.

7. Hutton, *Phil Sheridan*, pp. 184, 185.

8. Ibid., pp. 39, 41; Utley, *Cavalier*, pp. 59–60.

9. Hutton, *Phil Sheridan*, pp. 45–47.

10. Ibid., p. 42; Carroll, *Custer and Washita*, pp. xiii, 11.

11. Utley, *Cavalier*, p. 60; Merington, *Custer Story*, p. 216; P. H. Sheridan to G. A. Custer, September 28, 1868, telegram, GAC, Correspondence and Orders, LBBNM.

12. Frost, *General Custer's Libbie*, p. 172; Simon, *Papers*, 18:373.

13. Simon, *Papers,* 18:372–73; MSR/GAC, NA.

14. Frost, *General Custer's Libbie,* pp. 172–74; Utley, *Cavalier,* p. 60.

15. Burkey, *Custer,* pp. 1, 44; Special Field Orders, No. 16, October 4, 1868, GAC, Correspondence and Orders, LBBNM; Merington, *Custer Story,* p. 217; Utley, *Life,* p. 198; Ryan, "Ten Years," LBBNM.

16. Utley, *Life,* p. 198; Ryan, "Ten Years," LBBNM; Hutton, *Custer Reader,* p. 106.

17. Ryan, "Ten Years," LBBNM; Utley, *Life,* pp. 204, 205, 208; Hutton, *Custer Reader,* pp. 161, 162; Memorandum, GAC, Correspondence and Orders, LBBNM.

18. Merington, *Custer Story,* p. 217; GAC to Crosby, October 28, 1868, GAC Papers, YU; Custer, *Following,* p. 13.

19. Hutton, *Custer Reader,* p. 161; Utley, *Cavalier,* pp. 60, 61; Frost, *General Custer's Libbie,* p. 174.

20. Carroll, *Custer and Washita,* pp. 7, 8; Utley, *Cavalier,* pp. 60, 61; Hutton, *Phil Sheridan,* p. 52.

21. Hutton, *Custer Reader,* p. 161; Carroll, *Custer and Washita,* pp. 12, 13; Burkey, *Custer,* p. 45; Spotts, *Campaigning,* pp, 28, 45; *Outline Descriptions,* p. 169.

22. Hutton, *Custer Reader,* pp. 161–63; Hutton, *Phil Sheridan,* p. 52; *Outline Descriptions,* p. 169; Custer, *My Life,* pp. 210–13.

23. Hutton, *Custer Reader,* p. 164; Custer, *My Life,* p. 213; Utley, *Cavalier,* p. 63.

24. Utley, *Life,* p. 209.

25. Urwin and Fagan, *Custer,* p. 87.

26. Ibid., p. 85; Brill, *Conquest,* p. 16; GAC to Friend, November 8, 1868, Merington Papers, NYPL; Burkey, *Custer,* p. 49; Custer, *My Life,* pp. 192–93.

27. Hutton, *Custer Reader,* p. 165; Marshall, *Crimsoned Prairie,* p. 110; Custer, *My Life,* p. 215; GAC to Friend, November 8, 1868, Merington Papers, NYPL.

28. Hutton, *Custer Reader,* pp. 165–66; Utley, *Life,* pp. 213–14; Ryan, "Ten Years," LBBNM; Merington, *Custer Story,* p. 219.

29. Hutton, *Custer Reader,* pp. 166–67; Utley, *Life,* pp. 215–16; Ryan, "Ten Years," LBBNM; Merington, *Custer Story,* p. 219; Custer, *My Life,* pp. 216–24.

30. Hutton, *Custer Reader,* p. 167; Merington, *Custer Story,* p. 219; Custer, *My Life,* pp. 224–27.

31. Custer, *My Life,* pp. 231–33; Hutton, *Custer Reader,* pp. 167, 168; Carroll, *Custer and Washita,* p. 37; Utley, *Life,* pp. 216, 218.

32. Hutton, *Phil Sheridan,* pp. 56, 57, 59; Carroll, *Custer and Washita,* pp. 34, 36; Hutton, *Custer Reader,* p. 96; Utley, *Cavalier,* pp. 64, 65.

33. Utley, *Cavalier,* p. 65.

34. Utley, *Life,* p. 219; Hutton, *Custer Reader,* pp. 168, 169; Carroll, *Custer and Washita,* p. 37.

35. Utley, *Life,* p. 220; Utley, *Cavalier,* p. 65.

36. Custer, *My Life,* pp. 239–40; Carroll, *Custer and Washita,* p. 37; Hutton, *Custer Reader,* pp. 169, 170; Utley, *Life,* pp. 224, 225; Utley, *Cavalier,* p. 67.

37. Custer, *My Life,* p. 241–42; Utley, *Life,* p. 225; Carroll, *Custer and Washita,* p. xiv; Merington, *Custer Story,* p. 221.

38. Carroll, *Custer and Washita,* pp. 37, 38; Custer, *My Life,* pp. 241–44; Utley, *Life,* pp. 227–29, 243; *National Tribune,* August 22, 1901; Brill, *Conquest,* p. 25.

39. Carroll, *Custer and Washita,* pp. xix, xx, 43; Grinnell, *Fighting Cheyennes,* p. 304; Merington, *Custer Story,* p. 222.

40. Grinnell, *Fighting Cheyennes,* pp. 304–5; Carroll, *Custer and Washita,* pp. 43, 45, 68, 69.

41. Carroll, *Custer and Washita,* pp. xiv, xv, 37, 38; Hutton, *Custer Reader,* p. 170.

42. Hutton, *Custer Reader,* pp. 171–72.

43. Ibid., pp. 172–73.

44. Ibid., pp. 173–74; Custer, *My Life,* pp. 245–47; Merington, *Custer Story,* p. 222; Ryan, "Ten Years," LBBNM; Michno, *Mystery,* p. 14.

45. Custer, *My Life,* pp. 247–54; Carroll, *Custer and Washita,* pp. 38; Utley, *Cavalier,* pp. 69, 70.

46. Custer, *My Life,* pp. 258, 259; Merington, *Custer Story,* p. 223; Utley, *Cavalier,* p. 70.

47. Spotts, *Campaigning,* pp. 65, 66, 72; Custer, *My Life,* pp. 268–69.

48. Hutton, *Phil Sheridan,* p. 388n; Carroll, *Custer and Washita,* pp. xiii, 39.

49. Utley, *Cavalier,* pp. 70, 75; Carroll, *Benteen-Goldin,* pp. 252, 253; duBois, *Kick the Dead Lion,* pp. 30, 31; Frost, *Custer Legends,* p. 131; F. W. Benteen to D. F. Barry, September 28, 1895, Barry Papers, LBBNM.

50. Stewart, *Custer's Luck,* p. 165; Connell, *Son,* p. 193; Utley, *Cavalier,* pp. 75, 76; Hunt, *I Fought,* p. 8; Carroll, *Custer and Washita,* p. xi.

51. Carroll, *Custer and Washita,* p. xi; Spotts, *Campaigning,* p. 67.

52. Utley, *Cavalier,* p. 76; Koury, "Myth," *CBHMA,* 1992, p. 56.

53. Hutton, *Phil Sheridan,* pp. 95, 96; Hutton, *Custer Reader,* p. 93.

54. Carroll, *Custer and Washita,* pp. 53, 61; Custer, *My Life,* pp. 266–67, 271, 272; Utley, *Cavalier,* p. 71; Spotts, *Campaigning,* pp. 71–72; Monaghan, *Custer,* pp. 323, 324.

55. Urwin and Fagan, *Custer,* pp. 89, 90; Hutton, *Phil Sheridan,* pp. 79–81; Carroll, *Custer and Washita,* pp. 67, 68, 69, 70; Spotts, *Campaigning,* pp. 71–79; Custer, *My Life,* pp. 279–92.

56. Spotts, *Campaigning,* pp. 76–80; Stewart, *Penny,* pp. 8, 12, 13; Hutton, *Phil Sheridan,* pp. 82, 83; Custer, *My Life,* pp. 291–92.

57. Hutton, *Phil Sheridan,* p. 83; Custer, *My Life,* pp. 281–82, 290, 292–93; Spotts, *Campaigning,* pp. 79, 80.

58. Custer, *My Life,* pp. 297, 298; Hutton, *Phil Sheridan,* pp. 84, 85.

59. Custer contends that he and the others drew their revolvers and took the chiefs as prisoners, but other accounts do not support this version. Custer, *My Life,* pp. 298, 299, 300; Carroll, *Custer and Washita,* p. 70; Hutton, *Phil Sheridan,* pp. 85, 86; Spotts, *Campaigning,* pp. 80, 81.

60. Custer, *My Life,* pp. 304–11; Hutton, *Phil Sheridan,* pp. 88–89; Spotts, *Campaigning,* pp. 80, 81.

61. Custer, *My Life,* pp. 314, 316; Custer, *Following,* p. 46; Utley, *Cavalier,* pp. 72, 73; Hutton, *Phil Sheridan,* pp. 93, 94; Merington, *Custer Story,* p. 228.

62. Monaghan, *Custer,* p. 327; Frost, *General Custer's Libbie,* p. 181; Hutton, *Phil Sheridan,* p. 91.

63. Spotts, *Campaigning,* pp. 95–100; Hutton, *Phil Sheridan,* pp. 100, 101; Utley, *Cavalier,* p. 72.

64. Custer, *My Life,* pp. 317–318; Duncan and Smith, "Captives," *RR* 7 (2): 17; Spotts, *Campaigning,* p. 103; Hutton, *Phil Sheridan,* pp. 102, 103.

65. Duncan and Smith, "Captives," *RR* 7 (2): 18; Custer, *My Life,* pp. 319–38; Hutton, *Phil Sheridan,* pp. 103–4.

66. Custer, *My Life,* pp. 335–43; Duncan and Smith, "Captives," *RR* 7 (2): 18; P. H. Sheridan to GAC, January 31, 1869, Merington Papers, NYPL; Spotts, *Campaigning,* p. 118; Hutton, *Phil Sheridan,* pp. 104, 105.

67. GAC to EBC, February 9, 1869, Merington Papers, NYPL; Merington, *Custer Story,* pp. 226–27.

68. Merington, *Custer Story,* pp. 225, 226, 227; Hutton, *Phil Sheridan,* pp. 107, 108.

69. Merington, *Custer Story,* p. 228; Hutton, *Phil Sheridan,* p. 109.

70. Spotts, *Campaigning,* pp. 136–40; Custer, *My Life,* pp. 345–49; Duncan and Smith, "Captives," *RR* 7 (2): 18.

71. Custer, *My Life,* pp. 353–59; Spotts, *Campaigning,* pp. 151, 152; Duncan and Smith, "Captives," *RR* 7 (2): 18.

72. Custer, *My Life,* pp. 356–59; Duncan and Smith, "Captives," *RR* 7 (2): 18.

73. Urwin and Fagan, *Custer,* p. 96; Spotts, *Campaigning,* pp. 151–53; Utley, *Cavalier,* pp. 73, 74.

74. Duncan and Smith, "Captives," *RR* 7 (2): 5, 6, 9, 10, 19, 20; Spotts, *Campaigning,* pp. 156–58; Urwin and Fagan, *Custer,* pp. 88, 89; Hutton, *Custer Reader,* p. 363.

75. Custer, *My Life,* pp. 375–76; Spotts, *Campaigning,* pp. 162–72; Custer, *Following,* pp. 56, 57; Burkey, *Custer,* p. 74.

Chapter 16: NORTH TO DAKOTA

1. Armes, *Ups and Downs,* p. 291; Burkey, *Custer,* pp. 47, 50; Stallard, *Glittering Misery,* pp. 12, 15, 23.

2. Burkey, *Custer,* pp. 51, 52, 57; Frost, *Court-Martial,* p. 105n; Monaghan, *Custer,* p. 331; Custer, *Following,* pp. 71–77.

3. Custer, *Following,* chap. 7 and 8.

4. Ibid., pp. 91, 94, 95; Burkey, *Custer,* p. 65; Brill, *Conquest,* p. 46; Custer, *My Life,* pp. 281–84, 365–66.

5. Custer, *Following,* p. 91; Custer, *My Life,* p. 282; Zimmerman, "Mo-nah-se-tah," *CBHMA,* 1990, pp. 2, 4, 5; Utley, *Cavalier,* p. 107; Hutton, *Custer Reader,* pp. 94, 99n, 364; Miller, *Custer's Fall,* p. 67, 237; Carroll, *Benteen-Goldin,* pp. 258, 259; Kinsley, *Custer,* pp. 434–35; Monaghan, *Custer,* p. 324.

6. Utley, *Cavalier,* p. 108; Leckie, *Elizabeth Bacon Custer,* p. 110.

7. Zimmerman, "Mo-nah-se-tah," *CBHMA,* 1990, pp. 4, 5, 7, 8; Utley, *Cavalier,* pp. 106–8; Hutton, *Custer Reader,* pp. 94, 99n, 364; Connell, *Son,* pp. 200–202, 417–18; Kinsley, *Custer,* pp. 434–35; Monaghan, *Custer,* p. 324; Burkey, *Custer,* p. 68.

8. Custer, *Following,* pp. 105–7; Burkey, *Custer,* pp. 75, 76, 78, 79.

9. Levine, "Indian Fighters," *CWH* 31 (4): 329, 330; Utley, *Indian Frontier,* pp. 129, 130, 133, 134, 154, 155; Utley, *Frontier Regulars,* pp. 197, 198.

10. Burkey, *Custer,* pp. 81, 82; Johnson, *Jacob Horner,* pp. 4n, 5n; Warner, *Generals in Blue,* pp. 454, 486–87.

11. Merington, *Custer Story,* p. 228; Utley, *Cavalier,* pp. 104–5; duBois, *Kick the Dead Lion,* p. 97n.

12. Utley, *Cavalier,* p. 105; Frost, *General Custer's Libbie,* p. 183; Millbrook, "Big Game Hunting," *KHQ* 41 (4): 429n; Walker, *Campaigns,* p. 42.

13. Burkey, *Custer,* pp. 50, 51, 60; Millbrook, "Big Game Hunting," *KHQ* 41 (4): 431; Custer, *Following,* pp. 153, 154; Carroll, *Benteen-Goldin,* pp. 257, 258.

14. EBC to Laura, September 19, 1869, EBC Collection, MCLS; Custer, *Following,* pp. 113, 114, 120, 122, 324, 325, 328; Reynolds, *Civil War,* p. 102n.

15. Burkey, *Custer,* pp. 83, 84, 85, 85n; Custer, *Following,* pp. 243, 263–66; EBC to Laura, September 19, 1869, EBC Collection, MCLS; Dippie, *Nomad,* pp. xiv, 55; Ryan, "Ten Years," LBBNM; Millbrook, "Big Game Hunting," *KHQ* 41 (4): 435–40, 447, 448; A. T. O'Neil, "Custer Recollections," pp. 9, 10.

16. Leckie, *Elizabeth Bacon Custer,* pp. 86, 122, 247.

17. MSR/GAC, NA; warranty deed, August 4, 1869, GAC Collection, MCHMA; agreement, October 23, 1869, Special Orders No. 211, November 9, 1869, Section M: Other Collections Correspondence, LBBNM; Burkey, *Custer,* pp. 82, 88, 89.

18. GAC to EBC, November 27, December 6, fragment of letter [December] 1869, Merington Papers, NYPL; Merington, *Custer Story,* pp. 229–31; MSR/GAC, NA; Rosevear and Rosevear, *Canadians,* p. 4; T. E. O'Neil, *Custer Chronicles,* 1:33.

19. GAC to EBC, December 20, [1869], Merington Papers, NYPL.

20. Millbrook, "Rebecca," *KHQ* 42 (4): pp. 396–99, 400n, 401; Rebecca Richmond to Mother, March 16, 1870, Section M: Other Collections Correspondence, LBBNM: Burkey, *Custer*, pp. 89, 90.

21. Burkey, *Custer*, pp. 90–96, 98, 99; Ryan, "Ten Years," LBBNM.

22. Hutton, *Custer and His Times*, pp. 19, 26, 27; Burkey, *Custer*, pp. 99, 100; Millbrook, "Big Game Hunting," *KHQ* 41 (4): 449.

23. Pohanka, "George Yates," *GG* 8: 15–18; Hutton, *Custer and His Times*, pp. 9, 12–14, 32; Fougera, *With Custer's Cavalry*, p. 76.

24. Notes of Mrs. Annie Gibson Roberts Yates, typescript, Pohanka Collection.

25. MSR/GAC, NA; J. A. Williams, Certificate, February 15, 1871; Special Orders, No. 8, January 23, 1871; Special Orders, No. 100, March 11, 1871; Special Orders, No. 171, April 27, 1871, all in GAC, Correspondence and Orders, LBBNM; Frost, *General Custer's Libbie*, p. 191.

26. Frost, *General Custer's Libbie*, p. 191; Utley, *Cavalier*, p. 109.

27. Frost, *General Custer's Libbie*, pp. 191, 195; Utley, *Cavalier*, pp. 109, 110; J. J. Astor to GAC, April 7, 1871; J. W. Hall to GAC, April 7, 20, 25, 1871, July 26, August 8, 13, 1872; Theodore H. Lowe to J. W. Hall, August 14, 1872; J. W. Hall to W. A. Travis, February 23, 1875, all in GAC, Correspondence and Orders, LBBNM.

28. Merington, *Custer Story*, pp. 232–39; GAC to EBC, April 13, 29, 1871, Merington Papers, NYPL; Account Statement, Brooks Brothers, September 7, 1871, GAC, Correspondence and Orders, LBBNM; Frost, *General Custer's Libbie*, pp. 191, 195.

29. MSR/GAC, NA; Frost, *General Custer's Libbie*, p. 197; O'Neil and O'Neil, *Custers*, pp. 11, 12; Darling, *Custer's Seventh Cavalry*, pp. 18, 19.

30. Merington, *Custer Story*, pp. 240–42; Crackel, "Custer's Kentucky," *TFCHQ* 48: 144, 145, 146, 146n.

31. Foner, *Reconstruction*, pp. 422, 425–32, 434, 440, 454–59; Darling, *Custer's Seventh Cavalry*; Crackel, "Custer's Kentucky," *TFCHQ* 48: 144.

32. Hunt, *I Fought*, p. 5; Crackel, "Custer's Kentucky," *TFCHQ* 48: 148–50, 152; Burkey, *Custer*, p. 103; Frost, *With Custer in '74*, p. xxvi; O'Neil and O'Neil, *Custers*, p. 18.

33. Custer, *Boots*, pp. 139, 141, 142; Custer, *My Life*, pp. xxiii, xxiv; Urwin and Fagan, *Custer*, pp. 130, 133.

34. Darling, *Custer's Seventh Cavalry*, pp. 23, 27, 28, 29; Frost, *Custer's Seventh Cavalry*, p. xii; Utley, "War Houses," *Montana* 35 (4): 23.

35. Darling, *Custer's Seventh Cavalry*, pp. 36–38, 43–49.

36. Ibid., pp. 12, 56, 59–63; Kaufman, *Custer*, pp. 22, 136, 168; Hutton, *Custer Reader*, p. 182.

37. Darling, *Custer's Seventh Cavalry*, pp. 71–73; Hunt, *I Fought*, p. 10; Custer, *Boots*, pp. 10, 11.

38. Darling, *Custer's Seventh Cavalry*, pp. 73, 74, 75, 77; Kaufman, *Custer*,

p. 164; Custer, *Boots,* p. 12; Joseph Mills Hanson to Edward S. Godfrey, October 23, 1909, Godfrey Papers, USAMHI.

39. Darling, *Custer's Seventh Cavalry,* pp. 92–94; Hutton, *Custer Reader,* pp. 184, 185; Frost, *General Custer's Libbie,* p. 181.

40. Hutton, *Custer Reader,* pp. 184, 185.

41. Darling, *Custer's Seventh Cavalry,* pp. 121, 122, 142, 143, 145n.

42. Ibid., pp. 147–56, 173–78, 181–84, 191; Hunt, *I Fought,* p. 17.

43. Darling, *Custer's Seventh Cavalry,* pp. 175–78; Hutton, *Custer Reader,* p. 187.

44. Hutton, *Custer Reader,* p. 109.

45. Darling, *Custer's Seventh Cavalry,* pp. 181–84, 191; Piper, *Dakota,* p. 141; Hunt, *I Fought,* p. 6.

Chapter 17: LAKOTA GOLD

1. Hassrick, *Sioux,* pp. ix, 3, 61–66; Hedren, *Great,* p. 2; Utley, *Lance,* p. 4; King, "Cavalryman," *RR* 8 (1): 5; Hardorff, *Hokahey!,* p. 14.

2. Hassrick, *Sioux,* pp. 7, 11–14, 17, 25, 26, 36–39, 245; Utley, *Lance,* p. 13.

3. Hassrick, *Sioux,* pp. 32–34, 80; King, "Cavalryman," *RR* 8 (1): 6, 7; Utley, *Lance,* p. 106.

4. Hutton, *Custer Reader,* pp. 239, 240; Hedren, *Great,* pp. 1–4; Utley, *Lance,* p. 38; Miller, *Custer's Fall,* p. 218; Utley, "War Houses," *Montana* 35 (4): 20, 22.

5. Hutton, *Custer Reader,* p. 240; Hedren, *Great,* p. 4; Utley, *Lance,* pp. 26, 65; Graham, *Custer Myth,* p. 68.

6. Utley, "War Houses," *Montana* 35 (4): 20; Hutton, *Custer Reader,* p. 241; Utley, *Lance,* p. 106; Frost, *Custer's Seventh Cavalry,* pp. 3, 15, 16, 20.

7. Frost, *Custer's Seventh Cavalry,* pp. 22, 23, 28, 48; Stanley, *Personal Memoirs,* pp. 244, 245; Corliss, "Yellowstone Expedition," USAMHI.

8. Stanley, *Personal Memoirs,* p. 238; Custer, *Boots,* pp. 78–80.

9. Dustin, *Custer Tragedy,* p. 202; Thompson, "Custer's Last Fight," p. 9, USAMHI.

10. Stanley, *Personal Memoirs,* p. 249; Thompson, "Custer's Last Fight," p. 9, USAMHI; Dustin, *Custer Tragedy,* p. 202.

11. Warner, *Generals in Blue,* p. 470; Stanley, *Personal Memoirs,* p. 239; Connell, *Son,* p. 234.

12. Stanley, *Personal Memoirs,* pp. 238, 239, 240, 246, 247; Luther P. Bradley to Ione Bradley, July 1, 1873, Bradley Papers, USAMHI.

13. Stanley, *Personal Memoirs,* p. 240.

14. Frost, *Custer's Seventh Cavalry,* pp. 60, 61; Merington, *Custer Story,* p. 265.

15. Frost, *Custer's Seventh Cavalry,* pp. 61, 178; Merington, *Custer Story,* p. 265.

16. Merington, *Custer Story*, p. 266; Stanley, *Personal Memoirs*, p. 241; Utley, *Cavalier*, p. 119.

17. Frost, *Custer's Seventh Cavalry*, p. 185; Piper, *Dakota*, p. 77; Merington, *Custer Story*, pp. 254, 255; Luther P. Bradley to Ione Bradley, July 16, 1873, Bradley Papers, USAMHI.

18. GAC to EBC, July 19, 1873, undated fragment of letter, [June or July 1873], Merington Papers, NYPL; T. E. O'Neil and Vandenburg, "Modern Look," *RR* 8(2):p. 19; Carroll, *Custer and His Times*, p. 158.

19. Hutton, *Custer Reader*, p. 190, 191; Merington, *Custer Story*, pp. 248–50, 257, 264; Frost, *Custer's Seventh Cavalry*, pp. 57, 202.

20. Frost, *Custer's Seventh Cavalry*, p. 187; GAC to EBC, July 19, 1873, Merington Papers, NYPL; Merington, *Custer Story*, pp. 259, 260; Utley, *Cavalier*, p. 118.

21. Custer, *Boots*, pp. 268–69; Frost, *Custer's Seventh Cavalry*, pp. 64, 65, 68; Varnum, "Memoirs," USAMHI; Carroll, *They Rode*, p. 252; Hutton, *Custer Reader*, pp. 205, 206.

22. Custer, *Boots*, pp. 269–70; Hutton, *Custer Reader*, pp. 206, 207; Frost, *Custer's Seventh Cavalry*, p. 65; Varnum, "Memoirs," USAMHI.

23. Custer, *Boots*, pp. 269–70; Hutton, *Custer Reader*, pp. 207, 209–11, 213, 215, 217; Varnum, "Memoirs," USAMHI; Mangum, "Gall," *CBHMA*, 1991, p. 31.

24. Custer, *Boots*, pp. 269–71; Hutton, *Custer Reader*, pp. 213, 215, 217; Varnum, "Memoirs," USAMHI.

25. Custer, *Boots*, p. 272; Frost, *Custer's Seventh Cavalry*, pp. 187, 189; Liddic, *I Buried Custer*, p. 69.

26. Frost, *Custer's Seventh Cavalry*, pp. 79, 81, 189; Custer, *Boots*, pp. 272, 274; Lemuel C. Cherry to E. S. Godfrey, November 23, 1928, Godfrey Collection, LBBNM.

27. Custer, *Boots*, pp. 274–76; Frost, *Custer's Seventh Cavalry*, pp. 83–86; Stanley, *Personal Memoirs*, p. 242; Mangum, "Gall," *CBHMA*, 1991, p. 31.

28. Custer, *Boots*, pp. 276–79; Hutton, *Custer Reader*, pp. 196, 197; Frost, *Custer's Seventh Cavalry*, pp. 84, 86; Luther P. Bradley to Ione Bradley, August 19, 1873, Bradley Papers, USAMHI; Varnum, "Memoirs," USAMHI.

29. Custer, *Boots*, p. 270; Stanley, *Personal Memoirs*, p. 102.

30. Frost, *Custer's Seventh Cavalry*, pp. 189, 191; Nye, *Marching*, p. 13; Willert, *Little Big Horn Diary*, p. 71; Stewart, *Custer's Luck*, p. 112.

31. Merington, *Custer Story*, pp. 248–67; Frost, *General Custer's Libbie*, p. 204; fragment of a letter, [July 1873], Merington Papers, NYPL.

32. Fragment of a letter, [probably September 9–10, 1873], Merington Papers, NYPL; Frost, *Custer's Seventh Cavalry*, p. 191.

33. Frost, *Custer's Seventh Cavalry*, pp. 101, 102, 191; Stanley, *Personal Memoirs*, p. 241; Merington, *Custer Story*, p. 267.

34. Merington, *Custer Story,* pp. 264, 266, 267; Utley, *Cavalier,* p. 123.

35. Returns, Fort Abraham Lincoln; MSR/GAC, NA; *Outline Descriptions,* pp. 35, 38; Frost, *Custer's Seventh Cavalry,* pp. 16, 108, 114.

36. Returns, Fort Abraham Lincoln, NA; Custer, *Boots,* pp. 87–90; Fougera, *With Custer's Cavalry,* pp. 67, 68.

37. Custer, *Boots,* chap. 10, pp. 128, 133, 217, 218; Merington, *Custer Story,* p. 270; Urwin and Fagan, *Custer,* p. 133; Frost, *Custer's Seventh Cavalry,* pp. 16, 114.

38. Custer, *Boots,* pp. 105–7; Merington, *Custer Story,* p. 269; Frost, *General Custer's Libbie,* pp. 207, 210n.

39. Custer, *Boots,* pp. 164–67; Katz, *Custer,* p. 110.

40. Stewart, *Penny,* passim; Utley, *Cavalier,* p. 125; Frost, *General Custer's Libbie,* p. 218.

41. Stewart, *Penny,* passim; Frost, *General Custer's Libbie,* p. 218; Utley, *Cavalier,* p. 125.

42. Utley, *Cavalier,* pp. 125–26.

43. Ibid., pp. 133, 134; Jackson, *Custer's Gold,* pp. 4, 9.

44. Utley, *Lance,* p. 115; Ambrose, *Crazy Horse,* p. 37; Frost, *With Custer in '74,* pp. xi, xii; Jackson, *Custer's Gold,* p. 8.

45. Jackson, *Custer's Gold,* pp. 14, 15; Frost, *Custer's 7th Cav,* p. 128; Merington, *Custer Story,* pp. 221, 222.

46. Jackson, *Custer's Gold,* pp. 21, 22; Frost, *With Custer in '74,* pp. xviii, xix; Carroll and Frost, *Ewert's Diary,* pp. 5, 6.

47. duMont, *Custer,* pp. 23, 25, 26; duMont, "Firearms," *GG* 6: 27.

48. Jackson, *Custer's Gold,* p. 17, 22; Frost, *With Custer in '74,* pp. xv, 96n, 97n.

49. Frost, *With Custer in '74,* pp. 20–21; Carroll and Frost, *Ewert's Diary,* p. 8; Jackson, *Custer's Gold,* p. 25; *New York Times,* July 5, 1874.

50. Frost, *With Custer in '74,* pp. 20–87; Carroll and Frost, *Ewert's Diary,* pp. xi, 10–79; Hunt, *I Fought,* p. 33.

51. Frost, *With Custer in '74,* pp. 20–87; Carroll and Frost, *Ewert's Diary,* pp. 10–79; Merington, *Custer Story,* p. 272; Hunt, *I Fought,* p. 36.

52. Merington, *Custer Story,* pp. 272–73, 274; Jackson, *Custer's Gold,* pp. 73, 94.

53. Merington, *Custer Story,* pp. 273, 274; Carroll and Frost, *Ewert's Diary,* p. 34; Dippie, *Nomad,* p. xiii; W. A. Falconer to Charles Kuhlman, January 15, 1939, Kuhlman Papers, MTHS; Hunt, *I Fought,* p. 43; Stewart, *Custer's Luck,* p. 181.

54. Frost, *With Custer in '74,* pp. 53–56; Carroll and Frost, *Ewert's Diary,* pp. 43–47; Utley, *Cavalier,* pp. 136–37.

55. Frost, *With Custer in '74,* pp. 58–61; Carroll and Frost, *Ewert's Diary,* pp. 47, 53, 54; Utley, *Cavalier,* pp. 138, 139; Hunt, *I Fought,* pp. 40, 42.

56. Carroll and Frost, *Ewert's Diary,* pp. 59–79; Frost, *With Custer in '74,* pp. 70–87; Utley, *Cavalier,* p. 139.

57. *New York Times,* August 23, 1874; Utley, *Cavalier,* p. 140; Jackson, *Custer's Gold,* p. 108.

58. Utley, *Cavalier,* pp. 141–43; Frost, *General Custer's Libbie,* p. 214; Hedren, *Great,* p. 58.

59. Hutton, *Custer Reader,* p. 241; Utley, *Lance,* p. 145; Carroll and Frost, *Ewert's Diary,* p. 2; Hassrick, *Sioux,* p. 7.

Chapter 18: TOWARD LITTLE BIG HORN

1. Returns, Fort Abraham Lincoln, NA; Frost, *With Custer in '74,* pp. xx, xxi; Merington, *Custer Story,* pp. 274–75; *Monroe Evening News,* June 27, 1942.

2. Custer, *Boots,* pp. 205, 213; Utley, *Cavalier,* pp. 144, 145.

3. Returns, Fort Abraham Lincoln, NA; Custer, *Boots,* pp. 193–204; Utley, *Cavalier,* pp. 144, 145; Hunt, *I Fought,* pp. 29, 30.

4. Returns, Fort Abraham Lincoln, NA; Frost, *General Custer's Libbie,* p. 216; GAC to Augusta Ward, August 19, 1875, typescript, GAC Letters, RPL.

5. Monaghan, *Custer,* pp. 360, 361; GAC to Augusta Ward, August 19, 1875, GAC Letters, RPL; Returns, Fort Abraham Lincoln, NA; MSR/ GAC, NA.

6. Frost, *General Custer's Libbie,* pp. 216, 217; Utley, *Cavalier,* pp. 154, 155.

7. Warner, *Generals in Blue,* pp. 245–46; Utley, *Cavalier,* pp. 153, 154.

8. Utley, *Cavalier,* p. 154; Slotkin, *Fatal Environment,* pp. 421–24, although Slotkin mistakenly identifies Rufus Ingalls as Abraham Buford, a Kentucky horse breeder.

9. Utley, *Cavalier,* p. 154; Slotkin, *Fatal Environment,* pp. 421–24.

10. Leckie, *Elizabeth Bacon Custer,* p. 176; Slotkin, *Fatal Environment,* p. 424; Utley, *Cavalier,* pp. 154–55.

11. Carroll, *Benteen-Goldin,* pp. 254–57.

12. Merington, *Custer Story,* pp. 276, 277; Frost, *General Custer's Libbie,* p. 217; A. T. O'Neil, *Actor,* pp. 12, 13.

13. Merington, *Custer Story,* p. 277; J. R. Poncil to GAC, February 6, 1876, Merington Papers, NYPL.

14. MSR/GAC, NA; Custer, *Boots,* p. 240.

15. Custer, *Boots,* pp. 241–43.

16. Ibid., pp. 243–47; Returns, Fort Abraham Lincoln, NA.

17. Custer, *Boots,* pp. 246–47; Returns, Fort Abraham Lincoln, NA; Utley, *Cavalier,* p. 159; Merington, *Custer Story,* p. 281.

18. McFeely, *Grant,* pp. 428, 429; Frost, *Custer Legends,* pp. 180, 181.

19. McFeely, *Grant,* pp. 428, 429; Merington, *Custer Story,* p. 288.

20. Merington, *Custer Story,* p. 286; Frost, *General Custer's Libbie,* pp. 216, 221; Utley, *Cavalier,* pp. 151, 152, 164.

21. Merington, *Custer Story,* pp. 289, 290, 293; *Testimony,* passim; GAC to EBC, April 10, 1876, Merington Papers, NYPL; *New York Times,* April 4, 5, 6, 19, 1876.

22. Merington, *Custer Story,* pp. 292, 293; Utley, *Cavalier,* p. 161.

23. GAC to Augusta Ward, [April 30, 1876], GAC Letters, RPL; Merington, *Custer Story,* p. 293; Frost, *Custer Legends,* p. 183; GAC to U. S. Grant, May 1, 1876, GAC Collection, MCLS.

24. GAC to Augusta Ward, [April 30, 1876], GAC Letters, RPL; Frost, *Custer Legends,* pp. 104, 183; Kuhlman, *Did Custer Disobey,* p. 46; Merington, *Custer Story,* p. 294; Memorandum, May 5, [1876], GAC Collection, MCLS; Utley, *Cavalier,* pp. 161, 162.

25. Memorandum, May 5, [1876], GAC Collection, MCLS; Hutton, *Phil Sheridan,* p. 310; Merington, *Custer Story,* p. 294; Koury, "Myth," *CBHMA,* 1992, p. 61; Kuhlman, *Did Custer Disobey,* p. 46.

26. Frost, *Custer Legends,* p. 183; Hunt, *I Fought,* p. 50; Utley, *Cavalier,* p. 162; Darling, *Blunder,* pp. i, iii; Merington, *Custer Story,* p. 294.

27. Hutton, *Phil Sheridan,* pp. 308, 309; Utley, *Cavalier,* p. 163; Frost, *Custer Legends,* p. 183.

28. Darling, *Sad,* p. 17; Stewart, *Custer's Luck,* p. 138; Hutton, *Phil Sheridan,* p. 311.

29. Gray, *Centennial Campaign,* pp. 23–26; Hedren, *Great,* p. 5; Utley, *Cavalier,* p. 145.

30. Hutton, *Custer Reader,* p. 241; Hedren, *Great,* pp. 5, 46–48; Gray, *Centennial Campaign,* pp. 23–26.

31. Gray, *Centennial Campaign,* pp. 27–34; Hedren, *Great,* p. 6; Frost, *Custer Legends,* p. 149.

32. Stewart, *Custer's Luck,* pp. 81–82.

33. Ibid., pp. 84–96.

34. Ibid., chap. 5; Zimmerman, "Gibbon's Montana Column," *CBHMA,* 1991, pp. 1–4; Marquis, *Custer, Cavalry & Crows,* p. 21; Gray, *Custer's Last Campaign,* pp. 118, 148–49.

35. Utley, *Cavalier,* p. 170; Gray, *Centennial Campaign,* pp. 86–90, 94–95; Willert, *Little Big Horn Diary,* p. xxi.

36. Returns, Fort Abraham Lincoln, NA; Hunt, *I Fought,* p. 50; Utley, *Cavalier,* p. 165; Rosevear and Rosevear, *Canadians,* pp. 18, 20, 21.

37. Gray, *Centennial Campaign,* pp. 97–98; Stewart, *Custer's Luck,* pp. 178–79; Kuhlman, *Did Custer Disobey,* p. 33; Darling, *Sad,* p. 18.

38. Willert, *Little Big Horn Diary,* pp. 2, 5; Gray, *Centennial Campaign,* pp. 97, 98; Returns, Fort Abraham Lincoln, NA.

39. Willert, *Little Big Horn Diary,* p. 7; Willert, *Terry Letters,* pp. 1, 3; Hunt, *I Fought,* pp. 53, 54; Heski, "Trail," *RR* 9 (2): 22–30.

40. Willert, *Terry Letters,* pp. 3, 5, 7, 8, 9, 13, 45n; Custer, *Boots,* pp. 295–97; Willert, *Little Big Horn Diary,* pp. 65, 69, 70; Gray, *Centennial Campaign,* pp. 98–100.

41. Gray, *Centennial Campaign,* pp. 101, 102, 378; Willert, *Terry Letters,* pp. 13, 15; Stewart, *Custer's Luck,* pp. 220, 221; Custer, *Boots,* p. 297.

42. Willert, *Terry's Letters,* pp. 17, 19; Schneider, *Freeman Journal,* p. 53; Willert, *Little Big Horn Diary,* p. 98; Gray, *Custer's Last Campaign,* pp. 151,

152, 153, 157, 176, 181; Stewart, *Custer's Luck,* pp. 224, 225; Merington, *Custer Story,* p. 302.

43. Gray, *Custer's Last Campaign,* p. 182; Willert, *Terry's Letters,* p. 19; Gray, *Centennial Campaign,* pp. 125, 126.

44. Gray, *Custer's Last Campaign,* pp. 183, 184; Stewart, *Custer's Luck,* pp. 225, 226; Carroll, *Camp Talk,* p. 14.

45. Carroll, *They Rode,* p. 209; F. W. Benteen to D. F. Barry, September 28, 1895, Barry Collection; R. G. Carter to E. S. Godfrey, April 12, 1925, Godfrey Collection, LBBNM; Hagemann, *Fighting,* p. 252; Thompson, "Custer's Last Fight," pp. 4, 5, USAMHI; Hutton, *Custer Reader,* p. 245.

46. Gray, *Centennial Campaign,* pp. 127–30; Stewart, *Custer's Luck,* pp. 228–30; Urwin and Fagan, *Custer,* p. 227; Hunt, *I Fought,* pp. 63, 64; duMont, *Custer,* p. 23; Merington, *Custer Story,* pp. 302, 303.

47. Merington, *Custer Story,* pp. 303, 304.

48. Gray, *Custer's Last Campaign,* pp. 194, 195; Stewart, *Custer's Luck,* pp. 230–32.

49. A good account of Reno's scout is in Gray, *Custer's Last Campaign,* pp. 184–97; Thompson, "Custer's Last Fight," p. 13, USAMHI; Willert, *Little Big Horn Diary,* pp. 193, 194; Merington, *Custer Story,* p. 305; Upton, *Custer Adventure,* pp. 13, 14, 112n; Stewart and Luce, "Reno Scout," *Montana* 10 (3): 28; Liddic, *I Buried,* p. 13.

50. Gray, *Custer's Last Campaign,* p. 199; Hutton, *Custer Reader,* p. 243; Darling, *Blunder,* pp. 1, 2; Koury, "Myth," *CBHMA,* 1992, pp. 55, 56.

51. Edgerly, "A Narrative," pp. 15–16, NYPL; Darling, *Blunder,* pp. 68, 69, 71–75; Gray, *Custer's Last Campaign,* pp. 199, 200.

52. O'Neil and Vandenburg, "Modern Look," *RR* 8 (2): 19, 20; Carroll, *Custer and His Times,* pp. 158, 181; Frost, *Custer Legends,* p. 160; Hutton, *Custer Reader,* p. 244.

53. Hammer, *Custer,* pp. 53, 54; Carroll, *Camp Talk,* p. 85; Merington, *Custer Story,* p. 309.

54. Merington, *Custer Story,* pp. 306, 307; O'Neil, "Autie Reed's Last Letters," *NLBHA* 28 (3): 6.

55. Hammer, *Custer,* pp. 205, 209, 211, 212; Willert, *Little Big Horn Diary,* pp. 26, 39, 103.

56. Utley, *Lance,* pp. 137, 138; Utley, *Indian Frontier,* p. 181; Upton, *Custer Adventure,* pp. 60, 61.

57. Willert, *Little Big Horn Diary,* pp. 138, 139, 146, 155, 178; Stewart, *Custer's Luck,* pp. 199–207.

58. Hammer, *Custer,* p. 205; Willert, *Little Big Horn Diary,* pp. 178, 187, 248, 249; Utley, *Cavalier,* pp. 178, 179; Carroll, *Custer and His Times,* p. 217; Hutton, *Custer Reader,* pp. 281, 282, 365, 366; Hedren, *Great,* pp. 1, 6.

59. Kuhlman, *Legend,* p. 29; Hutton, *Custer Reader,* pp. 272, 273; Graham, *Custer Myth,* p. 16; Custer, *Boots,* p. 303; Dunlay, *Wolves,* pp. 77, 113; Plainfeather, "Role," *CBHMA,* 1990, pp. 34, 37; Hunt, *I Fought,* p. 19.

60. Gray, *Custer's Last Campaign,* pp. 3, 6, 8, 51, 59; Hammer, *Custer,* pp. 228, 241; Michno, *Mystery,* p. 160; Dunlay, *Wolves,* pp. 80, 140; Miller, *Custer's Fall,* p. 10; Nichols, *Reno Court,* p. 250; Carroll, *Benteen-Goldin,* p. 41; *New York Herald,* January 22, 1878; "Death of a Custer Scout," typescript, Camp Collection, LBBNM; Carroll, *They Rode,* p. 76.

61. Merington, *Custer Story,* p. 307.

62. Typescript copy of orders in Edgerly, "A Narrative," pp. 15–16, NYPL.

63. Ibid., p. 1; Gray, *Custer's Last Campaign,* pp. 203, 204; Hutton, *Custer Reader,* p. 244; Hammer, *Custer,* p. 26; Nichols, *Reno Court,* p. 465.

64. Hutton, *Custer Reader,* pp. 245, 324–30, 352; T. E. O'Neil, *Garry Owen,* 6:8; Michno, *Mystery,* p. 17; Fox, *Archaeology,* p. 261; Sills, "Recruits," *GG* 5: 5–7; *National Tribune,* March 23, 1893; duMont, *Custer,* pp. 32, 34; Hutton, *Custer and His Times,* p. 248.

65. Hammer, *Glory March,* p. 4; Darling, *Blunder,* pp. 2, 3, 6; Hammer, *Custer,* p. 53; Hunt, *I Fought,* pp. 70, 71; A. T. O'Neil, "Custer Recollections," p. 32; duBois, *Kick the Dead Lion,* p. 103n.

66. Hutton, *Custer Reader,* p. 275; Carroll, *They Rode,* p. 171; M. A. Reno to E. W. Smith, July 5, 1876, copy of report, Elder Papers, DU; Urwin and Fagan, *Custer,* p. 237; Gray, *Custer's Last Campaign,* pp. 204, 205.

67. Hutton, *Custer Reader,* pp. 275–77; Edgerly, "A Narrative," p. 2, NYPL; Merington, *Custer Story,* pp. 309, 310.

68. Merington, *Custer Story,* p. 310; Hutton, *Custer Reader,* p. 277.

69. Gray, *Custer's Last Campaign,* pp. 205, 210; Hammer, *Glory March,* p. 6; Hutton, *Custer Reader,* p. 278; Dustin, *Custer Tragedy,* p. 234; Darling, *Blunder,* p. 148.

70. Hammer, *Custer,* p. 59n; Gray, *Custer's Last Campaign,* pp. 211, 215; Hutton, *Custer Reader,* p. 279; Carroll, *They Rode,* pp. 252–53.

71. Hammer, *Custer,* pp. 59n, 60n; Hutton, *Custer Reader,* pp. 278, 279; Gray, *Custer's Last Campaign,* pp. 211–13.

72. Gray, *Custer's Last Campaign,* pp. 216–18; Hutton, *Custer Reader,* pp. 279–80; Hammer, *Custer,* p. 60n; Dustin, *Custer Tragedy,* p. 234.

73. Varnum, "Memoirs," USAMHI; Hammer, *Custer,* p. 60; Gray, *Custer's Last Campaign,* p. 218, 222; Graham, *Custer Myth,* p. 14.

74. There has been considerable discussion about Custer's decision at Busby; see, Stewart, *Custer's Luck,* p. 264; Calhoun, "Did Custer Disobey?," *GG* 6: 10, 14, 15; Walter M. Camp to Charles A. Varnum, April 28, 1909; and George Herendeen to W. M. Camp, May 15, 1909, Camp Collection, LBBNM; Hein, *Memories,* p. 144; Darling, *Blunder,* pp. 150, 154; *New York Herald,* January 22, 1878; T. E. O'Neil and Vandenburg, "Modern Look," *RR* 8 (2): 14, 19.

75. Hutton, *Custer Reader,* p. 280; Hunt, *I Fought,* p. 74; Edgerly, "A Narrative," pp. 2, 3, NYPL; Gray, *Custer's Last Campaign,* p. 226.

76. Hammer, *Custer,* p. 60n; Varnum, "Memoirs," USAMHI; Gray, *Custer's Last Campaign,* pp. 226, 227; Hutton, *Custer Reader,* p. 280.

77. Hammer, *Custer,* pp. 60n–61n; Varnum, "Memoirs," USAMHI.

78. Varnum, "Memoirs," USAMHI; Hammer, *Custer,* pp. 60n, 61n; Gray, *Custer's Last Campaign,* pp. 236, 237.

Chapter 19: MONTANA HILL

1. Hassrick, *Sioux,* p. 174

2. Hardoff, *Hokahey!,* pp. 27, 28; Kanipe, "Tarheel," *RR* 7 (2): 26.

3. Hammer, *Custer,* pp. 74, 75, 230; Edgerly, "A Narrative," pp. 3, 4, NYPL; Thompson, "Custer's Last Fight," p. 21, USAMHI; Gray, *Custer's Last Campaign,* pp. 241, 242.

4. Gray, *Custer's Last Campaign,* p. 243; duBois, *Kick the Dead Lion,* p. 81; Kuhlman, *Did Custer Disobey,* p. 16; Horn, "Custer's Turn," *RR* 8 (1): 14.

5. Stewart, *Custer's Luck,* p. 281; Thompson, "Custer's Last Fight," p. 20, USAMHI.

6. Hutton, *Custer Reader,* p. 248; Walter M. Camp to Charles A. Varnum, April 28, 1909, Camp Collection, LBBNM; Nichols, *Reno Court,* pp. 20, 541; Gray, *Custer's Last Campaign,* pp. 244–47; Hammer, *Custer,* p. 53; Church, "Did Custer Believe," *CBHMA,* 1991, p. 64.

7. M. A. Reno to E. W. Smith, July 5, 1876, copy of report, Edler Papers, DU; Hammer, *Glory March,* pp. 7, 8; T. E. O'Neil, *Custer to the Little Big Horn,* p. 11; Nichols, *Reno Court,* p. 405.

8. Hammer, *Custer,* pp. 54, 55; Nichols, *Reno Court,* pp. 421, 431; Edgerly, "A Narrative," p. 4, NYPL; Fougera, *With Custer's Cavalry,* p. 268; Darling, *Blunder,* p. 196; Carroll, *Benteen-Goldin,* p. 147; duBois, *Kick the Dead Lion,* p. 34; Hutton, *Custer Reader,* pp. 248, 249.

9. Gray, *Custer's Last Campaign,* pp. 248–50, 253; Horn, "Custer's Turn," *RR* 8 (1): 16; Hammer, *Custer,* pp. 64, 65; M. A. Reno to E. W. Smith, July 5, 1876, copy of report, Elder Papers, DU.

10. Stewart, *Custer's Luck,* pp. 322–25; Hammer, *Custer,* p. 65; Gray, *Custer's Last Campaign,* pp. 253–57; Hutton, *Custer Reader,* p. 249; Nichols, *Reno Court,* p. 561; Edgerly, "A Narrative," p. 5, NYPL.

11. Nichols, *Reno Court,* p. 561; Hammer, *Custer,* p. 65; Gray, *Custer's Last Campaign,* pp. 256–57; Stewart, *Custer's Luck,* p. 325, 325n.

12. Gray, *Custer's Last Campaign,* pp. 266, 270–71, 273; Nichols, *Reno Court,* p. 84; duBois, *Kick the Dead Lion,* p. 5; Bowen, "Notes," pp. 5, 6; Crow Scouts' Accounts, Battle of the Little Big Horn Papers, USAMHI.

13. Gray, *Custer's Last Campaign,* p. 275; Nichols, *Reno Court,* pp. 20, 21, 188, 541, 542; M. A. Reno to E. W. Smith, July 5, 1876, copy of report, Elder Papers, DU; *New York Herald,* January 22, 1878.

14. Varnum, "Memoirs," USAMHI; Horn, "Custer's Turn," *RR* 8 (1): 16.

15. M. A. Reno to E. W. Smith, July 5, 1876, copy of report, Elder Papers, DU; Nichols, *Reno Court,* pp. 46, 141, 199, 200, 203, 239, 380; Frost, *Custer Legends,* p. 187; Stewart, *Custer's Luck,* pp. 343, 344.

16. Hammer, *Custer,* pp. 198, 209; Hutton, *Custer Reader,* p. 337; Bowen, "Notes," p. 9, USAMHI; Stewart, *Custer's Luck,* pp. 346–49.

17. Hardoff, *Hokahey!,* pp. 106, 107; Utley, *Lance,* p. 149; Hammer, *Custer,* p. 181, 212; Hutton, *Custer Reader,* p. 248.

18. Utley, *Frontier Regulars,* p. 269.

19. Nichols, *Reno Court,* passim; T. E. O'Neil, *Custer to the Little Big Horn,* p. 15; Utley, *Cavalier,* pp. 198, 200; Edgerly, "A Narrative," p. 6, NYPL; Frost, *Custer Legends,* p. 100; Grinnell, *Fighting Cheyennes,* p. 356; Graham, *Custer Myth,* p. 305; Hammer, *Custer,* p. 232; M. A. Reno to E. W. Smith, July 5, 1876, copy of report, Elder Papers, DU; Stewart, *Custer's Luck,* pp. 351–52; Gray, *Centennial Campaign,* pp. 174–76.

20. Extensive descriptions of fighting on skirmish lines and in woods can be found in Nichols, *Reno Court,* passim; William E. Morris to Robert Bruce, May 23, 1928, typescript, Battle of the Little Big Horn Papers, USAMHI.

21. Nichols, *Reno Court,* passim; Fox, *Archaeology,* pp. 269, 270; duBois, *Kick the Dead Lion,* pp. 10, 11, 13; Utley, *Cavalier,* p. 200; T. E. O'Neil, *Garry Owen,* 8:18.

22. Nichols, *Reno Court,* p. 197, passim; William C. Sloper to Ruth Gibson, April 17, 1924, Glidden Papers, MTHS; Rosevear and Rosevear, *Canadians,* pp. 9, 11; Liddic, *I Buried Custer,* pp. 19, 20; Tuttle, "Who Buried," *CBHMA,* 1990, p. 9; Hardorff, *Lakota,* pp. 46n, 102n; Hardorff, *Custer Battle Casualties,* pp. 124, 125, 131, 135–37, 141–48, 154–56.

23. Gray, *Custer's Last Campaign,* p. 295; duBois, *Kick the Dead Lion,* pp. 14, 15; Hardorff, *Custer Battle Casualties,* pp. 137, 152; T. E. O'Neil, *Garry Owen,* 3:33.

24. duBois, *Kick the Dead Lion,* p. xix; Utley, *Cavalier,* p. 198; Stewart, *Custer's Luck,* pp. 381, 494; Gray, *Centennial Campaign,* pp. 178, 179.

25. A detailed analysis and timetable of Benteen's scout can be found in Gray, *Custer's Last Campaign,* pp. 258–65.

26. Ibid., pp. 263–64, 280; Hammer, *Custer,* p. 75.

27. Gray, *Custer's Last Campaign,* pp. 264, 280–84; Hammer, *Custer,* pp. 54, 55, 75, 80; Nichols, *Reno Court,* pp. 404, 405, 442, 479, 480; duBois, *Kick the Dead Lion,* pp. 36, 37; Urwin and Fagan, *Custer,* pp. 221, 223; Utley, *Cavalier,* p. 198.

28. Carroll, *Four on Custer,* p. 47; Nichols, *Reno Court,* pp. 191, 289, 407, 443, 482, 483; Forrest, *Witnesses,* p. 5; Henry Mechling to James Braddock, July 16, 1921, Mechling Papers, USAMHI; F. W. Benteen to D. F. Barry, March 1, 1895; and John Martin to D. R. Barry, April 7, 1907, Barry Collection, LBBNM; Gray, *Custer's Last Campaign,* pp. 308–12.

29. Nichols, *Reno Court,* pp. 79, 80, 160, 162, 163, 365, 408, 409, 444, 445, 490, 642; duBois, *Kick the Dead Lion,* p. 45; Edgerly, "A Narrative," pp. 9, 10, NYPL; Holmes, "Little Big Horn," *RR* 7 (1): 4; W. S. Edgerly to E. S. Godfrey, January 17, 1886, typescript, Dustin Collection, LBBNM;

Gray, *Custer's Last Campaign,* pp. 292, 312–18, 320–26; Hammer, *Custer,* pp. 143, 144; Hutton, *Custer Reader,* pp. 294, 295.

30. Nichols, *Reno Court,* p. 114–16; Hammer, *Custer,* pp. 231, 232; Sills, "Messages," *CBHMA,* 1990, p. 42; Horn, "Custer's Turn," *RR* 8 (1): 17–21; T. E. O'Neil, *Decision,* p. 58.

31. Horn, "Custer's Turn," *RR* 8 (1): 20, 21, 31; Hutton, *Custer and His Times,* p. 117; T. E. O'Neil, *Decision,* p. 58; Darling, *Blunder,* pp. 206–9.

32. Gray, *Custer's Last Campaign,* pp. 334–36; Nichols, *Reno Court,* pp. 43, 337, 338, 343; Horn, "Custer's Turn," *RR* 8 (1): 31; duBois, *Kick the Dead Lion,* p. 78; Hammer, *Custer,* pp. 155, 156; Kanipe, "Tarheel," *RR* 7 (2): 28.

33. Fox, *Archaeology,* p. 312; Edgerly, "A Narrative," pp. 17, 18, NYPL; Gray, *Custer's Last Campaign,* pp. 342–46, 354; Hammer, *Custer,* p. 104n; Darling, *Blunder,* pp. 210, 212, 215; Nichols, *Reno Court,* p. 388; Sills, "Crow Scouts," *CBHMA,* 1991, pp. 15, 16; Walter M. Camp to Dennis Lynch, January 2, 1909, and Walter M. Camp to Charles A. Woodruff, April 22, 1910, Camp Collection, LBBNM.

34. Michno, *Mystery,* p. 39; Hardorff, *Hokahey!,* p. 71; Gray, *Custer's Last Campaign,* pp. 268–69; Nichols, *Reno Court,* p. 549; Edward S. Luce to Charles Kuhlman, February 28, 1940, Kuhlman Papers, MTHS.

35. Fox, *Archaeology,* p. 141; Pohanka, "Myles Keogh," *Military Images* (1986): 15, 18, 20, 22.

36. Fox, *Archaeology,* p. 141; T. E. O'Neil, *Custer to the Little Big Horn,* p. 18; Fougera, *With Custer's Cavalry,* p. 132; Hammer, *Custer,* p. 207; Pohanka, "George Yates," *GG* 8: 11, 14–16.

37. Gray, *Custer's Last Campaign,* pp. 354, 355, 357; Graham, *Custer Myth,* p. 19; Hammer, *Custer,* pp. 166, 167; Hedley, " 'PS Bring Pacs,' " *CBHMA,* 1990, p. 52.

38. Fox, *Archaeology,* pp. 316, 317; T. E. O'Neil, *Decision,* p. 63; Gray, *Custer's Last Campaign,* pp. 358, 360.

39. Fox, *Archaeology,* pp. 142, 280, 284, 285, 290, 310, 317; T. E. O'Neil, *Decision,* p. 63; Gray, *Custer's Last Campaign,* pp. 362–64; Headly, " 'PS Bring Pacs,' " *CBHMA,* 1990, pp. 52, 55; Walter M. Camp to Charles A. Woodruff, April 22, 1910, Camp Collection, LBBNM.

40. Hardorff, *Lakota,* pp. 43n, 155–57; Urwin and Fagan, *Custer,* p. 235; T. E. O'Neil, *Decision,* p. 64; Fox, *Archaeology,* pp. 284, 318; J. W. Pope to E. S. Godfrey, January 9, 1892, Godfrey Family Papers, USAMHI; Nichols, *Reno Court,* p. 549; Hardorff, *Hokahey!,* p. 71; Gray, "Vindication," *CBHMA,* 1990, p. 22.

41. Fox, *Archaeology,* pp. 173–75; Sills, "Messages," *CBHMA,* 1990, p. 45.

42. Best description of Yates's wing's movement and initial combat is in Fox, *Archaeology,* pp. 173–80, 182, 183, 186, 187, 191, 192, 303–6; Buecker, "Clark's Sioux War Report," *GG* 7: 12, 18; T. E. O'Neil, *Decision,* p. 66; Graham, *Custer Myth,* p. 103.

43. Graham, *Custer Myth,* p. 54; Hutton, *Custer Reader,* pp. 338, 339; Scott et al. *Archaeological Perspectives,* p. 121; Scott and Fox, *Archaeological Insights,* pp. 45, 46, 108, 109; Urwin and Fagan, *Custer,* pp. 161, 162; Hammer, *Custer,* pp. 207, 215; Michno, *Mystery,* p. 50; Fox, *Archaeology,* pp. 251, 253, 299, 301, 302; Burdick, *David F. Barry's Indian Notes,* p. 27; Ambrose, *Crazy Horse,* pp. 14, 38; Bowen, "Notes," USAMHI.

44. Fox, *Archaeology,* pp. 146–47, 151, 153–55, 257, 258; Wells, "Little Big Horn," *GG* 5: 10; T. E. O'Neil, *Decision,* p. 68; Sills, "Recruits," *GG* 5: 7; Hardorff, *Lakota,* p. 44; Nichols, *Reno Court,* p. 67.

45. Finerty, *War-Path,* p. 132; Upton, *Custer Adventure,* p. 80; Hardorff, *Hokahey!,* pp. 61, 62, 69, 70, 74; Fox, *Archaeology,* pp. 157–60, 162.

46. Hammer, *Custer,* pp. 63, 96n; Fox, *Archaeology,* pp. 163–65; Hutton, *Custer Reader,* pp. 339, 340; Upton, *Custer Adventure,* pp. 81, 82; Hardorff, *Custer Battle Casualties,* p. 113.

47. Evidence of the panic among Keogh's three companies is convincing; see Hammer, *Custer,* pp. 95n, 102, 199, 199n, 200, 201, 211; Hardorff, *Lakota,* pp. 31, 31n, 69n, 86, 146, 167, 182; Hardorff, *Custer Battle Casualties,* pp. 108, 109, 114–16; Fox, *Archaeology,* pp. 166–72, 220, 229; statements of Two Eagles, Lone Bear, Hollow Horn Bear, Lights, and Thunder Hawks, Camp Collection, LBBNM; Wells, "Little Big Horn," *GG* 5: 13, 17.

48. Fox, *Archaeology,* pp. 195, 196; Wells, "Little Big Horn," *GG* 5: 13, 14; Trinque, "Defense," *RR* 8 (2): 25, 26.

49. Trinque, "Defense," *RR* 8(2): pp. 25, 26; Fox, *Archaeology,* pp. 196, 198; T. E. O'Neil, *Passing,* p. 17; Hutton, *Custer Reader,* p. 310; Hutton, *Custer and His Times,* pp. 164–66; Graham, *Custer's Battle Flag,* pp. 2, 3, 6, 11; Hardorff, *Custer Battle Casualties,* pp. 98–107, 112–17, 121, 122; Hammer, *Custer,* pp. 76, 77, 136, 250, 250n.

50. Fox, *Archaeology,* pp. 198–201; Trinque, "Defense," *RR* 8 (2):26, 27; Hammer, *Custer,* pp. 210, 213; Kuhlman, *Legend,* p. 3.

51. Hammer, *Custer,* pp. 72, 207; Fox, *Archaeology,* pp. 212–216, 218; Kuhlman, *Legend,* p. 8; Hardorff, *Hokahey!,* pp. 75, 76; Nichols, *Reno Court,* pp. 9, 237, 322–24; Scott et al., *Archaeological Perspectives,* pp. 34, 35, 46–48; Moore and Donahue, "Gibbon's Report," *GG* 7:30; Schneider, *Freeman Journal,* p. 65; Miller, *Custer's Fall,* p. 217.

52. Fox, *Archaeology,* pp. 15, 242, 247, 263, 264, 267–69, 322; Stewart, *Custer's Luck,* pp. 487–95; Hammer, *Custer,* p. 28; Connell, *Son,* p. 13; Hardorff, *Lakota,* p. 133.

53. Much detail of the fight on Reno Hill is in Nichols, *Reno Court,* passim; see also, Carroll, *Four on Custer,* pp. 46, 47; Hammer, *Custer,* pp. 62, 63, 71, 136, 208; Hutton, *Custer Reader,* pp. 296, 308; Fougera, *With Custer's Cavalry,* pp. 269, 270; Edgerly, "A Narrative," p. 11, 14, NYPL; Hunt, *I Fought,* pp. 76, 77, 101, 104, 105; Carroll, *Benteen-Goldin,* p. 207; Liddic, *I Buried Custer,* p. 18.

54. Willert, *March,* pp. 6–10; Schneider, *Freeman Journal,* pp. 56, 57; Hammer, *Custer,* pp. 242, 243.

55. Nichols, *Reno Court,* p. 535; Hammer, *Custer,* pp. 68, 79, 121, 248; Fougera, *With Custer's Cavalry,* pp. 271, 272; Liddic, *I Buried Custer,* p. 21; Moore and Donahue, "Gibbon's Route," *GG* 7: 27, 29, 31; Scott et al., *Archaeological Perspectives,* p. 84; Carroll, *Benteen-Goldin,* p. 155.

56. Carroll, *Custer and His Times,* pp. 42, 43; Brust, "Fouch," *GG* 7: 9; Michno, "Space Warp," *RR* 8 (1): 24; Jacob Adams to E. S. Godfrey, January 2, 1927, Godfrey Collection, LBBNM; T. E. O'Neil, *Passing,* p. 3; duBois, *Kick the Dead Lion,* pp. 46, 100n.

57. Hunt, *I Fought,* p. 1; Marquis, *Custer, Cavalry & Crows,* p. 82; McMurry, Correspondence, USAMHI; Hutton, *Custer Reader,* pp. 310, 317, 318; Hammer, *Custer,* p. 68; Miller, *Custer's Fall,* p. 255; Hardorff, *Hokahey!,* p. 130; White Swan's Story, Camp Collection, LBBNM; Lawrence, *His Very Silence,* pp. 39, 45; T. M. McDougall to E. S. Godfrey, May 18, 1909, typescript, Hagner Papers, NYPL.

58. T. E. O'Neil, "Newspapers," *NLBHA* 27 (9): 4, 6; Utley, *Cavalier,* p. 4; Hutton, *Custer Reader,* pp. 387, 388; Brininstool, *Troopers,* p. 34; "Some Monroe Memories," *BHCL,* pp. 10, 11; *New York Times,* July 7, 8, 1876; *Monroe Commercial,* July 18, 1876; *Monroe Evening News,* June 25, 1951, June 25, 1976.

59. Custer, *Boots,* p. 255; Fougera, *With Custer's Cavalry,* pp. 263–66; Frost, *General Custer's Libbie,* p. 227; Stallard, *Glittering Misery,* p. 41; Reynolds, *Civil War,* p. xi.

60. Hardorff, *Custer Battle Casualties,* pp. 41, 42, 44, 48; Barnard, "Custer Burial," *CBHMA,* 1992, p. 70; Hamilton, *Custer,* p. 253n; *Monroe Evening News,* September 18, 1948.

61. EBC to John Schofield, n.d. [c. 1877], EBC Collection, MCLS; Reynolds, *Civil War,* pp. 26, 35; Hedren, pp. 270, 271; Barnard, "Custer Burial," *CBHMA,* 1992, p. 73; Charles C. Martin to E. S. Godfrey, June 3, 1926, Godfrey Collection, LBBNM.

62. Leckie, *Elizabeth Bacon Custer,* p. xx, chap. 13 and 14; Nichols, *Reno Court,* passim; Hammer, *Custer,* p. 238; Hutton, *Custer and His Times,* pp. 143, 144; Custer, *Following,* p. xii.

63. Leckie, *Elizabeth Bacon Custer,* chap. 14 and 15, p. 307; A. T. O'Neil, "Custer's Recollections," p. 23; Frost, *General Custer's Libbie,* p. 325.

64. Dippie, *Custer's Last Stand,* passim; Whittaker, *Life,* passim; Utley, *Cavalier,* pp. 52, 56.

65. Utley, *Cavalier,* p. 210; Hutton, *Custer Reader,* p. 396.

66. Utley, *Cavalier,* pp. 211–12.

BIBLIOGRAPHY

UNPUBLISHED SOURCES

Alexander, Edward Porter. Papers. Southern Historical Collection. Wilson Library, University of North Carolina, Chapel Hill.

Alger, Russel A. Papers. William L. Clements Library, University of Michigan, Ann Arbor.

Andrews, Ray E., M.D. Interview with the author, December 14, 1994.

Baird, William. "Reminiscence." Baird Family Papers. Bentley Historical Library, University of Michigan, Ann Arbor.

Baker, I. Norval. Diary. *Civil War Times Illustrated* Collection. United States Army Military History Institute, Carlisle Barracks, Pa.

Ball, William. Letters. Ed Ridgeway Collection. Regional History Collections. Western Michigan University, Kalamazoo, Mich.

Barbour, George W. Diary. Bentley Historical Library, University of Michigan, Ann Arbor.

Barclay, Alexander. Letters. University Library, Washington and Lee University, Lexington, Va.

Barry, David F. Collection. Little Big Horn Battlefield National Monument Archives, Crow Agency, Mont.

Battle of Little Big Horn Papers. United States Army Military History Institute, Carlisle Barracks, Pa.

Benteen, Frederick W. Papers. United States Army Military History Institute, Carlisle Barracks, Pa.

Bowen, William H. C. "Notes on Custer Battle and Field." William H. C. Bowen Papers. United States Army Military History Institute, Carlisle Barracks, Pa.

———. Papers. United States Army Military History Institute, Carlisle Barracks, Pa.

Bradley, Luther P. Papers. United States Army Military History Institute, Carlisle Barracks, Pa.

Brininstool, E. A., to Col. Chas. E. T. Lull, June 22, 1932. Order of the Indian Wars Collection. United States Army Military History Institute, Carlisle Barracks, Pa.

Buck Family Papers. Bentley Historical Library, University of Michigan, Ann Arbor.

Camp, Walter M. Collection. Little Big Horn Battlefield National Monument Archives, Crow Agency, Mont.

Carr, Henry C. Diary, April 5, 1864–February 10, 1865 (typescript). Civil War Miscellaneous Collection. United States Army Military History Institute, Carlisle Barracks, Pa.

Christiancy-Pickett Papers. United States Army Military History Institute, Carlisle Barracks, Pa.

Clark, Benjamin. Clark Historical Library, Central Michigan University, Mount Pleasant, Mich. Letter of July 17, 1863.

Clark, John A. Papers. Schoff Civil War Collection. William L. Clements Library, University of Michigan, Ann Arbor.

Clapp, Albert A. Diary. *Civil War Times Illustrated* Collection. United States Army Military History Institute, Carlisle Barracks, Pa.

Compiled Records Showing Service of Military Units in Volunteer Union Organizations, Records Group 94 and 407, M 594. National Archives, Washington, D.C. Compiled Service Records, Records Group 109. National Archives, Washington, D.C.

Comte, Victor E. Papers (typescripts). Bentley Historical Library, University of Michigan, Ann Arbor.

Corliss, A. W. "The Yellowstone Expedition of 1873, Under Gen. D. S. Stanley, U.S.A." Indian Wars Miscellaneous Collection. United States Army Military History Institute, Carlisle Barracks, Pa.

Corselius, George. Papers. Bentley Historical Library, University of Michigan, Ann Arbor.

Crowninshield, Caspar. Papers. Massachusetts Historical Society, Boston.

Custer, Elizabeth B. Correspondence. Monroe County Library System, Monroe, Mich.

Custer, Elizabeth Bacon. Journal. Western Americana Collection. Beineke Rare Book and Manuscript Library, Yale University, New Haven, Conn.

Custer, G. A. Letters. Marguerite Merington Papers. New York Public Library.

Custer, General George A. Collection. Monroe County Historical Museum Archives, Monroe, Mich.

Custer, George A. Correspondence and Orders. Monroe County Library System, Monroe, Mich.

———. Correspondence and Orders, 1856–1876. Little Big Horn Battlefield National Monument Archives, Crow Agency, Mont.

———. Letters. Local History Division. Rochester Public Library, Rochester, N.Y.

———. Letters. United States Military Academy Library, West Point, N.Y.

Custer, George Armstrong. Letter. Montana Historical Society Library and Archives, Helena, Mont.

———. Letter, October 29, 1864. Bentley Historical Library, University of Michigan, Ann Arbor.

———. Letters. S-898–899. Western Americana Collection. Beineke Rare Book and Manuscript Library, Yale University, New Haven, Conn.

————, to "Dear Mollie." Letters. S-362. Western Americana Collection. Beineke Rare Book and Manuscript Library, Yale University, New Haven, Conn.

Del Vecchio, Richard, "With the First New York Dragoons: From the Letters of Jared L. Ainsworth." Jared L. Ainsworth Papers. Harrisburg Civil War Round Table Collection. United States Army Military History Institute, Carlisle Barracks, Pa.

Douglass-Nellis Family Papers. Bentley Historical Library, University of Michigan, Ann Arbor.

Dustin, Fred. Collection. Little Big Horn Battlefield National Monument Archives, Crow Agency, Mont.

Dye, Nathan G. Diary. William R. Perkins Library, Duke University, Durham, N.C.

Edgerly, W. S. "Narrative of the March of General Geo. A. Custer." Francis P. Hagner Papers. New York Public Library.

Elder, John Adams. Papers. William R. Perkins Library, Duke University, Durham, N.C.

Elliott Nellie Lock and Virginia Burleson. Interview with author, July 24, 1994.

Farr, Charles R. Diary. United States Army Military History Institute, Carlisle Barracks, Pa.

Ferguson, J. D. "Memoranda of the Itinerary and Operations of Major General Fitz. Lee's Cavalry Division of the Army of Northern Virginia, from May 4th to October 15, 1864, Inclusive by J. D. Ferguson Major & Asst. Adjutant General." William R. Perkins Library, Duke University, Durham, N.C.

Fiala, Anthony. "Records of Anthony Fiala Quar. M. Serg. and First Lieut, First New York (Lincoln) Cavalry." *Civil War Times Illustrated* Collection. United States Army Military History Institute, Carlisle Barracks, Pa.

Field Records of Hospitals, 1821–1912, Records Group 94, Records of the Adjutant General's Office, NARA. National Archives, Washington, D.C.

Fifth Michigan Cavalry File. Gettysburg National Military Park Library, Gettysburg, Pa.

First Michigan Cavalry File. Gettysburg National Military Park Library, Gettysburg, Pa.

Fisk, William. Letters. *Civil War Times Illustrated* Collection. United States Army Military History Institute, Carlisle Barracks, Pa.

Forsyth, John. Papers. William L. Clements Library, University of Michigan, Ann Arbor.

Frost, Dr. Lawrence A. Collection of Custeriana. Monroe County Historical Museum Archives, Monroe, Mich.

Furst, Luther C. Diary. Harrisburg Civil War Round Table Collection. United States Army Military History Institute, Carlisle Barracks, Pa.

Glidden, Ruth Gibson Papers. Montana Historical Society Library and Archives, Helena, Mont.

Godfrey, Edward, and C. A. Bach. Correspondence. Order of the Indian Wars Collection. United States Army Military History Institute, Carlisle Barracks, Pa.

Godfrey, Edward S. Collection. Little Big Horn Battlefield National Monument Archives, Crow Agency, Mont.

————. "Narrative of Part of the Little Big Horn—Lt. Hare's Participation." Order of the Indian Wars Collection. United States Army Military History Institute, Carlisle Barracks, Pa.

————. "Remarks of Brig. Gen. Edw. S. Godfrey at Annual Dinner of Order of Indian Wars, January 25, 1930." Order of the Indian Wars Collection. United States Army Military History Institute, Carlisle Barracks, Pa.

Godfrey Family Papers. United States Army Military History Institute, Carlisle Barracks, Pa.

Goldin, Theodore W. Papers. United States Army Military History Institute, Carlisle Barracks, Pa.

Greene, L. D. "Soldiering on the 'Old Frontier': Custer's Last Campaign." Order of the Indian Wars Collection. United States Army Military History Institute, Carlisle Barracks, Pa.

Hagner, Francis R. Papers. New York Public Library.

Hall, Clark B. Letter to the author, February 14, 1994.

Hannaford, Roger. "Reminiscences." Cincinnati Historical Society, Cincinnati, Ohio.

Hare, Luther R. Family papers. United States Army Military History Institute, Carlisle Barracks, Pa.

Harrington, George L. Diary. Dr. Allen Giddings Collection. Regional History Collections. Western Michigan University, Kalamazoo, Mich.

Haskell, John C. "Memoir" (typescript). William R. Perkins Library, Duke University Durham, N.C.

Hayes, Rutherford B. Papers. Rutherford B. Hayes Presidential Center, Fremont, Ohio.

Hooker, Joseph. Papers. Huntington Library, San Marino, Calif.

Humphrey, Milton W. Diary. Alderman Library, University of Virginia, Charlottesville.

Hunt, George W. "Custer and His Red Necks: A Brief Sketch of Incidents of the Civil War of 61 & 65." William L. Clements Library, University of Michigan, Ann Arbor.

Hurless, John W., Jr. "Where Was General Custer Really Born" (typescript). Monroe County Library System, Monroe, Mich.

Ireland, Oscar Brown. Papers. William R. Perkins Library, Duke University, Durham, N.C.

Ives, Lewis T. "Sketch of Genl. Custer." Special Collections Dartmouth College Library.

Jessup, Joseph. Civil War letters, 1861–1865. Bentley Historical Library, University of Michigan, Ann Arbor.

Kanipe, Daniel A. Memoirs and postwar correspondence on Little Big Horn. Order of the Indian Wars Collection. United States Army Military History Institute, Carlisle Barracks, Pa.

Kay, John B. Papers. Bentley Historical Library, University of Michigan, Ann Arbor.

Keiser, Henry. Diary. Harrisburg Civil War Round Table Collection. United States Army Military History Institute, Carlisle Barracks, Pa.

Kern, Todd. Interview with the author, July 24, 1994.

Kidd, James Harvey. Papers. Bentley Historical Library, University of Michigan, Ann Arbor.

Kuhlman, Charles. Papers. Montana Historical Society Library and Archives, Helena, Mont.

Longstreet, James. Papers. Emory University, Atlanta, Ga.

———. Papers. Georgia Department of Archives and History, Atlanta, Ga.

Macomber, Dexter M. Diary (typescript). Clark Historical Library, Central Michigan University, Mount Pleasant, Mich.

Mann, Wayne C. Letters to the author.

Martin, William H. Papers. Harrisburg Civil War Round Table Collection. United States Army Military History Institute, Carlisle Barracks, Pa.

Mattoon, Gershom W. Letter. Bentley Historical Library, University of Michigan, Ann Arbor.

McIntosh, Donald. Papers. United States Army Military History Institute, Carlisle Barracks, Pa.

McMurry, George J. Correspondence on the 7th U.S. Cavalry at Little Big Horn Burial Detail, 1876. Order of the Indian Wars Collection. United States Army Military History Institute, Carlisle Barracks, Pa.

Mechling, Henry. Papers. United States Army Military History Institute, Carlisle Barracks, Pa.

Military Service Records of George Armstrong Custer, 1856–1876. Records of the Adjutant General's Office, 1783–1917, Records Group 94. National Archives, Washington, D.C.

Monaghan, J. W. Diary (typescript). Monaghan Family Papers. Bentley Historical Library, University of Michigan, Ann Arbor.

Morey, John Rising. Papers. Bentley Historical Library, University of Michigan, Ann Arbor.

Morrison, Henry R. Letters and clippings. *Civil War Times Illustrated* Collection. United States Army Military History Institute, Carlisle Barracks, Pa.

Murphy, James Madison. Papers. William R. Perkins Library, Duke University, Durham, N.C.

O'Brien Family Papers. Bentley Historical Library, University of Michigan, Ann Arbor.

Official Register of the Officers and Cadets of the U.S. Military Academy, West

Point, N.Y., 1851–70. United States Military Academy Archives, West Point, N.Y.

O'Neil, Alice T. "Custer Recollections." Unpublished manuscript.

Other Collections Correspondence (Section M). Little Big Horn Battlefield National Monument Archives, Crow Agency, Mont.

Pell, Colonel Richard F., U.S. Army, Ret. Interview with the author, July 23, 1994.

Pleasonton, Alfred. Papers. Library of Congress, Washington, D.C.

Pohanka, Brian. Private collection.

Post Orders, No. 5, December 1, 1856 to February 23, 1861. United States Military Academy Archives, West Point, N.Y.

Register of Delinquencies, 1856–1861. United States Military Academy Archives, West Point, N.Y.

Register of Merit, 1853 to 1865, No. 3. United States Military Academy Archives, West Point, N.Y.

Returns from U. S. Military Posts 1800–1916: Fort A. Lincoln, N. Dak., December 1872–December 1880. M 617, Roll 618. National Archives, Washington, D.C.

Richmond, Rebecca L. Letters. Lewis Leigh Collection. United States Army Military History Institute, Carlisle Barracks, Pa.

Robertson, John. "Fifth Cavalry." Bentley Historical Library, University of Michigan, Ann Arbor.

Rowe, James D. "Camp Tales of a Union Soldier." Rowe Family Papers. Bentley Historical Library, University of Michigan, Ann Arbor.

Ryan, John. "Ten Years with Gen. Custer Among the Indians." Little Big Horn Battlefield National Monument Archives, Crow Agency, Mont.

Sanford, Charles Addison. Papers. William R. Perkins Library, Duke University, Durham, N.C.

Schorn, Charles. Papers. Civil War Miscellaneous Collection. United States Army Military History Institute, Carlisle Barracks, Pa.

Scott, Hugh L. Papers. United States Army Military History Institute, Carlisle Barracks, Pa.

Seventh Michigan Cavalry File. Gettysburg National Military Park Library, Gettysburg, Pa.

Sheridan, Philip H. Report, November 25, 1876, U.S. War Department, Division of the Missouri Records. National Archives, Washington, D.C.

Siebert, Jacob. Letters. Seibert Family Papers. Harrisburg Civil War Round Table Collection. United States Army Military History Institute, Carlisle Barracks, Pa.

Sixth Michigan Cavalry File. Gettysburg National Military Park Library, Gettysburg, Pa.

Special Orders, AGO, Engineer Orders, Mil. Acad. Orders, July–December 1861, No. 21. United States Military Academy Archives, West Point, N.Y.

Sperry, J. L. Papers. William R. Perkins Library, Duke University, Durham, N.C.

Stone, Addison Ray. Correspondence. Stone Family Papers. Bentley Historical Library, University of Michigan, Ann Arbor.

Suter, John P. Papers. Harrisburg Civil War Round Table Collection. United States Army Military History Institute, Carlisle Barracks, Pa.

Tarbell, Doctor. Diary, May 16–27, 1864. Civil War Miscellaneous Collection. United States Army Military History Institute, Carlisle Barracks, Pa.

Thayer, Edward A. Civil War Correspondence. Samuel Thayer Collection. New Hampshire Historical Society, Concord, N.H.

Thompson, Peter. "Custer's Last Fight: The Experience of a Private Soldier in the Custer Massacar" (typescript). Order of the Indian Wars Collection. United States Army Military History Institute, Carlisle Barracks, Pa.

Thompson, Stephen W. Papers. William R. Perkins Library, Duke University, Durham, N.C.

Thornton, Richard L. Letter to Allan L. Tischler, October 12, 1994 (in author's possession).

Tischler, Allan. Interview with the author, August 19, 1994.

———. Letters to author, June–November 1994.

U.S. Army Generals' Reports of Civil War Service, 1864–1886; Records of the Adjutant General's Office, 1780's–1917, Records Group 94, M 1098. National Archives, Washington, D.C.

Varnum, Charles A. "Memoirs of Service." Indian Wars Miscellaneous Collection. United States Army Military History Institute, Carlisle Barracks, Pa.

Walker, J. P. "Custer's Fatal Campaign." Dartmouth College Library, Hanover, N.H.

Waltz, Sylvester. Diaries. George A. Custer Collection. Monroe County Historical Museum Archives, Monroe, Mich.

Wells, William. Papers. Special Collections. University of Vermont Library, Burlington, Vt.

Whitaker, Edward W. Civil War Letters (typescript). Babcock Library, Ashford, Conn.

Whittle, B. F. Notebook, September 12, 1864–February 18, 1865. Alderman Library, University of Virginia, Charlottesville.

Woodbury, Eri D. Papers. Special Collections, Dartmouth College Library, Hanover, N.H.

NEWSPAPERS

Billings Gazette
Cadiz Republican
Charlotte Observer

Charlottesville Daily Progress
Detroit Advertiser & Tribune
Detroit Free Press
Monroe Commercial
Monroe Democrat
Monroe Evening News
National Tribune
New York Herald
New York Times
Toledo Blade
Washington Star
Winchester Star

PUBLISHED SOURCES

Agassiz, George R., ed. *Meade's Headquarters, 1863–1865: Letters of Colonel Theodore Lyman from the Wilderness to Appomattox.* Boston: Atlantic Monthly Press, 1922.

Alexander, Ted. "Gettysburg Cavalry Operations, June 27–July 3, 1863." *Blue & Gray Magazine* 6, no. 1 (October 1988).

Allen, Stanton P. *Down in Dixie: Life in a Cavalry Regiment in the War Days from the Wilderness to Appomattox.* Boston: D. Lothrop Co., 1893.

Ambrose, Stephen E. *Crazy Horse and Custer: The Parallel Lives of Two American Warriors.* Garden City, N.Y.: Doubleday & Co., 1975.

The Annals of the War Written by Leading Participants North and South. Reprint, Dayton: Morningside House, 1988.

Armes, George A. *Ups and Downs of an Army Officer.* Washington, D.C.: n.p., 1900.

Arner, Frederick B. *The Mutiny at Brandy Station: The Last Battle of the Hooker Brigade.* Kensington, Md.: Bates & Blood Press, 1993.

Athearn, Robert G., ed. "The Civil War Diary of John Wilson Phillips." *Virginia Magazine of History and Biography* 62 (1954).

Badwey, John D. "Ancient Milk Bill Stirs Interest in Kansas Role of General Custer." *Wichita Eagle Magazine,* July 1, 1956.

Bakeless, John. "The Mystery of Appomattox." *Civil War Times Illustrated* 9, no. 3 (June 1970).

Baltz, Louis J., III. *The Battle of Cold Harbor May 27–June 13, 1864.* Lynchburg, Va.: H. E. Howard, 1994.

Barnard, Sandy. "Custer's Burial Revisited: West Point, 1877." *6th Annual Symposium Custer Battlefield Historical & Museum Assn., Inc.,* 1992.

Barrett, O. S. *Reminiscences, Incidents, Battles, Marches and Camp Life of the Old 4th Michigan Infantry in War of Rebellion, 1861 to 1864.* Detroit: W. S. Ostler, 1888.

Barry, David. *Forty Years in Washington.* Reprint, New York: Beekman Publishers, 1974.

Beach, William H. *The First New York (Lincoln) Cavalry from April 19, 1861 to July 7, 1865*. Reprint, Annandale, Va.: Bacon Race Books, 1988.

Bearss, Ed, and Chris Calkins. *Battle of Five Forks*. Lynchburg, Va.: H. E. Howard, 1985.

Beauregard, Erving E. "The General and the Politician: Custer & Bingham." *Blue & Gray Magazine* 6, no. 1 (October 1988).

Bell, Raymond Martin. *The Ancestry of Maria Ward Kilpatrick Custer 1807–1882*. Washington, Pa.: Raymond Martin Bell, 1992.

Benedict, G. G. *Vermont in the Civil War: A History of the Part Taken by the Vermont Soldiers and Sailors in the War for the Union, 1861–5*. 2 vols. Burlington, Vt.: Free Press Association, 1886–1888.

Berthong, Donald J. *The Southern Cheyennes*. Paperback, Norman: University of Oklahoma Press, 1979.

Blackford, W. W. *War Years with Jeb Stuart*. New York: Charles Scribner's Sons, 1946.

Boudrye, Louis N. *Historic Records of the Fifth New York Cavalry, First Ira Harris Guard*. Albany, N.Y.: S. R. Gray, 1865.

Bowen, J. R. *Regimental History of the First New York Dragoons (Originally the 130th N.Y. Vol. Infantry) During Three Years of Active Service in the Great Civil War*. N.p.: J. R. Bowen, 1900.

Brewer, Wilmon. "The Capture of General Custer's Love Letters." *Yankee Magazine*, March 1969.

———. *Looking Backwards*, vol. 1. Francestown, N.H.: Marshall Jones Co., 1985.

Brill, Charles J. *Conquest of the Southern Plains: Uncensored Narrative of the Battle of the Washita and Custer's Southern Campaign*. Oklahoma City: Golden Saga Publishers, 1938.

Brininstool, E. A. *Troopers with Custer: Historic Incidents of the Battle of the Little Big Horn*. New York: Bonanza Books, 1952.

Brown, Kent Masterson. *Cushing of Gettysburg: The Story of a Union Artillery Commander*. Lexington: University Press of Kentucky, 1993.

Brust, James S. "Baldwin Talks with Reno, Writes About Custer's Final Battle." *Greasy Grass* 9 (May 1993).

———. "The Earliest Photograph of Custer Battlefield," *6th Annual Symposium Custer Battlefield Historical & Museum Assn., Inc.*, 1992.

———. "Fouch Photo May Be the First." *Greasy Grass* 7 (May 1991).

Buckeridge, J. O. *Lincoln's Choice*. Harrisburg, Pa.: Stackpole Co. 1956.

Buecker, Thomas R. "Lt. William Philo Clark's Sioux War Report and Little Big Horn Map." *Greasy Grass* 7 (May 1991).

———, ed. "A Surgeon at the Little Big Horn: The Letters of Dr. Holmes R. Paulding." *Montana: The Magazine Of Western History* 32, no. 4 (Autumn 1982).

Burdick, Usher L. *David F. Barry's Indian Notes on "The Custer Battle."* Baltimore: Wirth Brothers, 1949.

Burkey, Blaine. *Custer, Come at Once!* Chicago: Thomas More Press, 1976.

Busey, John W., and David G. Martin. *Regimental Strengths at Gettysburg.* Baltimore: Gateway Press, 1982.

Bush, Garry L. "Sixth Michigan Cavalry at Falling Waters: The End of the Gettysburg Campaign." *Gettysburg: Historical Articles of Lasting Interest,* no. 9 (July 1993).

Bushong, Millard Kessler, and Dean McKain. *Fightin' Tom Rosser, C.S.A.* Shippensburg, Pa.: Beidel Printing House, 1983.

Calhoun, Samuel W. "Did Custer Disobey?" *Greasy Grass* 6 (May 1990).

Calkins, Chris. "The Battle of Five Forks: Final Push for the South Side." *Blue & Gray Magazine* 9, no. 4 (April 1992).

———. *The Battles of Appomattox Station and Appomattox Court House April 8–9, 1865.* Lynchburg, Va.: H. E. Howard, 1987.

———. "With Shouts of Triumph and Trumpets Blowing: George Custer Versus Rufus Barringer at Namozine Church, April 3, 1865." *Blue & Gray Magazine* 7, no. 6 (August 1990).

Carpenter, George N. *History of the Eighth Regiment Vermont Volunteers, 1861–1865.* Boston: Press of Deland & Barta, 1886.

Carroll, John M. *Custer in the Civil War: His Unfinished Memoirs.* San Rafael, Calif.: Presidio Press, 1977.

———. *Custer's Cavalry Occupation of Hempstead & Austin, Texas: The History of Custer's Headquarters Building.* Glendale, Calif.: Arthur H. Clark Co., 1983.

———. *Four on Custer by Carroll.* New Brunswick, N.J.: Guidon Press, 1976.

———, ed. *The Benteen-Goldin Letters on Custer and His Last Battle.* Paperback, Lincoln and London: University of Nebraska Press, 1991.

———, ed. *Camp Talk: The Very Private Letters of Frederick W. Benteen of the 7th U.S. Cavalry to his Wife 1871 to 1888.* Mattituck, N.Y., and Bryan, Tex.: J. M. Carroll & Co., 1983.

———, ed. *Custer and His Times: Book Two.* Fort Worth: Little Big Horn Associates, 1984.

———, ed. *Custer in Texas: An Interrupted Narrative.* New York: Sol Lewis & Liveright, 1975.

———, ed. *General Custer and the Battle of the Washita: The Federal View.* Bryan, Tex.: Guidon Press, 1978.

———, ed. *General Custer and New Rumley, Ohio.* Bryan, Tex.: privately printed, 1978.

———, ed. *They Rode with Custer: A Biographical Directory of the Men That Rode with General George A. Custer.* Mattituck, N.Y.: J. M. Carroll & Co., 1993.

Carroll, John M., and Lawrence A. Frost. *Private Theodore Ewert's Diary of the Black Hills Expedition of 1874.* Piscataway, N.J.: Consultant Resources, 1976.

Carroll, John M., and W. Donald Horn, eds. *Custer Genealogies.* Bryan, Tex.: Guidon Press, n.d.

Cauble, Frank P. *The Surrender Proceedings: April 9, 1865 Appomattox Court House.* Lynchburg, Va.: H. E. Howard, 1987.

Chandler, Melbourne C. *Of Garry Owen in Glory.* Annandale, Va.: Turnpike Press, 1960.

Cheney, Norval. *History of the Ninth Regiment, New York Volunteer Cavalry, War of 1861 to 1865.* Poland Center, N.Y.: Martin Merz & Son, 1901.

Church, Robert. "Did Custer Believe His Scouts?" *5th Annual Symposium Custer Battlefield Historical & Museum Assn., Inc.,* 1991.

Civil War: Sketches and Incidents. Military Order of the Loyal Legion of the United States, Nebraska. Reprint, Wilmington, N.C.: Broadfoot Publishing Co., 1992.

Clark, Archie L. "John Maguire Butte's 'Belasco.' " *Montana: The Magazine of Western History* 2, no. 1 (January 1952).

Clark, Orton S. *The One Hundred and Sixteenth Regiment of New York State Volunteers.* Buffalo: Printing House of Matthews & Warren, 1868.

Coddington, Edwin B. *The Gettysburg Campaign: A Study in Command.* New York: Charles Scribner's Sons, 1968.

Colt, Margaretta Barton. *Defend the Valley: A Shenandoah Family in the Civil War.* New York: Orion Books, 1994.

Confederate Veteran. Reprint, Wilmington, N.C.: Broadfoot Publishing Co., 1987–1988.

Connell, Evan S. *Son of the Morning Star.* San Francisco: North Point Press, 1984.

Conrad, W. P., and Ted Alexander. *When War Passed This Way.* Shippensburg, Pa.: Beidel Printing House, 1982.

Crackel, Theodore J. "Custer's Kentucky: General George Armstrong Custer and Elizabethtown, Kentucky, 1871–1873." *Filson Club History Quarterly* 48 (April 1974).

Crary, Catherine S. *Dear Belle: Letters from a Cadet & Officer to his Sweetheart, 1858–1865.* Middletown, Conn.: Wesleyan University Press, 1965.

Croffut, W. A., and John M. Morrison. *The Military and Civil History of Connecticut During the War of 1861–65.* New York: Ledyard Bill, 1869.

Crowninshield, Benjamin W. "Sheridan at Winchester." *Atlantic Monthly* 42 (1878).

Crozier, Emmet. *Yankee Reporters 1861–65.* New York: Oxford University Press, 1956.

Custer, Elizabeth B. *"Boots and Saddles"; or, Life in Dakota with General Custer.* New York and London: Harper & Brothers, 1913.

———. *Following the Guidon.* Reprint, Norman: University of Oklahoma Press, 1966.

———. *Tenting on the Plains; or, General Custer in Kansas and Texas.* New York: Charles L. Webster & Co., 1889.

Custer, George A. *My Life on the Plains; or, Personal Experiences with Indians.* Reprint, Norman: University of Oklahoma Press, 1976.

Darling, Roger. *Custer's Seventh Cavalry Comes to Dakota*. El Segundo, Calif.: Upton & Sons, 1989.

———. *A Sad and Terrible Blunder: Generals Terry and Custer at the Little Big Horn: New Discoveries*. Vienna, Va.: Potomac-Western Press, 1992.

Day, Carl. "If You Want to Know . . ." *Greasy Grass* 9 (May 1993).

DeForest, John William. *A Volunteer's Adventures: A Union Captain's Record of the Civil War*. Edited, with Notes, by James H. Croushore. With an Introduction by Stanley T. Williams. New Haven: Yale University Press, 1946.

Delauter, Roger U., Jr. *Winchester in the Civil War*. Lynchburg, Va.: H. E. Howard, 1992.

Denison, Frederic. *Sabres and Spurs: The First Regiment Rhode Island Cavalry in the Civil War, 1861–1865*. Central Falls, R.I.: Press of E. L. Freeman & Co., 1876.

Devin, Thomas C. "Fierce Resistance at Appomattox." *Civil War Times Illustrated* 17, no. 8 (December 1978).

Dippie, Brian W. *Custer's Last Stand: The Anatomy of an American Myth*. Paperback, Lincoln and London: University of Nebraska Press, 1994.

———, ed. *Nomad: George A. Custer in Turf, Field, and Farm*. Austin and London: University of Texas Press, 1980.

Downey, Fairfax. *Indian-Fighting Army*. New York: Charles Scribner's Sons, 1941.

duBois, Charles G. *Kick the Dead Lion: A Casebook of the Custer Battle*. Reprint, El Segundo, Calif.: Upton & Sons, 1987.

duMont, John S. *Custer Battle Guns*. Ft. Collins, Colo.: Old Army Press, 1974.

———. "Firearms at Little Big Horn." *Greasy Grass* 6 (May 1990).

Duncan, Charles, and Smith, Jay. "The Captives." *Research Review: The Journal of the Little Big Horn Associates* 7, no. 2 (June 1993).

Dunlay, Thomas W. *Wolves for the Blue Soldiers: Indian Scouts and Auxiliaries with the United States Army, 1860–90*. Lincoln and London: University of Nebraska Press, 1982.

Dunphy, James J. "West Point Class of '61." *Research Review: The Journal of the Little Big Horn Associates* 7, no. 1 (January 1993).

DuPont, Henry A. *The Campaign of 1864 in the Valley of Virginia and the Expedition to Lynchburg*. New York: National Americana Society, 1925.

Dustin, Fred. *The Custer Tragedy: Events Leading Up To and Following the Little Big Horn Campaign of 1876*. Introduction by Frank Mercantante. El Segundo, Calif.: Upton & Sons, 1987.

Emerson, Edward W. *Life and Letters of Charles Russell Lowell*. Reprint, Port Washington, N.Y.: Kennikat Press, 1971.

Encounter at Hanover: Prelude to Gettysburg. Reprint, Shippensburg, Pa.: White Mane Publishing Co. 1988.

Everett, John P. "Bullets, Boots, and Saddles." *Sunshine Magazine* 11, no. 1 (September 1930).

Farrar, Samuel Clarke. *The Twenty-Second Pennsylvania Cavalry and the Ringgold Battalion, 1861–1865.* Pittsburgh: New Werner Co. 1911.

Finerty, John F. *War-Path and Bivouac; or, The Conquest of the Sioux.* Norman: University of Oklahoma Press, 1961.

Foner, Eric. *Reconstruction: America's Unfinished Revolution 1863–1877.* New York: Harper & Row, 1988.

Forrest, Earle R. *Witnesses at the Battle of the Little Big Horn.* Introduction by John M. Carroll. Monroe, Mich.: Monroe County Library System, 1986.

Forsyth, George A. *The Story of the Soldier.* New York: D. Appleton & Co., 1900.

———. *Thrilling Days in Army Life.* New York and London: Harper & Brothers, 1900.

Foster, Alonzo. *Reminiscences and Record of the 6th New York V. V. Cavalry.* N.p.: Alonzo Foster, 1892.

Fougera, Katherine Gibson. *With Custer's Cavalry.* Reprint, Lincoln and London: University of Nebraska Press, 1986.

Fox, Richard Allan, Jr. *Archaeology, History, and Custer's Last Battle: The Little Big Horn Reexamined.* Norman and London: University of Oklahoma Press, 1993.

Frost, Lawrence A. *The Court-Martial of General George Armstrong Custer.* Norman: University of Oklahoma Press, 1968.

———. *Custer Legends.* Bowling Green, Ohio: Bowling Green University Popular Press, 1981.

———. *Custer Slept Here.* Monroe, Mich.: Garry Owen Publishers, 1974.

———. *Custer's Seventh Cavalry and the Campaign of 1873.* El Segundo, Calif.: Upton & Sons, 1986.

———. *General Custer's Libbie.* Seattle: Superior Publishing Co., 1976.

———. *With Custer in '74: James Calhoun's Diary of the Black Hills Expedition.* Provo, Utah: Brigham Young University Press, 1979.

Furgurson, Ernest B. *Chancellorsville 1863: The Souls of the Brave.* New York: Alfred A. Knopf, 1992.

Gallagher, Gary W. *Stephen Dodson Ramseur: Lee's Gallant General.* Chapel Hill and London: University of North Carolina Press, 1985.

———, ed. *Fighting for the Confederacy: The Personal Recollections of General Edward Porter Alexander.* Chapel Hill and London: University of North Carolina Press, 1989.

Gardiner, William. *Operations of the Cavalry Corps Middle Military Division, Armies of the United States, from February 27 to March 8, 1865, Participated in by the First Rhode Island Cavalry.* Providence: Rhode Island Soldiers & Sailors Historical Society, 1896.

Gause, Isaac. *Four Years with Five Armies.* New York and Washington: Neale Publishing Co., 1908.

Glazier, Willard. *Three Years in the Federal Cavalry.* New York: R. H. Ferguson & Co., 1874.

Glimpses of the Nation's Struggles: A Series of Papers Read Before the Minnesota Commandery of the Military Order of the Loyal Legion of the United States. Reprint, Wilmington, N.C.: Broadfoot Publishing Co., 1992.

Godfrey, E. S. "Some Reminiscences, Including the Washita Battle, November 27, 1868." *Cavalry Journal* 37, no. 153 (October 1928).

Goree, Langston James, V., ed. *The Thomas Jewitt Goree Letters,* vol. 1: *The Civil War Correspondence.* Bryan, Tex.: Family History Foundation, 1981.

Gracey, S. L. *Annals of the Sixth Pennsylvania Cavalry.* Philadelphia: E. H. Butler & Co., 1868.

Graham, W. A. *The Custer Myth: A Source Book of Custeriana.* Harrisburg, Pa.: Stackpole Co., 1953.

————. *Custer's Battle Flags: The Colors of the Seventh at the Little Big Horn.* Brooklyn, N.Y.: Arrow & Trooper, n.d.

————. *The Story of the Little Big Horn: Custer's Last Fight.* New York: Bonanza Books, 1959.

Grant, Ulysses S. *Personal Memoirs of U. S. Grant.* 2 vols. New York: Charles L. Webster & Co., 1886.

Gray, John S. *Centennial Campaign: The Sioux War of 1876.* Paperback, Norman and London: University of Oklahoma Press, 1988.

————. *Custer's Last Campaign: Mitch Boyer and the Little Bighorn Reconstructed.* Lincoln and London: University of Nebraska Press, 1991.

————. "A Vindication of Curly." *4th Annual Symposium Custer Battlefield Historical & Museum Assn., Inc.,* 1990.

Green, Wharton J. *Recollections and Reflections: An Auto of Half a Century and More.* N.p.: Presses of Edwards & Broughton Printing Co., 1906.

Greiner, H. C. *General Phil Sheridan as I Knew Him: Playmate-Comrade-Friend.* Chicago: J. S. Hyland & Co., 1908.

Grimes, Bryan. *Extracts of Letters of Major-Gen'l Bryan Grimes, to His Wife, Written While in Active Service in the Army of Northern Virginia.* Compiled by Pulaski Cowper. Raleigh, N.C.: Edwards, Broughton & Co., Steam Printers and Binders, 1883.

Grinnell, George Bird. *The Fighting Cheyennes.* Norman: University of Oklahoma Press, 1956.

Hagemann, E. R., ed. *Fighting Rebels and Redskins: Experiences in Army Life of Colonel George B. Sanford, 1861–1892.* Norman: University of Oklahoma Press, 1969.

Haines, Alanson A. *History of the Fifteenth Regiment New Jersey Volunteers.* New York: Jenkins & Thomas, 1883.

Hall, Clark B. "Season of Change: The Winter Encampment of the Army of the Potomac, December 1, 1863–May 4, 1864." *Blue & Gray Magazine* 8, no. 4 (April 1991).

Hall, Hillman A., et al., comps. *History of the Sixth New York Cavalry (Second Ira Harris Guard), Second Brigade—First Division—Cavalry Corps, Army of the Potomac, 1861–1865.* Worcester, Mass.: Blanchard Press, 1908.

Hall, James O., ed. " 'An Army of Devils': The Diary of Ella Washington." *Civil War Times Illustrated* 16, no. 10 (February 1978).

Hammer, Kenneth. *The Glory March.* Monroe, Mich.: Monroe County Library System, 1980.

———, ed. *Custer in '76: Walter Camp's Notes on the Custer Fight.* Provo, Utah: Brigham Young University Press, 1976.

Hanaburgh, D. H. *History of the One Hundred and Twenty-eighth Regiment, New York Volunteers (U.S. Infantry) in the Late Civil War.* Pokeepsie, N.Y.: Enterprise Publishing Co., 1894.

Hardorff, Richard G. *The Custer Battle Casualties: Burials, Exhumations, and Reinternments.* El Segundo, Calif.: Upton & Sons, 1991.

———. *Hokahey! A Good Day to Die!: The Indian Casualties of the Custer Fight.* Spokane, Wash.: Arthur H. Clark Co., 1993.

———. *Lakota Recollections of the Custer Fight: New Sources of Indian-Military History.* Spokane, Wash.: Arthur H. Clark Co., 1991.

Harris, Nathaniel E. *Autobiography: The Story of an Old Man's Life with Reminiscences of Seventy-five Years.* Macon, Ga.: J. W. Burke Co., 1925.

Harris, Samuel. *The Michigan Brigade of Cavalry at the Battle of Gettysburg and Why I Was Not Hung.* Reprint, Rochester, Mich.: Rochester Historical Commission, 1992.

———. *Personal Reminiscences of Samuel Harris.* Chicago: Rogerson Press, 1897.

Hassrick, Royal B. *The Sioux: Life and Customs of a Warrior Society.* Norman: University of Oklahoma Press, 1972.

Hatton, Robert W., ed. "Just a Little Bit of the Civil War, as Seen by W. J. Smith, Company M, 2nd O. V. Cavalry—Parts 1 and 2," *Ohio History* 84, nos. 3 and 4 (Summer and Autumn 1975).

Haven, E. Amy. "In the Steps of a Wolverine: The Civil War Letters of a Michigan Cavalryman." Unpublished manuscript.

Hedley, William. " 'ps Bring Pacs': The Order That Trapped the Custer Battalion." *4th Annual Symposium Custer Battlefield Historical & Museum, Assn., Inc.,* 1990.

Hedren, Paul L., ed. *The Great Sioux War 1876–77: The Best from Montana: The Magazine of Western History.* Helena: Montana Historical Society Press, 1991.

Heidenreich, C. Adrian. "The Native Americans' Yellowstone." *Montana: The Magazine of Western History* 35, no. 4 (Autumn 1985).

Hein, O. L. *Memories of Long Ago.* New York & London: G. P. Putnam's Sons, 1925.

Henderson, William D. *The Road to Bristoe Station: Campaigning with Lee and Meade, August 1–Ocotber 20, 1863.* Lynchburg, Va.: H. E. Howard, 1987.

Heski, Thomas M. "The Trail to Heart River and the Rediscovery of James N. DeWolf," *Research Review: The Journal of the Little Big Horn Associates* 9, no. 2 (June 1995).

Hewitt, William. *History of the Twelfth West Virginia Volunteer Infantry: The Part It Took in the War of the Rebellion 1861–1865*. N.p.: Twelfth West Virginia Infantry Association, [1892].

Hixon, John C. "Custer's 'Mysterious' Mr. Kellogg." *North Dakota History* 17, no. 3 (July 1950).

Holmes, Thomas A. "The Little Big Horn—Benteen: An Unpublished Letter," *Research Review: The Journal of the Little Big Horn Associates* 7, no. 1 (January 1993).

Horn, W. Donald. "Custer's Turn to the North at the Little Big Horn: The Reason." *Research Review: The Journal of the Little Big Horn Associates* 8, no. 1 (January 1994).

———. *"Skinned": The Delinquency Record of Cadet George Armstrong Custer U.S.M.A. Class of June 1861*. Short Hills, N.J.: W. Donald Horn, 1980.

———. "Tom Custer's Civil War Wounds Considered." *Newsletter, Little Big Horn Associates* 24, no. 3 (1995).

Horst, Samuel. *Mennonites in the Confederacy: A Study in Civil War Pacifism*. Scottdale, Pa.: Herald Press, 1967.

Hunt, Frazier, and Robert Hunt. *I Fought with Custer: The Story of Sergeant Windolph, Last Survivor of the Battle of the Little Big Horn*. Lincoln and London: University of Nebraska Press, 1987.

Hutton, Paul A., ed. *Custer and His Times*. El Paso, Tex.: Little Big Horn Associates, 1981.

———. *The Custer Reader*. Lincoln and London: University of Nebraska Press, 1992.

———. *Phil Sheridan and His Army*. Lincoln and London: University of Nebraska Press, 1985.

Hyde, George. "Custer in Virginia: A Glance at the General's Early Campaigns." *The Frontier*, c. 1906.

Indians at Greasy Grass: Statements by: Kills Eagle, Yellow Nose, Joseph White Bull, Two Moon. Brooklyn, N.Y.: Arrow & Trooper, n.d.

Isham, Asa B. *An Historical Sketch of the Seventh Regiment Michigan Volunteer Cavalry: From Its Organization, in 1862, to Its Muster Out, in 1865*. New York: Town Topics Publishing Co., [1893].

Jackson, Donald. *Custer's Gold: The United States Cavalry Expedition of 1874*. New Haven and London: Yale University Press, 1966.

Johnson, Robert Underwood, and Clarence Clough Buel, eds. *Battles and Leaders of the Civil War*. Reprint, New York and London: Thomas Yoseloff, 1956.

Johnson, Roy P. *Jacob Horner of the Seventh Cavalry*. Reprint, Bismarck, N.D.: State Historical Society of North Dakota, 1964.

Jones, Douglas C. *The Treaty of Medicine Lodge: The Story of the Great Council as Told by Eyewitnesses*. Norman: University of Oklahoma Press, 1966.

Kanipe, J. E. "Tarheel Survivor of Custer's Last Stand: The North Carolina Cavalryman Describes the American Thermopylae." Edited by Bill

Boyles. *Research Review: The Journal of the Little Big Horn Associates* 7, no. 2 (June 1993).

Kanitz, Jay F. "Varnum: The Later Years of Custer's Last Lieutenant." *5th Annual Symposium Custer Battlefield Historical & Museum Assn., Inc.,* 1991.

Katz, D. Mark. *Custer in Photographs.* Gettysburg, Pa.: Yo-Mark Production Co., 1985.

Kaufman, Fred S. *Custer Passed Our Way.* Aberdeen, S. Dak.: North Plains Press, 1971.

Keenan, Jerry. "'Rosebud, Oh Rosebud': Crook, Custer, and Conjecture." *6th Annual Symposium Custer Battlefield Historical & Museum Assn., Inc.,* 1992.

Kidd, James H. *Historical Sketch of General Custer.* Reprint, Monroe, Mich.: Monroe County Library System, 1978.

——. *Personal Recollections of a Cavalryman with Custer's Michigan Cavalry Brigade in the Civil War.* Reprint, Alexandria, Va.: Time-Life Books, 1983.

King, A. Barnes. "The Cavalryman & Strong Elk." *Research Review: The Journal of the Little Big Horn Associates* 8, no. 1 (January 1994).

Kinsley, D. A. *Custer: Favor the Bold, A Soldier's Story.* Reprint, New York: Promontory Press, 1992.

Kleese, Richard B. *Shenandoah County in the Civil War: The Turbulent Years.* Lynchburg, Va.: H. E. Howard, 1992.

Koury, Mike. "The Myth of the Indian Warrior; or, Why Did George Do That?" *6th Annual Symposium Custer Battlefield Historical & Museum Assn., Inc.,* 1992.

Krolick, Marshall D. "Forgotten Field: The Cavalry Battle East of Gettysburg on July 3, 1863." *Gettysburg Magazine,* no. 4 (January 1991).

Krause, Wesley. "The Guns of '76." *6th Annual Symposium Custer Battlefield Historical & Museum Assn., Inc.,* 1992.

Kuhlman, Charles. *Did Custer Disobey Orders at the Battle of the Little Big Horn?* Harrisburg, Pa.: Stackpole Co., 1957.

——. *Legend into History: The Custer Mystery.* Harrisburg, Pa.: Stackpole Co., 1952.

Lawrence, Elizabeth Atwood. *His Very Silence Speaks: Comanche—The Horse Who Survived Custer's Last Stand.* Detroit: Wayne State University Press, 1989.

Leckie, Shirley A. *Elizabeth Bacon Custer and the Making of a Myth.* Norman and London: University of Oklahoma Press, 1993.

Lee, William O., comp. *Personal and Historical Sketches and Facial History of and by Members of the Seventh Regiment Michigan Volunteer Cavalry 1862–1865.* Detroit: 7th Michigan Cavalry Association, [1902].

Levine, Richard R. "Indian Fighters and Indian Reformers: Grant's Indian Peace Policy and the Conservative Consensus," *Civil War History* 31, no. 4 (December 1985).

Levstik, Frank. "'Our Brother Tom.'" *North South Trader* 3, no. 4 (May–June, 1976).

Liddic, Bruce R., ed. *I Buried Custer: The Diary of Pvt. Thomas W. Coleman, 7th U. S. Cavalry.* Introduction by John M. Carroll. College Station, Tex.: Creative Publishing Co., 1979.

Lloyd, William Penn. *History of the First Reg't Pennsylvania Reserve Cavalry, from Its Organization, August, 1861, to September, 1864.* Philadelphia: King & Baird, Printers, 1864.

Long, E. B. *The Civil War Day by Day: An Almanac 1861–1865.* Garden City, N.Y.: Doubleday & Co., 1971.

Longacre, Edward G. *The Cavalry at Gettysburg: A Tactical Study of Mounted Operations During the Civil War's Pivotal Campaign 9 June–14 July 1863.* London and Toronto: Associated University Presses, 1986.

Lothrop, Charles H. *A History of the First Regiment Iowa Cavalry Veteran Volunteers.* Lyons, Iowa: Beers & Eaton, Printers, 1890.

Lowry, Thomas P. *The Story the Soldiers Wouldn't Tell: Sex in the Civil War.* Mechanicsburg, Pa.: Stackpole Books, 1994.

Luce, Edward S. "The Diary and Letters of Dr. James M. DeWolf, Acting Assistant Surgeon, U.S. Army; His Record of the Sioux Expedition of 1876 as Kept Until His Death." *North Dakota History* 25, nos. 2 and 3 (April and July 1958).

Mangum, Neil. "Gall: Sioux Gladiator or White Man's Pawn?" *5th Annual Symposium Custer Battlefield Historical & Museum Assn., Inc.,* 1991.

Marquis, Thomas, ed. *Custer, Cavalry & Crows: The Story of William White as told to Thomas Marquis.* Ft. Collins, Colo.: Old Army Press, 1975.

Marshall, S. L. A. *Crimsoned Prairie: The Wars Between the United States and the Plains Indians During the Winning of the West.* New York: Charles Scribner's Sons, 1972.

May, George S. *Michigan and the Civil War Years 1860–1866: A Wartime Chronicle.* N.p.: Michigan Civil War Centennial Observance Commission, 1964.

McCann, Donald C. "Anna E. Jones: The Spy Who Never Was." *Incidents of the War* 2, no. 1 (Spring 1987).

McClellan, George B. *McClellan's Own Story: The War for the Union.* London: Sampson, Low, Marston, Searle & Rivington, 1887.

McDonald, William N. *A History of the Laurel Brigade, Originally the Ashby Cavalry of the Army of Northern Virginia and Chew's Battery.* Reprint, Arlington, Va.: R. W. Beatty, 1969.

McFeely, William S. *Grant: A Biography.* New York and London: W. W. Norton & Co., 1981.

Melton, A. B. *Custer's Last Fight and Other True Indian Stories.* N.p.: Guynes Printing Co., 1963.

Merington, Marguerite, ed. *The Custer Story: The Life and Intimate Letters of General George A. Custer and His Wife Elizabeth.* New York: Devin-Adair Co., 1950.

Meyer, Henry C. *Civil War Experiences Under Bayard, Gregg, Kilpatrick, Custer, Raulston, And Newberry 1862, 1863, 1864.* New York: Knickerbocker Press, 1911.

Michno, Gregory. *The Mystery of E Troop: Custer's Gray Horse Company at the Little Bighorn.* Missoula, Mont.: Mountain Press Publishing Co., 1994.

———. "Space Warp: The Effects of Combat Stress at the Little Big Horn." *Research Review: The Journal of the Little Big Horn Associates* 8, no. 1 (January 1994).

Millbrook, Minnie Dubbs. "Big Game Hunting with the Custers, 1869–1870." *Kansas Historical Quarterly* 41, no. 4 (Winter 1975).

———. "Custer's First Scout in the West," *Kansas Historical Quarterly* 39, no. 1 (Spring 1973).

———. *A Study in Valor: Michigan Medal of Honor Winners in the Civil War.* Lansing: Michigan Civil War Centennial Observance Commission, 1966.

———, ed. "Mrs. General Custer at Fort Riley, 1866." *Kansas Historical Quarterly* 40, no. 1 (Spring 1974).

———, ed. "Rebecca Visits Kansas and the Custers: The Diary of Rebecca Richmond." *Kansas Historical Quarterly* 42, no. 4 (Winter 1976).

Miller, David Humphreys. *Custer's Fall: The Indian Side of the Story.* New York: Duell, Sloan & Pearce, 1957.

Moffett, Mary Conner, ed. *Letters Of General James Conner C.S.A.* Columbia, S.C.: Presses of the R. L. Bryon Co., 1950.

Monaghan, Jay. *Custer: The Life of General George Armstrong Custer.* Boston and Toronto: Little, Brown & Co., 1959.

Moore, James O. "Custer's Raid into Albemarle County: The Skirmish at Rio Hill, February 29, 1864." *Virginia Magazine of History and Biography* 79, no. 3 (July 1971).

Moore, Michael, and Michael Donahue. "Gibbon's Route to Custer Hill." *Greasy Grass* 7 (May 1991).

Morris, Roy, Jr. *Sheridan: The Life and Wars of General Phil Sheridan.* New York: Crown Publishers, 1992.

———. "Sweltering Summer Collision." *Military History* 9, no. 6 (February 1993).

Morrison, James L. "The Struggle Between Sectionalism and Nationalism at Ante-Bellum West Point, 1830–1861." *Civil War History* 19, no. 2 (June 1973).

Moyer, H. P., ed. *History of the Seventeenth Regiment Pennsylvania Volunteer Cavalry.* Lebanon, Pa.: Sowers Printing Co., n.d.

Myers, Frank M. *The Comanches: A History of White's Battalion, Virginia Cavalry, Laurel Brig., Hampton Div., A.N.V., C.S.A.* Reprint, Gaithersburg, Md.: Butternut Press, 1987.

Nettleton, A. Bayard. "How the Day Was Saved at the Battle of Cedar

Creek." *Glimpses of the Nation's Struggle, Minnesota Commandery, Military Order Loyal Legion of the United States, First Series.* St. Paul: St. Paul Book & Stationery Co., 1887.

Nevins, Allan, ed. *A Diary of Battle: The Personal Journals of Colonel Charles S. Wainwright 1861–1865.* Reprint, Gettysburg, Pa.: Stan Clark Military Books, n.d.

Nichols, Ronald H., ed. *Reno Court of Inquiry: Proceedings of a Court of Inquiry in the Case of Marcus A. Reno Concerning His Conduct at the Battle of the Little Big Horn River on June 25–26, 1876.* Crow Agency, Mont.: Custer Battlefield Historical & Museum Association, 1994.

Norton, Chauncey S. *"The Red Neck Ties"; or, History of the Fifteenth New York Volunteer Cavalry.* Ithaca, N.Y.: Journal Book & Job Printing House, 1891.

Norton, Henry, ed. *Deeds of Daring; or, History of the Eighth N. Y. Volunteer Cavalry.* Norwich, N.Y.: Chenango Telegraph Printing House, 1889.

Nye, Elwood L. *Marching with Custer.* Glendale, Calif.: Arthur H. Clark Co., 1964.

O'Neil, Alice T. *The Actor and the General: The Friendship Between Lawrence Barrett and George Armstong Custer.* Brooklyn, N.Y.: Arrow & Trooper, 1994.

————. "Custer and Politics." *Newsletter, Little Big Horn Associates* 28, no. 4 (May 1994).

————. *My Dear Sister: An Analysis of Some Civil War Letters of George Armstrong Custer.* Brooklyn, N.Y.: Arrow & Trooper, 1993.

O'Neil, Thomas E. "Custer's First Romance Revealed," *Newsletter, Little Big Horn Associates* 28, no. 2 (March 1994).

————. *Custer to the Little Big Horn: A Study in Command.* Brooklyn, N.Y.: Arrow & Trooper, 1991.

————. *Decision at Little Big Horn: A Custer Retrospective.* Brooklyn, N.Y.: Arrow & Trooper, 1994.

————. *Passing into Legend: The Death of Custer.* Brooklyn, N.Y.: Arrow & Trooper, 1991.

————. "Two Men Of Ohio: Custer & Bingham." *Research Review: The Journal of the Little Big Horn Associates* 8, no. 1 (January 1994).

————. ed. "Autie Reed's Last Letters," *Newsletter, Little Big Horn Associates* 28, no. 3 (April 1994).

————, ed. *Custer Chronicles.* Vol. 1. Brooklyn, N.Y.: Arrow & Trooper, 1994.

————, ed. *Custer's Civil War.* Arrow & Trooper, 1992.

————, ed. *Garry Owen Tid Bits.* 9 vols. Brooklyn, N.Y.: Arrow & Trooper, 1991–1993.

————, ed. "Hero, to Anti-hero, to Hero: George Armstrong Custer in Monroe's Newspapers." *Newsletter, Little Big Horn Associates* 28, no. 6 (August 1994).

————, ed. *Letters from Boston Custer.* Brooklyn, N.Y.: Arrow & Trooper, 1993.

————, ed. "Newspapers React to Custer's Last Stand." *Newsletter, Little Big Horn Associates* 27, no. 9 (November 1993).

————, ed. "A Sister's Letter." *Newsletter, Little Big Horn Associates* 27, no. 2 (March 1993).

O'Neil, Thomas E., and Alice A. O'Neil. *The Custers in Monroe.* Monroe, Mich.: Monroe County Library System, 1991.

————, eds. *A Custer Time Line: Important Dates in the Life of George A. Custer.* Brooklyn, N.Y.: Arrow & Trooper, 1995.

O'Neil, Thomas E., and Hoyt S. Vandenberg. "A Modern Look at Custer's Orders." *Research Review: The Journal of the Little Big Horn Associates* 8, no. 2 (June 1994).

O'Neill, Robert F., Jr. *The Cavalry Battles of Aldie, Middleburg, and Upperville: Small but Important Riots June 10–27, 1863.* Lynchburg, Va.: H. E. Howard, 1993.

Outline Descriptions of the Posts in the Military Division of the Missouri, Commanded by Lieutenant General P. H. Sheridan. Reprint, Bellevue, Nebr.: Old Army Press, 1969.

Page, Charles A. *Letters of a War Correspondent.* Boston: L. C. Page & Co., 1899.

Parson, John E., and John S. duMont. *Firearms in the Custer Battle.* Harrisburg, Pa.: Stackpole Co., 1953.

Personal Narratives of Events in the War of the Rebellion, Military Order of the Loyal Legion of the United States, Rhode Island. Reprint, Wilmington, N.C.: Broadfoot Publishing Co. 1993.

Personal Recollections of the War of the Rebellion: Addresses Delivered Before the Commandery of the State of New York, Military Order of the Loyal Legion of the United States. Reprint, Wilmington, N.C.: Broadfoot Publishing Co., 1992.

Pickerill, W. N. *History of the Third Indiana Cavalry.* Indianapolis: Aetna Printing Co., 1906.

Piper, Marion J. *Dakota Portraits: A Sentimental Journal of Pictorial History.* Mohall, N.D.: Marion J. Piper, 1964.

Plainfeather, Mardell. "The Role of the Native American Indian in the Interpretation of Military History." *4th Annual Symposium Custer Battlefield Historical & Museum Assn., Inc.,* 1990.

Pohanka, Brian. "George Yates: Captain of the Band Box Troop." *Greasy Grass* 8 (May 1992).

————. "Letter to the Editor," *Blue & Gray Magazine* 6, no. 3 (February 1989).

————. "Myles Keogh," *Military Images,* September–October 1986.

————. "Schooled for Conflict: "Seventh Cavalry Officers at West Point, 1863–1875." *6th Annual Symposium Custer Battlefield Historical & Museum Assn., Inc.,* 1992.

Preston, N. D. *History of the Tenth Regiment of Cavalry New York State Volunteers August, 1861, to August, 1865.* New York: D. Appleton & Co., 1892.

Pyne, Henry R. *The History of the First New Jersey Cavalry.* Trenton: J. A. Beecher, 1871.

Quarles, Garland R. *Some Old Homes in Frederick County, Virginia.* Winchester, Va.: Winchester-Frederick County Historical Society, 1990.

Rawle, William Brooke, ed. *History of the Third Pennsylvania Cavalry, Sixtieth Regiment Pennsylvania Volunteers in the American Civil War 1861–1865.* Philadelphia: Franklin Printing Co., 1905.

Regulations for the U. S. Military Academy, at West Point, New York. New York: John F. Trow, Printer, 1857.

Revised Regulations for the Army of the United States, 1861. Reprint, Harrisburg, Pa.: National Historical Society, 1980.

Reynolds, Arlene. *The Civil War Memories of Elizabeth Bacon Custer.* Austin: University of Texas Press, 1994.

Rhodes, Robert Hunt, ed. *All for the Union: The Civil War Diary and Letters of Elisha Hunt Rhodes.* New York: Orion Books, 1991.

Roberts, Richard A. *Custer's Last Battle: Reminiscences of General Custer.* Monroe, Mich.: Monroe County Library System, 1991.

Robertson, Jno. *Michigan in the War.* Lansing: W. S. George & Co., 1880.

Rockwell, A. D. *Rambling Recollections: An Autobiography.* New York: Paul B. Hoeber, 1920.

Rodenbough, Theodore F., Henry C. Potter, and William P. Seal, eds. *History of the Eighteenth Regiment of Cavalry Pennsylvania Volunteers (163d Regiment of the Line) 1862–1865.* New York: Wynkoop Hallenback Crawford Co., 1909.

Roe, Charles Francis. *Custer's Last Battle.* New York: Robert Bruce, 1927.

Ronsheim, Milton. *The Life of General Custer.* Reprint, Monroe, Mich.: Monroe County Library System, 1991.

Rosenberg, Bruce A. *Custer and the Epic of Defeat.* University Park and London: Pennsylvania State University Press, 1974.

Rosevear, Bernie, and Stephen Rosevear. *Canadians with Custer in 1876.* Monroe, Mich.: Monroe County Library System, 1992.

Schaff, Morris. *The Spirit of Old West Point 1858–1862.* Boston and New York: Houghton, Mifflin Co., 1907.

———. *The Sunset of the Confederacy.* Boston: John W. Luce & Co., 1912.

Schmitt, Martin F., ed. *General George Crook: His Autobiography.* Norman: University of Oklahoma Press, 1946.

Schneider, George A. *The Freeman Journal: The Infantry in the Sioux Campaign of 1876.* San Rafael, Calif.: Presidio Press, 1977.

Schultz, Fred L. "A Cavalry Fight Was On." *Civil War Times Illustrated* 23, no. 10 (February 1985).

Scott, Douglas D., and Richard A. Fox, Jr. *Archaeological Insights into the Custer Battle: An Assessment of the 1984 Field Season*. Norman and London: University of Oklahoma Press, 1987.

Scott, Douglas D., et al. *Archaeological Perspectives on the Battle of the Little Bighorn*. Norman and London: University of Oklahoma Press, 1991.

Scrymser, James A. *Personal Reminiscences of James A. Scrymser in Times of Peace and War*. N.p.: James Scrymser, 1915.

Sears, Stephen W. *George B. McClellan: The Young Napoleon*. New York: Ticknor & Fields, 1988.

———. *Landscape Turned Red: The Battle of Antietam*. New Haven and New York: Ticknor & Fields, 1983.

———. *To the Gates of Richmond: The Peninsula Campaign*. New York: Ticknor & Fields, 1992.

———, ed. *The Civil War Papers of George B. McClellan: Selected Correspondence, 1860–1865*. New York: Ticknor & Fields, 1989.

———, ed. *For Country, Cause & Leader: The Civil War Journal of Charles B. Haydon*. New York: Ticknor & Fields, 1993.

Sergent, Mary Elizabeth. *The Lie Forgotten: The United States Military Academy 1856–1861 Together with a Class Album for the Class of May, 1861*. Middletown, N.Y.: Prior King Press, 1986.

Shannon, Denise E. "Custer's Texas Home." *Texas Highways* 33, no. 2 (February 1986).

Sheridan, Philip H. *Personal Memoirs of P. H. Sheridan, General United States Army*. New York: Charles L. Webster & Co., 1888.

Shevchuk, Paul M. "The Battle of Hunterstown, Pennsylvania, July 2, 1863." *Gettysburg: Historical Articles of Lasting Interest,* no. 1 (July 1989).

Shillinburg, Eva. "More About Ella." *Research Review: The Journal of the Little Big Horn Associates* 8, no. 2 (June 1994).

Sills, Joe, Jr. "The Crow Scouts: Their Contributions in Understanding the Little Big Horn Battle." *5th Annual Symposium Custer Battlefield Historical & Museum Assn., Inc.,* 1991.

———. "Messages and Messengers." *4th Annual Symposium Custer Battlefield Historical & Museum Assn., Inc.,* 1990.

———. "The Recruits Controversy: Another Look." *Greasy Grass* 5 (May 1989).

Simon, John Y. *The Papers of Ulysses S. Grant*. 18 vols. Carbondale and Edwardsville: Southern Illinois University Press, 1967–1991.

Slease, William Davis. *The Fourteenth Pennsylvania in the Civil War*. Pittsburgh: Art Engraving & Printing Co., n.d.

Sloan, W. Eugene. "Goodbye to the Single-Shot Musket." *Civil War Times Illustrated* 23, no. 3 (May 1984).

Slotkin, Richard. *The Fatal Environment: The Myth of the Frontier in the Age of Industrialization 1800–1900*. New York: Atheneum, 1985.

"Some Monroe Memories." *Burton Historical Collection Leaflet,* May 1939.

Southern Historical Society Papers. 52 vols. Richmond, Va.: Southern Historical Society, 1876–1927.

Spotts, David L. *Campaigning with Custer and the Nineteenth Kansas Volunteer Cavalry on the Washita Campaign, 1868–'69.* Reprint, New York: Argonaut Press, 1965.

Stallard, Patricia Y. *Glittering Misery: Dependents of the Indian Fighting Army.* Fort Collins, Colo.: Old Army Press, 1978.

Stanley, David S. *Personal Memoirs of Major-General D. S. Stanley, U.S.A.* Reprint, Gaithersburg, Md.: Olde Soldier Books, 1987.

Stanton, Bill, ed. "A Letter from General Custer." *Newsletter, Little Big Horn Associates* 27, no. 3 (April 1993).

Starr, Stephen Z. *The Union Cavalry in the Civil War.* 3 vols. Baton Rouge: Louisiana State University Press, 1979–1985.

Steere, Edward. *The Wilderness Campaign.* Reprint, Gaithersburg, Md.: Olde Soldier Books, 1987.

Stevenson, J. H. *"Boots and Saddles": A History of the First Volunteer Cavalry of the War, Known as the First New York (Lincoln) Cavalry, and Also as the Sabre Regiment. Its Organization, Campaigns, and Battles.* Harrisburg, Pa.: Patriot Publishing Co., 1879.

Stewart, Edgar I. *Custer's Luck.* Paperback, Norman and London: University of Oklahoma Press, 1989.

———, ed. *Penny-an-Acre Empire in the West.* Norman: University of Oklahoma Press, 1968.

Stewart, Edgar I., and E. S. Luce. "The Reno Scout." *Montana: The Magazine of Western History* 10, no. 3 (July 1960).

Sutton, J. J. *History of the Second Regiment West Virginia Cavalry Volunteers, During the War of the Rebellion.* Reprint, Huntington, W. Va.: Blue Acorn Press, 1992.

Swank, Walbrook Davis. *Battle of Trevilian Station: The Civil War's Greatest and Bloodiest All-Cavalry Battle, With Eyewitness Memoirs.* Shippensburg, Pa.: Burd Street Press, 1994.

Sylvia, Steve. "Custer: Portrait of a Soldier." *North South Trader* 3, no. 4 (May–June 1976).

Taylor, James E. *The James E. Taylor Sketchbook: With Sheridan up the Shenandoah Valley in 1864. Leaves from a Special Artist's Sketch Book and Diary.* Dayton: Morningside House, 1989.

Tenney, Luman Harris. *War Diary of Luman Harris Tenney 1861–1865.* Cleveland: Evangelical Publishing House, 1914.

Testimony: Custer on the Sale of Post Traderships, The Clymer Committee. Brooklyn, N.Y.: Arrow & Trooper Publishing, n.d.

Thomas, Emory M. *Bold Dragoon: The Life of J. E. B. Stuart.* New York: Harper & Row, 1986.

Townsend, George Alfred. *Rustics in Rebellion: A Yankee Reporter on the Road to Richmond 1861–65.* Chapel Hill: University of North Carolina Press, 1950.

Tremain, Henry Edwin. *Last Hours of Sheridan's Cavalry.* New York: Bonnell, Silver & Bowers, 1904.

Trinque, Bruce A. "The Cartridge Case Evidence on Custer Field: An Analysis and Re-interpretation." *5th Annual Symposium Custer Battlefield Historical & Museum Assn., Inc.,* 1991.

———. "The Defense of Custer Hill." *Research Review: The Journal of the Little Big Horn Associates* 8, no. 2 (June 1994).

Trudeau, Noah Andre. *The Last Citadel: Petersburg, Virginia June 1864–April 1865.* Boston: Little, Brown & Co. 1991.

Tuttle, Jud. "Who Buried Lieutenant Hodgson?" *4th Annual Symposium Custer Battlefield Historical & Museum Assn., Inc.,* 1990.

Upton, Richard, ed. *The Custer Adventure, as Told by Its Participants.* Fort Collins, Colo.: Old Army Press, 1975.

Urwin, Gregory J. W. *Custer Victorious: The Civil War Battles of General George Armstrong Custer.* Rutherford, N.J.: Associated University Presses, 1983.

Urwin, Gregory J. W., and Roberta E. Fagan, eds. *Custer and His Times: Book Three.* Paperback, N.p.: University of Central Arkansas Press, 1987.

U.S. War Department. *Atlas to Accompany the Official Records of the Union and Confederate Armies.* Reprint, Gettysburg, Pa.: National Historical Society, 1978.

———. *The War of the Rebellion: A Compilation of the Official Records of the Union and Confederate Armies.* 128 volumes. Washington, D.C.: U.S. Government Printing Office, 1880–1901.

Utley, Robert M. *Cavalier in Buckskin: George Armstrong Custer and the Western Military Frontier.* Norman and London: University of Oklahoma Press, 1989.

———. *Custer and the Great Controversy: The Origin and Development of a Legend.* Pasadena, Calif.: Westernlore Press, 1980.

———. *Frontier Regulars: The United States Army and the Indian, 1861–1891.* New York and London: Macmillan Publishing Co., 1973.

———. *The Indian Frontier of the American West 1846–1890.* Albuquerque: University of New Mexico Press, 1984.

———. *The Lance and the Shield: The Life and Times of Sitting Bull.* New York: Henry Holt & Co., 1993.

———. "Sitting Bull." *Greasy Grass* 10 (May 1994).

———. "War Houses in the Sioux Country: The Military Occupation of the Lower Yellowstone." *Montana: The Magazine of Western History* 35, no. 4 (Autumn 1985).

———, ed. *Life in Custer's Cavalry: Diaries and Letters of Albert and Jennie Barnitz 1867–1868.* New Haven and London: Yale University Press, 1977.

Van de Water, Frederic F. *Glory-Hunter: A Life of General Custer.* Indianapolis and New York: Bobbs-Merrill Co., 1934.

Viola, Herman J., ed. *The Memoirs of Charles Henry Veil: A Soldier's Recollections of the Civil War and the Arizona Territory.* New York: Orion Books, 1993.

Walker, Judson Elliott. *Campaigns of General Custer in the North-west, and the Final Surrender of Sitting Bull.* Reprint, New York: Promontory Press, 1966.

Wallace, Charles B. *Custer's Ohio Boyhood: A Brief Account of the Early Life of Major General George Armstrong Custer.* Freeport, Ohio: Freeport Press, 1978.

War Papers: Being Papers Read Before the Commandery of the State of Wisconsin, Military Order of the Loyal Legion of the United States. 4 vols. Reprint, Wilmington. N.C.: Broadfoot Publishing Co., 1993.

War Papers: Being Papers Read Before the Commandery of the State of Michigan, Military Order of the Loyal Legion of the United States. 2 vols. Reprint, Wilmington. N.C.: Broadfoot Publishing Co., 1993.

War Papers and Personal Reminiscences 1861–1865: Read Before the Commandery of the State of Missouri, Military Order of the Loyal Legion of the United States. One volume Reprint, Wilmington, N.C.: Broadfoot Publishing Co., 1992.

Warner, Ezra J. *Generals in Blue: Lives of the Union Commanders.* Baton Rouge: Louisiana State University Press, 1964.

———. *Generals in Gray: Lives of the Confederate Commanders.* Baton Rouge: Louisiana State University Press, 1959.

Wayland, John W. *A History of Rockingham County, Virginia.* Dayton, Va.: Ruebush-Elkins Co., 1912.

———. *A History of Shenandoah County, Virginia.* Strasburg, Va.: Shenandoah Publishing House, 1927.

———. *Virginia Valley Records: Genealogical and Historical Materials of Rockingham County, Virginia and Related Regions.* Reprint, Baltimore: Genealogical Publishing Co., 1965.

Welch, James, with Paul Stekler. *Killing Custer: The Battle of the Little Bighorn and the Fate of the Plains Indians.* New York and London: W. W. Norton & Co., 1994.

Wells, Wayne. "Little Big Horn Notes: Stanley Vestal's Indian Insights," *Greasy Grass* 5 (May 1989).

Wert, Jeffry D. *From Winchester to Cedar Creek: The Shenandoah Campaign of 1864.* Carlisle, Pa.: South Mountain Press, 1987.

———. *General James Longstreet: The Confederacy's Most Controversial Soldier.* New York: Simon & Schuster, 1993.

———. *Mosby's Rangers.* New York: Simon & Schuster, 1990.

———. "Old Jubilee's Last Battle." *Civil War Times Illustrated* 16, no. 5 (August 1977).

Whittaker, Frederick. *A Complete Life of General George A. Custer.* New York: Sheldon & Co., 1876.

Wildes, Thomas. F. *Record of the One Hundred and Sixteenth Regiment Ohio Infantry Volunteers in the War of the Rebellion.* Sandusky, Ohio: I. F. Mack & Brothers, Printers, 1884.

Willert, James. *Little Big Horn Diary: Chronicle of the 1876 Indian War.* La Mirada, Calif.: James Willert, 1977.

———. *March of the Columns: A Chronicle of the 1876 Indian War June 27 September 16.* El Segundo, Calif.: Upton & Sons, 1994.

———, ed. *The Terry Letters: The Letters of General Alfred Howe Terry to His Sisters During the Indian War of 1876.* La Mirada, Calif.: James Willert, 1980.

Williams, Charles Richard, ed. *Diary and Letters of Rutherford Birchard Hayes,* vol. 2. Columbus: Ohio State Archaeological and Historical Society, 1922.

Williams, Robert A. "Haw's Shop: A 'Storm of Shot and Shell.'" *Civil War Times Illustrated* 9, no. 9 (January 1971).

Wooster, Robert. *The Military and United States Indian Policy 1865–1903.* New Haven and London: Yale University Press, 1988.

Wright, Steven. "Edward Settle Godfrey and the Custer Myth." *6th Annual Symposium Custer Battlefield Historical & Museum Assn., Inc,* 1992.

Zimmerman, Barbara. "Gibbon's Montana Column." *5th Annual Symposium Custer Battlefield Historical & Museum Assn., Inc.,* 1991.

———. "Mo-nah-se-tah: Fact or Fiction." *4th Annual Symposium Custer Battlefield Historical & Museum Assn., Inc.,* 1990.

INDEX